Jerusalem
Gaza
el-Arish

ISRAEL

Eilat

SINAI ✪

Nuweiba

Dahab

el Tor

GULF OF
AQABA AND
THE RED SEA ✪

Hurghada

Port Safaga

Qoseir

K

ANK:
UXOR

nbo

N

75   150 km
45   90 miles

DENDERA ▲ 388

LUXOR ▲ 397

THEBES ▲ 416

EDFU ▲ 448

ASWAN ▲ 456

ABU SIMBEL ▲ 464

Commandments.

**GULF OF AQABA
AND THE RED SEA**
Nature at its purest:
the most beautiful
seas in the world and
landscapes with varied
reliefs, rich in color.

CAIRO
The capital of Egypt,
Cairo contains a
thousand and one
marvels – pharaonic,
coptic and islamic.

**THE PYRAMIDS
AND THE SPHINX**
The highlight of
a trip to Egypt, the
seventh wonder of
the world still has the
power to intrigue.

SAQQARA
An impressive collection
of funerary monuments
from every epoch of
Egyptian history, from
earliest times to the
Christian era.

DENDERA
The temple to the
Goddess Hathor,
conserved just
as it was when it
was built in the time
of the pharoahs.

LUXOR
Especially prized
by tourists, Luxor
owes its fame to
its two temples
and the nearby
necropolis of Thebes.

THEBES WEST BANK
The immense
funerary buildings
and, even more
impressive, the
temples dedicated
to past kings.

EDFU
From the monumental
entrance to the secret
sanctuary, here are all
the components of a
temple of the pharaohs.

ASWAN
Situated at the
crossroads of Africa and
India, this Nubian city
boasts an abundance of
monuments.

ABU SIMBEL
The restored temples
of Ramesses and
Nefertari occupy
a dominant site
overlooking the Nile.

EGYPT

EVERYMAN GUIDES

● Encyclopedia section

■ **NATURE** The natural heritage: species and habitats characteristic to the area covered by the guide, annotated and illustrated by naturalist authors and artists.

HISTORY, LANGUAGE AND RELIGION The impact of international historical events on local history, from the arrival of the first inhabitants, with key dates appearing in a timeline above the text.

ARTS AND TRADITIONS Customs and traditions and their continuing role in contemporary life.

ARCHITECTURE The architectural heritage, focusing on style and topology, a look at rural and urban buildings, major civil, religious and military monuments.

AS SEEN BY PAINTERS A selection of paintings of the city or country by different artists and schools, arranged chronologically or thematically.

AS SEEN BY WRITERS An anthology of texts focusing on the city or country, taken from works of all periods and countries, arranged thematically.

▲ Itineraries

Each itinerary begins with a map of the area to be explored.

✪ **SPECIAL INTEREST** These sites are not to be missed. They are highlighted in gray boxes in the margins.

★ **EDITOR'S CHOICE** Sites singled out by the editor for special attention.

INSETS On richly illustrated double pages, these insets turn the spotlight on subjects deserving more in-depth treatment.

◆ Practical information

All the travel information you will need before you go and when you get there.

SIGHTSEEING A handy table of addresses and opening hours.

USEFUL ADDRESSES A selection of the best hotels and restaurants compiled by an expert.

APPENDICES Bibliography, list of illustrations and general index.

MAP SECTION Maps of all the areas covered by the guide, followed by an index; these maps are marked out with letters and figures making it easy for the reader to pinpoint a town, region or site.

Each map in the map section is designated by a letter. In the itineraries, all the sites of interest are given a map reference (for example: **F** B2).

● ▲ ◆
The above symbols within the text provide cross-references to a place or a theme discussed elsewhere in the guide.

The mini-map pinpoints the itinerary within the wider area covered by the guide.

▲ ASWAN

1 ASWAN ○ 2 KITCHENER'S ISLAND 3 ELEPHANTINE ISLAND 4 TOMB OF THE AGA KHAN 5 MONASTERY OF ST SIMEON 6 SEHEL ISLAND 7 FIRST DAM 8 PHILAE 9 HIGH DAM

10 KERTASSI 11 KALABSHA 12 MAHARRAKA 13 DAKKA 14 WADI EL-SEBUA 16 ABU SIMBEL ○

A TASTE OF AFRICA ○
At Aswan the desert closes in again on the Nile, changing the ambience and scenery – now you are truly in Africa! A stay of two to three days is ideal to look around the town on foot, explore the spice market, supplied by caravans for millennia, go on an excursion to the island of Aqilqila to see the temple of Philae, tired from the water, and examine at close quarters the famous Aswan dam, constructed by the builders of the pyramids.

ASWAN
Aswan is situated about 130 miles south of Luxor on what was once the southern border of Ancient Egypt. It lies on the east bank of the Nile at a point where the river cuts its way through the granite rock of the first of the cataracts

surrounding the ISLAND OF SEHEL, where Anukis (daughter of Khnum) was worshipped. About 250 inscriptions (dating from the 4th Dynasty to the Ptolemaic period), engraved on the rocks of the island, commemorate particular expeditions and events: for example, the famine which raged for seven years during the reign of Djoser was ended only by the intervention of the god Khnum. At Aswan the green, fertile belt of the Nile Valley is interrupted and replaced in mid-desert, behind the great dam, by the vast LAKE NASSER. Sandstone is replaced by granite in the form of two rocky barriers which hold back the Nile and also harbor the quarries

exploited early on in history by the great builder-pharaohs. Khnum is the lord of the cataract and master of a gulf which was believed to be the source of the Nile floods. From ancient times Aswan was a huge market situated at the crossroads of the routes from Africa, the western deserts of Egypt and India. This frontier trading-post, visited by people from a number of different countries, was also an important strategic point. It has served as a base for Roman garrisons, for the Turkish troops of the Ottoman sultan Selim in 1517, for the army of General Kitchener during the conquest of the Sudan (1896–8) and is now a major garrison for the modern Egyptian army.
ELEPHANTINE ISLAND ★. Syene, the Ancient Egyptian name of Aswan, was derived from "syenite" (the name was wrongly applied to granite and today reserved for another type of rock). It is the modern counterpart of the first market town situated on the island of Elephantine (from the Egyptian word *abu* meaning "elephant") so called because of the extensive trade in ivory during antiquity. The island, with its Nubian villages, is reached by *felucca*. The ancient quays and landing-stage on the eastern side of the island once gave access to the temples of Thutmose III and Amenhotep III, destroyed in 1822 by the Turkish government. Only the Roman NILOMETER remains. Near the Nilometer the ELEPHANTINE MUSEUM houses objects discovered on the island and in the surrounding area, including prehistoric schist basins and the mummies of the sacred rams of Khnum, with their richly decorated and gilt casings. The ruins of the ancient city were discovered beyond the museum, in the south part of the island. They include the temples dedicated to Khnum and Satis by Queen Hatshepsut and the temple built in honor of Hekayib (governor of Elephantine Island during the 6th Dynasty and deified posthumously) by his successor Sarenput I (whose tomb is at Gharbi Aswan). Several chapels containing statues represent the largest complex devoted to private worship.

NILOMETER
The Nilometer on Elephantine Island was described by Strabo in the 1st century AD as "a steeply graded staircase that plunges down into the river". The graduated scale on the walls was used to measure the flood levels which were certified by inscriptions in demotic script, Greek, Arabic and French.

Four days
◆F C4-B5-B6-A6

456

457

At the beginning of each itinerary, the distance, the suggested means of travel and the time it will take to cover the area are indicated beneath the maps:
By foot
By car

The itinerary map shows the main sites, the editor's choices and the places of special interest.

○ This symbol indicates places of special interest.

★ The star symbol signifies sites singled out by the editor for special attention.

03

FRONT MAP Sites of special interest
END MAP The Republic of Egypt
02 How to use this guide
06 Introduction to the itineraries
07 The authors

● Encyclopedia section

15 NATURE
16 The Nile Valley
24 Climate
26 Lake Nasser
28 Coral reef
30 Mangrove forests
32 Sinai
34 Animals of Ancient Egypt
36 Fauna of the archeological sites

**37 HISTORY, LANGUAGE AND
     RELIGION**
38 Pre-Pharaonic Egypt
46 The Nile in Pharaonic times
54 Life and death in Ancient Egypt
66 From the Arab conquest to
   modern times
72 Language
74 Religion

77 ARCHITECTURE
Pharaonic architecture:
   78 Construction techniques
   82 Religious architecture
   86 Funerary architecture
   90 Civil architecture
   92 Military architecture
 94 History of excavations
102 Restoration techniques
106 Coptic monastic architecture

Islamic architecture
   108 Mosques
   112 Religious establishments
   114 Funerary architecture
   116 Domestic architecture
   118 "Wakala"

119 ARTS AND TRADITIONS
120 Boats
124 Rituals and ceremonies
126 Festivals and pilgrimages
128 Music and dance
130 Craft trades
132 Cafés
134 Food: "fuul"
136 Horses
138 Falconry

139 EGYPT AS SEEN BY PAINTERS
140 Egypt Expedition's scientific mission
142 Early Orientalists
144 Orientalists
146 Contemporary artists
148 Egyptian artists

149 EGYPT AS SEEN BY WRITERS

▲ Itineraries in Egypt

171 ALEXANDRIA
174 The city of Alexandria
186 Graeco-Roman Museum
192 Catacombs
200 Around Alexandria

205 NILE DELTA
206 Cairo to Rosetta
216 Champollion and hieroglyphics
220 Cairo to Damietta

224 Cairo to Tanis
228 Suez Canal

237 SINAI
240 South Sinai
243 Sinai mountains
244 St Catherine's Monastery
246 Mount Sinai
248 Gulf of Aqaba and the Red Sea
250 North Sinai

253 DESERTS
254 Libyan Desert
256 Siwa Oasis
260 Kharga Oasis
264 Arabian Desert

269 CAIRO
272 The city center
276 Egyptian Museum, Cairo
286 El-Hussein and Khan el-Khalili
294 El-Azhar
300 Darb el-Ahmar
304 The Citadel
308 Midan Salah ad-Din
316 Islamic Museum
318 Old Cairo
322 Coptic Museum
326 Cemeteries
332 Memphis
344 Saqqara

353 MEMPHIS TO THE FAIYUM
354 Dahshur
356 Lisht
357 Meidum
359 Illahun
360 Ihnasiya el-Medina

361 THE FAIYUM
366 Kom Ushim
368 Medinet el-Faiyum

371 EL-MINIA TO THEBES
372 El-Minia
374 Beni Hassan
376 Hermopolis
377 Tuna el-Jebel
378 Tell el-Amarna
380 Assiut

386 Abydos
388 Dendera

393 THEBES
398 Temple of Luxor
404 Temple of Karnak
416 Valley of the Kings
418 Tomb of Tutankhamun
424 Temple of Sety I
426 Deir el-Bahari
430 Necropolis of Sheikh
    Abd el-Qurna
432 Ramesseum
434 Medinet Habu
438 Deir el-Medina
440 Valley of the Queens
442 Qurna

443 THEBES TO ASWAN
446 Esna
447 El-Kab
448 Edfu
452 Kom Ombo

455 ASWAN AND ABU SIMBEL
456 Aswan
460 Aswan High Dam
462 Philae
464 Abu Simbel

**467 EGYPT IN THE MUSEUMS OF
    THE WORLD**
468 Italy
470 Germany
472 United States
474 United Kingdom
476 France
478 Europe
480 Obelisks

◆ Practical information

482 Getting there
484 Getting around
486 Daily life
493 Useful words and phrases
494 List of addresses
507 Places to visit
516 Bibliography
517 Table of illustrations
528 Index

539 MAP SECTION
540 Cairo street index
A-B Alexandria
C Northeast Egypt
D Northwest Egypt
E Libyan desert
F Southeast Egypt
G Nile Delta
H Cairo
I North Cairo
J South Cairo
K Thebes
L Luxor
M Aswan

ALEXANDRIA ▲ 171
A look around the port, town center, catacombs, Graeco-Roman Museum, as well as a trip by tram along the coast.

NILE DELTA ▲ 205
Three trips exploring the regions and villages of the Nile Delta, along its channels as far as the isthmus of Suez.

SINAI ▲ 237
A varied landscape of coastal plains, deserts and mountains, it is home to ancient and mythological sites.

LIBYAN DESERT ▲ 254
To the east of the Nile, visits to five oases in the stretch of desert that covers two-thirds of the country.

ARABIAN DESERT ▲ 264
This arid region encircled by the Nile and the Red Sea includes two monasteries and ancient quarries.

CITY CENTER ▲ 269
Modern Cairo, its districts and museums, the islands of Roda and Gezira, the suburbs and surrounding area.

ISLAMIC CAIRO ▲ 286
The districts of el-Hussein and Khan el-Khalili as well as the area surrounding the el-Azhar mosque.

THE CITADEL ▲ 304
Inside the ramparts, visits to palaces, museums and mosques; outside, Midan Salah ad-Din and Shari' Saliba.

COPTIC CAIRO ▲ 318
Today the ancient city houses several churches, including the famous el-Muallaqa, as well as the Coptic Museum.

CEMETERIES ▲ 326
Guided tour of the necropolis of the Mamelukes in the east of the city, and the Imam as-Shafi'i necropolis to the south.

MEMPHIS TO THE FAIYUM ▲ 353
Leaving Cairo, this trip takes in the lesser-known pyramids, including Meidum, Lisht and Hawara.

THE FAIYUM ▲ 361
Near Cairo, this region has a salt lake, Birket Qarun, and numerous archeological sites from the Ptolemaic period.

EL-MINIA TO THEBES ▲ 371
Middle Egypt includes several famous Pharaonic sites, such as Tell el-Amarna, Abydos and Dendera.

THEBES ▲ 393
The town of Luxor, the temples of Luxor and Karnak and, on the opposite bank, the funerary monuments of the valley of Thebes.

THEBES TO ASWAN ▲ 443
Several stops on the road to Aswan including the temples of Esna, el-Kab, Edfu and Kom Ombo.

ASWAN AND ABU SIMBEL ▲ 455
A trip rich in discoveries: the town of Aswan, the High Dam, the temples of Philae and Abu Simbel.

Numerous specialists and academics have contributed to this guide.

●

Encyclopedia section

NATURE: Philippe Dubois, Dominique Bénard
(The Nile Valley), Peter Meininger
(Climate, Sinai)
HISTORY (PHARAONIC): Alain Zivie
LIFE AND DEATH IN ANCIENT EGYPT:
Guillemette Andreu Lanoë
HISTORY (POST PHARAONIC): Robert Ilbert
LANGUAGES AND RELIGION: Robert Ilbert
ARTS AND TRADITIONS: Eglal Errera,
Mercédès Volait, Ghislaine Alleaume,
Christian Gaubert, Nessim Henein (Bateaux)
PHARAONIC ARCHITECTURE:
Nathalie Vaillant, Jean-Pierre Lange
HISTORY OF EXCAVATIONS:
Nathalie Vaillant, Jean-Pierre Lange
COPTIC AND ISLAMIC ARCHITECTURE:
Mercédès Volait
EGYPT AS SEEN BY PAINTERS:
Eglal Errera, Mercédès Volait
EGYPT AS SEEN BY WRITERS:
Lucinda Gane

▲

Itineraries in Egypt

ALEXANDRIA:
Eglal Errera, Mercédès Volait
NILE DELTA: Ghislaine Alleaume,
Jean-Luc Bovot
SINAI: Olivier Sanmartin
DESERTS: Nicole Levallois
CAIRO:
Christine Roussillon (coordination)
MODERN CAIRO:
Alain Roussillon, Mercédès Volait
ISLAMIC CAIRO: Sawsan Noweir,
Hanaa Farid (Islamic Museum)
OLD CAIRO: Sawsan Noweir,
Alain Roussillon (History)
Hanaa Farid (Coptic Museum)
NECROPOLIS: Galila el-Kadi
MEMPHIS, GIZA AND SAQQARA: Alain Zivie
MEMPHIS TO THE FAIYUM: Jean-Luc Bovot
THE FAIYUM: Pierre Gazio
EL-MINIA TO THEBES: Vincent Rondot
THEBES: Jean-Pierre Golvin,
Paul Geday (City Center)
THEBES TO ASWAN: Catherine Graindorge
ASWAN AND ABU SIMBEL: Catherine Graindorge
EGYPT IN THE MUSEUMS OF THE WORLD:
Ester Coen

◆

Practical information

Jean-Luc Berger, Thierry Beaurepère

EVERYMAN GUIDES

EVERYMAN GUIDES
Published by Everyman Publishers Plc

First published 1995
Further editions, revised and updated:
August 1996 and June 2000

© 2000 Everyman Publishers Plc

Originally published in France by
Nouveaux-Loisirs, a subsidiary of
Editions Gallimard, Paris, 1994
© 1994 Editions Nouveaux-Loisirs.

Egypt – ISBN 1-84159-002-9

TRANSLATED BY
Wendy Allatson

EDITED AND TYPESET BY
Book Creation Services Ltd, London

SPECIAL THANKS TO
CEDEJ (Centre d'études documentaires et
juridiques), The Press Office of the
Egyptian Embassy, Christine Roussillon,
Jacques Livet.

EGYPT
■ **EDITOR**
Soraya Khalidy
■ **PRACTICAL INFORMATION**
Philippe Gallois, Veronika Vollmer
■ **LAYOUT**
Natacha Kotlarevsky, Michelle Bisganbiglia
(Nature), François Chentrier (Practical
information)
■ **PICTURE RESEARCH**
Marielle Blanc
■ **COORDINATION**
Eglal Errera
■ **ILLUSTRATIONS**
NATURE: François Desbordes, Gilbert
Houbre, Bruce Pearson, Claire Felloni, Jean
Chevalier, Anne Bodin
ARCHITECTURE : Philippe Biard, François
Brosse, Philippe Cande, Claude Quiec,
Jean-Claude Séné, Françoise Gastineau,
Jean-Pierre Lange
ARTS AND TRADITIONS: Maurice Pommier,
Nathalie Fonteneau, Philippe Biard
ITINERARIES: Jean-Benoît Héron, Jean-Pierre
Lange, Philippe Biard, Gilbert Houbre,
Jean-Claude Séné
MAPS : Stéphane Girel
COMPUTER GRAPHICS: Paul Coulbois,
Emmanuel Calamy, Patrick Alexandre,
Kristof Chemineau
■ **PHOTOGRAPHY**
Wessam Amin, Patrick Godeau, Dylan
Doyle.

Printed in Italy by Editoriale Lloyd

EVERYMAN GUIDES
Gloucester Mansions, 140a Shaftesbury Avenue,
London WC2H 8HD
guides@everyman.uk.com

Encyclopedia section

15 Nature
37 History, language and religion
77 Architecture
119 Arts and traditions
139 Egypt as seen by painters
149 Egypt as seen by writers

Boats on the Nile with skysails.

Tourists returning from Karnak.

Tourists picnicking in a temple (c. 1900).

Sculpture in the Temple of Philae.

NATURE

THE NILE VALLEY, *16*
CLIMATE, *24*
LAKE NASSER, *26*
CORAL REEF, *28*
MANGROVE FORESTS, *30*
SINAI, *32*
ANIMALS OF ANCIENT EGYPT, *34*
FAUNA OF THE
ARCHEOLOGICAL SITES, *36*

■ THE NILE VALLEY

The Nile is the longest river in the world, stretching for a distance of 4,163 miles. The Great – Egyptian – Nile is formed by the merging of the White Nile, which rises in the Ruwenzori range in Zaire, and the Blue Nile, which rises in the high plateaux of Ethiopia. It flows into the Mediterranean via a vast delta system. Alluvium deposited over the centuries has helped to create an extremely fertile strip of land (up to 12½ miles wide) which has given rise to a rich and diversified agriculture. This "linear oasis" has also favored the development of a very specific flora and fauna.

Winter plumage

Breeding plumage

Cattle egret

Felucca

CATTLE EGRET
Flocks of cattle egrets are a common sight as they search for insects, frogs and small rodents among the crops.

Many of the Nile's reed-covered islands contain large breeding colonies of cattle egrets.

A "percussion" instrument (usually a metal can or drum) is used to drive the fish into the net.

16·

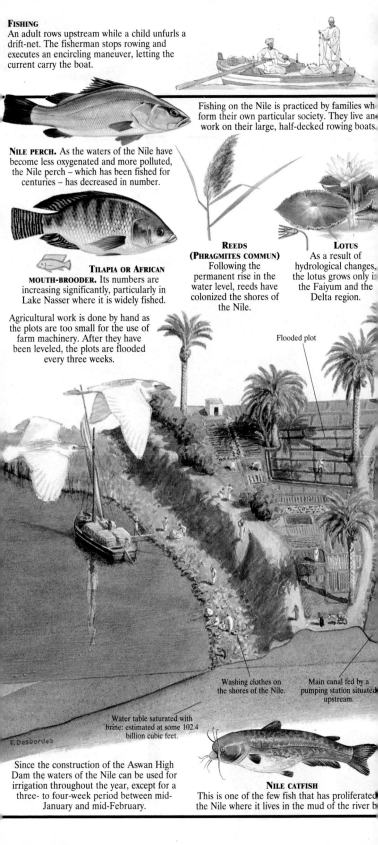

FISHING
An adult rows upstream while a child unfurls a drift-net. The fisherman stops rowing and executes an encircling maneuver, letting the current carry the boat.

Fishing on the Nile is practiced by families wh form their own particular society. They live an work on their large, half-decked rowing boats.

NILE PERCH. As the waters of the Nile have become less oxygenated and more polluted, the Nile perch – which has been fished for centuries – has decreased in number.

REEDS (PHRAGMITES COMMUN)
Following the permanent rise in the water level, reeds have colonized the shores of the Nile.

LOTUS
As a result of hydrological changes, the lotus grows only i the Faiyum and the Delta region.

TILAPIA OR AFRICAN MOUTH-BROODER. Its numbers are increasing significantly, particularly in Lake Nasser where it is widely fished.

Agricultural work is done by hand as the plots are too small for the use of farm machinery. After they have been leveled, the plots are flooded every three weeks.

Flooded plot

Washing clothes on the shores of the Nile.

Main canal fed by a pumping station situated upstream.

Water table saturated with brine: estimated at some 102.4 billion cubic feet.

F.Desbordes

Since the construction of the Aswan High Dam the waters of the Nile can be used for irrigation throughout the year, except for a three- to four-week period between mid-January and mid-February.

NILE CATFISH
This is one of the few fish that has proliferated the Nile where it lives in the mud of the river b

WATER HYACINTH
This South American plant, favored by the changing conditions in the Nile, has colonized and obstructed 80% of its canals.

The *noria* or Persian wheel is a hydraulic device whose blades (or buckets) are activated by the waters of a canal.

PAPYRUS
Papyrus, the Pharaonic symbol of Lower Egypt, was widely cultivated for paper until the 10th century. It was believed to have died out by the beginning of the 19th century until a remaining site was found at Wadi Natrun ▲ 208.

ACACIA
A common sight on the banks of the Nile, with its eye-catching balls of small, yellow flowers.

Secondary canal

Bersim

Saqia: an animal-operated, double wheel system.

Cabbages

Secondary canal   Flooded plot   Siphon beneath secondary drainage canal.   Underground can

Bersim – used for covers third o

Since the filling of the Aswan High Dam there are three annual seasons, apart from permanent crops (crops grown on trees, sugar cane). The main winter (October to April) crops are *bersim*, wheat, broad beans, barley, garlic and onions. Mealtimes in January are a monochrome study in various shades of green.

Onion

Fuul   Garlic

in
d.

The Ancient Egyptians buried their dead in rock-cut tombs on the edge of the desert.

BLACK-WINGED KITE
For reasons as yet unclear, the numbers of this pretty little bird of prey have increased dramatically, especially in the Delta region.

REED WARBLER
Easily recognized by its grating cry in spring. This is another bird which has benefited from the extension of the reed beds.

PIED KINGFISHER
This large kingfisher captures its prey by hovering over and diving into the waters of canals and the Nile.

SWALLOW
The Egyptian race of the barn swallow is characterized by its brick-red breast and underbelly.

PYGMY SUNBIRD
This small bird, commonly found in Upper Egypt, is a reminder that the country is not far from the tropics.

Every part of the palm tree is used. The wood from its trunk is burned or transformed into roofing (**1**) or gutters (**2**). The branches are used for fuel, wind-breaks (**3**), or to make mats (**4**), furniture or baskets (**5**).

HOOPOE
In Egypt the hoopoe tends to be associated with the Nile as it is rarely seen beyond the Nile Valley.

COMMON BULBUL
The bulbul is found close to human habitation. Its bubbling calls are a common sound among crops and in oases.

■ CLIMATE

Although apparently uninhabited, the most arid desert regions harbor a flora and fauna well adapted to the harsh conditions.

Egypt has a total surface area of over 386,000 square miles and a predominately desert climate.

In fact 96 percent of the country is covered by desert and only the northern coastline has a Mediterranean climate. Although Egypt is part of Africa, the Sinai Peninsula encroaches upon Asia. The Egyptian part of the Nile covers a distance of 750 miles and marks the "border" between the Libyan Desert in the west and the Arabian Desert in the east. Rainfall is minimal and occurs mainly in winter in the Delta region where the northwest winds prevail.

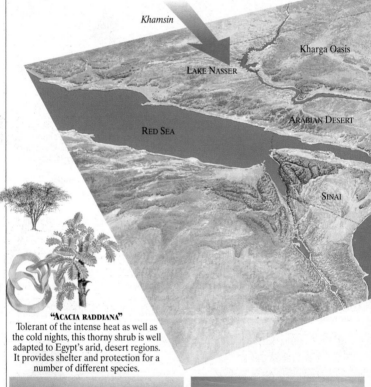

Khamsin

Kharga Oasis

LAKE NASSER

ARABIAN DESERT

RED SEA

SINAI

"ACACIA RADDIANA"
Tolerant of the intense heat as well as the cold nights, this thorny shrub is well adapted to Egypt's arid, desert regions. It provides shelter and protection for a number of different species.

The silt once deposited in the Nile Delta is retained by the Aswan High Dam. The result is the erosion of the Mediterranean shores.

It rarely rains in the Arabian Desert. The regular mists which occur at high altitude are the main source of water for flora and fauna.

24

Wadis are seasonal desert rivers. After the rains, flowers and grasses bloom briefly on their banks. Only a few well-adapted plants survive during periods of drought.

Its position in the center of the desert and its altitude (70 feet below sea level) make Kharga Oasis ▲ 260 one of the hottest places on earth.

Male

BLACKBIRD **COLLARED DOVE**
These two species are now found as far south as Israel due to the increasing number of artificial oases. This has meant they are beginning to be seen in Egypt.

LIBYAN DESERT

Farafra Oasis

Bahriya Oasis

THE FAIYUM

DELTA

MEDITERRANEAN SEA

In spring a dry, burning wind – the *khamsin* – blows from the south and causes sandstorms. The *khamsin* (which means "fifty" in Arabic) is so called because it can last for up to fifty days. Summer is the season of drought in Upper Egypt and of high humidity in the Nile Delta.

The high peaks of Sinai are the only place in Egypt where snow is found.

Isohyets (in mm) of average annual precipitation. Only the Mediterranean region has any degree of rainfall.

Average maximum temperature in °C (July).

Average maximum temperature in °C (January).

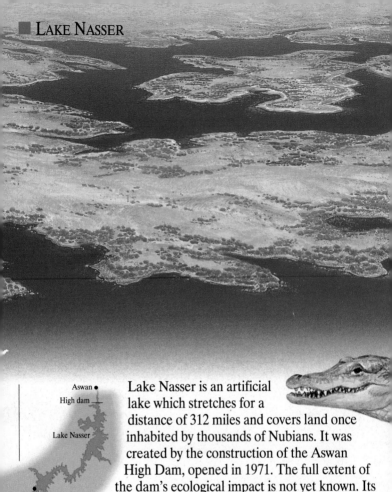

Aswan ●
High dam
Lake Nasser
● Abu Simbel

Lake Nasser is an artificial lake which stretches for a distance of 312 miles and covers land once inhabited by thousands of Nubians. It was created by the construction of the Aswan High Dam, opened in 1971. The full extent of the dam's ecological impact is not yet known. Its positive effects include putting an end to the devastating Nile floods, more extensive cultivation as a result of irrigation, the production of electricity and improved navigation. However the fact that the silt is now retained by the dam may well lead to impoverished soil below the dam and the need to use chemical fertilizers. Also the river is no longer powerful enough to repel the inflow of salt water from the sea which is sterilizing the soil, while the banks of the Nile in the Delta region are becoming badly eroded.

Lake Nasser's many creeks (*khors*) represent almost 80% of the surface area when the lake is full. The shoreline covers an overall distance of 4,875 miles.

SOFT-SHELL TURTLE
This extremely rare, fish-eating turtle appears to be surviving in small numbers in the waters of Lake Nasser.

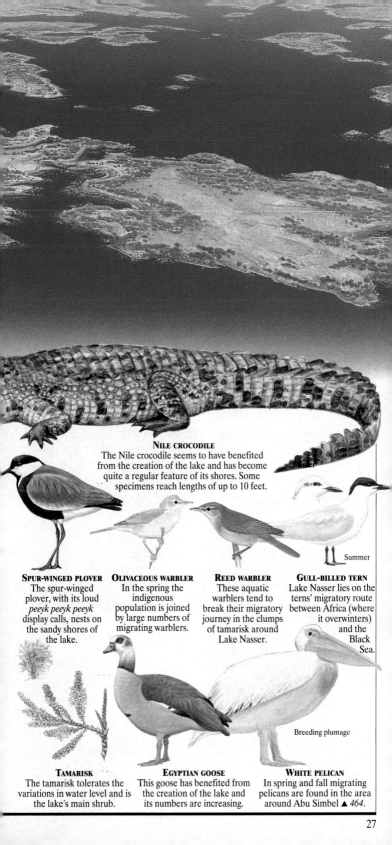

NILE CROCODILE
The Nile crocodile seems to have benefited from the creation of the lake and has become quite a regular feature of its shores. Some specimens reach lengths of up to 10 feet.

Summer

SPUR-WINGED PLOVER
The spur-winged plover, with its loud *peeyk peeyk peeyk* display calls, nests on the sandy shores of the lake.

OLIVACEOUS WARBLER
In the spring the indigenous population is joined by large numbers of migrating warblers.

REED WARBLER
These aquatic warblers tend to break their migratory journey in the clumps of tamarisk around Lake Nasser.

GULL-BILLED TERN
Lake Nasser lies on the terns' migratory route between Africa (where it overwinters) and the Black Sea.

Breeding plumage

TAMARISK
The tamarisk tolerates the variations in water level and is the lake's main shrub.

EGYPTIAN GOOSE
This goose has benefited from the creation of the lake and its numbers are increasing.

WHITE PELICAN
In spring and fall migrating pelicans are found in the area around Abu Simbel ▲ 464.

27

■ CORAL REEF

This colony of *Acropora* coral or *Stagshorn* coral has formed a clump which looks like a sunshade.

Egyptian coral reefs are found along the Red Sea coast and to the south and east of the Sinai Peninsula. This region of the world forms part of the Syro-African fault and is famed for the wealth and variety of its fish, corals and other invertebrates of Indo-Pacific origin. Coral reefs can only develop properly in warm, clear waters with a high salt content, little sediment and relatively little wave movement.

The scales of the emperor angelfish go through several stages before reaching the full beauty of adulthood.

Blue-speckled parrot fish

The masked puffer fish is a member of the puffer family, which can inflate themselves at the slightest hint of danger.

Soft coral *Dendronephtia*

Organ-pipe sponge

Red sponge

Sea slug *Chromodoris*

Sea urchin

Slingjaw wrasse

Giant clam

Fan-worm *Sabella*

Sea anemone *Gyrostoma*

Banded *Amphiprion* or anemone-fish

Banded reef prawn

During the day the gray moray stays hidden in a crevice in the reef.

The biological diversity of coral reefs is truly remarkable. Corals, sponges, sea anemones, sea urchins, molluscs, and prawns live together in harmony or even – as in the case of sea anemones with the anemone-fish or *Amphiprion* – in symbiosis. Other species such as sponges act as filters.

The flying scorpion fish swims slowly through the semi-darkness of the reef in search of its prey.

28

"Fire" coral

The greatest variety of fish is found near the reef, which provides both food and shelter.

Barrier reef (terrace)   Breakers

Sea level

Coastal rocks   Lagoon   Rim

Reef wall   Fringing reef

Sandy slope

The three types of reef – terrace, fringing reef and bottom rock – are defined in terms of depth. The intermediate reef has the widest variety of fauna.

POLYPS
Polyps live in huge communities, growing on the calcareous skeletons of their predecessors. Over time, they form the coral reef.

Acropora Coral

The surgeon fish, endemic to the Red Sea, has a sharp spike at the end of its tail.

Butterfly fish – also known as "tobies" – live in shoals.

Blue tang, an endemic species, belongs to the "surgeon" family.

Anthias teaniatus

The red or tropical grouper – which rarely grows to more than 30 inches long – lives in the cracks and crevices of the reef.

Lyretail coralfish

Egypt's mangrove forests are typical of the coastal forests of tropical regions. They are found along the Red Sea coast and southeast coast of Sinai where they reach their most northerly latitude in the world (28° 13' N). This bushy, partly submerged forest – consisting mainly of salt-water mangroves (*Avicennia marina*) – is teeming with life. By retaining sediment its root system favors the development of a rich and abundant community of animals. It is a breeding ground and nursery for fish and many invertebrates, such as prawns, as well as a nesting site for several rare species of birds.

In 1989 the site of Ras Mohammed ▲ 248 was designated a national park to protect one of the most northerly growing mangrove forests in the world.

SALT-WATER MANGROVE
Avicennia marina is the most commonly found mangrove along the shores of the Red Sea. Mangroves have a specialized system of aerial roots which enables them to draw the nutrients they need from the soil.

DUGONG
The dugong has become extremely rare as a result of intensive hunting and pollution. Today the population is limited to a few sites along the south coast of the Red Sea.

Migrating shorebirds feed on the muddy foreshore of the mangrove forests.

Ghost crab

HAWKSBILL TURTLE
Every year this large marine turtle lays its eggs on the beaches along the eastern coast of Egypt.

GHOST CRAB
The best indication of the presence of these nocturnal crabs are the little mounds of sand formed at the entrance to their newly dug burrows.

OSPREY

This bird of prey feeds entirely on fish.
On the Red Sea coast it has developed the
habit of nesting on the ground, in low bushes
or on uninhabited islands where it will be
undisturbed. Elsewhere it nests high in
the trees.

GOLDEN ACANTHODACTYL

This diurnal lizard is often found on sandy
ground at the foot of mangroves.

The western reef heron builds its
nest in the tallest mangroves.

Western reef heron (white form)

Western reef heron
(dark form)

The green-
backed heron is found in
warmer areas worldwide, including
the Americas.

The white spoonbill nests
on the inaccessible islands of the
Red Sea.

Breeding
plumage

Winter
plumage

Summer
plumage

BLACK-BELLIED PLOVER

This shorebird from the
arctic tundra winters on the
Red Sea coast. It has a black
belly in breeding plumage.

WHITE-EYED GULL

A native of the Red Sea. Almost
two thousand pairs nest on the
islands off the coast of
Hurghada ▲ 267.

HERON

The – strictly coastal –
western reef heron is a
common sight in the
mangrove forests.

31

LORANTHUS ACACIAE
This semi-parasitic plant lives on acacias, the most predominant shrub in the desert.

The Sinai Peninsula constitutes the only land "bridge" between Africa and Asia. The high mountain ranges in the south – which rise to a height of 8,650 feet with Mount Catherine (Jebel Katherina) and 7,497 feet with Mount Sinai (Jebel Musa or Mountain of Moses) – constitute some of the most spectacular scenery in Egypt. The Alpine topography produces exceptional variations in climate, flora and fauna. For example, the average minimum temperature at St Catherine's Monastery is 34°F while the maximum August temperature is 86°F. In the mountains above the monastery the annual precipitation – mainly in the form of snow – can be in excess of 11½ inches.

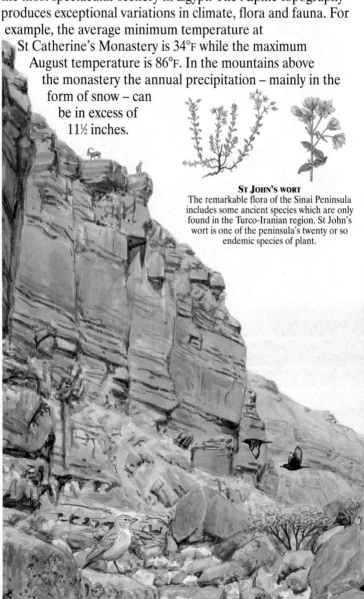

ST JOHN'S WORT
The remarkable flora of the Sinai Peninsula includes some ancient species which are only found in the Turco-Iranian region. St John's wort is one of the peninsula's twenty or so endemic species of plant.

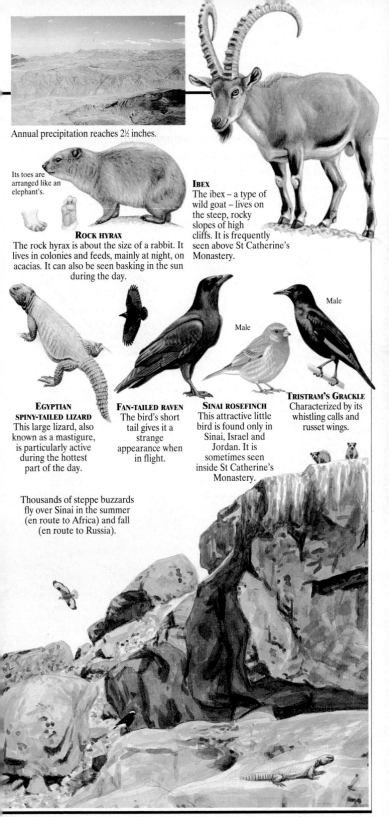

Annual precipitation reaches 2½ inches.

Its toes are arranged like an elephant's.

ROCK HYRAX
The rock hyrax is about the size of a rabbit. It lives in colonies and feeds, mainly at night, on acacias. It can also be seen basking in the sun during the day.

IBEX
The ibex – a type of wild goat – lives on the steep, rocky slopes of high cliffs. It is frequently seen above St Catherine's Monastery.

Male

Male

EGYPTIAN SPINY-TAILED LIZARD
This large lizard, also known as a mastigure, is particularly active during the hottest part of the day.

FAN-TAILED RAVEN
The bird's short tail gives it a strange appearance when in flight.

SINAI ROSEFINCH
This attractive little bird is found only in Sinai, Israel and Jordan. It is sometimes seen inside St Catherine's Monastery.

TRISTRAM'S GRACKLE
Characterized by its whistling calls and russet wings.

Thousands of steppe buzzards fly over Sinai in the summer (en route to Africa) and fall (en route to Russia).

33

SCARAB. The demi-god Khepri took the form or the head of a scarab. The ideogram represents the sound *hpr*.
BEE. Its ideogram represents the sound *bit*.

References to animals and plants were an important part of Ancient Egyptian civilization, whether on bas-reliefs, in the ideograms of hieroglyphs or through the sounds they represented. In addition to their linguistic and philosophical significance, they are also of great scientific interest since they are among the few pieces of historical evidence which provide detailed information on the composition of the flora and fauna which existed in the last few centuries BC.

EGYPTIAN VULTURE (PHARAOH'S CHICKEN)
The Egyptian vulture is a common sight in the desert regions. The vulture goddess Nekhbet (the symbol of Upper Egypt) and the cobra adorned the pharaoh's forehead. The ideogram represented the sound *tyw*.

LANNER FALCON
The god Horus was often represented as a falcon, as were Re, Montu and Sokar (mummified falcon) ● *60*. The ideogram represents the sound *hr(w)*.

GRIFFON VULTURE
The griffon vulture – once common in Egypt – no longer breeds there and is seen only occasionally during migration. The ideogram represents the sound *mwt*.

QUAIL
For some unknown reason the ideogram of the quail chick and not the adult is used to represent the sound *w*.

HORNED VIPER
The horned viper gave its name to the 12th nome of Upper Egypt. Today this nocturnal viper is found in desert regions.

EGYPTIAN COBRA (ASP)
The rearing cobra which adorns the pharaoh's forehead is an angry female cobra, the Delta goddess Wadjet, symbol of Lower Egypt.

HAMADRYAS BABOON. The baboon is not part of Egypt's indigenous fauna, due to the lack of forests and trees. Nevertheless, the Delta god Thoth ● *62* was sometimes depicted as a baboon. The ideogram represents the sounds *nd*, *ky* and *knd*.

HIPPOPOTAMUS. Now disappeared from the Nile Valley, it was considered to be a manifestation of negative forces because it devastated crops. It represented "heaviness", while the female symbolized fertility in the form of the hippopotamus goddess Taweret ● *60*.

White-fronted and red-breasted geese on a bas-relief in an Old Kingdom tomb at Meidum ▲ *357*.

Male

Male

RED-BREASTED GOOSE
Breeding in small numbers in a few places in Siberia , this pretty little goose is today unknown in Egypt as it only winters as far south as the Black Sea. It appears that it used to overwinter in Egypt three thousand years ago.

PINTAIL AND TEAL
Bas-reliefs suggest that these ducks – still seen in Egypt today – were also found in Ancient Egypt, probably in winter.

Breeding plumage

GREATER FLAMINGO. In the past large numbers of flamingos nested in Egypt whereas today they are simply passing visitors. The flamingo symbolizes the sound *dsr*.

SACRED IBIS. The sacred ibis, which represented the god Thoth, is no longer found in Egypt. Although the rare hermit ibis – which symbolized the word "resplendent" – has also disappeared, the glossy ibis still exists.

GREAT CORMORANT
A common winter visitor, particularly on Lake Manzala ● *123*. Its ideogram represents the sound *k*.

GOLDEN JACKAL
The incarnation of the funerary god Anubis, embalmer and guide of the dead ● *61*. Jackals used to haunt the valleys in which the dead were buried. Its ideogram represents the sounds *zb* and *sb*.

WILD CAT
A variety of bob-tailed, wild cats lived in Egypt in Ancient times. The domestic cat appeared in 2100 BC. The cat goddess Bastet ● *62* symbolized femininity and love.

AFRICAN LION. Lions lived in the desert and came to drink and hunt at the mouths of *wadis*, where the temples dedicated to the lion goddess Sekhmet ● *63* are usually found. The sphinx is derived from the lion, the epitome of the royal animal.

DOMESTIC COW
The milch cow, mother and wife of the Sun, was worshipped in the form of Hathor ● *63*. She protected the world and suckled the pharaoh. The hieroglyph for the cow suckling her calf was the symbol of tenderness.

35

■ FAUNA OF THE ARCHEOLOGICAL SITES

SPINY DESERT MOUSE
Although never far from human habitation, this nocturnal mouse is rarely seen.

Most pyramids and temples in Egypt are situated in a desert, and sometimes even a hostile, environment. A particular type of fauna has established itself on these sites which, abandoned by human beings, afford shelter from the heat and a daytime refuge for nocturnal species. The rugged cavities of the rock provide nesting places for certain types of birds, while rodents find enough to live on and in turn provide a source of food for their predators.

BROWN-NECKED RAVEN. Groups of these large birds are often seen wheeling and diving high above the pyramids and temples.

DESERT LARK
A native of hot deserts, this lark is well camouflaged by its dull-colored plumage.

WHITE-CROWNED BLACK WHEATEAR
This bird nests in the nooks and crevices of the stones of Abu Simbel ▲ *464*.

ROCK MARTIN
The pyramids and temples provide an alternative environment for this swallow, usually found near rocks and cliffs.

AGAMA OR GRAY LIZARD
Although this large lizard (up to 8½ inches long) is harmless to human beings, visitors are often alarmed by its size.

HISTORY

PRE-PHARAONIC EGYPT, *38*
THE NILE
IN PHARAONIC TIMES, *46*
LIFE AND DEATH
IN ANCIENT EGYPT, *54*
FROM THE ARAB CONQUEST
TO MODERN TIMES, *66*
LANGUAGE, *72*
RELIGION, *74*

Cartouches of Snefru and Khufu (4th Dynasty).

Egyptology enjoys the paradoxical distinction of being a relatively recent historical science (barely two hundred years old) applied to a field which is as ancient as it is vast. It was first acknowledged as a science when Jean-François Champollion ▲ 216 provided the key to the wealth of texts and inscriptions by deciphering Egyptian hieroglyphs. From then on Egyptologists tried to define the history of Egypt within an exact chronological framework, in spite of the uncertainty which still surrounds the very early periods (up to and including 3000 BC). They grouped the dynasties (royal houses with a common geographical origin and possibly a common line of descent) into periods known as "kingdoms" and "intermediate periods". However, in so doing they in fact used the old dynastic divisions established by the Egyptian priest and historian, Manetho, who lived during the so-called "Greek period". His chronicles on Egypt (of which only fragments have survived) were based on sacerdotal sources which have long since disappeared. But although much more is now known about certain periods, it should not be forgotten that many centuries remain shrouded in mystery.

Pre-Dynastic knife from Jebel el-Arak.

PRE-PHARAONIC EGYPT

Cartouche of Khafre (4th Dynasty).

Vase and figurine of a woman from the Nagada I period.

CIRCA 7000–3100 BC. Egyptian history proper was preceded by a prehistoric period which lasted tens of thousands of years. Increasing numbers of field studies and research projects are constantly renewing and extending our knowledge of this period which had many connections – climatic, hydrological and ecological changes, population migration – with other developing African cultures. Although changes were slow they were continuous and had far-reaching effects. The main constituent traits of what was to become the Egyptian (also known as Pharaonic) civilization and culture – in the fields of politics, religion, technical progress and art – were formed during the period from 7000 to 4000 BC. The Egyptian population – both coherent and heterogeneous as a result of racial intermixing – was also established within a framework which changed very little for several thousand years. It is possible to identify several major stages during this long pre-Dynastic period which tend to take their name from the sites with which they were particularly associated. The best known are the Badarian, Amratian and Gerzean (or Nagada) in the Nile Valley and Merimde and Omari in the Delta region. One of the outstanding characteristics of this pre-Dynastic period was the progressive organization of the country into principalities or "nomes" which were mostly gathered together into two kingdoms: the (culturally dominant) Lower (north) and Upper (south) Kingdoms. This was a period that was marked by numerous wars and challenges to unification before a truly unified, if not united, Egypt finally emerged.

Cartouches of Menkaure (4th Dynasty) and Unis (5th Dynasty).

Circa 3100–2700 BC: Archaic or Thinite period.
Egypt was governed by a single pharaoh who was king of Upper and Lower Egypt. Its constituent elements were organized into a culture which, as a rule, transcended de-centralizing and divergent influences. The birth of writing, after a long period of gestation, had far-reaching consequences. Egypt took its place in History. However, little is known of the first two Thinite Dynasties, so called because the first Thinite pharaohs came from the town of Thinis where they were either entombed or had their cenotaphs. But Memphis ▲ 332, on the border of Upper and Lower Egypt, was soon to play a central role.

Limestone statue of Djoser from the king's funeral complex at Saqqara.

Cartouche of Djoser (3rd Dynasty).

OLD KINGDOM

Circa 2700–2600 BC: 3rd Dynasty.
The reign of Djoser saw the beginning of a period of power and success which was symbolized by the introduction of a spectacular and ambitious stone architecture, illustrated by the impressive complex of the Step Pyramid ▲ 346 at Saqqara. The architect of the complex, the writer and scholar Imhotep remains one of the first great names in history. This period marked the development of a strongly centralized monarchy which governed Egypt from Memphis, controlling the nomes via the nomarchs, or representatives of royal power.

Circa 2600–2450 BC: 4th and 5th Dynasties.
Judging by the magnificence of their pyramids, the reigns of Snefru, Khufu and Khafre (4th Dynasty) would appear to mark the apogee of this period. The construction of the pyramids of Dahshur ▲ 354, Meidum ▲ 357 and Giza ▲ 334 suggests a flourishing and well-organized administration and economy. The 5th Dynasty witnessed the development of a "solar ideology" (Abusir and Abu Ghurob ● 82) and the inscription of the famous Pyramid Texts on the walls of the Pyramid of Unis at Saqqara.

Stele of the Serpent-King (c. 3000 BC) from Abydos.

Cartouche of Tety (6th Dynasty).

Circa 2450–2200 BC: 6th Dynasty.
Although the 6th Dynasty was powerful and well represented in the neighboring regions, and organized military and commercial expeditions to the southern tip of Africa, the increasing power of certain local nomarchs challenged the centralized power of Memphis and led to serious upheavals.

Cartouche of Pepy I (6th Dynasty).

Casket and cylindrical seals of King Mentuhotep.

FIRST INTERMEDIATE PERIOD

Cartouche of Mentuhotep (11th Dynasty).

CIRCA 2200–2050 BC. In less than two hundred years, Egypt experienced what has sometimes been defined as a social revolution, but very little is in fact known about it. Asiatic peoples appear to have controlled part of the Delta region while weak and sometimes overlapping dynasties continued to rule from Memphis, but particularly from Heracleopolis in Middle Egypt ▲ 360 and later from the small town of Thebes ▲ 394 in Upper Egypt. It would seem that, during this period, the monarchy was a victim of the deep-rooted, de-centralizing tendencies of Egyptian society and its "feudal lords" and suffered changes of fortune that had longlasting effects. The progressive development of the concept and practice of funeral rites, according to which the dead were identified with the god Osiris, is one possibility.

MIDDLE KINGDOM

Cartouche of Senwosret III (12th Dynasty).

Black granite statue (right) and cartouche of Amenemhet III (12th Dynasty).

CIRCA 2050–1990 BC: 11TH DYNASTY. With the reunification of Mentuhotep II in c. 2050 BC, the 11th-Dynasty Theban kings ruled over the whole of Egypt. Although this gave their town of origin an increasing prominence it did not detract from the importance of Memphis. In fact the Theban rulers traveled and, during the 12th Dynasty, readily built residences and new towns such as Ity-Tawy at the entrance to the Faiyum ▲ 362. This transfer of power toward the north, without abandoning Thebes, marked the return to strong, centralized government.

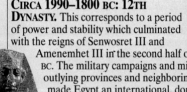

CIRCA 1990–1800 BC: 12TH DYNASTY. This corresponds to a period of power and stability which culminated with the reigns of Senwosret III and Amenemhet III in the second half of the 19th century BC. The military campaigns and mining expeditions to outlying provinces and neighboring countries (which made Egypt an international, dominant and almost imperial power), the development of the Faiyum and its economy, and achievements in its sculpture, architecture and literature made this a classic period (lasting almost two hundred years) whose writings became the authoritative texts of later centuries.

SECOND INTERMEDIATE PERIOD

Statue of Senwosret III.

CIRCA 1800 BC: 13TH DYNASTY. The periods of balance and stability alternated, in Egypt as elsewhere, with periods of unrest. De-centralizing, provincial forces (combined with other factors that have, for the most part, defied historic analysis) helped to undermine the Theban rulers who succeeded their 12th-Dynasty counterparts. Egypt broke up into several kingdoms and principalities.

1730–1530 BC. According to later chronicles and Manetho a large part of Egypt came under the control of the Hyksos, an originally Asiatic people who had settled long before in the Delta region and become "Egyptianized".

They had been joined by new arrivals following the population migrations which occurred in the Near East. From their eastern Delta capital of Avaris the Hyksos rulers proclaimed themselves fully-fledged pharaohs and extended their power to Middle Egypt, even trying to form an alliance with the Nubians in an attempt to weaken the power of the Theban rulers. This partly foreign domination provoked a reaction from Thebes and inspired a feeling of "national identity" among the Egyptians. The wars against the Hyksos (identified with the traditional and continually renewed struggle of the sun god against his enemies and the maintenance of order and their subsequent expulsion, which marked the end of the 17th Dynasty, constituted an event of considerable importance as well as the founding myth for the New Kingdom and beyond.

Scarab seals dating from the Hyksos period.

Cartouche of Thutmose I (18th Dynasty).

Cartouche of Thutmose II (18th Dynasty).

NEW KINGDOM

CIRCA 1550–1350 BC: IMPERIAL EGYPT.

The capture of Avaris by the Theban ruler Ahmose in c. 1530 BC marked the beginning of an extraordinary era of successive or concurrent periods of power, brilliance and crisis in Egypt. A very different Egypt emerged during the 18th Dynasty with the Ahmosids (Thutmose I–IV, Amenhotep I–III and the famous Hatshepsut ▲ 426), which reached the height of its splendor, as well as its breaking point, at the end of the long reign of Amenhotep III (c. 1390–50 BC). The expulsion of the Hyksos and a desire for maximum security soon put the new rulers on a war footing. But these were wars of expansion and acquisition which would guarantee an almost uninterrupted period of prosperity for Egypt lasting for several decades. This was achieved by a policy of direct domination or, more cooperatively, by vassal sovereigns positioned throughout the east as far as the Euphrates, and by expeditions and straightforward annexation in the south. Thebes (at the origin of this period of glory) and Memphis prospered. Trade expanded and acculturation was at its height. The army was extended, but improved living standards meant recruiting foreign mercenaries or levying a colonial force. Certain social groups became increasingly important, particularly the priests of Amun, the god of Thebes. The Temple of Karnak and its dependencies throughout Egypt became a power in their own right and an indispensable ally of the monarchy.

Cartouche and bust of Queen Hatshepsut (18th Dynasty).

The beginning of the New Kingdom heralded a period of exceptional brilliance with regard to civilization, culture and art, as well as the daily life of Egypt's ruling minority.

Cartouche of
Amenhotep IV (18th
Dynasty).

Akhenaten, Nefertiti
and their daughters
worshipping the Aten.

Cartouche of
Ramesses II (19th
Dynasty).

Painted wood coffin
of Ramesses II,
discovered in Thebes
in 1875.

Ramesses II fighting
the Hittites on the
shores of the
Orontes.

CIRCA 1350–30 BC: THE AMARNIAN PERIOD.

Beneath its apparent success lay the elements of a serious crisis, and the eastern Egyptian empire was under threat from the growing power of the Hittites. By his increasingly exclusive worship of the Aten, the physical manifestation of the sun god (which he reinforced by taking the name Akhenaton or Akhenaten), and by progressively distancing himself from Amun and Thebes, Amenhotep IV broke with tradition. This was further aggravated by his foundation of a new capital – Akhetaton (also Akhetaten) – in Middle Egypt ▲ *378* and from which his priests were excluded. During this period Egyptian domination in Syria and Palestine was showing signs of weakening. The reign of Akhenaten stands apart in the history of Egypt, with its theological and artistic innovations. But Akhenaten's successors did not pursue his ideology. The defenders of the old order prevailed, starting with the priests of Amun. The army decided the matter and their commander-in-chief, Horemheb, became pharaoh.

CIRCA 1300–1100 BC: THE RAMESSIDE DYNASTIES.

Ramesses I and Sety I, the rulers from the eastern Delta region who succeeded Horemheb, were also generals. The situation in Egypt had changed and the Hittites had become a force to be reckoned with. The long reign of Ramesses II (a large part of the 13th century BC) represented one of the last periods of Egyptian power. The pharaoh built monuments throughout the country and developed the northern capital of Piramesse (The Estate of Ramesses) near Avaris. During the reign of his son, Merneptah, the situation became even more precarious and external threats (from the Libyans and Sea Peoples) were only just repelled. The 19th Dynasty was overtaken by problems of succession.

Cartouches of Tutankhamun (18th Dynasty), Sety I (19th Dynasty) and Necho (26th Dynasty).

The 20th Dynasty (c. 1200–1100 BC) was dominated by a succession of Ramesses (ending with XI). The only exception in this period of political decline was the reign of Ramesses III. The repulsion of foreign invasions, an increasing number of mercenaries, economic problems, corruption, the increasing influence of the priests of Amun and struggles for succession all added to the weakening of political power.

Cartouche of Taharqa (25th Dynasty) and statue (Tanis).

THIRD INTERMEDIATE PERIOD

CIRCA 1100–750 BC. Although the high priest of Thebes was crowned sovereign, a strong, parallel power was established in Tanis ▲ 226, in the eastern Delta region, which set itself up as the northern equivalent of Thebes. Military commanders who had originally come from Libya also increased their influence and eventually ruled as pharaohs over a fragmented Egypt.

However, extensive architectural and artistic activity proved that political problems were not everything. In spite of a few more successes in the Near East, Egypt suffered the repercussions of the political and military upheavals of its neighbors and became a tempting prey for rival powers.

Statuette of Taharqa worshipping the falcon god, Horus.

CIRCA 750–600 BC: 25TH DYNASTY. The Kushites (inhabitants of Nubia and modern Sudan), steeped in Egyptian culture after centuries of domination and acculturation, finally conquered Egypt under Pi(ankh)y. These southern pharaohs (especially Taharqa) restored Egypt to its former unity and strength. Taharqa was finally defeated by the Assyrians in 664–3 BC.

"LATE" PERIOD

CIRCA 600–525 BC: 26TH DYNASTY. A new dynasty, which originated in the town of Sais ▲ 212, in the Delta region, seized power and gradually managed to free Egypt from Assyrian domination. Although Egypt was once again independent and ruled by indigenous sovereigns, the country was not out of danger and the age of power was over. However the reigns of Necho, Psamtik, Apries and Ahmose were far from marking the decline of Egyptian civilization. In some respects this period has even been referred to as the "Saite renaissance" and one only has to consider its remarkable statuary to understand why. Although no longer a great power, Egypt enjoyed considerable prestige, inspired envy and, like it or not, opened up to the winds of change sweeping the Mediterranean. Greek mercenaries, merchants or simply visitors came flocking to Egypt.

Painted limestone stele of the god Apis, dating from the Late period.

Cat wearing the cartouche of the pharaoh Psamtik I (26th Dynasty).

CIRCA 525–404 BC: 27TH DYNASTY.
The Persian empire exerted its conquering power, Egypt became a satrapy and the rulers of Susa became its new pharaohs.

CIRCA 380–43 BC: 30TH DYNASTY. Renewed efforts for Egyptian independence culminated in the reigns of Nectanebo I and II. But the country continued to remain at the center of Greek and Persian rivalry and became a major strategic and economic asset.

THE GREEK PERIOD

Cleopatra VII (above) and Alexander the Great (right).

332–30 BC. The Persians regained control of Egypt but lost it less than ten years later when it was conquered, along with the rest of the Achemenid empire, by Alexander the Great and the Macedonians in 332 BC, and thus became part of the Greek empire. Alexander, who was legitimized by the oracle of Amun at Siwa ▲ 256, founded the town of Alexandria – destined for a glorious future – on the western coast of the Delta. Alexander's generals shared out his empire and the ancient Land of the Pharaohs fell to Ptolemy, son of Lagos, founder of the Ptolemaic dynasty which ruled Egypt (and occasionally part of the Near East) for three centuries until the last ruler in the Macedonian line, Cleopatra VII, was forced to surrender to Octavian (Augustus) and the Romans in 30 BC.

THE ROMAN PERIOD

30 BC–AD 313. The political change was abrupt. From this point on the seat of government lay beyond Egypt's borders, in Rome. However, for the sake of political expediency, the Roman emperors succeeded in establishing themselves as the successors of the pharaohs, even going as far as to have their names inscribed in a royal cartouche. In fact Egypt became a province which was directly answerable to the emperor. Its strategic and economic importance (among other things as the granary of the Roman empire) were considerable. But many things remained unchanged, particularly at administrative and cultural levels, and with regard to the use of Greek, the language of the ruling classes and elites. Alexandria continued to occupy a prominent position in all respects. Building was still carried on extensively throughout Egypt: sanctuaries and public buildings but also entire new towns which were important in the protection of the *limes* (the fortified frontier of the empire and its glacis). But the Roman empire developed and began to show signs of breaking up. Egypt was not indifferent to the process, particularly as it did not welcome an exploitation which was

Roman emperor represented as a pharaoh (1st century BC).

Statue of the god Osiris.

in many respects colonial. Rebellions were sporadic and often violent. The spiritual crisis represented, in particular, by the development of religions preaching salvation, also affected Egypt, whose ancient, indigenous forms of worship had long been established in a modified form in Rome. The theme of Osiris, the god who died and was resurrected, proved extremely successful and was complemented by the parallel theme of Isis, protectress and comforter, the divine mother of the god Horus. But it was emergent Christianity, initially rejected and eradicated and subsequently accepted and triumphant, that marked the end of the crisis and the break with the ancient world.

Roman mosaic with Nile scenes (1st century BC).

AD 313. Although the Emperor Constantine restored a certain unity within the Roman empire by ending the conflict with Christianity, theological (and political) quarrels were violent, especially with the heresy of Arius which enjoyed a degree of success in Egypt. Arianism finally lost the struggle under Theodosius, whose edict condemning paganism (AD 383) led to the temples being closed or converted into churches. This heralded the end of Ancient Egyptian culture, intrinsically associated with the Pharaonic monarchy (which had long since disappeared) and the temples of the gods which were now either burned or closed.

Title page of the (northern) Bohairic Coptic gospel-book.

THE BYZANTINE PERIOD

AD 395. Egypt became part of the eastern Roman empire. The Mono- versus Dyophysitic dispute (as to whether Christ had one or two natures) and its inherent religious and political implications led to uprisings and the ultimate defeat of Monophysitism. An edict issued by the emperor Justinian in AD 551 ordered the closure of the Temple of Philae ▲ 462 where the last defenders of the pagan faith, protected by the remoteness of Nubia, were still practicing the ancient cults, and the cult of Isis in particular. However, the Monophysites of Egypt joined forces and an indigenous, national church was established: the Coptic Church. Coptic also describes the final stage of the Ancient Egyptian language and the writing used to transcribe it which consisted of the Greek alphabet with seven additional symbols borrowed from the Egyptian demotic script ▲ 219.

The Roman emperor Justinian.

AD 619–40. The power of Byzantium declined and when the Persians invaded Egypt in AD 619 they encountered very little resistance. The process was repeated in AD 639 when Amr Ibn el-As, at the head of the army of the caliph Omar, took Babylon from Egypt ▲ 318. Alexandria fell in AD 640. Egypt became an Arab country and this marked the turning point in its history and the end of Ancient Egypt.

THE NILE IN PHARAONIC TIMES

ABU SIMBEL

WADI ES-SEBUA

QASR IBRIM

MAHARRAQA

DAKKA

DENDUR

KALABSHA

KERTASSI

ELEPHANTINE

DABUD

PHILAE

ASWAN

BAHARIYA

MEDINET MADI

DIONYSIAS

ARSINOE

DIMAI

GIZA

NAUCRATIS

HAWARA

KARANIS

SAQQARA

ILLAHUN

MEMPHIS

HELIOPOLIS

TANIS

PELUSIUM

MADIN

DAKHLA

DUSH

FAR

ABYDOS

LE OF SETY I

ARMANT

ANTÆOPOLIS

JE

SERABIT EL

ALEXANDRIA

BEHBEIT EL-HAGAR

LIFE AND DEATH IN ANCIENT EGYPT
FARMING, HUNTING AND FISHING

Everyday life in Ancient Egypt, governed by the Nile floods which irrigated crops and perpetuated myths, changed very little during the three thousand years of Pharaonic rule. The Egyptians respected their gods and their laws, anxious to ensure an eternal life in the Hereafter and pass on to their children the land and beliefs of their ancestors. From the beginning of the 3rd millennium BC they developed a complete system of written and figurative forms of expression which today constitutes the wealth of information that has enabled Egyptologists to reconstruct the life of these ancient Nile-dwellers. The population, which consisted mainly of peasants, lived under the double law of the Nile and the pharaoh, the respective guarantors of fertility and order. The Nile floods, coupled with the patient toil of the peasant-farmers, brought prosperity to the land of Egypt, while the ebb and flow of the great river determined not only the three four-month seasons of the year but also the main events of the Egyptian calendar.

The beginning of the Egyptian year coincided with the heliacal rising of Sirius, about July 19, and marked the beginning of *akhet* (the season of floods) during which the Nile inundated the

land, covering it with fertile mud. The season of *peret* followed *akhet* four months later, when the waters receded and the land was visible once again, ready for ploughing and sowing.

Fruit trees (figs, date palms, sycamores, acacias and pomegranates) and a wide variety of vegetables (onions, lentils, runner beans, broad beans, chick peas, lettuce, cucumbers, cabbages

and horseradish) grew in abundance in orchards and gardens. Crops shown in ploughing scenes tend to be mainly flax and cereals; men drive teams of oxen.

The Ancient Egyptians were fond of the meat of certain desert animals, which were tracked down in their dens by experienced hunters. Fishing was also an important activity for the inhabitants of the Nile shores and the marshlands of the Delta region. Nearly all the fish caught were edible, and a number of recipes have been found which prescribe a variety of methods for drying, salting and seasoning fish. The papyrus clumps and thickets favored by fishermen were also an ideal place to hunt the noisy flocks of wild ducks and other birds which circled above them.

This was a time of great activity in the fields. There was not a moment to lose. Crops had to be sown and the precious water saturating the land had to be stored.

By careful management of the floods, the Egyptian peasants could dedicate the third, dry season (*shemu*), lasting from mid-March to mid-July, to gathering and harvesting their crops.

Cattle and poultry breeding was also a part of traditional Egyptian iconography. Farmyards abounded with ducks, geese, pelicans and pigeons, which were plucked and roasted on smoking wood fires. Vines occupied pride of place on pergolas and were grown as much for the bunches of grapes as for the wine, which was drunk at family celebrations.

An Egyptian "marriage" was private, unmarked by any ceremony. It took the form of two young people deciding to live together as the concrete expression of their relationship. The house had to be provided by the man, who was responsibl for the respectability of his household.

Houses are thought to have been about 95 square yards in area, made of sun-dried mudbrick. They consisted of four connecting rooms, a kitchen and a terrace.

The furniture of the Ancient Egyptians was simple, and consisted of stools, chairs, beds and storage chests, not forgetting the

Egyptian middle-class houses stood in an airy garden with a pool and consisted of reception rooms, bedrooms and bathrooms.

The Egyptian ideal of a large family not only ensured the social status of the parents but also guaranteed the funerary rites due to their ancestors' and that upon their death their own tombs would be observed. In spite of a high rate of infant mortality, the average family had between four and eight children.

Greeks who came to Egypt after the conquest of Alexander the Great were struck by the fact that Egyptian women enjoyed legally recognized, independent status. In the event of a "divorce", brought about by the breakdown of the relationship for reasons of infertility, adultery or "re-marriage" (for although polygamy was in fact legal, it was not widely practiced), the woman maintained her rights over her inheritance unless she had committed adultery.

uncomfortable but very common wood and stone head-rests which served as pillows.

18th-Dynasty make-up applicator (right).

WRITING. Papyrus sheets, made from the stem of the plant, were prepared using a papyrus-cutter and a smoothing tool. Reeds soaked in black ink, made with smoke-black, were used for writing. An ocher-based red ink was used for headings.

As the custodians of the arts and sciences, scribes stood apart from the peasant majority. Every Egyptian family wanted their sons to become scribes so that they could escape a life of agricultural labor and become servants of the pharaoh's administration. In addition to peasants and scribes, artisans occupied an important position in Egyptian society. The Egyptian vocabulary does not distinguish between the terms "artist" and "artisan" since "art for art's sake" was not an Egyptian concept. Architects, sculptors, painters and goldsmiths all worked to eternalize physical existence and immortalize life in a form that transcended the biological reality.

"Ostraca". *Ostraca* were limestone chips or terracotta shards used to make a sort of "rough draft".

Papyri and cloth scrolls were kept in wooden chests.

Artisans. The Egyptian middle class, created at the end of the Old Kingdom, included artisans whose highly esteemed skills were passed from father to son.

Although Egyptian society recognized the specialist skills of artisans, it did not acknowledge their independence. They were employed by the government, by temples or as part of wealthy households. They worked in workshops, in small groups, and formed corporations headed by high-ranking government officials.

Once a surface was smoothed and leveled for decoration, the designers drew a grid. An outline was sketched and corrected by the team leader. Then the sculptor carved out the relief with his bronze chisel. He was followed by the painter with his palette of colors.

BES
A strangely mutated dwarf,
patron saint of childbirth.

TAWERET
Hippopotamus-goddess of
mothers and children.

RE
Sun-god associated with Horus, who
often assumed the form of a falcon.

RENENUTET
The serpent-goddess who
presided over the harvest.

KHEPRI
Scarab-beetle demiurge
representing the rising sun.

ANUBIS. The embalmer of Osiris who became the patron of embalmers. This jackal-headed god introduced the dead into the other world and watched over their tombs.

SOBEK
The crocodile-god, symbol of fertility.

NUT. Nut, wife of the earth-god, Geb, was the embodiment of the celestial vault. She was the mother of the sun-god Re, swallowing the solar disk in the evening and giving birth to it each morning.

MUT
Goddess of Thebes and consort of Amun.

ASTRONOMICAL CALENDAR. The calendar divides the year into three four-month seasons. The figures below each month represent the stars and planets which appear in the sky at that time of year.

NEKHBET
Vulture-goddess, protectress of Upper Egypt. (Wadjet is the goddess of Lower Egypt.)

NEPHTHYS, ISIS AND OSIRIS
Nephthys, sister of Isis, took part in the ritual protection and resurrection of Osiris, murdered by his brother Seth.

BASTET
The cat-goddess Bastet is the embodiment of joy.

HAPI
The "spirit of the Nile" and the rising waters of the *nun*, the source of all life.

HORUS
The mythical first pharaoh of Egypt and the son of Isis and Osiris.

THOTH
God of wisdom and knowledge, patron of scribes and recorder of the Judgement of the Dead.

PTAH
God of Memphis, where he was believed to be the creator of all things.

HATHOR
Wife of the sun-god Horus. In the form of the cow she was goddess of joy and music.

ALLEGORY OF THE WORLD
The goddess Nut, symbolizing the celestial vault, is arched above the earth represented by the god Geb. The sun-god Re sails between them.

KHNUM
Ram-headed creator of life, who fashioned mankind on his potter's wheel.

MA'AT
Embodiment of universal order and harmony, depicted with a feather on her head.

AMUN
A Theban divinity worshipped during the New Kingdom, who became the supreme god.

SEKHMET
The lion-goddess who unleashes her anger on the last five days of the year.

MIN
God of fertility, represented with an erect phallus, his right arm bent and holding a whip.

FLIGHT OF THE "BA"
The *ba* (spiritual element) left the body of the deceased and was able to wander at will.

MUMMIFICATION
Mummification prevented the decomposition of the earthly remains, enabling the deceased's spiritual and physical elements to be reunited, intact, after death.

FAREWELL CEREMONY
Funeral processions accompanied the deceased to the tomb where they were buried, surrounded by familiar objects likely to add to the comfort of their future life. Such preparations enabled the dead to enter the kingdom of Osiris, god of the Hereafter and symbol of resurrection and rebirth.

SARCOPHAGI
The sarcophagus was placed inside a casket. A door painted on the outer casing enabled the dead to observe the world of the living.

BANDAGING
Bandaging was carried out according to a strict ritual. Embalmers had to recite the appropriate sacred formulae at each stage of the process.

CANOPIC JARS
The stomach, intestines, liver and lungs were removed and preserved in the Canopic jars.

The sarcophagus was taken across the Nile by boat. Once on the far shore the procession went on to the necropolis, where priests performed the customary rites.

"BOOK OF THE DEAD"
This collection of texts (hymns and magic formulae), placed in the tomb, was believed to ensure the survival of the dead in the Hereafter.

JUDGEMENT
The deceased were led by Anubis into the presence of Osiris and his associated gods where they were "judged". First they had to declare themselves innocent of a series of wrong-doings against the gods and mankind. This was followed by the "weighing of the heart" which had to be as light as the feather of Ma'at, goddess of truth and justice. Ammit "the Devourer" waited to consume the deceased if their heart was too heavy. The results were recorded by Thoth.

Abbasid coins from the time of Baybars.

EGYPT UNDER THE ARAB GOVERNORS

540–46
Amr Ibn el-As conquers Egypt.

540
Foundation of Fustat.

642
Fall of Alexandria.

660–750
Ommiad caliphate of Damascus.

706
Arabic becomes the official administrative language.

725
First Coptic rebellion.

750–868
Abbasid caliphate of Baghdad.

868–905
Egypt under Tulunid control.

When Amr Ibn el-As (580–664), who had been sent to Egypt by the caliph Omar, seized the Byzantine fortress of Babylon, he became master of the Nile Valley. The siege of Alexandria (and the destruction of the Great Library) brought the Greek chapter of Egypt's history to a close. Egypt became an Arabic colony administered by governors nominated by the caliphs, and although the first elected caliphate was replaced by the Ommiad dynasty, neither this, nor the subsequent accession of the Abbasids of Baghdad, altered the post-Arab-conquest status of Egypt: it remained a province of the caliphate, mainly organized by the Ommiads who were responsible for imposing Arabic as the language of administration. The introduction of the land tax known as the *kharadj* was accompanied by the widespread Islamization of minor officials. It was during this dynasty that the town of Fustat ▲ *324*, originally the encampment of the conquering Arab tribes, became an important center. A new state was born in Egypt, based (as the Copts discovered) on religion, in which the only way to survive was to embrace the language and faith of the new masters. Although the Copts initially enjoyed greater freedom than they had under Byzantine rule, the heavy taxation incurred by their protected status led to large-scale conversions to Islam.

THE GREAT EGYPTIAN DYNASTIES

879
Inauguration of the Ibn Tulun Mosque.

905–36
Baghdad regains direct control of Egypt.

936–69
Egypt under Ikshidid control.

969–1169
Egypt under Fatimid control.

969
Foundation of El-Qahira.

Salah ad-Din's cavalcade (right and below).

THE TULUNIDS. The political and artistic history of Muslim Egypt really began with Ahmed Ibn Tulun (835–84) ▲ *312*, who seized power in 868. For almost four centuries after this, a series of dynasties, including several of foreign origin, established themselves firmly in Egypt. The struggle with the caliphate of Baghdad brought about the collapse of the Tulunids (who were originally only governors). But the rivalries which divided the caliphate brought new masters to the country. These were the Turkman Mohammed Ibn Tuglij, who was founder of the Ikshidid dynasty, the Fatimids, who were the new masters in North Africa, and the Ayyubids, whose empire extended as far as Syria. The crises associated with the Crusades highlighted changing alliances and the possibilities of autonomy. Fustat, which was Egypt's key town, was later re-founded by the Fatimids.

THE FATIMIDS. Royal palaces and mosques were built to the north of Fustat, where the Fatimids founded El-Qahira ("the Triumphant One"). Egypt subsequently became one of the centers of international trade. Warehouses, palaces and

Map of Egypt from the manuscript of El-Idrissi (12th century).

mosques provide evidence of the dynamic exchanges that took place in spite of the internal crises of the Fatimid regime and the despotic reign of the sultan El-Hakim (985–1021) ▲ 291 in particular. The Fatimids also made Cairo the capital of a Shi'ite caliphate, an occupation which led to a complete break with ancient traditions (although it did foster, for a while at least, remarkable intellectual activity). The subsequent return to power of the Sunni Muslims, who were led by Salah ad-Din el-Ayyubi, or Saladin (1138–93), did not destroy these achievements. Salah ad-Din built the imposing Citadel ▲ 304 which stands above Cairo on the boundary between the Tulunid and Fatimid cities. He also encouraged the development of the great medersa ● 112, which were religious colleges.

THE MAMELUKE EMPIRE IN EGYPT

Under the Mameluke sultans Egypt experienced another brutal revolution linked to the attacks of the Crusaders that the last of the Ayyubids were unable to repel. Baybars founded a regime which lasted for almost three centuries and presented some very distinctive characteristics: Turkish and Circassian soldiers who maintained a non-hereditary power until the end of the 14th century and who, in spite of their bloody power struggles and famed violence, created the only great modern Egyptian empire. In addition to stability of power the Mamelukes also ensured the prosperity and greatness of Egypt and Cairo, especially during the 14th century. As protectors of the Abbasid caliph and the two holy cities of Arabia, the Mamelukes, a vast foreign legion, became indissolubly linked to the history of Egypt, expressing their influence through the magnificence of their palaces and mosques. Above and beyond their defeat by the Ottomans, they continued to be the true masters of Egypt until the accession of Mohammed Ali in the 19th century. The majority of the indigenous Egyptian population had been of the Muslim faith since the 13th century and eventually seemed more Arabian than their Bahrite and North African masters, who were soldiers from the Black Sea or the outlying parts of the Empire.

1167
Frankish support to prevent the Syrians conquering Egypt.

1169–1250
Ayyubid control.

1169
Restoration of Sunni Islam.

1193
Death of Salah ad-Din.

1249
Louis IX of France (St Louis) lands at Damietta (Seventh Crusade).

1251–1382
Bahrite Mamelukes.

1260
Baybars comes to power.

1279
Qala'un becomes sultan.

1291
St John of Acre is captured.

1366
Alexandria is plundered by Pierre de Lusignan.

1382–1517
Circassian Mamelukes.

1382
Sultan Barquq comes to power.

1467
Qaitbay becomes sultan.

1501
Sultanate of Qansu el-Ghuri.

Inauguration of the Suez
Canal: arrival of the
imperial yacht, *L'Aigle*,
at Ismaïliya.

1517–1798: EGYPT, AN OTTOMAN PROVINCE

1517
Selim conquers Egypt.

1524
*Egypt's new status:
administered by a
pasha.*

1528
*Renewal of the
capitulations of 1507.*

1569
*Sinan Pasha's
expedition to the
Yemen.*

1623
*First overt rebellions
against Istanbul.*

Alexandria captured
by Napoleon
Bonaparte.

1707
*Mameluke conflicts in
Cairo.*

1725
*Rebellions and loss of
pashas' authority.*

1765–98
*Mameluke opposition
to the Ottomans.*

1768
*Ali Bey separates
Egypt from the
Ottoman empire.*

When the Mameluke regime fell to the Ottomans Egypt once again became a province, a status which had never before been so clearly defined. The Ottomans mistrusted Egypt's autonomous aspirations and installed a *pasha*, an administrative governor, while the *aga,* or commander, of the Janissaries was responsible for the military. Egypt suffered crises or enjoyed long periods of prosperity according to the particular *pasha* appointed. In real terms the reins of power were held by the *beys* of Cairo, supported by an army that included a large body of Mamelukes who thus recovered much of their former power. During the 18th century the latter were the true masters of Egypt, at a time when Egypt was playing a less prominent role in the history of the eastern Mediterranean, although its continued economic prosperity

was borne out by its architecture as well as the account books of local merchants. Egypt's early commercial links with Europe served as a further indication of this sustained vitality. The accession of Ali Bey, however, in the second half of the 18th century, plunged Egypt into anarchy and left the country teetering on the brink of economic strangulation. The appearance of Bonaparte's fleet on July 1, 1798 came as a complete surprise, and the last Ottoman *pasha* barely had enough time to flee the country.

1798–1805: EUROPEAN INTERLUDE

1773
Death of Ali Bey.

1786
*An Ottoman fleet is
sent to Alexandria.*

1788
*The beys' return to
power is followed by
anarchy.*

Mohammed Ali.

1798–1803
*French
occupation.*

1803–5
*Political
vacuum. British
presence.*

The main advantage of the French presence was that it enabled Egypt to complete the break with Istanbul, even though it nominally remained an Ottoman province until 1914. It also facilitated the establishment of the initial elements of a centralized administration and an awareness of the importance of Egypt's past. The French occupation was too short-lived to make a lasting impression, however. It led, above all, to the installation of mercenaries sent from Istanbul to restore a basic level of order. They included Mehemet-Ali (Mohammed Ali) (1769–1849), the son of a tobacco merchant from Kavala, in Epirus, who seized power after the withdrawal of British troops. Mohammed Ali was the leader of an army of mercenaries who almost became emperor . . . but instead became viceroy.

1805–49: MOHAMMED ALI

After he had successfully managed to eliminate the last of the Mamelukes, Mohammed Ali played the part of the sultan's faithful servant. He went to Mecca to combat the Wahhabi "heretics", and he restored order in the rest of Egypt and conquered the Sudan. In 1819 he began to form a conquering army, officially to restore the sultan's authority in Greece and Syria, but clearly intended to be used to conquer the entire Ottoman empire. The fundamental reforms carried out in Egypt made the country a model of social and economic development. The Syrian campaign, however, finally provoked an international response. With the support of Great Britain the sultan managed to obtain Mohammed Ali's surrender, in return for which he was offered the hereditary viceroyalty of Egypt. Mohammed Ali's dynasty lasted until 1952.

1831
Syrian campaign.

1840–1922: BRITISH CONTROL

Mohammed Ali's successors were the prisoners of new international relations. Egypt's frontiers had been opened by a free-trade treaty and no longer protected the national economy. The construction of the Suez Canal ▲ 228 pushed the country into an economic dependency which was further aggravated by the cotton boom. Paradoxically the inauguration ceremonies of the Suez Canal in 1869 marked the end of an era and placed the finances of Egypt under Franco-British supervision. The national reaction precipitated the British bombardment of Alexandria and occupation of Cairo. Although Egypt's political and administrative structures remained officially intact, the country was effectively placed under the direct control of Europe. British control assumed two (successive) forms. Until 1914 Egypt remained an Ottoman province, governed by a virtually independent viceroy but under British supervision. In 1914 all links with Istanbul were finally severed but, although Egypt became a monarchy, British control became official and Egypt was declared a protectorate. At the same time this control brought about an unusual political calm. Egypt became a veritable Mediterranean retreat and entered a period of great prosperity and

1862
Cotton boom.

1875
Franco-British financial control.

1881
Orabi Pasha's nationalist movement.

1882
British occupation.

Battle of Tell el-Kebir.

1902
First Aswan Dam.

1907–8
The first Egyptian nationalist parties are founded.

1914
British protectorate.

1919
Saad Zaghlul's national revolution.

Banner used in a demonstration by Egyptian women at the opening of the first Parliament in December 1924.

INSTRUISEZ VOS FILLES RESPEC-TEZ LES DROITS DE VOS FEMMES PAR LA FEMME ON JUGE DE LA CIVILISATION D'UN PEUPLE.

Egyptian ministers in December 1924 and Saad Zaghlul.

modernization. The Egyptian social elite grew rich and became aware of their need for independence. In 1907 they formed multicultural, liberal nationalist parties whose members were united in their rejection of the British presence. World War One was scarcely over when their leader, Saad Zaghlul ▲ 281, declared his intention of demanding full independence for Egypt. The British refusal to receive his delegation (*wafd*) provoked a series of disturbances and strikes. After three years of delays and excuses Great Britain finally decided to declare the end of the protectorate, but the British occupation and control of Egypt continued.

1922–52: LIBERAL EGYPT

1922
End of the protectorate. Fuad I becomes king.

1928
Muslim brotherhoods founded.

1936
Anglo-Egyptian treaty.

1949
Defeat in the war against Israel.

The years that followed were known as Egypt's "liberal" era. The Wafd Party made repeated efforts to renegotiate and find an area of common ground with the British, finally succeeding in 1936. The multicultural Egyptian society of the 19th century was gradually disappearing and local elites were clearly Egyptian. However an increasingly corrupt regime condemned the ideology of the liberal model. The voice of Islam was raised in protest and the Muslim brotherhoods were born. Those in power sought legitimacy via the struggle with Israel and the creation of the Arab League, but the contradictions were too obvious and the defeat of 1949 too bitter. Individual acts of violence were followed by riots and, in 1952, the Cairo fire emphasized the powerlessness of the government. Within six months, a few young officers had taken over, abolishing the monarchy before taking up the reins of power. For the first time in its history, the future of Egypt was in the hands of the "sons of Nile *fellaheen*".

1952–70: THE NASSER YEARS

The 1973 Arab-Israeli War.

1952
The Cairo fire and the Free Officers' coup d'état.

1956
Suez Crisis.

The movement away from "liberal" Egypt took place gradually. After offering power to Mohammed Nejib (1901–84), Colonel Gamal Abd el-Nasser (1918–70) assumed total power in 1954 and became the representative of the Third-World countries in Bandung. He declared independence for the Sudan and obtained the departure of the last of the British troops before announcing the nationalization of the Suez Canal, his response to the American refusal to finance the

NOUS SOMMES PRETS !

construction of the Aswan High Dam ▲ *460*. Continued tension led to the military operation of October 1956 which ended with the withdrawal of the combined Israeli, French and British forces and the radicalization of the Egyptian regime, expressed internally by nationalization and the execution of the Muslim brotherhoods, and externally by expulsions and projects for Arab unions. Nasser became the mouthpiece of the Arab world and, in this capacity, prioritized the war with Israel. The Six-Day War in June 1967 ▲ *234* dealt the final blow. Nasser was maintained in power by popular demand but died just as a truce had finally been agreed. However, Arab socialism also brought radical economic changes: there were more big industrial projects, and large towns destroyed the agricultural balance of the Nile Valley. In 1970, in spite of Soviet counsel, Egypt was unable to meet its accumulated deficits and imbalances.

Gamal Abd el-Nasser.

1960
Nationalization.

1961
Agricultural reform.

1967
Six-Day War.

1970
Nasser dies.

1971
Inauguration of the Aswan High Dam.

1972
Expulsion of Soviet advisors.

1973
Fourth Arab-Israeli (October) War.

1974
"Open door" policy.

Camp David Agreements.

1971–81: U-TURNS

This series of difficulties led Egypt to turn to the West and the new Gulf States. Anwar el-Sadat (1918–81) began to open up the economy to the West (*infitah*). By liberalizing the markets he risked destabilizing the middle classes on whose support Nasser had depended, but he intended to counter this weakness with rapid economic growth. Peace with Israel was a vital part of the process and the fourth Arab-Israeli War in October 1973 ▲ *235*, in which neither side managed to procure victory, provided an opportunity for the necessary negotiations which ended with the Camp David Agreements and the return of Sinai to Egypt. An economic upturn, however, was not forthcoming; or at least not for everyone. Inequalities became more pronounced and gave rise to violent social tensions. The Islamic movements re-emerged and Sadat paid with his life.

AT THE CROSSROADS. From this point onward Egypt has tried to overcome its contradictions. The peace with Israel did not prevent its reintegration into the Arab-Muslim camp. Its neighbors are intent on avoiding a destabilization which could plunge the region into uncontrollable chaos. Meanwhile the number of Western loans is increasing, accompanied by a policy of liberalization and control. But growing social unrest is matched by the mounting strength of the Islamic groups which represent the only form of structured opposition. Although briefly tempted by reconciliation, the government of Hosni Mubarak has been forced to adopt a confrontational stance since 1990. Today Egypt stands at a crossroads.

1978
Camp David.

1981
President Sadat is assassinated.

1981
The Sharia becomes the primary source of judicial law.

1991
Confrontations between Copts and Muslims.

1992
Demonstration over the cost of living.

Bilingual Coptic prayer book. The text written in the right-hand column is in Arabic, while the left-hand column is in Coptic.

FROM COPTIC TO ARABIC

The Arab conquest represents a fundamental break in the history of Egypt which is reflected in its language. During the next thousand years Arabic spread throughout Egypt, not only keeping pace with conversions to Islam but also explaining them. In 706 Arabic became the language of official documents. Whereas the early conquerors had Coptic prayers translated to ensure that they were not offensive to Islam, the lessons of the Scriptures, which, during services, were read in Greek and explained in Coptic, were soon read in Coptic and explained in Arabic. Coptic became a devotional language, which saved it from oblivion but did not prevent its irreversible decline. It was only kept alive by the monastic tradition. Place names are the only surviving evidence of the Coptic revenge on the Greeks during the Arab conquest: Akhmim ▲ 383 and Ashmunein, for example, both take their origin from their original Coptic names. The Jewish community was also Arabized, since from the 19th century onward commercial texts were written in Judeo-Arabic, which is Arabic that has been transcribed into Hebrew characters.

Covers of novels written in Arabic by Naguib Mahfouz ● 160. Although he makes extensive use of the Cairene dialect, his novels are read throughout the Arab world.

CLASSICAL AND DIALECTICAL ARABIC

As a result, Egypt became one of the main centers of Arabic culture, as evidenced not only by an extremely active academy of the Arabic language but also by the screening of Egyptian films in cinemas throughout the world. The growing importance of the Nile Valley, bordered by Arab countries, has finally relegated the traditional division between classical and dialectical Arabic to a position of secondary importance. But as well as being understood well beyond Egypt's natural borders (a phenomenon largely due to the media), this Arabic dialect also has a written form. The work of Naguib Mahfouz, winner of the Nobel Prize for Literature, is a famous example: his extremely "classical" approach is interspersed with many so-called "Egyptianisms". Opposition to this predominance of dialect is either ideological or political. For example, the language of the Koran must be jealously protected because it alone can strengthen the union of all Arabs, be they Muslim or non-Muslim. It should be pointed out, however, that the debate on the "levels of language" is, generally speaking, inappropriate. On the one hand modern classical Arabic is significantly different from the language of the Koran and, on the other, the dialects have borrowed from the terms and structures of modern Arabic. Apart from that, all that remains are the phonetic and semantic differences which make it possible to distinguish between the dialects of Upper and Lower Egypt, and the relative poverty or richness of vocabulary according to social class and background.

A MULTILINGUAL SOCIETY

In spite of the absolute dominance of Arabic, several European languages are strongly represented. Most well-to-do Egyptian families are bi- or even tri-lingual. The education system and the legacy of liberal Egypt are mainly responsible. In the 19th century French enjoyed second-language status in Egypt and was used in mixed courts and all administration. It was only between 1936 and 1949 that all references to French, English and Italian were excluded from official documents. However, the future of these multilingual skills, which constitute one of the riches of Egyptian culture, is guaranteed by religious teaching establishments and language schools.

THE TWENTY-EIGHT LETTERS OF THE ALPHABET.
From top to bottom, starting on the left: alif, ba, ta, tha, jim, ha, kha, dal, zal, ra, za, sin, shin, sad, daad, ta, za, aïn, ghaïn, fa, qaf, kaf, lam, min, nun, ha, waw, ya.

73

THE COPTIC CHURCH

A few traces of Egypt's ancient religious traditions have survived. Although the "Night of the Tear" has disappeared with the Nile floods, the Festival of Spring is

Since the 12th and 13th centuries Egypt has been a predominately Muslim country. As the number of Arab garrisons increased the Coptic Christians gradually converted to Islam, often to escape the financial penalties and social restrictions imposed on non-Muslims. Initially the Coptic Church welcomed the Arabs, who were seen as liberators.

still celebrated throughout Egypt, and in Luxor the Nile boatmen still carry the barque of their saint just as the Ancient Egyptians carried the sacred barque of Amun ▲ 408. But these surviving remnants are few and far between. Saint Mark preaching in Alexandria (above).

The adoption of the Monophysite doctrine was probably, and primarily, a means of opposing the Byzantines who, by way of reprisal, gradually closed the Coptic churches and monasteries. By marginalizing Alexandria's Hellenized (Jewish and Greek) elite and maintaining local administration, the Arabs enabled the exiled bishops to return to their sees, allowing freedom of worship and authorizing synods. The burden of financial penalties and the increasingly clear affirmation of Muslim sovereignty ruined many monasteries and led to rebellions and conversions. Christians had to wear a distinguishing mark, and the rebuilding of ruined churches was forbidden. There were several mass conversions (in particular in 725, 832 and 1171), which continued throughout the following centuries, with another significant conversion in Upper Egypt in 1750. Since the 13th century the Copts have tended to congregate in Middle and Upper Egypt.

The Coptic abbot Shenute officiating at a Christmas mass in a Coptic church.

ISLAM IN EGYPT

The Sunni branch of Islam was subsequently imposed throughout Egypt. In spite of two centuries of Shi'ite domination (969–1169) by the Fatimids, Egyptian Islam was an orthodox form whose principal rite was that of the Shafi'ite school. The only remaining Shi'ites were the Persian traders in Cairo. The El-Azhar ▲ 294 Mosque perpetuated this

At prayer in the mosque (right) and a prayer mat embroidered with the one hundred names of Allah (below).

orthodox form of Islam by educating most of the doctors of Islamic law (*ulama*) destined to become prayer leaders in Egypt. From the Mameluke period onward, the major issues that had troubled Islam in its early stages were resolved. Religious teaching decided on its line of approach and mystical theology was included in the technical and moral teaching disseminated by the intermediaries of the *ulama* class. The Jewish and Christian minorities enjoyed a clearly defined protected status.

FRACTURES AND DIVISIONS

This balance was maintained until the 19th century, which saw the abolition of protected status for Armenian orthodox minorities by Mohammed Ali in an attempt to guarantee their support, and the sudden arrival of the European powers in Egypt, who introduced a number of new and competitive religious communities.

RELIGION

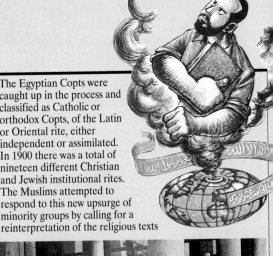

"El-Azhar was gradually waking up, roused from its torpor by the sound of the sheikhs' voices as they taught their lessons, punctuated by the discussions that arose, often acrimoniously, between them and their pupils. The students crowded round, voices were raised, sounds became merged and

The Egyptian Copts were caught up in the process and classified as Catholic or orthodox Copts, of the Latin or Oriental rite, either independent or assimilated. In 1900 there was a total of nineteen different Christian and Jewish institutional rites. The Muslims attempted to respond to this new upsurge of minority groups by calling for a reinterpretation of the religious texts

the sheikhs were obliged to raise their voices even higher in order to make themselves heard. They were sometimes even forced to adopt stentorian tones to pronounce the phrase 'God is all-knowing', which brought the lesson to a close."

Taha Hussein

and the modernization of the Islamic doctrine. Two main fracture lines were appearing around the constitution of the national movement, however: on the one hand, opposition between Egyptians (Copts and Muslims) and foreigners and, on the other, the less apparent opposition between Muslims and other groups. There seemed to be an initial movement away from a liberal Egypt toward Nasser's Egypt. Religious matters were relegated to a position of secondary importance as successive regimes became increasingly secular in outlook, in spite of a very strong Islamic representation.

DEMANDS OF ISLAM. With the creation of the Muslim brotherhoods in 1928, the religious demands of Islam were very much in evidence, reaching a climax in the early 1980's when Islamic law was declared the primary source of judicial law. A parallel Coptic movement was established, while the expulsions of the Nasser regime considerably reduced the status of other communities. In 1956 the disappearance of the ancient Jewish community, the direct descendant of Alexandrian gnosis, was closely linked to the development of Islam. Against this background the future of the Coptic Church in Egypt and its four million worshippers became the symbol of Islamic-Christian cohabitation. It encountered increasingly bitter antagonism from the Islamic groups, who favored a return to the original hierarchy that recognized the protected status but not the equality of other religious groups. It should, however, be remembered that this exclusive form of Islam is in the minority, while the brotherhoods (*turuq*) and traditional structures of Azharist Islam continue to be the mainstays of religion in Egypt.

FRIDAY PRAYERS AT THE EL-HUSSEIN MOSQUE
Friday is a public holiday in Egypt and the day when Muslims gather at the mosque for their weekly prayer meeting.

ARCHITECTURE

PHARAONIC ARCHITECTURE
CONSTRUCTION TECHNIQUES, 78
RELIGIOUS ARCHITECTURE, 82
FUNERARY ARCHITECTURE, 86
CIVIL ARCHITECTURE, 90
MILITARY ARCHITECTURE, 92
HISTORY OF EXCAVATIONS, 94
RESTORATION TECHNIQUES, 102

COPTIC MONASTIC ARCHITECTURE, 106

ISLAMIC ARCHITECTURE
MOSQUES, 108
RELIGIOUS ESTABLISHMENTS, 112
FUNERARY ARCHITECTURE, 114
DOMESTIC ARCHITECTURE, 116
"WAKALA", 118

The earliest Egyptian constructions, which dated from the end of the Neolithic age, appear to have been made of branches and wattle daubed with clay. There is evidence to suggest that brick was used to build houses in c. 4000 BC. The desire to create "mansions of eternity" for their dead led the Egyptians to replace mudbrick with stone in the funerary architecture of the Thinite period, a process which culminated in the construction of the funerary complex of Djoser at Saqqara in c. 2700 BC. From then on stone was used in all funerary architecture, while brick continued to be used for more utilitarian structures. Egyptian technology in the field of architecture was thus established during the Old Kingdom and lasted until the Roman period.

MAKING MUDBRICK
The coarse impurities were removed from the clay soil, which was mixed with water to form a paste. Straw or grass was added to the paste to limit shrinkage and prevent cracking during drying. The mixture was kneaded, molded and dried in the sun.

BRICK
During the annual floods the Nile carried and deposited the silt used to make bricks, thus providing a simple and inexpensive material for domestic architecture. The Egyptians used different types of bonding, such as that based on regular curves (above). Two types of roof were used in mudbrick architecture: the flat roof and the softfitless vault.

Today it is possible to date excavated remains more accurately using the cartouches found on the bricks.

SOFTFITLESS VAULT
By using bricks added in successive, sloping layers it was possible to construct a softfitless vault. The arched vault was not transposed into stone architecture.

FLAT ROOFS
Flat roofs were made from reeds placed across beams and covered with clay.

STONE QUARRIES

Stone was extracted from two types of quarries, which were often a long way from the building site. Hard rock (sandstone and granite) was extracted from open quarries and soft rock (limestone and tufa) from closed quarries. The quarriers chipped out a groove along the line of the blocks to be extracted. Wooden wedges were then inserted and kept well soaked so that they swelled and shattered the stone, separating it from the rock face. The blocks were then rough hewn and taken to the point of embarkation.

Well-soaked wooden wedges were used to shatter the stone.

TRANSPORTING OBELISKS

According to an account by Pliny – and contrary to the symbolic representation (below) – the Nile floods were used to transport obelisks, which were carried submerged between two boats. This reduced their weight by one third.

On sandy or stony ground the sled was pulled over wooden rollers.

On clay soil the ground was soaked to make it slide more easily.

CONSTRUCTION TECHNIQUES

WATER LEVEL
The Egyptians used water and the principle of communicating vessels to ensure that foundations were horizontal.

LEVELING
A channel, which was either built of clay or hewn out of the rock, was dug around the perimeter of the site and filled with water to determine the overall horizontal level.

Secondary channels were also built to create a second point of reference. A cord and two stakes made it possible to apply this horizontal to any point on the site.

FOUNDATIONS
Once the horizontal was established, it was a matter of leveling the rock or building low, parallel brick walls and filling the space between them with sand to the required level.

1   2   3

BONDING
The Egyptians used a regular, isodomous type of bonding with (mortarless) open butt joints (1). Where economy was a priority, due to the need to transport the stone, irregular bonding was used (2). For wide walls (pylons) a dry-stone infill was used between two facings (3).

ERECTING AN OBELISK
The obelisk was hoisted horizontally, by means of a continuous series of balanced levers, onto a purpose-built platform which incorporated a sand-filled groove. The block was raised to its vertical position by draining away the sand on which it rested. Under the effect of its own weight, the obelisk gradually righted itself and slid into place. The most delicate operation involved removing the sled which separated it from its pedestal. This was done by using sacks of sand which were gradually emptied.

TOOLS

Most of the tools used for cutting and hewing stone were made of copper or diorite (a very resistant stone). A wooden level square, a vertical level, diorite chisels, a mallet, a brace, a wedge and a cord, which was used for marking out and measuring (above).

LIGHTING

To create enclosed spaces the Egyptians used light from the roof rather than the façade. The light filtered in through gaps or stone tracery.

CEILINGS

Ceilings were made of flagstones. The span of the flags was no greater than the size of the stones used (13–16 feet). A system for draining away water was introduced during the Late period.

CONSTRUCTION

The Egyptians had a limited number of lifting mechanisms at their disposal. The simplest way of raising stone blocks was by means of a ramp which was built using successive layers of sand infill.

Each layer of sand corresponded to a layer of blocks and the height of the ramp increased with each new layer. The last two layers consisted of lintels and flagstones together, which formed the ceiling.

FINISHINGS

The building was gradually cleared so that the finishing of the columns and decoration of the walls could be carried out from the ceiling downward. The fragile bas-reliefs, reserved for the interior walls, were rough-hewn with an adz, carved with copper, wood and stone tools and finally polished with an abrasive paste.

Religious Architecture in Pharaonic Egypt

Archaic chapels, the predecessors of the naos.

The temple was both the house of a particular god and a symbolic representation of the universe. The columns with their plant-inspired decorations symbolized the terrestrial world which supported the cosmic world, represented by starred ceilings. The focal point of the edifice evoked the place where the universe was created and where the divinity resided. The sacred precinct was isolated by an enclosure wall. There were two main types of temple: the open, solar temples of the Old Kingdom (which have mostly disappeared) and the so-called "classic" temples, with enclosed sacred areas, which are typical of the New Kingdom and subsequent periods.

Alabaster altar, situated in the center of the court in front of the obelisk, at Abu Ghurob. The four offering tables faced the four points of the compass.

TEMPLE OF ABU GHUROB
(1st Dynasty)
The temple, built by Niuserre on the edge of the desert, consists of an obelisk (115 feet) standing on a truncated, pyramidal base (65 feet). The complex is surrounded by an enclosure wall (360 feet x 262 feet) and is reached via a triple-porticoed access temple and an ascending causeway. About 30 yards to the south is a painted brick replica of a barque.

82

TEMPLE OF MENTUHOTEP AT DEIR EL-BAHRI (11th Dynasty)

The sepulcher of Mentuhotep introduced a new dimension to funerary architecture.

An access ramp leads to the two terraces supported by square-columned porticos. It is thought that the

complex was once surmounted by a pyramid. To the west was a temple reserved for private worship

which consisted of a sanctuary and a hypostyle hall as well as a porticoed court.

TEMPLE OF QASR ES-SAGHAH (Middle Kingdom) This incomplete sanctuary to the north of the Faiyum ▲ 361 has retained its archaic appearance: its limestone bonding consists of alternate header and front blocks. Inside the seven adjacent chapels are flanked by pillars.

TEMPLE OF MEDINET MADI (12th Dynasty)
This small temple, built to the south of the Faiyum ▲ 361 by Amenemhet III and Amenemhet IV, is the only Middle-Kingdom temple that can be dated with any certainty. It is less than 33 feet wide. It was dedicated to Sobek, god of the Faiyum, and Renenutet, goddess of the harvest ● 60. A portico with two papyrus columns and closed capitals precedes the sanctuary hall where three niches contain statues of the divinities.

KIOSK OF SENWOSRET I AT KARNAK
(12th Dynasty)
The kiosk or barque shrine was discovered by Henri Chevrier inside one of the pylons of the Great Temple of Amun-Re ▲ 404. This beautifully proportioned edifice, with grooved cornices and square pillars, was designed to

act as a "way station" during processions. The sacred barque was carried up the slipway situated in the center of the steps. With its four rows of sixteen pillars decorated with religious scenes, the kiosk foreshadowed the temples of later periods.

83

RELIGIOUS ARCHITECTURE IN PHARAONIC EGYPT

The naos of Horus at Edfu. From the Late period onward, naos were constructed from stone and monoliths.

TEMPLE OF KHONSU AT KARNAK ▲ *412*
The sandstone structure (246 x 98 feet) was built toward the end of the reign of Ramesses III, on the site of a temple dating from the reign on Amenhotep III. The sloping, outer walls surrounded a closed area whose architecture was dedicated to the service of things sacred.

With the establishment of a colonial empire (New Kingdom), the religious domain became increasingly wealthy. Amun, divine protector of Thebes, became the imperial divinity of Egypt, and his priests of Amun enjoyed significant political power. Mudbrick buildings and annexes (warehouses, silos, stables, schools and accommodation) were added to the temples. The religious complex became an economic, cultural and political center which played an important part in everyday life. The Temple of Khonsu in Karnak provided the archetype for temples which prevailed until the Byzantine period.

PYLON
The pylon formed the façade of the temple and consisted of two piers closed by a monumental gate, symbolizing the horizon.

ESPLANADE
The esplanade or colonnade which preceded the pylon was used to celebrate the rites of entry, which could be attended by ordinary citizens.

Hypostyle hall

1st court

The campaniform capitals of the Ptolemaic period can be simple or multilobate. Several rows of papyrus umbels are carved on the bell of the capital, while their stems and the cord which binds them are carved on the shaft of the column.

RAMESSEUM (20th Dynasty)

The Osiride colossi which punctuate the façade of the Ramesseum ▲ *432* are an indication of the funerary nature of the Temple of Ramesses II.

HYPOSTYLE HALL
A raised portico opens onto the hypostyle hall which was reserved for divine appearances.

DIVINE APARTMENTS
These included the shrine of the ceremonial barque, a vestibule lit by a light well and the naos containing the god's statue.

"DROMO"
The monumental causeway leading to the Temple of Khonsu was guarded by stone crio-sphinxes (sphinxes with rams' heads).

COURT
The court was the public part of the temple where the elite were admitted during festivals. It was surrounded by a double row of columns, whose papyrus capitals were decorated with closed buds.

TEMPLE OF THE ATEN AT TELL EL-AMARNA

The political and religious reforms of Amenhotep IV imposed the Aten as the unique and universal solar god. The king revived the principle of the cult of ancient Heliopolis in an open-air temple consisting of two main sections: the "jubilee house" (*per haï*), with a pylon and a sixteen-columned hypostyle hall, and the "discovery of the Aten" (*Gem Aten*), consisting of six consecutive courts with three hundred and sixty-five offering tables. The elongated proportions of the temple, which was constructed from small stone blocks (*talatat*) reflect a new architectural concept ▲ *378*.

2nd court   3rd court   4th court   5th court   6th court

Necropolises were always set apart from the world of living and were situated outside the towns and cities, on the edge of the desert. The very first tombs consisted of an underground burial chamber and a superstructure for the purpose of funeral worship. The form of the proto-Dynastic tombs, constructed in perishable materials, was reproduced in the brick mastabas (bench-like tombs) of the Thinite period. From the 3rd Dynasty onward the use of stone and research into the superposition of several mastabas resulted in the development of the pyramids, which were still exclusively royal.

During the Middle Kingdom mastabas were replaced by rock tombs.

CENOTAPH OF QUEEN MER-NEITH AT UMM EL-QA'AB (1st Dynasty) These so-called royal burials in the region of Abydos ▲ *386* are surrounded by secondary tombs.

The mudbrick superstructure, which no longer exists, was probably in the form of a tumulus.

The entrance was flanked by two funeral stelae.

Mudbrick vault with an overhanging arch.

SATELLITE TOMB OF A FAMILIAR Familiars of the royal family were buried in small tombs near the royal sepulcher. Mudbrick vaults were constructed for the first time.

PYRAMID OF DJOSER AT SAQQARA (3RD DYNASTY) ▲ *346* To recreate the shape of the original tumulus , the architect Imhotep built a first, four-step, pyramid above an initial mastaba where several stages of construction are evident.

TOMB OF QUEEN MER-NEITH AT SAQQARA (1st Dynasty)
In the edifice above the underground burial chamber, several rooms contained the funeral paraphernalia. The façades echo the fortified, wood enclosure walls of the period. The structure was stuccoed and painted in symbolic colors. A false door in the façade overlooking the Nile allowed the soul of the deceased to escape.

BURIAL FIELDS
Private sepulchers, grouped together in vast cemeteries, were designed along the same lines. A rectangular stone or brick structure with sloping walls contained several decorated rooms, including a chapel with a stele, a false door, an offering table and the *serdab*, a sealed chamber which housed statues of the deceased. A shaft in the roof of the mastaba gave access to the burial chamber.

FUNERAL COMPLEX OF PEPY II
(5th Dynasty)
From the 4th Dynasty royal funeral complexes consisted of a "lower" or access temple linked by an ascending, covered causeway to the "upper" temple and pyramid. The funeral temple consisted of a public area, outside the enclosure wall, and a private area adjoining the pyramid. The king's three wives each had their own pyramid and funeral temple.

COVERED CAUSEWAY
The ascending causeway was covered along its entire length. The few inches left between the ceiling flags let in a little light.

TOMB OF PRINCE AMENEMHET AT BENI HASSAN ▲ *374*
(12th Dynasty)
A portico with two grooved columns precedes this new type of sepulcher, hewn out of the rock. A four-columned hall gives access, via a double door, to the sacred niche. The access shaft to the burial chamber runs along the south wall.

BONDING ON THE PYRAMID OF DJOSER
To ensure the solidity of the structure, Imhotep invented a system of bonding in which the layers of stone (consisting of 8-foot thick slabs) were inclined and parallel to the outer wall. During the final stage of construction a six-step pyramid was built around the entire structure.

FUNERARY ARCHITECTURE IN PHARAONIC EGYPT

From the 18th Dynasty onward the places of worship and burial in royal tombs were clearly separated. The principle of the rock-cut tomb or hypogeum is simple: an axial corridor, sloping downward into the cliff, serviced a series of small and large pillared halls. During the Saïte period the structure of the tombs became more complicated and veritable funerary palaces were constructed. To prevent plundering, which had become a common occurrence, the tomb entrance was filled with sand and debris. Under the Ptolemies tombs were dug beneath towns and cities and the principle of separating the world of the living from that of the dead was abandoned.

NEW-KINGDOM ROYAL TOMBS IN THE VALLEY OF THE KINGS
The tomb of Amenhotep I was built according to the characteristic angular design of the 18th Dynasty.

From the 19th Dynasty onward an axial plan was adopted for tombs. A system of protective shafts replaced the granite portcullises of the pyramids.

ARTISAN'S TOMB AT DEIR EL-MEDINA
(19th and 20th Dynasties)
The artisans' tombs at Deir el-Medina
▲ *438* were individual or family tombs.
A two-columned porch, surmounted by a small, constructed pyramid, opened onto a vaulted chamber beneath which lay the burial chamber. At the far end of the burial chamber was a niche containing a statue of the deceased.

TOMB OF THE VIZIER BOCHORIS AT SAQQARA
▲ *344* (16th Dynasty)
Like the Theban tombs of the same period, the tomb was based on the design of a rock temple but with a noticeably greater number of underground rooms and galleries.

TOMB OF PSUSENNES
(21st Dynasty)
The royal tombs of the Saïte period were all built within the enclosure wall of the Temple of Tanis ▲ *226*. These small tombs were built of limestone, granite and mudbrick.

NECROPOLIS OF KOM ES-SHOGAFA
(1st–2nd century BC)
The necropolis, with its complex arrangement of galleries around a circular shaft ▲ *192*, is a fine example of a collective tomb based on the Roman family principle.

GRAECO-ROMAN TOMB AT TUNA EL-JEBEL ▲ *377*
(c. 330 BC)
During the Graeco-Roman period tombs were built like funerary chapels. The false, vaulted walls of their façades were inspired by contemporary temples such as Dendera ▲ *388*.

CIVIL ARCHITECTURE IN PHARAONIC EGYPT

Tiling in the palace of
Ramesses II.

Floods and continual re-occupation have
destroyed all trace of ordinary mudbrick
dwellings. Stone was reserved for thresholds,
column bases and door and window frames,
while doors and columns were in wood.
The layout of Egyptian houses, however
prestigious or humble they may have been,
was bi-polar, with the reception area separate
from the living accommodation. All that
remains today are the ruins of new towns built on
the edge of the desert and suddenly abandoned,
and the occasional remains of palaces which
attest to the past splendor of these
edifices.

**ARTISAN'S HOUSE IN
DEIR EL-MEDINA**
(13th–20th Dynasties)
The consecutive
rooms are rectangular
in design. The living
room, supported by
two or three wooden
columns, was
preceded by a
reception area. At the
rear of the house a
kitchen, with an oven
and a cellar, opened
onto a bedroom.
Steps led up to the
roof-terrace.

**THE
TOWN OF
KAHUN**
(12th Dynasty)
The town was built to
accommodate the
workforce used to construct
the Pyramid of Senwosret III. It
was surrounded by an enclosure wall
and geometrically divided into districts,
with a brick wall separating administrative
workers and artisans.

**THE
VILLAGE OF DEIR
EL-MEDINA**
(19th–20th Dynasties)
Deir el-Medina
▲ 438 is an example
of a village created
from scratch, in
response to a
particular demand. It
was built to
accommodate the
artisans working in
the Valley of the
Kings ▲ 417. The
level
of urban
planning
achieved by the
Egyptians can be seen
in the dense network
of rows of adjoining
houses, dissected by a
north–south axis. The
village was
surrounded by an
enclosure wall (426 x
164 feet).
The houses
were all built
according to a similar
layout. A warden's
lodge stood at the
town's only entrance.

1. Main entrance
2. Garden
3. Entrance hall
4. Living room
5. Bathroom
6. Bedrooms

7. Courtyard and grain silos
8. Outhouses and stables
9. Servants' quarters
10. Kitchens

HOUSE OF THE VIZIER NAKHT AT TELL EL-AMARNA
(18th Dynasty) ▲ 378
Like all prestigious dwellings, the house of Nakht stood in a vast enclosure which incorporated ornamental gardens. The outbuildings, reached through a service entrance, stood together in an area set apart from the house. The house itself consisted of private apartments and reception rooms.

THE PALACE OF RAMESSES III
(20th Dynasty)
The structure of the palace, which adjoins the funeral temple of Ramesses III at Medinet Habu ▲ 434, is organized around the throne room and echoes the principles of Egyptian houses.

CEILING IN THE PALACE OF AMENHOTEP III AT MALKATTA
The polychrome decoration, punctuated with floral motifs, alternates geometric spirals and heads of horned animals on a whitewashed, mortar revetment.

MILITARY ARCHITECTURE IN PHARAONIC EGYPT

Military architecture first appeared during the Archaic period and was developed during the Old Kingdom. The techniques of this type of architecture can be observed in the 12th-Dynasty Nubian fortresses built along Egypt's southern border to combat the threat from the kingdom of Kush. Built of mudbrick and strengthened by beams, they consisted of a glacis broken by a dry moat at the foot of the walls. The forts were designed to house a barracks, an administrative center and a temple. With the great conquests of the New Kingdom, Egyptian colonies were established in Lower Nubia and military structures became larger, more numerous and enriched by examples copied from the peoples of the Levant. They housed or defended Egyptian villages built in foreign lands.

FORTRESS OF BUHEN
The fortress stands at the northernmost point of a defensive line, dating from the Middle Kingdom, which stretched from the second cataract to the forts of Semna and Kumma in the south. These three mudbrick forts made use of the natural relief of the terrain which was partially recut.
Diagrammatic façade of a pre-Dynastic palace.

GATE IN THE ENCLOSURE WALL OF MEDINET HABU
(19th Dynasty)
This type of crenelated entrance tower ▲ *436* was based on Oriental examples. Their name (*migdol*) means "tower" in Hebrew. Here, it has no defensive role: apartments fill the two upper-level apartments. The outer façade of the sloping walls is reinforced by banquettes.

Plan of the fortifications of Buhen.

FORTRESS OF SEMNA

The fortress of Semna and its counterpart Kumma, on the opposite bank of the Nile, controlled access to Egypt from the south. The bastioned wall, built on constructed granite foundations, follows the relief of the terrain. The defenses are completed by a large moat.

FORTIFICATIONS OF BUHEN

A low wall precedes the moat. Then comes a defense wall with a glacis, built on the slope of the moat and flanked by semicircular bastions pierced by a number of loopholes. The last fortification (about 16 feet thick) is punctuated at regular intervals by square towers. A rampart walk, protected by crenelations, runs around the top of the two walls. Two oblong towers protect the main entrance and stand either side of an inner moat crossed by a footbridge.

93

HISTORY OF ARCHEOLOGICAL EXCAVATIONS
EARLY TRAVELERS
AND THE EGYPT EXPEDITION

Experts from the
Egypt Expedition's
scientific mission.

From the time of the Crusades the Orient and Egypt became a popular destination for many travelers who wanted to see the lands of the Bible for themselves. The 16th-century fascination for the ancient world and the advances made in understanding led to an increased interest in past civilizations. Religious, diplomatic and business expeditions were joined by people in search of exoticism or with a thirst for discovery. One such military and scientific expedition, led by Napoleon Bonaparte in 1798, heralded the birth of archeology in Egypt. As well as leading his troops in a campaign to free Egypt from the Ottoman oppressor, Bonaparte also took with him a scientific and artistic mission led by Dominique Vivant Denon.

EGYPT EXPEDITION'S SCIENTIFIC MISSION

The Egypt Expedition's scientific mission consisted of several famous European scientists, sixteen cartographers and topographers, and more than 160 artists and technicians. Their task was to methodically collect information in areas as widely varied as architecture, geography, natural science and the humanities. This information was published collectively in 1809 as *La Description de l'Egypte* and consisted of eleven volumes of plates (three thousand drawings) and nine of text.

Following Champollion's decipherment of hieroglyphics in 1822, interest in the mysteries of Egyptian civilization increased even further. There followed a period during which European consuls organized the systematic plunder of the most important archeological sites, either on their own account or on behalf of their governments who wanted to enhance their country's museum collections. The most famous of these were the (Italian) French consul Bernadino Drovetti ▲ 468, the British consul Henry Salt ▲ 474 and the

PURVEYORS OF MUSEUMS

Swedish consul Anastasi. To ensure the success of their treasure hunt, they recruited such adventurers as Jean-Jacques Rifaud, who worked for Drovetti and who can be considered as the forerunner of modern archeology. He was the first to take interest in the less spectacular urban sites such as the houses of Arsinoe, and to try to identify the different layers he encountered, thus introducing the concept of stratigraphy.

Henry Salt (above) and Champollion (right).

94

CHAMPOLLION

As a member of the Franco-Tuscan expedition (1828) Champollion ▲ 216 was not exempt from this thirst for scientific discovery. With the Italian Rossellini he combed the length and breadth of the Nile Valley as far as Abu Simbel ▲ 464, carrying out architectural and epigraphic surveys of the monuments they discovered.

They acquired bas-reliefs from the tomb of Sety I and several bronzes found in Thebes. On his return he submitted a report to the *pasha* of Cairo on the "conservation of the monuments of Egypt", which suggested that excavations should be controlled and sites protected from damage caused, in particular, by the Egyptian *fellaheen* (archeological sediment in fact made excellent fertilizer for crops). At the same time (in 1821) John G. Wilkinson, the founding father of British Egyptology, compiled an inventory of the sites and drew the first plan of Thebes during his excavations in and around the city. Prussia was also affected by this passion for Ancient Egypt. In 1842 Frederick William IV sent the philologist Karl Richard Lepsius to compile a catalogue of monuments and gather a collection of predominately epigraphic texts for the Agyptisches Museum in Berlin ▲ 470. In 1866 he made a return visit. Champollion's German counterpart, Lepsius was the founder of the German School of Egyptology.

BELZONI
At the beginning of the 19th century the Italian Giovanni Battista Belzoni undertook several archeological investigations on behalf of Henry Salt. In 1817 he discovered the tomb of Sety I in Thebes ▲ 424 and, in 1818, the entrance to the Pyramid of Khafre (Chefren) ▲ 340. Drawings by Belzoni during his excavations (opposite and above). Drawing by Jean-Jacques Rifaud (left).

HISTORY OF ARCHEOLOGICAL EXCAVATIONS
FROM PHILOLOGY TO ARCHEOLOGY

The director of excavations entering the Tomb of Amenhotep III, discovered in Thebes in 1898.

During the second half of the 19th century Auguste Mariette, or "Mariette Pasha" (1821–81), introduced a more systematic approach to field research and a hitherto non-existent concern for Egypt's national heritage. Mariette, a former grammar lecturer, was above all a committed field researcher who, from 1851 until his death, led numerous pioneering excavations. An important first discovery (the Serapeum at Saqqara) encouraged him to increase the number of on-site projects. Although his methods may be questionable, he was instrumental in founding the Egyptian Department of Antiquities in 1859 (which centralized and supervised archeological research) and the Bulaq Museum in Cairo in 1863. From then on all antiquities found on Egyptian soil had to be preserved in the museum. This was a watershed in the history of Egyptian archeology.

GASTON MASPERO

When Mariette died in 1881 he was replaced as head of the Department of Antiquities by Gaston Maspero (1846–1916), professor of archeology at the Collège de France. Maspero continued his work in the field (excavation and restoration) and gathered around him an international team of researchers.

Toward the end of the 19th century the first archeological organizations were created and, in 1890, Maspero founded the École d'Archéologie Orientale, forerunner of the IFAO. Two years later the British set up the Egypt Exploration Fund which was followed in 1898 by the German Deutsche Oriental-Gesellschaft. For more than fifty years, Egyptian archeology was a colonial affair and it was not until 1952 that an Egyptian actually became head of the Department of Antiquities which, until then, had been under French direction.

Bulaq Museum (left) and Mariette Pasha (right).

BIRTH OF EGYPTOLOGY

It was during this period that archeology became a science in its own right and not just a source of supply for epigraphists. The key figure in this development was incontestably the British archeologist Flinders Petrie (1853–1942), engaged by the Egypt Exploration Fund in 1882, whose methods gained a following and who formed an entire generation of researchers. As a prehistoric specialist he favored the less spectacular sites of the pre- and proto-Dynastic periods. He was a meticulous and methodical man who considered the slightest clue indispensable to an understanding of ancient civilizations. He drew plans and cross-sections of the smallest architectural structures, recorded successive levels of occupation and compiled indexes and made drawings of shards, flint tools and other objects he

discovered. He was the first to realize that pottery, which developed in form and decoration over the ages, could act as a sort of "A–Z of ancient ruins" and provide chronological indicators of the different archeological layers. The concepts of typology and stratigraphy, which

are the central principles of modern archeology, were thus applied to Egyptology and enabled Petrie to establish comparative chronologies with neighboring civilizations. Petrie's methods were perfected throughout the 20th century and,

in 1958, UNESCO's Nubian rescue project provided an ideal opportunity for the further development of research specialisms, whether in specific periods of Egyptian history (Byzantine and Arabic civilizations) or indeed in particular areas of specialist information which contributed to the overall fund of archeological knowledge (palynology, paleontology and the study of ceramics).

The British archeologist Flinders Petrie (above) and the excavations of Dahshur, which took place in 1894 (left).

In 1954 Gamal Abd el-Nasser decided, for economic reasons, to build the Aswan High Dam, which would mean flooding the Nile Valley for a distance of over 312 miles, in other words the whole of Nubia as far as the second cataract. Christiane Desroches-Noblecourt and Sarwat Okasha called upon the international community to intervene, with a view to surveying and protecting the region that would be affected by the flooding. In January 1955 the director of UNESCO went to Nubia and, a few months later, the CEDAE (Centre d'Étude et de Documentation sur l'Égypte Antique) was established. An international rescue program was launched which involved carrying out surveys (to compile a complete inventory of sites under threat), making drawings, excavating specific sites and mounting rescue operations for the most important monuments.

Moving the blocks from the Temple of Abu Simbel.

The movable dam used to dismantle the flooded Temple of Philae.

PHILAE

The Temple of Philae, already partially flooded by the construction of earlier barrages, was rescued in the same way as the Temple of Abu Simbel. The stone blocks were simply dismantled and rebuilt on Agilkia, which was redesigned (with the help of dynamite) to reproduce the topography of Philae. The bas-relief texts made it possible to reconstruct the gardens of Isis to whom the temple was dedicated.

Some of the rescued monuments were given to countries taking part in the project. Others (the temples of Amada, Kalabsha, Abu Simbel and Philae ▲ 462), were moved and rebuilt well above the water level. Still others, such as the fortress of Buhen, were left to their fate.

Outline plan for dismantling the north wall of Abu Simbel.

ABU SIMBEL RESCUE OPERATION

In 1955 the CEDAE carried out photographic and photogrammetric surveys of the façades, paintings and epigraphic texts of Abu Simbel. Three rescue plans were considered. The first involved constructing a barrage to protect the site of Abu Simbel, while the second proposed raising each temple in a single block above the 200 elevation mark. The third (which was adopted) meant cutting the monuments into blocks and moving them 210 feet further up the cliff. The first stage of the operation involved getting the buildings out of the water. This was achieved by installing an 82-foot-high movable dam and pumping stations. The façades of the temples were then covered with sand to protect them from possible damage by falling rocks during the next stage: the leveling of the cliffs above the temples. During the actual dismantling of the monuments the blocks were often cut by hand because of the fragility of the sandstone, in spite of its being strengthened by injections of epoxy resin. Weighing over 11 tons each, 1,036 blocks were cut, numbered and transported further up the cliff. During reconstruction they were fixed to a concrete superstructure according to their original position and orientation. Each temple was then protected by a reinforced concrete vault to support the weight of the debris of rocks used to reconstruct the two hillocks which had originally surmounted them. It took three years and a 3,000-strong workforce to complete the operation. The temples were officially opened on September 22, 1968.

Marking the blocks of the Temple of Philae during the rescue operation.

A photogrammetric survey (left) of part of the entrance to the Temple of Ramesses II at Abu Simbel ▲ 464 and a photograph (right) of the same section. Photogrammetry makes it possible to *determine the dimensions of a photographed object by measuring photographic perspectives. The process was used by UNESCO during the Abu Simbel rescue operation to facilitate the cutting and reconstruction of the temple blocks.

The monuments of Pharaonic Egypt are several thousands of years old and often badly disfigured by the ravages of time. The work of the archeological architect is slow and painstaking and consists of "unraveling" the architectural history of the monuments, curing the disorders from which they are suffering and restoring their original appearance. Restoring a monument is not simply a matter of patching up or rebuilding a badly damaged wall. It means taking it apart stone by stone in order to understand the circumstances in which it was constructed and the materials used. The work of the architect is therefore indissociable from that of the archeologist, and a piece of restoration often leads to a major archeological discovery.

Before undertaking any form of restoration work architects carry out systematic photographic and graphic surveys of each of the monument's façades. They then dismantle it, using a crane, stone by stone and layer by layer, from the top. Each of the dismantled blocks, as well as those found near the edifice, is recorded, numbered, photographed and stored in the so-called "stone museum".

SUBSIDENCE
The sandstone and limestone used at Karnak ▲ 404 contain high levels of sea salt. When the stone comes into contact with dampness the salt crystals lose their stability and re-crystallize on the surface of the stone blocks. The crust thus formed causes several inches of the stones to crumble or subside.

AREA OF EVAPORATI⚊

sol

▓ CAPILLARY FRINGE
▤ WATER TABLE
▦ DAMPNESS CONTACT

> "Although an architect's life is, of course, spent on site,
> it is also spent in an office or laboratory."
>
> Jean Vercoutier

CONSOLIDATING STONES

As a general rule, restorers consolidate crumbling stones with ethyl silicate injections and restick broken ones.

Any blocks which prove too badly damaged to be reused are replaced by new, made-to-measure blocks.

RECONSTRUCTING A FAÇADE

The fragments of carved stone are collected and identified. Once the blocks have been

CLEANING A STATUE

The surface of the statue is cleaned by means of a high-pressure jet, which is made up of a mixture of sand and water.

reconstructed, they are then assembled like a giant jigsaw puzzle. This was the method used to rebuild the sections of one of the walls of the tomb of Montuemhet in the Valley of Asasif, Thebes ▲ *425*.

RE-ASSEMBLING A MONUMENT

Monuments are re-assembled in accordance with the Charter of Venice, which states that the final state of a building must be respected and must therefore incorporate all the changes that it has undergone during its history. The stones found near the monument are sometimes used. Ruined foundations are replaced by red-brick masonry.

"TALATTAT"

During the restoration of the ninth pylon of the Temple of Karnak ▲ 404, thousands of stones used in its foundations were found to have come from monuments dating from the Amarnian period ● 42 which were destroyed after the reign of Akhenaten. Twelve thousand of these standard-sized (10.2 x 9.8 x 19.7 inches), sandstone blocks (*talattat*) were saved. Most of them had extremely well-preserved carved and painted decorations.

RESTORING A STATUE

The various fragments found scattered inside the tomb of Montuemhet, in Thebes, were identified and assembled to reconstruct the statues shown above.

"WHITE CHAPEL" OF SENWOSRET I

The blocks of this 12th-Dynasty chapel ▲ 413 were reused in the 18th Dynasty foundations of the third pylon of the Temple of Karnak. They were discovered in 1938 by the architect Henri Chevrier. After patiently reconstructing the chapel on paper (anastylosis) he was able to rebuild the complete edifice.

RESTORING A SARCOPHAGUS

After the difficult task of identification, the wooden sarcophagus is painstakingly cleaned and reassembled piece by piece. The next stage is concerned with replacing the fragments of *pâte de verre* which together form the decoration.

SORTING "PÂTE DE VERRE" FRAGMENTS

The fragments of *pâte de verre* inlay found in a tomb are carefully sorted, identified and replaced.

CLEANING A MUMMIFIED CAT

Cats' mummies are often badly damaged. The sand must be cleaned away before they can be studied and sometimes X-rayed.

RESTORING COLORS

Carved and painted wall decorations are reproduced on transparent, plastic film as well as being photographed. Polychrome decorations are cleaned by micro-abrasion and the painted surface sprayed with a chemical fixative.

IDENTIFYING SHARDS

Pottery fragments and shards which have been found inside a tomb are carefully laid out so that they can be sorted, classified and identified.

Coptic Monastic Architecture

Desert monasteries and hermitages constitute one of the main components of Coptic architecture. This essentially monastic architecture, with its well-defended entrances, was built of sun-dried or burnt brick which blended remarkably well with the desert environment in which it evolved. Unfortunately its formal development remains obscure. The longstanding state of ruin of most of these complexes and the many modifications undergone by others over the ages make it impossible to obtain a precise impression of their original structure, which is also difficult to date.

TROGLODYTE HERMITAGE
This type of hermitage consisted of an open courtyard, reached via a flight of steps, which opened onto various rock-cut chambers. Large numbers of these hermitages, most of which were occupied during the 6th and 7th centuries, were discovered near Esna ▲ 446.

DETAIL OF STONEWORK IN THE KELLIA HERMITAGES
The bricks were laid in horizontal layers, or in a herringbone pattern, and covered with a clay revetment which was decorated with wall paintings.

"QASR"
Inside the enclosure wall of certain fortified monasteries – for example the Deir es-Suriani ▲ 208 (Wadi Natrun) – was a large square courtyard (*qasr*), reached via a drawbridge. *Qasr* were designed to withstand long sieges and consisted of cellars, kitchens, quarters (cells) and a chapel.

PULLEY LIFT
The pulley lift was another means of defending the entrance of a monastery. It was also used to hoist provisions over the walls as was the case, for example, at the Monastery of St Anthony ▲ 265.

MONASTERY OF ST SIMEON AT ASWAN ▲ *459*
The monastery, surrounded by a high enclosure wall, is one of the largest in Egypt. Its main buildings were a church, refectory and a multistoried structure containing the monks' cells and various outbuildings.

MEDIEVAL MONASTERY
The Deir Mari Girgis (Monastery of St George) ▲ *359* is situated on the edge of the desert and enclosed by a high wall. Apart from its religious function, it once served to protect the Christian peasants who farmed the surrounding land. Until the early 20th century their dwellings occupied the first court of the monastery. The second court housed the church with its five naves flanked by side chapels. The complex was covered by irregularly shaped domes and vaults of varying heights. The choir was located on the axis of the entrance to the church and consisted of three apsidal rooms (*haykal*) with iconostases and niches. A funerary enclosure and various outbuildings completed the complex.

WALLED HERMITAGE
Numerous examples of another type of (walled) hermitage were discovered on the site of Kellia ▲ *209* which was inhabited during the 4th and 5th centuries.

Niche of the mihrab.

The religious architecture of Muslim Egypt is characterized by three main types of mosque. The earliest of these was built around a central, open courtyard surrounded by arcades on four sides, with a deeper portico on the side indicating the direction of Mecca. Alongside this classic-style mosque (subsequently reserved for the great mosques), the mosque with *iwan* was a very different and specifically Egyptian type of mosque which became widespread during the second half of the 15th century. The third type, inspired by the mosques of Istanbul, was introduced during the Ottoman period.

CLASSIC-STYLE MOSQUE
The classic-style mosque, governed by the direction of Mecca, was often subjected to ingenious distortions to ensure that it followed the alignment of the streets. The El-Aqmar (Gray) Mosque in Cairo (1125) ▲ *290* is the oldest example of this type of mosque.

OTTOMAN-STYLE MOSQUE
The Malika Safiyya Mosque in Cairo (1610) is a fine example of an Ottoman-style mosque with its characteristic, domed sanctuary preceded by a open, porticoed courtyard.

MINBAR AND MIHRAB
The carved wood or sometimes marble minbar is the "pulpit" from which the *imam* preaches. The mihrab, the niche indicating the direction of Mecca, is richly decorated with polychrome marble, painted tiles and an archway whose festooned voussoirs are in alternately colored stone (a technique known as *ablaq*).

MOSQUE OF AS-SALIH TALAI (1160) ▲ *299*
This perfectly regular, classic-style mosque is the only example of a mosque with a porticoed facade.

OASIS MOSQUES
In less densely built, urban areas mosques are more regular in design. The minarets of oasis mosques tend to be squat, and in this aspect they resemble those that can be found along the Mediterranean coast.

NUBIAN MOSQUE
The mudbrick mosque of the village of El-Khallassab, with its straight staircase leading to the minaret, inspired Hassan Fathi's design for the mosque of Qurna el-Gedida ▲ *442*.

MOSQUE WITH "IWAN"
The mosque with *iwan* became widespread throughout Cairo from the 14th century onward. It consists of a central, covered area opening onto four *iwan* (vaulted areas) of unequal depth. The layout is reminiscent of the great halls of the Mameluke palaces ● *116*, from which the term *qaa* layout is derived. Since they were built at a time when towns and cities were already dense, most mosques with *iwan* are fairly modest in size. They often have several outbuildings, like the Qijmas el-Ishaqi Mosque (1480) ▲ *300* in Cairo, a remarkable example of the adaptation of this layout to a triangular plot of land at the tip of an island.

MINARETS

The tip of most minarets is surmounted by a brass crescent. On the minaret of the Imam as-Shafi'i Mosque – as formerly on the minaret of the Ibn Tulun Mosque – this has been replaced by a boat.

It is from the top of the minaret, a functional element attached to every Islamic religious building, that the *muezzin* issues his call to prayer. Generally speaking Egyptian minarets are characterized by three clearly defined, vertical sections. The first section is based on a square, the second on an octagonal and the third on a circular layout. Some scholars have associated this arrangement with the famous Alexandrian Pharos Lighthouse.

MINARET OF THE IBN TULUN MOSQUE (879)
▲ *312*
The minaret with its external, spiral staircase is the only one of its kind in Egypt. It was inspired by the great Mosque of Samarra, in Mesopotamia, where Ibn Tulun was born.

MINARET OF THE SULTAN HASSAN MEDERSA (1363)
▲ *309*
The minaret, one of the most elegant in medieval Cairo, stands about 260 feet high. Apart from a square base, its sections are octagonal.

MINARET OF THE FARAG IBN BARQUQ KHANQA (1411)
▲ *329*
The arrangement of the sections of this minaret defies the established order. The square section is followed abruptly by the circular section, while the transitional, octagonal section is at the top.

MINARET OF THE EL-MU'AYYAD MOSQUE (1419)
▲ *298*
This is in fact a pair of minarets which do not stand at a corner of the mosque but on either side of the entrance adjoining the Bab Zuwaila.

MINARET OF THE ISKANDAR PASHA MOSQUE (1556)
This was one of the earliest Ottoman minarets in Cairo. Although it no longer exists, its details were preserved for posterity in a diagram by Pascal Coste (1787–1879) ▲ *190*.

BALUSTRADES AND PARAPETS

Balustrades and parapets are a characteristic feature of Mameluke-style minarets. They appear in each of the sections and consist of stone panels with an openwork design or sunk or bas-relief carving based on a technique used for the first time on the screens of the Sangar el-Gawli Mausoleum.

STALACTITES

Stalactites form one of the principal decorative elements of minarets. These small, cellular pendentives were used in particular to decorate the transitional area between sections.

CROSS-SECTION OF THE SECTIONS OF THE FARAG IBN BARQUQ MINARET

MINARET OF THE ABU EL-DAHAB MOSQUE (1774) ▲ *295*
Although in fact Ottoman, the minaret harks back to the Mameluke style and was mainly inspired by the unusual square minaret of the nearby El-Ghuri Mosque.

There were two main types of monastic establishment built in Muslim Egypt: the *khanqa* of the Mameluke period and the *takiya* of the Ottoman period. *Khanqa*, intended to accommodate the members of a Sufi brotherhood, were very often (like *medersa*) also an excuse to erect an impressive mausoleum. *Khanqa* and *medersa* were built along similar lines: a cruciform layout with *iwan* of unequal sizes. *Takiya* were closely based on the layout of the *medersa* of Istanbul.

"TAKIYA"
The *takiya* – introduced during the Ottoman period – was an independent building which consisted of a raised, open courtyard surrounded by an arcade and overlooked by domed cells. The *iwan* was located more or less along the axis of the entrance and its far wall indicated the direction of Mecca. The *takiya* could be combined with another religious establishment (a *sabil-kuttab*, for example) as with the Mahmudiya *takiya* of 1750 (right).

"KHANQA"
The Baybars el-Jashankir *khanqa*, which dates from 1310, is the oldest in Cairo. It is a fine example of the distorted open-court, cruciform layout (below) which developed in Egypt and which was characterized by a tendency to extend the axial at the expense of the lateral *iwan*. In this case, the difference in the size is particularly noticeable: the lateral *iwan* are much reduced, while the *iwan* containing the niche of the mihrab is the more spacious of the two broad axial *iwan*.

"SABIL-KUTTAB"
The *sabil-kuttab* was a specifically Egyptian form of architecture which fulfilled the dual function of providing free drinking water and offering local children a basic education. Although the *sabil-kuttab* was sometimes combined with other establishments such as mosques, mausoleums or *medersa*, it was also an independent building. Large numbers of *sabil-kuttab* were built during the Ottoman period and in c. 1800 there were around three hundred in Cairo.

"KUTTAB"
The Koranic school occupied the upper-floor loggia and was reached through a separate entrance. A teacher, paid by the establishment, taught the Koran, reading and writing to local children.

"SHAZARWAN"
Some fountains had a built-in cooling system which involved running the water over a carved marble plaque (*shazarwan*) placed at an angle in a support in the fountain (*sabil*) room.

The Baybars el-Jashankir *khanqa* ▲ 292 was designed to house around two hundred Sufis. Some resided in the adjoining living accommodation (which no longer exists) while others lived in the three-storied cell block which overlooked the courtyard.

113

ISLAMIC FUNERARY ARCHITECTURE

Aerial view of a Muslim necropolis. Egyptian necropolises extend for distances of over a mile. One of the most impressive is Cairo's "city of the dead"
▲ 326.

In spite of opposition from orthodox Islam (according to which a simple tombstone is sufficient), a monumental style of funerary architecture developed within the city walls in Cairo during the Fatimid period. It was introduced by the Shi'ite rulers and initially took the form of independent, square mausoleums surmounted by a cupola. The early cupolas were built in brick and later in stone. From the 13th century onward mausoleums were often attached to a *medersa* (college of religious education), according to a formula adopted long before in Syria. As time passed royal sepulchers gave rise to the construction of huge funerary complexes, which combined several different types of structures, usually situated in the "cities of the dead" on the outskirts of the city.

KIOSK
The cenotaphs of important (especially religious) people are placed in square kiosks whose roofs are supported by four marble columns.

SIMPLE CENOTAPH
Simple cenotaphs mark the entrance to an underground tomb where the bodies are buried. They always consist of a horizontal stone flanked by two stelae, one of which ends in a "cap" indicating the rank and sex of the deceased.

FUNERARY COMPLEXES
These edifices sometimes achieve impressive dimensions, as in the case of the adjoining complexes of the Emir Qurqumas (1506) and Sultan Inal (1456).

INDEPENDENT, CUPOLATED MAUSOLEUM

Unlike their more modest predecessors, situated in necropolises on the outskirts of the city, these monuments often reached monumental proportions and were built within the city walls.

Although mausoleums have an invariable basic structure – a square building surmounted by a circular cupola resting on a (usually) octagonal drum – their cupolas and drums became the object of widely varying architectural techniques.

Cupola sculpted with a zig-zag or "herringbone" design.

Striated or ribbed cupola.

SCULPTED CUPOLAS

From the Mameluke period onward, cupolas on tombs and mausoleums were built of sculpted stone, an art which had no equivalent in the Muslim world. Striations were the first motif used but these were soon replaced by a "herringbone" design. Both were soon superseded by starbursts which were subsequently combined with various kinds of arabesques. This skilled art form disappeared with the Ottoman conquest.

Cupola decorated with starburst motifs.

Cupola decorated with arabesques.

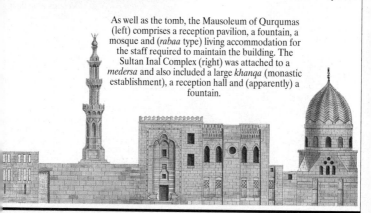

As well as the tomb, the Mausoleum of Qurqumas (left) comprises a reception pavilion, a fountain, a mosque and (*rabaa* type) living accommodation for the staff required to maintain the building. The Sultan Inal Complex (right) was attached to a *medersa* and also included a large *khanqa* (monastic establishment), a reception hall and (apparently) a fountain.

115

Contrary to many preconceived ideas of "Arab" houses as inward-looking spaces which are strictly private and always built around an open courtyard, Egyptian domestic architecture offers a wide range of different layouts which combine semi-public and private areas reserved for family life. For this reason many houses were not built with a courtyard, a feature reserved for the wealthiest households. However, all houses were organized around one central element: the main hall or *qaa*, which dictated the arrangement of the other rooms and was the center of the family's private life.

Layout of Beit as-Suhaymi ▲ *290*.

OFFSET ENTRANCE
Access to houses was through an offset entrance with a stone porters' bench (*mastaba*).

COURTYARD
The entrance led into a courtyard, which was usually left unpaved. Opening onto the courtyard were various outbuildings: storerooms and stables, in particular, and sometimes an open reception room or *tahtabuch* for more modest visitors.

URBAN DEVELOPMENT
Courtyards in houses were a source of air and light as well as a semi-public area which compensated for the narrow streets and absence of public squares. The intensive urban development of the Mameluke period was accompanied by a reduction in the size of courtyards and the emergence of a vertical style of architecture.

"QAA"
Depending on their size, houses sometimes had several *qaa* (also known as *mandara*) situated on the first or second floor. The *qaa* was the focal point of family life: it provided the setting for meals and everyday activities as well as doubling as a reception room.

"MAQAAD"
More important visitors were received in the *maqaad* (literally "the room for sitting in"). This north-facing, mezzanine loggia was mainly used during the summer months. It was reached via a staircase leading from the courtyard to the *qaa*.

In the ceiling of one of the *iwan* was a north-facing air captor (*malqaf*), designed to capture the cool evening breezes. This ancient ventilation system was already in use in Pharaonic Egypt.

LAYOUT OF THE "QAA"

Qaa, which were sometimes impressive in size and always richly decorated, consisted of three sections. The slightly sunken, central section (known as a *durqaa*) usually had an ornamental basin with a fountain (*fasqiya*) and was lit by an octagonal lantern. It was flanked by two lateral *iwan* whose ceilings were not as high as that of the *durqaa*.

MAMELUKE "MAQAAD"

During the Mameluke period *maqaad* often took the form of huge loggias, like the one built in 1496 by the emir Mamay el-Saïfi. It opened onto an equally vast courtyard which is today the Midan Beit el-Qadi ▲ 288. When houses were near a canal or lake the *maqaad* usually overlooked the water rather than the inner courtyard.

● "WAKALA"

DESIGN OF FAÇADES
The façades of the *riwaq* were identical in design: a low window with a small, overhanging balcony decorated with moucharabieh work (turned wood panels) and surmounted by three openings closed by wooden grilles.

Caravanserais (known as *khan, fonduq* or *wakala* depending on the period) were vast establishments which served as inns for traveling merchants, warehouses for imported merchandise and places in which to do business. They also provided accommodation for foreign residents and soldiers. Over the years their residential function was reinforced by the addition of a *rabaa*, a block of identical tenements, several stories high reached via a gallery.

ORGANIZATION OF A "RABAA WAKALA"
Caravanserais were organized around a large, central courtyard. The first floor was reserved for shops, some opening onto the street and others onto the courtyard. The accommodation for traveling merchants was on the upper floors. The *rabaa* proper might occupy several stories and had one or two separate entrances.

LAYOUT OF "RABAA" ACCOMMODATION
Rabaa accommodation consisted of duplex (or triplex) apartments. The main room (*riwaq*) overlooked the street or courtyard and was always on two levels. The first level also included the service areas (kitchen, etc.). The upper level(s) were occupied by bedrooms which opened onto the *riwaq*.

ENTRANCE
The entrance to the *wakala* was marked by a richly decorated, monumental gateway.

ARTS AND TRADITION

BOATS, *120*
RITUALS AND CEREMONIES, *124*
FESTIVALS AND PILGRIMAGES, *126*
MUSIC AND DANCE, *128*
CRAFT TRADES, *130*
CAFÉS, *132*
"FUUL", *134*
HORSES, *136*
FALCONRY, *138*

The River Nile and the marshes which were formed by its floods, the lakes of northern Egypt and the Faiyum, the Red Sea and the Mediterranean all provided the setting for navigation in Egypt. The scarcity of wood (acacia, sycamore and mulberry), coupled with the abundance of aquatic plants, were the determining factors in the construction of the many different and original types of boats used for fishing and hunting, transportation and war. Even divinities and the deceased took to the waters in their own sacred barques.

In 1954 one of the (dismantled) funeral barques of Khufu (Cheops) ▲ 335 was discovered. The 140-foot-long cedar-wood boat is a fine example of one of the methods of construction used by Old-Kingdom carpenters.

The keel-less hull was made of broad, jointed planks bound together with cords. On contact with the water the cords shrank and the wood swelled, thus ensuring that the boat was watertight.

From prehistoric times rafts were made from papyrus stems bound together with ropes made from plants. They were easily carried by hunters and fishermen and could be used in shallow water and marshes. The upswept prow and stern were the prototype for the characteristic design used over the centuries.

Drawings of boats were discovered on pieces of pottery from the Nagada period. They were probably made of papyrus and propelled by poles or oars. The prow and stern of this wooden pilgrim's boat (above), dating from the Old Kingdom, are made from papyrus clumps.

The transportation of Queen Hatshepsut's ▲ 409 two granite obelisks from Aswan to Thebes is illustrated in the bas-reliefs of the Deir el-Bahri. They were attached to a huge vessel made of sycamore with a specially reinforced deck to support their weight (410 tons), pulled by three rows of ten rowing boats.

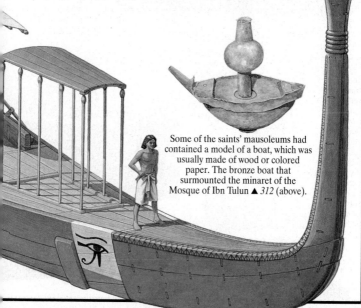

Some of the saints' mausoleums had contained a model of a boat, which was usually made of wood or colored paper. The bronze boat that surmounted the minaret of the Mosque of Ibn Tulun ▲ 312 (above).

There is evidence of the traditional use of ceremonial boats in Mameluke and Ottoman Egypt. During festivals such as the opening of the El-Khalig Canal ▲ 315, the 15th-century sultans used an *ashari* or *dahabiya* (above), which was lavishl decorated for the occasio In the 19th century the *dahabiya* was extremely popular among travelers sailir up the Nile to visit the sites of Middle and Upper Egypt.

Today transport vessels are made of iron rather than wood and traditional techniques are disappearing, except in the case of small fishing and pleasure boats.

Feluccas are still used for transporting stones and bricks used for building, sand, pottery and sometimes even animals.

The development of the Egyptian sail: with the increased transport of bulky freight, the central mast inclined toward the stern has been replaced by two or three masts; the hull has become much larger and a boom has been added to each sail to improve maneuverability.

Today there are more than four hundred of these fishing boats on Lake Manzala. Fish are caught with a rod, or with a net held flat just above the surface of the water, into which the mullet jump.

This simply designed, decked boat, or *zeheri*, is only found on Lake Manzala, whose shallow waters (you can stand up in them) require boats with a shallow draft. The *zeheri* enables fishermen to reach the marshy corners of this lagoon, which is teeming with fish. The vaulted cabin fitted with side ledges provides shelter for the crew in bad weather.

Felucca used for transporting stones.

123

● RITUALS AND CEREMONIES

Everyday life in Egypt is punctuated by rites of passage, as it is throughout the rest of the Muslim world. These mark the major stages in a person's life: birth, circumcision, marriage and death. In this respect religious and social ceremonies are still influenced by past rituals, which explains, in particular, the importance of funeral rites. The Copts, who have been in Egypt since time immemorial, still observe certain Pharaonic traditions as well as adopting Muslim customs such as circumcision.

Modern marriage ceremonies are becoming more "Westernized" and are often celebrated in public.

THE BRIDAL CARAVAN
The bride used to ride on a camel, while her dowry was carried by a caravan and thus exposed to public view. Today a car decorated with flowers and followed by a procession of vehicles has replaced this ancient tradition.

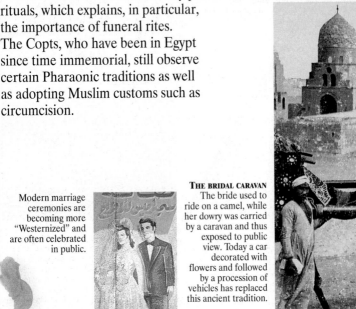

THE MARRIAGE CEREMONY
The signing – by the men – of the marriage contract (*katb el-kitab*) is followed by the payment of the dowry and, a week to ten days later, by a ceremony during which the day of the marriage (*khotba*) is arranged. On that day, according to tradition, the bride arrives in a procession to the sound of oboes and percussion instruments.

CIRCUMCISION

Boys are usually circumcized, between the ages of five and twelve, by a barber. It is the occasion of great celebration during which a procession is organized. Today the *mutahar* (boy to be circumcized) is dressed up, as if for a Western carnival.

COPTIC BAPTISM

Boys are baptized at forty days old and girls at eighty days. The ceremony is held earlier if the child is sickly. According to Coptic belief, if a child dies without baptism it will be reborn blind.

FUNERAL PROCESSION

The coffinless body of the deceased, wrapped in a white or green shroud, is carried by four close relatives. They are preceded by male relatives and friends and schoolboys carrying the Koran. The women of the family can be distinguished by a blue ribbon or scarf.

The social life of Egyptian people, whatever their religion or beliefs may be, is governed by religious festivals and pilgrimages. The only exception is Sham el-Nessim, which is a festival that marks the arrival of spring. The most festive period is Ramadan, the ninth month of the Muslim calendar (during which the Koran was revealed to the prophet Mohammed) and the month of the ritual fast. Another high point on the Muslim calendar is the last month of the year when the pilgrimage to Mecca is made. The worship of saints, whose anniversaries are commemorated by their *muled*, is another important and fairly characteristic aspect of popular Egyptian religion.

SHAM EL-NESSIM
This ancient festival corresponds to the first Monday after Easter. It is a day for family gatherings, traditionally celebrated in the open air, and a meal of *fshi* (salt fish), with eggs and green onions, is served.

"MULED"
The annual saints' festivals are the occasion for huge popular gatherings which may last for two or three days or as long as two weeks! From Cairo to the provinces, each town and village has its own *muled*, like the *muled* of El-Hagag celebrated in Luxor ▲ *397* (left), which is also the occasion for meetings of the Sufi brotherhoods. Muslim Egypt's most venerated saint is Sidi Ahmed el-Badawi who is buried in Tanta ▲ *211*. The Coptic community also has its own *muled*.

Pilgrims (*hajj*) from Upper Egypt returning from Mecca find the façade of their houses decorated with a fresco consisting of conventional images of holy places, illustrations of their journey, scenes from everyday life and symbolic animals.

"MULED" PROCESSIONS

Muled are celebrated by processions and dazzling displays of lights in the towns and cities. The most impressive of these is the procession that passes through Cairo on the occasion of the Muled el-Nabi (festival of the Prophet's birthday).

"MAHMAL"

The *mahmal*, a richly decorated, empty litter symbolizing the power of Egypt, was carried by a camel at the head of the official caravan that set out every year for Mecca. The tradition ceased in 1926 when the Egyptian government stopped sending the black carpet (made every year in Egypt) which covered the four walls of the Kaaba.

RAMADAN

Before the cannon announces nightfall and the breaking of the fast, tables are set out in the streets of Cairo to serve the *iftar*, the first meal of the day during Ramadan.

The classic repertoire of Egyptian music and dance was compiled during the 19th century. Abdu el-Hamuli (1845–1901), who was the official singer of the khedive Ismaïl, revolutionized traditional music by making it accessible to the general public. Umm Kalsum, Farid el-Atrach, Mohammed Abd el-Wahab and Abd el-Halim Hafez, the popular idols of the Arab world, are his direct descendants, while Oriental dancers such as Leila Murad and Fifi Abdu have followed in the footsteps of the great singer and dancer, Almaza, the darling of 19th-century Egyptian high society. Ancient folkloric customs, together with a traditional orchestra and segregated dancing (the men in public and the women among themselves), are still practiced during the religious festivals and marriages.

"RABBABA"
The *rabbaba* is a wood instrument similar to the viol. There are two sorts: the two-stringed *rabbaba* of the *mughani* (singer) and the single-stringed *rabbaba* of the *shaer* (poet).

UMM KALSUM
Umm Kalsum (1898–1975) was a symbolic figure in the 20th-century Arab world. She sang of love, the glory of Egypt and the Muslim faith, and was extremely skilled at arousing the ecstatic emotion (*tarab*) experienced by Arabs when listening to poetry and music.

The *darbuka*, a drum made of skin and terracotta or metal, and the *dof*, which consists of skin stretched over a frame bordered with cymbals, are used to beat time for the dancers.

SAMIA GAMAL
Samia Gamal was a musical comedy star of the big screen during the 1940's and 1950's.

"OUD"
The *oud* is the ancestor of the lute, which dates back to early Egyptian antiquity. It is the key instrument of classical Arab music.

"QANUN" AND "NAI"
Together with the *oud*, the *qanun* and *nai* form the *taht*, the ancient orchestra which is today part of Egypt's classical repertoire. The *qanun*, which belongs to the cithara (zither) family, is placed horizontally across the player's knees and plucked with two finger guards worn on the index fingers. The *nai*, a reed flute even older than the *oud*, is the favorite instrument of the dancing dervishes.

Musical group from Siwa Oasis ▲ 256 celebrating a local festival.

129

BASKETS
Baskets are woven from small palm leaves.

During the 19th century it was difficult to gain access into private homes so Orientalist writers tended to concentrate on descriptions of streets and local life: craft trades, artisans and street sellers. Although some of these are tending to disappear, the conviviality and industrious animation described by such writers as Gustave Flaubert, E.M. Forster and Lawrence Durrell can still be found at the heart of the crowds and traffic jams of modern towns and cities. Contemporary Egyptian writers such as Naguib Mahfouz, Yussef Idriss and Sonallah Ibrahim have used such settings as a background for their novels.

DONUT SELLER
Donuts are fried in oil and plunged into sugar syrup.

"FUUL" SELLER
The traditional Egyptian breakfast consists of well-boiled broad beans.

KNIFE GRINDER
The whine of blades against steel wheels is a familiar sound.

LICORICE-SYRUP SELLER
He rattles metal cups in his hand and carries a copper-plated metal pitcher slung on a strap across his shoulder.

PUBLIC SCRIBE
Love letters, business letters, legal letters: in spite of the increase in literacy, the public scribe is never short of customers.

MAT MAKER
Reed-fiber mats became popular during the 19th century, especially in Minuf, in the heart of the Delta region ▲ *205*.

SHOE SHINER
Shoe shiners (often young children) work in stations, restaurants, barbers' shops and on street corners.

LIME-JUICE SELLER
The magnificently accoutered lime-juice seller.

POTTER
Clay pottery is made by both men and women.

IRONER
With his iron attached to his foot, he sprinkles the cloth with water as he works.

BARBER
He circumcizes young boys, shaves bridegrooms on their wedding day and gives the local men their daily shave.

MARQUETRY WORK
This craft is still used for tourist items and musical instruments.

> "With its tea, the Orient enters middle-class sitting rooms; with its coffee it enters the brain."
>
> Paul Morand

"KANAKA"
The *kanaka* is used in the preparation of coffee.

During the Ottoman rule new products were introduced into Egypt: coffee appeared at the beginning of the 16th century, and tobacco arrived from Persia in the 17th century. Coffee soon became extremely popular in spite of the reservations that were expressed concerning this new beverage by certain religious authorities. The first cafés proved so successful that, in 1650, Cairo already had around 650 of these establishments and only a century later twice as many could be found. Nowadays there are around five thousand of them. These new meeting places have remained central to the social life of the urban male population in Egypt.

DRINKS
Coffee used to be drunk sweetened and scented with ambergris. Today it tends to be drunk *ziada* (which is extremely sweet) or *mazbut* (fairly sweet), occasionally *ariha* (with the merest hint of sugar) or alternatively *sada* (without any sugar) and sometimes scented with cardamom. Cafés also serve tea, which is not as heavy, and a variety of other infusions such as *karkade* (a hibiscus-based infusion), *yansun* (which is aniseed-based) and *erfa* (cinnamon-based). They do not serve alcoholic drinks.

STORYTELLERS AND MUSICIANS
In the past cafés were a place to listen to storytellers and musicians who used to turn up particularly just before major religious festivals. Nowadays customers can watch television and possibly an Egyptian or foreign film on video.

Cafés are an ideal place to while away the afternoon or evening hours. The choice of a regular café is based on political, professional and intellectual affinities.

CAFÉS BY ANY OTHER NAME
Egyptian cafés were traditionally known as *qahwa*. Over the years and according to their particular function they have acquired different names. Some are still known as *nadi* (clubs), while others have become *cafitiria* (cafeteria) with a generally mixed clientele. The derivation of the term *borsa*, the cafés situated along the Mediterranean shore, remains unknown.

Various board games such as backgammon, dominoes and draughts are played in cafés. It is also the place to hear the latest *nokat* (funny stories) and, of course, to smoke the hookah.

The aluminum *edra* has replaced the old copper pot of bygone days.

Fuul is an Egyptian specialty sold on corners by street sellers, and in shops. It is especially popular at breakfast time, although the Egyptians eat it at any time throughout the day. Traditionally *fuul* was simmered overnight on the embers of wood fires, particularly those used to heat the water pipes in the *hammam* (bath house). In fact *fuul* sellers used to leave their *edra* (the copper container in which the *fuul* was prepared) at the *hammam* in the evening and collect it the following morning.

1. Clean the broad beans and rinse under the cold tap. Dissolve the bicarbonate of soda in about 4 pints of water and soak the beans for 24 hours.

2. Rinse the beans and place in an earthenware casserole in twice their own volume of water. Cover and bring quickly to the boil.

5. Put the garlic purée into a dish and add the lemon juice and olive oil. Add the warm beans with some of their liquid.

6. Mix together and sprinkle with salt, chopped parsley and paprika.

INGREDIENTS

2 cups dried broad beans (Egyptian variety),
1 oz bicarbonate of soda, ¾ oz garlic, sea salt,
5 lemons, ¾ cup olive oil, table salt.

2 rounded tbs chopped parsley, paprika,
radishes, spring onions, hard-boiled eggs.

3. Leave to simmer gently until completely cooked
(approximately 2 hours), adding more boiling water
if necessary.

4. Peel the cloves of garlic and place
them in a mortar with some sea salt.
Crush to a fine purée.

Serve hot with Arabic
bread, radishes,
spring onions and
hard-boiled eggs.

The horse, which according to Arab legend was created from a handful of the south wind, was introduced into Egypt at the end of the Middle Kingdom during the Hyksos invasions. Under the pharaohs horses were mainly used as draft animals, and it was not until the Graeco-Roman period that a cavalry was formed. From the time of the Arab conquest the cavalry became the supreme military weapon and the horse, unlike its European counterpart, which was beginning to be used for agricultural labor, was reserved exclusively for fighting. Equestrian skill reached its peak during the Mameluke period, and at this time Arabic literature also acquired its great treatises on horsemanship.

MAMELUKE EQUESTRIAN SKILLS
Once they had mastered the art of mounting bareback, the Mamelukes practiced vaulting onto their horse with and without a saddle, both with and without weapons. They continued their training with the twelve skills of classical horsemanship: use of the lance, use of the gourd, use of the mace, archery, swordsmanship, polo, jousting, hand-to-hand combat, the Mahmal ▲ *126*, hunting, use of the crossbow and racing.

Until the 18th century horses were reserved for warriors and members of the aristocracy. They only became more generally used during the 19th century, as illustrated by these drawings from *La Description de l'Egypte* (1809) showing different types of horsemen.

Illustrations from Ibn Ahnaf's *The Book of Horses* (1277): grooming (above) and schooling with the aid of a stick.

Arab tribesmen were less concerned with the training of the rider. Their traditional methods for rearing and schooling horses focused on the meticulous training of the animal, from which they required strength and obedience.

A pilgrim on his way to Mecca and a *muhasseb*, a member of the police responsible for the security of markets (above). Throwing the lance (right), one of the skills practiced by Mameluke horsemen.

● FALCONRY

The falcon, the symbol of the god Horus, occupied an important place in the imagery of Ancient Egypt.

In medieval Egypt, as in all eastern Arabic countries at that time, falconry was the most highly prized mode of hunting. Although birds of prey were used in Arabia well before the arrival of Islam, the art of falconry was mainly developed after the great conquests which brought the Arabs into contact with the Persians and Byzantines. With the first Ommiad caliphs, falconry became a veritable institution. Skills were passed on through the rural and nomadic populations, however, for falconry was not reserved merely for the privileged classes.

Birds of prey trained for hunting traditionally fell into one of two categories: "black-eyed" and "yellow-eyed" birds. The "yellow-eyed" birds used for hawking, such as the goshawk or *baz* (right), were low-flying hawks of the fist. The "black-eyed" birds belonging to the falcon family (above) are the only birds of prey with black irises. These high-flying hawks were used for hunting herons and cranes.

In Egypt the traditional techniques of falconry have survived in the regions bordering the deserts and are still as described in medieval texts.

EGYPT AS SEEN
BY PAINTERS

EGYPT EXPEDITION'S SCIENTIFIC MISSION

La Description de l'Egypte, which contained nine volumes of text and eleven volumes of plates (some three thousand illustrations), was the first systematic inventory of a country whose mysteries had intrigued travelers since the days of the 16th century. It was compiled from the endless notes, accounts and original sketches made by the scientists and artists who composed the Egypt Expedition's scientific mission. One such illustration is this view of the ruins on *Elephantine Island* (1), in which the figure in the foreground disappeared in the final reproduction; the remains from different periods (3) are another example, including jewelry and clothing whose color could not be restored for publication. One of the members of the mission was Dominique Vivant Denon (1747–1825), who was to be the creator of the Louvre Museum. Vivant published his own drawings including this watercolor of *Pompey's Pillar* (2) in 1802, several years ahead of his colleagues, whose work did not begin to appear until 1809.

| 1 |
| 2 | 3 |

140

During the 1830's the establishment of an "Oriental" school of artists was accompanied by a period of artistic or so-called "picturesque" voyages to the Orient and to Egypt in particular. One of the first arrivals in 1830 was Adrien Dauzats (1804–68), an architectural artist renowned for his exactitude. In 1845 he painted this *Outisde View of St Catherine's Monastery* (3), based on his traveling sketches, which was considered one of his most successful works. He was followed a few years later by the Scottish painter David Roberts (1796–1864), the best known of this first generation of painter-travelers. Roberts traveled in Egypt between September 1838 and June 1839 and, although he tended to concentrate on ancient monuments, he also drew several general views of Cairo (1) during his stay as well as interiors of mosques and medersat, including that of Sultan Hassan ▲ *308* (2) for which he had to obtain special official authorization.

	1	
2		3

143

The predominant
themes of the
Oriental artists were
bazaars and interiors.
The markets of Cairo
were a favorite theme
of the British
watercolorist Charles
Robertson (1844–91),
who painted this
street scene in the
Khan el-Khalili (1)
▲ 286. They were
also the subject of
several paintings by
Jean-Léon Gérôme
(1824–1904) whose
depiction of a Cairo
carpet seller entitled
*Le Marchand de tapis
au Caire* (3) is an
imaginary
composition in which
the background is
based on
photographs. Western
artists painting
official
portraits
were often
inspired by
the
domestic

interiors of their subjects. For example the English artist Frank Dillon (1823–1909) painted several watercolors of the residence of Sheikh el-Mahdi (2), an important religious figure. The skillfully painted interiors of his compatriot John Frederick Lewis (1805–76), lit by the light from courtyards or turned-wood screens, were set in the artist's own house in Cairo where he lived from 1840 to 1850. Lewis was the master of the genre, which included *The Midday Meal in Cairo* (4). These interiors, however, tend to be eclipsed by the abundant but seldom alluring imagery of the harem, which was so popular among the Orientalists.

1	2
3	4

Paul Klee (1879–1940) owes his very individual mastery of color and light to the Orient, which he discovered in the spring of 1914 during a brief stay in Tunisia. According to his journal, it was North Africa that gave his art a more definitive form: "I am obsessed by color. . . I am an artist." A journey to Egypt in 1928–9 proved no less decisive, as is evidenced by his painting, which became steadily more abstract and increasingly incorporated signs and symbols. New elements began to appear in the work of the German painter: horizontal streaks of color intersecting vertical or diagonal lines, a pictorial language composed of personal "hieroglyphs". *Ad Parnassum* (2), an oil painting completed in 1932, represents the sacred mountain of Apollo in the form of a pyramid. *Pyramid* (3), a watercolor painted in 1934, was directly inspired by the Pyramids of Giza ▲ *334*. It was three years after this that he produced the

famous pastel on cotton and jute, which was entitled *The Legend of the Nile* (4). Here Klee relived (as he confided in his journal) "the event from a distance", which represented "the point at which reality and the abstract meet". The work is the culmination of the symbolic

language which he valued so highly. It uses a form of hieroglyphs representing barques, fish and aquatic plants against a background of blue rectangles of varying intensity and unusual luminosity. For Kees van Dongen (1877–1968) it was India that represented the artist's decisive encounter with the Orient of his dreams. His "Indian period"

(1922–32) was contemporary with the period of Negro influence on the works of Picasso, Derain and Braque. In 1909 Van Dongen had attended a performance of the ballet *Cleopatra* in Paris, which had inspired a painting. In March 1913 he was profoundly affected by a visit to Egypt, so much so, in fact, that it was to transform his style. His lines became purer and his forms became increasingly elongated. He returned in 1928–9 after he had completed several new paintings. Amongst these was a work entitled *Cairo* (1), a stunning oil painting of the city at night.

1	2
	3
	4

The 1920's saw the development of an Egyptian school of artists, headed by the Alexandrians Mohammed Naghi (1888–1956) and Mahmud Saïd (1897–1964). Naghi moved away from an early Impressionist influence to explore other styles, but returned to it toward the end of his life in this *View of the Nile in Cairo* (2) painted in 1942. The paintings of Mahmud Saïd, inspired by classical culture, are more realistic. They consist mainly of portraits which try to capture the sensuality and opulence of Egypt, as well as several landscapes which give a more personal and fantastic view of the country. This painting of Mersa Matruh (1) painted in 1950 belongs to his final period of lunar landscapes bathed in an unreal light.

EGYPT
AS SEEN BY WRITERS

ANCIENT SITES

FROM A NILE STEAMER

It is said that nobody can fail to be impressed by the first sight of the pyramids, but William Makepeace Thackeray (1811–63) also had other concerns.

"At dawn in the morning we were on deck; the character had not altered of the scenery about the river. Vast flat stretches of land were on either side, recovering from the subsiding inundations: near the mud villages, a country ship or two was roosting under the date trees; the landscape everywhere stretching away level and lonely. In the sky to the east was a long streak of greenish light, which widened and rose until it grew to be of an opal colour, then orange then, behold, the round red disk of the sun rose flaming up above the horizon. All the water blushed as he got up, the deck was all red; the steersman gave his helm to another, and prostrated himself on the deck, and bowed his head eastward, and praised the Maker of the sun: it shone on his white turban as he was kneeling, and gilt up his bronzed face, and sent his blue shadow over the glowing deck. The distances, which had been grey, were now clothed in purple; and the broad stream was illuminated. As the sun rose higher, the morning blush faded away; the sky was cloudless and pale, and the river and the surrounding landscape were dazzlingly clear.

Looking a-head in an hour or two, we saw the Pyramids. Fancy my sensations, dear M——; – two big ones and a little one:

! ! !

There they lay, rosy and solemn in the distance – those old majestical, mystical, familiar edifices. Several of us tried to be impressed; but breakfast supervening, a rush was made on the coffee and cold pies, and the sentiment of awe was lost in the scramble for victuals."

W.M. THACKERAY, *NOTES OF A JOURNEY FROM CORNHILL TO GRAND CAIRO*,
PUB. SMITH, ELDER & CO., 1865

DAWN

Eric Newby (b. 1919) paid a visit to the pyramids at dawn.

"Around 6.15 a.m., the terrible wind suddenly ceased, as if whoever was in charge had switched it off at the main, the sand fell back to earth where it belonged, the sky over the Gulf of Suez and Sinai turned an improbable shade of mauve, overhead the morning star shone down brilliantly out of a sky that had suddenly become deep indigo, and the Pyramids of Giza – two huge ones, of King Cheops and King Chephren, a lesser one of King Mykerinos and three little ones, one behind the other – appeared to rise up out of the ground with the rapidity of mushrooms in a slow-motion film, the only Wonders of the Seven Wonders of the ancient world – first designated by Antipater of Sidon in the second century BC, six of which were on the shores of the Mediterranean (the other, which was not, was the Hanging Gardens of Babylon) – to survive more or less intact.

Looking at them, under a sky that was now rapidly turning from mauve to apple green and lower down was the colour of honey, with the lights of Cairo glimpsed shining between them until they were either switched off or made invisible by the strengthening light of day, there was no doubt that these were among a select body of man-made wonders of any date which in spite of having all the attributes of follies and having suffered severely from over-exposure, actually came up to expectations, if for nothing else, for their shapeliness. **"**

ERIC NEWBY, *ON THE SHORES OF THE MEDITERRANEAN*,
PUB. HARVILL PRESS, 1984

A PATIENT PEOPLE

The work of excavating tombs was long and laborious, as Vita Sackville-West (1892–1962) was quick to note.

"A patient people. I had watched them working at some excavations, a long stream of them, ascending and descending like the angels on Jacob's ladder, carrying little baskets of sand and rubbish on their heads. So must the children of Israel have laboured under the lash of the taskmaster, for even now in the twentieth century the taskmasters stood by, curling their knotted thongs round the ragged limbs of the laggards. Nothing could have given so poignantly the sense of cheapness and abundance of labour as the size of the little baskets; not much bigger than a punnet of strawberries, they were scarcely a load for a child, yet young men and women fetched them from out of the deep tomb, carried them up, and emptied them on the growing heap where the sun glared on the rocks. As they climbed and descended, they chanted a monotonous song; when the lash fell on them, they skipped into the air, but very good-humouredly, as though the lash were all in the day's work and fell with impartiality, more to keep the ranks on the move than to chastise the individual; so they gradually emptied the tomb which their forefathers had dug, and which time had silted up until the day should come for the curious foreigner to expose again the underground chambers, the rigid images of god and Pharaoh; only when the sunset whistle suddenly blew did they turn from beasts of burden into human beings, breaking their ranks and scattering like a flock of starlings at the clapping of hands. Then they ran and leapt over the rocks, some going away to ease themselves, others to drink thirstily from pannikins, but all joyful at their release, and childish in their demonstrations of pleasure. **99**

VITA SACKVILLE-WEST, *PASSENGER TO TEHERAN*,
PUB. THE HOGARTH PRESS, 1926

A PETRIE DIG

T.E. Lawrence (1888–1935) took part in a dig at this site, some forty miles south of Cairo in the middle of the desert.

66No one but I would have achieved a letter at all from a Petrie dig. A Petrie dig is a thing with a flavour of its own: tinned kidneys mingle with mummy-corpses and amulets in the soup: my bed is all gritty with prehistoric alabaster jars of unique types – and my feet at night keep the bread-box from the rats. For ten mornings in succession I have seen the sun rise as I breakfasted, and we come home at nightfall after lunching at the bottom of a 50 foot shaft, to draw pottery silhouettes or string bead-necklaces. In fact if I hadn't malaria to-day I could make a pretty story of it all: – only then I wouldn't have time. . . .

About the digging: 'we' have stumbled on what is probably the richest and largest prehistoric cemetery in Egypt, and in our first week have dug out about 100 graves: these contain wooden coffins and bedsteads, boxes of alabaster jars, dozens of pots of new and known types, some little ivory, (spoons and gaming pieces and scraps of caskets) a good many bronze implements, axes, adzes, chisels, and other trifles. Also a good many baskets, and the shrouds and cloths in which the bodies were wrapped. We have found very few flints, and those not of the best, since the bronze was in general use. The graves are usually about 5 feet deep, and as all the soil is pure sand, digging is merely child's play. Owing to a hitch in his arrangements the Professor has all his workmen here, and so twice as many graves are found than we can record properly: with plenty of time it would be delightful, whereas now we are swamped with the multitude. We have about 900 pots (complete: – all broken ones are thrown away) about 120 alabasters, and a matter of twenty bedsteads. Also we have preserved a number of bodies and skeletons complete by soaking them with boiling parafin wax. These will go to Museums. **99**

THE LETTERS OF T.E. LAWRENCE,
ED. BY DAVID GARNETT,
PUB. JONATHAN CAPE, 1938

LETTERS HOME

POMPEY'S PILLAR

Herman Melville (1819–91) recorded his impressions of Egypt in a journal. The following observations date from December 1856 and January 1857.

66At early morning came in sight of Alexandria Light house, and shortly after, saw Pompey's Pillar. Landed at 10. AM. Donkey to hotel, near which garden of the date palm. Pompey's pillar looks like huge stick of candy after having been long sucked. Cleopatra's

Needles – one of them down & covered over. Rode along banks of Canal of Mahammed, and to Garden of the Pasha. . . .

Alexandria. Seems Mcadamed with the ruins of thousand cities. Every shovel full of earth dug over. The soil, deep loam, looks historical. The Grand Square. Lively aspect. Arabs looking in at windows. The sea is the principal point. Catacombs by it. R.R. extension driven right through. Acres. Wonderful appearance of the sea at noon. Sea & sky molten into each other. . . . One down & covered. Sighing of the waves. Cries of watchmen at night. Lanterns. Assassins. Sun strokes. A daub of Prussian blue.**99**

HERMAN MELVILLE, *JOURNAL OF A VISIT TO EGYPT AND THE LEVANT*,
ED. HOWARD C. HORSFORD,
PUB. PRINCETON UNIVERSITY PRESS, 1955

CAIRO

Rudyard Kipling (1865–1936) wrote the following description to his children Elsie and John in February 1913.

66Cairo itself is a cross between Rome and Florence with touches of Cape Town thrown in. *But* it is cold – beastly cold and Mother and I are surprised and annoyed. The train that met us at Port Said was, as Sunshine T. remarked, exactly like a South African train – I looked for the big coat of arms and the springbuck on the outside. The men (there are no women in the street) are attired in long blue petticoats . . . When they do anything that requires exertion – such as pushing baggage trucks – they hold one end of the petticoat between their teeth. This has the great advantage of reducing them to silence. The colours of their garments are mostly blue or black, with occasional white or orange. We have not seen more than half a dozen women in the streets and they are of course veiled.

The nice thing is to see the camel again – passing unconcernedly between motor cars and trams. Cairo bristles with motor cars and all the luxuries. Our hotel here is full of the latest appliances down to a glorious lift, worked by an Arab in gold-embroidered jacket. It stuck this morning, when I was in it and the Arab panicked. The notice in the bedroom about bells says:–

> Once for the waiter.
> Twice for the chambermaid.
> Three times for the Arab!

This gives one a spacious feeling – as though, if one rang six times a Pyramid would enter. You never saw anything in the world so like their photographs as the Pyramids. We saw them this morning, across the Nile with the tawny grey desert behind 'em, and I only said:– 'Huh! Of course. Those are the pyramids.' Only when one looks at 'em for some time one realizes their enormous size. They dwarf the low hills behind 'em, and they change with the changing lights exactly like mountains. . . .

Our window attracts us . . . There are always camels or dahabeeyahs [large sailing boats] or donkeys to look at. Our balcony looks slap on to the great brown silent Nile. Somewhere round the corner is a barrack of English troops (Sunshine discovered it first) and we can hear bugles and drums.**99**

O BELOVED KIDS – RUDYARD KIPLING'S LETTERS TO HIS CHILDREN,
ED. BY ELLIOT L. GILBERT,
PUB. WEIDENFELD & NICOLSON, 1983

TOURIST AMENITIES

Evelyn Waugh (1903–66) found the service adequate in some areas but lacking in others during his visit to Cairo.

❝We arrived at Cairo in the late afternoon and went to look for an hotel. All the hotels in Egypt are bad, but they excuse themselves upon two contrary principles. Some maintain, legitimately, that it does not really matter how bad they are if they are cheap enough; the others, that it does not really matter how bad they are if they are expensive enough. Both classes do pretty well. We sought out one of the former, a large, old-fashioned establishment under Greek management in the Midan el-Khaznedar, called the Hotel Bristol et du Nil, where rooms even in the high season are only 80 piastres a night. My room had three double beds in it under high canopies of dusty mosquito netting, and two derelict rocking chairs. The windows opened onto a tram terminus. None of the servants spoke a word of any European language, but this was a negligible defect since they never answered the bell. . . .

The journey was unremarkable except to Juliet, who was not used to the ways of Egyptian porters. These throw themselves upon one's baggage like Westminster schoolboys on their Shrove Tuesday pancake, with this difference, that their aim is to carry away as small a piece as possible; the best fighter struggles out happily with a bundle of newspapers, a rug, an air-cushion, or a small attaché case; the less fortunate share the trunks and suitcases. In this way one's luggage is shared between six or seven men, all of whom clamorously demand tips when they have finally got it into the train or taxi. Juliet was shocked to see her husband and myself defending our possessions from attack with umbrella and walking-stick; when the first onslaught was thus checked and our assailants realised that we had not newly disembarked, we were able to apportion it between two of them and proceed on our way with dignity. . . .

One Friday, Solomon came to tell us about some religious dances that were to be performed in the neighbourhood; did we want to see them? Juliet did not feel up to it, so Geoffrey stayed at home with her and I went off alone with Solomon. We rode to the farther end of the plateau on which the pyramids stand, and then down into a sandy hollow where there were the entrances to several tombs. Here we left our camels in charge of a boy and climbed into one of the holes in the hillside. The tomb was already half full of Arabs; it was an oblong chamber cut in the rock and decorated in places with incised hieroglyphics. The audience were standing round the walls and packed in the recesses cut for the coffins. The only light came through the door – one beam of white daylight. The moment we arrived the dance began. It was performed by young men, under the direction of a sheik; the audience clapped their hands in time and joined in the chant. It *was* a dull dance, like kindergarten Eurythmics. The youths stamped their feet on the sandy floor and clapped their hands and swayed slowly about. After a short time I signed to Solomon my readiness to leave, and attempted to make as unobtrusive a departure as possible so as not to disturb these ungainly devotions. No sooner, however, had I reached the door than the dance stopped and the whole company came trooping out crying for 'bakshish.' I asked Solomon whether it was not rather shocking that they should expect to be paid by an infidel for keeping their religious observances. He said, rather sheepishly, that some tip was usual to the sheik. I asked where the sheik was. 'Sheik. Me sheik,' they cried, all running forward and beating their chests. Then the old man appeared. I gave him the piastres and they promptly transferred their attention to him, seizing his robes and clamouring for a share. We mounted our camels and rode away. Even then two or three urchins pursued us on foot crying, 'Bakshish! Bakshish! Me sheik!'

As we went back I asked Solomon, "Was that a genuine religious dance?"

He pretended not to understand.

'You did not like the dance?'

'Would they have done that dance if you had not brought me?'

Solomon was again evasive. 'English and American lords like to see dance. English lords all satisfied.'

'I wasn't satisfied,' I said.**

> EVELYN WAUGH, *LABELS –*
> *A MEDITERRANEAN JOURNEY,*
> PUB. DUCKWORTH, 1930

THE DESERT

MOVEMENT AND SHADOW

English writer, traveler and social reformer Harriet Martineau (1802–76) wrote enthusiastically of riding in the desert.

Our first ride in the Desert, was full of wonder and delight. It was only about three miles: but it might have been thirty from the amount of novelty in it. Our thick umbrellas, covered with brown holland, were a necessary protection against the heat, which would have been almost intolerable, but for the cool north wind. – I believed before that I had imagined the Desert: but now I felt that nobody could. No one could conceive the confusion of piled and scattered rocks, which, even in a ride of three miles, deprives a stranger of all sense of direction, except by the heavens. These narrow passes among black rocks, all suffocation and glare, without shade or relief, are the very home of despair. The oppression of the sense of sight disturbs the brain, so that the will of the unhappy wanderer cannot keep his nerves in order. . . . The presence of dragon-flies in the Desert surprised me; – not only here, but in places afterwards – where there appeared to be no water within a great distance. To those who have been wont to watch the coming forth of the dragon-fly from its sheath on the rush on the margin of a pool, and flitting about the mountain watercourse, or the moist meadows at home, it is strange to see them by dozens glittering in the sunshine of the Desert, where there appears to be nothing for them to alight on: – nothing that would not shrivel them up, if they rested for a moment from the wing. The hard dry locust seemed more in its place, and the innumerable beetles, which everywhere left a net-work of delicate tracks on the light sand. Distant figures are striking in the desert, in the extreme clearness of light and shade. Shadows strike upon the sense here as bright lights do elsewhere. It seems to me that I remember every figure I ever saw in the Desert; – every veiled woman tending her goats, or carrying her water-jar on her head; – every man in blue skirting the hillocks; every man in brown guiding his ass or his camel through the sandy defiles of the black rocks, or on a slope by moonlight, when he casts a long shadow. Every moving thing has a new value to the eye in such a region. **99

HARRIET MARTINEAU, *EASTERN LIFE, PRESENT AND PAST*,
PUB. EDWARD MOXOM, 1848

THE DROMEDARY

Alexander Kinglake (1809–91) wrote the following lively account of his journey across the desert from Cairo to Suez.

66The 'Dromedary,' of Egypt, and Syria is not the two-humped animal described by that name in books of natural history, but is in fact of the same family as the camel, to which it stands in about the same relation as a racer to a cart-horse. The fleetness, and endurance of this creature are extraordinary. It is not usual to force him into a gallop, and I fancy from his make that it would be quite impossible for him to maintain that pace for any length of time, but the animal is on so large a scale, that the jog-trot at which he is generally ridden implies a progress of perhaps ten or twelve miles an hour, and this pace, it is said, he can keep up incessantly without food, or water, or rest for three whole days, and nights.

Of the two dromedaries which I had obtained for this journey, I mounted one myself, and put Dthemetri on the other. My plan was, to ride on with Dthemetri to Suez as rapidly as the fleetness of the beasts would allow, and to let Mysseri (who was still weak from the effects of his late illness) come quietly on with the camels, and baggage.

The trot of the Dromedary is a pace terribly disagreeable to the rider, until he becomes a little accustomed to it; but after the first half hour I so far schooled myself to this new exercise, that I felt capable of keeping it up (though not without aching limbs) for several hours together. Now, therefore, I was anxious to dart forward, and annihilate at once the whole space that divided me from the Red Sea. Dthemetri, however, could not get on at all; every attempt which he made to trot seemed to threaten the utter dislocation of his whole frame, and indeed I doubt whether any one of Dthemetri's age (nearly forty I think,) and unaccustomed to such exercise could have borne it at all easily; besides, the dromedary which fell to his lot was evidently a very bad one; he every now and then came to a dead stop, and coolly knelt down as though suggesting that the rider had better get off at once, and abandon the attempt as one that was utterly hopeless. **99**

ALEXANDER KINGLAKE, *EOTHEN; OR TRACES
OF TRAVEL BROUGHT HOME FROM THE EAST*,
PUB. JOHN OLLIVIER, 1844

THE KNACK OF RIDING CAMELS

Edward Lear (1812–88) wrote to his wife Ann about the problems entailed in a relationship with a camel.

66Thus far we have come quite safely & with great pleasure. I wrote to you from Cairo – on the 12th – just before we were going to start, & I told you that I had already tried my camel, which conveyance both Cross & myself found admirably easy & pleasant. I cannot tell why people write such nonsense about the East as they do: regarding the camel, you have only to sit quite still when it rises, & hold fast by the saddle – & you are lifted up on the long necked monster – & away you go *just as if on a rocking chair.* – But the great beauty of the camelriding is the size of the sort of table you sit on – made up of pillows, & coats, & carpets & saddlebags: – we sit crosslegged – or opposite each other, or we turn round – just as we please, & we lunch or read as quietly as if we were in a room. Nothing can be more charming. As for the camels themselves – I cannot say much for them: – they *are* quite harmless & quiet, but *seem* the most odious beasts – except when they are moving. The sort of horrible way in which they growl & snarl if you only go 6 feet near them – is quite frightful – & if you did not know them – you would suppose they were going to eat you. They do the same to their own masters the Arabs – & appear to have the most unsociable disposition in the world – even among themselves. I give my camel a bunch of green morning & evening – but all attempts at making friends are useless: When I put the vegetable within a yard of him, he yells & grunts as if I were killing him – & after he has taken & eaten it he does just the same. – They all seem to say – 'Oh! bother you! can't you let me alone!' —— & are certainly uninteresting quadrupeds as to their social qualities. – Their pace is *just* 3 miles an hour – like clockwork: If you try to make them go faster – they growl: if you stop them or try to go slower – they growl also. – They will have their own way. It is a wonderful thing to see the long long strings of these strange creatures crossing the desert – silently striding along – laden with bales of goods. One & all have the same expression – 'I am going from Suez to Cairo to please you – but don't speak to me or come near me:– I shall go on well if you let me alone – but if you only look at me I'll growl – '– At night, when our tent is pitched, all the camels stride away – just where they please – looking for little thorny shrubs they feed on – till quite out of sight: but after sunset – when the Arabs call them, they all appear in 2s and threes – & are soon round the tent fires – where they are all tethered & have a lot of beans given them – & there they stay till morning. Most of them make a nasty noise as if they were sick all night long. – At sunrise, they are disturbed to be loaded, & then the groans & grumblings begin & go on till we are fairly off.**"**

EDWARD LEAR, *SELECTED LETTERS*,
ED. BY VIVIEN NOAKES,
PUB. CLARENDON PRESS, 1988

WOMEN IN EGYPT

EGYPTIAN CUSTOMS

Greek historian Herodotus (c. 480–c. 425 BC) writes entertainingly about the social mores of his day in Book Two of his "Histories", which is titled "Odd Practices of the Egyptians".

"About Egypt itself I shall have a great deal more to relate because of the number of remarkable things which the country contains, and because of the fact that more monuments which beggar description are to be found there than anywhere else in the world. That is reason enough for my dwelling on it at greater length. Not only is the Egyptian climate peculiar to that country, and the Nile different in its behaviour from other rivers elsewhere, but the Egyptians themselves in their manners and customs seem to have reversed the ordinary practices of mankind. For instance, women attend market and are employed in trade, while men stay at home and do the weaving. In weaving the normal way is to work the threads of the weft upwards, but the Egyptians work them downwards. Men in Egypt carry loads on their heads, women on their shoulders; women pass water standing up, men sitting down. To ease themselves they go indoors, but eat outside in the streets, on the theory that what is unseemly but necessary should be done in private, and what is not unseemly should be done openly. No women holds priestly office, either in the service of goddess or god; only men are priests in both cases. Sons are under no compulsion to support their parents if they do not wish to do so, but daughters must, whether they wish it or not. Elsewhere priests grow their hair long; in Egypt they shave their heads. In other nations the relatives of the deceased in time of mourning cut their hair, but the Egyptians, who shave at all other times, mark a death by letting the hair grow both on head and chin. They live with their animals – unlike the rest of the world, who live apart from them. Other men live on wheat and barley, but any Egyptian who does so is blamed for it, their bread being made from spelt, or *Xea* as some call it. Dough they knead with their feet, but clay with their hands – and even handle dung. They practise circumcision, while men of other nations – except those who have learnt from Egypt – leave their private parts as nature made them. Men in Egypt have two garments each, women only one. The ordinary practice at sea is to make sheets fast to ring-bolts fitted outboard; the Egyptians fit them inboard. In writing or calculating, instead of going, like the Greeks, from left to right, the Egyptians go from right to left – and obstinately maintain that theirs is the dexterous method, ours being left-handed and awkward. They have two sorts of writing, the sacred and the common. They are religious to excess, beyond any other nation in the world, and here are some of the customs which illustrate the fact: they drink from brazen cups which they scour every day – everyone, without exception. They wear linen clothes which they make a special point of continually washing. They circumcise themselves for cleanliness' sake, preferring to be clean rather than comely.**

HERODOTUS, *THE HISTORIES*,
TRANS. AUBREY DE SÉLINCOURT,
PUB. PENGUIN CLASSICS, 1954

AN ENGINEER'S WIFE

Freya Stark (1893–1993) was saddened to come upon the following example of an unemancipated marriage.

**We had done our work, and there were some hours to spare, and our hosts took us driving through the soft roads of this Arcadia, on which orange trees and mangoes and the feathery peppers threw their shade, – to where a small slope has the distinction, they told us, of generating the only water power in the flat Egyptian land. An engineer was in charge, and lived with his young wife in a brown detached villa as new as a new pin, with everything modern about it. We called, and found a drawing-room as polished as all the rest, with satin cushions of every size, shape and colour scattered wherever a cushion could be. On the middle of the sofa sat a doll, almost life-size and very richly dressed; we were left to admire it for a long time, while the engineer's wife got ready to receive us – not an everyday labour, as we saw when she came in, resplendent in Cairo fashions, with waved hair and face made up to match, and tea approaching behind her, in thin Japanese cups, shepherded hesitatingly by a very small maid.

As we talked, she told us what a lonely life she led: there was no one to call upon at all.

'Do you ever go walking?' said we, trying to find a bright side.

'Sometimes, when my husband has time. I could not go alone in the fields.'

There seemed nothing to be said; we admired the doll on the sofa.

She gave it a wistful little glance. 'I had it before I was married,' she said (I suppose she was about eighteen). 'I keep it. It is a sort of company.'

Poor young effendis. Their professions oblige them to live in country places, and when they marry, their wives, surrounded by exported modernity in chilly splendour, have nothing in the world to do. No wonder they all ask to be transferred to a metropolis, where they may once more see a smile by the domestic hearth, and not feel that the whole social existence of their dear ones depends on them alone. **99**

FREYA STARK, *WEST IS EAST*,
PUB. JOHN MURRAY, 1945

THE ROOF GARDEN
Egyptian Nobel Prize-winning novelist Naguib Mahfouz (b. 1911) included the following description in Book 1 of the "Cairo Trilogy".

66The most amazing aspect of the roof was the southern half overlooking al-Nahhasin Street. There in years past she had planted a special garden. There was not another one like it in the whole neighbourhood on any of the other roofs, which were usually covered with chicken droppings. She had first begun with a small number of pots of carnations and roses. They had increased year by year and were arranged in rows parallel to the sides of the walls. They grew splendidly, and she had the idea of putting a trellis over the top. She got a carpenter to install it. Then she planted both jasmine and hyacinth bean vines. She attached them to the trellis and around the posts. They grew tall and spread out until the area was transformed into an arbor garden with a green sky from which jasmine flowed down. An enchanting, sweet fragrance was diffused throughout.

This roof, with its inhabitants of chickens and pigeons and its arbor garden, was her beautiful, beloved world and her favorite place for relaxation out of the whole universe, about which she knew nothing. As usual at this hour, she set about caring for it. She swept it, watered the plants, fed the chickens and pigeons. Then for a long time, with smiling lips and dreamy eyes, she enjoyed the scene surrounding her. She went to the end of the garden and stood behind the interwoven, coiling vines, to gaze out through the openings at the limitless space around her.

She was awed by the minarets which shot up, making a profound impression on her. Some were near enough for her to see their lamps and crescent distinctly, like those of Qala'un and Barquq. Others appeared to her as complete wholes, lacking details, like the minarets of the mosques of al-Husayn, al-Ghuri and al-Azhar. Still other minarets were at the far horizon and seemed phantoms, like those of the Citadel and Rifa'i mosques. She turned her face toward them with devotion, fascination, thanksgiving, and hope. Her spirit soared over their tops, as close as possible to the heavens. Then her eyes would fix on the minaret of the mosque of al-Husayn, the dearest one to her because of her love for its namesake. She looked at it affectionately, and her yearnings mingled with the sorrow that pervaded her every time she remembered she was not allowed to visit the son of the Prophet of God's daughter, even though she lived only minutes away from his shrine. **99**

NAGUIB MAHFOUZ, *PALACE WALK*,
TRANS. BY WILLIAM MAYNARD HUTCHINS
AND OLIVE E. KERRY,
PUB. DOUBLEDAY, 1991

THE EFFECTS OF LANGUOR

E.D. Clarke (1769–1822) wrote of the effects on visiting Europeans of the atmosphere of the city.

❝*Denon* speaks of the pleasurable sensations daily excited by the delicious temperature of *Caïro*, causing *Europeans*, who arrive with the intention of spending a few months in the place, to remain during the rest of their lives, without ever persuading themselves to leave it. Few persons, however, with whom we associated, were disposed to acquiesce in the opinion of this very amiable writer. Those who are desirous of uninterrupted repose, or who are able to endure the invariable dulness which prevails in every society to which strangers are admitted, may, perhaps, tolerate, without murmuring, a short residence in the midst of this dull and dirty city. The effect, whether it be of climate, or of education, or of government, is the same among all the settlers in *Egypt*, except the *Arabs*; namely, a disposition to exist without exertion of any kind; to pass whole days upon beds and cushions; smoking, and counting beads. This is what *Maillet* termed *Le vrai génie Egyptienne*; and that it may be acquired by residing among the native inhabitants of *Caïro*, is evident from the appearance exhibited by *Europeans* who have passed some years in the city.❞

E.D. CLARKE, *TRAVELS IN VARIOUS COUNTRIES*
OF EUROPE, ASIA AND AFRICA, VOL. VI,
PUB. T. CADELL & W. DAVIES, 1818

THE GROTESQUE

Gustave Flaubert (1821–80) wrote to his friend Louis Bouilhet from Cairo in December 1849.

❝I am sure that as an intelligent man you don't expect me to send you an account of my trip ... In a word, this is how I sum up my feelings so far: very little impressed by nature here – i.e. landscape, sky, desert (except the mirages); enormously excited by the cities and the people. Hugo would say: 'I was closer to God than to mankind.' It probably comes of my having given more imagination and thought, before coming here, to things like horizon, greenery, sand, trees, sun, etc., than to houses, streets, costumes and faces. The result is that nature has been a rediscovery and the rest a discovery. There is one new element which I hadn't expected to see and which is tremendous here, and that is the grotesque. All the old comic business of the cudgeled slave, of the coarse trafficker in women, of the thieving merchant – it's all very fresh here, very genuine and charming. In the streets, in the houses, on any and all occasions, there is a merry proliferation of beatings right and left. There are guttural intonations that sound like the cries of wild beasts, and laughter, and flowing white robes, and ivory teeth flashing between thick lips, and flat negro noses, and dusty feet, and necklaces, and bracelets! Poor you! The pasha at Rosetta gave us a dinner at which there were ten negroes to serve us – they wore silk jackets and some had silver bracelets; and a little negro boy waved away the flies with a kind of feather-duster made of rushes. We ate with our fingers, the food was brought one dish at a time on a silver tray – about thirty different dishes made their appearance in this way. We were on divans in a wooden pavilion, windows open on the water. One of the finest things is the camel – I never tire of watching this strange beast that lurches like a turkey and sways its neck like a swan. Their cry is something that I wear myself out trying to imitate – I hope to bring it back with me – but it's hard to reproduce – a rattle with a kind of tremulous gargling as an accompaniment.**99**

THE LETTERS OF GUSTAVE FLAUBERT,
ED. AND TRANS. BY FRANCIS STEEGMULLER,
PUB. FABER & FABER, 1981

BAKSHISH BOYS
Writing in the 1980's, William Golding (1911–93) does not lament the passing of the young hashish salesmen.

66An aspect of any Egyptian town that is bound to surprise a westerner – northerner – is how the children swarm everywhere. They seemed healthy enough to me as did the population generally. There were no ghastly cripples begging beside the road, no children too listless to move. Even so, the children stopped their playing as we approached and waited. They did not bother us, however, but only examined us curiously and from a distance. This is a change that has happened in the last ten years. It was not because we were 'convoyed' by Alaa and Rushdie, who look as Egyptian as anyone can. It is the result of a push by the authorities to get the bakshish boys off the backs of foreigners. Ten years before we had been plagued by them and they have been notorious for generations. But as far as my experience goes, from one end of Egypt to the other the bakshish boys are gone. So in Abu Tig we were able to walk free and unhindered. The streets were a little untidy but not dirty. There were small shops which seemed to stock only a few goods, except the tobacco kiosk which was loaded down with every kind of tobacco product. The Egyptians make 'hubble-bubbles' out of a can and a length of bamboo. Those who could afford the earlier, ornate versions of the hubble-bubble now smoke western style. But the average Egyptian if he is not dragging at his bamboo pipestem is smoking a cigarette. Everybody smokes hash now and then. Officially the police are supposed to stop it, but wink.**99**

WILLIAM GOLDING, *AN EGYPTIAN JOURNAL,*
PUB. FABER & FABER, 1985

AFTER THE WAR
Lawrence Durrell (1912–90) describes the atmosphere in Alexandria after World War Two.

66Even the war had come to terms with the city, had indeed stimulated its trade with its bands of aimless soldiers walking about with that grim air of unflinching desperation with which Anglo-Saxons embark upon their pleasures; their own demagnetised women were all in uniform now which gave them a ravenous air – as if they could drink the blood of the innocents while it was still warm. The brothels had overflowed and gloriously engulfed a whole quarter of the town around the old square. If anything the war had brought an air of tipsy carnival rather than anything else; even the nightly bombardments of the harbour were brushed aside by day, shrugged away like nightmares, hardly remembered as more than an inconvenience. For the rest, nothing had fundamentally changed. The brokers still sat on the steps of the Mohammed Ali club sipping their newspapers. The old horse-drawn gharries still clopped about upon their listless errands. The crowds thronged the white Corniche to take the frail spring sunlight. Balconies crowded with wet linen and tittering girls. The Alexandrians still moved inside the murex-tinted cyclorama of the life they imagined. ('Life is more complicated than we think, yet far simpler than anyone dares to imagine.') Voices of girls, stabbing of Arab quarter-tones, and from the synagogue a metallic drone punctuated by the jingle of a sistrum. On the floor of the Bourse they were screaming like one huge animal in pain. The money-changers were arranging their currencies like sweets upon the big squared boards. Pashas in scarlet flower-pots reclining in immense cars like gleaming sarcophagi. A dwarf playing a mandolin. An immense eunuch with a carbuncle the size of a brooch eating pastry. A legless man propped on a trolley, dribbling. **"**

Lawrence Durrell, *Clea*,
pub. Faber & Faber, 1960

The Rue Rosette

E.M. Forster (1879–1970) was sent to Alexandria in 1915 with the Red Cross, and he later published a history and a guide to the city.

"Of the three streets that dispute the honour of being Alexandria's premier thoroughfare the Rue Rosette undoubtedly bears the palm for gentility. The Bond Street (I refer to Rue Chérif Pacha) is too shoppy to be genteel, and the Boulevard de Ramleh competes from this particular aspect not at all. In its length, its cleanliness, and the refined monotony of its architecture, Rue Rosette outdoes either of its rivals. They are tainted with utility: people use them to get something or somewhere. But Rue Rosette is an end in itself. It starts in the middle of the town and no man can tell where it stops: a goal it may have but not one discoverable by mortal leg. Its horizon, narrow but uninterrupted, ever unrolls into a ribbon of blue sky above the wayfarer's head, and the ribbon of white beneath his feet corresponds, and right and left of him are the houses that he thought he had passed a quarter of an hour before. Oh, it is so dull! Its dullness is really indescribable. What seem at first to be incidents – such as the trays of worthies who project from the clubs – prove at a second glance to be subdued to what they sit in. They are half asleep. For you cannot have gentility without paying for it.

The poor street does not want to be dull. It wants to be smart, and of a Parisian smartness. Eternally well-dressed people driving infinitely in either direction – that is its ideal. It is not mine, and we meet as seldom as possible in consequence.**"**

E.M. Forster, *Pharos and Pharillon*,
pub. Michael Haag, 1983

By train to Aswan

In an essay entitled "Nasser's Egypt", Gore Vidal (b. 1925) describes a meeting with a young poet named Ahmed, on the banks of the Nile, and then a conversation about the Egyptian economy on a train to Aswan.

❝'Are you German, sir?' A small, dark youth stepped from behind a palm tree into the full light of the setting sun which turned scarlet the white shirt and albino red the black eyes. He had been watching me watch the sun set across the Nile, now blood-red and still except for sailboats tacking in a hot, slow breeze. I told him that I was American but was used to being mistaken for a German: in this year of the mid-century, Germans are everywhere, and to Arab eyes we all look alike. He showed only a moment's disappointment.

'I have many German friends,' he said. 'Two German friends. *West* German friends. Perhaps you know them?' He pulled a notebook out of his pocket and read off two names. Then, not waiting for an answer, all in a rush, he told me that he was a teacher of Arabic grammar, that he was going to Germany, *West* Germany (he emphasized the *West* significantly), to write a book. What sort of book? A book about West Germany. The theme? He responded with some irritation: 'A Book About West Germany.' That was what the book would be about. He was a poet. His name was Ahmed. 'Welcome,' he said 'welcome!' His crooked face broke into a smile. 'Welcome to Luxor!' He invited me to his house for mint tea.

As we turned from the bank of the Nile, a long, haunting cry sounded across the water. I had heard this same exotic cry for several evenings, and I was certain that it must be of ancient origin, a hymn perhaps to Ikhnaton's falling sun. I asked Ahmed what this lovely aria meant. He listened a moment and then said, 'It's this man on the other side who says: will the ferryboat please pick him up?' So much for magic.❞

❝In the diner on the train south to Aswan I had breakfast with a young government official from the Sudan. He was on his way home to Khartoum. He had a fine smile and blue-black skin. On each cheek there were three deep scars, the ritual mark of his tribe – which I recognized, for I had seen his face only the day before on the wall of the Temple of Luxor. Amenhotep III had captured one of his ancestors in Nubia; five thousand years ago the ritual scars were the same as they are now. In matters of religion Africans are profound conservatives. But otherwise he was a man of our time and world. He was dressed in the latest French fashion. He had been for two years on an economic mission in France. He spoke English, learned at the British school in Khartoum.

We breakfasted on musty-tasting dwarfish eggs as dust filtered slowly in through closed windows, covering table, plates, eggs with a film of grit. A fan stirred the dusty air. Parched, I drank three Coca-Colas – the national drink – and sweated. The heat outside was already 110 degrees, and rising. For a while we watched the depressing countryside and spoke very little. At some points the irrigated land was less than a mile wide on our side of the river: a thin ribbon of dusty green ending abruptly in a blaze of desert where nothing at all grew, a world of gray sand as far as the eye could see. Villages of dried-mud houses were built at the desert's edge so as not to use up precious land. The fellahin in their ragged clothes moved slowly about their tasks, quite unaware of the extent of their slow but continual decline. In the fifth century B.C., Herodotus was able to write: 'As things are at present these people get their harvest with less labor than anyone else in the world; they have no need to work with plow or hoe, or to use any other of the ordinary methods of cultivating their land; they merely wait for the river of its own accord to flood the fields.' But all that has changed. Nearly thirty million people now live in a country whose agriculture cannot support half that number.❞

GORE VIDAL, *COLLECTED ESSAYS 1952–72*,
PUB. HEINEMANN, 1974

Itineraries in Egypt

171 Alexandria
205 Nile Delta
237 Sinai
253 Deserts
269 Cairo
353 Memphis to the Faiyum
361 The Faiyum
371 El-Minia to Thebes
393 Thebes
443 Thebes to Aswan
455 Aswan and Abu Simbel
467 Egypt in the museums
    of the world

▲ Pyramids of Giza

▼ Temple of Wadi es-Sebua

▼ Necropolis of Thebes

▲ Temple of Philae on the island of Agilkia

▲ Deir el-Bahri

▼ Temple of Horus at Edfu

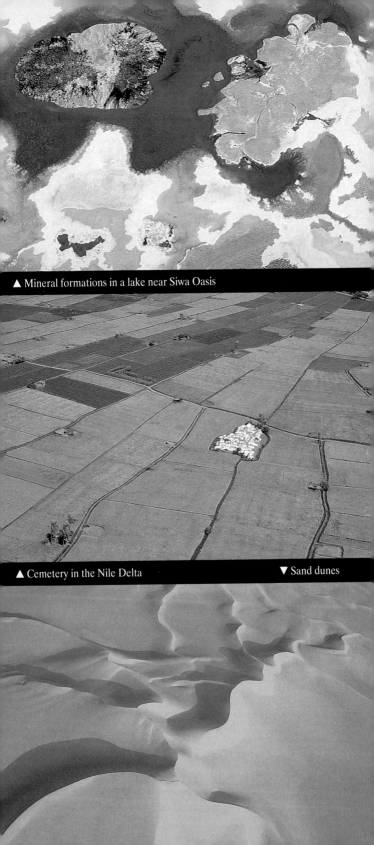

▲ Mineral formations in a lake near Siwa Oasis

▲ Cemetery in the Nile Delta   ▼ Sand dunes

▲ On the shores of Lake Nasser

▲ Harvest

▼ Valley of the Kings

▲ The Citadel, Cairo

▼ Market in Medinet el-Faiyum

▼ Cemetery in Aswan

ALEXANDRIA

THE PORT, *174*
TURKISH QUARTER, *176*
MANSHIYA, *180*
THE CITY CENTER, *182*
GRAECO-ROMAN MUSEUM, *186*
MAHMUDIYA CANAL, *190*
KOM ES-SHOGAFA
CATACOMBS, *192*
CAPE SILSILA, *196*
AROUND ALEXANDRIA, *200*
KARM ABU MENAS, *202*
THE COASTAL REGION, *204*

"It is an arid desert, and between the two chains of mountains that it forms lies a wonderful land. To the west, the chain has the appearance of a line of sand hills; to the east it looks like the belly of a lean horse or the back of a camel. That, O Commander of the Faithful, is Egypt; all its wealth stems from the blessed river that flows through this land with the dignity of a caliph. It waxes and wanes as regularly as the sun and the moon."

Amr Ibn el-As

173

▲ ALEXANDRIA

1 RAS EL-TIN **2** ANFUSHI **3** ABU EL-ABBAS MOSQUE **4** FORT QAITBAY **5** TERBANA MOSQUE **6** EL-SHORBAGI MOSQUE **7** TOMB OF THE UNKNOWN SOLDIER **8** ATTARINE MOSQUE **9** MIDAN SAAD ZAGHLUL **10** NABI DANIEL MOSQUE **11** RAMLEH STATION **12** EL-QAID MOSQUE **13** ENGINEERING FACULTY **14** GRAECO-ROMAN MUSEUM

🏊 **Two days**

🚌 **One day**

◆ A B

According to Plutarch's account of the founding of Alexandria, Homer appeared to Alexander the Great in a dream and described the site of the future city, where:

"An island set in ocean deep, Lies off fair Egypt's rich and fertile land, And the name of the island is called Pharos". "Alexander's dream" was realized when the future capital of the Lagides and second largest city in the Roman empire, and the great commerical port of the late 19th and early 20th centuries, was founded in 331 BC on the site of the Ancient Egyptian village of Rakhotis. It was designed by the architect Dinocrates and lay between the Mediterranean coast in the north and Lake Mareotis (now Lake Mariut) in the south ▲ *203*. Although Alexandria has retained little of its ancient glory, it is still a legendary city which has been continually enriched by the numerous cultural influences exerted throughout its history. To many, it is the symbol of open-mindedness and cosmopolitanism.

EGYPT'S LEADING PORT. Since the construction of Heptastadion, a causeway built between Pharos and the mainland by Dinocrates, Alexandria has had two harbors. The EASTERN HARBOR is the oldest of the two, and was very active in the Middle Ages. During the Ottoman period it underwent a gradual decline caused by competition from the ports of Rosetta and Damietta, whose position at the mouth of two branches of the Nile meant they were directly linked with the hinterland. The WESTERN HARBOR, previously known as Eunostos ("safe return"), dates from the time of the Ptolemies and was the harbor that Mohammed Ali decided to develop. The creation of infrastructures and the improved links with Cairo following the

THE HARBORS OF ALEXANDRIA
Today the eastern harbor is only used by a few fishing boats and yachts. Boats can be hired for trips around the bay.

174

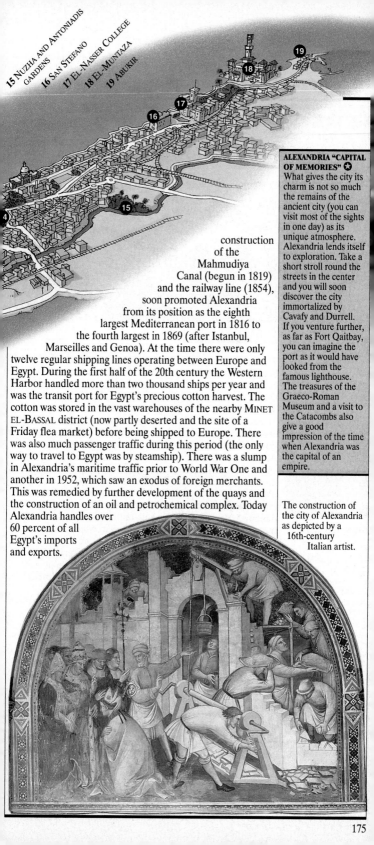

15 NUZHA AND ANTONIADIS GARDENS
16 SAN STEFANO
17 EL-NASSER COLLEGE
18 EL-MUNTAZA
19 ABUKIR

ALEXANDRIA "CAPITAL OF MEMORIES" ✪

What gives the city its charm is not so much the remains of the ancient city (you can visit most of the sights in one day) as its unique atmosphere. Alexandria lends itself to exploration. Take a short stroll round the streets in the center and you will soon discover the city immortalized by Cavafy and Durrell. If you venture further, as far as Fort Qaitbay, you can imagine the port as it would have looked from the famous lighthouse. The treasures of the Graeco-Roman Museum and a visit to the Catacombs also give a good impression of the time when Alexandria was the capital of an empire.

construction of the Mahmudiya Canal (begun in 1819) and the railway line (1854), soon promoted Alexandria from its position as the eighth largest Mediterranean port in 1816 to the fourth largest in 1869 (after Istanbul, Marseilles and Genoa). At the time there were only twelve regular shipping lines operating between Europe and Egypt. During the first half of the 20th century the Western Harbor handled more than two thousand ships per year and was the transit port for Egypt's precious cotton harvest. The cotton was stored in the vast warehouses of the nearby MINET EL-BASSAL district (now partly deserted and the site of a Friday flea market) before being shipped to Europe. There was also much passenger traffic during this period (the only way to travel to Egypt was by steamship). There was a slump in Alexandria's maritime traffic prior to World War One and another in 1952, which saw an exodus of foreign merchants. This was remedied by further development of the quays and the construction of an oil and petrochemical complex. Today Alexandria handles over 60 percent of all Egypt's imports and exports.

The construction of the city of Alexandria as depicted by a 16th-century Italian artist.

175

Fort Qaitbay, built on
the site of the Pharos
Lighthouse.

The capture of
Alexandria by
Bonaparte's army in
1798 (above).

SHARI' RAS EL-TIN
The last corbeled
houses, so
characteristic of late
Ottoman
architecture, can still
be seen in the Shari'
Ras el-Tin, as can
some of the first
European-style
apartment blocks,
with their profusion
of Italianate
decorations.

TURKISH QUARTER

The oldest part of Alexandria, lying along the causeway
linking the former island of Pharos with the mainland,
consists of the districts of Anfushi, Gumrok (the customs
district) and Ras el-Tin ("cape of figs"). For a long time, these
districts were collectively known by Western travelers as the
"Turkish Quarter". They were only established, at the very
earliest, during the 16th century. GUMROK, the oldest of the
three, flourished as a result of the decline of medieval
Alexandria, which lay further south on the site of the ancient
city. Although the medieval city had became quite important
during the Mameluke period, its population was decimated by
plague in the 17th century and by 1658 the city was little more
than a heap of ruins punctuated by a few dilapidated
dwellings. New houses were built outside the city walls, and
these constituted the nucleus of a new city which was to
expand rapidly in the early 18th century before it, too, was hit
by plague. When the French landed in Alexandria in 1798 the
"Turkish Quarter" was little more than a small town of eight
thousand inhabitants centered around the Gumrok district
and subsisting mainly from fishing. The later urban
development of RAS EL-TIN and ANFUSHI BAY dates from the
reign of Mohammed Ali (1805–49), whose expansionist
aspirations, which hinged on the development of a naval
fighting force, led him to choose Alexandria as the center of
his Mediterranean policy. This was the beginning of a period
of major construction for the city. In 1818 the great pasha
began to build the huge PALACE OF RAS EL-TIN, of which

certain sections, especially the *haramlik*, were reminiscent of his native Macedonian architecture. The present palace, which was built in 1925 by Italian architects, houses the Admiralty and is closed to the public. A military hospital and camps were built to the east of the palace. In 1825 Mohammed Ali commissioned the French engineer Lefèbure de Cerisy to construct an arsenal, whose workshops soon employed more than four thousand workers. Several years later he undertook the relocation of the cemeteries that were scattered along Anfushi Bay, so that the land could then be sold by lots and used for the establishment of a new district. The site revealed some of the most ancient necropolises in Alexandria.

RAS EL-TIN NECROPOLIS. Three hypogea were discovered in the gardens of the Palace of Ras el-Tin during the renovation work carried out on the building in 1913–14. Eight more were discovered in 1939–40. They date from the early 2nd to the 3rd centuries BC, and their design is significantly different from those of the neighboring Anfushi Necropolis. A quadrilateral well provided access to three long galleries. Within the galleries, dozens of burial niches had been hollowed out. Nowadays the necropolis is not open to the public.

ANFUSHI NECROPOLIS. The necropolis lies to the south of the esplanade leading to the Palace of Ras el-Tin and consists of five tombs, all dating from the first half of the 3rd century, discovered in 1901 and 1921. The first and most remarkable of the tombs is reached by way of a vaulted stairway hewn out of the rock, leading down into a square courtyard which is open to the sky and provides access to two tombs. The walls of the stairway and tombs have a painted stucco revetment imitating alabaster and marble. The vaulted ceiling of the funeral chamber is decorated with geometric trompe l'oeil designs reminiscent of the coffered ceilings in certain ancient villas. The funeral motifs are a fine example of the combined influence of Greek art and the traditional forms of Egyptian art.

SHARI' RAS EL-TIN. The long Shari' Ras el-Tin is one of the new streets which were built in the Turkish Quarter during the 19th century. It runs from the palace esplanade, crossing through the Turkish Quarter to arrive at the Midan Manshiya.

FORT QAITBAY. The fort (above) was built at the end of the 15th century on the site of the Pharos Lighthouse which, because of its height, was one of the Seven Wonders of the World.

**ABU EL-ABBAS
EL-MURSI MOSQUE**
The high, central
dome of the mosque
(79 feet beneath the
keystone) is
supported by eight
monolithic pink
granite columns
quarried, cut and
polished in Italy, and
flanked by four small
cupolas.

ABU EL-ABBAS EL-MURSI MOSQUE. The main mosque in
Alexandria is named after Sidi Abu el-Abbas el-Mursi, a holy
man from Andalusia who died in the 13th century. It stands
midway between Fort Qaitbay and the city center, in a square
set slightly back from the Corniche called the Midan el-
Gawamaa (Square of the Mosques). The square also contains
several other sanctuaries, including the ABU EL-FATAH, EL-
BUSEIRI, YAQUT and NASR AD-DIN mosques, which were
either restored or rebuilt when the square was renovated after
World War One. Although they tend to date from the 18th
century, the Abu el-Abbas el-Mursi Mosque was constructed
relatively recently, since it was started in 1928 and completed
in 1945 after work had been suspended during the war years.
It replaced a structure, built in 1767, which had been
destroyed by fire a few years earlier, and this has caused some
confusion over the age of the mosque. The building, which
covers an area of over 32,000 square feet, has an extremely
unusual octagonal design. Although such a design was not
unprecedented in the Islamic architectural tradition (the most
famous example being the Rocher dome in Jerusalem), it
tended to be reserved for mausoleums and had never been
used in Egypt. The building was designed by the Italian
architect Mario Rossi (1897–1961), who for many years
headed the architects' department of the Waqf ▲ *302* ministry
which commissioned the mosque, and who is said to have
converted to Islam shortly before his death. He also designed
several other Alexandrian mosques, including the Ras el-Tin
and Ibrahim el-Qaïd mosques.

TERBANA MOSQUE. The Terbana Mosque (1677) is one of the
few remaining ancient mosques in Alexandria. It stands on
the corner of the Shari' Terbana and the Shari' Suq el-
Tabakhin and is reached by following the
Shari' Ras el-Tin toward Manshiya. The
first-floor façade is occupied
by shops and a *sabil*
● *113.*

The entrance consists of a portal of bicolored bricks. Particularly worthy of note are the two enormous granite columns with Corinthian capitals, which stand to the left of the steps, and a number of ancient columns (some of which, unfortunately, are very badly damaged), which have come from other sites. The mihrab ● *108* is covered with Maghrebi-style ceramics.

THE SUQ DISTRICT ★. As it nears Manshiya the last section of the Shari' Ras el-Tin, still known as the Shari' Faransa, becomes a busy shopping street. The district around the Shari' Ras el-Tin and Shari' Midan which runs parallel to it is Alexandria's traditional *suq* district. At the turn of the century mainly duty-free goods, including items of clothing, cloth, gold and silver jewelry, could be found on sale here. Each section of the *suq* has its own speciality. For example, the SUQ EL-MAGHARBA (Maghrebi *suq*) has row upon row of medicinal plants which are used to make infusions with healing or supposedly miraculous properties, while the SUQ EL-LIBIA (Libyan *suq*)

sells the famous embroidered costumes worn by the Bedouins. In the Shari' Midan one of Alexandria's few surviving *wakala* ● *118* attests to the age of these *suq*. It forms part of the EL-SHORBAGI MOSQUE COMPLEX, which was founded in 1757 and has a distinctive gallery on the second floor that overlooks the street. Some of the stonework of this architectural complex, which also includes shops and living accommodation, bears hieroglyphic inscriptions. The Shari' Midan was also renowned as the home of a large section of Alexandria's Jewish community. Many Jewish families lived in *okelles* ● *181* like the huge EL-LAYMUN OKELLE, built round a central courtyard with galleries leading to the apartments. There was a continuous Jewish presence in Alexandria from the time of its foundation (as evidenced by the Greek and Aramean inscriptions found in the necropolis of the Ibrahimiya district) to the period following World War Two when the community totaled about forty thousand. After this time, however, came the waves of emigration, in the years 1948, 1956, 1962 and finally in 1967 when the last Jews were expelled from Egypt in the aftermath of the June 1967 Arab–Israeli War. As one approaches Manshiya, the streets become increasingly narrow. This area is known as the ZANQAT EL-SITTAT (or "Ladies' Alley"). The confined space is packed with both shops and stalls which sell the cloth, trinkets and perfumes that find so much favor not only with native Alexandrian women, but also with increasing numbers of tourists. Popular myth would have it that men and women alike come here to enjoy the close contact imposed by the narrowness of the streets.

THE JEWISH COMMUNITY
Most of the synagogues belonging to Alexandria's Jewish community have been destroyed (above).

SHORBAGI MOSQUE
The second-floor gallery looks over the shops at street level. A fruit market such as one might find anywhere in the city.

179

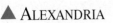

The Alexandria Stock Exchange was destroyed by fire in 1977.

MANSHIYA

The Manshiya district grew up around a vast esplanade some 350 yards long, built on the edge of the Turkish Quarter during the 1830's on the site of an old training ground where Bedouins and oasis-dwellers came to sell their goods. The successive names given to the esplanade evoke the various stages of its history. When it was first built it was known as the PLACE DES CONSULS because the adjacent land was divided up to provide sites for the consulates of the major

BRITISH BOMBARDMENT
In July 1882, after a violent bombardment which destroyed vast areas of the city, a British squadron landed in Alexandria and managed to wipe out the army of Colonel Orabi Pasha, the leader of the Nationalist Party and Egyptian Minister for War, who wanted to put an end to Anglo-French economic control.

foreign powers. It became the MIDAN MOHAMMED ALI following the inauguration (1873) of the equestrian statue of the great pasha (by the French sculptors Jacquemart and Cordier), which was placed in the center of the esplanade, and then the MIDAN MANSHIYA when the area around the esplanade was rebuilt after the 1882 bombardment. The only building that did not have to be rebuilt was the Anglican Church of St Mark, founded in 1844. Most of these buildings have survived and form a remarkably homogenous architectural complex rarely to be seen in Egyptian cities, which are usually a hotch-potch of different architectural styles and buildings from a huge variety of different periods. Some are modern versions of the *okelle*, a type of apartment block characteristic of Alexandrian architecture. The ALEXANDRIA STOCK EXCHANGE, the nerve center of the city, stood at one end of the square for almost a century. It was burnt during the 1977 hunger riots and subsequently demolished; since then the site has remained a piece of waste ground. Manshiya, now known as MIDAN AT-TAHRIR (Liberation Square), was the scene of President Gamal Abd el-Nasser's famous announcement in 1956, informing the people of Alexandria that the Suez Canal had been nationalized.

"OKELLE". The *okelle* was a rental apartment block, organized in much the same way as a *wakala* ● *118*, which provided residential and commercial accommodation. The first floor opened onto the courtyard and street and was reserved for shops and workshops, while the upper floors were given over to living accommodation. Two examples of modern *okelle* are the PASSAGE MENASCE, built in 1883 and designed by Lasciac ▲ *281*, and the MONFERRATO BUILDING, also built in 1883 and designed by Piattoli, which are both situated in the Midan at-Tahrir. The interior of each of these huge edifices is dissected by a narrow, cruciform street.

"OKELLES"
These buildings housed Alexandria's ethnic minorities. In the 18th century, each European nation had its own *okelle*.

TRIBUTE FROM THE ITALIAN COMMUNITY. Manshiya opens onto the sea via the MIDAN ORABI, an enormous planted area which was formerly known as the "French Gardens" because they were established on land given to the city by France. At the end of the square, a monument in the form of an exedra (which is now dedicated to the Unknown Soldier) was a tribute given by the Italian community to the khedive Ismaïl. It was designed by the architect Verrucci and erected in 1937. In the period between the wars, the Italian population of Alexandria, which was second in size only to that of the Greek community, reached 25,000; yet although the Italians had been living in Egypt for quite a considerable time, they had never really become established there. They were usually Italian émigrés expatriated for one or, at most, two generations. During the first half of the 19th century, Italian immigration was essentially politically motivated. After the Risorgimento the reasons behind it became economic. The community was usually of modest status, commonly excelling in the field of construction work. Until the 1950's Alexandria, like many other Egyptian cities, had a good supply of monumental masons, cabinet makers, building contractors, architects and engineers. The tall, smoked-glass tower beyond the monument has housed the new French-speaking Léopold Sédar Senghor University since late 1990.

Midan Manshiya (below) at the turn of the century, now the Midan at-Tahrir (Liberation Square).

Map of 17th-century Alexandria.

The Attarine Mosque, where Saïd Mohammed, a friend of Abu el-Abbas ▲ *178*, is buried.

THE CITY CENTER

At the turn of the century the center of Alexandria, which for some time had been focused around the Midan Manshiya, shifted toward the new suburbs to the west of the city. From then on it developed on the site of the ancient city which had subsequently become the site of the medieval city after the Arab conquest. An amphitheater, fragmented ramparts and a few cisterns are all that remains of these successive occupations, although parts of the original layout such as the ancient Canopic Way, now the Shari' Hurriya (formerly the Shari' Bab Rosetta), survived and could still be seen in the 19th century. The so-called "Arab" fortifications, a huge five-mile-long perimeter wall fortified with towers which had protected the city since the 13th century, were still intact when the French landed in Alexandria and remained so until the declassification of fortifications decreed in 1885. The same was true of the famous Alexandria cisterns. In 1800 the engineers of the Egypt Expedition recorded over three hundred, while in 1846 Colonel Barthélemy Gallice counted 896. Today there are only half a dozen.

ATTARINE ANTIQUES DISTRICT ★. The district is reached by crossing the Midan Manshiya and taking the Shari' Ahmed Orabi, turning right into the Shari' Senwosret and finally into the Shari' Attarine. The district takes its name from the mosque on the corner of the Shari' Attarine and the Shari' Sidi-Metwali. This former church was dedicated to Saint

Athanasius in 370 and converted into a mosque at the beginning of the Arab conquest. In the early 19th century it was used as a naval hospital before being destroyed in 1830 and subsequently rebuilt. Behind the mosque lies the SUQ EL-ATTARINE (Perfume Market) where, at the end of the last century, perfumes and spices from Syria and Lebanon were sold. Today dealers sell antique and second-hand furniture, sometimes beautiful opalines, chandeliers, ancient weapons and more modern wrought-iron work. Lovers of French literature may be interested to know that it is not uncommon to come across an early edition on the shelves of the French bookshop *Librairie des Amis des Lettres*. One of the district's specialties are the roasted quail and pigeons on sale in the evenings in a tiny square only a few yards from the French bookshop. If you follow the Shari' Attarine in the direction of Cairo station and turn left into the Shari' Ismaïl-Mehna, you will come to an intersection and the amphitheater.

KOM EL-DIKKA. The Roman amphitheater was discovered in 1964 by archeologists from Warsaw University and the Graeco-Roman Museum. The discovery followed the demolition of the remains of a fort dating from the Napoleonic expedition, and the leveling of the artificial hill on which it was constructed. Its present horseshoe shape is the consequence of a series of modifications made between the 2nd and 4th centuries when it was converted into a church. Next to the amphitheater are the remains of two necropolises (13th–14th and 8th–9th centuries). The tombs had been incorporated into a recently discovered ancient Roman bath complex which was one of the biggest in Alexandria and indeed in Egypt.

THE AMPHITHEATER
The thirteen gray and white marble tiers of the terrace lead down to the arena. The buttressed wall of the semicircular passageway which ran beneath the early theater constitutes the perimeter of the new amphitheater. Nearby are the ruins of the Roman baths (above).

"CLEOPATRA'S NEEDLES"
Today the two obelisks that the Alexandrians called "Cleopatra's Needles", illustrated (left) by Vivant Denon, can be seen in London and New York. They used to stand near one of the towers of the Arab fortifications.

View of the rooftops of Alexandria with, in the foreground, the cupolas of the Nabi Daniel Mosque.

SHARI' NABI DANIEL. The first street on the right after the Amphitheater is the Shari' Nabi Daniel, which leads down to the Corniche. It is a perfect example of Alexandria's cultural and religious heterogeneity. On the left, below the street, are several columns which were probably part of the ancient Roman road. Nearby the NABI DANIEL MOSQUE houses the tombs of the khedivial family, including that of Saïd Pasha, the son of Mohammed Ali. As part of the controversy surrounding the location of the tomb of Alexander the Great, the so-called Soma, which is one of the great unsolved mysteries of Alexandrian archeological exploration, some historians have maintained that it lies beneath the Nabi Daniel Mosque. Modern archeologists tend to situate the Soma about half a mile further east, in the Graeco-Roman cemeteries. A little further on, before you cross the Shari' el-Hurriya, is the elegant villa of the FRENCH CULTURAL CENTER and, below that, the huge ELIAHU HANABI SYNAGOGUE, the only synagogue which still holds religious services. It was founded in the late 19th century on the site of an earlier synagogue built in 1354 and destroyed by fire during the 19th century. It houses the combined treasures of the seven (now nonexistent) Alexandrian synagogues. The Shari' Nabi Daniel opens onto the Shari' Saad Zaghlul near the Midan Saad Zaghlul and the central tram station.

Midan Saad Zaghlul, the nerve center of Alexandria.

CINEMAS AND RESTAURANTS. Alexandria's liveliest entertainments spots, both by day and night, are found near the vast Midan Saad Zaghlul and the streets leading from the square to the Shari' Hurriya. The intercity bus terminus and the Ramleh (Ar-Raml) tram station make the MIDAN SAAD ZAGHLUL one of Alexandria's busiest thoroughfares. The square stands on land reclaimed from the sea when the city's new quays were built, beginning in 1907. It is dominated by a huge monument to the great nationalist leader Saad Zaghlul ▲ 281 by the Egyptian sculptor Mahmud Mukhtar ▲ 282. Several luxury hotels overlook the square, including the famous *Cecil Hotel* (1928), which provided the setting for part of Lawrence

The façade (right) and interior (below) of the Eliahu Hanabi Synagogue.

Durrell's ● *162 Alexandria Quartet*. The square also boasts two of the city's best-known coffee houses: the *Délices*, still run by the descendants of its Greek founder, and the *Trianon*, whose superb Art Nouveau-style frescos on wood have been recently restored. A little further on, in the Shari' Safiya-Zaghlul, leading up to Kom el-Dikka, are several of Alexandria's more prestigious cinemas. They include the *Strand* (owned for a long time by the founder of the Dores Studios, a portraitist who was extremely popular with prominent Alexandrians at the turn of the century), the *Rialto* with its name written in Greek lettering, the luxurious *Metro* built in 1950 by Metro-Goldwyn-Mayer (its décor, carefully maintained by successive managers, is well worth seeing) and the *Rio*, the only cinema with a second, open-air auditorium on the terrace. The *Elite* restaurant, the last gastronomic stronghold of French-speaking Alexandrians, is to be found in the same street. Its Greek patronne, who is known to her regulars as Madame Cristina, has had the walls covered with paintings, in the style of the bistros of Montparnasse. One of the paintings is a portrait of the poet Constantine Cavafy.

CAVAFY MUSEUM. Constantine Cavafy (1863–1933), the great poet born in Alexandria to Greek parents, is buried in the Greek cemetery near his house at no. 4 Shari' Sharm el-Sheikh. In 1933 his apartment was converted into a museum, a place of pilgrimage for his admirers where various rare editions of his books are on display. Visitors can also see family photos, his funeral mask and pieces of furniture which are supposed to have belonged to him but are probably copies. A new room is devoted to another Greek writer, Stratis Tsirkas.

GRAECO-ROMAN MUSEUM ★. The Graeco-Roman Museum is reached by way of the Shari' Safiya-Zaghlul and Shari' el-Hurriya. When it was founded in 1891 by the Italian archeologist Botti the museum occupied the five rooms of an apartment in the Shari' Rosetta. In 1894, in response to a growing interest in the history and archeology of Ancient Egypt, the khedive Abbas II decided to found a museum devoted to the ancient splendor of Alexandria. The newly established Graeco-Roman Museum received gifts from such great private collectors as Antoniadis, Gianaclis and Glymenopoulos and rooms were named after them until the Free Officers' coup in 1952. Since then the collection has been enriched by exhibits which have come mainly from excavations carried out in the city and its environs as well as from the Faiyum ▲ *361*, the Nile Delta ▲ *205* and Middle Egypt ▲ *371*. The museum's collection serves as an admirable illustration of the influence of Alexandrian culture throughout Egypt.

"You will find no other countries, no other seas. The city will always be with you: you will be walking along these same streets, growing old in these same, familiar districts and your hair will turn white beneath these same roofs. You will always find yourself in this city. As for leaving – vain hope – there is no boat, no road that you can take. As you have ruined your life in this corner of the earth, so you have destroyed it everywhere else in the world."
  Constantine Cavafy

Façade of the Graeco-Roman Museum.

Today the modern city stands on the site of ancient Alexandria and there are few visible remains of this former capital of the ancient world. The remains of Ptolemaic palaces, temples, baths and other public buildings are constantly being discovered and added to the collections of the city's Graeco-Roman Museum. Its twenty connecting rooms, arranged around a central garden containing statues, stelae, sarcophagi and a temple dedicated to Sobek, house the legacy of ancient Alexandrian civilization. The museum is a remarkable synthesis of Egyptian, Greek and Roman cultures, which echoes the symbolic cosmopolitanism of the city.

Bronze head of Hadrian with eyes in *pâte de verre*, found at Qena.

Marble statue of the god Harpocrates (naked and with a finger in his mouth), son of Isis. Found at Ras el-Soda.

Fragment of colored *pâte de verre* from the Roman period. Alexandria had a flourishing glass industry famed for its iridescent *millefiori* glass.

Plaster head (probably a Libyan) from Cyrenaica.

"TANAGRA"
The museum has a collection of terracotta figurines known as *tanagras*, named after the Greek town where a similar collection was discovered. They all come from Alexandrian necropolises, mainly Shatby, Hadra and Ibrahimiya.

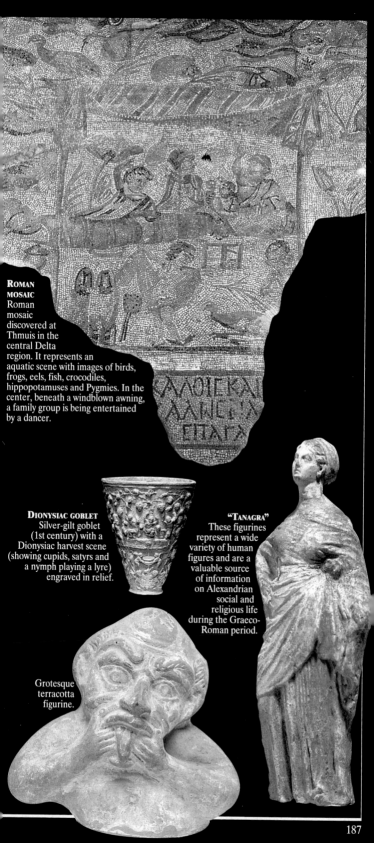

ROMAN MOSAIC
Roman mosaic discovered at Thmuis in the central Delta region. It represents an aquatic scene with images of birds, frogs, eels, fish, crocodiles, hippopotamuses and Pygmies. In the center, beneath a windblown awning, a family group is being entertained by a dancer.

DIONYSIAC GOBLET
Silver-gilt goblet (1st century) with a Dionysiac harvest scene (showing cupids, satyrs and a nymph playing a lyre) engraved in relief.

"TANAGRA"
These figurines represent a wide variety of human figures and are a valuable source of information on Alexandrian social and religious life during the Graeco-Roman period.

Grotesque terracotta figurine.

The district was named after the (now destroyed) Bab Rosetta.

THE CISTERNS
Alexandria's network of cisterns impressed many Europeans and in particular elicited the following remark from Saint-Génis, a member of the Egypt Expedition: "Here the ingenuity of the Greeks, inspired by the most pressing of all needs when founding a city without [a natural source of] water, equaled the momentous efforts of the Ancient Egyptians in terms of the exacting nature of their undertaking, while endowing it with their natural taste for elegance. They succeeded in creating a second, subterranean city which was quite as vast as the first, and its remains are certainly one of the greatest and most beautiful works of Antiquity".

BAB ROSETTA DISTRICT

GREEK QUARTER. One of the most beautiful residential districts in Alexandria stretches along the Shari' el-Hurriya beyond the Graeco-Roman Museum. Its luxury villas and elegant residential blocks include the monumental MICLAVEZ BUILDING opposite the Town Hall (a prize-winner in the 1927 façade competition organized by the city) and the impressive ADDA COMPLEX, which was built in 1929 by the architect Nahman. It is undoubtedly the best maintained district in Alexandria; it is also the only district to have escaped the disfiguring modern construction suffered by the rest of the city. It used to be known as the Greek Quarter because, at the turn of the century, the wealthiest members of the Greek community chose to live in these streets, which are still named after the Ptolemies, Pharaohs, Abbasids and Fatimids. It was neither the only nor the oldest Greek quarter in the city, however. The first site of the city's largest foreign community, which could claim a population of over fifty thousand in the years between the wars, lay further east in the area around the Greek Orthodox patriarchate and the old Church of St Saba, in close proximity to which the Greek hospital (now used as warehouses) was built in 1887. Greeks of more modest status moved into the less expensive housing developments of Ibrahimiya.

REMAINS OF THE SHALLALAT GARDENS. Beyond the Greek Quarter the Shari' el-Hurriya opens onto a vast green area, which are the public gardens created by the Alexandria Town Council in 1905 on the site of the old fortifications around the Bab Rosetta. The debris was used to create relief and build the waterfalls (*shallalat*) after which the gardens were named. The remains of one of the rampart towers (the west tower) were excavated and incorporated into the design of the gardens, which also have the only CISTERN in Alexandria open to the public: the so-called IBN EL-NABI. The three levels of this square cistern

> "Alexandria seems paved with the crumbling ruins of a thousand cities. Every acre of earth has been turned and turned again. The ground appears thick with the humus of its history."
>
> Herman Melville

are supported by granite columns taken from earlier structures.

THE CISTERNS OF ALEXANDRIA. These enormous reservoirs were constructed below ground level mainly when the city was founded to ensure that its houses always had a fresh supply of drinking water; some, however, were built at a later date. They were all linked by a complex, intercommunicating system of conduits and drew their water from a canal leading from the Canopic branch of the Nile about 17 miles from Alexandria, in the locality of Schedia. According to the engineer and historian Ali Mubarak, many cisterns were artificially filled with water brought in water skins and were cleaned out once a year to ensure that they remained hygienic. Most were filled in during the 19th century, although a few were still being used in 1888 to supply water to private citizens and public buildings. The five other surviving cisterns in Alexandria are closed to the public. One of these is situated nearby, on the corner of the Shari' el-Hurriya and a street that takes its name from the Ptolemies, and was used as a shelter during World War Two. Rumor has it that other cisterns still exist and may be the cause of certain unexplained disappearances.

FINE ARTS MUSEUM. The Fine Arts Museum, which is housed in a villa in the district of Muharram Bey, is the subject of a long-standing and so far unresolved controversy between the Governorate, on which it depends in principle, and the Ministry of Culture, which claims responsibility for the supervision of the museum. The consequence of this, however, is that most of its richly stocked collections are kept in reserve and are only occasionally brought out for temporary exhibitions.

The Museum of Modern Art is housed in a beautiful villa donated in 1954 by the Menasce family.

Engraving (1802) by Louis Mayer of the ancient columnated mosque of the (now nonexistent) Bab Rosetta.

The tent occupied by the chief engineer in charge of the construction of the Mahmudiya Canal. The plans for the canal were drawn up by Pascal Coste.

"Alexander found the Nile at Abukir (Canopic Mouth); then you had to go to Rosetta (ancient Bolbitine Mouth). So Mohammed Ali built a 45-mile-long canal, the Mahmudiya Canal, named in honor of Mahmud, the then ruler of Turkey, which was completed in 1820. It was badly constructed and its banks were continually collapsing, but the opening of the canal led to the rapid expansion of Alexandria and the decline of Rosetta."
E.M. Forster

MODERN ARCHITECTURE. The so-called "water traffic circle" is a must for lovers of modern architecture. Among the interesting old installations preserved by the Alexandria Water Company is the VILLA AGHION (1926), a fine piece of avant-garde architecture designed by the French architect Auguste Perret (1874–1954). On the way back to the Shari' el-Hurriya, which is particularly impressive just beyond the city walls, is the former GREEK HOSPITAL, built in 1945 by the French architect Jean Walter. Opposite the hospital is found the ENGINEERING FACULTY, built in 1950–2 by the architects' department of the Egyptian Ministry for Construction.

WALK ALONG THE MAHMUDIYA CANAL

From the point at which it leaves the Nile, the Mahmudiya Canal winds over a distance of about 50 miles before entering the roadstead of the western harbor. To some extent it can be seen as the successor to the canal which once brought water to Alexandria's cisterns and which was also constructed in the bed of the former Canopic branch of the Nile. The Mahmudiya Canal was built between 1817 and 1820 on the orders of Mohammed Ali, who envisaged a canal which would act as a navigable waterway to Cairo as well as supplying Alexandria's drinking water and irrigating the land of Bahayra province. The project was so important to Mohammed Ali that, having entrusted it for some time to a Turkish engineer who was soon overcome by the sheer scope of the task, he called upon the French architect Pascal Coste (1787–1879), who went on to complete the work, which was in fact his greatest construction project in Egypt. The Mahmudiya Canal can be reached from the Shallalat Gardens by way of a street that takes its name from the Suez Canal. At the

turn of the century a number of Alexandrian families owned beautiful canal-side residences in luxuriant garden settings. Unfortunately almost nothing remains of these today, apart from the occasional palm-lined driveway leading to factories and warehouses in the now industrialized zone traversed by the canal. It is still possible to walk the entire length of the canal along the old paved road bordered by sycamores which runs along its banks. Although the walk may not be as romantic as it once was, it is still a very original way to discover the working-class and industrial districts of Alexandria.

NUZHA AND ANTONIADIS GARDENS. About 1½ miles upstream, the canal runs along the edge of the Nuzha and Antoniadis Gardens. The Nuzha district is steeped in history. In 268 BC the poet Callimachus lived and taught here, in c. AD 640 the Roman general Pompilius thwarted the King of Syria's attempt to capture Alexandria, while in the same year the cavalry of the Arab conqueror Amr Ibn el-As ● *66* pitched camp here before entering the city. The gardens were redeveloped by the Alexandria Town Council at the turn of the century. They originally belonged to a Marseilles trader by the name of Pastré before they were bought by the khedive Ismaïl. It was Ismaïl who opened them to the public. Today they comprise ZOOLOGICAL GARDENS, a small MUSEUM OF NATURAL HISTORY and a ROSE GARDEN. The magnificent neighboring property, also a public garden, used to belong to Sir John A. Antoniadis (1815–95), a prominent Alexandrian of Greek origin. The gardens could be visited during his lifetime and the entrance fee of two piasters was donated to charity. In 1918 his son gave the gardens to King Fuad, who in turn donated them to the city. Beyond the ANTONIADIS PALACE, which was the venue for the 1951 Anglo-Egyptian negotiations, a Roman tomb hewn out of the rock is of the same design as the tombs in the Anfushi Necropolis ▲ *177*, with three funeral chambers opening onto a central hall. It is impossible to know what type of paintings decorated the walls because the tomb is in a very bad state of disrepair. The originality of these remains lies in the total absence of Egyptian influence and its exclusively Greek architecture and decoration.

The massive Engineering Faculty, built in neo-Pharaonic style (1950–2) by the Egyptian Ministry for

Construction, has aged particularly well because it was so carefully finished.

KOM ES-SHOGAFA ★

On the side walls of the vestibule two niches carved out of the rock contain statues of a man and

a woman which combine Egyptian (clothes and general bearing) and Greek (hair and headdresses) sculptural styles.

Take the Shari el-Khediwi from Ramses Station and turn left into the Shari' el-Awud as-Sawari. Continue past Pompey's Pillar and take the Shari' Bab el-Muluk on the right and then the Shari' el-Nasriya, which leads to the catacombs. The Kom es-Shogafa ("hill of tiles") is a rocky plateau situated between the ancient villages of Karmuz and Minia el-Bassal, now densely populated districts of Alexandria, where Christian catacombs and chapels were first discovered. The exploitation of the quarries, in addition to Mohammed Ali's ● *68* use of the hill as a bastion to defend the modern city, destroyed any remaining traces. In 1900, almost fifty years later, a donkey accident led to the discovery of another necropolis, an enormous hypogeum which is the largest in Alexandria and probably dates from the 2nd century AD. It is a remarkable example of the Alexandrian blend of Graeco-Roman and Egyptian styles.

INTERIOR. The catacombs were hewn out of the rock on three superposed levels. The dead were lowered by ropes down the central well of a spiral staircase. The vestibule has two semi-circular niches, each containing a bench surmounted by a shell carved in the vaulted upper half of the niche. This opens onto a rotunda built around a central well covered with a sort of domed kiosk supported by eight pillars. The adjoining burial chambers contain sarcophagi and niches for funeral urns have been hollowed out of the rock. On the left is the TRICLINIUM or banqueting hall where, on the days dedicated to remembrance of the dead, relatives and friends gathered for a funeral banquet in memory of their loved ones. The ceiling is supported by stone pillars and there are three stone couches (on which mattresses were piled) arranged in a semi-circle. The table, most probably wooden, stood in the center.

On the right is the so-called HALL OF CARACALLA, named in remembrance of that emperor's massacre of Christians invited to the amphitheater of Alexandria. Particularly interesting are the four tombs decorated with paintings on stuccowork where the bones of young men and horses were found. A staircase, decorated with a large relief carving of a shell, leads from the rotunda to the lower story, which consists of a vestibule and a burial chamber. Here the decoration is reminiscent of the Pharaonic tombs of Luxor and Saqqara in the Valley of the Kings. In the vestibule the capitals of the pillars are decorated with papyrus and acanthus leaves and the cornice with a winged sun flanked by two falcons. The statues have Greek hairstyles and headdresses and Egyptian clothes. A door set in the far wall leads into the funeral chapel, where both Greek and Egyptian religious symbols are found. On a bas-relief sculpture positioned on both sides of the door, two bearded serpents wearing the double crown of Upper and Lower Egypt rear up on their coils next to the serpent staff of Hermes and the pine cone of Dionysus. Above them two gorgons can be seen, which were probably intended to terrify unwelcome visitors. The burial chamber contains three enormous sarcophagi, hewn out of the rock and decorated with festoons of flowers, fruit and gorgons' heads. It is interesting that the representations of the Egyptian gods Anubis, Thoth, Ptah, Horus and Apis show a marked lack of understanding of both Pharaonic style and symbolism. The archeologist Gaston Maspero was struck by the Egyptian style of this funeral chapel, which caused him to comment: "Nothing is more curious to study than this hybrid form of documentation and the way in which it has been executed. The idea that comes immediately to mind as you examine it is that it was commissioned by members of the Egyptian nobility who were still deeply attached to their national form of worship. [. . .] However, if we remember the degree of popularity enjoyed by Isis throughout the Roman empire toward the end of the 2nd century AD, there is nothing to stop us supposing that this Egyptian décor housed the remains of a foreigner in some way associated with the worship of that goddess, perhaps an Isiac of Greek origin." Nothing remains of the structure that once surmounted the hypogea, except for a mosaic with geometric designs.

A passageway hewn out of the rock leads to a circular chamber supported by pillars. The tombs are arranged around the central chamber.

Some historians believe that Pompey's Pillar was part of the portico of the "sister" library of the Great Alexandria Library housed in the Serapeum. The 88-foot pillar is made of pink Aswan granite and tapers slightly from the 9-foot diameter of its base to one of 7½ feet at the top. It was dedicated in c. AD 297 by the prefect of Egypt to the emperor Diocletian for his victory in 296 over the Christian Achilles, who had usurped the title of emperor. On the west face of the granite base, the following four lines in Greek characters can still be deciphered: "To the most just of emperors, the divine protector of Alexandria, Diocletian the invincible: Postumus, prefect of Egypt." The pillar was wrongly named Pompey's Pillar by the Crusaders who believed that it marked the site of the tomb of the Roman general.

POMPEY'S PILLAR. By retracing your steps along the Shari' el-Nasriya and Shari' Bab-el-Muluk you come to Pompey's Pillar (El-Awud as-Sawari, "horseman's pillar") on the left. It is the most important surviving element of the SERAPEUM, the ancient temple of Serapis, which certain ancient writers described as the most beautiful in Alexandria and second only to the Capitol in Rome. The temple was built on a platform reached by a flight of one hundred steps. In the sanctuary was a richly decorated statue of Serapis, a Graeco-Roman deity combining the attributes of Osiris and Apis. Excavations carried out in 1943–4 in the southeast and southwest corners of the Ptolemaic enclosure yielded remains of the foundations of the temple containing plaques made of gold, silver, bronze, opaque glass and ceramic tiles which bore the inscription in Greek and in Egyptian hieroglyphics: "King Ptolemy [III Euergetes], son of Ptolemy and Arsinoe, divine siblings, [has dedicated] the temple and sacred enclosure to Serapis". The Serapeum was destroyed toward the end of the century during the reign of Trajan (98–117) and a new temple was probably built in the following decade, during Hadrian's reign. In 391 the Christians destroyed it and built a monastery and a church dedicated to Saint John the Baptist. These were destroyed in their turn, probably in the 10th century. The remains of Roman baths and various statues of the Sphinx and Ramesses II brought to Alexandria from Heliopolis (date unknown) can still be seen on the site of Pompey's Pillar. The function of the two long, underground galleries set with niches to the west of the pillar is not known for certain. One theory is that funeral urns were placed in the niches; another maintains that birds and other sacred animals were buried there. Another somewhat ludicrous hypothesis would have it that they were used as shelves for the books of the "sister" library of the Great Alexandria Library. They were most probably dedicated in some way to the worship of Serapis. From here, it is possible to regain the city center via the canal or the Sidi Gaber district.

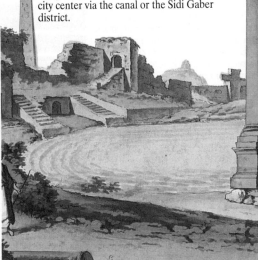

Engraving (1820) depicting the entirely imaginary site of Pompey's Pillar with one of "Cleopatra's Needles" in the distance.

> "Alexandria, the morning dew, the down of white clouds, slanting rays of sunlight washed by the rain, the heart of memories steeped in honey and tears."
>
> Naguib Mahfouz

THE CORNICHE ★

Alexandria did not have a corniche until the early 20th century. At the time the old isthmus residences faced inland while the rest of the bay was bordered by the remains of fortifications. Their declassification (1885) was followed by a seawall project, whose purpose was to reclaim a large area of land from the sea (a strip of land with an average width of about 100 yards). The new quays between Fort Qaitbay and Cape Silsila were begun in 1907 and completed ten years later. In 1934 the Corniche was extended as far as El-Muntaza.

CASINOS, BEACHES AND BEACH HUTS. Because Alexandria's beaches were either unsuitable or inaccessible, bathing (a popular pastime among European residents) was practiced throughout the 19th century in special bathing establishments. The most famous of these was the *Zuro*, later known as the *Cleopatra*, situated on the present site of the *Grand Trianon*. It had long, floating landing stages which lay at right angles to the beach, and wooden huts on stilts so that the women could bathe shielded from prying eyes. Although nothing remains of these establishments, they have to some extent been superseded by the many stilted "casinos" dotted along the Corniche. Nobody bathes here any more but people come to drink tea, even in bad weather, and for wedding celebrations. Dances were held here in the postwar years, especially at the *Ship* (now the *Saraya*), a casino that looked like a steamer, which was built in 1945 by the Alexandria Town Council but somewhat disfigured by successive renovation work. The development of the Corniche was accompanied by the construction of row upon row of beach huts, which were intended to offer the bathers the best possible facilities.

BEACH HUTS
The famous rows of beach huts (above) built along Alexandria's Corniche. They could be rented seasonally from the town council

and were initially a huge success. In 1945 demand was three times greater than the number of huts available because it was considered the "in thing" to have your own beach hut. Today the four thousand huts are enjoyed by a very different type of clientele for whom bathing in a swimsuit would be unthinkable.

CAPE SILSILA AND THE SITE OF THE NEW LIBRARY. In the fall of 1989 the foundation stone of the new Alexandria Library was laid on Cape Silsila (formerly Lochias, the site of the palaces of the Ptolemies). The goal of the project's sponsor, UNESCO, was to reconstruct the "temple of learning" represented by the original Great Alexandria Library, whose 500,000 volumes will be part of the new library's data base. Founded by Ptolemy I Soter, the Great Library was the most important element of the Mouseion (museum) whose vast premises housed amphitheaters, laboratories, observatories, a refectory, a park and a zoo. It was the great intellectual achievement of the Ptolemaic dynasty, and the work conducted within its walls had a profound influence on Western thought. It appears that the museum and library, of which nothing now remains, were situated on the Canopic Way. The causes of the great fire that destroyed the library at the time of the conquest of the city by Amr Ibn el-As ● 66 in 640, and those responsible for it, remain the subject of heated historical debate.

ALEXANDRIA BY TRAM

One of the best ways of discovering Alexandria is by tram. The main Ramleh line, which is also the oldest, leaves from the Midan Saad Zaghlul in the city center and follows a route which runs more or less parallel to the Corniche. It was originally a railway line, built and operated by a British company to service various coastal towns and villages scattered among the dunes from which the name "Ramleh" (*ar-raml*, "sands") is derived. At the time the area to the east of the city had a population of at most five hundred inhabitants, but the beauty of the site and the reputedly therapeutic value of the climate soon encouraged prominent Alexandrians to establish their summer residences there. Over the years the Ramleh suburb became a permanent residential district and the population increased to such an extent that today only a few of the old villas have survived the high-rise construction of the last few decades. The observant visitor will, however, notice the few surviving remnants of extravagant early 20th-century architecture. The Ramleh line opened in 1863 and operated for the first year with horse-drawn carriages. The following year steam engines were introduced. The terminus was on the present site of the Bulkeley Station, and there were departures every hour. In 1868 the line was extended to Schutz Station, and, twenty years later, to San Stefano; in 1891 new stations (Saroit Pasha, Laurens, Saraya) were added. In 1904 the line was electrified and a new branch line was constructed to create a more direct link between Bulkeley and San Stefano. Finally the line was extended in 1910 to Victoria Station, which is now the terminus.

RAMLEH STATION AND "CLEOPATRA'S NEEDLES". The tram terminus is in an extremely busy part of the city, invaded from dawn until dusk by a host of street vendors and small craftsmen such as the traditional shoe-shiners. Near the present site of the station and opposite the modern *Hotel Metropole*, the CAESAREUM once stood, a sumptuous temple built by Cleopatra for Mark Antony and completed, after their double suicide, by Octavian (Augustus), who dedicated it during his lifetime to imperial worship. The temple was sacked by Constantius II in AD 356, rebuilt, razed to the ground once more and converted into a church before finally disappearing in 912. It was here that the

STATION NAMES
Although a committee was formed in 1963 to give "Egyptian" names to all the stations on this line, most of them are still known by their original name, which was often associated with the district in which they were located, evoking the topography and cosmopolitanism of Alexandria.

Imaginary representation of the site of the Great Library.

Fort and harbor at Abukir.

HYPOGEUM AT MUSTAFA PASHA
There is a first-century tomb near the Mustafa Pasha Tram Station.

SHATBY CEMETERY
High walls surround the areas reserved for the members of each faith. View of the Jewish cemetery and the Suarez family mausoleum (below).

famous mathematician Hypatia was killed by being stoned to death in 415. Her murder marks the height of the persecution of nonbelievers by the Christians of Alexandria. In his writings, Pliny the Elder made mention of the obelisks (the deceptively named "Cleopatra's Needles") that decorated the temple, and which remained in Alexandria until they were transported to London's Embankment (in 1877) and New York's Central Park (in 1879), where they still stand. The pink Aswan granite "needles" had originally been erected in front of the temple of Heliopolis in Cairo by Thutmose III before being transported to Alexandria on the orders of Julius Caesar.

STATIONS. "MAZARITTA", the name of the first station on the tram line, is a corruption of "lazaretto" (built nearby by Mohammed Ali in 1831 and subsequently transferred to the other end of the city). En route to the station the line passes the IBRAHIM EL-QAÏD MOSQUE, which was built in 1951 by Mario Rossi. Shatby, named after a Muslim saint who died in 1272, is situated outside the old city walls. It is here that the cemeteries for members of the city's non-Muslim faiths (the main Muslim cemetery is at Bab Sidra) can be found, which were built in the mid-19th century near an ancient necropolis of little interest. IBRAHIMIYA services a district constructed on agricultural land belonging to Prince Ibrahim Ahmed, which was sold off in lots in 1888 by a real estate company. Sporting is named after the 100-acre Sporting Club, founded in 1889, and still remains one of the city's more fashionable districts. SIDI-GABER is the name not only of the tram station, but also of the railway station on the main Alexandria–Cairo line and the district surrounding the nearby mausoleum of Sidi Gaber (1145–1217), who was an Andalusian traveler. The tramline forks after MUSTAFA PASHA and BULKELEY stations, and merges again at San Stefano. The more direct, northern line passes through SABA PASHA, GLYMENOPOULOS, ZIZINIA, LAURENS, SARAYA and SIDI BISHR. Sidi Bishr is renowned for its unspoiled beaches, and it was here that the remains of the 2nd-century RAS EL-SODA TEMPLE were discovered in 1936. VICTORIA was named after Victoria College, founded by the British in 1899. The college was renamed the El-Nasser College after the Suez Crisis. In 1909 it moved its premises to the far end of the Ramleh line, but only after it had managed to ensure that the line would be extended to one of its entrances.

EL-MUNTAZA, EL-MAMURA AND ABUKIR GARDENS

EL-MUNTAZA. El-Muntaza lies about 15 miles east of
Alexandria along the Corniche. This vast estate was gradually
acquired by the khedive Abbas II who chose it as the site for
the SALAMLIK, one of his residences, built in 1892 and later

converted into a hotel. In 1932 King Fuad built the
HARAMLIK, a larger palace which was converted into a
museum after 1952 but which is now closed to the public.
King Farouk's contribution to El-Muntaza was the bridge to
the island where he built a tea-house. The complex is now
reserved for the Free Officers and their families. In the vast,
115-acre park asphalted pathways cross the gardens, follow
the edge of a pinewood and link pavilions and rotundas. The
luxury *Palestine Hotel* overlooks the beach. Next to the
El-Muntaza estate is the resort of EL-MAMURA with its ultra-
modern architecture, which was very popular in the 1960's.

ABUKIR ★. The fishing village of Abukir has a fine beach and
is renowned for its fish restaurants. Legend has it that ancient
Canopus took its name from the tomb of Canopus, one of
Menelaus' pilots who had returned from the Trojan War
and was buried near Fort Tawfiqiya. The few remnants
of the temples of Serapis and Isis, destroyed
by Theophilus, Bishop of Alexandria, are in
the Graeco-Roman Museum ▲ 186. Reputed
to have miraculous properties, the relics of
Saint John and Saint Cyr (after whom
modern Abukir was named) were
transported to Canopus by Cyril, another
bishop of Alexandria. All that now remains
are the ruined baths near the fort, the Greek
catacombs, a granite statue and a recently
discovered statue of Isis.

ANCIENT CANOPUS
Canopus is associated
with the pleasure and
debauchery described
by Seneca (hence the
expression "Canopic
pleasures"): "There,
pleasure is given free
rein, there, as if a
certain licence were
due to the very place
itself, everything is
unrestrained".

**THE BATTLE OF
ABUKIR**
On July 25, 1799, the
French drove back
the Turkish army who
had landed in the Bay
of Abukir. But on
March 8, 1801, Sir
Ralph Abercromby
succeeded in
defeating the
Ottoman army, which
was forced to leave
Egypt in September.

These painted
carrioles are a feature
of Abukir.

☒ **Half a day**
◆ C

AROUND ALEXANDRIA

EL-MEX. Leave Alexandria via the Midan at-Tahrir and take the Shari' Bab el-Akhdar, which crosses the Minet el-Bassal district to the industrial suburb of Gabari, named after the venerable sheikh. The western cemetery of the ancient city, which stretched along this section of the coast, is now mainly submerged and eroded by currents. Some of the remains are in the Graeco-Roman Museum. Beyond the cemetery lies the former fishing village of El-Mex, a popular vacation resort with middle-class Alexandrians at the beginning of the century and now one of the city's industrial suburbs. Today the shoreline is occupied by warehouses, tanneries, oil refineries and a military camp. The extensively damaged remains of a small PTOLEMAIC NECROPOLIS, hewn out of the limestone rock and probably dating from the 1st century BC, was discovered in the El-Wardian district. Stone taken from the El-Mex quarries was used to construct both the ancient and modern cities of Alexandria.

EL-DIKHEILA. El-Dikheila lies on the coast road between Alexandria and Mersa Matruh. Excavations carried out near the military camp of El-Dikheila uncovered the remains of the ENATON MONASTERY, founded in the 5th century by a community of monks whose traces were also found further west in the desert near Lake Mariut and Wadi Natrun.

Detail of the interior of the Ptolemaic necropolis of El-Wardian.

AGAMI. Agami, the Egyptian St-Tropez further along the coast road, is still the most fashionable resort on the Mediterranean coast and, from the end of June, welcomes several hundred thousand visitors and holiday-makers. The Cairo and Alexandria "smart set" still gather there every summer, but nowadays they are forced to share the resort with the middle and even the working classes as a result of the building boom experienced by Agami over the last decade. The resort was founded in the 1950's when two Alexandrians, Bianchi and Bless, acquired substantial areas of land on this virtually deserted site (only a few Bedouin families camped there), which owed its beauty to the fig trees growing in abundance and the long bay with its small fort, built by the French army

Gabari Palace near El-Mex, which was built by the viceroy Saïd and subsequently used as a quarantine center.

during their Egypt campaign. Bianchi and Bless offered the land (fairly unsuccessfully) for sale in two lots which are still named after them. Throughout the next twenty years Agami comprised only a few stone villas (in the Bianchi district) and wooden chalets (in the Bless district) scattered among the dunes. With no running water or electricity, spending the summer there was more like going on safari than on holiday. For the early "settlers", modern Agami is barely recognizable. Few of the original buildings remain, most having been replaced by residential blocks, each one taller than the one before, where the apartments are extremely expensive. However, there is the occasional exception: for example, the VILLA LASHIN, built in 1962 by the architect Ali Azzam, or the award-winning (Aga Khan Foundation in 1980) BEIT EL-HALAWA (1975) designed by Abd el-Wahid el-Wakil, a disciple of Hassan Fathi ▲ *442*. The coast road passes through the resorts of Hannoville and Sidi Kheir, which are extremely popular in summer with local tourists, before it eventually reaches Abusir.

ABUSIR. Abusir is the site of the Ptolemaic temple of Taposiris Magna, probably built shortly after the foundation of Alexandria. All that remains of the temple, dedicated to Osiris, is the outer wall and the pylons. It appears that sacred animals were worshipped there, as is evidenced by an animal necropolis that was found nearby. Inside the walls can be found the remains of a Christian church and, below these, what is left of the public baths built by the emperor Justinian, a seawall, quays and a bridge. To the north of the hill the tower, which was built by Ptolemy II Philadelphus but is now ruined, has a square base surmounted by an octagonal and then a circular story. It is supposedly a replica of the destroyed Alexandrian Pharos Lighthouse. The BURG EL-ARAB, otherwise known as the Arab Tower, gave its name to the nearby village.

BURG EL-ARAB. At the center of Burg el-Arab, a village built on a small hill, is a sort of citadel which is in fact a carpet factory founded by the British after World War One. In close proximity to the village a quarry can be seen, which was exploited in ancient times.

The Villa Lashin, whose design was inspired by the hull of a ship.

KARM ABU MENAS

The 3rd-century Monastery of Abu Menas lies west of the city, midway between Alexandria and Wadi Natrun, on the road that used to lead to the Oasis of Amun and Cyrenaica. The site commemorates Saint Menas, an Alexandrian soldier serving in the army of Diocletian who, having refused to persecute the Christians and publicly declared his Christian faith, was martyred in 296. Legend has it that his remains were brought back from Phrygia by camel and buried at the spot where the animal stopped and refused to go any further. A spring whose waters possessed miraculous properties immediately welled up on the spot.

Today ruins are all that remain of this once bustling town. Its walls were covered with inscriptions made by pilgrims who had come here to find a cure for their pain or illness.

SAINT MENAS VINEYARDS. Today only ruins and desert remain where once vines and olive trees flourished in a fertile oasis whose four basilicas (discovered at the turn of the century by Monsignor Kaufmann) were reputedly the most beautiful in Egypt, famed for the richness of their marble, the majesty of their paintings and the splendor of their mosaics and gold. The impressive ruins of the sanctuary were destroyed in the 9th century by the Abbasid caliph el-Mutawakkil who dismissed the clergy, seized the ornamental tiling and plundered the treasure, thus beginning the acts of coercion perpetrated against the Copts during the Middle Ages.

BASILICA OF ARCADIUS. The most noticeable thing about the Basilica of Arcadius is its sheer size. It was built in the early 5th century and constitutes the heart of this vast monastic complex. The bases of the fifty-six marble columns that supported its roof can still be seen today. The gallery stood at the intersection of the transept and the main nave in an enclosed area containing the altar, the bishop's throne and the pews of the officiating priests. At the western end of the basilica stood a baptistry whose "corners" were rounded into semicircular, polychrome marble niches. This independent element, which was usually incorporated into the main structure, is the only example of its kind in ancient Christian architecture. A CHURCH to the west of the basilica (which it pre-dates) was built above the crypt containing the saint's tomb. Its capitals have a strong Egyptian and Byzantine influence. A staircase led down to the crypt from the central nave. To the west is an underground drain connected to the "miraculous" cistern which supposedly collected the curative waters but which in reality collected rainwater.

GRAPE PRESS
To the north of the site was a large monastery complex whose cells, shops, vast reception halls and a vat for pressing grapes (above) can still be seen today.

THERMAL BASILICA. In the 5th century another basilica was built to accommodate the growing numbers of pilgrims and infirm. The so-called "Thermal Basilica" was intended to house the source of the curative waters. Some of the heated baths and one of the pools (230 x 130 feet) attest to the size and importance of the structure. Pilgrims would fill their tiny terracotta flasks, usually stamped with the seal of Saint Menas (depicting the saint standing between two kneeling camels), at the source which rose beside the basilica.

> "Amidst the harsh austerity of the desert, the monks washed away their sins."
>
> Rufinus of Aquileia

ADDITIONAL BUILDINGS. During the 5th and 6th centuries additional buildings were constructed around the second "Thermal Basilica". To the north a huge monastery, a veritable business complex, covered an area of almost 48,000 square yards. Ramparts strengthened by bastions surrounded the sanctuary, which was guarded by more than twelve thousand soldiers. An entire town, complete with houses and cemeteries, was excavated. The most surprising discovery was the house of one of the potters who made the flasks. The walls were covered with strange designs, and the workshop, shop, and remains of flasks, lamps and even toys were found.

LAKE MARIUT. Lake Mariut, ancient Mareotis, lies below sea level and separates Alexandria from the desert. It used to be linked to the River Nile by canals which brought products from all over Egypt to Alexandria.

Lake Mariut (below).

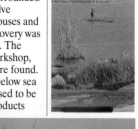

During the Middle Ages the waters of the lake dried up. In 1801, during the siege of Alexandria, the British breached the dyke which separated Lake Mariut from Lake Abukir (which no longer exists), flooding thousands of acres and destroying 150 villages.

THE COASTAL REGION

EL-ALAMEIN. Various tanks, pieces of artillery, uniforms and operational maps can be seen in the town's Military Museum. The Italian and German military cemeteries stand on the Tell el-Eisa Hill a few miles outside the town. Further along the coast, the village of Sidi Abd el-Rahman is renowned for its beautiful beaches.

MERSA MATRUH. Now the administrative capital of the Libyan Desert, Mersa Matruh is ancient Paraetonium where Alexander the Great stopped before moving on to the Oasis of Jupiter Amun ▲ *256*. It was also the port where the Egyptian fleet lay at anchor during the war between Octavian (Augustus) and Cleopatra and Mark Antony. It is still possible to see the remains of Cleopatra's quay to the west of the ancient lagoon on which the town is built. On a hill to the

north are the remains of a church dating from the early centuries AD. Along the bay to the east, ROMMEL'S CAVE, now a museum, stands on a spit of land. The cave was Field Marshall Rommel's base and headquarters before

the Battle of El-Alamein. One of the region's most beautiful beaches, Cleopatra Beach, lies 3 miles to the west. On a rocky islet about 50 yards offshore is CLEOPATRA'S BATH, a pool said to have been hewn out of the rock so that the queen could bathe in safety. In early June the Bedouin tribes of the Libyan Desert come to Mersa Matruh to honor their saint on the occasion of his *muled*. AGUIBA BEACH, 15 miles from Mersa Matruh, is one of the most famous beaches on this stretch of coast but the bathing is dangerous. EL-NAGUILA, an ancient Roman town whose remains can still be seen, was renowned for its gardens and figs. In 1916 EL-MAKTELA was the scene of a decisive battle between the British forces and the Sanusi Bedouins.

SALLUM. Sallum was once the ancient Roman port of Baranis, and the remains of wells in the town and surrounding area are still in evidence. Sallum is the last Egyptian town before the border with Libya. It is a trading center for Bedouin peoples from all parts of the region. The soldiers who were killed during the battle with Rommel's Afrika Korps are buried in the British and Commonwealth forces' military cemetery.

BATTLE OF EL-ALAMEIN
The Battle of El-Alamein ("the two worlds"), fought between Field Marshall Montgomery's Eighth Army under General Alexander and Rommel's Afrika Korps, lasted from October 23 to November 4, 1942. It stopped the German advance in North Africa and marked the beginning of their retreat. Military cemeteries and monuments to the memory of the soldiers killed at El-Alamein were built on the battlefield. About 66 miles from Alexandria is the memorial to the British and Commonwealth soldiers. The British cemetery with its impeccably aligned graves lies to the left of the road.

Nile Delta

Cairo to Rosetta, *206*
Champollion and

▲ CAIRO TO ROSETTA

1 CAIRO
2 DELTA BARRAGE
3 DEIR AMBA BARAMUS
4 DEIR ES-SURIANI
5 DEIR AMBA BISHOI
6 DEIR ABU MAKARYUS
7 SHATANUF
8 EL-BAGUR
9 TANTA
10 KAFR EL-SHEIKH
11 TELL EL-FARAÏN
12 DISUQ

DELTA BARRAGE: THE EARLY STAGES
Linant de Bellefonds, aware of the instability of the substratum, suggested constructing the barrage several miles downstream of the river's point of divergence. There were to be two barrages, one on the Rosetta branch of the Nile and one on the Damietta branch, with three navigable canals fed from a point above the barrage. Work began in 1834, but stopped the next year because of plague.

This itinerary leaves the main "agricultural route" between Cairo and Tanta and crosses an ancient, wooded landscape which provides a striking contrast to the vast cotton-producing regions of the eastern Delta.

DELTA BARRAGE. The Delta barrage, or El-Qanatir el-Qahiriya, was constructed at the southern tip of the Nile Delta, about 12 miles downstream from Cairo, to control the supply of water to Lower Egypt. The idea was first conceived in 1833 and the project study initially entrusted to Linant de Bellefonds, a French naval officer who had joined the staff of Mohammed Ali. The site was closed by a plague epidemic two years later. In 1842 Bellefonds was replaced by another French engineer, Dieudonné-Eugène Mougel. Construction began in 1843 and lasted for almost twenty years, through three khedivial reigns. The barrage was completed in 1863 but was so badly designed that it had to be constantly repaired and, by 1883, it was very nearly abandoned. However, a group of British engineers, led by Sir Colin Scott-Moncrieff, came to the rescue, which is a matter of some historical interest since, at the time, the Delta barrage was the largest hydraulic construction in the world.

206

🚃 **Four/five days**
◆ **D G**

CITADEL OF SAID.
Mougel was also responsible for designing the fortress surrounding the barrage. EL-QAL'A EL-SAÏDIYA was built between 1856 and 1859 at the request of Saïd Pasha, the son of Mohammed Ali, who reigned from 1854 to 1863. The park and zoological gardens were designed in the late 19th century by Sir William Willcocks, a British engineer and keen botanist.

MOHAMMED ALI BARRAGE. Mougel's barrage never really fulfilled its purpose and the water supply to Lower Egypt is today controlled by another barrage, built in 1936–9 about 200 yards downstream from the first, according to recommendations made for the initial project in 1833.

MUSEUM OF IRRIGATION. The Museum of Irrigation occupies the former residence of the engineer-in-chief of the barrage project and houses a collection of models of the region's major hydraulic projects. They trace the development of "barrage technology" from 1860 to the present day.

COMPLETION OF THE DELTA BARRAGE
Work on the barrage was resumed in 1836. In 1842 the French engineer Dieudonné-Eugène Mougel (1808–90) suggested constructing the barrage on the river bed at the most southerly tip of the Delta. The instability of the substratum on the Rosetta branch of the Nile hindered progress. By 1853 a total of 47 million francs had been poured into the project. Exasperated, the khedive Abbas called upon Mohammed Mazhar (1810–73) to help with the project.

207

Deir es-Suriani, Deir
Abu Makaryus, Deir
Amba Bishoi and Deir
Amba Baramus (top
to bottom).

DEIR AMBA BISHOI
Legend has it that
Father Bishoi was led
to the ascetic life
through the call of an
angel, and founded
the community which
inhabits the
monastery bearing his
name. The building is
distinguished by its
well-preserved
entrance loggia and a
mill which stands to
the northeast. The
Deir Amba Bishoi
and Deir Amba
Baramus are the only
two monastries with
baptisteries.

REMAINS OF KELLIA
All that remains of
the mudbrick
architecture of Kellia
(made from sand
compressed with
saline soil) are a few
mounds covering the
hermitages that have
escaped the
bulldozers.

THE MONASTERIES OF WADI NATRUN

In the early 4th century AD a monastic order, which favored
retreat beyond the Nile Valley, was founded in the western
Delta region. The solitude of the desert retreat soon became
the Christian heroic ideal and the image of the "white martyr"
replaced the "red martyr" of the persecutions which marked
the reign of Diocletian in the early 4th century and ended in
AD 313 when Constantine made Christianity the official
religion of the Roman empire ● 74. In 325 Saint Amun
founded the first monastic establishment at
Nitria (El-Barnudji) with a view to practicing the
doctrine of renouncement, austerity
and prayer advocated by the Scriptures
to obtain eternal salvation and escape
the temptations of the secular world.
THE RETREATS OF WADI NATRUN. Five
years later Saint Makarios, who aspired
to a more rigorous form of asceticism,
decided to found the eremitic retreats of
Scete, now Wadi Natrun, which
comprises four functioning monasteries:
Deir Amba Baramus, Deir Amba Bishoi,
Deir Abu Makaryus, founded in the 4th
century, and the 6th-century Deir es-
Suriani. On the death of a Desert Father
whose life was considered to have been
exemplary, a chapel was built in front of
his cell, and the first monasteries came into being.
DEIR AMBA BARAMUS. Deir Amba Baramus, or Monastery of
the Romans (named after the Roman monk Arsenius who
lived there), was Wadi Natrun's first religious community. The
western section, the nucleus of the monastery, contains the
church dedicated to the Virgin Mary whose nave is divided by
19th-century wood paneling. The south wing has some
beautiful Corinthian pillars and the northeastern section
contains the living accommodation, library and garden. Some
beautiful frescos have also been uncovered.

DEIR ES-SURIANI. Deir es-Suriani, or Monastery of the Syrians, was named after the Syrian merchants who acquired it at the beginning of the 8th century for the community of Syrian monks living in Egypt at the time. The community remained in Egypt until the 16th century when Syria fell to the Turks. The great EL-ADRA CHURCH is dedicated to the Virgin Mary and its frescos tell the story of her life. The iconostasis (the so-called "Door of Symbols") of the sanctuary consists of six leaves, each with seven ebony panels inlaid with ivory representing (from top to bottom) the seven periods of the Christian era. The library contains several hundred manuscripts and over three thousand printed works.

DEIR ABU MAKARYUS. From the 6th century the Deir Abu Makaryus, or Monastery of St Makarios, assumed considerable importance as the official residence of the bishops of Alexandria, the heads of the Coptic Church, who were forbidden to reside in Alexandria itself by the Byzantine rulers. It was here that Wadi Natrun's first library, widely dispersed in the 17th century, was founded. The dungeon-tower, the most developed of the towers, is truly remarkable. It incorporates no less than four churches and a wine vat. The second-floor church has an iconostasis and sculptures dating from the 4th and 5th centuries.

THE KELLIA HERMITAGES. The community of Kellia, founded by Saint Amun, consists of 1,500 hermitages (cells) arranged in five clusters over a distance of about 12 miles. Situated about one third of the way along the track linking Nitria with Wadi Natrun, the Kellia hermitages were originally a staging post before becoming an ascetic retreat, although they did not break all ties with the secular world. Abandoned toward the 9th century, the site was rediscovered in 1964 by Guillaumont. However, cultivation has changed the landscape where once there was little more than shrubs and bushes. The two 5th-century ecclesiastical centers of Qasr Waheida and Qusur Isa are, apart from the church of the White Monastery (440), the earliest monastic buildings that can be dated with any certainty.

FORTIFICATIONS
These desert communities originally had no form of defense against the raids organized by Libyan tribes, and their history is one long series of plunder and destruction (during which their inhabitants were exiled or sold into slavery), followed by phases of reconstruction. In the 9th century a fortified enclosure about 30 feet high, in the form of an ark symbolizing Noah's ark, was constructed to protect the rectangular dwellings and basilical churches. It

also included a garden where olives and vines were grown. On the north side a single gate was surmounted by a guardroom with a trap door through which provisions and visitors were hoisted by means of a pulley. The square guard tower, which reached across a drawbridge, was between two and four stories high and represents the oldest part of the complex. With their cellars, shops, kitchen, cells and chapel the inmates were well equipped to withstand a siege.

Between the barrage and Tanta the landscape becomes fragmented: enclosed fields separated by hedges and large villages hidden among the trees. The tiny region of Batn el-Baqara ("belly of the cow"), which lies between the two branches of the Nile and the ancient Bahr Firuniya, gives an idea of what the landscape must have looked like before the major hydraulic projects of the 19th century changed the face of agriculture.

SHATANUF. According to French-speaking Egyptians Shatanuf is a corruption of "Châteauneuf" and was named by the soldiers of Napoleon Bonaparte. In fact it is an ancient village whose name was of Coptic origin. ASHMUN, an industrial center renowned for its ceramics, lies off the main route. Its brickworks produce the polychrome bricks which give the regional architecture its distinctive appearance.

EL-BAGUR. El-Bagur is an unprepossessing town whose only claim to fame is to have been the birthplace of Sheikh Ibrahim el-Baguri (1783–1860), rector of El-Azhar ▲ *294* and a renowned theologian. He is better known today, however, as the organizer of the first student demonstration to be held in modern times, against military conscription during the reign of Saïd (1854–63). Since 1826 SHIBIN EL-KOM has been the capital of Minufiya province. President Anwar el-Sadat ● *71* was born (1918) a few miles away in MIT ABU EL-KOM.

TANTA

Tanta, which nestles at the heart of the rich Gharbiya province, is both the provincial capital and one of the largest towns in the Nile Delta (335,000 inhabitants in 1986). During the Byzantine period this ancient city was the seat of a bishopric, but little evidence is left of its long history. Today the town is especially famous for the mausoleum of Egypt's greatest Muslim saint, Sidi Ahmed el-Badawi, born in Fez, Morocco, in 1199. In 1237 he was told in a vision to go to Tanta, where he began to lead the life of an ascetic. He installed himself on the

"We left Mehallet-Kebir this morning, and took the road to Tanta. [. . .] Travelers often make endless detours to cover a relatively short distance. Here you count miles in terms of the number of hours' walking they represent and assess routes in relation to the number of villages along the way. As you get further away from the Nile, the landscape becomes less wooded; in some places there is not a tree in sight, with cultivated fields stretching as far as the eye can see and a few palms, mimosa, sycamores, willows and the occasional vine providing the only shade near the houses and villages."
Joseph Michaud

roof of a house (which is why his disciples became known as Sutuhiya, or Ashab el-Sath, "people of the terrace") where he remained without eating or drinking for forty days. He died on June 8, 1276, and was buried in the house on top of which he had lived. Several years later his disciple and successor, Abd el-Al, built a *qalua* (a sort of cell to which ascetics could retreat) above his tomb, and this was later converted into a *zawia* (a center for religious teaching). The first mosque, which incorporated the mausoleum, was not built until the 18th century, but all that remains today is the minaret and the *naqsura* (the bronze grille surrounding the catafalque). It bears an inscription, dated 1773, which traces the saint's genealogy. The present building dates from the reign of Abbas (1848–54). The MUSEUM OF TANTA contains several collections ranging from Pharaonic times to the present day.

Xois. Not far from KAFR EL-SHEIKH (the town's Egyptian name), capital of the Sixth Nome of Lower Egypt, the village of Pa-Khasu ("village of the pothole") stands on the site of the remains that have managed to survive. Excavations have revealed the *agora* of the Graeco-Roman town, with its public baths and pottery workshops. On the road between Tanta and Alexandria a lake to the west of the El-Khandaq el-Gharbi Canal marks the site of ancient NAUCRATIS (el-Nibeira), originally a Pharaonic village that later became a Greek military fortress and then a commercial center. Imau, the capital of the Third Nome of Lower Egypt, is situated not far from here on the KOM EL-HISN.

THE TANTA PILGRIMAGE
Three *muled* are celebrated in honor of Sidi Ahmed el-Badawi. The first, or "great *muled*", which coincides with the *muled* of the Prophet ● *126*, gave rise to the Tanta pilgrimage. The other two, the "little *muled*" and the "*muled* of the month of Ragab",

were introduced later by the sheikhs of the various branches of the Ahmediya Brotherhood, founded after the death of Ahmed by his successor. Because the three festivals were also huge agricultural fairs, their dates were later incorporated into the old Nilotic calendar inherited from Pharaonic Egypt and preserved to the present day by the Coptic liturgy. They were replaced by similar fairs, in particular at Disuq ▲ *212* and Damanhur (between Alexandria and Cairo), and became part of a cycle of traveling fairs which were a blend of popular piety and agrarian rites. The pilgrims would start their pilgrimage to Mecca with a visit to the saint of Tanta, which became known as "the gate of the Prophet" (Bab el-Nabi).

TELL EL-FARAÏN. Tell el-Faraïn, or Pharaohs' Hill, is near the village of Shaba (7½ miles from Disuq). According to Herodotus, "Leto" (Buto) was the seat of an important oracular divinity during the Persian period. On one of the site's three *tells* is the enclosure wall of the temple of

the serpent-goddess Wadjet, symbol of Lower Egypt and mistress of the site. The town was divided into two sections known as Pe and Dep, and occupied the other two hills.

DISUQ. Like Tanta, Disuq is a place of pilgrimage and is mainly renowned for its patron saint, Sidi Ibrahim el-Disuqi (1235–78), founder of the Burhamiya, or Disuqiya, the brotherhood named after him and one of the four largest in Egypt, who are distinguished by their green turbans. He is thought to have been Sheikh el-Islam during the reign of El-Zahir Baybars, who had a *zawia* built for him where he taught and was buried. The present 19th-century mosque is a vast edifice, covering an area of almost 24,000 square yards, whose prayer hall is adorned with seventy white marble columns. Further west the route follows the winding course of the Rosetta branch of the Nile and offers the double advantage of enabling visitors to journey across a beautiful landscape and visit the town of Saïs.

SAÏS. Saïs, or Zaou, the capital of the Fifth Nome of Lower Egypt, lies north of the town of Sa el-Hagar on the right bank of the Damietta branch of the Nile.

It has been a religious center since the beginning of the Pharaonic period and houses the sanctuaries of Neith, its principal divinity, and various associated divinities. Saïs was one of the compulsory destinations for funerary rites. It became a bishopric during the Christian era and remained active until the 12th century. The site is somewhat disappointing since all that remains of the Pharaonic capital are mudbrick walls and a few scattered blocks of stone.

FUWA. Fuwa is an ancient town which probably stands on the site of ancient Metelis. Its position opposite the mouth of the Alexandria Canal made it the offloading point for maritime and river traffic, and it became such an important trading center that in the 15th century many European countries established consulates there. The gradual silting-up of the canal, however, diverted trade to Rosetta and indirectly brought about the decline of Fuwa. Prospects improved slightly in the 19th century when the construction of the Mahmudiya Canal ▲ 190 restored some of Fuwa's former activity, but it was the opening of a large tarboosh factory that really revitalized the town. Yet, like most of the factories established by Mohammed Ali, it fell into disuse during the reign of Saïd, and the town had to diversify into other areas of industrial activity (rice-growing and flour-milling). Its location, off the main road networks, has meant that Fuwa has remained a sleepy little town (114,000 acres in 1986) but this has enabled it to retain a certain old-fashioned charm. Fuwa was also the birthplace of Saad Zaghlul ● 70 ▲ 281.

VISITING FUWA. The MOSQUE OF NASR AD-DIN, founded by Hassan ben Nasr Allah el-Ustadar, a Mameluke emir born in Fuwa in 1365, gives some idea of the town's medieval grandeur. The oldest mosque in Fuwa is the MAUSOLEUM OF SIDI ABD ALLAH EL-BURULLUSI. It was renovated in 1860 by Mohammed Pasha, brother of Ismaïl. The ABU EL-NAGA MOSQUE (opposite), on the banks of the river, is in an advanced state of ruin.

BRIDGE OF MUTUBIS. Built in the 1940's along the lines of the Mohammed Ali barrage ▲ 207, this is the most northerly of the barrages which cross the Nile.

PALM GROVE OF ROSETTA. The vast palm grove of Rosetta stretches from the shores of the Nile to Lake Idku. Its dates (there are several carefully selected and artificially sown varieties) ripen a month later than in other regions and are reputedly Egypt's best.

TELL EL-FARAÏN
Several architectural elements from the reign of Ramesses II and a stele donated by Shoshenq V (AD 38) stand side by side with a number of objects from the Late Period. Recent soundings around the *tell* have revealed the remains of a pre-dynastic civilization.

213

ROSETTA

Rosetta, the "city of a thousand palm trees", is situated about 9 miles from the mouth of the Nile. It is one of the most attractive of the Delta cities and has the richest selection of monuments. According to Arab chroniclers it was founded in AD 870 by Ibn Tulun ● *66* ▲ *312*. In fact the site has been occupied since prehistoric times and the town's Arabic name (Rashid) is derived from the Ancient Egyptian via the Coptic name (Rikhit). Its foundation by Ibn Tulun corresponds to a relocation of the town, slightly further south. Rosetta, for a long time a town of modest proportions, housed the garrison responsible for defending the Boghaz (mouth of the Nile) which today lies about 7 miles away. The town began to assume greater importance during the Ottoman period, reaching its peak in the 17th century when it benefited from the developing trade with Constantinople and the Aegean, and remaining prosperous until the 19th century. With the construction of the Mahmudiya Canal ▲ *190* it began to move into slow decline and once again became a small town (52,000 inhabitants in 1986) relying for its livelihood on traditional fishing and food industries. But this relative decline has in fact meant that Rosetta has preserved its architectural heritage.

The minaret of one of the many mosques, and a café in Rosetta.

THE OTTOMAN TOWN. Built along the river, the town has maintained a regular, almost orthogonal, urban development and offers a remarkable overview of domestic Ottoman architecture. Twenty-two of the thirty-eight houses originally classified by the Committee for the Conservation of Arab Monuments have survived. Bought and restored by the Egyptian Department of Antiquities, they were all built between the 16th and 18th centuries and form a homogenous series of buildings in terms of their layout, exterior design and interior decoration. Rosetta's houses are characterized by their height (two or three stories above the first floor), which contrasts with their relatively narrow façades overlooking the street, and the use of visible brickwork which is often outlined with mortar to create polychrome patterning in black, red and white. The layers of bricks are intersected by horizontal wood clamps which are also visible.

MOSQUES. The mosques of Rosetta are also characteristic of the region. The (often tiny) courtyard has been reduced to a simple square which has been made into a garden and forms a small atrium at the center of the extremely simple prayer hall. Only the entrance and the mihrab are richly decorated, with polychrome marble or tile mosaics. Everything of interest can be seen by taking a few leisurely walks around the town. The northwest district has four of the most beautiful houses in Rosetta: the AMACIALI, HASSIBA GHAZAL and MAKKI HOUSES (today occupied by a women's aid organization) and the partially restored THABET HOUSE, which is a training center for carpenters and wood turners. The SHEIKH QINDIL

MOSQUE is a particularly delightful sanctuary. The main market street runs from the Midan el-Gumhurriya through the old part of the town. The ARAB KELI MUSEUM occupies an 18th-century house and traces the history of Rosetta. The EL-MAHALLI MOSQUE (1721) has a distinctive prayer hall whose beamed ceiling is supported by ninety-nine columns taken from other sites. The EL-GINDI MOSQUE is of the same type but smaller, while the ruined ZAGHLUL MOSQUE is Rosetta's largest and oldest mosque. The AZZUZ BATHS (a beautiful 18th-century *hammam*) have remained intact with all their original installations. At the southern end of the town is the EL-ABBASI MOSQUE, built in 1809, while the Turkish tiles and finely carved marble columns of the DUMAQSIS MOSQUE (1704), which is situated in the Shari' Port Said, are of particular interest.

FORT QAITBAY. This small fort was built in about 1470 on the banks of the River Nile by the Sultan Qaitbay to defend the Boghaz. Its twin, Fort Rashid (renamed Fort Julien by the French), was built across the river. It was here that the French army captain Bouchard discovered the Rosetta Stone in 1799.

THE HOUSES OF ROSETTA ● *116*
The many large doors and windows of the houses are covered by turned-wood grilles or *mashrabiya* work. The doorway opening onto the street is wide enough to allow a fully loaded camel to pass through since in most of the houses, which were mainly owned by merchants, the first floor was used for business, with shops, cellars, warehouses, stables and sometimes a *mandara* for receiving customers. There is often a well, fed by an underground cistern, which sometimes opens onto the street via a *sabil* ● *113*. The living accommodation was on the upper floors, with the second-floor *salamlik* reserved for the men and the third-floor *haramlik* for the women and family. All the houses are built according to the same layout.

Egyptian belongs to the family of Hamito-Semitic (or Afro-Asiatic) languages. When it first appeared in c. 3150 BC Egyptian writing contained all the theoretic principles that would last throughout its development until it disappeared in the 4th century AD.

Jean-François Champollion (le Jeune) was born in Figeac in 1790. Fascinated by Egypt from an early age, he went on to study Oriental languages (Hebrew, Coptic and Arabic) and was the first to interpret Egyptian hieroglyphs (1822) from the Rosetta Stone. He dedicated his entire life to improving his knowledge of the Ancient Egyptian language and civilization. In 1826 he founded the Department of Egyptology of the Louvre Museum and, in 1831 (one year before his death), he was appointed professor of the Collège de France by Louis-Philippe.

"MONUMENTS DE L'EGYPTE ET DE LA NUBIE"
This collection of Champollion's work in Egypt was published between 1835 and 1845 by his brother.

THE ROSETTA STONE
This bilingual decree by Ptolemy V Epiphanes (196 BC) was discovered in Rosetta in 1799 by a French officer of the Egypt Expedition. It was written in hieroglyphs, demotic script and Greek.

Lettres Grecques	Signes Démotiques	Signes Hieroglyphiques
A	ↄ . ↄↄ .	
B	4 . ⊥⊥ .	

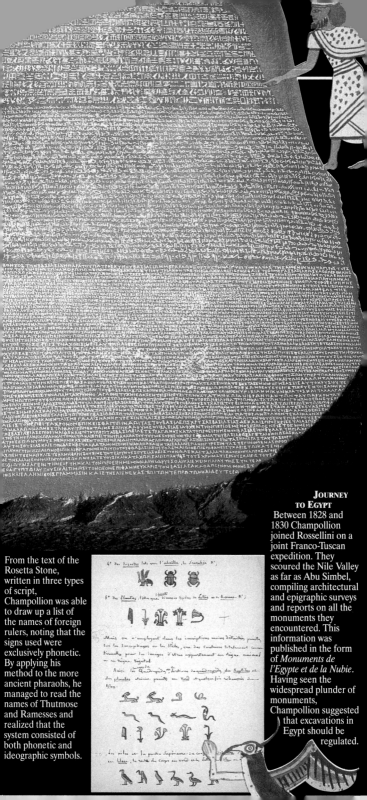

From the text of the Rosetta Stone, written in three types of script, Champollion was able to draw up a list of the names of foreign rulers, noting that the signs used were exclusively phonetic. By applying his method to the more ancient pharaohs, he managed to read the names of Thutmose and Ramesses and realized that the system consisted of both phonetic and ideographic symbols.

JOURNEY TO EGYPT

Between 1828 and 1830 Champollion joined Rossellini on a joint Franco-Tuscan expedition. They scoured the Nile Valley as far as Abu Simbel, compiling architectural and epigraphic surveys and reports on all the monuments they encountered. This information was published in the form of *Monuments de l'Egypte et de la Nubie*. Having seen the widespread plunder of monuments, Champollion suggested that excavations in Egypt should be regulated.

HIEROGLYPHS READ HORIZONTALLY FROM RIGHT TO LEFT

HIEROGLYPHS READ HORIZONTALLY FROM LEFT TO RIGHT

The hieroglyphs are not aligned in sequence, one after the other, but arranged in the form of an imaginary square.

HIEROGLYPHS READ VERTICALLY FROM RIGHT TO LEFT

HIEROGLYPHS READ VERTICALLY FROM LEFT TO RIGHT

There are no spaces between words and no punctuation.

DECIPHERING HIEROGLYPHICS

Egyptian hieroglyphs were written from right to left or from left to right, horizontally or vertically. The direction from which the hieroglyphs should be read is indicated by the direction in which the "living" symbols, represented in profile, are facing.

Detail (above) of a color plate from *Monuments de l'Egypte et de la Nubie*, showing bas-reliefs from the Temple of Amenhotep III at Wadi Hellal. A detail from the manuscript of Champollion's *Grammaire égyptienne* is shown at the bottom of the page.

HIERATIC SCRIPT

Hieratic script is a cursive form of hieroglyphics, used during the early dynasties for everyday documents. It was written with a calamus (reed pen) on papyrus, leather or pottery. From the 21st Dynasty it was used to transcribe religious texts on papyrus.

DEMOTIC SCRIPT

Demotic script is a simplified form of hieratic script. It became the popular form of writing during the 25th Dynasty. Like hieratic script it is always written horizontally, from right to left.

COPTIC SCRIPT

Coptic script was the last stage in Pharaonic Egyptian writing and the only written language used between the 3rd and 17th centuries AD since when it has been reserved for the Coptic liturgy. It was written using the Greek alphabet with seven additional symbols taken from demotic script.

The first of the two itineraries from Cairo to Damietta follows the right bank of the Nile, while the second crosses the river at Mit Ghamr to Zifta and follows the left bank to Damietta.

ZIFTA. The town of Zifta is proud of having been the scene of an unusual event. In the spring of 1919, at the Congress of Versailles, the world powers confirmed the British protectorate of Egypt and rejected the Egyptian demand for independence ● 70. In Zifta a demonstration of secondary-school students was supported by the entire town and a revolutionary group proclaimed independence. The incident lasted only a few weeks as British troops eventually surrounded the town.

ABU SIR BANA. Modern Abu Sir Bana is named after the ancient town of Busiris mentioned by the Greek historian Herodotus (although nothing remains of the Temple of Osiris to which he referred).

EL-MAHALLA EL-KUBRA. El-Mahalla el-Kubra ("the great warehouse"), already an important trading center in the 10th century, developed significantly in the 14th century when the administrative reforms of the reign of the sultan Barquq made it the capital of the central Delta region. It was relieved of this function in the 19th century and entered a decline from which it did not recover until the 1930's when the establishment of the Misr Group factories made it the largest industrial textile center in Egypt. Today it is Egypt's fourth largest city (359,000 inhabitants in 1986). It still has many of its mosques although, unfortunately, most are damaged. The GAMIA EL-NASSER, or Victory Mosque, in the old town, was founded at the time of the Arab conquest, while the nearby KHAWKHAT EL-YAHUD ("the postern of the Jews") has replaced one of the oldest synagogues in Egypt. The 13th-century EL-MITWALI MOSQUE is remarkable for its sheer size, and the Coptic Church of SUEIQAT EL-NASARA for its two superposed structures (although only the lower of the two is of any great age).

The ruins of Iseum, the ancient town of Hebet or Per-Hebet, meaning "the house of the god Hebet" (Horus), look like a huge pile of stone blocks and are for the most part inaccessible.

The port of Talkha at Mansura.

BEHBEIT EL-HAGAR. The ruins of Iseum are situated midway between Semenud and Mansura. The temple probably dates from the Saïte period, while the monument (the sanctuary of Isis) was mainly built by Ptolemy II and completed by Ptolemy III. A block of stone used in the construction of the Iseum in Rome suggests that it was destroyed during the first century AD. The temple was surrounded by a mudbrick wall built during the Ptolemaic period and an avenue of sphinxes would once have led to the main entrance. Today gardens cover the area between the enclosure wall and the inscribed blocks of stone. The western façade of the temple is decorated with images of the Nile and dedicated to Osiris ▲ 386. A colonnade, with Hathor capitals, bounded to the south by a flight of steps leading to the roof, precedes the sanctuary of Isis (for which it is at present proving difficult to reconstruct the layout). In a rear chapel, the god Osiris is depicted as a king with divine attributes, not as a mummy.

SEMENUD. The town has retained the Greek name (Sebbenytos) of the Egyptian town of Tchebnetcheret (the Divine Calf), capital of the Second Nome of Lower Egypt. It was the birthplace of the historian Manethon ● 66, author of the first history of Egypt, according to whom it was the land of the 30th-Dynasty pharaohs. The few, scattered blocks of stone on the ancient *tell* to the west of the town are not really worth visiting.

MANSURA. Today the town of Mansura is the capital of Daqahliya province and an important industrial center. It was founded as a fortified camp in 1219 by the Ayyubid sultan El-Malik el-Kamil to oppose the Crusaders after the capture of Damietta in 1218. Built along the River Nile and the Bahr el-Saghir ("little river"), one of its former branches, it was surrounded by water and made an ideal entrenched camp. In July 1221 an offensive led by John of Jerusalem was stopped before the city walls and the crusade of Louis IX of France ended at Mansura after a long and fruitless siege punctuated by skirmishes (1249–50). The French king was taken prisoner on April 7, 1250 and released a month later in return for the restoration of Damietta and payment of a ransom. With the end of the Crusades the town was able to pursue a more peaceable existence. It became a provincial capital during the Ottoman period and its rapid expansion in the second half of the 19th century made it one of the leading cotton centers in the Delta region. About 19 miles southeast of Mansura, two important *tells* mark the ancient sites of MENDES (Tell el-Rub' in the north) and THMUIS (Tell el-Tmei in the south). Mendes, capital of the Sixth Nome of Lower Egypt and an important town from the time of the Old Kingdom to the 29th Dynasty, was superseded by Thmuis in the 1st century AD. Among its ruins are the enclosure wall of the temple (dedicated to Be, the god of fertility embodied in the form of a ram) dominated on one side by a monolithic naos (over 25 feet high) in pink granite. The site of Thmuis is littered with shards, architectural stone fragments and remains of mosaics.

EL-MUAFI MOSQUE
The El-Muafi Mosque (below) stands in the heart of the old town of Mansura. The mosque, built by El-Salih Ayyub in 1188 and refurbished at the end of the 16th century, houses the mausoleum of Sidi Abd Allah el-Muafi. The small, old house to the south (the so-called house of Ibn Loqman) is said to have been the prison of Saint Louis (Louis IX). It is in fact all that remains of a public kitchen used during the *muled* to prepare and distribute food to the town's inhabitants.

During the siege of Mansura (1249) the Muslims used gunpowder for the first time. They made incendiary devices and sowed terror among the ranks of the Crusaders.

Unlike Mansura, Damietta is an ancient town, renowned for its textile industry during the Byzantine period. Its wealth and its strategic position on the eastern mouth of

DAMIETTA. Damietta was one of the main Muslim objectives during the Arab conquest of Egypt. During the first two centuries of Arab domination, the Byzantines launched frequent naval attacks against the town and it was after one such raid, in 853, that Damietta was fortified for the first time. Protected by its walls, the city expanded rapidly and became extremely prosperous during the Fatimid period as a result of the growth of the textile industry. Damietta is in fact famed for its brocades and its *tiraz* industry. The wearing of this extremely expensive ceremonial garment, reserved for princes and monarchs, was probably a revival from the Sassanid empire. The extremely complex figurative, floral and geometric designs of the silk embroidery decorating these linen or cotton robes often included epigraphic borders which

the Nile made it a key town during the Crusades. Damietta never recovered its early prosperity and today it is a modest-sized town (ninety thousand inhabitants in 1986) by Egyptian standards.

make some of these garments not only works of art but also valuable historic documents. During the Crusades the town was the focus of a bitter and drawn-out struggle. It was subjected to a long and unsuccessful siege on the accession of Salah ad-Din as part of an attack launched by Amaury I of Jerusalem in December 1169. In 1218 the Crusaders succeeded in capturing the town and occupied it for almost three years. But they failed to resist El-Kamil, who withdrew to the fortified town of Mansura, and were forced to surrender it to the Muslims in 1221.
Recaptured by Saint Louis in 1249,

just before the death of El-Salih, Damietta came under Christian control once more until the French king was defeated at Mansura in 1250. The following year, the Bahrite Mamelukes, convinced that the town was too vulnerable, destroyed its fortifications. In 1261 Baybars closed the Boghaz to ocean-going vessels for the same reason. Damietta fell into decline and was abandoned in favor of a new town which was founded a little further south on the site that it still occupies today.

VISITING DAMIETTA. The ABU EL-MAATI MOSQUE can still be seen in the old town of Damietta. The mosque is surrounded by a huge cemetery where pigeon enthusiasts discuss turtle- and ring-doves at the pigeon market held there every week. Pigeon fancying is still a highly regarded sport in Egypt and its techniques perpetuate the memory of the prestigious pigeon post organized by the Mameluke sultans to maintain communications between Egypt and Syria, the two provinces of their empire. Damietta was one of the main staging posts on the Cairo–Palestine route. The fragile-looking boxes on reed racks which adorn the balconies of Damietta are in fact the urban equivalent of the earthen pigeon lofts seen in rural areas. The MADBULIYA MOSQUE, founded by Qaitbay in the 15th century for Sidi Ibrahim el-Madbuli, is a fine example of a medersa from the Mameluke period.

MONASTERY OF ST DAMIENNE. In addition to its monastic buildings and accommodation, this 6th-century Coptic complex also has four churches, although only one is of any great age. Saint Damienne, the daughter of a governor of the Delta region, vowed to remain celibate and retreated with forty companions to a palace built for her by her father. She and her companions were martyred during the great persecutions of the reign of Diocletian for refusing to pay homage to the emperors. Her festival, celebrated from May 5 to 20, is the occasion of a vast gathering. In the far north of the region, the RAS EL-BARR ("cape of the world") dominates the Boghaz of Damietta.

ABU EL-MAATI MOSQUE
The Abu el-Maati Mosque was built during the Fatimid period on the site of the Gamia el-Fath (Mosque of Conquest), founded when the town was captured by the Muslims, and has several points in common with the Amr Ibn el-As Mosque in Cairo ● *325*. It stands outside the modern town on a hill whose ruins mark the site of the first town. The mosque has been closed down and is falling into ruins.

Although the area of archeological interest extends along both sides of the road, the most remarkable remains lie to the north. At the western end the remains (from north to south) of a palace, a pre-Dynastic tomb, various cemeteries (Old Kingdom, Coptic and Muslim) and cat cemeteries have been identified. Of the two chapels dedicated to Qa'a, only the white limestone pillars of the chapel of Pepy I (to the south) are still standing. At the eastern end the ruins of several Middle and New Kingdom palaces, a New Kingdom necropolis and two tombs belonging to the viceroy of Kush stand near a pile of basalt blocks marking the site of the Temple of Bastet.

CAIRO TO TANIS

The itinerary from Cairo to Zagazig follows the Ismaïliya Canal and makes a pleasant excursion that can be extended to the isthmus of Suez. The route passes through Heliopolis ▲ *285* and the village of MUSTURUD where the Holy Family is said to have stayed in Egypt, now a place of pilgrimage from August 5 to 22.

BIRKET EL-HAGG. This dried-up "pilgrims' lake" was, for many centuries, an assembly point for the pilgrimage to Mecca. It was for these pilgrims that Sultan Barsbey built the EL-KHANQA MOSQUE in 1427.

TELL EL-YAHUDIYA. Tell el-Yahudiya ("the hill of the Jews") lies about 12 miles northeast of Heliopolis. From the 20th Dynasty the site was named after territory owned by Ramesses III and a sanctuary dedicated to Re. It was extended during the Middle Kingdom and the Second Intermediate period. The great enclosure wall has been attributed, without evidence, to the Hyksos. The high priest of Jerusalem, Onias IV, who sought the protection of Ptolemy VIII, is said to have built a temple to Yahweh in the disused sanctuary in 160 BC. Today the site is of little interest.

BILBEIS. Situated on the boundary of the eastern Delta region, this ancient city has always been one of the region's fortresses. Captured during the Arab conquest, the city's strategic importance increased with the creation of the Hejaz route. During the Crusades it became the rallying point for the Muslim armies leaving for Palestine. At the entrance to Bilbeis are the barrage built during the reign of Baybars and the EMIR EL-GEISH MOSQUE (640, renovated in 1593).

TELL BASTA. The ruins of Tell Basta extend on either side of the road to the northeast of Zagazig. Its Greek name, Bubastis, echoes the Egyptian name Per-Bastet, meaning "House of Bastet". It was the capital of the Twelfth Nome of Lower Egypt until the 18th Dynasty, and became capital of Egypt in the 22nd and 23rd Dynasties. The sacred animals of its principal divinities, the cat for Bastet and the Pharaoh's rat for Atum, were buried by the thousands in special cemeteries.

ZAGAZIG. The capital of Sharqiya province was originally a camp which housed the workers requisitioned around 1830 to construct barrages on an ancient branch of the Nile, the Bahr Moïs. The center of the town has retained some beautiful examples of 19th-century architecture and the museum has some interesting regional collections. About 2 miles west of Abu Kebir, HORBEIT has been recognized as the Pharaonic town of Shednu (Pharbaethos in Greek), and about 2 miles southeast of Horbeit, ABU YASSIN was the late necropolis of the sacred bulls of Pharbaethos. The excavation of the mausoleum of the bulls by the OAU (Organization of African Unity) in 1938 discovered several granite sarcophagi, which can still be seen today. TELL TUKH (one mile south of Tukh el-Qaramos), ancient Bekhnu or Dekyt, is thought to have been active from the time of the New Kingdom. The first excavations of the site revealed structures built on sand embankments forming a rectangular rampart and a temple surrounded by a brick enclosure wall. The activity of the *sebakhin*, increased by important discoveries (the Zagazig treasure in 1905), has cleared the northwestern part of the site and only a tiny part of the ramparts can still be seen. Between the villages of KHATANA and QANTIR (about 4 and 5 miles north of Fakus), a series of *tells* marks the sites of the ancient Pharaonic cities of Avaris (capital of the Hyksos) and Piramesse (the estate of Ramesses). Avaris already existed at the time of the Middle Kingdom. It was colonized by the Canaanites and became the capital of the kingdom of the Hyksos. Ramesses II came from Avaris, and decided to build temples and palaces there. His successors preferred the site of Tanis, stripped the nearby town of its monuments and reused them elsewhere. In El-Husseiniya, the TELL NABASHA occupies the site of the ancient Imet, eastern Buto.

The name of Bilbeis (above) is derived from the Coptic "Phelbes". Views of the eastern Delta with one of the region's many pigeon lofts (below).

TANIS
The Temple of Amun has been reduced to a pile of granite blocks by the extensive exploitation of limestone used to manufacture lime. The reconstructed entrance, a statue of Ramesses II and a head (below).

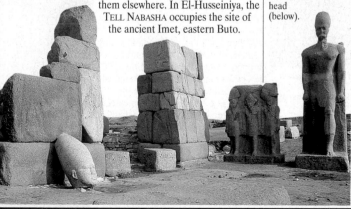

TANIS

Tanis (Djane in Egyptian, Zoan in Hebrew and Tanis in Greek), capital of the Fourteenth Nome of Lower Egypt, appears with some certainty to have been founded at the end of the 20th Dynasty and became capital of Egypt in the 21st and 22nd Dynasties ● *43*. Psusennes I made it the replica of Karnak, while his successors increased the number of sanctuaries dedicated to Theban deities. Although the town occupied a large area during the Ptolemaic period, the gradual submersion of the region led to its decline during the Roman occupation. Tanis was a bishopric until the 5th century and little more than a village by the end of the 7th. In the 14th century the region was almost deserted. The development of San el-Hagar, founded in 1821, was largely a result of the land reclamation policy.

EXCAVATIONS. Although it was mentioned in the Bible, Tanis was not identified with San el-Hagar until the map produced in 1722 by a French priest, Father Claude Sicard ▲ *264*. Auguste Mariette ● *96* ▲ *350* excavated the great temple between 1859 and 1864 and his work laid the foundations for the erroneous theory that Tanis was Piramesse (the estate of Ramesses), which had already been identified with Avaris, the Hyksos capital. In 1884 Flinders Petrie ● *96* excavated the site for five months. In 1939 Pierre Montet discovered the miraculously preserved royal necropolis of the kings of the Third Intermediate period, which he worked until 1946. In 1964, after the interruption caused by the Suez Crisis ▲ *234*, Jean Yoyotte resumed excavations which were taken over in 1985 by Philippe Brissaud, who steered the mission's activities toward their present direction. After the MUSEUM (note, in particular, the exhibits outside) visit the central part of the *tell* from west to east.

GATE OF SHOSHENQ III. The avenue leading to the main temple is bordered by carved stone blocks and fragmented colossi of Ramesses II. The huge gate has no foundations and is made of inscribed stone blocks brought from other sites. On the right is a pink granite triad of Re, Ramesses and Ptah-Tatenen. Beyond are the remains of the columns of Ramesses II.

ENCLOSURE WALLS. Part of the double enclosure (two successive and independent mudbrick walls), lies to the left of the gate. The corners of the enclosure of Psusennes I, built around the temple, can be seen from the hill that it formed. A bigger enclosure was built in the 30th Dynasty.

In his tomb (detail above) Psusennes I, protected by a golden mask, lay on a silver leaf inside a silver coffin contained in an anonymous Ramesside sarcophagus in black granite. This was enclosed in another huge granite sarcophagus inscribed with the name of Merneptah.

TOMB OF OSORKON
As well as the vault of the king and his son, the tomb also contained four limestone rooms with painted walls. One of these rooms, whose walls were decorated with the "Field of Cyperus" (detail above), contained the tomb of Takelot II.

226

THE GREAT TEMPLE. The Great Temple of Amun is nothing more than a heap of granite blocks. In the absence of any remains we are left to imagine the rows of pylons preceded by obelisks, and colonnaded courtyards with palm capitals. The scattered monuments include a recumbent colossus of Ramesses II, said to favor procreation.

THE ROYAL NECROPOLIS. The necropolis lies, surprisingly, within the enclosure of Psusennes. It appears that the 21st Dynasty ranged its tombs against a sandy hill. The 22nd Dynasty extended the complex until the reign of Shoshenq III, who leveled the area and enclosed the tombs in a mudbrick platform on which he built his own tomb. The tombs of (north to south) Shoshenq III, Amenemope, Psusennes I and Osorkon II, and three anonymous tombs, built of reused materials (especially Ramesside granite), can still be seen.

TOMB OF PSUSENNES I. A vertical shaft leads to an antechamber decorated with images of protective spirits and one of the king worshipping Osiris. It contained the sepulcher of an unknown 22nd-Dynasty king, Heqakheperre Shoshenq. Two chambers opening toward the east contained the kings Psusennes and Amenemope (south chamber, intended for Queen Mutnedjemet). Another chamber contained the sepulcher of Ankhefenmut, while a blind chamber contained that of the General Wundebawdjed.

TOMB OF OSORKON. The granite vault contained the huge granite sarcophagus of Osorkon II and the sepulcher (found intact) of his son, Prince Hornakht.

TOMB OF SHOSHENQ III. The rectangular tomb, built of limestone blocks from the 21st Dynasty (including inscribed blocks taken from private tombs), consisted of a central shaft and a chamber containing two granite sarcophagi (the king's had been taken from another site). Only the chamber is decorated, with scenes from the *Book of the Dead* and the *Book of Night*. To the north of the Great Temple the remains of a TEMPLE OF NECTANEBO, dedicated to Khonsu, were excavated. To the east, beyond the enclosure of Psusennes, stands the TEMPLE OF THE EAST, a kiosk-like structure with ten or so palmiform columns (Ramesses II usurped by Osorkon II). To the south, opposite the gate of Ptolemy I, is a 30TH-DYNASTY TEMPLE. To the southwest of the precinct a 21st Dynasty temple dedicated to Mut was discovered and named the TEMPLE OF ANTA. It had been rebuilt during the Saite and Ptolemaic periods.

Recent excavations have revealed the remains of the town and two other temple complexes. A large enclosure and the outline of a temple dismantled during the Ptolemaic period were discovered at the southern end of the *tell*. Further west a later necropolis, built on the site of a Third Intermediate period cemetery, was identified. In the center of the *tell* a line of granite blocks marked the site of a (destroyed) temple, which was almost as vast as the Great Temple of Amun.

The fault that is today
occupied by the Gulf
of Suez and the Red
Sea was formed at the
end of the Eocene,
during the folding
process which created
the Sinai peninsula.
The fault was filled by
the waters of the
Mediterranean
during the Miocene
and the connection
with the Indian
Ocean was
established toward
the middle of the
Pliocene. Less is
known about the
formation of the
isthmus separating
the Gulf of Suez from
the Mediterranean. It
is the result of a slow
upthrust affecting the
whole of the eastern
Delta. It could have
begun at the end of
the Pliocene, but was
never completed.

Geologically speaking
the isthmus is almost
indistinguishable
from the Arabian
Desert, of which it
forms the northern
extremity. In the
north the aridity is
slightly tempered by
the proximity of the
coast and the
presence of lakes and
marshland, today
being reclaimed. The
plateau slowly rises
toward the south until
the rocky sub-stratum
surfaces between the
Bitter Lakes and
Suez.

SUEZ CANAL

CANAL FROM THE NILE TO THE RED SEA. A
legend based on Greek and Latin texts (Strabo
and Pliny) attributes the first project for the construction of a
direct link between the River Nile and the Red Sea to
Senwosret I. There is no supporting archeological evidence
for this, however. It was not until the Saïte period and the
reign of Necho II (610–595 BC) that the first canal was dug
from the Pelusian branch of the Nile to the northern end of
the Bitter Lakes. It was restored and completed almost a
century later by Darius I (522–486 BC) and traces of this canal
can still be seen today along the Wadi Tumilat, between Saft
el-Hinna and Ismaïliya. It was extended to the Red Sea during
the reign of Ptolemy II Philadelphus (285–46 BC), abandoned
at the beginning of the Roman occupation and re-excavated
during the reign of Trajan (AD 98–117). A new point of supply
was established on the Nile a few miles north of Cairo, and it
was this canal that was restored by Amr Ibn el-As ● 66 and
became known as the "Canal of the Commander of the
Faithful". In AD 767 the Abbasid caliph El-Mansur closed the
canal to cut off supplies to the insurgent towns of the Hejaz.
EARLY PROJECTS. The engineers of the EGYPT EXPEDITION
● 94 were the first to develop the full-scale project of a direct
link between Pelusium and Suez. By opening up the Suez
route, Napoleon Bonaparte hoped to "deal a blow to England
which was as fatal as the discovery of the Cape of Good Hope

had been to the Genoese and Venetians". However, the leveling of the site, begun in January 1799 under the supervision of Charles Le Père, only lasted a few months. An error in calculating one of the positions led Le Père to conclude that, at high tide, there was a significant difference in level (about 33 feet) between the two seas and that, as a result, locks would have to be incorporated into the ship canal. In spite of opposition from theorists, Le Père's hypothesis was accepted unquestioningly for almost fifty years. It was supported by the Saint-Simoniens (a group of revolutionary French intellectuals) who arrived in Cairo in 1833 and who saw the Suez Canal as the first in a series of similar interoceanic links which would promote economic and financial exchanges. However, Mohammed Ali preferred to involve the group's twenty or so engineers and technicians in the Delta barrage ▲ 206 project. In 1835 a plague epidemic closed the site and dispersed the Saint-Simoniens, although they did leave behind them disciples such as Linant de Bellefonds ▲ 206 and Ferdinand de Lesseps. Lesseps, then French vice-consul in Alexandria, was attracted by their views and convinced of the feasibility of the Suez Canal project. He adopted their idea of forming a public company and launching a public loan to raise funds for its completion.

RESEARCH ASSOCIATION. The creation of a transit service and the establishment of the Overland Road (transit via Egypt of the India packet) in 1839 revived enthusiasm for the Mediterranean–Red Sea link. In Paris the Saint-Simoniens formed an association in 1846 to research the Suez project, which brought together English, German, Austrian and French industrialists and entrepreneurs. In 1847 the leveling work carried out by Bourdaloue confirmed that there was no significant difference in level between the two seas. Linant de Bellefonds compiled the technical report. The implementation of the project was delayed by Turkish opposition, British skepticism and the illness of Mohammed Ali. The khedive Abbas, who succeeded his grandfather in 1849, was not particularly pro-European, as he was afraid of a further increase of their influence in the region.

The Suez Canal, built between 1859 and 1869 to link the Mediterranean and the Red Sea, was one of the major construction projects of the 19th century and the first in a series of similar links that would revolutionize the world geography of trade. It covers a distance of over 100 miles between Port Said and Suez, crossing the sands of the northern coastal region and then the series of lagoons formed by Lake Timsah and the Bitter Lakes (which are an extension of the Gulf of Suez) separating the eastern Delta region from the Sinai peninsula.

The political situation was altered by the accession of Saïd (1854) who, unlike his predecessor, was very open to European ideas and counted Ferdinand de Lesseps among his friends. He immediately approved the Suez project, presented for the first time on November 15, 1854, and ratified the act of concession a fortnight later. The pilot study estimated that a total of 2,613 million cubic feet of earth would have to be excavated: 600 million on land by manpower and 2,013 million in water by dredgers. The total cost was estimated at two hundred million francs.

PORT-SAID - Palais de la Compagnie du Canal de Suez

The act of concession granted the Universal Company of the Suez Ship Canal the right to manage and develop the canal for ninety-nine years from the time it was filled with water. The profits were to be shared between the founders (10 percent), the Egyptian government (15 percent) and the shareholders (75 percent).

FERDINAND DE LESSEPS
Ferdinand de Lesseps (1805–94), son of a diplomat who was French consul-general in Egypt, spent part of his boyhood in Alexandria and was a friend of the sons of Mohammed Ali. He returned to Egypt as a trainee at the French Consulate in Cairo in 1833 and was vice-consul in Alexandria from 1834 to 1838 where he met the Saint-Simoniens and learned about their Suez Canal project. The accession of his childhood friend, Saïd, to the throne of Egypt offered him an unexpected opportunity.

A mobile machine used during the excavation of the Suez Canal.

THE CANAL PROJECT

Work on the canal began on April 25, 1859, near Port Said, but soon ran into political and financial difficulties. Lesseps was forced to launch a Europe-wide campaign to sell over half of the four hundred thousand 500-franc shares issued. He managed to sell the remainder to Saïd, who became the holder of 44 percent of the capital. This concerned the British and the Turks, who succeeded in having work on the project suspended. The intervention of Napoleon III brought the crisis to an end. From 1860 twenty thousand Egyptian *fellaheen* worked day and night on the site. They were requisitioned by the army (many traveling long distances) and were replaced every month. The freshwater canal was completed in 1862 and in November of the same year, the waters of the Mediterranean entered Lake Timsah. Ismaïl, who succeeded Saïd in 1863, was less enthusiastic about the project. The Turks reminded him that he had not approved the work on the canal and would not allow him to use enforced labor. Lesseps once again appealed to Napoleon III. An international commission, formed in March 1864 to resolve these differences, pronounced in favor of the company. The sultan issued a decree on March 19, 1866, approving the concession and the work was completed three years later.

CELEBRATIONS
The ceremonial inauguration of the Suez Canal at Port Said, preceded by an extravagant firework display and a ball attended by six thousand people, was the start of celebrations that lasted several weeks and included the opening of the Cairo Opera House built by the khedive Ismaïl.

THE FINAL BLOW
On November 17, 1869 Ali Pasha delivered the final blow which breached the barrage of the Suez plain reservoir and let the waters of the Mediterranean flow into the Red Sea.

AT ANCHOR IN THE BITTER LAKES
The convoy left Port Said for the new town of Ismailiya where it dropped anchor for the night before continuing its journey to the port of Suez.

INAUGURATION CELEBRATIONS
Lavish celebrations were held to commemorate the inauguration of the Suez Canal. Among the khedive Ismaïl's six thousand guests were several of the crowned heads of Europe, including the Empress Eugenie, the Emperor of Austria, the Prince of Wales, the Prince of Prussia and the Prince of the Netherlands, as well as a host of journalists, artists and businessmen. When the sluices closing the Bitter Lakes were opened and the waters of the Mediterranean flowed to Suez, the first convoy of forty-eight ships bedecked with flags sailed through.

PORT SAID
"There is nothing
worthy of note about
Port Said. It admits to
a bad reputation and
has, for its size, an
even larger stock
of improper
photographs
than Brussels or
Buenos Aires."
    Richard Curle

THE THREE SUEZ CANAL WARS

NATIONALIZATION. The Suez Crisis erupted during the
summer of 1956 against a background of international
tension. On July 19, 1956, the United States announced that,
contrary to pilot agreements negotiated in Cairo, they would
not be making a financial contribution to the Aswan High
Dam ▲ 460. Great Britain and the World Bank also withdrew
from the agreement. On July 26, 1956, President Nasser
responded by announcing the nationalization of the Suez
Canal. A series of negotiations and talks were held
throughout the summer to no avail. On October 29 the
Israelis invaded Sinai, on the pretext of dismantling
Palestinian bases. France and Great Britain
issued an ultimatum to the two parties
which stipulated a ceasefire and
withdrawal to a distance of 10 miles
on either side of the canal. Israel,
which had not reached the ten-
mile limit, agreed to the
ceasefire while Egypt rejected
it. The French and British
bombed the canal towns and
airlifted troops into Port
Said. Under pressure from
the United States the three
aggressors accepted a
ceasefire and authorized the
deployment of an international
security force, which had evacuated
the canal zone by March 1, 1957.

THE FRONT LINE. In spring 1967, after
several months of tension running high, Syria
called upon her Egyptian ally in accordance with
the joint defense agreement signed by the two countries. At
the end of the month Jordan, which had just suffered a series
of Israeli attacks, also signed a joint defense agreement with
Egypt. At the beginning of June 200,000 troops were on a war
footing in Egypt and Syria and ready to face the 264,000-
strong Israeli force. On June 5 the Israeli government took
American diplomats unawares by launching a huge air
attack on Egyptian, Syrian and Jordanian airports,
followed by a ground offensive the next day. When
the ceasefire was signed on June 8, Egypt had lost
Sinai and the Suez Canal was in ruins, while Syria
was cut off from Golan and Jordan from the left
bank of the River Jordan. In spite of an
armistice negotiated under the auspices of the
United Nations, Egypt and Israel installed
themselves on either side of the Suez
Canal and began a war of attrition
punctuated by isolated incidents. For the
next eight years the Suez Canal became
the front line between the two armies
and was closed to navigation.

The town of Suez was
badly damaged by the
three "canal wars".
A reconstruction
campaign has
been underway for
several years.
A street in Suez.

234

BREAKING THE DEADLOCK. On October 6, 1973, Egypt initiated the hostilities by launching a surprise attack on the Suez Canal and the reputedly impregnable fortified defense (the so-called Bar-Lev Line) constructed by the Israelis on the east bank. The Badr plan, prepared down to the last detail during the previous two years, was carried out to perfection in the first few days of the conflict, but the Israeli counter offensive, launched on October 8, was swift and equally effective. When the ceasefire was signed on October 22 the Egyptians had recaptured a large part of Sinai but the Israelis still held the canal zone between Ismaïliya and Suez. Neither side was the victor. Egypt, however, was able to reestablish her sovereignty over both

banks of the canal with the first disengagement agreement, which was signed in January 1974.

A MAJOR TRADE ROUTE. It took two years to clear the canal of the accumulated wreckage and rubble of eight years of war. The canal was reopened to shipping on June 5, 1975, and gradually reestablished its position in international trade, but only after extensive redevelopment. The increased tonnage of cargo ships meant that the channel had to be widened. The first phase of the work, completed in December 1980, extended the overall length of the canal to 122 miles, and the width was expanded to 399 yards (208 yards for the channel) with a maximum draft of 56 feet. A new phase was begun in 1990 to deepen and widen the channel so that it could now accommodate ships with a draft of up to 68 feet.

The main attraction of Port Said is its port, which consists of four huge harbors and an outer port. It is worth a visit just to see the ships waiting to go through the Suez Canal. The distinctive green-domed offices of the Suez Canal Company (above right), built in 1967.

PORT TAWFIQ
Port Tawfiq lies southeast of Suez and is linked to the town by a jetty. It stands on an artificial peninsula created from the sand excavated during the construction of the Suez Canal.

▲ Cairo to Suez

Today the former villa of Ferdinand de Lesseps in Ismaïliya is used to receive the Egyptian government's VIP guests.

The bazaar of Suez in about 1870.

Ismaïliya, founded in the 1860's, was named in honor of the khedive Ismaïl on the initiative of Ferdinand de Lesseps, who lived there until work on

the canal was complete. A street in early 20th-century Ismaïliya and the Suez Canal (above).

THE CANAL TOWNS

SUEZ. Suez was built in the 15th century when Qolzum, whose ruins form a *tell* at the entrance to the freshwater canal, was abandoned. The town developed during the 19th century when it was used by the British as a staging post on the route to India, and a railway line linking it with Cairo (constructed in 1857) contributed to its further expansion. The town was badly damaged during the wars with Israel and most of its factories (fertilizer and refineries) were destroyed from the 1960's onward. Today they are being rebuilt with financial aid from Saudi Arabia.

ISMAÏLIYA. Ismaïliya, which now has more than 500,000 inhabitants, was founded on the shores of LAKE TIMSAH (Crocodile Lake) during the construction of the Suez Canal. It consisted mainly of houses for the engineers and technicians working on the site. In a Pharaonic-style building Ismaïliya's MUSEUM OF ANTIQUITIES houses collections put together by the French conservationist Jean Clédat. The Ramesside stelae which used to stand in the Garden of Stelae are now in the Port Said Museum.

PORT SAID. Port Said was originally nothing more than a camp consisting of huts on stilts, founded in 1859 by Saïd Pasha to house the Suez Canal workforce. The sand excavated during dredging was used to fill in part of Lake Manzala and level the reclaimed land. By the late 19th century it was already an important port and all the major maritime powers had a consulate there. The new Port Said MUSEUM houses Pharaonic, Graeco-Roman, Coptic and Islamic antiquities. On the other side of the canal is PORT FUAD, founded in 1925.

SINAI

SOUTH SINAI, *240*
SINAI MOUNTAINS, *243*
ST CATHERINE'S MONASTERY, *244*
MOUNT SINAI, *246*
GULF OF AQABA AND THE
RED SEA, *248*
NORTH SINAI, *250*

BEDOUINS

The Bedouins were the original inhabitants of Sinai and still represent the largest section of the total population (200,000) of the peninsula. They belong to different tribes governed by customary laws. Tribal confederations, in both North and

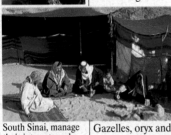

South Sinai, manage their interests and organize their social life. This mainly sedentary population is today being marginalized by new economic trends and the development of their territory. Although their nomadic lifestyle may have disappeared they continue to maintain their traditional activities and there is a thriving Bedouin craft industry.

SINAI

Bordered by the Mediterranean in the north, the Gulf of Suez in the west and the Gulf of Aqaba in the east, the Sinai peninsula covers an area of almost 24,000 square miles between Africa and Asia. It is the other face of Egypt, a far cry from the Pharaonic sites of the Nile Valley. Sinai is an area of contrasts. The northern coastal plain, where most of the peninsula's population is concentrated, stretches from the Suez Canal ▲ 228 to the Gaza Strip and gradually gives way in the south to a limestone plateau, the El-Tih Desert. South of El-Tih are the Sinai Mountains, a vast range of crystalline mountains rising to heights of over 6,500 feet. Here, traditional farming and stock breeding are carried on in the many oases of its *wadis*. Finally the Red Sea, where the mountains fall steeply into the turquoise waters, is teeming with marine life, whose beauty and variety is equal to that of the famous tropical reefs found in the Southern Hemisphere. While he was visiting Egypt in 1850, Gustave Flaubert wrote: "The sea bed with its wealth of different shells and corals was more colorful than a primrose meadow, while the surface of the sea shimmered and sparkled with every possible shade of color, blending from chocolate to amethyst, from pink to lapis-lazuli and the palest of pale green. It was truly unbelievable . . ."

CLIMATE. The climate is varied, although aridity is the common factor in these vast desert wastes. There is a very definite Mediterranean influence in the north where the coastal strip has a much higher winter rainfall and temperatures are much cooler than the regional average. The central plateau is the most arid region, while in the fall and early spring the Sinai Mountains often suffer torrential and devastating rainstorms. In mid-winter the highest peaks are regularly covered in snow. The Gulf of Aqaba has a fairly constant climate throughout the year, with milder winters resulting from the temperature of the Red Sea (68 to 77 degrees Fahrenheit) and cooler summers resulting from the north-northeasterly winds which blow down this natural corridor.

FAUNA. Sinai's once richly varied fauna has become much impoverished. Gazelles, oryx and jackals are now rare and leopards have completely disappeared. However, original species such as the hyrax (a strange rodent-like creature) and the ibex (a type of wild goat) still populate the peninsula. Steps have been taken to safeguard the wildlife of Sinai and special reserves have been created. Camels, the traditional symbol of the Bedouin way of life, are now gradually being replaced by Japanese jeeps.

LOOKING TO THE FUTURE: PROJECTS AND PROSPECTS. Since it was restored to Egypt in 1982 Sinai has been the subject of a number of tourist, agricultural and industrial development projects. In fact Egypt sees this vast territory as a potential solution to its problem of overpopulation. Work is currently underway on the El-Salam Canal, which will link the Nile with North Sinai and ultimately irrigate about 495,000 acres. This is surely an indication of the intention to

🗓 Five days
◆ D

populate this previously neglected region and make it productive. Now that there are real prospects of peace in the region, Sinai should also be able to resume its traditional function as a bridge between Egypt and Lebanon, Syria and Israel.

GETTING TO SINAI. There are several ways of getting to Sinai by means of public transport, including bus and taxi, but visitors who are short of time may prefer to fly. However, given the vast distances that have to be covered, the best solution, if possible, is to have your own vehicle. Good road maps are available and the road signs in Sinai are better than anywhere else in Egypt. If you plan to leave the main highways, it is essential to have a four-wheel drive. Alternatively you can join one of the excursions organized by local Bedouins, and these can be either in their own vehicles, by camel or on foot.

A MYTHICAL PLACE ✪
The visit to St Catherine's Monastery does not take long, but it would be a pity to leave without trying the ascent of Mount Sinai, where Moses is said to have received the Ten Commandments. Go in the early morning or evening, using the goat track, then climb back down the 750 steps. If you are feeling brave you can spend the night at the summit in order to see dawn rising.

239

SOUTH SINAI

The first route into South Sinai suitable for motor vehicles was opened in 1929 by King Fuad who wanted to visit St Catherine's. The route followed the Suez Canal before winding up into the mountains and continuing along a track as far as El-Tor, today the regional capital of the Governorate of South Sinai. It was used by pilgrims on their way to St Catherine's as well as servicing the quarantine center for the pilgrimage to Mecca. The center was set up in El-Tor at the end of the 19th century when sea routes to places of pilgrimage gradually replaced the traditional *darb el-hajj* route across the center of the peninsula. Until the Israelis invaded Sinai in June 1967 ● *71* the peninsula remained a marginal area which was virtually cut off from the rest of Egypt, the real frontier of the country being the Suez Canal ▲ *228*. The 1979 Camp David Agreements and the restoration of Sinai to Egypt marked the beginning of a new era, symbolized by the opening of the Ahmed Hamdi Tunnel (named after an officer killed during the 1973 Arab–Israeli War) in 1980. The tunnel, which is about 10 miles north of Suez and about 88 miles from Cairo, was intended to open up Egypt's Asiatic territory. On the Sinai side the road heads south along the Suez Canal.

Aïn Musa. "They took us to the oasis of the Springs of Moses which is the starting point of the desert routes and where our tents, which had left Cairo two days before us, had been put up beneath the slender palm trees." (Pierre Loti, *Le Désert*, 1896). Aïn Musa (Springs of Moses), the largest oasis in South Sinai, was planted with palm trees, mimosa and tamarisk and fed by a hot (104 degrees Fahrenheit) spring. According to the Bible the oasis was the site of Marah (which in Hebrew means "bitter") where Moses is said to have thrown a piece of wood into the bitter-tasting waters and made them sweet (Exodus 15, 24–5). Until the freshwater canal between the valley and Suez was built, in 1863, Aïn Musa constituted one of the main freshwater supplies for the town and the ships that docked there, as well as

Moses receiving the Ten Commandments.

"And the people murmured against Moses, saying, What shall we drink? And he cried unto the Lord; and the Lord shewed him a tree, which when he had cast into the waters, the waters were made sweet."
(Exodus 15, 24–5).

one of the main way stations on the Sinai route. The members of the Egypt Expedition recorded a total of nine springs and during the 19th century the oasis was a popular vacation resort among foreign diplomats. Today it is a mere shadow of its former self. Only one of its sources is still maintained, and a good proportion of the pools are now filled in; the palm grove remains only partly cultivated. The wreckage of the successive Arab–Israeli wars fought in this region is the only legacy from an era which sealed the fate of this once prosperous oasis.

RAS EL-SUDR AND QAL'AT EL-JUNDI. Ras el-Sudr is the second most important town on the Gulf of Suez after El-Tor. It originally developed as a result of the oil industry, but now it is becoming increasingly popular as a tourist center mainly because of its proximity to both Suez and Cairo. A road leads northeastward from Ras el-Sudr to Qal'at el-Jundi, the former citadel of Salah ad-Din, at a distance of about 30 miles. The 12th-century citadel, which was built to protect the route of pilgrimage and also to repel the attacks of the Crusaders, stands at the top of an outlier of the Jebel el-Raha several hundred yards above the vast expanses of the El-Tih plateau. For centuries it stood forgotten among the surrounding rocks, until it was rediscovered in 1909 by the French geologist Jules Barthoux, who was traveling from Suez to El-Tor. Among the buildings that can be found enclosed by the walls of the citadel are cisterns and shops with particularly beautiful, vaulted rooms which have been hewn out of the rock. There is also an old observation post.

THE WILDERNESS
The biblical description of Sinai as the "wilderness" always evokes the image of Moses leading the Jews out of Egypt along the valleys known as "the most ancient routes in the world". These routes took them to Mount Sinai (Jebel Musa, or the Mountain of Moses) where the prophet received the Ten Commandments. The Bible seems to have identified the spot (which subsequently became mythical) where over the centuries scholars, holy men and women and pilgrims have come to seek salvation. Until the early 20th century the route of the Exodus was the subject of many scientific and theological debates. It is now widely thought that Moses led the Children of Israel from Goshen (the eastern Delta) via the Bitter Lakes to the Isthmus of Suez, along the Gulf of Suez and Wadi Feiran to Mount Sinai.

The Oasis of Feiran extends almost 3 miles and includes a truly magnificent palm grove and a number of orchards.

The temple of Sarabit el-Khadim, partly built into the rock, probably dates from the Middle Kingdom. It has a number of upright stelae dedicated to Hathor and the rulers of the Nile Valley.

Remains of Qal'at el-Jundi. Texts carved on some of the stone lintels recount the history of the fortress.

The mosque, with its Fatimid-style mihrab, dominates the complex. The climb from the road takes about 20 minutes and the effort is rewarded by a magnificent view of the central Sinai Desert.

HAMMAM FARA'UN. The road runs south from Ras el-Sudr along the Gulf of Suez to Jebel Hammam Fara'un (approximately 69 miles from the tunnel), which stands 1,620 feet above the Red Sea. The main road turns into the mountains while a track continues along the coast for a further 2 miles to the Fara'un Hot Springs (158 degrees Fahrenheit), which rise in a cave at the foot of the mountain before tumbling into the sea. The local Bedouins are familiar with the medicinal properties of these sulphurous waters, which they call "Hammam Fara'un Malun" (meaning "the baths of the accursed pharaoh"). Legend would have it that the Egyptian army pursuing the Jews was drowned on this very spot, said to be haunted by the spirit of the pharaoh.

TEMPLE OF SARABIT EL-KHADIM. The main road follows the Wadi Tayiba ("pleasant valley") for about 20 miles before rejoining the coast at Abu Zenima, a small oil and mining center. To the south of the town the road running along the Wadi Matalla to the temple of Sarabit el-Khadim is surfaced for the first 22 miles and then replaced by a track for about 7½ miles. The temple is situated at the top of a hill about 45 minutes' walk from the track. It was dedicated to Hathor, "Mistress of the Turquoise", and was built to protect the many mines in the area from which the Egyptians of the Old Kingdom extracted turquoise and copper during winter campaigns. Visitors are shown round by the Barakat family, who have been the temple guardians for as long as anyone can remember.

MAGHARA TURQUOISE MINES. Abu Rudeis, which is situated about 103 miles from the tunnel, is an oil center to the south of Abu Zenima. From here a track follows the Wadi Sidri for about 13½ miles to the Maghara turquoise mines. The entrance to the mines is marked by stelae dedicated to the rulers of the Old Kingdom.

WADI MOQATTEB. From the mausoleum of Sheikh Suleyman, south of the mines, the track heads southeast for about 4½ miles before joining the Wadi Moqatteb, otherwise known as the Written Valley. The valley has derived its name from the

Nabatean inscriptions which are cut into the sandstone face of its western slopes. About 6 miles further on the track joins the Wadi Feiran road leading to St Catherine's Monastery. These two excursions can be combined by using the road between Sarabit el-Khadim and the turquoise mines, but should not be undertaken without a guide and four-wheel drive.

242

Beyond Feiran (left), the road follows the Wadi el-Sheikh to the Watia Pass gorge, bordered by granite cliffs, before emerging onto the plateau of St Catherine's Monastery. The typical mountain village of St Catherine looks incongruous in this desert landscape. The village has almost four hundred inhabitants, mainly Bedouins originating from the Jebaliye ("mountain") tribe, who are said to be the descendants of two hundred Walachian and Bosnian families sent by Justinian to defend the monastery when it was founded.

THE SINAI MOUNTAINS

About 27 miles south of Abu Rudeis the main road continues toward El-Tor while a secondary road turns eastward toward the Oasis of Feiran and St Catherine's.

OASIS OF FEIRAN ★. The oasis of Feiran lies midway between the Red Sea and St Catherine's and is an ideal place to break your journey. It is the largest oasis in South Sinai and lies at the narrowest point of the valley at the foot of the Jebel Serbal, which rises to a height of 6,790 feet to the south of the oasis. This is traditionally the site of Rephidim, where the Jews stopped on the last stage of their journey before reaching Mount Sinai (Exodus 17, 1–16). The oasis flourished in the early centuries of the Christian era and a bishop's palace was founded there in 400. In the 7th century the conquering army of Caliph Omar brought about its decline by putting an end to its religious ascendancy in favor of St Catherine's. The ruins of ancient Pharan stand on a hill, El-Meharret, at the center of the oasis. At its foot is a small hermitage, a dependency of St Catherine's. Today Feiran has about 650 inhabitants, mainly Qararsha or Awlad Saïd Bedouin.

The first thing you see as you approach the monastery, built between 527 and 565 on the orders of the emperor Justinian on the site of the "Burning Bush", at an altitude of 5,150 feet, are its gardens surrounded by cypresses and its impressive walls. It has the double distinction of being the smallest diocese in the world and the oldest working monastery. It is named after Saint Catherine, an Alexandrian martyr who died in 307. Her body was supposedly carried away by angels and discovered five centuries later at the top of the mountain which today bears her name.

The monastery belongs to the Greek Orthodox Church and most of the monks are Greek. Although the principal church and the site of the "Burning Bush" are open to the public, the monks guard their tranquillity and do not allow visitors into the treasure-house, the museum or the library, which has the largest collection of manuscripts in the world after the Vatican Library.

During times of instability and unrest, the normal access route to the monastery was closed and a basket-and-pulley was used to hoist visitors and provisions over the walls.

A short ascent opposite the entrance leads to a vantage point overlooking the interior of the monastery. It is a heterogeneous complex consisting of buildings from different periods and even includes a 10th-century mosque built as a mark of allegiance to the Muslim powers that had promised to protect it. Inside the Byzantine-style church, originally dedicated to the Transfiguration of Christ, a fine collection of icons from different periods gives some idea of the extent of the monastery's treasures.

"And Mount Sinai was altogether on a smoke, because the Lord descended upon it in fire: and the smoke thereof ascended as the smoke of a furnace, and the whole mount quaked greatly. And when the voice of the trumpet sounded long, and waxed louder and louder, Moses spake, and God answered him by a voice." (Exodus 19, 18–19)

It was on Mount Sinai (Jebel Musa, or the Mountain of Moses) that Moses received the Ten Commandments. It lies south of St Catherine's Monastery and rises to a height of 7,497 feet. It can be reached along a track to the east of the monastery walls or via a flight of three thousand steps hewn out of the rock to the south. Both lead to an amphitheater (known as the "Seventy Elders of Israel") where St Stephen's Hermitage stands in a garden planted with cypresses. A flight of some 750 steps leads to the summit where a chapel built in 1934 is reminiscent of the original (AD 363) rebuilt by Justinian in 530.

It is advisable to take the gently sloping track to the top of Mount Sinai and leave the steps for the descent.

There is a breathtaking view from the chapel (above) and on a clear day you can see the Gulf of Aqaba and the coast of Saudi Arabia. To the

southwest Mount Catherine (Jebel Katherina), the highest point on the Sinai peninsula, dominates Mount Sinai from a height of 8,650 feet.

The remarkable rock formations of the Colored Canyon (below).

GULF OF AQABA AND THE RED SEA ★

The road continues eastward toward the Gulf of Aqaba through 44 miles of breathtaking landscapes, where the combined effect of the limestone mountains and sedimentary deposits has produced some remarkable variations of form and color, as well as some truly spectacular views. About 56 miles from St Catherine's Monastery, a main intersection leads southward toward Dahab, Sharm el-Sheikh and Ras Mohammed and northward to Nuweiba and Taba on the Israeli border.

DAHAB. The "Bedouin village" of Assalah forms the southern half of Dahab. Its palm-fringed bay is bordered by cafés, restaurants and campsites, which offer basic facilities at competitive prices. A little further on, the Israeli-built village of Dahab is a business and administrative center. The many beaches and diving sites that can be reached from both villages include the famous "Blue Hole" about 5 miles from Assalah.

SHARM EL-SHEIKH. About 12½ miles from Ras Mohammed is the peninsula's most developed tourist center, which all underwater enthusiasts must visit. Sharm el-Sheikh is divided into two parts, the southern half where the town stands on a cliff overlooking the port, and Na'ama Bay, situated 4½ miles to the north, which is the center for hotels and diving clubs. The 10-mile stretch of coast between Sharm el-Sheikh and Ras Nusrani has many diving sites randomly dotted along its length, and these are easily accessible from the road. Beyond Ras Nusrani the main road heads northward and the diving sites are reached along coastal tracks.

RAS MOHAMMED. Ras Mohammed (*ras* is the Arabic word for "cape" or "head") is the most southerly point of the Sinai peninsula. It was declared a conservation site in 1983 and became a national park in 1989 in order to protect and preserve the region's marine and desert flora and fauna. Foxes and gazelles have been reintroduced and the park also has a large migratory and sedentary bird population. The

NATURE LOVER'S PARADISE ✪
There are few architectural sites to visit here but instead a natural paradise to explore: a blue sea with translucent depths, home to thousands of marine species and more than 150 types of corals; spectacular desert landscapes. The Ras Mohammed National Park covers much of the area. Several marked-out itineraries (identified by different colors) gives one the opportunity to discover the region's ecosystem.

mangrove forests in the south provide an ideal habitat and have the most northerly growing mangroves in the Northern Hemisphere. The park is renowned for its diving sites where a pair of flippers and a snorkel are all you need to discover the wonders of its underwater marine life. Among the shoals of multicolored fish, the lucky diver may encounter the Napoleon fish (up to 6 feet in length but the most peaceable of diving companions), the reef shark, the manta ray or the green turtle. Maps of the park are available at the entrance.

NUWEIBA. From Dahab the road cuts through the mountains, rejoining the coast in sight of the port of Nuweiba from where there is a daily ferry service to the Jordanian port of Aqaba. Nuweiba lies either side of the Wadi Watir delta, with the port and Muzeina Bedouin fishing village to the south and 2½ miles to the north the tourist and Tarabiin Bedouin villages, separated by the remains of an 18th-century Turkish citadel. The road running westward between the two will take you to the COLORED CANYON. It follows the Wadi Watir to the oasis of Aïn el-Furtaga where a track, to the right, runs along the bottom of the valley for 7½ miles and comes out onto a plateau above the canyon. Nuweiba also has a number of beaches and diving sites.

TABA. For six years Taba was the stumbling block in Israeli–Egyptian relations. It was only restored to Egypt in 1989 following international arbitration. Plans for the development of a major resort on the Israeli–Egyptian border are currently under consideration. At present Taba has restaurants and beach cafés and one luxury hotel. The frontier post (about 100 yards from the hotel) can be crossed on foot and there is a bus service to Eilat.

RETURN ROUTE VIA DARB EL-HAJJ. The road leading westward from between the fjord and the Geziret Fara'un (Pharaoh's Island) winds for about 19 miles along a *wadi* to the central plateau of the Sinai peninsula, the El-Tih Desert. It follows the ancient pilgrim's route, which crossed the peninsula to the Hejaz mountains in present-day Saudi Arabi. The route, which was much frequented until the early 20th century, was used for an annual pilgrimage, accompanied by an army escort to protect the *mahmal* ● *126*. Today it is still the main overland link between Egypt, the Arabian peninsula, Lebanon, Syria and Israel, via the port of Nuweiba. The Bedouin village of EL-THAMAD, the first settlement on the route, is gradually becoming an important way station. Nakhl lies at the center of the peninsula and has for a long time been a crucial staging post. A road leads from the center of Nakhl to El-Arish, 94 miles to the north. About 37½ miles west of NAKHL the road climbs to the top of the Mitla Pass and then down toward Suez in the west across dunes dotted with the wreckage of armored vehicles, evidence of the conflicts that have taken place in the area.

There are some truly beautiful landscapes between Nuweiba and Taba. The road borders a sea whose transparent colors range from deep blue to turquoise. On the opposite shore is the Saudi Arabian and Jordanian coast and the port of Aqaba. About 6½ miles before you get to Taba the road climbs above the fjord, where the turquoise waters of the inlet are dominated by cliffs. After crossing the bed of the Wadi

Morakh, Geziret Fara'un (Pharaoh's Island) can be seen beyond a hill, dominated by its recently restored fortress, begun in 1170 by Salah ad-Din.

THE SUEZ CANAL AT EL-QANTARA

In 1916 El-Qantara was the departure point for the Palestine railway line that ran along the Mediterranean coast toward Gaza and Jerusalem. It was built for military purposes by the British and linked Cairo and Jerusalem until 1948. It continued to run as far as Gaza between 1948 and 1967. It was dismantled at the time of the Israeli invasion and its lines and sleepers used to construct the Bar-Lev Line, a defensive rampart erected by Tsahal along the Suez Canal during the occupation. A mobile bridge (above), destroyed in 1967, enabled trains to cross the canal at El-Firdan, about 12½ miles south of El-Qantara.

NORTH SINAI

The route across North Sinai, known as the "Ways of Horus", has linked Egypt and Palestine since ancient times and served as both an invasion and trade route. Before the Suez Canal was built, the isthmus acted as a bridge between Africa and Asia.

EL-QANTARA. El-Qantara ("the passage"), which lies about 22 miles north of Ismaïliya ▲ 236 between the Bitter Lakes and Lake Timsah in the south and the marshlands of the ancient Pelusian branch of the Nile in the north, has always been a place of passage into Sinai. Dissected by the Suez Canal, El-Qantara el-Garbiya in the west and El-Qantara el-Sharkiya in the east are two fairly uninteresting towns which suffered during the Arab–Israeli conflicts from 1956 to 1973. A ferry service links the two towns. About 3 miles outside El-Qantara the road runs north to El-Arish (100 miles) and south to Ismaïliya (25 miles).

PELUSIUM. The ancient site of Pelusium, about 19 miles north of El-Qantara, can be reached via a minor road which turns off near the village of BALUZA, whose name is reminiscent of the ancient port. Pelusium dates from the time of the Hyksos invasion in c. 1700 BC. The Hyksos were initially going to found their capital on the site of Pelusium, on the mouth of a branch of the Nile, but instead decided to settle further up the Delta. However, an important port was established at Pelusium and became, under the Ptolemies, the eastern counterpart of Alexandria. As a major Egyptian port it fell prey to invaders and gradually declined as the Pelusian branch of the Nile moved and dried up. In 1118 it finally fell to the Crusaders led by King Baldwin I of Jerusalem and was burned and razed to the ground. The only remains that can be seen at Tell el-Farama, the site of ancient Pelusium, are several hundred yards of the outer walls and the Aswan granite columns scattered on the ground on the site of the ancient port.

LAKE BARDAWIL. Beyond Baluza the road runs eastward, parallel to the coast, along the shores of Lake Bardawil, which can be reached via a number of minor roads. The 52-mile-long lagoon occupies half the northern coastline of the Sinai peninsula and is separated from the sea by a narrow sandbank only a few dozen yards wide in places. It is an important staging post for migratory birds who rest there when crossing the Mediterranean. It is classified as a protected site and is considered one of the richest waterfowl reserves in the Mediterranean Basin. Fishing plays an important part in the region's economy and employs 15 percent of the working population. The fishing season is at its height between January and May when the 999 gaily colored fishing boats, following local tradition, are dotted across the glittering waters of the lagoon. Sole constitutes the main catch and is exported as far afield as Europe. The lake supposedly takes its name from the nearby tomb of Crusader King Baldwin, even though the king's remains were

Legend attributes the name of Lake Bardawil to the Crusader King Baldwin I of Jerusalem, who died at El-Arish in 1118. His body was embalmed and his entrails buried near the lagoon, beneath a small mound of stones known as the Turbet el-Bardawil.

"The Bedouins wear a tunic with pointed sleeves which sweep the ground and which they tie behind their backs so that they can walk unhindered; the tunic is fastened at the waist with a broad, embroidered leather belt in which they insert a curved dagger.... Some throw a brown-and-white-striped woollen blanket over the tunic; they drape a piece of soft, dark-colored cloth elegantly over the tarboosh and turban covering their head, to protect them from the heat of the sun. They are all tanned ... and all have noble features."
Valérie de Gasparin, 1850

EL-ARISH
The capital of North Sinai, which has one of the most beautiful palm groves in Egypt, today has a population of 70,000. Until fairly recently, the less wealthy Cairenes used to holiday in palm beach huts rented from the Bedouins. Today hotels and villas occupy several miles of the seafront. The population of this important commercial center on the main Palestine

later taken back to Jerusalem.

EL-ARISH. Today the capital of North Sinai is being extensively developed. FUAKHARIYA, the oldest part of the town, which used to stand on a hill overlooking the palm grove, has the remains of a Pharaonic fortress, rebuilt by the Ottomans in 1560, occupied and restored by Bonaparte's troops in 1799 and destroyed by British bombardments during World War One. The remains of the fort can be seen at the end of the Shari' Suq el-Khamiss ("Thursday market") where a Bedouin market is held every Thursday morning. There is a permanent exhibition of the arts and traditions of the Bedouins of the Sinai peninsula near the zoological gardens on the outskirts of El-Arish.

route is made up of Egyptians, Palestinians and Bedouins. Some of the town's inhabitants claim to be descended from the Bosnian soldiers sent by Süleyman the Magnificent to build the fortress in 1560.

RAFAH. The 27-mile trip to Rafah can easily be made from El-Arish. As you approach the border with the Gaza Strip the rapidly changing landscape resulting from much heavier rainfall and more developed agriculture can be considered as an "introduction to Palestine". About 19 miles from El-Arish the village of SHEIKH ZUAYED holds a Bedouin market every Tuesday morning. About 6 miles further on, at a point where an arch stands above the road, a minor road leads to the coastal village of EL-FAIRUZ, built on the site of Yamit, an Israeli settlement which symbolized the resistance of Jewish settlers during the Israeli withdrawal in 1982. A few miles further on the town of Rafah is dissected by the border and partly inhabited by Palestinian refugees from the 1967 war, some of whom cross the border every day to work in the Gaza Strip. There is a Saturday market in Rafah.

RETURN JOURNEY BY THE INLAND ROUTE. From El-Arish a road leading south (follow the signs to Ismaïliya) into the interior offers an opportunity to see the desert which was once the preserve of nomadic tribes. A few grazing camel herds are a reminder of a way of life that has virtually disappeared. The road, which forks west to El-Arish (37½ miles), skirts round the Jebel Maghara with its open-cast coal mines, passes through the village of Bir Gifgafa and crosses the Khatmia Pass before heading down toward the Suez Canal across some beautiful sand dunes. There is a ferry service to Ismaïliya.

DESERTS

LIBYAN DESERT, *254*
SIWA OASIS, *256*
KHARGA OASIS, *260*
ARABIAN DESERT, *264*

🚗 🚶 **Ten days**
◆ **C E**

The date palm is ideally suited to this desert region, which produces a wide variety of dates.

LIBYAN DESERT

The Libyan Desert stretches from the eastern bank of the Nile to the Libyan border over an average distance of 500 miles, and covers two thirds of the total surface area of Egypt. It is an inhospitable region with hardly any rainfall, high summer temperatures and treacherous winds. The Ancient Egyptians likened this vast desert to the sea and the oases to islands. In fact several deep depressions in the Libyan plateau actually lie below sea level and have created the five great oases: Siwa, Farafra, Bahariya, Dakhla and Kharga. These low-lying areas make it easy to reach the water table, which lies above an impermeable layer of clay. Kharga, the largest of the five oases, stretches for nearly 120 miles.

POPULATION. In ancient times foreign influence (Egyptians, Greeks, Romans and Libyans) destroyed the basic stock of the indigenous oasis-dwellers. During the Islamic period the population was further modified by slaves brought from Darfur (Sudan). According to Roman records the Kharga Oasis in fact became a vast slave market which sold oasis-dwellers into slavery in the Nile Valley. Aspects of Bedouin culture have survived among the population (which has been sedentary for centuries); that place particular emphasis on blood ties, animist beliefs grafted onto Islam and a poetic tradition which speaks of nostalgia for the desert in a language similar to classical Arabic. Unlike the Sinai tribes ▲ *238*, who have inherited the traditions of the Arabian peninsula, the Bedouins of the Libyan Desert (with the exception of Siwa) live according to the traditions of the Egyptian civilization handed down by the original oasis-dwellers. However, their main forms of activity, driving caravans and collecting tributes from sedentary populations (in return for their protection), have died out.

CARAVAN ROUTES. Since the time of the Old Kingdom the desert has been crossed by a network of caravan routes linking Egypt with her neighbors. Ivory, ebony, rhinoceros hide, panther skins and slaves were brought into Egypt across this harsh and arid wasteland. In order to protect the borders and control the wealth arriving from Libya and Darfur, the Egyptians colonized the western oases, while the Greeks built Ptolemaic temples and the Romans constructed fortresses.

CROPS. Crops were cultivated in the oases of the Libyan Desert between the 1st and 4th centuries AD. These included olive trees, grown for their oil, vines, thought to have disappeared with the arrival of Islam (the vineyard which exists today dates from the reign of Mohammed Ali), corn, barley, millet, cotton and cardamom. However, the date

The palm date, and the papyrus.

palm so characteristic of this desert region is rarely mentioned. Of the fifty or so varieties of dates produced in Egypt, the oases grow mainly tamars, faligs, hamrawis and, best of all, the delicious saïdis.

MONASTIC CELLS. Christian mummies dating from the second half of the 3rd century AD were discovered in the oases of the Libyan Desert. This new religion was introduced very early on and began to develop within the lower strata of Egyptian society. The environment of the desert was favorable to the creation of monastic cells, which were often the victim of attacks by Barbarian tribes such as the Blemmyes. The Arab conquest finally put an end to Christianity in the desert region.

FAUNA. In Pharaonic times the donkey was Egypt's most widely used pack animal. It was gradually replaced in caravans by the dromedary, introduced into Egypt in 525 BC during the invasion led by the son of Hystaspes, later Darius I, King of Persia, who reigned from 521 to 486 BC. The country's population of camels has decreased significantly, owing to the development of the railway and the automobile.

Sand dunes cover 40 percent of the total surface area of the Libyan Desert. They can reach heights of up to 500 feet and change shape and direction with the winds. The pure, clean lines and gentle slopes of these sand mountains can be treacherous, gradually engulfing anything that lies in their path.

255

SIWA OASIS

To reach the Siwa Oasis from Cairo, take the toll expressway that crosses the desert to Alexandria and turn off left toward Burg el-Arab ▲ *201*. Siwa is situated nearly 190 miles southwest of Mersa Matruh, and the road linking them has a surprisingly good surface. For those who like the desert, the "oasis route" runs south from Giza ▲ *334* to Siwa and south-southwest to the oases of Bahariya, Farafra, Kharga and Dakhla. Siwa lies 187½ miles from the shores of the Mediterranean and 312½ miles from the Nile in a depression about 60 feet below sea level. Several million years ago the Libyan Desert was entirely covered by the waters of the Mediterranean, and there are still some salt-water lakes, such as El-Zeitun. Although these may add to the mystery of the landscape, it is the freshwater springs (nearly three hundred of them) flowing beneath palm- and olive-shaded paths that constitute the true beauty and wealth of the oases. Dates and olives are gathered by *zaggala* (stick bearers) who must remain celibate until the age of forty. The oases' ten thousand inhabitants are divided into nine tribes who are all descended from the Zenatiya Berbers. In spite of extensive intermarriage they continue to speak the Berber Siwi dialect. The Berber influence is also apparent in the craftsmanship which is unique throughout Egypt. The women continue to embroider yellow, orange and green geometric designs on *milaya* (large shawls), although synthetic materials have replaced traditionally woven cloth.

SHALI. This fortified town, whose outer wall was pierced by only three gates, was founded in 1203 following a violent Bedouin attack which left only forty survivors in the entire oasis. The steep, winding streets of Shali (the Berber word for "town") have been abandoned since 1926 when, for three days and nights, the rains beat down on the *karshif* (salt-caked mud) houses, making them uninhabitable.

TEMPLE OF AGHURMI. Of the many visitors who came to Siwa in ancient times to consult the oracle of Jupiter Amun (Darius), it was Alexander the Great who, in 331 BC,

CRAFTSMANSHIP
Traditionally the women of the Siwa Oasis used to wear all their wealth in the form of heavy silver jewelry: bracelets and different sorts of necklaces as well as rings and chains. Today these items of jewelry are becoming increasingly rare and their precious metal content is decreasing. Siwa is also renowned for basketwork and embroidered cloth. A wedding dress (above) embroidered with colored threads and decorated with buttons.

The Siwa Oasis has many lakes and over three hundred (freshwater or therapeutic) springs.

> "The utter barrenness and desolation that often encompass scenes and spots of exquisite fruitfulness and beauty . . . are almost peculiar to Egypt."

> John Carne

All that remains of the Temple of Umm el-Ubeyda is one wall, richly decorated with funeral scenes.

TEMPLE OF JUPITER AMUN
Although the houses which concealed the edifice (below) were cleared away in 1970, the temple is in an advanced state of disrepair. It is still possible to make out the Egyptian-style Ismail Hellenized by two Doric demi-columns (only one remains). Two rooms lead to the sanctuary where a corridor less than 32 inches wide must have been used to hide the priest who delivered the oracle.

immortalized both the oracle and the oasis. The young Macedonian had just been proclaimed pharaoh in Memphis and was greeted as such by the high priest of the oracle. The temple stands to the northwest of the rock of Aghurmi, the ancient town. Cartouches of Amasis dating from the 26th Dynasty have been deciphered in spite of their very damaged condition, and these have established the date of the construction of the monument as the 6th century BC. At the foot of the rock of Aghurmi there is a second Temple of Amun, built during the 30th Dynasty and known as UMM EL-UBEYDA.

JEBEL EL-MAWTA. The ancient site of Jebel el-Mawta ("mount of the dead") was unknown to the 19th-century explorers. This huge limestone mass contains tombs from the 26th Dynasty and Ptolemaic period. The most beautiful sepulcher belongs to Si-Ammon, a rich oasis-dweller of Greek origin, and dates from the 3rd century BC. The image of the sky-goddess Nut with a halo of sycamore leaves (to the right of the entrance) is particularly impressive. The tombs were plundered by the Romans and subsequently reused. The oasis-dwellers were obliged to use them as shelters during the Italian air raids at the beginning of World War Two.

CLEOPATRA'S POOL. The most famous spring at Siwa Oasis is the Aïn el-Hammam, otherwise known as "Cleopatra's Pool". The dark-green waters are collected in a circular pool, carpeted with algae and moss. Other well-known features of the Siwa Oasis include the sand baths where it is believed that rheumatism sufferers can relieve their pain by being buried up to their necks in the sands of JEBEL DAKRUR.

FARAFRA
Farafra, which lies on a plain rather than in a depression, is surrounded by a stone wall (above). About 19 miles to the north is the so-called White Desert where huge, dazzlingly white limestone formations assume weird and wonderful shapes (below).

EL-AREG

A hard track (nearly 190 miles long) linking the Bahariya and Siwa oases was opened in 1991 (military authorization must be obtained before using it). It passes through the uninhabited oases of SITRA (90 miles from Bahariya), NUA MISSA (125 miles) and BAHREIN (nearly 140 miles) before reaching El-Areg. About 160 miles from Bahariya the track joins the foothills of a plateau which it follows northward. After 5 miles leave the track and turn due east (follow the tire marks in the sand). After 4½ miles on a rocky plateau, you reach the top of the depression. Although the descent to the oasis is easy, the ascent is a much more delicate operation because of the soft sand. Unlike the other oases in the desert El-Areg ("the lame man") cannot be seen from a distance. Its green palms are surrounded by high, white cliffs in which the Romans dug out forty or so tombs. The harsh brilliance of the sheer, white rock rises steeply from a mother-of-pearl carpet of fossilized shells covering the bottom of a depression. Purity of color and a sense of vastness and space make this one of the most striking oases in Egypt.

BAHARIYA

Although Bahariya is the nearest oasis (225 miles) to the Egyptian capital, it has been least affected by modern development in spite of its proximity to an important iron mine. Its palm groves cover a 60-mile long, undulating basalt depression which is quite literally overflowing with hot springs. According to the Arab archeologist Ahmed Fakhri, El-Bawiti (which has

16,000 of Bahariya's 26,000 inhabitants) is the site of the most beautiful of these springs, the AïN EL-BISHMU. Unfortunately many of the lovely freestone basins which contained the soft waters have been replaced by concrete tanks. The few archeological remains in the oasis (which converted to Christianity in the 4th century) are virtually inaccessible.

FARAFRA

Farafra has all the features of a traditional oasis: groups of palm trees emerging from a sea of sand dunes and mysterious, narrow alleyways bordered by blind walls. The inhabitants have a reputation for being skilled hunters and kill jackals, hyenas, gazelles and even fennecs.

DAKHLA

The villages of Dakhla ("inner") Oasis, which lies in a rocky landscape punctuated by sand flows, have preserved their traditional architecture. The oasis extends over a distance of about 40 miles and most of its archeological sites are near the Kharga–Dakhla–Farafra road.

DEIR EL-HAGAR. A winding track leaves the road 4½ miles before El-Qasr and leads to the ruins of Deir el-Hagar ("monastery of the rock"), which lie in a shallow depression. The temple dedicated to the Theban Triad, which was one of the few Roman ruins in the oasis, was damaged by an earthquake.

EL-MUZAWAKA TOMBS. The tombs of Pelusis and Petosiris, hewn out of the Jebel el-Muzawaka, are decorated with scenes of traditionally Egyptian funeral rites. Petosiris, however, is dressed in Greek clothes and the ceiling is decorated with a bull from the Persian Mithras cult.

EL-QASR. This ancient fortified town, about 17 miles from Mut, was established in the Middle Ages on the foundations of a Roman village. It is one of the oldest inhabited sites in the oasis.

BALAT. Balat, with Mut and El-Qasr, is one of the three villages of Dakhla Oasis. Nearby, excavations are presently being carried out by the Institut Français d'Archéologie Orientale (IFAO) on the complex of AïN ASIL and the necropolis of Qila el-Dabba. A row of five mastabas, which comprised the main elements on the site, were discovered during a *khamsin* (sandstorm) by the archeologist Ahmed Fakhri. The mastaba of the governor Medunefer, who was a contemporary of Pepi II, was still intact and revealed some beautiful funeral paraphernalia, which included gold jewelry.

EL-QASR
The four- and five-story houses which border the narrow, winding village streets have carved doors, locks and lintels. The oldest lintel (1518) decorates the Beit Ibrahim. The mosque has retained its Ayyubid minaret (below) and stands next to a medersa housing several ancient texts. Small, individual mausoleums (above) stand side by side in the Muslim cemetery.

These stones, known as "melons", can be seen between Assiut and the Kharga Oasis.

EL-BAGAWAT
The 120 Nestorian chapels built between the 4th and 10th centuries are scattered across the sandy slopes of Jebel el-Teir, about 1¼ miles northwest of Kharga. Only five of these domed, mudbrick monuments still have their painted decorations.

KHARGA OASIS

The capital of Kharga ("outer") Oasis, which, at 116 miles long, is the largest of the five oases, is also called Kharga. The oasis can be reached from Dakhla or via the new DESERT ROAD (completed in 1991), which follows the right bank of the Nile toward Assiut (244 miles). Make sure you don't miss the badly marked turnoff at Koreimat (56 miles from Cairo) and then continue due south, crossing the Nile at Assiut and then following a resurfaced road for 150 miles until you come to Kharga. The region, known as New Valley, is also serviced by an airline. Most of the archeological remains in the Libyan Desert are to be found in this oasis along the road running north–south between Kharga and Baris.

NEW VALLEY. In 1959 the Egyptian government announced its desert colonization program, which aimed to develop agriculture in the oases and exploit the region's industrial potential as well as its natural resources of ore and water. The "New Valley" project was centered around the town of Kharga and included the oases of Dakhla and Farafra, thus covering an area of roughly 176,800 square miles, with a population of 120,000. In 1967 Hassan Fathi ▲ *442* launched the New Baris project but the expected population movement just did not happen, no doubt because of the *fellaheen*'s age-old mistrust of the desert. Development initiatives have therefore been focused on more reliable ventures, with tourism benefiting from substantial investments and the promotion of such events as the "Pharaoh's Rally". Mining is centered around the phosphates of Abu Tartur, between Dakhla and Kharga. A new museum in the Shari' Gamal-Abd el-Nasser houses Pharaonic objects discovered at Balat by the IFAO.

TEMPLE OF HIBIS. The temple, which stands about 1¼ miles north of the present capital, is the only Persian temple of any size in Egypt. It was built by Darius I, according to Egyptian architectural tradition, with a quay, an avenue of sphinxes, monumental entrances and three hypostyles leading into a naos. The eight-columned pavilion with its extremely beautiful capitals dates from the reign of Nectanebo II (30th

Dynasty), while the main entrance, decorated with Greek legal inscriptions, was built by the Ptolemies. In spite of these additions, the edifice has a fine unity of style.

EL-BAGAWAT. Christianity, the official religion from the reign of Constantine until the Islamic conquest, spread rapidly through the oases and gradually replaced the social structure of the Pharaonic period. Pagan temples were replaced by monasteries, churches, chapels and monastic complexes. However, the worship of the dead continued to be practiced with the same degree of fervor, as evidenced in the 120 Nestorian chapels of El-Bagawat. In ancient times religious and political opponents of established power were banished to the oases. One such opponent was Nestorius, a heretical bishop who was exiled to El-Bagawat for having maintained that of the two natures of Christ (divine and human) only the human was earthly and suffered on the cross. From this it followed that Mary, mother of the "human" Christ, was not the mother of the Son of God. Cyril, Bishop of Alexandria, opposed this doctrine and Nestorius was condemned and removed from office in 431 by the Council of Ephesus. He died twenty years later.

TEMPLE OF NADURA. About 1¼ miles northeast of Kharga is the ruined Temple of Nadura, built by the Romans during the reign of Antoninus Pius or his predecessor Hadrian (117–38). Although it was badly eroded by the wind, a scene representing female musicians playing percussion instruments and sistra can still be made out on the few remaining wall sections. This would seem to suggest that the temple was in fact not dedicated to the Egyptian god Amun but to his divine spouse.

DARB EL-SINDADIYA. To defend themselves against attack from hostile tribes, all too frequent before the reign of Mohammed Ali, the inhabitants of the Western Desert lived in underground fortresses. In the ancient village of Darb el-Sindadiya the mudbrick houses have palm-trunk beams. The dark, narrow streets wind around the spring of Aïn el-Dar, which

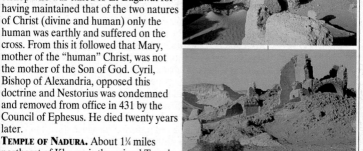

AÏN UMM EL-DABADIB
The village of Aïn Umm el-Dabadib is dominated by trapezoid towers. In the distance are the sandy slopes of the north escarpment of the oasis. The village once had a very sophisticated irrigation system, built by the Romans, which consisted of four underground aqueducts each 3 miles long, running from the escarpment to the fort. The aqueducts can be reached via the air shafts, dug every 30 or 40 yards and covered at ground level with huge, flat stones.

261

FORTRESS OF AïN UMM LABAKHA
The fortress's round towers make it look more like a castle. The beauty of its proportions is enhanced by the sand-covered cliffs.

Markets in the town of Kharga.

has dried up. This 10th-century site is now used to stable animals and should be visited with a guide.

AïN UMM EL-DABADIB ★. A rough track runs south from Kharga across the foothills of Jebel el-Sheikh before turning north to Umm el-Dabadib. Another track (17½ miles) skirts westward round JEBEL EL-SHEIKH and JEBEL EL-TARIF to Kharga. This expedition should be undertaken with a guide as the going is often difficult across the sand dunes. Under Diocletian, the temples, surrounded by vast, square mudbrick enclosures, were replaced by fortresses which sometimes had a church outside the walls. Communities grew up around the churches with their attendant houses, necropolis and crops. This was how the Romano-Byzantine village of Aïn Umm el-Dabadib was founded. The site is typical of the caravan oases, which were situated near a spring at the end of the caravan routes and also served as staging posts on the Libyan Desert routes. They had the cisterns and irrigation systems so vital in places where water is scarce. The Ptolemies exploited the agricultural wealth of the oases and were succeeded by the Romans, whose irrigation systems were unsurpassed. At El-Deir water is drawn using a system of hand-operated levers and directed along drainage channels leading from the well in the courtyard of the fort to irrigate the crops.

AïN UMM LABAKHA ★. The Romans built Aïn Umm Labakha at the other end of the caravan route about 19 miles from Aïn Umm el-Dabadib. Leave the road about 2 miles north of Munira and head westward, skirting south round the village of Aïn Sabba and then leaving the track altogether to head across country toward a cliff about 3 miles to the northwest. The Roman fort can be seen at the foot of the escarpment.

EL-DEIR. The Roman fortress of El-Deir lies about 15 miles north of Kharga. Follow the Assiut road northward to Munira (10 miles). Turn right (eastward) about 200 yards before the road checkpoint and follow the track, which is an old tarmacked road. The last mile or so can only be negotiated in a four-wheel drive. El-Deir ("the monastery"), an impressive rectangular structure supported by twelve towers, stands at the foot of JEBEL UMM EL-GHANAYIN.

QASR EL-GHUEIDA. This is one of the few temples (250–80 BC) in the oasis which was constructed and decorated entirely during the Ptolemaic period, between the reigns of Ptolemy III and Ptolemy X. The outline of its fortifications, built by the Greeks at the intersection of the Sudan and Libyan routes, can be seen to the east of the road. The wooden roof covering the hypostyle has disappeared, exposing the columns with their Composite capitals. The flat roof of the naos and the vaulted roof of the lateral chapels were a characteristic architectural feature of oasis temples. Qasr el-Ghueida was dedicated to the Theban Triad: Amun, Mut and Khonsu.

QASR EL-ZAIYAN. In the village of Qasr el-Zaiyan (15 miles south of Kharga) is a small temple dedicated to Amenebis, god of the town of Tchnonemyris, which was built under the Ptolemies and flourished until the Byzantine period. A Greek inscription commemorates the restoration of the temple during the reign of the emperor Antoninus (138–61).

DUSH. Beyond the village of Baris a track leads eastward (56 miles) to the temple and excavations of Dush. About 1½ miles to the north is the unfinished and now abandoned "show town" of NEW BARIS designed by the architect Hassan Fathi ▲ *442*. The remarkable religious, military and civilian complex of Dush developed, to a large extent, as a result of the slave trade. It is situated at the end of the Darb el-Arbaïn ("the road of forty days", the time it took to travel from Sennar in the Sudan back into Egypt). At Dush the caravans either headed for Kharga and rejoined the Nile Valley at Assiut or turned off toward the Nile at Esna. The IFAO has been excavating the site since 1967. The temple, entirely cleared of sand, is in pure Pharaonic tradition. Built during the reigns of Domitian and Trajan (1st century) it was decorated during the reign of Hadrian (2nd century). The sanctuary, which comprises two interconnecting rooms with a vaulted ceiling, is flanked by two chapels. On the outside of the far wall are images of Osiris-Huy (Serapis) and Isis. The wall, which has a window communicating with the interior, constituted the (gold-plated) back wall of an adjoining chapel. The fortress and its civilian buildings are also Roman, but stratigraphic studies show that the site was occupied from the beginning of the Ptolemaic period.

263

MONASTERY OF ST ANTHONY

In spite of successive restorations, the monastery has retained its original appearance, surviving the Arab conquest as a result of its isolated position. The

intellectual life of the monastery flourished between the 12th and 15th centuries until it was plundered in 1454 by Bedouin servants. Today it still has about one hundred icons (the oldest dating from the 9th century) housed in the library and the seven churches whose white domes stand out against the green of the palm groves. In the Church of the Virgin Mary a wooden iconostasis, inlaid with ivory crosses and motifs, separates the nave from the sanctuary.

Map of the deserts of Lower Thebaid, produced in 1717 by an icon artist using information provided by Claude Sicard, who was given the task of locating and drawing the monuments of Ancient Egypt by Philippe d'Orléans. The map includes plans of the monasteries of St Paul (right) and St Anthony (left).

ARABIAN DESERT

The Arabian Desert is an arid, mountainous region which lies between the Nile and the Red Sea. Several thousand nomadic Bedouins (the Ababdeb and the Bichariya) live amidst the austere beauty of its mountains and gorges, a mineral world of metamorphic rocks where a few thorn-bushes and sebaceous plants manage to grow. The fauna is also limited since the hordes of gazelle that once populated the region have been decimated by hunters, while social change has got the better of the herds of dromedaries. However, rodents and foxes can survive in this vast, empty wasteland, which every spring welcomes huge flights of migrating birds, especially storks. All forms of life depend on the winter precipitation (less than 118 inches per year), which often falls within the space of a few hours. The Arabian Desert is also a vast mining region which has been exploited since ancient times, its quarries providing the building materials for many great edifices in Upper Egypt and Rome. Since the advent of Christianity it has also served as a refuge for anchorites seeking communion with God in the solitude of the desert. Two monasteries were built by the disciples of Saint Anthony and Saint Paul on the sites where the saints had chosen to live. Today these fortresses are occupied by Coptic Orthodox monks. Leave Cairo via the Katamia road, which joins the coast road north of Aïn Sukhna. Turn south in the direction of Hurghada. About 20 miles west of Ras Za'farana, on the road between the coast and the Nile Valley, a track forks off to the Monastery of St Anthony. The Monastery of St Paul can be reached by way of the tarmacked road which leaves the main Suez–Hurghada route about 15½ miles south of Ras Za'farana.

From the top of the promontory, the magnificent view of the monastery complex of St Paul compensates for the mass of recent concrete constructions outside the walls.

1 MONASTERY OF ST PAUL
2 MONASTERY OF ST ANTHONY
3 MONS PORPHYRITES
4 HURGHADA
5 MONS CLAUDIANUS
6 SAFAGA
7 WADI HAMMAMAT HIEROGLYPHS
8 QUSEIR

MONASTERY OF ST ANTHONY.

Saint Anthony the Great was born in 251 near Beni Suef and orphaned at the age of eighteen. He sold all his worldly possessions and retired into the mountains of the Arabian Desert. The founder the Desert Fathers died at the age of 105 and is buried beneath the ancient church of the monastery. About 300 yards away is the cliff cave in which he lived. The monastery (Deir Mari Antonios), built by his disciples in 361–3, is the oldest monastery in Egypt and has retained its original appearance in spite of successive restorations.

MONASTERY OF ST PAUL.

Saint Paul was born into a wealthy Alexandrian family in 228. In his attempt to find his way in life he sought refuge in the Arabian Desert where he remained alone for eighty years, wearing garments made out of palm fibers and living on the half-loaf of bread brought to him every day by a raven. It was Saint Anthony who revealed his saintliness to him. The 5th-

🎞 **Five days**

◆ **F**

265

"Walked and walked for hour after hour across the plains, in the burning sun and the icy wind, continually crushing the pale, embalmed plants [beneath our feet]. The desert is both as monotonous and as changing as the sea. The day before yesterday it was monumental blocks of granite; yesterday smooth, flat sand, and today we are entering a region of millstones and are surrounded by a new and surprising world of hitherto unseen landscapes. A gloomy maze of valleys, made of these yellowish and white stones, has just opened up before us; the horizontal layers of rock look like regular courses in a wall built by a human hand. You have the impression of walking through a destroyed city, walking along streets, giant streets, between ruined palaces and citadels."
Pierre Loti

TEMPLE OF SERAPIS
On the site of Mons Porphyrites a flight of steps leads to the temple whose various elements (pediments, architraves, bases of Ionic columns) lie scattered on the ground.

century Monastery of St Paul has three churches. It was plundered several times during the 15th and 16th centuries and abandoned for a long time before being reinhabited by monks from the Monastery of St Anthony. In St Paul's Church the knightly saints, Saint George, Saint Theodorus and Saint Michael the Archangel, are depicted on horseback fighting devils. The icons include an image of Saint George of Cappadocia, dressed in a purple habit, mounted on a white horse. The monastery also has such ancient, illuminated manuscripts as the Coptic version of the Divine Liturgy and the Commentary on The Epistle of Saint Paul the Apostle to Titus by Saint John Chrysostom. Outside the monastery there can still be seen an ancient grain mill, olive press and the pulley that was used to hoist visitors and provisions over the walls during times of unrest.

IMPERIAL QUARRIES. The Arabian mountains had two Roman penal colonies or "quarry farms", enterprises involved in the extraction from these desert quarries of monoliths weighing several hundred tons used in the construction of temples.

The quarries were exploited by a private entrepreneur, known as the "quarry farmer", but were supervised by an imperial representative and a soldier such as the centurion Avitus, who commanded the first cohort of the Sicilian cavalry. The emperor Claudius is generally considered to have been the first to exploit these mines. The archeological sites of Mons Porphyrites and Mons Claudianus can be reached via the Red Sea coast or the Nile Valley. The first route follows the coast in the direction of Hurghada, a small resort with an underwater diving center. At RAS GHARIB a long mountain ridge known as the JEBEL EL-ZEIT, or Mountain of Oil (petroleum), runs parallel to the shore. In the second millennium BC the Egyptians exploited two mines here to extract galena (natural lead sulphide) or kohl, which was applied around the eyes. Mons Porphyrites is reached by turning off the main coast road just over 11 miles north of Hurghada and following a newly tarmacked road for about half a mile and then a well-marked track to the right. After nearly 18 miles you suddenly leave the track and head northward for about 7 miles. A Roman discharge ramp will become visible at the foot of a fairly steep slope. Head into the mountains along the Wadi Sidri (which runs from east to west) and after five rather stony miles you eventually come to an ancient Roman site shaded by four acacia trees. Follow the valley to the left, which runs west and then south for 4½ miles, and you will finally arrive at the Roman camp of Mons Porphyrites.

Mons Porphyrites. The stone on this site is a pinkish-purple porphyry which comes from JEBEL ABU DUKHAM ("father of smoke"). In the arid valley of Abu Ma'mmal, between the Nile and the Red Sea, the Romans built a veritable town, with a fort, two temples, stables, cisterns and wells. Five columns arranged in a semi-circle, which form the remains of a cistern with a circular roof and *saqia* (water wheel), stand among the smooth stones of the *wadi*. The castellum (fort) and baths were built against a rock opposite the cistern. A flight of steps leads to the remains of the Temple of Serapis. A stele, discovered in 1823, provides the only surviving evidence of a Christian church, which was commissioned and undoubtedly financed by a high-ranking official by the name of Flavius Julius.

Mons Claudianus ★. Turn onto the Port Safaga–Qena road and follow it for about 24 miles. A roadside stopping-place with a refreshment stall indicates the direction (due north) of the Mons Claudianus. Follow the badly maintained, tarmacked road for 14 miles. At the end of the tarmac take the second *wadi* to the right of the track after some trees and small houses. The Roman fort stands to the left of the *wadi*, about 1½ miles from where you turned off. The Roman penal colony of Mons Claudianus, nestling at the foot of JEBEL FATIRA, supplied Rome with black granite columns, some of which still support the Pantheon today, while others can be seen in Trajan's forum. According to certain archeologists the workforce consisted of *damnati in metallum* (men sentenced by common law) and included early Christians. The grandiose ruins of the penal colony are in keeping with the scope of the undertaking. The fort, with its massive walls flanked by beautifully rounded towers, and the outline of the inner buildings which housed the Roman garrison can be seen from a distance, like a mirage in this arid valley. Today hot springs still well up inside the ruins. This was an extremely sophisticated complex for a penal colony in the middle of the desert. A bath is set into the ground and underground heating systems called hypocausts lead to the *sudatoria*

otherwise known as the "sweating baths". Outside the walls stables big enough to house horses and bullocks were covered with a thatched roof supported by thirty or so pillars. A flight of twenty steps leads up to the Temple of Mons Claudianus, which was begun during Hadrian's reign, but never completed.

Quarries. The actual quarries are on the opposite slope of the *wadi*. The fragments of granite and geometric designs carved in the rock illustrate the method used to extract the columns. Quarriers dug oblong holes along the line to be cut and drove in wooden wedges which were then soaked with water. As the wood expanded, the granite shattered. A cracked column rests on a thick layer of granite fragments, and makes the quarry look as though it has been only recently abandoned.

Port of the popular resort of Hurghada.

Mons Claudianus quarries
The perfectly cylindrical shaft of a polished granite column lies between the fort and *wadi*. On the opposite slope of

the mountain an apparently perfect column (200 tons) cracked as it was transported and was abandoned on the spot. The columns were dragged across the desert by draught animals and then transported down the Nile to Rome where they arrived more than a year later.

The Wadi Sakait emerald mines were exploited by the pharaohs and Mameluke sultans.

Detail of the cartouche of Irwywrta (17th Dynasty), one of the rock carvings in the Wadi Hammamat.

WADI HAMMAMAT. In Pharaonic times Wadi Hammamat, at the foot of Jebel Hammamat, was known as the Valley of the Rohamnu. Its quarries, exploited since the time of the Old Kingdom, provided much of the *bekhen* (hard stone) used to build the temples of Thebes and Upper Egypt. The deposits lie in long, narrow layers midway between the Nile and the Red Sea. On the northern bank of the *wadi* is the classic *bekhen*, a sort of sandstone schist with reddish reflections, whereas the stone in the *wadi* bed is of inferior quality. A third type of stone, more finely grained and lighter in color but with a dull finish, was also used. Extracting the stone and transporting it across the desert to build the sacred edifices of the pharaohs was a glorious undertaking which deserved to be recorded for posterity. To this end a number of hieroglyphic tablets were carved along the southern slope of the Wadi Hammamat gorge over a distance of 2½ miles (milestone 96 on the Qift–Quseir road, opposite the wooden hut selling Egyptian antiques). The rock carvings, representing men, hunting scenes and dancing, are next to some truly remarkable inscriptions dating from the Old to the New Kingdom. The thirty-seven Middle Kingdom inscriptions include the stele of Senwosret I, carved during the reign of Senwosret I by Ameni, an inspector of naval recruits and infantry commander. It confirms the vast size of some of the expeditions, which involved over seventeen thousand free men crossing these desert gorges to build monuments to the greater glory of the pharaoh. Among the representations of animals and hieratic inscriptions, an early Aramean alphabet and eight inscriptions illustrating the period of the New Kingdom, there are scenes dedicated to Min-Amun executed in a more classical style.

TRADE ROUTES. Once the ancient trade routes with Punt (southern Arabia and the coast of Somalia), the routes linking the Nile with the Red Sea coast have been much less frequented since the construction of the Suez Canal. Spices and perfumes were brought to the Egyptian ports of Myos Hormos (Abu Shar el-Kibli), Leukos Limen (Quseir) and Berenice.

GOLD MINES. Gold was found in the quartz seams of the mountain ranges of the Arabian Desert, in the region of Qift (otherwise known as Koptos). Iron ore and emeralds were two of the other resources to be found in the Arabian Desert which were mined during ancient times.

"The sand leads us to Kosseïr [Quseir]. It is as if the sand from the shore has been blown into this broad valley by the wind; it is like the abandoned floor of a gulf. From a distance you can see the foremasts of the ships which are laid up like those on the Nile."
Gustave Flaubert

CAIRO

THE CITY CENTER, *272*
EL-HUSSEIN AND
KHAN EL-KHALILI, *286*
EL-AZHAR, *294*
DARB EL-AHMAR, *300*
THE CITADEL, *304*
MIDAN SALAH AD-DIN, *308*
OLD CAIRO, *318*
CEMETERIES, *326*
MEMPHIS, *332*
SAQQARA, *344*

CAIRO: A MIXTURE OF CIVILIZATIONS ✪
You could spend weeks, even months, here: each district is a new discovery. Allow at least three days to visit the city, with one reserved for an exploration of the Egyptian Museum, a veritable treasure-trove of Pharaonic marvels, including the treasures of Tutankhamun. After the Citadel and its alabaster mosque, visit the churches of old Cairo and the Coptic Museum. Take time also to visit the districts of el-Hussein and el-Azhar. Walk through the maze of streets bordered with wakala, mosques and ancient houses, linger in the shops of Khan el-Khalili and taste the pleasures of smoking the *chicha* in the Café des Mirrors.

ANTIQUITY

Bounded in the west by Jebel Moqattam and in the east by the River Nile, the site of modern Cairo had not always been the chosen location for the foundation of a capital. There are in fact three major landmarks in the city's evolution: HELIOPOLIS ▲ *285*, the capital (in c. 3100 BC) of the first, short-lived, united kingdom of Upper and Lower Egypt; MEMPHIS ▲ *332*, which as the majestic capital of the Old Kingdom has perhaps the most legitimate claim to the title of the "great ancestor" of modern Cairo; and the Fort of Babylon ▲ *318*, built by Trajan (98–117).

FROM FUSTAT TO EL-QAHIRA

The capture of the Fort of Babylon by the armies of Amr Ibn el-As in 640 marked the beginning of the various stages of the construction of the "Mother of the World" (Umm el-Dunya), as Cairo was called by its chroniclers and inhabitants, as well as the establishment of Islam in Egypt. Amr founded a mosque at the apex of the Nile Delta, where he began to build the first Arab settlement in Egypt. Centered around the mosque, FUSTAT ▲ *324* ("encampment"), as it later became known, had the outward appearance of a military camp, in which the various Arab tribes that made up his army were divided into *khittat* (districts). With the emergence of the Abbasid dynasty a new military and administrative district known as EL-ASKAR ("army") was established to the north of Fustat, now the modern district of Sayyida Zeinab ▲ *314*. The Abbasid governor of El-Askar, Ahmed Ibn Tulun, who was of Turkish origin, sought to free himself from the control of Baghdad. In 868 he founded, around the mosque named after

Two Mameluke horsemen practicing with lances (below).

View of the aqueduct, built by Salah ad-Din, which brought water from the River Nile to the foot of the Citadel.

16TH-CENTURY CAIRO
With the Ottoman conquest Egypt became one of the provinces of a vast empire whose capital was Istanbul. The spice and later coffee trade ensured Cairo's remarkable prosperity throughout the 16th and 17th centuries. A 16th-century French map of Cairo (left).

him, the new district of EL-QATAI' ("the wards", a reference to the districts allocated to the various contingents of his army). El-Qatai' was recaptured and burned by the Abbasids, gradually abandoned and finally used as a "quarry" for the construction of the Fatimid capital of El-Qahira (originally Kahira, "The Triumphant One"), built on the site of the "Islamic City" and, for the first time, fortified.

THE MEDIEVAL CITY

Salah ad-Din (Saladin) commissioned the Citadel. It took 89 years to build (1116–1207) and became the new seat of power, opening up the city of El-Qahira which became (and continues to be) populated by craftsmen, laborers and *harafish* (beggars). In the 16th century the Ottoman governors who occupied the Citadel pursued the construction projects begun by the Mameluke sultans.

THE MODERN CITY

Mohammed Ali ● *68* began the major construction work, which entailed draining the lakes of El-Ezbekiya ▲ *274* and building new roads, and the Cairo of today finally began to take shape. His successors carried out a series of projects to extend the city which involved building new districts such as Heliopolis ▲ *285* in 1905, mostly financed by private foreign interests. Today Cairo has a population of twelve million (one quarter of the entire population of Egypt), with an average density of 130,000 inhabitants per square mile and as many as 250,000 in some districts.

NAPOLEON BONAPARTE IN CAIRO
After defeating the army of Murad Bey at the Battle of the Pyramids (below) in 1798, Bonaparte remained in Egypt until returning to France in November 1799. The most tangible evidence of the French presence

in Cairo was, on Bonaparte's orders, the shutting of the gates which closed each *hara* (district) at night.

The Obelisk of Senwosret I (left) is one of the few remaining monuments of the so-called Thinite ● *39* period of the city of Heliopolis.

271

🏃 Two days

◆ H

QASR AN-NIL PALACE
Ibrahim planted olive and fruit trees on the lands cleared by his father. He also built the first palace complex on the banks of the Nile (which had been strengthened by a dyke). His brother Saïd, who ruled from 1854 to 1863, continued the tradition by building the Qasr an-Nil Palace (below) on his accession.

The district designated by modern Cairenes as the city center lies between Old Cairo and the River Nile. In the early 19th century it was nothing more than a stretch of land which was submerged during the Nile floods and partially cultivated when the waters subsided. It was cleared and leveled by Mohammed Ali ● *68* and planted with trees by his son Ibrahim. In 1867 the rows of trees were converted into avenues and the plots of land thus created were sold to anyone who agreed to use it for the (immediate) construction of a private residence. Hastily built, this district, named Ismaïliya after its promoter Ismaïl, was slow in attracting inhabitants. The rate of building increased at the turn of the century with an influx of foreign capital and residents. New suburbs also sprang up to the north and

1 Museum of Egyptian Civilization **2** Opera **3** Mukhtar Museum **4** Marriott Hotel **5** Pharaonic Village **6** Geographical Society **7** Sabil el-Walda **8** Ramses Station **9** Midan el-Ataba **10** El-Ezbekiya **11** Abdin Palace **12** Islamic Museum **13** Manyal Palace

northeast with the extension of the tram network, begun in 1897.

BAB EL-HADID

RAMSES STATION. First built in 1856, the main railway station was reconstructed in traditional Arabic style in 1892. Its façade was refurbished in the same style in 1955 and its esplanade renovated the following year, when a statue of Ramesses II, standing above a fountain, replaced the famous statue depicting the *Awakening of Egypt* by the sculptor Mahmud Mukhtar ▲ *282* erected in 1928.

RAILWAY MUSEUM. The museum, founded in 1933, stands at the far end of the station and houses seven hundred exhibits (scale and life-size models). At the station end of the SHARI' EL-GUMHURRIYA stands Cairo's last *sabil-khuttab* ● *113*, the SABIL EL-WALDA (Fountain of the Queen-Mother), built in 1869 by the Italian architect Ciro Pantanelli (1833–84).

SHARI' IMAD AD-DIN. Cairo's first investment properties were built along the main thoroughfare of the city center, formerly the theater and nightclub district. The oldest are the KHEDIVIAL BUILDINGS (1910) inspired by Haussmann. Several of Cairo's largest clubs were situated in the Shari' Imad ad-Din, including the CLUB DES PRINCES built in 1897 by Lasciac ▲ *281*. All that remains of the original décor with its distinctive masonic symbolism are heads crowned with a diadem, reminiscent of the Statue of Liberty.

BAB EL-HADID
The Bab el-Hadid (Railway Gate) once gave its name to the square in front of the station (now Ramses Square) and to one of Cairo's old districts. It also inspired the title of a film by Yussef Shahin. Shahin (above) with actress Hind Roustom during shooting.

THE "DIANA" CINEMA
Of the several cinemas in the Shari' Imad ad-Din, the *Diana* (1933), a fine example of pure Art Deco, is undoubtedly the best preserved.

273

CAIRO OPERA HOUSE
The Cairo Opera House, which opened in 1871 with a performance of Verdi's *Aïda*, was destroyed by fire in 1971 and replaced by a car park.

EL-EZBEKIYA

Equestrian statue of Ibrahim Pasha in the Midan el-Opera.

Some of the arcaded buildings in north El-Ezbekiya still remain in the Shari' Wagh el-Birka and the Shari' Mohammed Ali.

A VAST LAKE
Following the Egypt Expedition, most of Cairo's European residences and several royal palaces, including one belonging to Mohammed Ali, were built on the shores of what was once the lake of El-Ezbekiya (below).

Once a vast lake, El-Ezbekiya is today one of the most important communications centers in Cairo. The area was drained in 1837, and took shape from 1868 onward. The northern section was sold by lots and arcaded buildings constructed in accordance with a rigidly enforced plan. In the center the khedive Ismaïl had the El-Ezbekiya Gardens designed along the lines of Parisian parks by Delchevalerie, a horticulturalist from Paris. They had many attractions, including a waterfall, bandstands, cafés-concerts and carousels. The khedive, who was particularly fond of entertainment, also had a circus, theater and opera house built in the southern part of the gardens, all within a few months. Finally, he ordered several new streets to be built through the old districts, including the Shari' Clot-Bey, which was intended to give easy access to the station, the Shari' Abd el-Aziz, which led to the Abdin Palace ▲ *281,* and the Shari' Mohammed Ali, the road to the Citadel ▲ *304*. Almost fifty years later the Shari' el-Azhar and Shari' el-Geish were built to open up the old center of Cairo.

HOTELS AND DEPARTMENT STORES. These elaborate projects made El-Ezbekiya the favorite haunt of European visitors and residents for many years afterward. A number of countries initially had their consulates here and it was also Cairo's leading café, brasserie and hotel district, with such establishments as the NEW HOTEL (now the *Hotel Continental*) and the famous SHEPHEARD'S. Tourists who were not so wealthy stayed in the many boarding houses in the SHARI' CLOT-BEY where the nights were reputedly extremely "hot". Several department stores, SEDNAWI (1913), TIRING & STEIN (1908), OMAR EFFENDI (1911) and the CICUREL chain, were opened on the edge and in the neighborhood of El-Ezbekiya.

MODERN EL-EZBEKIYA. Since the 1960's the El-Ezbekiya Gardens have become neglected and dusty. They were dissected by the extension of the Shari' 26 Yulyo, and were gradually encroached upon by a number of different buildings.

MIDAN EL-ATABA EL-KHADRA

Cairo's largest fresh food market is held in the Midan el-Ataba el-Khadra or Ataba ("threshold") Square, situated (as its name suggests) between the old and modern cities. Beneath the arcades of the adjacent buildings, traders sell all kinds of bric-a-brac. Since the 1930's the northern side of the square has traditionally been the preserve of the booksellers.

POSTAL MUSEUM. Situated on the second floor of the Central Post Office, the museum is a hotch-potch of artefacts, pictures and documents illustrating the ways in which messages have been sent in Egypt over the centuries.

THE "GROPPI" CAFÉ. The SHARI' ADLI is worth a visit, if only to stop off at one of Cairo's three *Groppi* cafés (the second is in the Midan Suleyman-Pasha and the third in Heliopolis), founded by a Swiss caterer who settled in Cairo in the 1920's.

TURN-OF-THE-CENTURY ARCHITECTURE. In the same street, the widely diverse styles of a group of more or less contemporary buildings reflect the heterogeneity of turn-of-the-century Cairene architecture: a SYNAGOGUE (1907) of Secessionist inspiration standing next to a block of rented apartments of Italianate design (GATTEGNO), and the ST DAVID'S BUILDING, a neo-Gothic, brick apartment block. Next to these are the head office of the government-controlled building society (1905) and the neoclassical CLUB RISOTTO (1899).

SHARI' QASR AN-NIL. The buildings in the Shari' Qasr an-Nil are more recent (1930–50) and therefore taller. The IMMOBILIA (1937) was, for over a decade, the tallest building in Cairo. Two impressive 1930's apartment blocks, the BAEHLER and the SEDNAWI, stand either side of the far end of the Shari' Qasr an-Nil where it leads into the MIDAN TAL'AT HARB, officially renamed in 1952 but still generally known as the MIDAN SULEYMAN-PASHA.

"SHEPHEARD'S"
This famous hotel, the epitome of European colonialism, was destroyed by fire during the riots of January 26, 1952.

The Egyptologist Auguste Mariette (1821–81) was instrumental in the foundation of Cairo's Museum dedicated to Pharaonic antiquities, which provided an indispensable complement to the Egyptian Department of Antiquities established by the viceroy of Egypt, Saïd Pasha, in 1859. The original collection was housed in the suburb of Bulaq and then transferred to Giza in 1891 before re-crossing the Nile in 1902 to its present building in the Midan at-Tahrir (Liberation Square). This tailor-made museum encompasses every aspect of Ancient Egyptian civilization. The concealed basement area is as large as the section open to the public and houses an equally large collection of treasures.

On the west wall of the so-called treasure-chamber of the Tomb of Tutankhamun are twelve turquoise monkeys, the benevolent spirits of the First Hour of the sun's nocturnal voyage.

Chair belonging to the royal princess and queen, Sitamun, Daughter of Amenhotep III. It is decorated with five plaster and gilt scenes in relief and two sculpted heads in front of the arm rests.

THE TREASURE OF TUTANKHAMUN ▲ 418

Scene decorating one of the sides of a stuccoed and painted wooden chest found in the antechamber of the Tomb of Tutankhamun (above). It shows the king in his chariot, driving back the Nubian enemy from the south. On the other side the king is shown crushing the Syrian enemy from the north. The famous funerary mask of Tutankhamun (right).

Colossal limestone group (23 feet high and 13 feet wide) found in several pieces at Medinet Habu ▲ 434. It represents the pharaoh Amenhotep III, Queen Tiyi and three of their daughters.

One of the sides of a chest showing Tutankhamun seated, stringing his bow, with Queen Ankhesenamon sitting at his feet.

Sculpted alabaster head, inspired by the face of Tutankhamun, used as a cover for one of the Canopic jars which contained the king's entrails.

HEAD OF NEFERTITI
Quartzite head
thought to be of
Nefertiti found near
the Palace of
Merneptah in
Memphis. It was part
of a group of several
sculpted elements
ultimately intended to
form a statue.

Akhnaton, l'hérétique.

Étrange personnage

**BLAKE AND
MORTIMER**
In the Amarnian
room, Mortimer and
Professor Ahmed
admire a statue of
Akhenaten from
Karnak.

**RAHOTEP AND
NOFRET**
Painted limestone
statues of the high
priest Rahotep, one
of the sons of Snefru,
and his wife Nofret,
from the mastaba of
Rahotep at Meidûm
▲ *357*.

HEAD OF NEFERTITI
Unfinished head in brown quartzite, from a sculptor's workshop at Tell el-Amarna
▲ 378.

INSPECTION OF CATTLE
A model (representing cattle inspection by the owner and his scribes) from the tomb of the chancellor Meketre to the south of the Temple of Deir el-Bahri ▲ 426.

Rebuilt after 1952, the Midan at-Tahrir is an important communications center. The freeways of the 6 October Bridge, a major overpass, end at the square, which is also the terminus for a number of bus routes.

MIDAN AT-TAHRIR

Over the years the Midan at-Tahrir (Liberation Square), which was for a long time peripheral to the city center, has become a major communications nucleus. Several important public buildings stand on the approaches to the square. The MUGAMAA ("conglomerate") or Central Government Building (1950) is the nerve center of Cairene bureaucracy. All government ministries and departments have offices and representatives there. In 1960 the LEAGUE OF ARAB STATES moved into premises designed by Mahmud Riad

THE GEOGRAPHICAL SOCIETY
The Geographical Society was founded by the khedive Ismaïl as the scientific

(1905–86), who also designed the offices of the ARAB SOCIALIST UNION which, after its dissolution in 1977, became the headquarters of the National Democratic Party.

THE AMERICAN UNIVERSITY. This private establishment, founded in 1920, occupies the Khayri Palace, which formerly housed the Gianaclis cigarette factory and then the first Egyptian University.

THE GEOGRAPHICAL SOCIETY. Founded in 1875 by Ismaïl, the society has a library, a cartographic collection and a series of relief maps of Egypt. It also houses an ethnographical museum with a collection of objects depicting everyday life in 19th-

instrument of his imperial aspirations in East Africa. In reality it was used as a staging post by the European explorers who came in search of the sources of the Nile, and later by the many geographers whose research it financed during the interwar years (as illustrated by its well-stocked library, consisting mainly of works in French). The main hall (above).

century Egypt. Situated in the same complex, the PARLIAMENT building was built in only a few months after the unilateral Declaration of Independence on February 28, 1922, by the British government.

Boats on the Nile: detail of an engraving in the Geographical Society collection.

ABDIN

ABDIN PALACE. The construction of this vast palace, on the outskirts of the old city, was begun by Ismaïl on his accession in 1863. The khedive wanted to transfer the seat of government from the Citadel to a more open site. The work was supervised by two French engineers, De Curel and Rousseau, and lasted for ten years. Initially constructed with a traditional wooden framework, the palace was destroyed by fire on several occasions. Between 1909 and 1911 it was entirely rebuilt in stone by Antoine Lasciac (1856–1946), who, for more than fifty years, was one of the key figures in Egypt's architectural circles. Various alterations made during the 1930's by Verrucci included a luxurious Byzantine throne room.

BEIT EL-UMMA. Built at the turn of the century, this eclectic residence was the home of the nationalist leader of modern Egypt and founder of the Wafd party, Saad Zaghlul (1857–1927). When it became a museum, the so-called Beit el-Umma (House of the People) was carefully preserved in its original state. With its Art Nouveau dining room, Louis XV reception rooms, "Arab" living room, Turkish baths and magnificent library, the villa is a rare example of the tastes and lifestyle of the early 20th-century Egyptian political elite. The nearby SAAD ZAGHLUL MAUSOLEUM, built in neo-Pharaonic style between 1928 and 1931, was based on plans by the Egyptian architect Mustafa Fahmi.

After 1952, the Abdin Palace (above) was opened to the public. The curious collection of clocks and watches put together by Farouk I was of particular interest. Today the palace houses various government departments and can no longer be visited.

GARDEN CITY

In spite of the sweeping curves of its boulevards, this residential district, designed in 1906, does not really resemble a "garden city". Its promoters, the Bacos, who were property developers of Syro-Lebanese origin, acquired what was left of Ibrahim Pasha's estate on the banks of the Nile at a very reasonable price. Apart from a few villas constructed in 1910 most of the buildings date from between 1925 and 1935, a period which saw the spectacular development of the Art Deco style in Egypt. Among the most remarkable are the VILLA WAHBA, designed in 1925 by the French architect Edrei, and three large apartment blocks by the Italian architect Mazza.

THE "WAFD"
In 1919 a *wafd* (delegation) headed by Saad Zaghlul (left) declared its intention of visiting London to try to secure Egyptian independence. The delegation was not received by the English, but it gave its name to the Wafd nationalist party led by Zaghlul. Certificate of

subscription (above) for the construction of the Saad Zaghlul Mausoleum.

When the Abdin Palace was built, a broad esplanade was created in front of the main façade.

281

Abu el-Ela Bridge,
Gezira.

GEZIRA

This 14th-century island with its changing shoreline remained uninhabited until 1830 when Mohammed Ali built a palace and quarters for the royal guard at its northern tip. Because of the precariousness of its construction the complex soon became known as As-Zamalik, which in Turkish means "makeshift dwelling". Since it could only be reached by boat it was intermittently occupied and it was not until the accession of Ismaïl that it was extensively refurbished. The shores of the island were raised to prevent flooding, a jetty was constructed to facilitate access and most of the land was cultivated. In the center of the island the khedive built a palace surrounded by botanical and zoological gardens with exotic plants, a fine menagerie of African wildlife, fountains and various pavilions, including the monumental GEZIRA SALAMLIK. The island became the favorite residence of the khedive and in 1872 was linked to Cairo by the Qasr an-Nil Bridge, which was guarded at either end by lions sculpted by André Jacquemart (1824–96). Although Gezira has lost the elegance it had during the interwar years, it still has some very fine buildings, including some impressive villas in a wide variety of architectural styles.

The Gezira *salamlik* (above) where the Empress Eugenie stayed during her visit to Cairo, now the *Marriott Hotel*.

MUKHTAR MUSEUM. The Mukhtar Museum, designed by Ramesses Wissa Wassef for the sculptures of Mahmud Mukhtar (1891–1934), one of the greatest Egyptian sculptors, houses eighty-five works in bronze, stone, marble, basalt, granite and plaster. In the Shari' at-Tahrir renovation work is currently being carried out on the building (designed in 1936 by Mustafa Fahmi ▲ 281) which houses the PLANETARIUM, the MUSEUM OF EGYPTIAN CIVILIZATION and the GEZIRA MUSEUM, whose collection includes thousands of objets d'art collected by the royal family, housed in the Agricultural Pavilion of the Gezira Exhibition Grounds.

OPERA COMPLEX. This cultural complex (left), a gift to Egypt from Japan in 1988, was inaugurated in 1993. It comprises two concert halls, the *hanager* (multi-purpose exhibition and theater areas) and the Museum of Modern Art which, when it opened in 1991, housed thirteen thousand works by Egyptian artists. In the ANDALUSIAN GARDENS, or MASPERO GARDENS, near the Ramesses Bridge, is an obelisk discovered at Tanis ▲ 226.

CAIRO TOWER
The 614-foot tower was built in 1961 with the three million dollars paid by the Americans to President Nasser as compensation for their refusal to participate in the construction of the Aswan Dam.

GEZIRA SPORTING CLUB. In 1882 the British established their first institution in Egypt on a piece of land given to them by the khedive Tawfiq. The Gezira Sporting Club, which was based on London's Hurlingham Club, was reserved for British officers. Although now half its original size, it is still very exclusive.

THE GEZIRA CENTER FOR MODERN ART. The museum is housed in a *salamlik* ● 116 that was once owned by Ibrahim Pasha, and contains a modern art gallery as well as the Mohammed-Khalil collection. The collection includes works by major Impressionist painters such as Monet, Van Gogh and Gauguin, which were acquired in Paris from 1919 onward.

RODA

Roda Island was formed earlier than Gezira. It has not changed significantly since the time of the Arab conquest (7th century) when some impressive buildings were constructed: an arsenal, a Nilometer and a fortress. The last Ayyubid sultan even decided to transfer the seat of his government to the island and, to this end, had a new fortress, palaces and barracks built in 1240. Under the Mamelukes the seat of government returned to the Citadel and Roda became a district of beautiful waterside residences built in garden settings by the ruling classes. The few remaining examples of this trend, which continued into the 20th century, include the MANISTERLI SALAMLIK, built in the middle of the 19th century and originally part of the home of a Turkish official, and the MANYAL PALACE. Built between 1901 and 1933 by Mohammed Ali Tawfiq in the "neo-Islamic" style, it comprised five different buildings, one of which was a mosque. The present Manyal Gardens represent a tiny part of the gardens created, at enormous expense, by Ibrahim and which originally covered most of the island. They disappeared as a result of the post-Zamalik urbanization during the 1930's.

Map of Roda Island made by members of the Egypt Expedition.

The Manyal Palace was converted into a museum in 1955. Since 1964 part of the grounds has been occupied by Club Méditerranée chalets and a swimming pool.

NILOMETER
The Nilometer or *miqyas* was first constructed in 715 and completely rebuilt in 861. It consisted of a stone-lined well connected to the river bed which was used to measure the rise in the water level that occurred during August and September, as well as to regulate the distribution of water and determine the tribute to be paid by Egypt to the caliph. The central, calibrated column acted as a graduated scale, with its nineteen divisions corresponding to so many cubits.

283

THE INNER SUBURBS

BULAQ. During the Ottoman period Bulaq was an extremely
busy port with many warehouses. Today the ruined
caravanserais and the SINAN PASHA MOSQUE (1571) are
surrounded by slums. The EL-BALAH WAKALA (date
caravanserai), now a combined cloth, military surplus and
scrap-iron market, is a dealers' paradise.
THE PRESS DISTRICT. On the outskirts of
Bulaq, halfway between Ramses Station
and the Egyptian Museum, is the "press
district" where several leading Egyptian
dailies have their offices. The most
famous of these, *Al-Ahram* (*The
Pyramids*), was founded in 1876 by the
Takla brothers, Lebanese refugees who
fled to Cairo to escape the Ottoman
repression of the first "Arab nationalists". With a daily
circulation of almost one million copies and over six thousand
employees, including one thousand journalists, the unofficial
Al-Ahram has become the jewel in the crown of the largest
newspaper group in the Arab world as well as one of the
leading international newspapers.
SHUBRA. This densely populated suburb, linked by a tram
service to the city center since 1903, has developed along the
Shari' Shubra which, in the early 19th century, was one of the
few roads in Cairo suitable for motor vehicles. It was built by
Mohammed Ali to facilitate access to his favorite residence
where pavilions were scattered in a garden setting. The most
extravagant of these pavilions was a NYMPHAEUM, a large
ornamental lake fed by a central fountain and surrounded by
a colonnade (1826).
AS-SAKAKINI. Sold by lots in the 1880's, the As-Sakakini
district, named after the Syrian family who owned the land,
also owes its development to the tram service. At the center
of this radially designed district is the palace built by Habib
Sakakini in 1897. It is characterized by its overornate exterior
and, among other curiosities, one of Cairo's first ever lifts.
Temporarily closed for restoration, it houses the collection of
the Hygiene Museum.

THE OUTER SUBURBS

The spa town of Helwan was the first realized example
of the 19th-century idea of building cities in the
desert. Today it is an important industrial
center. At the turn of the century a Belgian
finance group founded the city of Heliopolis to the
north of Cairo while the garden city of Maadi was
established to the south at about the same time. Such
initiatives had previously been the prerogative of private

developers. Since the first plan for the development of Cairo in 1958, the authorities have focused on the urbanization of the eastern desert plateau as the best way to prevent the progressive loss, through building, of the agricultural land surrounding the capital to the north and west. This has resulted in the creation of the suburbs of Medina Nasr and Medina el-Moqattam. The eastward extension of the city was again incorporated into the 1970 and 1981 urban planning programs and gave rise to the construction of such new towns as 10 Ramadan, 6 October, 15 May (named after victories against Israel) and Medina el-Sadat.

HELIOPOLIS

Heliopolis, or Misr el-Gadida (New Cairo) as it is known by the Cairenes, is a unique example of urban development which owes a great deal to the personality of its promoter, Baron Empain. After successfully developing Cairo's first tram network, for which he obtained the concession in 1894, the baron had the idea of building a new town in the desert on land bought cheaply from the Egyptian government in 1905. It was several decades before the project, which was for prestige rather than profit, became viable. Heliopolis is different from other contemporary developments in every aspect: within an area of 6,250 acres, it is a composite urban development based on a garden-city layout with buildings which combined the French architectural tradition (apartment blocks above arcades built flush with the façade) with the neo-Arabic style used by the development company. A hierarchy of districts and types of housing to suit the future population (manual workers, office workers, and the wealthy middle class) was established, and strict building regulations were imposed on potential buyers. Palm groves, advanced infrastructures for the time such as a sewer system which Cairo did not have, sports facilities, schools and hotels helped to make Heliopolis a cohesive urban development which has retained most of its original characteristics.

"EXOTIC" ARCHITECTURE
As well as the villas and arcaded apartment blocks which line the main streets (above), other monumental constructions include the *Heliopolis Palace Hotel* (detail below). With its eight hundred bedrooms, it was once the largest hotel in the Middle East; today, however, it houses the central offices of the Egyptian Presidency and is not open to the public. In the city center the neo-Byzantine basilica containing the tomb of Baron Empain was designed by Marcel (1860–1928), who also designed a series of villas in different architectural styles.

THE "HINDU VILLA"
Baron Empain stayed in this extravagant building, inspired by the temples of India, during his visits to Heliopolis.

1 ASHRAFIYA MEDERSA
2 SHEIKH MUTAHAR MOSQUE
3 GAMAL AD-DIN WAKALA
4 GAWHARA MOSQUE
5 TAGHRI BARDI MOSQUE
6 QALA'UN MOSQUE-MEDERSA
7 AN-NASIR MOHAMMED MOSQUE
8 BARQUQ MEDERSA
9 BAYBARS MEDERSA
10 ISMAÏL PASHA SABIL-KUTTAB
11 KAMILIYA MEDERSA
12 UTHMAN KATKHUDA PALACE
13 BESHTAK PALACE
14 KATKHUDA SABIL-KUTTAB
15 SHEIKH SINAN MAUSOLEUM
16 EL-AQMAR MOSQUE
17 EL-SILAHDAR MOSQUE
18 MITHQAL MOSQUE
19 EL-HIGAZIYA M
20 BAZA
W

One day
◆ I F2-F3-F4

Cover of *El-Suqariya*,
a novel by
Naguib Mahfouz.

EL-HUSSEIN MOSQUE
In principle the
mosque is out-of-
bounds to non-
Muslims. It is the

main focal point for
religious gatherings,
especially Friday
prayer meetings and
the major Islamic
festivals.

EL-HUSSEIN AND KHAN EL-KHALILI

The El-Hussein and Khan el-Khalili districts are as
popular with tourists as they are with the
Egyptians, particularly during Ramadan
and the *muled* ● *126* of El-Hussein
(629–80), the grandson of the
Prophet and holy martyr of the
Shi'ites who was killed by the
Ommiads at the Battle of
Karbala.

**THE EL-HUSSEIN
MOSQUE.** The mosque,
entirely rebuilt under the
khedive Ismaïl, was erected
on the site of the cemetery
of the Fatimid caliphs.
Remains of the cemetery
were discovered during
work carried out on the
mosque's foundations earlier
this century. Inside are forty-
four white marble columns;
the wood ceiling is supported
by arches and pierced by three
lanterns. To one side of the mosque
is the MAUSOLEUM, the oldest part of the
complex (built in 1154 and
modified in 1236), containing the remains
of El-Hussein. It is surmounted by a cupola
whose ceiling is decorated and inlaid with gold.
The complex has two minarets, one to the southwest
dating from the same period as the mosque, and the other
built in a different style which is contemporary with the
mausoleum.

AHMED PASHA "SABIL-KUTTAB". Built in 1864, the *sabil* ● *113*
has a rounded façade surmounted by a wooden canopy.

KHAN EL-KHALILI. The Khan el-Khalili was named after the
great *khan* (caravanserai) ● *118* built in 1380 by the Emir
Djaharks el-Khalili. It can be reached via the Shari' Sikka
el-Badistan opposite the minaret of the El-Hussein Mosque.
A series of early 20th-century housing blocks have replaced

two great *wakala* ● *118,* one of which was
the famous carpet *wakala.* The first
narrow street on the left leads to the
El-Fishawi Café, or *Café of Mirrors,*
which, at the turn of the century, was
the meeting place for Cairene artists,
writers and intellectuals, and is the
favorite haunt of the writer Naguib
Mahfouz (pictured opposite). Half
the café was demolished in 1968 when
the Midan El-Hussein was extended.

SHARI' EL-BADISTAN. The long, narrow Shari' el-Badistan and
the Shari' Khan el-Khalili are the district's two main
thoroughfares. Once two gates controlled access to the
streets, but now only the west gate remains.

EL-GHURI GATE. In 1511 the sultan El-Ghuri replaced the
Khan el-Khalili with a larger *khan* whose gate and wide,

BEIT AS-SUHAYMI
22 SAÏD EL-SAADA MOSQUE
23 EL-USTADAR MOSQUE
24 BAB EL-FUTUH
25 QITASBAY SABIL-KUTTAB
26 ODA BASHI SABIL-KUTTAB
27 QARA SUNOUR MEDERSA
28 SULEYMAN AGA SABIL
29 EL-JASHANKIR MOSQUE
30 EL-HAKIM MOSQUE
31 BAB AN-NASR
32 MUSAFIRKHANA MOSQUE
33 ODA BASHI WAKALA
34 MUHARRAM MOSQUE
35 EL-AHMEDI MOSQUE
36 EL-HUSSEIN MOSQUE
37 AHMED PASHA SABIL
38 BAB EL-BADISTAN
39 EL-SILAHDAR WAKALA
40 AYYUB MEDERSA

"EL-FISHAWI" CAFÉ
Naguib Mahfouz, winner of the Nobel Prize

vaulted entrance can still be seen today.

EL-SILAHDAR "WAKALA". El-Silahdar *wakala* was constructed in 1837 on the site of an older *wakala* and restored in 1985. The second floor of the *wakala* houses numerous workshops reached along an external gallery. Most of the items sold in the streets below are made on the upper floors of the district's *wakala.* The Shari' el-Badistan becomes the SHARI' EL-MUIZZ, which is bordered from end to end by *wakala,* including the former slave market, the EL-GALLABA WAKALA. The Shari' el-Muizz crosses the SHARI' EL-MUSKI, built in 1845 to link El-Ezbekiya ▲ *274* with the El-Hussein district. On the corner of the two streets stands the SHEIKH MUTAHAR MOSQUE, built by Abd el-Rahman Katkhuda in 1744. It still has its original entrance, minaret and *sabil-kuttab*.

for Literature, is one of the "regulars" at the *El-Fishawi Café.*

ASHRAFIYA MEDERSA. The complex was constructed in 1425 by the sultan El-Ashraf Barsbey, and comprises a mosque-medersa, a mausoleum and *sabil-kuttab*. Inside the complex, the *iwan* of the *qibla* has a remarkable marble-covered floor, while the west *iwan* has a wood ceiling inset with ivory and an inlaid *minbar*.

Detail (above) of
the minaret of the
An-Nasir
Mohammed
Medersa.

SHARI' EL-MUIZZ

This three-mile-long street forms the kasbah, the backbone of
the city. During the time of the pharaohs it linked Heliopolis
▲ 285 and Memphis ▲ 332. In the 10th century it was
incorporated into the city founded by the Caliph el-Muizz
(931–75) after whom it was named.

As-Salih Nagm ad-Din Ayyub Medersa. Built between 1242
and 1250 this is one of the first Ayyubid medersat and one of
the few to have survived from this period. All that remains is a
wall surmounted by a minaret. To the north of the medersa is
the nearby KHUSRU PASHA SABIL-KUTTAB (1535).

Shari' Beit el-Qadi. This 19th-century street was built on
the site of the Zahiriya Medersa (1263). On the left as you
leave the Shari' el-Muizz is the QAA MUHIB AD-DIN or
UTHMAN KATKHUDA PALACE ● 116, once a Mameluke
residence (1350). The street leads into
the MIDAN BEIT EL-QADI (the Judge's
House, which stands on the site of the
former courthouse). To the south the so-
called MAMAY MAQAAD is the only
surviving element of a house built in
1496. Today it stands in isolation and
consists of a five-arched colonnade
and a doorway. The great porch on
the eastern side of the square was one
of the entrances to the
house.

THE COMPLEX OF SULTAN QALA'UN. The complex, built along the Shari' el-Muizz in 1284 by Sultan el-Mansur Qala'un comprises a mosque-medersa, a mausoleum and a *mauristan* (hospital), which was replaced by a modern hospital in the 1920's. The main entrance, surrounded by Gothic columns

and surmounted by an inscribed lintel, opens onto a long corridor. To the left the mosque-medersa comprises a rectangular courtyard with four *iwan*. The mausoleum stands opposite the medersa and consists of a partially covered entrance hall and a funeral chamber. The entrance to the *mauristan* was at the end of the corridor.

THE COMPLEX OF SULTAN AN-NASIR MOHAMMED. To the right of the Qala'un minaret are the medersa and tomb of An-Nasir Mohammed, the son of Qala'un, who died in 1340. The Gothic-style entrance came from the 13th-century Christian Church of St John of Acre, destroyed by Sultan El-Ashraf Khalil, brother of An-Nasir. Built in 1295, it was the first cruciform medersa in Cairo.

THE COMPLEX OF SULTAN BARQUQ. Built in 1384 by Sultan Barquq, who ruled from 1382 to 1399, the complex comprises a medersa, a *khanqa* ● 112 and a tomb. The façade has a distinctive stone entrance, a plain cupola and a minaret with three balconies. The bronze-plated entrance door with its polygonal decorations opens onto a square chamber. A corridor links the chamber with an extremely regularly designed courtyard where a central fountain is surrounded by four *iwan* with almost symmetrical façades. A door next to the north *iwan* leads to the tomb of the sultan's daughter. The sultan is buried in the Eastern Cemetery ▲ 327.

KAMILIYA MEDERSA. The medersa of Sultan el-Kamil (1180–1238), built in 1225, is the second largest medersa in the world after that of Zinki in Damascus. During the Mameluke period, it became the prototype for the development of some of the most beautiful examples of Cairene urban architecture. All that remains of the original edifice is the monumental entrance and the west *iwan*, the rest having been replaced by modern buildings.

ABD EL-RAHMAN KATKHUDA "SABIL-KUTTAB". The street forks just beyond this series of monuments. The Shari' an-Nahassin, on the left, leads to the Bab el-Futuh ▲ 291 and the Shari' Tombukshiya to the Bab an-Nasr ▲ 292. In the angle of the fork the Katkhuda *Sabil-kuttab* (1744) can be found, a blend of Mameluke and Ottoman architecture and one of the most spectacular *sabil-kuttab* ● 113 in Cairo. One of the square, faïence plaques decorating the first-floor chamber represents a view of Mecca (right), while the second-floor chamber has a carved wood loggia overlooking the street, whose decorated wood roof is supported by fine wooden pillars.

QALA'UN MAUSOLEUM
The funeral chamber is in the shape of a square enclosing an octagon described by eight monolithic granite pillars and columns (four of each), all richly decorated (left). The mihrab is surrounded by columns and has a revetment of marble and mother-of-pearl mosaic panels (above).

The fountain of the Barquq Medersa is virtually identical to that of the Sultan Hassan Medersa ▲ 309.

▲ Shari' el-Muizz

Bab el-Futuh (right), the Gate of Conquest.

BEIT AS-SUHAYMI
The *qaa* (chambers) of this 17th-century house ● *116* are in two different styles: the more or less enclosed, classic style of the great *mandara*

in the east wing to the right of the entrance, where the lantern is the only source of light, and the more open style of the *salamlik* (reception suite) ● *116* in the west wing, whose wide, turned-wood bays overlook the courtyard. The *tahtabuch* on the first floor and the *maqaad* on the second floor (rooms reserved for the menfolk and their guests) both look onto the courtyard. The *maqaad* faces north to take advantage of the cooler air, while the south-facing *tahtabuch* is ideal for receiving guests or relaxing in winter. Opposite the *maqaad* the harem chamber, with its Turkish faïence, *mashrabiya* and wood paneling, is a true museum piece.

SHARI' DARB EL-QIRMIZ. In 1973 the German Archeological Institute in Cairo undertook the restoration of the Islamic monuments in the Shari' Darb el-Qirmiz. In the space of 165 yards, there are five buildings dating from the 14th and 18th centuries: the Katkhuda *Sabil-kuttab*, the Beshtak Palace, the SHEIKH SINAN MAUSOLEUM (1585–6) and the Sabiqiya Medersa. The restoration of the street won the 1983 Aga Khan Award for Architecture.

BESHTAK PALACE. Built by Emir Beshtak in 1334, the palace has distinctive projecting windows covered with *mashrabiya*. The proportions of the main *qaa* (chamber) on the second floor, its pointed arches, stained-glass windows and gilt and painted wood paneling make it one of the most beautiful chambers of its period. The palace houses a museum which traces the history of the city of Cairo. A small, outer door leads to the 13th-century BESHTAK or EL-FIJL MOSQUE on the first floor of the palace.

SABIQIYA MEDERSA. The Sabiqiya Medersa, otherwise known as the Mithqal Medersa, was built in 1368. A vaulted passage runs beneath the medersa and into a narrow street leading to the Midan Beit el-Qadi.

EL-AQMAR OR GRAY MOSQUE. The mosque, built in 1125 on the site of a Coptic monastery, is one of the few surviving examples of Fatimid architecture. Its design is extremely interesting, with the thickness of the outer wall compensating for the constraints imposed by the direction of *qibla*, the geometry of the layout and the direction of the street. The residual space was occupied by the entrance hall, the staircase to the minaret and two rooms opening onto the courtyard. On the corner of the Shari' el-Muizz and DARB EL-ASFAR is the BEIT MUSTAFA GAAFAR (1713), which today houses the Egyptian Antiquities Organization.

BEIT AS-SUHAYMI. Beit as-Suhaymi, the most impressive of what was once a large group of houses reached via a network of narrow streets and culs-de-sac, was built in 1648. It was bought in 1796 by Sheikh Ahmed as-Suhaymi who extended it by converting several of the adjacent houses. The various parts of the building have separate staircases and in the region of thirty *qaa*.

SULEYMAN AGA EL-SILAHDAR MOSQUE AND "SABIL". The complex (1839), which comprises a *sabil*, medersa and mosque, has a single façade overlooking the street. The distinctive, rounded façade of the *sabil*, which conforms to no particular school, is in inscribed marble. The complex is surmounted by a Turkish-style canopy decorated in relief.

EL-HAKIM MOSQUE. The second largest Fatimid mosque after El-Azhar ▲ 294 was begun in 990 by the Caliph El-Aziz and completed in 1013 by his son El-Hakim (who reigned from 996 to 1021), founder of the Egyptian Druze sect. It was abandoned, converted into a market, then into an Islamic museum and finally restored in 1981 by the Indian Bahai sect, which completed the modification of the small remaining section of the original edifice. An interior staircase leads to the remains of the city's 12th-century ramparts and a well-preserved rampart walk.

BAB EL-FUTUH (GATE OF CONQUEST). In 1087 Badr ad-Din el-Gamali (1010–94), the vizier of El-Mustansir, sent for three Syrian architect-brothers from Edessa to build the three main gates of the city: the Bab el-Futuh, Bab an-Nasr and Bab Zuwaila ▲ 298. The Bab el-Futuh consists of a huge block of stone pierced by a huge vaulted opening and flanked by two rounded towers. The squat proportions of the vault result from the base being about 16 feet below street level.

EL-AQMAR MOSQUE This was the first mosque in Cairo to have a decorated stone façade and a shell-like sculpted pediment.

EL-HAKIM MOSQUE The architectural features of this huge mosque (395 x 370 feet) are similar to those of the Ibn Tulun Mosque ▲ 312: a large courtyard surrounded by porticos in two or three naves and a hypostyle prayer hall. The El-Hakim Mosque in the 19th century (left) and after it was restored in 1981 (above).

Entrance to the
Baybars el-Jashankir
khanqa (above).

QAITBAY "WAKALA"
Each first-floor bay
of the *wakala* is
occupied by a stall
which backs onto a
shop opening onto
the interior. The
windows of the
second and third
floors each represent
separate apartments.

The entrance
(above), in the center
of the façade, has
maintained its
monumental aspect
in spite of the fact
that the ground level
has risen.

SHARI' EL-GAMALIYA

BAB AN-NASR (VICTORY GATE). The two
square towers flanking the gate, built at the
same time as the Bab el-Futuh, have an
upper story with barbicans and
machicolations.

QAITBAY "WAKALA". Built in 1480 by Sultan
Qaitbay, the *wakala* ▲ *118* is one of the most
interesting examples of Circassian civil
architecture. The extremely regular external façade of the
edifice is created by the repetition of the identical, vertical
bays consisting of a first-floor opening, a *mashrabiya* panel
surmounted by a lattice window on the second floor and a
group of three windows on the third floor. Inside the four
main sections of the building surround a fairly large
courtyard. The first floor (whose openings have slightly
pointed arches) is in stone, while the upper floors are brick.

BAYBARS EL-JASHANKIR "KHANQA". Baybars el-Jashankir only
ruled for one year. He was executed by An-Nasir Mohammed,
whose power he had usurped, and his name was removed
from the façade of the *khanqa* (1306–10), one of the oldest in
Cairo. As well as a funeral chamber it also contains a *ribat*
(monastery) designed to house soldiers. The minaret is one
of the few to have a revetment of turquoise faïence. The
QITASBAY SABIL-KUTTAB opposite dates from 1630.

QARA SUNQUR MAUSOLEUM. The mausoleum was part of a
medersa built in 1300. A section of the façade still exists today
and the coat of arms of Emir Qara Sunqur, master of polo to
Sultan Qala'un, can be seen above one of the windows.
Next to the BAB HARA EL-MABAYDA, one of the old
city gates, is the ODA BASHI SABIL-KUTTAB (1673)
whose façade is decorated
with green and blue tiles
and surmounted by a
wood canopy.

ZULFIQAR "WAKALA". The separate accommodation for
traveling merchants above this impressive *wakala* (1673)
is reached through an entrance next to the *sabil-kuttab*.
During the 17th century coffee was sold in the *wakala*.
Today the first floor, which used to be a storage and wholesale
warehouse, contains workshops which make furniture from
recycled wood. The upper floors comprise over sixty
apartments. The windows of the interior and exterior
façades have been modified and the *mashrabiya* work
replaced by simple windows.

THE GAMAL AD-DIN EL-USTADAR MEDERSA. Reached via the
Shari' Wakala el-Tuffah, the medersa was built in 1408 on the
site of one of the gates (Gate of the Wind) of the great
Fatimid Palace. This probably explains its unusual design,
with the dimensions of the *qibla* chamber reduced to a
minimum and the building extended in the opposite direction.
Beyond the medersa is the *mashrabiya* façade of the 17th-
century BAZARAA WAKALA, the sole survivor of the street's
several cloth and tobacco *wakala*, which still existed at the
turn of the century.

TATAR EL-HIGAZIYA MEDERSA. South of the Ustadar Medersa
in Atfa el-Qaffasin, the Tatar el-Higaziya Medersa was built
between 1348 and 1360 by Qunad Tatar el-Higaziya, daughter
of the sultan An-Nasir Mohammed, near the so-called
"Palace of the Emeralds". Its plain façades and interior
design, however, make it look more like a
private residence. On the corner of Atfa
el-Qaffasin and the Shari' el-Gamaliya
the MAHMUD MUHARRAM MOSQUE
(1539) can be found, and on the corner of
the Shari' Darb el-Tabalawi is the
MARZUQ EL-AHMEDI MOSQUE, built in
the 7th century.

MUSAFIRKHANA PALACE. The palace
stands in the Shari' Darb el-Tabalawi and
has a second entrance in the Shari' Darb el-Masmat. Built
between 1779 and 1788, this fine example of an Ottoman
residence was the birthplace of the khedive Ismaïl in 1830.
It was bought by Mohammed Ali at the turn of the century
and used for receiving important guests, hence the name
"Musafirkhana" ("House of Guests"). Today it houses
artists' and sculptors' studios. It has several rooms decorated
with various types of intricately carved *mashrabiya* panels,
while the interiors of the rooms, especially the second-floor
harem chamber, are full of richly decorated and painted
wood paneling.

Bab an-Nasr and, in
the background, the
minaret of the
El-Hakim Mosque.
"In the maze of
narrow, winding
streets, beneath the
endless, overhanging
balconies in finely
carved wood lattice-
work, we are forced
to slow our pace as
we join the tightly
packed throng of
people and animals
. . . An occasional
encounter with the
more delightful face
of the Orient as,
above the tiny
houses decorated
with *mashrabiya* and
arabesques, you
catch a sudden
glimpse of tall
minarets soaring
skyward in the dusk."
Pierre Loti

Two doors of the
Musafirkhana Palace
open onto the
courtyard; the
windows are closed
with wood lattice
(above). The palace
is situated in the
Qasr el-Shawq
district, which existed
before the city was
built.

▲ EL-AZHAR

1 INAL EL-YUSUFI MOSQUE
2 EL-MU'AYYAD MOSQUE
3 RADWAN BEY KASBAH
4 QAITBAY PALACE
5 MAHMUD EL-KURDI MOSQUE
6 FARAG IBN BAROUQ ZAWIA
7 BAB ZUWAILA
8 AS-SALIH TALAI MOSQUE
9 NAFISA EL-BEIDA WAKALA
10 MOHAMMED ALI SABIL
11 EL-FAKAHANI MOSQUE
12 EL-GHURI MEDERSA
13 BEIT SHABSHIRI
14 EL-GHURI MAUSOLEUM

EL-AZHAR

Until the turn of the century El-Azhar, which took its name from the mosque built by General Gawhara in 971, was one of the most famous districts in Cairo. Since then it has undergone many changes, particularly with the construction of the SHARI' EL-AZHAR in the 1920's, which divided the city in two. Almost from the outset the El-Azhar Mosque served a dual purpose as a place of worship and learning. The desire of successive rulers to make their mark has meant that the present building, which is very different from the original porticoed mosque, is a mixture of architectural styles from different periods. The mosque has six entrances and five minarets. The main entrance, the 18th-century BAB EL-MUZAYINI (Barbers' Gate), so called because students used to be shaved beneath its porch, opens onto a tiny courtyard which leads into the AQBUGHAWIYA MEDERSA (built in 1340 and now a library) on the left and into the TAYBARSIYA

⚑ One/two days
◆ I E4-E5-F4-F5

THE UNIVERSITY OF THE ARAB WORLD
The El-Azhar Mosque-University used to house around ten thousand students. Today students are taught in faculties and the mosque is reserved strictly for prayer.

MEDERSA (1310) on the right. The QAITBAY ENTRANCE (1469), surmounted by a minaret, opens onto a vast central courtyard (275 x 112 feet) surrounded by porticos supported by more than three hundred marble columns which have come mainly from ancient monuments. The prayer hall, to the east, is larger than the courtyard (262 x 164 feet) and consists of several rows of columns whose arrangement conceals the various alterations. Although the mihrab has been modified several times, the Kufic inscription decorating the interior is original. The section of the hall behind the mihrab was added by Abd el-Rahman Katkhuda in 1753. At the northern end is the tomb-medersa of Gawhara Qunqubay (1440).

ABU EL-DAHAB MOSQUE. The mosque (1774), built in typical Ottoman style with a central cupola ● *108*, consisted of a mausoleum and a *takiya*. Today it provides living accommodation for the students of the El-Azhar University.

QAITBAY "WAKALA" AND "SABIL-KUTTAB". Built in 1447, four years before the identical *wakala* built by the same sultan near the Bab an-Nasr ▲ *291*, the Qaitbay *wakala* and *sabil-kuttab* is in a sorry state today. Only the wing overlooking the street and *sabil-kuttab* are used. The ABLUTIONS FOUNTAIN on the corner is part of the complex. The BEIT ZEINAB KHATUN ● *116* at the far end of the Shari' Atfa el-Azhari, which runs along the side of the El-Azhar Mosque, was built in 1468 and refurbished in 1713. The characteristics of the two periods are illustrated by the difference in style between the first-floor rooms, which reflect the severity of Mameluke architecture, and the more extravagant style of the Ottoman period in the second-floor rooms. Opposite the Beit Zeinab Khatun and beyond the El-Ayni Mosque, two old houses stand at the far end of the Shari' Atfa el-Ayni: the BEIT SITT WASSILA, probably built before 1637 and now in ruins, and the BEIT EL-HIRAWI (1731), which was recently restored by the French mission set up in 1983 to help preserve Islamic Cairo.

The five minarets of the El-Azhar Mosque (left and above).

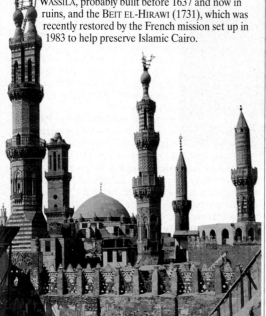

"[Their minarets] have small balconies and columns which are so intricately carved that you can see through them; some are a long way off and some quite close pointing skyward above your head."

Pierre Loti

295

EL-GHURI COMPLEX

The complex, built by the sultan El-Ghuri (1501–16), the last great Mameluke sultan, comprises five buildings: a medersa and mausoleum, which stand opposite each other in the Shari' el-Muizz, a *sabil-kuttab* ● *113*, a *maqaad 116* and a *wakala* ● *118*.

EL-GHURI "WAKALA". Built in 1504–5, this is the most complete and best-preserved *wakala* in Cairo. The regularity of the external façade and the uniformity of the windows of this stone edifice are extremely impressive. The first floor has a few small, high, square windows, while the upper stories have three rows of different types of windows, arranged in groups of three. This last row is closed by *mashrabiya* panels, each the width of three windows. The great door with its trilobate arch leads into a central courtyard where the surrounding sections of the building echo its external regularity, with the exception of the first floor, which consists of wide arcades intersected by a gallery. Today the *wakala* houses a craft center.

The central courtyard of the El-Ghuri *wakala*, the interior of the mosque and the entrance (below).

EL-GHURI MAUSOLEUM. The mausoleum (1503–4), distinguishable from the mosque by its unfinished cupola and a *sabil-kuttab*, includes a funeral chamber to the right and, to the left, a prayer hall with three *iwan* ● *116* evenly distributed around the central, raised and covered part of a lantern, which was once part of a *khanqa* ● *112*. The SABIL-KUTTAB forms the front section of the mausoleum and is a particularly fine example of Mameluke architecture. It has three latticed bays framed by moldings and surmounted by stone panels, while the interior is richly decorated with marble floors and walls and a ceiling with rounded, painted and gilt beams. The entrance to the MAQAAD can be found in the Shari' el-Azhar. The richly decorated walls and ceiling of this large, rectangular room provide a striking contrast with the simplicity of the limestone floor.

EL-GHURI MOSQUE. Built in 1504, the mosque has four *iwan* and a central, sunken courtyard open to the sky. The two large *iwans* are pierced by large Moorish arches; the lateral *iwans*, which are smaller, have raised arches. The base of the bicolored stone façade is occupied by cloth merchants' shops. The formerly covered street between the mosque and the mausoleum used to be the home of the famous silk market. An enormous entrance with a trilobate arch decorated with stalactites opens onto a corridor lit by a central well. The interior decoration has distinctive polychrome marble dados (whose rectangular design is reproduced to infinity), flagging laid in geometric patterns and gilt and painted wood paneling. The southern section of the Shari' el-Muizz is the extension of the main thoroughfare that crossed the city to Old Cairo ▲ *320* and which is now intersected by the Shari' el-Azhar.

> **"Streets of private houses are like tunnels from meeting overhead of projecting windows . . . Sometimes high blank walls – mysterious passages – dim peeps at courts and wells in shadow."**
>
> Herman Melville

BEIT GAMAL AD-DIN EL-DAHABI. The only surviving house in this once extensive residential district, no. 6 Hara Hoch Qadam was built in 1637. The rectangular, interior courtyard is surrounded by four architecturally distinct façades. The second-floor harem chamber is remarkable for its balanced proportions and the almost perfect symmetry of its spatial organization. The *mashrabiya* walls of the north *iwan* adjoin the loggias at mezzanine level. This allowed the womenfolk to be present and yet remain unseen when (male) guests were received. On the corner of the Shari' el-Muizz and the Shari' Hara Hoch Qadam, the EL-FAKAHANI MOSQUE, constructed in 1145 and rebuilt during the 17th century, still has its original carved wood doors.

HARA EL-RUM. To the east of the Shari' el-Muizz, the Hara el-Rum or "Christian Quarter" was originally located outside the city walls. It became part of the city when the walls were moved during the 11th century and, until the 19th century, was the seat of the Coptic patriarchate and housed several churches and monasteries. Today all that remains are the Church and relatively recent MONASTERY OF ST TADROS, and the 6th-century El-Adra (CHURCH OF THE VIRGIN), which was entirely rebuilt after the district was ravaged by fire during the 11th and 14th centuries. At the end of Atfa el-Tateri the 17th-century BEIT SHABSHIRI can be recognized by the projecting *mashrabiya* work on its façade. Although small, the house includes all the elements of a grand aristocratic residence: *tahtabuch*, *maqaad*, various *qaa* (six on three floors) and several staircases which give separate access to each part of the house.

BEIT GAMAL AD-DIN
A typical 17th-century residence of a Cairene notable. The house was saved from demolition by the Cairo Conservation Committee, which classified it as an historic monument in 1899. The external façade has two projecting *mashrabiya* panels overlooking the street. The entrance is through a curved arch set deep in the ground (detail below).

BEIT SHABSHIRI
The small, interior courtyard of the house (above) is overlooked by four richly decorated façades with projecting *mashrabiya* panels, lattice windows and galleries. The harem chamber occupies the entire east wing of the house. It is well lit by large, lateral bays covered with *mashrabiya*, which overlook both street and courtyard.

EL-MU'AYYAD MOSQUE

The prayer hall of the mosque looks directly onto a courtyard which has been converted into a shady garden (right and below). The arcades incorporated into the walls of the garden are surmounted by blind niches in the form of Persian-style arches reminiscent of the El-Azhar Mosque ▲ 294.

The El-Mu'ayyad Mosque was built by Sultan el-Mu'ayyad on the site of a prison in which he had endured such suffering that he vowed, if he ever regained his freedom, to replace it with a mosque. The fulfillment of this promise gave rise to one of the most beautiful mosques in Cairo. Although the prison was demolished, the site was still used for executions and the heads displayed in accordance with tradition. It was here that the sultan Selim had his enemy Tomanbay, the last of the Mameluke sultans, hanged in the 16th century. Exterior of the mosque (right), the sanctuary (center right) and the prayer hall with the mihrab and minbar (far right).

TUSSUN PASHA "SABIL". The *sabil* ● 113 was built in 1820 by Mohammed Ali in memory of his son, Ahmed Tussun, who died at the age of twenty. Its marble-clad, rounded façade surmounted by a wooden canopy observes the criteria of contemporary Turkish architecture. The rooms of the *kuttab* are scattered throughout the building.

NAFISA EL-BEIDA "WAKALA". This 18th-century *wakala* ● 118 specialized in the manufacture and sale of sweetmeats. Today various structures have encroached upon the large, rectangular courtyard. The *rabaa* section is still inhabited and has around fifty apartments accessible via an interior passageway. The southern section of the building is occupied by a *sabil-kuttab* ● 113 with an overornate façade.

EL-MU'AYYAD OR RED MOSQUE. The mosque was built (1415–20) by Sultan El-Mu'ayyad against the south wall of the city. The bronze-plated entrance door, which bears the titles and name of Sultan Hassan, is from his medersa ▲ 309. An entrance hall leads into the mausoleum containing the tombs of the sultan and his sons. Its walls are completely covered with a polychrome marble revetment forming several geometric patterns. The prayer hall looks directly onto the courtyard, which has been converted into a garden. The columns of the hall are surmounted by two rows of superposed arches which are reminiscent of the great Ommiad mosque in Damascus, where El-Mu'ayyad was governor. The mihrab has a remarkably fine central, marble-covered decoration and festooned archstones, while the minbar is decorated with polygonal panels inlaid with mother-of-pearl and ivory. The two minarets, which stand on the two salient angles of the BAB ZUWAILA (1092), offer a panoramic view of Cairo. To the east is the outline of the city wall and its towers buried beneath the rubble.

AS-SALIH TALAI MOSQUE ★. The mosque, which stands to the south of the Bab Zuwaila, was founded in 1160 by the emir As-Salih Talai, vizier to the last of the Fatimid caliphs. Around the interior courtyard the columns supporting the arches of the porticos are surmounted by ancient capitals from Christian churches. A subtle combination of stained glass and stuccowork decorates the windows in the upper part of the wall of the *qibla*. The wooden minbar (1300) is engraved with star motifs repeated to infinity. Opposite the mosque, all that remains of the FARAG IBN BARQUQ ZAWIA, which was built in 1408, are two reception rooms, one of which is used as a mausoleum.

RADWAN BEY KASBAH. Opposite the Bab Zuwaila is Cairo's only surviving example of a covered market. It was built during the 17th century by the emir Radwan Bey who dominated Egypt's political life for a quarter of a century and renovated the district, building *rabaa* (apartment blocks), a *wakala*, two *zawia*, a *sabil* and a palace. The market is a covered street whose wooden roof is pierced by lanterns which let in a soft, filtered light. Today it is occupied by manufacturers of tent fabric who have given the market its name (Khayamiya, which means "tentmakers' bazaar"). The living accommodation above the first-floor shops and stalls is virtually abandoned. On the left, beyond the Radwan Bey Kasbah, is the MAHMUD EL-KURDI MOSQUE, built in 1395, which comprises a mosque-medersa and a mausoleum. About 20 yards to the south, the INAL EL-YUSUFI ATABAKI MOSQUE also includes a mausoleum and a *sabil-kuttab*. Built in 1392–3 it is in the same style as the Mahmud el-Kurdi Mosque-Medersa with two *iwan* and a covered courtyard. The difference lies in the shape of the minaret and the minor decorative details. The interior of the second of the two mosques is better preserved with painted ceilings and marble-clad walls.

All that remains of the palace (above) built by Radwan Bey in 1650 is the triple-arched *maqaad* ● *116*. The *wakala*, to the north, is now occupied by a sawmill and the courtyard is used as a wood depot.

AS-SALIH TALAI MOSQUE
The five Persian arches of the freestone façade of the mosque (above) are closed to the street by *mashrabiya* panels which were added in 1303. When the mosque was built in 1160 the shops, which are today below the building, were at street level.

299

EL-MIHMANDAR MOSQUE
The mosque is reached through a gateway with a lobed arch decorated with stalactites (above).

UMM EL-SULTAN SHA'BAN MEDERSA
The medersa contains the mausoleums of the sultan and his mother. Each tomb has a door with sculpted wood panels (above) leading into the prayer hall.

DARB EL-AHMAR

The districts surrounding the Shari' Suq el-Silah and Shari' Darb el-Ahmar were established in the 12th century. They reached the peak of their urban development under the Mamelukes when they were centered around particular activities and markets such as the Suq el-Silah (Weapons Market).

EL-ISHAQI MOSQUE ★. This cruciform mosque ▲ *108* was built in 1480–1 by the Emir Qijmas el-Ishaqi, head of the Sultan Qaitbay's stables. It stands above street level and the lower level is occupied by shops. The complex includes an ablutions room and a drinking fountain in a building across the street, linked to the mosque by a covered gallery surmounted by *mashrabiya* work. The entrance is decorated with marble and Koranic inscriptions and leads into a square entrance hall with a painted wood ceiling surrounded by an epigraphic frieze. A lattice window looks onto the mausoleum. The wall of the *qibla* is decorated with red and white marble and the beautifully carved minbar is inlaid with ivory.

EL-MIHMANDAR MOSQUE ★. Built in 1324–5, the mosque comprises a central courtyard and four *iwan*. The west *iwan* has a mezzanine loggia with a turned wood balustrade and stained-glass windows. The wood ceilings have decorated beams. The mausoleum, in the northeast corner, has a fluted-stone exterior.

EL-MARIDANI MOSQUE ★. The mosque was founded in
1339–40 by Prince Altanbugha el-Maridani. The work was
carried out under the supervision of Ibn el-Suyufi, chief
architect to Sultan an-Nasir Mohammed. The central
courtyard, surrounded by porticos, is separated from the
prayer hall by an attractive wood lattice. Inside, four rows of
raised arches are supported by ancient columns. The mihrab,
inlaid with geometrically arranged green, red and yellow
marble, is one of the most beautiful in Cairo, while the carved
minbar is a work of art in its own right. The wall of the *qibla*
has a marble revetment and a series of stained-glass, gemel
windows with rounded arches. The arch of the main entrance
in the Shari' el-Tabbana is decorated with stalactites.

QAITBAY PALACE. All that remains of this luxurious palace,
built in 1485, is the *maqaad*, which consists of three Gothic
arches resting on two ancient columns.

BEIT ER-RAZZAZ. This grand, 15th-century palace with two
courtyards was built by Sultan Qaitbay and converted by
Ahmed Katkhuda er-Razzaz in 1778. The present entrance is
near the ablutions fountain, which stands between the PALACE
and the SULTAN SHA'BAN MEDERSA built in 1369. A passageway leads into an irregularly shaped courtyard surrounded by
buildings. On the right the QAITBAY ENTRANCE leads to the
upper floors, which consist of several *qaa*, including a beautiful
harem chamber. Its originality lies in the carved openwork of
the huge vertical wood bays which reach from floor to ceiling.
The part of the building overlooking the second courtyard has
a first-floor reception room and second-floor *maqaad*.

**EL-MARIDANI
MOSQUE**
Unusually, the wall of
the *qibla* is separated
from the rest of the
mosque by a turned
and carved wood
screen (above). It is
one of the earliest
examples of
mashrabiya work in
Cairo.

The Beit er-Razzaz
has two entrances.
Today one of them is
actually inside the
shops on the Shari'
el-Tabbana.

301

AQSUNQUR OR BLUE MOSQUE. The mosque was founded in 1346 by the Emir Shams ad-Din Aqsunqur, a member of Sultan an-Nasir Mohammed's entourage, and was restored and slightly modified in 1652 by Ibrahim Aga el-Mustahfizan who had the interior walls covered with blue tiles, thereby giving the mosque its alternative name. The arches of this porticoed mosque are supported by square and octagonal pillars rather than columns, which lends it a very distinctive appearance. The porticos were originally covered by groined vaults instead of the usual wood ceiling, but some of these have been replaced. The first of the mosque's three mausoleums, at the northwest corner, is dedicated to the son of Sultan an-Nasir Mohammed. The second, between the minaret and the south entrance, has the same tiled decoration and is dedicated to Ibrahim Aga, while the third is of more recent construction and contains the tomb of Aqsunqur.

THE BLUE MOSQUE
The Iznik tiles used to cover the interior of the mosque were imported from Istanbul and Damascus. The mihrab is in polychrome marble, while the minbar, the oldest marble minbar in Cairo, is inlaid with precious stones. The minaret offers a panoramic view of the city.

THE WAQF. The Waqf is a religious foundation which converts or acquires property in perpetuity for religious or charitable purposes. The income from a Waqf building is used to ensure the continuation of the foundation. During the Mameluke period the Waqf became widespread and resulted in the creation of a private version of the foundation. The ingenious exploitation of the system has enabled major construction companies to participate effectively in the urban development of the city.

THE OMAR AGA WAQF. The complex (1621) occupies the west façade of the street and comprises, from north to south, a *sabil-kuttab*, a mausoleum, an ablutions fountain and a *rabaa*.

KHAYRBAY MOSQUE. Khayrbay, governor of Aleppo during the reign of El-Ghuri, was made commander-in-chief of the army during the conquest of Syria by Sultan Selim I into whose hands he delivered the country. His complex comprises a mausoleum, built in 1502, a mosque and a *sabil-kuttab* added in 1520. The mosque is built according to the irregular layout of a medersa with *iwan*, with the prayer hall occupying a central position flanked by two *iwan*, although the direction of Mecca is not strictly observed. The funeral chamber, surmounted by a cupola, is surprisingly high.

ALIN AQ PALACE. Built in 1293, the palace is also known as the Palace of Khayrbay (Khayrbay lived there after being appointed Pasha of Cairo under the Ottomans). All that remains of this once luxurious palace are the freestone walls of the four façades pierced by arched windows. The main entrance in the Shari' Bab el-Wazir is a wide, rectangular opening decorated with stalactites and flanked by two stone benches.

TARABAY AS-SHARIFI MAUSOLEUM AND GATE. About one hundred yards further on in the Shari' Bab el-Tureb is the Tarabay as-Sharifi Mausoleum and Gate built in 1503 on the site of the Bab el-Wazir (Cemetery Gate). The *sabil-kuttab* to the right of the gate used to lead to a medersa (which no longer exists), while the façade of the beautifully constructed mausoleum is composed of vertical panels crowned with stalactites.

AYTMISHI MOSQUE. Built in 1383 by Seif ad-Din Aytmish el-Baghasi, a member of Sultan Barquq's entourage, the structure comprises a *sabil-kuttab* on the corner where only the first floor remains, a mosque and a mausoleum. The mosque consists of a single *iwan* leading off a central area with a wood ceiling pierced by a lantern. The mausoleum is surmounted by a small dome of a type virtually exclusive to Cairo. It is decorated with raised ribs which are vertical at the base and become suddenly helicoidal.

EL-MU'AYYAD "MAURISTAN". The impressive ruins of the El-Mu'ayyad *mauristan* (1418) are reached by following the Shari' el-Tabbana southward into the Shari' el-Mahgar and turning right into the Shari' Sikka el-Kumi. The *mauristan* replaced the 14th-century Ashrafiya Medersa founded by Sultan Sha'ban and was once a huge building which covered a vast area. Today much of this area is occupied by apartment blocks. It was Cairo's second largest hospital after the one founded by Sultan Qala'un ▲ *289*. Inside the ruins huge arcades, whose façades are pierced by arched windows surmounted by oculi, can still be seen around a courtyard.

An arch in one of the walls surrounding the courtyard of the ruined El-Mu'ayyad *mauristan*.

⚔ **Half a day**
◆ I F1-F2

The Lions' Tower (below), today transformed into the Military Museum.

THE CITADEL

The site, formed by the foothills of Jebel Moqattam, was first occupied in 810 when the governor Hatim Ibn Hartama built the so-called "Dome of the Wind" pavilion. Since then the Citadel has continually attracted the attention of the governors of Egypt. In 1176 Salah ad-Din ▲ *270* enclosed it with fortifications to protect it against attack by the Crusaders. The Mameluke sultans made it their headquarters and built a number of structures, including the vast QASR EL-ABLAQ PALACE and an 11,000-foot aqueduct with four pumping stations. During the Ottoman period, the Citadel became a real city with two residential districts occupied by Janissaries and *azab* (celibates). It became the main residence and seat of government of Mohammed Ali, who modified the walls and constructed civil and military buildings as well as the mosque named after him. The Citadel has three distinct sections, each surrounded by walls punctuated with towers and gates: the Lower Enclosure (El-Azab), the Northern

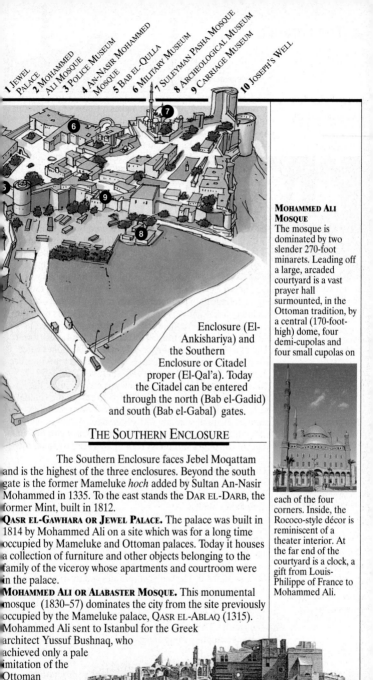

1 JEWEL PALACE 2 MOHAMMED ALI MOSQUE 3 POLICE MUSEUM 4 AN-NASIR MOHAMMED MOSQUE 5 BAB EL-QULLA 6 MILITARY MUSEUM 7 SULEYMAN PASHA MOSQUE 8 ARCHEOLOGICAL MUSEUM 9 CARRIAGE MUSEUM 10 JOSEPH'S WELL

MOHAMMED ALI MOSQUE
The mosque is dominated by two slender 270-foot minarets. Leading off a large, arcaded courtyard is a vast prayer hall surmounted, in the Ottoman tradition, by a central (170-foot-high) dome, four demi-cupolas and four small cupolas on each of the four corners. Inside, the Rococo-style décor is reminiscent of a theater interior. At the far end of the courtyard is a clock, a gift from Louis-Philippe of France to Mohammed Ali.

Enclosure (El-Ankishariya) and the Southern Enclosure or Citadel proper (El-Qal'a). Today the Citadel can be entered through the north (Bab el-Gadid) and south (Bab el-Gabal) gates.

THE SOUTHERN ENCLOSURE

The Southern Enclosure faces Jebel Moqattam and is the highest of the three enclosures. Beyond the south gate is the former Mameluke *hoch* added by Sultan An-Nasir Mohammed in 1335. To the east stands the DAR EL-DARB, the former Mint, built in 1812.

QASR EL-GAWHARA OR JEWEL PALACE. The palace was built in 1814 by Mohammed Ali on a site which was for a long time occupied by Mameluke and Ottoman palaces. Today it houses a collection of furniture and other objects belonging to the family of the viceroy whose apartments and courtroom were in the palace.

MOHAMMED ALI OR ALABASTER MOSQUE. This monumental mosque (1830–57) dominates the city from the site previously occupied by the Mameluke palace, QASR EL-ABLAQ (1315). Mohammed Ali sent to Istanbul for the Greek architect Yussuf Bushnaq, who achieved only a pale imitation of the Ottoman

An-Nasir Mohammed
Mosque

The great interior courtyard of the An-Nasir Mohammed Mosque

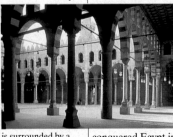

is surrounded by a double row of stone arcades in alternate red and black bricks, supported by ancient Pharaonic, Byzantine and Coptic columns.

BAB EL-AZAB
The Bab el-Azab (below), which opens onto the Midan Salah ad-Din, was built by Abd el-Rahman Katkhuda in 1754. Today it is surrounded by 19th-century walls. It was on a road somewhere between the Bab el-Azab and the upper part of the Citadel that Mohammed Ali ordered the massacre of five hundred Mameluke chieftains on March 1, 1811.

mosques. However its position makes it Cairo's most famous and most frequented mosque.

AN-NASIR MOHAMMED MOSQUE ★. Built by Sultan an-Nasir Mohammed in 1335, it is the only well-preserved Mameluke building in the Citadel. The mosque has two minarets and two entrances. The first entrance, inscribed in an arch decorated with stalactites, was reserved for the sultan, while the second, in the form of a trilobate arch, was situated opposite the Bab el-Qulla and used by the soldiers stationed in the Citadel. The marble panels covering the interior of the mosque were removed and sent to Istanbul by Sultan Selim I when he conquered Egypt in 1517. Their absence accentuates the characteristically sober interior decoration of Mameluke architecture. A gateway opposite the mosque leads onto the esplanade of the POLICE MUSEUM, which occupies the old Artillery School built in 1830 on the site of the Lions' Tower. The museum traces the history of the Egyptian police force from Pharaonic to modern times. On the left is the MILITARY PRISON, built by the British in 1880 and used until 1983.

JOSEPH'S WELL. The 270-foot well was carved out of the rocky hillside by Salah ad-Din in 1183 to ensure the Citadel's water supply. The water was brought up by two pumping stations. A spiral staircase with observation windows winds around the outside of the well. The additional width (about 6 feet) of the upper section is taken up by an access ramp for the first pumping station.

THE INNER WALL. The wall separating the Northern and Southern Enclosures was built by the Mameluke sultan Baybars el-Bunduqari (1223–77) to isolate his palace from the rest of the Citadel.

NORTHERN ENCLOSURE

The Northern Enclosure is surrounded, for the most part, by the fortifications erected by Salah ad-Din and rebuilt by Mohammed Ali. The wall incorporates twenty or so towers and two gates: the Bab el-Gadid (1826) and the Bab el-Qulla, the central gate built in the 16th century and modified by Mohammed Ali, who added the upper sections reserved for the guards. This part of the Citadel has for a long time been used as a military camp and garrison. Behind the Bab el-Qulla, in the open space in front of the Harem Palace, stands a statue of Ibrahim Pasha (one of Mohammed Ali's sons) which is a copy of the one in the Midan el-Opera ▲ 274. To the left of the gate is the DIWAN, which is the equivalent of a ministry of education, built during the reign of Mohammed Ali.

THE HAREM PALACE. The palace (1827) consists of three wings whose interior decoration and painting reflect the Levantine style adopted by Mohammed Ali. It was the residence of the royal family until 1874 when the khedive Ismaïl transferred the seat of government to the Abdin Palace ▲ 281. It was used as a military hospital during the British occupation and, in 1946, was converted into a museum which traces the military history of Egypt. In the central wing visitors can see the former alabaster-covered *hammam*, while the exit in the left wing leads into a courtyard where the statue of Colonel de Sèves (previously in the Midan Suleyman Pasha ▲ 275) now stands. On the right, halfway between the palace and the Suleyman Pasha Mosque, stands the 16th-century tomb of Sheikh Mohammed el-Kahaki and, on the left, part of the wall built by Salah ad-Din and circumscribed by the later, 19th-century wall.

SULEYMAN PASHA MOSQUE ★. Built in 1528 by an Ottoman governor, Suleyman Pasha (who had no connection with Colonel de Sèves), the Suleyman Pasha Mosque is not only Egypt's first cupolated Ottoman mosque, but also its most beautiful. It stands in a small garden, which is enclosed by an outer wall, and can be reached by way of a courtyard whose arcades are surmounted by small cupolas. The prayer hall has a large central cupola and three demi-cupolas, all richly decorated with floral and geometric motifs. The extremely fine, marble-covered mihrab illustrates the influence of Mameluke art. The mosque is also known as the Sariya el-Gabal Mosque after the Fatimid saint, Sayyid Sariya, whose tomb stands at the eastern end of the surrounding wall. Several of its rooms are surmounted by cupolas and decorated with 19th-century naive designs.

CARRIAGE MUSEUM. Housed in the building used as the British Officers' Mess during the colonial period, the museum has a collection of eight carriages, the majority of which date from the reign of the khedive Ismaïl; indeed, the collection includes the carriage he used for the opening of the Suez Canal ▲ 232 in 1869. To the south of the museum, the BURG EL-TURFA (1207) is one of the few towers in Cairo which is open to the public. Columns from the Ottoman period and the remains of a 15th-century minaret can be seen in the open-air archeological museum.

The dome of the Suleyman Pasha Mosque, decorated with Koranic verses.

The French officer Colonel de Sèves (1788–1860) (left) was employed by Mohammed Ali to reorganize the Egyptian army. He was promoted to general and converted to Islam, taking the name Suleyman Pasha.

Interior of the Suleyman Pasha Mosque (below).

"... the immense city of Cairo, with its citadels and towers, and walls, and minarets stretching away for miles, the splendid ancient city, and beyond it, modern Cairo, with its turmoil of tramways, railroads, and other modernities."
Wilfred Scawen Blunt

307

MIDAN SALAH AD-DIN

The Midan Salah ad-Din, built in the 12th century at the same time as the Citadel, became a parade ground around which a number of great monuments were constructed.

⚑ One day
◆ J D1-D2-E1-E2-F1-F2

The wooden minbar inlaid with mother-of-pearl, and detail of the interior decoration (above) of the Qanibey Emir Akhur Medersa.

One of the streets leading off the Midan Salah ad-Din (right). In the distance is the Mahmudiya Mosque.

MAHMUDIYA MEDERSA. Founded in 1567–8 by the governor Mahmud Pasha, this medersa has four different façades. The interior is about 65 feet square and consists of two *iwan* and a long, narrow courtyard.
QANIBEY EMIR AKHUR MEDERSA ★. The medersa (1503), whose façade overlooks the square, comprises a *sabil-kuttab*, an entrance at the top of a flight of steps and a mausoleum with a high-pitched cupola decorated with geometric and floral motifs. The building is entirely of stone and consists of a central courtyard open to the sky and four *iwan*. Near the Citadel, the HARA DARB EL-LABBANI was bordered on either side by houses whose upper stories overhung the street. Today only one of these remains, the (probably) pre-18th-century BEIT ALI EFENDI LABIB, situated at no. 4, on the right. This former residence of Hassan Fathi ▲ *442* is now owned by the Aga Khan Foundation.
EL-GAWHARA EL-LALA MOSQUE ★. Although small (about 2,000 square feet), the mosque (1430) comprises an ingeniously designed medersa, *sabil-kuttab* and mausoleum where every inch of space has been used to advantage.
AR-RIFA'I MOSQUE. The mosque was founded in 1869 on the site of the Sheikh ar-Rifa'i *zawia* (1122). Designed by the architect Mustapha Fahmi ▲ *281* and completed in

13 DERVISH THEATER
14 AR-RIFA'I MOSQUE
15 EL-GAWHARA EL-LALA MOSQUE
16 QANIBEY MEDERSA
17 MAHMUDIYA MEDERSA
18 SULTAN HASSAN MEDERSA
19 QAITBAY SABIL-KUTTAB
20 QANIBEY EL-MOHAMMEDI MOSQUE

MIDAN ▲
SALAH AD-DIN

rectangular area of about 75,350 square feet and has four monumental façades. As well as the tomb of Sheikh ar-Rifa'i the mosque also contains those of King Fuad (1868–1936), his mother, and Mohammed Reza Pahlavi (1919–80), the last Shah of Iran.

SULTAN HASSAN MEDERSA. Founded by Sultan Hassan, son of An-Nasir Mohammed, the medersa (1356–63) is one of the finest examples of Mameluke architecture. A corridor leads from the entrance hall into an almost square courtyard surrounded by four *iwan*, in the center of which is an ablutions fountain. The four doors leading to the medersa correspond to the four Muslim orthodox schools. The *iwan* of the *qibla* is decorated with stuccowork friezes inscribed with Kufic script and has a mihrab, flanked by eight marble columns and preceded by a marble *dikka* (platform), and a minbar. Behind the minbar the mausoleum, surmounted by a once gold and silver-plated cupola, houses the tombs of Sultan Hassan's two sons (the assassinated sultan's body was never recovered); there is also an ancient wooden Koran case inlaid with ivory.

SHARI' SUYUFIA. Part of the ancient thoroughfare which

Everything about the Sultan Hassan Medersa is impressive: its area (about 850, 350 square feet), its façade surmounted by a projecting cornice, its monumental entrance (39 x 125 feet) and its sober interior where every corner is perfect.

Remains of the Emir Qusun Palace, which still has a vaulted entrance decorated with stalactites.

"MAQAAD" OF THE EMIR TAZ PALACE
The *maqaad* appears to have been added by Ali Aga Dar el-Saada who built the *sabil-kuttab* (1677) at the southern end.

The cupola of the Hassan Sadaqa Mausoleum is covered with plaster decorations.

used to cross the city to Old Cairo, it extends beyond the Ibn Tulun district in the direction of the Imam as-Shafi'i cemetery.

EMIR QUSUN PALACE. The palace, which stands to the west of the Sultan Hassan Medersa, was built between 1330 and 1337 by Emir Qusun and has been renovated several times, in particular by Yashbak Min Mahdi. The existing ruins cannot be visited because they are in a bad state of disrepair.

EMIR TAZ PALACE. The palace, built in 1352 by Emir Taz on his marriage to the daughter of Sultan An-Nasir Mohammed, was significantly modified at the end of the 19th century when it became the first Egyptian girls' school. Today it is used as an educational supplies depot and the interior has been badly damaged. The *qaa* overlooking the west entrance and the entrance itself have collapsed, while the courtyard was divided in two by a wall built in the 19th century at the same time as most of the buildings surrounding the northern section.

EL-ABAR "ZAWIA". The *zawia* (1248) stands on the corner of the Shari' Suyufia and the Shari' Qaraqol el-Manshiya. It was originally part of a complex consisting of a *khanqa* and a medersa, of which only the mausoleum remains. This now forms part of the façade of the Emir Taz Palace and houses the tombs of Sheikh Ala ad-Din el-Abar and his wife.

QIZLAR "SABIL-KUTTAB" AND "RABAA". The façade of this complex, founded in 1618 by Ali Aga Dar el-Saada, consists of a *sabil-kuttab* entirely surrounded by identical bays (each corresponding to a *rabaa*) pierced at first-floor level by wide openings and, on the upper floor, by pairs of superposed, oriel windows.

HASSAN SADAQA MAUSOLEUM. The mausoleum houses the tombs of its founder, Sunqur Saadi, and Hassan Sadaqa. It was part of a complex (1315) consisting of a medersa which no longer exists, a *takiya* ● *112* and a *ribat* (monastery) which was replaced during the 19th century by a Dervish theater.

DERVISH THEATER. The theater, also known as Sama Khana, is dedicated to the dancing dervishes of the Mawlawiya sect. It was restored between 1979 and 1989 by the Italian Cultural Center and houses an Italian-Egyptian restoration training center and an exhibition hall. The 19th-century building includes some older sections. Excavations have revealed the remains of the Sunqur Saadi Medersa, which were used as foundations. The interior includes a monastery complex and a huge circular chamber with a special women's gallery, whose walls and dome are decorated with flowers and landscapes. The first floor is all that remains of the YUSSUF BEY SABIL-KUTTAB (1772) on the opposite side of the Shari' el-Muzafar, while on the corner of the Shari' el-Helmiya the El-Muzafar Mausoleum (1322) forms part of the adjacent building.

DERVISH THEATER
The monastery cells of the Sufis occupied a vast complex built around gardens.

SHARI' SALIBA

In the Shari' Sheikhu, to the west of the Midan Salah ad-Din, the QAITBAY SABIL-KUTTAB (1479) is, unlike its contemporaries, completely autonomous: an innovation which became popular during the Ottoman period. On the corner of Shari' Sheikhu and Shari' Darb el-Samak stands the QANIBEY EL-MOHAMMEDI MOSQUE (1413). The interior consists of a single *iwan* whose wide arch opens onto a covered courtyard with a wood ceiling.

SHEIKHU MOSQUE AND "KHANQA" ★. The mosque and *khanqa* were built (1349–55) opposite each other by Emir Sheikhu. The absence of any decoration accentuates the strength of the architectural form. The design of the mosque combines the characteristics of mosques with *iwan* and porticoed mosques ● 108 as it consists of two porticoed *iwan* and a central courtyard open to the sky. At the northeast corner of the *khanqa* stands the EMIR ABDALLAH SABIL-KUTTAB (1719). The 19th-century UMM ABBAS SABIL-KUTTAB, built by the mother of the khedive Abbas, has replaced the Sheikhu *sabil*.

TAGHRI BARDI MEDERSA. The complex, founded in 1440 by Emir Taghri Bardi el-Rumi, comprises a medersa, a *sabil-kuttab* and a mausoleum surmounted by an impressive stone cupola decorated with interwoven fluting.

SHEIKHU "KHANQA"
The *khanqa* was designed to house needy pilgrims. The courtyard (left) is surrounded at second-floor level by wooden galleries leading to the study cells on the west and south sides. The other two sides consist of two *iwan*, one of which is reserved for prayer.

▲ IBN TULUN MOSQUE

IBN TULUN MOSQUE
The mosque's main mihrab consists of a stone niche surrounded by a simple frame. Others were added

subsequently in the prayer hall, including a marble mihrab with a wooden arch, flanked by four columns.

The Ibn Tulun Mosque before it was restored in 1918.

EL-QATAI'. In 868 Ahmed Ibn Tulun seized power and founded the city of El-Qatai' ▲ *271*. He erected a fortress-like mosque on a small hill in the center of the new city, as well as a huge castle on the Jebel Moqattam, at the foot of which lay a vast *midan*. In 1069, following a terrible famine, the city was sacked and abandoned. In 1168 Cairo was besieged by the Francs and the vizier Shawar ordered Fustat and El-Qatai' to be burned. Today the Ibn Tulun Mosque is all that remains of this legendary city. The site, upon which a vast lake lay until the mid-19th century, was occupied by the Mamelukes who builts palaces, mosques and medersat. It was totally transformed following the draining of the lake, after which modern buildings were constructed.

IBN TULUN MOSQUE. Built in 876–9 by Ahmed Ibn Tulun on the Jebel Yashkur, this is the oldest original mosque in Cairo. It was converted into a military hospital by Ibrahim Pasha in the 19th century, and was subsequently used as a salt warehouse and a beggar's prison before being classified as a historic monument in 1882. It was restored, in 1918. The rectangular building is entirely constructed in brick (including the strange-looking merlons on top of its walls) and surrounded by a "rampart" walk. It is a porticoed mosque ● *108* (the porticos rest on pillars) consisting of five naves on the *qibla* side and two on the other three sides. The plaster of the intrados of the arches is decorated with inscribed geometric designs. The long foliate frieze which runs the length of the porticos is surmounted by a carved wood inscription of Koranic verses. The minaret, a square tower with an external, spiral staircase, is the only one of its kind in Egypt. Faithfully restored by the sultan Lajin in the 18th century, it is reminiscent of the minaret of the Samarra Mosque in Mesopotamia, which is believed to have been the inspiration behind the design of the Ibn Tulun Mosque.

GAYER-ANDERSON MUSEUM. The museum houses the private collection of Major Gayer-Anderson and includes furniture, silks, glassware, crystal, carpets, carved wood paneling and embroidered Arab costumes. It was founded in 1937 in two ancient residences, the BEIT EL-KIRIDILIYA (1632) and BEIT AMNA BENT SALIM (1540), reached via a narrow, private street. The first has a *sabil* at the southwest corner and a *maqaad* with a monumental entrance. The *qaa* situated between the two buildings has been furnished in its original style. The second residence has a small courtyard with a single-arched *maqaad* and a magnificent *qaa* with an extremely high ceiling which runs the length of the house. Several third-floor rooms have been organized to accommodate the collections and include a reconstruction of a Syrian room. Beyond the Ibn Tulun Mosque the Shari' el-Khalifa leads to the cemeteries ▲ *326*.

SARGHATMISH MEDERSA. The medersa was built in 1356 by Emir Seif ad-Din Sarghatmish against the northwest wall of the Ibn Tulun Mosque. It has a central courtyard open to the sky, formed by four *iwan* surrounded by study cells. The cupola, supported by wooden pendentives, covering the main *iwan* in front of the mihrab, was rebuilt in 1940 to replace the original which had been destroyed. The mausoleum is situated next to the west *iwan*. In front of the medersa are the recently renovated MOSQUE AND MAUSOLEUM OF EL-KHODARI, built in 1767. Inside, the arcaded prayer hall has a painted wood ceiling.

SANGAR SALAR MOSQUE AND MAUSOLEUM. The complex (1304) is situated to the west of the Sarghatmish Medersa, in the Shari' Abd el-Magid el-Labbani. It houses two similar mausoleums, one dedicated to its founder, Emir Alam ad-Din Sangar el-Gawli, and the other to his comrade, Emir Seif ad-Din Salar. A staircase leads (right) to the mausoleums along a corridor surmounted by groined vaults and (left) to the mosque with its single *iwan*. The eastern gate of the courtyard opens onto the Qal'at el-Kabch district.

"Allah is the one and only God and Mohammed is his Prophet."
The *shahada* (profession of faith) inscribed above the main mihrab in the Ibn Tulun Mosque.

Napoleon Bonaparte visiting the French Institute in Egypt.

During the Ommiad period the modern working-class district of QAL'AT EL-KABCH was one of the most exclusive districts in Cairo. It experienced its Golden Age during the reign of Sultan An-Nasir Mohammed who carried out extensive renovations and constructed a water supply. At the end of the 14th century the district was destroyed and abandoned as a result of a power struggle between Prince Yalbugha and Sultan Sha'ban. Land and property were subsequently divided into plots and today buildings stand on sites once occupied by gardens.

QAITBAY MEDERSA. The medersa is situated in a square on the Shari' Qal'at el-Kabch. Founded by Sultan Qaitbay in 1475, one year after the construction of the mausoleum-medersa ▲ *328* on which it was based, it is characterized by a profusion of stalactites and honeycomb decorations, especially on the façade and below the balconies of the minaret. Inside there are four *iwan* and a courtyard covered by a wood ceiling. The wood casing of the mihrab is decorated with intricately carved polygonal stars. On the left, in the Shari' Abd el-Magid el-Labbani, the two stone benches in front of the (now condemned) wooden entrance of the YUSSEF BEY SABIL-KUTTAB (1634) are a favorite resting place for peddlers. The stone consoles that used to support the second floor can still be seen. Opposite the *sabil* the mosque founded by Sultan el-Malik el-Zahir Jaqmaq is named after Lajin el-Seifi who rebuilt it in 1449. Behind the mosque is a recently created GARDEN, reached via the Shari' Qadri opposite the Sarghatmish Medersa, which won the 1992 Aga Khan Award for Architecture.

AS-SAYYIDA ZEINAB MOSQUE. The mosque houses the shrine of Sayyida Zeinab, granddaughter of the Prophet and patron saint of Cairo, whose primitive mausoleum is said to be contemporary with that of El-Hussein ▲ *286*. The mosque, renovated in 1549 and rebuilt by Abd el-Rahman Katkhuda in 1761, used to have a columned prayer hall and was surmounted by small, flat domes. It was entirely rebuilt at the end of the 18th century and extended and restored in 1884 and again in 1942. The main façade, minaret and cupola are typical of the Mameluke architectural style.

The interior is richly decorated with arabesques and inscriptions, while the colonnaded prayer hall has a painted wood ceiling and is surmounted by a cupola in front of the mihrab. The mausoleum, to the west, is also surmounted by a cupola supported by a pendentive of stalactites. The cenotaph is surrounded by a finely worked bronze grille. Opposite is the SULTAN MUSTAFA SABIL-KUTTAB (1759).

BEIT AS-SINNARI. The Beit as-Sinnari is reached by taking the first street on the right after the *sabil*, turning left into the Shari' Hassan el-Kashef and then right into a narrow alleyway named after a former president of the French Institute, Gaspard Monge (1746–1818). Built in 1794 by Prince Ibrahim Katkhuda as-Sinnari, the house was requisitioned in 1798 (as were the now nonexistent houses of Hassan Kashef and Qasim Bey) as a residence for the scientists and scholars of the Egypt Expedition's scientific mission.

The building has all the characteristic elements of Cairene houses ● *116* of that period. To the north the *tahtabuch* forms a wide loggia which opens onto a courtyard, and is surmounted by a *maqaad* with a separate entrance. The harem suite comprises several rooms and *qaa* which are interconnected by a series of stairways and passages. The main *qaa* overlooks both the street and the

courtyard, while the huge *mashrabiya* bays of the second *qaa*, to the west, look onto the courtyard.

SHARI' PORT SAID OR EL-KHALIG. Today it is difficult to imagine the former charm of this district, which was totally transformed by the urban development of the early 20th-century. The El-Khalig Canal was first dug during the Pharaonic period to link the Nile and the Red Sea and was subsequently filled in and re-dug many times. In the 14th century it was rebuilt and opened to navigation by An-Nasir Mohammed and soon became a popular place for boating. The canal, fed by the Nile opposite Roda Island ▲ *283*, crossed the city from north to south. It was navigable almost all year, when the waters of the Nile were high. During the Nile floods (between August 10 and 20), a special ceremony was held to let the water into the canal by breaking the small dyke at its mouth. The event was followed by a great public celebration during which the Cairenes took to the stretch of water between the Nile and the El-Khalig Canal. In 1897 the canal was filled in once again to make way for a tram line. It was replaced by the Shari' el-Khalig el-Masri, which was later widened and renamed Shari' Port Said.

THE FRENCH INSTITUTE IN EGYPT
On July 12, 1798, Napoleon Bonaparte landed in Alexandria with 38,000 men, including a scientific mission consisting of a team of mathematicians, engineers, scientists, economists, artists and writers. The leading members of the mission formed a society, based on the French Institute, with the aim of studying the resources and development of Egypt. The results of their work were published in *La Description de l'Egypte* (1809), which included more than three thousand illustrations.

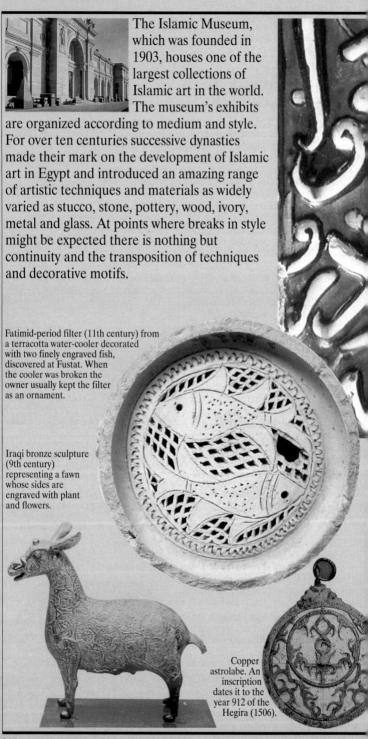

The Islamic Museum, which was founded in 1903, houses one of the largest collections of Islamic art in the world. The museum's exhibits are organized according to medium and style. For over ten centuries successive dynasties made their mark on the development of Islamic art in Egypt and introduced an amazing range of artistic techniques and materials as widely varied as stucco, stone, pottery, wood, ivory, metal and glass. At points where breaks in style might be expected there is nothing but continuity and the transposition of techniques and decorative motifs.

Fatimid-period filter (11th century) from a terracotta water-cooler decorated with two finely engraved fish, discovered at Fustat. When the cooler was broken the owner usually kept the filter as an ornament.

Iraqi bronze sculpture (9th century) representing a fawn whose sides are engraved with plant and flowers.

Copper astrolabe. An inscription dates it to the year 912 of the Hegira (1506).

Elaborately worked bronze lamp (Mameluke period) from the Sultan Hassan Medersa ▲ *308*.

Detail of a wood-paneled room, inlaid with decorative motifs in mother-of-pearl.

Glass lamp (14th century) from the Sultan Hassan Medersa ▲ *308*, decorated with Koranic verses and phrases honoring the sultan.

Page from an Arabic manuscript (1582) describing the beneficial effects and medicinal properties of certain plants and herbs.

Ancient Coptic religious community (above)

BABYLON
At the time of the Arab conquest in 640, Babylon was a large fort with huge towers, bastions and a 40-foot-high outer wall with a moat. It had a port, and two Nilometers, and was linked to the Red Sea by a canal which had existed in the days of Ancient Egypt. The Nile, which now lies 400 yards or so further west, flowed at the foot of these fortifications, whose remains can still be seen today. The fort

was also known as Qasr el-Shamaa (Castle of the Candle), *shamaa* (candle) being in fact a corruption of the Coptic word *khemi* (Egyptian).

Remains of the Fort of Babylon (above).

THE COPTS

Traditionally, the Apostle Mark is said to have preached Christianity in Egypt in c. AD 40. Within the context of the Roman and Byzantine occupations, Egypt became one of the main theaters of a schismatic activity which culminated in the appearance of Arianism in Alexandria in c. AD 318. As the object of Roman persecution, Christianity in Egypt took to the desert and gave rise to the cenobite monasticism preached by Saint Pachomius at the beginning of the 3rd century. During the reign of Constantine (324–37) the Egyptians converted en masse but, in response to Byzantine oppression, adopted the Monophysite doctrine which affirms the one, primarily divine, nature of Christ. This hostility toward Byzantium helps to explain the ease with which the Persians (in 619) and later the Muslim armies ● 66 were able to capture Memphis and Babylon. A century later there was a major movement to convert to Islam, but this was accompanied by major uprisings against Arab domination in 725 and 739. Egypt remained predominately Christian until the mid-9th century, but between the 12th and 14th centuries the present proportion of a 90-percent Muslim population was established. The Delta has a small Coptic population concentrated in Middle Egypt, between Minya and Assiut. Social and religious life is centered around the church, presided over by priests (who are allowed to marry), but it is the monasteries, especially Deir Amba Baramus ▲ *208*, which constitute the focal points of the Coptic community and the seat of its episcopal hierarchy.

1 NILOMETER
2 ST GEORGE'S CHURCH
3 ST GEORGE'S CONVENT
4 AMR IBN EL-AS MOSQUE
5 CHURCH OF ST SERGIUS
6 ST GEORGE'S CHURCH (COPTIC)
7 BEN-EZRA SYNAGOGUE
8 EL-MUALLAQA
9 COPTIC MUSEUM
10 ST BARBARA'S CHURCH

⏳ Half a day
◆ **J** B5-B6

OLD CAIRO

FORT OF BABYLON. The name Babylon is a corruption of the ancient name Pi-Hapi-n-On, meaning "the home of Hapi" (the Nile god). The site of Old Cairo is believed to have been occupied, well before the arrival of the Romans, by an important settlement which was the forerunner of the towns founded subsequently on the site.

EL-MUALLAQA OR ST MARY'S CHURCH. El-Muallaqa, dedicated to the Virgin Mary, is said to have been built between the end of the 3rd and beginning of the 4th century. The name Muallaqa ("suspended") is derived from the fact that its floor was constructed on two of the

Exterior, interior and icons in El-Muallaqa (St Mary's Church).

319

**GATE OF
ST GEORGE'S
CONVENT**
A wooden gate
leads onto a small
courtyard and
St George's Convent,
today inhabited by
thirty or so nuns.

towers of the ancient Roman fortress, covered with palm
trunks and a layer of stone. The church originally consisted of
the southeastern section or "upper church", now appearing as
an addition. The main church is said to have been built
between the 5th and 6th centuries. Destroyed in the 9th and
rebuilt in the 11th century, the church became the seat of the
Coptic patriarchate until the 14th century. The set of twenty-
nine steps leading to the entrance so impressed 14th- and
15th-century travelers that it became known as the "staircase
church". The interior is divided into four naves by three rows
of marble columns and has seven sanctuaries, six in the two
side aisles and one in the upper Church of St Mark. In front
of the central sanctuary is an 11th-century pulpit supported by
fifteen marble columns. A wooden staircase leads to the
chapel of the Ethiopian saint, Takla Haymanot, built on one
of the bastions of the fortress. The craftsmanship of the 10th-
and 13th-century iconostases, in cedar, ebony and walnut
inlaid with ivory, is truly remarkable, as is the collection of
over one hundred icons, the oldest of which dates from the
8th century. Other objects belonging to the church, such as
icons and manuscripts, are preserved in the Coptic Museum.
THE GREEK CHURCH OF ST GEORGE. A long set of steps leads
to one of the few round churches which still exist in the East,
built on part of the outer wall and the Roman towers.
Although rebuilt in 1904 and extensively restored after several
fires, it has retained some of its beautiful stained-glass
windows.

COPTIC QUARTER. A huge, studded
wooden gate opens onto Hara Mari
Girgis, a narrow street which still has its
original paving stones.
ST GEORGE'S CONVENT. The
convent is situated at no. 17 Hara
Mari Girgis. Only the chapel, the
oldest part (10th century) of the
convent, can be visited. Its old wooden ceiling has been
replaced, but it still has several original wood fixtures,
including three doors, one 23 feet high, with beautiful
decorations in relief.

**CHURCH OF THE
VIRGIN**
In Coptic and Arab
manuscripts from the
17th century onward,
the church (above)
was known as
Keniset el-Adra
Qasriyet el-Rihan
(Church of the
Virgin and the Pot of
Basil). It can no
longer be visited as it
was ravaged by fire
in 1975.

KENISET MARI GIRGIS OR ST GEORGE'S CHURCH. A
small porchway, beyond no. 9 Hara Mari Girgis,
leads into Atfa Mari Girgis. St George's Church,
on the right, was founded in 684 by Athanasius,
a wealthy scribe, and rebuilt in 1857. The
church has one ancient section, the Qaa el-
Arsan (wedding chamber), which dates from
the 4th century. Formerly reserved for the
Coptic marriage ceremony, the chamber
houses some real works of art: turned-wood
lattice windows, walls decorated with
paintings and elements in relief, and a
ceiling painted with colored frescos.
EL-ADRA OR CHURCH OF THE VIRGIN.
The 9th-century Church of the Virgin,
rebuilt in the 18th century, stands at
the far end of Atfa Mari Girgis.
**ABU SARGA OR THE CHURCH OF
ST SERGIUS.** The Church of St
Sergius is a typical example of

The tower of the
Church of the
Virgin (right).

> "This country is a palimpsest, in which the Bible is written over Herodotus, and the Koran over that."
>
> Lady Duff Gordon

Coptic churches and monasteries. Its façade is no different from those of the neighboring houses. Founded at the end of the 4th century and rebuilt at the beginning of the 11th century, it stands on a crypt that is said to have sheltered the Holy Family during their flight from Egypt. It is a place of pilgrimage for Christians of all denominations and is named after Saint Sergius and Saint Bacchus, soldiers martyred during the reign of Maximian. The church, built along the lines of an Eastern basilica with a single nave, three sanctuaries separated by iconostases and two side aisles delimited by arches resting on columns, houses some extremely fine examples of marquetry work inlaid with ivory, especially in the sanctuaries. The original altar can be seen in the Coptic Museum.

The 14th-century Arab geographer Maqrizi (1364–1442) described Sitt Barbara, or St Barbara's Church (above), as the largest and most beautiful Coptic church of its time. Most of the woodwork is now in the Coptic Museum and the only piece remaining in the church is a 13th-century carved wood iconostasis inlaid with ivory (left).

SITT BARBARA OR ST BARBARA'S CHURCH. The church, originally constructed between the 4th and 5th centuries and rebuilt during the 11th century, still has an ancient chapel in which the relics of Saint Cyrus and Saint John (to whom it was originally dedicated) are preserved. It also has some remarkable wood paneling, some of which is in the Coptic Museum, and a series of icons. At the far end of Hara Sitt Barbara, the CONVENT OF ST BARBARA stands in a pleasant garden setting with a view of the ancient fortifications and part of the cemeteries. The convent comprises several buildings, including a school built in 1960 by the architect Ramesses Wissa Wassef.

BEN-EZRA SYNAGOGUE. The synagogue was built on the site of the 8th-century Church of St Michael, which was in turn built on the ruins of an ancient synagogue said to have been founded in c. 605–562 BC by Jews led back into Egypt by Jeremiah, on the very spot where Moses prayed in the 13th century BC. In 1115 the Rabi Abraham Ben-Ezra persuaded the Coptic patriarchate to restore the land, without tribute, to the Jewish community and had the synagogue rebuilt. Its recently restored, relatively simple exterior contrasts with the intricacy and richness of the interior decoration, the 12th-century woodwork in particular. During reconstruction work carried out in 1894 a GENIZA (a repository for documents) was discovered. It had been designed to store all the documents containing a reference to God and which could therefore not be destroyed without

The Ben-Ezra Synagogue houses a large number of antiques, including several ancient Torah (above).

321

In 1910 Marcos Simaïka Pasha, aware of the very specific nature of an art belonging to a period which extended from early Christian times to the Arab conquest in the 7th century, collected funds by subscription and founded Cairo's first Coptic Museum on land belonging to the Coptic Church. The simple lines of the building are emphasized by the elaborately carved *mashrabiya* work from ancient palaces and houses. A new wing was added in 1947 to accommodate the collection of Coptic antiquities put together by Gaston Maspero (1846–1916), which had previously been exhibited in the Cairo Museum.

One of the five pieces of a linen and wool wall hanging (above) whose central section represents Leda and the swan.

Detail from a parchment of magical texts.

Wall fresco.

Painted wooden icon (18th century) showing the two Coptic saints, Abrakaad and Ogbani, who are wearing animal masks.

SAINT ANTHONY AND SAINT PAUL
Painted wooden icon (18th century) illustrating a visit by Saint Anthony to the white-bearded Saint Paul. Beside him is the raven which brought him bread every day in its beak.

Bronze oil lamp of the type used to illuminate Coptic churches, with a handle in the form of an imaginary animal.

Details from a piece of Coptic fabric (4th or 5th century) on which flute players (above), dancers and Amazons carrying shields are embroidered with wool and silk threads.

Detail of a 3rd- or 4th-century linen curtain showing a centaur inside a medallion.

Napoleon Bonaparte is said to have built the first windmills in Egypt (their remains can still be seen today) on the plateau of Fustat (above). Their number was subsequently increased, reaching seventy-five by the end of the 18th century. They survived until 1982 when they began to disappear as the area (which today has thirty thousand inhabitants) began to be populated.

sacrilege. According to legend, the scribe Ezra concealed Moses' incomplete Torah there. Among the (now widely dispersed) documents more than 250,000 are said to have dated from 1002 to 1266, including at least 7,000 of great historical value. They constitute a valuable source of information on Cairo during the Fatimid period seen through the eyes of the Jewish community of Fustat.

FUSTAT AND THE ARAB CONQUEST. When he arrived in Egypt in 640 Amr Ibn el-As ● *66* pitched camp in a large vineyard on the banks of the river to the north of the Fort of Babylon and thus founded Fustat ("encampment"), the first Arab settlement in Egypt. Legend has it that as he was striking camp to move on to Alexandria, Amr discovered a pair of doves nesting on his tent and ordered them to be left untouched. Upon his return the tent was replaced by a mosque around which the *khittat* (districts) were established, as a result of the military concessions granted to each of the ethnic and tribal groups represented among the thousands of soldiers who had fought in the campaign. For three centuries Fustat continued to expand, incorporating the old Fort of Babylon and the town of El-Askar ▲ *270* and finally becoming part of the city of El-Qatai' ▲ *312*. It reached the height of its glory at the end of the 9th century when it (and not Alexandria) became one of the major commercial centers and one of the largest cities (with 120,000 inhabitants over an area of 750 acres) in the Mediterranean Basin. In 1175 the vizier Shawar ordered the city to be razed to the ground to prevent it falling into the hands of the Crusaders. Today all that can be seen is the black smoke from the kilns of the potters who have moved onto this vast wasteland. The last of the several excavation projects carried out at Fustat between the Amr Ibn el-As Mosque and the Greek Orthodox cemetery were the Gayraud excavations which began in 1982 at Istabl Antar, a former powder magazine built on top of the plateau.

AMR IBN EL-AS MOSQUE. The mosque stands in the Shari' Mari Girgis about 350 yards north of the Coptic district. Built by Amr Ibn el-As in 642, it was Africa's first mosque. It was originally a simple rectangle (197 x 118 feet) of clay bricks with a low ceiling supported by palm trunks. It was used for teaching long before the El-Azhar Mosque ▲ *294* was built and could hold up to five thousand students. The mosque has been destroyed, rebuilt and renovated many times, particularly in 1798 by Murad Bey, who gave it its present form: a parallelogram (394 x 360 feet) with four porticos supported by 150 white marble columns, 8 doors and 3 minarets. It was extensively restored and almost entirely rebuilt in reinforced concrete in the 1970's.

CHURCH AND CONVENT OF ST MERCURIUS. The Church and Convent of St Mercurius or Abu Seifein are situated to the north of the Amr Ibn el-As Mosque, outside the Roman fortifications but inside the rectangle formed by the Coptic, Maronite, Anglican and Protestant cemeteries. After several fires this extremely ancient church was used as a sugar-cane warehouse before being reconsecrated in the 11th century. Inside a painting of Christ and the twelve Apostles hangs in front of the 10th-century sanctuary whose wooden dome is supported by demi-cupolas decorated with biblical scenes. The walls of the second-floor Chapel of St George have revealed several layers of paintings from different periods. A staircase on the north side of the church leads to a crypt where Saint Barsum is said to have lived for twenty years during the 14th century. The 6th-century convent, one of the oldest in Egypt, was entirely rebuilt in the 10th century. Today it is occupied by nuns and is not open to the public. Its wealth of artistic treasures, including an extraordinary collection of icons, makes it a real school of Coptic art.

CHURCH OF AMBA-SHENUDA. The 7th-century church was converted into a mosque in the 11th century. Three centuries later it was restored and reverted to its original function. It has three naves, separated by two rows of marble columns. The iconostasis, in red cedar inlaid with ivory, contains a series of seven extremely valuable icons. It also possesses a triptych of Greek origin and a 14th-century glass lamp.

Icon depicting Saint Mercurius.

Details of marquetry work (below) from the Church of St Mercurius.

🗓 **One day**
◆ J F3-F4-F5-F6

THE COMPLEX OF SULTAN QAITBAY
The complex once comprised several buildings, but now only the mosque and the medersa (interior, above), which houses the tomb of the sultan, remain.

KHUND TUGHAY MAUSOLEUM
Khund Tughay, also known as Umm Anuk, favorite wife of An-Nasir Mohammed and mother of his son Anuk, died in 1348. Today all that remains of the original complex, which consisted of a *khanqa* with two *iwan* and a mausoleum surmounted by a cupola, is the vaulted *iwan* and the drum of the cupola with its (now largely destroyed) richly decorated faïence frieze.

The area (about 2,500 acres), cultural wealth and ancient history of Cairo's Muslim cemeteries make them an important part of the city. Their position on its immediate outskirts, extending for a distance of about 7 miles from north to south, constitutes a barrier to Cairo's eastward expansion.

A CITY WITHIN A CITY. At first glance the cemeteries are characterized by a rich and varied use of space and building styles, and it would be no exaggeration to refer to them in terms of cities and urban planning. The plots on which the tombs are built vary from a few square yards to several hundred square yards or more. They form a network which combines a regular, orthogonal framework born of a desire for order and economy of space with a remarkable freedom and complexity of organization: two extremes which not only coexist but interpenetrate.

The diversity of the plots has given rise to a similar diversity of architectural forms: the tombs can be simple stone parallelepipeds decorated with two stelae, mausoleums surmounted by cupolas in garden settings, intricately carved wood "kiosks" or even "towns" with several buildings.

LIVING AMONG THE DEAD. Cairo currently has two necropolises and four cemeteries used by Muslims. Together they represent 6.4 percent of the surface area of Cairo itself and 3.6 percent of its suburbs. The vast "City of the Dead" is also inhabited by the living. The two great necropolises have a permanent population of 179,000 inhabitants, of whom almost 20,000 live inside the perimeters while the rest live on the outskirts of these two great burial sites. It is worth taking a closer look at two of Cairo's cemeteries in particular: the Mameluke Cemetery, to the east of the medieval city, and the Southern or Imam as-Shafi'i Cemetery.

1 PRINCESS TOLBIYA
2 KHUND TUGHAY
3 GUZAL
4 TOMB OF AZDUMUR
5 ROYAL CHAPEL
6 QAITBAY MOSQUE-MAUSOLEUM
7 SHEIKH YUSSEF TAKIYA
8 BARQUQ COMPLEX
9 QAITBAY RABAA
10 INAL COMPLEX
11 QURQUMAS MEDERSA-MAUSOLEUM
12 BARSBEY MEDERSA
13 QOBBET AR-RIFA'I
14 TOMB OF QURQUMAS

THE MAMELUKE TOMBS

THE FUNERARY COMPLEX OF SULTAN QAITBAY
The buildings which comprised the funerary complex of Sultan Qaitbay were surrounded by a wall.

The Eastern Cemetery contains the tombs of the Circassian Mamelukes, including those of five sultans: Barquq, El-Ashraf Barsbey, El-Ashraf Inal, Abu Saïd Qunsua and Qaitbay. There were twenty-one other monuments, made up of the tombs of Mameluke princes and princesses and nine mosques.

SOUTHWEST OR AZROMOK COMPLEX. The tomb of EL-ASHRAF AZROMOK (1505), recognizable by the blue enamel ribs of the cupola, is reached by carrying straight on after the flyover at the end of the Shari' El-Azhar and taking the first street on the right, the Shari' Qarafet Bab el-Wazir. By retracing your steps, the SULTAN MOHAMMED KUZ EL-ASSAL (said to have existed only in the popular imagination) cupola or "honey pot" can be seen on the right. Further north the street takes the name of the Sultan Ahmed, and, 100 yards or so further on, on the left, stands the monument of KHUND TUGHAY (1348). Opposite the monument is the cupola of the PRINCESS TOLBIYA MAUSOLEUM (1363), Sultan An-Nasir's principal wife. To the north the TOMB OF GUZAL (1403) stands on the right while, on the left, behind the *hochs*, is the TOMB OF AZDUMUR and, as you turn into the Shari' el-Afifi, the TOMB OF TASCTUMUR (1334). Three hundred yards or so further on a tiny square leads to the ROYAL CHAPEL, dedicated to the sons of Mohammed Ali. The complex, which occupies an area of about 242,000 square feet, was designed in 1894 by Fabricius Bey. It includes several different types of tombs, from the simple marble tombstones in the gardens reserved for the princesses to the chapel surmounted by a cupola housing the tombs of the khedives Tawfiq and Abbas Helmi.

Two different views of the Sultan Barsbey Complex (above). The Sultan Inal Complex and Ounas Mausoleum (opposite page).

QAITBAY MAUSOLEUM
The overall harmony of the proportions of the last mausoleum to be built in this Mameluke wasteland by Sultan Qaitbay (1418–96) is striking. The richly decorated prayer hall with its marble-covered floor and a detail of the mihrab (above).

QAITBAY CEMETERY

The Qaitbay Cemetery is reached by following the Shari' el-Afifi westward. On the right between two apartment blocks, the QAITBAY GATE leads into the heart of a suburb established at the end of the 19th century on the waste ground surrounding the Mameluke tombs. It extends from the Qaitbay to the Barquq complex and in 1986 had a population of 17,255 (compared with 2,287 in 1897). To the north lies a small square bordered on the west by the QAITBAY MOSQUE. The building, which consists of a mosque-medersa, a *sabil-kuttab* and a mausoleum, is only the central unit of a remarkable complex linked by some historians with a "royal suburb". By continuing northeast you come to the 15th-century SHEIKH YUSSEF TAKIYA on the left, while directly opposite, on the other side of the street, a block of houses conceals a brick cupola, the QOBBET KHANDIJA UMM EL-ASHRAF (1430).

SULTAN BARSBEY COMPLEX. A 985-foot-long wall, pierced by a double row of windows, identifies the complex of Sultan Barsbey (1432), who reigned for sixteen years (1422–38). The complex covered an area of about 32,000 square feet and consisted of four buildings situated on either side of the central street. On the east side, the medersa and *khanqa* share the same façade and are linked by an interior communicating passage leading from the main entrance, although each has a separate, secondary entrance. The other buildings, about 300 yards from the first two, are a *zawia*

(whose ruins can still be seen today) dedicated to the poor and, opposite, the 16th-century Qobbet ar-Rifa'i convent surmounted by a cupola. Beyond the complex lies a flatter and less densely built-up area where the tombs of Gani Beik el-Ashrafi (1430) and Qurqumas (1511), which until 1981 stood in front of the El-Hakim Mosque ▲ *291*, are surrounded by railings.

SULTAN BARQUQ "KHANQA". This was the first and largest monument to be built (1400–11) in the necropolis. The square building (50,000 square feet in area) is surmounted by two symmetrical minarets and two symmetrical cupolas at both ends of the northeast façade. Between them a smaller, third cupola heightens the central mihrab. The north cupola houses the tombs of the sultan and his sons, while the south cupola contains the tombs of his wives. The northern corner of the building is occupied by a triple-arched SABIL-KUTTAB on the two loggia sides, which offers a general view of the complex. The northern section of the cemetery consists of a network of roads, small squares and gardens laid out in the 1950's, which provide the setting for the two adjoining burial sites: the EMIR QURQUMAS MEDERSA AND MAUSOLEUM (1506–7), mainly inspired by the COMPLEX OF SULTAN QAITBAY, whose equerry he was, and the Sultan Inal Complex (1451–6). The cupola at the center of a five-road intersection is all that remains of the last monument in this necropolis, that of SULTAN QUNSUA ABU SAÏD, who reigned for a year in 1798.

329

▲ CEMETERIES

Exterior view of the
Mameluke tombs.

**IMAM AS-SHAFI'I
AVENUE**
This broad avenue,
which runs between
two rows of "palace-
tombs", is the main
thoroughfare through
the Imam as-Shafi'i
Cemetery. With its
interwoven
patchwork of old and
more recent
residential blocks,
which have filled
every available space,
and the constant
noise of passing
traffic, the cemetery
is a busy place. The
hubbub reaches its
peak on Fridays when
visitors come to the
cemetery and one of
the largest
fleamarkets in Cairo
is held.

SOUTHERN CEMETERY

The Southern Cemetery has been Cairo's main burial site
since the Arab conquest in 640. Today it covers an area of
around 1,375 acres and contains twenty-six monuments to
ascetics, canonists, holy men and descendants of the Prophet,
as well as the forty-seven funerary monuments of the emirs
and sultans from the Ikhshidid, Fatimid, Mameluke and
Ottoman periods. Since the early 1980's the necropolis, which
once formed a continuation of the city, has been cut off by a
network of motorways, freeways and flyovers which has
surrounded it and cut through it, leaving only a few links in
the north.

IMAM AS-SHAFI'I CEMETERY. The BAB EL-QARAFA, built in
1499 by the sultan Qaitbay, marks the entrance to the
cemetery at the intersection of the Shari' Salah Salim freeway
and the Imam as-Shafi'i Avenue. Take the Shari' el-Qadiriya,
named after the descendants of Sheikh Abd el-Qader el-
Ghilani who settled (date unknown) around the ZEIN AD-DIN
YUSSEF MEDERSA AND MAUSOLEUM (1298), the first
monument on the right. The Shari' el-Qadiriya bends slightly
to the right and then to the left before joining the Imam as-
Shafi'i Avenue.

IMAM AS-SHAFI'I MAUSOLEUM. The south end of the avenue
leads into a small square formed by the demolition of tombs
and *hochs*. On the right stands the tomb of Imam as-Shafi'i,
the founder of one of the four orthodox schools of Sunni
jurisprudence and creator of the social philosophy of Islam, a
retiring man who devoted himself to prayer. He died in 820.
The rectangular mausoleum, commissioned by Salah ad-Din
● 66 and built in 1211, is one of the largest in Egypt and
measures 49 feet along the inside and 67 feet along the
outside wall. The stone structure supports a wood cupola
which is similar to the Rocher dome. It houses the
cenotaphs of the imam, the sultan el-Kamel Ayyub
(1218–38) and Sayyed Mohammed Abd el-Hakam, who
shared the former tomb of the imam. The present
structure is very different from the
original.

EL-BASHA "HOCH". Turn
right as you leave the
avenue and join
the Shari' el-

**EL-SULTANIYA
MAUSOLEUM**
The mausoleum
(1350) houses the
tomb of the mother
of Sultan Hassan
(1347–61) ▲ 309.
The recently restored,
rectangular structure
consists of a vaulted
iwan flanked by two
identical cupolas.

Imam el-Leisi (which runs parallel to the avenue) via a network of narrow streets. Follow it northward, turning right after about 300 yards, and you come to the tiny, white-painted mausoleum of MOHAMMED EL-HASSWATI (1160), whose square tomb is surmounted by a brick cupola. To the north the five cupolas of the El-Basha *hoch* can be seen outlined against the sky. The royal chapel, which dates from 1820, contains the khedivial tombs of Tussun, Ibrahim, Abbas and Farouk, Mohammed Ali's sons and grandsons who succeeded him on the throne of Egypt, as well as the tombs of their wives, children and servants.

All that remains of the Menufi *iwan*, once part of a magnificent late 13th-century edifice, is the huge cupola and vaulted *iwan*.

MAMELUKE CEMETERY

The Mameluke Cemetery lies to the south of the Citadel and is part of the Southern Cemetery. As you leave the Imam as-Shafi'i Cemetery, turn right into a narrow alleyway about 50 yards after the NUR AD-DIN MOSQUE (1575). This leads to the Mameluke Cemetery, which is devoid of roads and where the tall, isolated minarets serve as landmarks among the ruins. The first of the twelve funerary monuments is the EL-SULTANIYA MAUSOLEUM (1350), while further on, on the right, stands the EMIR QUSUN MINARET (1335), which is all that remains of what was one of the first burial complexes built in the cemetery under the Bahrid Mamelukes. To the west is a complex comprising the small BADR AD-DIN EL-QARAFI MAUSOLEUM (1300) surmounted by a cupola, and the 14th-century south minaret. Further on, to the southeast, the EL-RIHAN IWAN (1534), the stone cupola of the SUDUN MAUSOLEUM (1504) and the small, brick cupola of EL-SAWABI MAUSOLEUM (1286) stand around a small square.

TOMBS OF THE MAMELUKES
The El-Basha *hoch* (above) also houses the tombs of the Mamelukes that Mohammed Ali had assassinated on his accession ● 68.

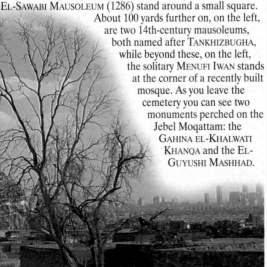

About 100 yards further on, on the left, are two 14th-century mausoleums, both named after TANKHIZBUGHA, while beyond these, on the left, the solitary MENUFI IWAN stands at the corner of a recently built mosque. As you leave the cemetery you can see two monuments perched on the Jebel Moqattam: the GAHINA EL-KHALWATI KHANQA and the EL-GUYUSHI MASHHAD.

The Gahina el-Khalwati *khanqa* (left), built in 1538, is the more northerly of the two funerary monuments on Jebel Moqattam. The other, the El-Guyushi *mashhad*, was built in 1085 by the Fatimid vizier Badr el-Gamali (also known as Emir el-Guyushi) who governed Egypt between 1074 and 1094. It is considered the most important shrine of the Fatimid period.

331

Artist's impression of the site of Memphis as it might have looked in about 800 BC.

EMBLEMS OF EGYPT ✪
Classic symbols of Egypt, the Sphinx and the Pyramids of Giza are the high points of a visit to the country. The gigantic monuments impress as much by their size as by the mystery they represent. In half a day it is possible to cover the site at Memphis, explore the interior of the Pyramid of Cheops and visit the museum of the Solar Barque. But for an even more spectacular sight, you should come back in the evening and see the *son et lumière* show.

The ruins of the ancient city of Memphis are situated on the left bank of the River Nile about 19 miles south of Cairo. Although most of the visible remains are not particularly spectacular, Memphis really should be visited before the Pyramids of Giza and Saqqara for two reasons: firstly, because these sites are in fact the two main necropolises of Memphis; and secondly, because Memphis played a key role in Egyptian history for over three thousand years. The city was founded by the first 1st-Dynasty king Menes (or Narmer) and, although it was not the capital as such (this is too modern a concept), it has almost always been the center of Egypt. Its role as such has been favored by its geographical location on the boundary between Lower and Upper Egypt and almost at the apex (point of divergence) of the Nile Delta. As a result Memphis and its immediate environs became known, among other things, as the juncture of the Two Lands. The name Memphis was derived from the Greek form of the Egyptian *Men-neter*, which was an abbreviation of the name of the Pyramid of Pepy I at Saqqara and its dependency. The main part of the ruins, which corresponds in general terms to the city's largest sanctuary, the so-called Sanctuary of Ptah and its dependencies, are situated near the village of MIT RAHINA. Part of the village is perched on a vast, high hill (*kom* or *tell* in Arabic) formed from accumulated and stratified archeological layers. To the east of the hill can be found the buildings of the village of BEDRASHEIN.

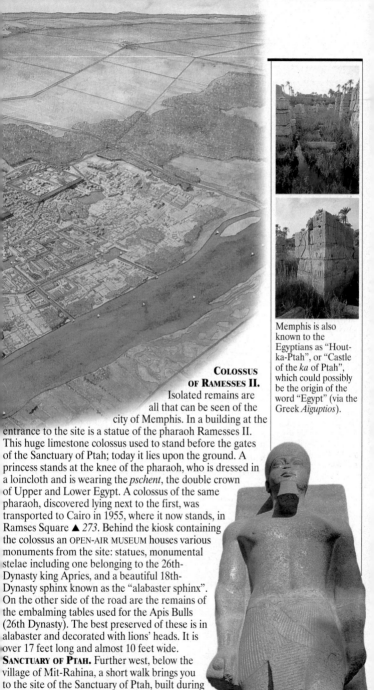

Memphis is also
known to the
Egyptians as "Hout-
ka-Ptah", or "Castle
of the *ka* of Ptah",
which could possibly
be the origin of the
word "Egypt" (via the
Greek *Aiguptios*).

**COLOSSUS
OF RAMESSES II.**
Isolated remains are
all that can be seen of the
city of Memphis. In a building at the
entrance to the site is a statue of the pharaoh Ramesses II.
This huge limestone colossus used to stand before the gates
of the Sanctuary of Ptah; today it lies upon the ground. A
princess stands at the knee of the pharaoh, who is dressed in
a loincloth and is wearing the *pschent*, the double crown
of Upper and Lower Egypt. A colossus of the same
pharaoh, discovered lying next to the first, was
transported to Cairo in 1955, where it now stands, in
Ramses Square ▲ *273*. Behind the kiosk containing
the colossus an OPEN-AIR MUSEUM houses various
monuments from the site: statues, monumental
stelae including one belonging to the 26th-
Dynasty king Apries, and a beautiful 18th-
Dynasty sphinx known as the "alabaster sphinx".
On the other side of the road are the remains of
the embalming tables used for the Apis Bulls
(26th Dynasty). The best preserved of these is in
alabaster and decorated with lions' heads. It is
over 17 feet long and almost 10 feet wide.
SANCTUARY OF PTAH. Further west, below the
village of Mit-Rahina, a short walk brings you
to the site of the Sanctuary of Ptah, built during
the reign of Ramesses II. All that remains of this
vast edifice, which is on the scale of Karnak
▲ *404*, are the bases of columns and walls
standing in mud. However, research is still being
carried out on the site of Memphis and some
important archeological and historical results are
currently emerging.

THE MAGIC OF THE PYRAMIDS
The Great Pyramid, the largest of the three Pyramids of Giza, is the only one of the Seven Wonders of the World (as defined by classical antiquity) to have survived to the present day. With its two neighbors and the Sphinx, ever watchful at the foot of the plateau, the Great Pyramid continues to fire the imagination of all those who see it. It owes its survival to the simplicity and perfection of its design.

PYRAMIDS OF GIZA

The "Pyramids" are situated on the desert plateau which marks the boundary of the vast urban complex of Giza (pronounced with a hard "g"), which is in fact a suburb of Cairo. Today there is a tendency to refer to the "Pyramids of Giza" even though the Egyptian name for the site is *El-Ahram* ("the Pyramids"), a name which was also used by Western visitors prior to the meteoric rise of the village of Giza. Although the site extends beyond the plateau of Giza and despite the fact that there are many other pyramids in the Libyan Desert (in an area extending from Abu Rawash in the north to Lisht ▲ *356* in the south), the exclusivity of the name is justified by the sheer magnificence of these three pyramids, which have been renowned since classical antiquity and even from the time of the Ancient Egyptians. The pyramids are in fact the tombs of three 4th-Dynasty pharaohs: Khufu (Cheops in Greek), Khafre (Chephren) and Menkaure (Mycerinus).
PYRAMIDS. The Egyptian pyramids, from the Pyramid of Khufu (an unrivaled architectural masterpiece) to the more modest pyramids belonging to less powerful or less ambitious pharaohs, were tombs reserved for the pharaohs of the Old Kingdom (3rd–6th Dynasties) and part of the Middle Kingdom

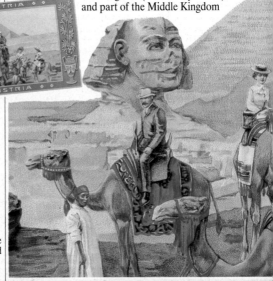

"I know that philosophers may groan or smile at the thought that the greatest monument ever created by mankind is a tomb; but why see the Pyramid of Cheops merely as a pile of stones and a skeleton."

François René de Chateaubriand

(11th–12th Dynasties) and their queens. They are the principal element of a large architectural complex which, in addition to the actual pyramid, consisted of a funerary or "upper" temple, a small pyramid or "annex" (of religious or symbolic significance), and a causeway leading to a valley or "lower" temple which stood at the foot of the plateau, on the edge of the desert, and was linked to the Nile by a dock and a canal. The perfect and to some extent elementary design of the Pyramids of Giza in particular was the product of a long process which took place over several centuries incorporating various stages of development: superposed mastabas and the so-called "step" pyramids ● 84. The form of the monument also has several levels of symbolic significance. The pyramid was in fact the means by which the dead pharaoh rose to the firmament and joined the sun, far from the shadows of the tomb. It was also seen as an emanation of this heavenly body, the mineral concretization of the sun's rays. These are only two interpretations from an entire spectrum of symbolic images that the Ancient Egyptians associated with the pyramid. In spite of the many remaining obscurities (a situation which is not helped by the lack of any pre-5th Dynasty inscriptions in these sometimes gigantic monuments), there is still sufficient information to identify the occupants of the pyramids, even though most traces of them and their funeral paraphernalia have long since disappeared from the monuments they commissioned.

PYRAMID OF KHUFU. The pyramid is 755 feet square at its base, was originally 482 feet high (it lost 33 feet when the apex was removed) and has a total superposed volume

AVENUE OF THE PYRAMIDS

Once a pleasant, tree-lined avenue (left) led to the Pyramids of Giza. Today they are reached via a very ordinary and seemingly endless approach road, which has developed haphazardly and uncontrolledly, with its constant stream of traffic, hotch-potch of apartment blocks and bars interspersed with a few fields, and the gilt grandiloquence of the *Mena House Hotel*, formerly one of the grand palaces which marked the main staging posts on the India and Far East route.

WHAT IS A PYRAMID?

An Egyptian pyramid is nothing more than a tomb, in spite of what may have been or may be said by those lovers of false mysteries, the so-called "pyramidologists" and the adherents of a similar bogus form of Egyptology. But this is neither disheartening nor disappointing if it is considered within the context of Ancient Egyptian culture and its view of life, death and the divine monarchy. Nor does it detract from the often huge merit of those who designed and constructed these monuments.

CORRIDORS AND GALLERIES
A descending gallery leads from the entrance of the pyramid to an unfinished underground chamber hewn out of the living rock of the plateau. At one point it intersects an ascending corridor that widens and

opens out, a little further on, into the 28-foot-high Grand Gallery with its striking corbeled courses.

(assuming it were solid) of about 88 million cubic feet. According to tradition the entrance was on the north side and the corridors were aligned with the circumpolar stars ever-present on the horizon to ensure immortality. The present ENTRANCE, lower than the original entrance, is linked by a passageway to the "real" access corridor. There is "nothing to see" in the pyramid apart from the pyramid itself, whose interior construction and remarkable atmosphere (although the stale air can sometimes be tiring) make it a true architectural masterpiece.

INSIDE THE PYRAMID. The layout of the chambers and passageways inside the pyramid has been modified over the years. The descending gallery intersects an ascending corridor that opens out into the Grand Gallery. From the bottom of the gallery a horizontal passage leads into the so-called QUEEN'S CHAMBER (these traditional names have no factual basis). At the top of the Grand Gallery a sort of antechamber with granite portcullises leads into the main chamber, known as the KING'S CHAMBER. The precision and perfection of its construction make the chamber, which is almost 20 feet high, 34 feet long and 17 feet wide, an unrivaled piece of architecture. It is entirely sheathed in granite and the ceiling consists of granite monoliths. Above the chamber five "discharge" compartments were built to relieve the enormous weight above the ceiling. There is no doubt that this was the burial chamber of Khufu himself. The king's lidless granite sarcophagus is still in the chamber, although entirely empty, most probably plundered toward the end of the Old Kingdom. The architectural complex of Khufu is not limited to these underground chambers. The funerary or "UPPER" TEMPLE with its basalt flagging can still be seen on the east side of the pyramid. Recent (1992–3) discoveries have also made it possible to excavate part of the valley or "lower" temple, as well as a so-called "annex" pyramid in the village of Nazlet el-Saman.

SOLAR BARQUE. The so-called "Solar Barque" is preserved in an unprepossessing building, on the south side of the pyramid, above the 100-foot boat pit in which it was discovered, completely dismantled, in 1954. It

> "To the west stood the Pyramids, swathed in gold dust and the fire of the setting sun."
>
> Auguste Mariette

took several years to restore the 140-foot, cedar-wood barque to its original elegance, complete with cabin and long oars. All the elements are joined with ropes and pegs, with not a nail in sight. The significance of such grandiose vessels is still the subject of much discussion. They may have actually been used, in particular for the king's funeral, or they may have been a representation of the Night- and Day-Barques of the Sun: a promise of immortality or at least of resurrection. Near the Pyramid of Khufu are two other monuments which, although they cannot be visited and are relatively unattractive, form part of the history of the site. The TOMB OF QUEEN HETEPHERES, the mother of Khufu, is one of the few royal tombs left untouched by grave robbers. The funerary treasures, discovered by an American expedition led by George Reisner, can be seen in the Cairo Museum ▲ *276*. Also near the Great Pyramid, the temple of one of the smaller

Climbing to the top of the pyramid was for a long time an obligatory if dangerous pastime among (even some of the most illustrious) tourists. This is now strictly forbidden.

Akhet-Khufu (the Ancient Egyptian name for the monument and architectural complex, meaning "the Horizon of Khufu") dates, like its two neighbors, from c. 2500 BC (it is impossible to give a more precise date for these early periods).

Although the climb to the top of the Pyramid of Khufu (Cheops) was perilous, it still proved a very popular undertaking among travelers and tourists. Each block of stone measured between 2 and 3 feet and the climb was far from easy.

The Pyramid of Khufu (surmounted by a pyramidion made of a single granite or basalt block) stood 479 feet high and covered an area of 12 acres. It consisted of 2½ million stone blocks, each 35 cubic feet, arranged in 201 courses.

In the center of the King's Chamber (33 feet long by 16 wide and 16 high) the pharaoh once lay in his sarcophagus surrounded by his now non-existent treasures. In spite of the many precautions taken by the tomb builders to obstruct and conceal the corridors, grave robbers managed to find their way into the tomb on several occasions.

"Suddenly the corridor rose steeply. The torch illuminated an imposing gallery, about 26 feet high, with corbeled upper courses. Breathing became easier and we might have been at the entrance to a magnificent temple were it not for the steps carved in this slippery slope. But they were only shallow notches about three feet apart and we advanced with great difficulty, often falling, unless supported by the Bedouins who climbed like cats along this eerie corridor. The dry stone blocks are so marvellously positioned that you would not get a pin between them."

Edouard Schuré

Drawings by Belzoni ● 95 showing the exposed entrance of the Pyramid of Khafre and the interior of the great burial chamber which he discovered in 1818.

(queens' or princesses') pyramids in the complex of Khufu was later converted into the SHRINE OF ISIS, "Mistress of the Pyramid" and *paredra* of Osiris, "Lord of Su-menu", whose own shrine was situated not far from the Sphinx, on the edge of the desert.

PYRAMID OF KHAFRE. Although the pyramid of Khafre (Chephren) is not quite as big (originally over 470 feet high, today over 446 feet) as his father's, it is nonetheless a striking sight with its white "cap" at the apex, the remains of the dazzling limestone casing which once completely covered the pyramids of both Khufu and Khafre. The interior is less complicated but just as impressive as that of Khufu. The Pyramid of Khafre, however, is renowned not so much just for itself but for the entire pyramidal complex: the partly preserved ascending causeway (descending if you approach it from the pyramid) and, lower down, at the entrance to the valley (where there is now a Sound and Light Auditorium), the impressive and extremely well-preserved valley or "lower" temple. Abu Hol, the Great Sphinx, which has become indissociably linked with the Pyramids, is also a "must" for all visitors to Egypt.

THE SPHINX. The Sphinx of Giza was undoubtedly carved out of a rocky spur which suggested its shape. Although it has long been the victim of erosion, and damage from upsurges of underground water, it has been cleared of sand and restored several times since antiquity, and remains one of the undisputed wonders of a civilization renowned for its architectural achievements. This colossus of Khafre (240 feet long and 65 feet high) is both the guardian and symbol of royalty. Other meanings have been attributed to it over the ages. During the New Kingdom it was seen as a representation of Re-Harakhti, the falcon-headed sun god, or Horem-Akhet (Horus on the Horizon, Harmachis in

Greek), whom everyone came to worship and entreat. Young princes raised in Memphis came here either to meditate upon the concept of power or in search of legitimacy. Legend has it that the future Thutmose IV built a stele between the feet of the Sphinx following a dream that he had there in which the god Harmachis asked him to clear away the sand from his feet in return for his royalty. During the New Kingdom the Sphinx was also seen as a representation of the Syro-Canaanite god Hurun: an illustration of the ambient cosmopolitanism and the cultural and religious parallels of the period.

PYRAMID OF MENKAURE. The Pyramid of Menkaure (Mycerinus), which is much smaller than the other two, is beautifully constructed, distinguished by its red granite lower courses and extremely well-preserved underground chambers. An enormous stone sarcophagus that was found inside the pyramid and sent to England in the 19th century was unfortunately lost when the ship transporting it sank off the coast of Spain. Visitors leaving Menkaure are reminded of the semi-legendary tradition that the pyramid was built by Nitocris, the queen of the last of the 6th-Dynasty pharaohs (who is sometimes confused with the Saite courtesan Rhodopis). Until the 19th century it was generally believed that the pyramid was haunted and that as it approached noon the ghostly figure of a beautiful, naked woman would appear and cause the downfall of overzealous visitors.

"View of the Sphinx, Abu Hol (Father of Terror). The gray of the sand, the Pyramids and the Sphinx are steeped in a deep rosy hue; in the intensely blue sky eagles glide and circle slowly round the summits."
Gustave Flaubert

341

Head of the Great Sphinx,
by Luigi Mayer (1755–1803).

Oedipus, oil on canvas
by Jean-Léon Gérôme (1824–1904).

Profile of the Head of the Great Sphinx,
by Frederik Ludvig Norden (1708–42).

*View of the Head of the Great Sphinx and the
Second Pyramid,* by L.F. Cassas (1756–1827).

For a long time the Sphinx
(which dates from c. 2500 BC)
remained engulfed by sand. In
1853 Auguste Mariette ● *96*
began to clear it, a task which
was completed over forty
years later. *The Sphinx*
(right), by David
Roberts.

The Sphinx, watercolor
by Emile Prisse d'Avenue (1807–79).

*Head of the Great Sphinx and the Pyramids of
Giza*, print by David Roberts (1796–1864).

The Sphinx and the Pyramid of Giza, drawing
by Louis-Amable Crapelet (1822–67).

"Simoon" in the Desert, print
by David Roberts (1796–1825).

"Its head, neck, shoulders, and breasts
are still uncovered; its face, though
worn and broken, is mild, amiable,
and intelligent, seeming, among the
tombs around it, like a divinity
guarding the dead."

John Lloyd Stephens

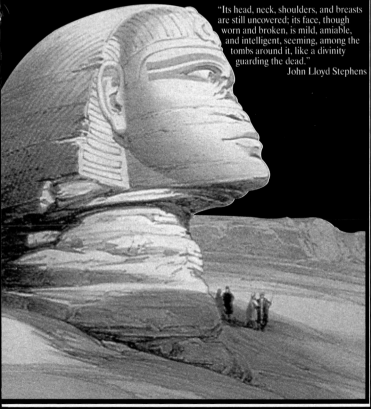

▲ SAQQARA

🖼 🏃 One/two days
◆ G D5

**SAQQARA, AN
IMMENSE
NECROPOLIS** ✪
A visit to the
Memphis necropolis
can take from half
to a whole day. It
means an early start,
as the trip involves a
lot of walking: the
tombs are in the open
desert, set far apart
from each other.
Start with the
spectacular funeral
complex at Djoser
and the intriguing
Step Pyramid, then
visit the catacombs at
Serapeum and finish
with a visit to
whichever tombs
are open that
particular day.

HARRANIA
The architect
Ramesses Wissa
Wassef ▲ 282 trained
young artists (in
whom he recognized
spontaneity and an
innate sense of
beauty) who, from
early childhood, had
revived an extremely
ancient tradition and
achieved total mastery
of design and color in
their carpets. His
work was continued
after his death and
the carpets produced
in his workshop are
unrivaled, in spite of
many imitations.

SAQQARA

With Giza ▲ 334, Saqqara is one of the two main necropolises
of Memphis ▲ 332. Its monuments cover every period of
Egyptian history, including the Archaic period (these are now
engulfed by sand), the 3rd Dynasty and the Christian era.
Stretching across the desert is a string of non-royal pyramids
and cemeteries which also depended on Memphis. Although
these sites may not feature on many tourist itineraries (some
are in any case military zones and therefore out of bounds),
they are an important part of understanding Ancient Egypt
and especially the Old Kingdom. North of Giza, at the point
where the Nile Delta begins to diverge, the remains of the
Pyramid of Djedefre, the son of Khufu, can be seen at ABU
RAWASH. To the south is the site (out of bounds) of ZAWIYET
EL-ARYAN with its unfinished pyramid, which is in fact a vast,
preliminary excavation.
ABUSIR. The Abusir cemetery contains the pyramids of the
principal 5th-Dynasty pharaohs: (from north to south)
Sahure, Niuserre, Neferirkare and
Neferefre, all closely associated with the
worship of the solar god Re (who forms part

of each of their names). The pyramids are of average size and badly preserved although some still have their causeway (access ramp) and part of their funerary temple. The vast TOMB OF PTAHSHEPSES, situated between the Pyramids of Sahure and Niuserre, has been excavated and restored by an expedition from Czechoslovakia, which has worked regularly on the site for many years. The tomb is well worth a visit. A short walk across the desert brings you to the site of the sun temples of ABU GHUROB, to the north of Abusir. The TEMPLE OF NIUSERRE is open to the sky and has a central obelisk (known as a *benben*) symbolizing the light of the sun. Much further south are the Pyramids of Dahshur ▲ *354*.

▲ *354*

NECROPOLIS OF MEMPHIS
Generally speaking the various branches of the Necropolis of Memphis correspond to a fairly recent (19th-century) breakdown which linked each site to a modern village in the valley, although these subdivisions are not always well founded. For example, north and central Saqqara are more closely linked to Abusir than to South Saqqara. And it should not be forgotten that the site is in the desert "west of Memphis".

GETTING TO SAQQARA. Most people travel to Saqqara by road. Alternatively you can cross the desert on horseback from the Pyramids of Giza. As you turn west at Bedrashein (not far from Memphis) it soon becomes obvious, whether you are following the road along the canal or the main highway leading toward Upper Egypt, that the region is becoming an albeit distant and partly agricultural suburb of Cairo. The landscape becomes increasingly urban: factories, poultry farms, houses, highways, private villas and "carpet schools" (which are nothing

more than workshops and shops centered around the mass tourist industry). The village of HARRANIA, a few miles from the main pyramid route is an interesting place to stop. It is the home of the famous carpet weavers who work in the Wissa Wassef ▲ *282* workshop (which also has a shop). As you leave the road which follows the canal and fork right (toward the west), the plateau will gradually come into view with the summit of the Step Pyramid over to the left. Once through the ticket barrier the road (which soon becomes a track) takes you into the heart of this vast site whose archeological and artistic wealth is truly overwhelming. As there are usually only a few hours allowed for this visit, it is important to be selective and well organized. The many monuments at Saqqara are often some distance apart, but you will find it extremely rewarding if you take your time walking across the plateau.

Necropolis of Abusir: the pyramids of Niuserre and Neferirkare (right), and the Pyramid of Sahure.

The funeral complex of Djoser with the remains of the Monastery of St Jeremiah in the foreground.

JUBILEE CHAPELS
The pavilions and chapels (in fact a series of décors and façades whose stone

doors are permanently open onto passageways suitable for ghostly processions) were built by Imhotep to immortalize Djoser's jubilee celebrations.

STEP PYRAMID. The visit usually starts with the Step Pyramid and vast funeral complex of Djoser, the 3rd-Dynasty pharaoh. The complex is truly remarkable, if only for its building materials, as this was the first monumental structure to be built entirely of stone. It is also one of the most ancient monuments in Egypt, and even the world, as it dates from c. 2500 BC. Imhotep, the highly talented architect and master of works of Djoser, was also a vizier, doctor of medicine and literary scholar. Over the centuries the figure of Imhotep assumed a superhuman dimension, becoming a sort of demigod of medicine and healing whom the Greeks associated with Asclepius (Aesculapius). The Step Pyramid of Djoser is the culmination of an entire stage of development. Originally the pharaoh's tomb looked like a huge mastaba which was subsequently altered several times until it looked like several superposed mastabas, hence the six "steps" of the pyramid. Small stone blocks replaced the mudbrick used in the construction of previous royal tombs. The pyramid stands above a vast network of underground galleries, with stelae and blue-tiled chambers. Only the so-called Saïte gallery, refurbished for technical reasons at a later date, can be visited.

THE FUNERAL COMPLEX OF DJOSER. The funeral complex, the only one of its kind in the world, includes a funerary temple (now in ruins), situated on the north (and not the east) side of the pyramid. This is less interesting, however, than the impressive statue of Djoser (the original is in the Cairo Museum ▲ 276) which can be seen through two holes drilled in the wall of the *serdab* (hiding place). The temple and pyramid stood in a vast, rectangular precinct (1,820 feet long, 100 feet wide and about 33 feet high) whose redans and beautiful, honey-colored limestone can still be seen near the southeast corner. Here, too, is the only entrance into this vast complex. A long, narrow colonnade leads into the courtyard dominated, on the right, by the Step Pyramid and, on the left, by the southern mass of the enclosure wall.
Incorporated into the

wall is the access shaft to the SOUTH TOMB (reminiscent of the ancient royal burials of Abydos) whose apartments, which are decorated in the same way as those of the pyramid, are unfortunately closed to the public. From the top of the walls there is a magnificent view of south Saqqara with the Pyramids of Dahshur to the south. An inset in the courtyard side of the wall is decorated with a frieze of cobras.

JUBILEE CHAPELS. Back across the courtyard is the purely symbolic (and to some extent fictitious) complex built in beautiful bonded stone, a permanent monument to Djoser's royalty and so-called *heb-sed* (jubilee) celebrations. Royal jubilees, which were usually held to celebrate the thirtieth anniversary of a monarch's reign, dated back to early Pharaonic times. They were usually held in temporary structures built for the occasion. Djoser wanted to immortalize the occasion with permanent structures, hence the Jubilee Court and chapels and the simulated structures representing buildings associated with the dual monarchy of Upper and Lower Egypt: the House of the South and House of the North, whose capitals are decorated with the heraldic plants of both kingdoms.

PYRAMID OF UNIS. A flight of steps on the south side of the enclosure wall brings you down into the precinct where you can walk along the "streets" of tombs to the pyramid of the last of the 5th-Dynasty pharaohs. The pyramid, which has lost most of its outer casing, was the first to have its chambers and underground galleries decorated, or rather inscribed. In fact the regular columns of blue-painted hieroglyphics inscribed on the walls are the earliest known version of the so-called Pyramid Texts. The only other pyramids containing these texts (those of Tety, Pepy I, Mernere, Pepy II and the queens of Pepy II) are all at Saqqara and date from the 6th Dynasty.

Only the texts of Unis and Tety are accessible. Follow the ruins of the covered causeway which once linked the pyramid and Upper Temple to the Valley Temple to see the remains of the reliefs which once decorated its walls.

The funeral complex of Djoser (above), workmen on the site of the Saqqara excavations and the reopening of the Step Pyramid in 1987.

THE FUNERAL COMPLEX OF DJOSER
You will be encouraged to take your time when visiting the vast architectural complex of the Pyramid of Djoser if you spare a thought for the difficult and painstaking task of excavating, studying and partially restoring it. The French architect Jean-Philippe Lauer (left, standing behind the wall), the master of works for almost seventy years and undisputed pyramid expert, returns to work on the site every winter.

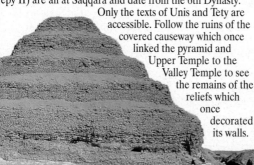

Colonnaded entrance

South tomb and "cobra" wall

This vast funeral complex is the work of the architect Imhotep, minister of Djoser, the 3rd-Dynasty pharaoh who founded the capital of Memphis. The complex was innovative in its use of stone as a building material and in the form of its pyramid. The systematic excavation of the site was begun in 1927 by the Egyptian Department of Antiquities and continued by Jean-Philippe Lauer, who also instigated a large-scale restoration program.

Granite statue of King Djoser, found on the Saqqara site.

Imaginary reconstruction of the construction of the Step Pyramid.

Step Pyramid   North court   Enclosure wall

Heb-sed (jubilee) court

uth court

ENCLOSURE WALL
The outer wall,
punctuated with redans and
the traditional decoration of false
doors, encloses an area of about 37 acres.

**COLONNADED
ENTRANCE**
The first court is
reached along a
covered gallery
supported by engaged
semi-columns,
sometimes joined in
pairs. The so-called
"fasciculate" columns
represent the stems of
plants bound in
bundles.

"COBRA" WALL
On the interior façade of the enclosure wall is
a series of "dummy" doors with their blinds
rolled up, surmounted by a frieze of
protective cobras.

"HEB-SED" (JUBILEE) PAVILION
The solid stonework is surmounted by an
arched roof. Slender columns with double-
arched capitals decorate the façade which is
preceded by a low wall.

One of the granite sarcophagi (above), which contained the mummified bulls. Mariette recorded twenty-four, placed in chambers dug on either side of an underground corridor.

Although the causeway no longer extends as far as the Valley Temple (whose few remains can be seen near the barrier closing off the site), it is still flanked, about midway along, by mastabas: the rock-cut TOMB OF NEFER with its fresh-looking, colored scenes (limited access: ask for information) and the impressive, constructed tombs of NYANKH-KHNUM and KHNUMHOTEP with their perfect colors. The MONASTERY OF ST JEREMIAH (Apa Jeremias) lies to the southeast, beyond the "boundary" represented by the causeway of Unis. Many of the architectural elements of the building have been taken from Pharaonic monuments.

CEMETERY OF THE NEW KINGDOM. Excavations begun by an Anglo-Dutch mission about twenty years ago, in a vast area to the west, revealed a cemetery of the New Kingdom (late 18th and 19th Dynasties). Some impressive and often superbly decorated tombs, which have lain forgotten beneath the sand since they were plundered by 19th-century grave robbers, are being gradually uncovered. They include the TOMB OF HOREMHEB, the general who became king. He was one of the successors of Amenhotep IV (Akhenaten) who, after becoming pharaoh, had a tomb constructed in the Valley of the Kings ▲ 417 where he was buried. However, his Memphite tomb remained an important monument for funeral worship. The surviving reliefs are remarkable for their blend of idealization and "realistic" observation of scenes of mourning, tributes and prisoners of war. It is also possible to visit the so-called Persian Tombs, more than 65 feet deep, which date from the 26th (Saïte period) and 27th Dynasties. On the way back to the Pyramid of Djoser are the TOMBS OF PRINCESS IDUT (6th Dynasty) and the VIZIER MEHU, both decorated with beautiful scenes in relief. In an area to the northwest, where MARIETTE'S HOUSE once stood (it has since been destroyed), a tent serves as a makeshift cafeteria.

SERAPEUM. The Serapeum was a vast religious complex which extended from the eastern edge of the site to

the tombs of the Apis Bulls, via a long avenue of sphinxes. To a certain extent it also represented the religious, intellectual and cultural convergence of two civilizations: Egypt and Greece. The Serapeum (the Latin form of the Greek "Serapeion") is dedicated to Serapis, a hybrid or "synthesized" divinity created by the early Ptolemies in an attempt to bring Egyptians and Greeks closer together. Serapis is, as it were, a compound of Osiris and Apis, the sacred animal of Ptah; hence the association between the Serapeum and the tombs of the Apis Bulls. A very badly damaged HEMICYCLE (a semicircle of Greek statues),which includes such illustrious figures as Plato, Heraclitus, Homer, Hesiod and Pindar, stands near the entrance to the catacombs. It is a fine example of the Graeco-Egyptian relationship, which was more than just a close association.

MASTABA OF TI. Near the tombs of the Apis Bulls is the remarkable 5th-Dynasty mastaba of Ti, the largest in the necropolis. The decorations in the courtyard, vestibule and chapels depict the activities of a high-ranking figure of the Old Kingdom. Other mastabas which are well worth a visit include the TOMBS OF PTAHHOTEP and AKHETHOTEP, to the

Scene from the tomb of Nefer and Qa'a-Hay depicting the making and baking of bread.

SERAPEUM
This is one of the most incredible sites in Egypt: mummified bulls were buried in monolithic sarcophagi in vast underground chambers. The practice went on for centuries and, in the tombs open to the public, until the early Christian era.

NEW DISCOVERIES
The recently
discovered tomb of
the vizier Aper-El
(below). The domed
interior of the
Pyramid of Mernere,
discovered by the
Archeological
Mission at Saqqara, is
decorated with stars
(below, bottom).

northwest of the Pyramid of Djoser. Further south is the "Street of Tombs", which lies beyond the PYRAMID OF USERKAF (5th Dynasty) and PYRAMID OF TETY (6th Dynasty) where the walls of the burial chambers are inscribed with Pyramid Texts. Then there are the MASTABAS OF MERERUKA (sometimes known as Mera), which has reliefs and a magnificent statue set within a niche, KAGEMNI (or Memi) and ANKHMAHOR. The latter is also known as the "Doctors' Tomb" because some of its images represent surgical operations. This is the end of the "standard" tour of the site. But Saqqara is not just a cemetery of the Old Kingdom (although monuments from this period tend to be in the majority) and the later Egyptian and Greek periods are well represented. There are also the cliff tombs, which include, for

example, the tomb of the vizier Bakenrenef (Bocchoris) excavated by the Pisa Mission, and the many animal necropolises (for the cows that bore the Apis Bulls, dogs, cats, ibis, baboons and falcons) associated with shrines which flourished here in the later centuries BC. The New Kingdom is also represented on the site. For example, the cliff just north of the road, dominated by an official rest house, contains a series of New-Kingdom rock tombs dating mainly from the 18th Dynasty. For ten or so years the French Bubasteion Mission (named after the shrine of the goddess Bastet, which stood on the site at the time of the Serapeum) has been excavating the tombs of such important figures as the CHANCELLOR MERY-RE and the VIZIER APER-EL (the jewelry from the tomb is on display in the Cairo Museum) from the reigns of Amenhotep III and Amenhotep IV (Akhenaten). Finally it should be remembered that the site of Saqqara extends much further south. Two groups of monuments are well worth a visit, even though they are not on most tourist itineraries. On the edge of the desert are the PYRAMIDS OF DJEDKARE-ISESI and

TOMB OF APER-EL
The burial chamber
of Aper-El was
discovered, at a great
depth, by the
Bubasteion Mission.
In spite of the
plundering of the
monuments of
antiquity, the tomb
contained the
remains of the vizier
Aper-El (his statue is
seen on the right), his
wife and son
(General Huy) and
much of their
remarkable funeral
paraphernalia.

PEPY I and, further west, the PYRAMID OF MERNERE. The chambers of the last two (6th-Dynasty) pyramids are inscribed with Pyramid Texts and are being studied and restored by the French Mission at Saqqara. The mission, which is also excavating the religious complex of Pepy I, has made a recent discovery of pyramids belonging to the king's wives to south of the complex. Much further south the site of the MASTABA EL-FARA'UN (Pharaoh's Bench) can be found, as well as the unusual sarcophagus-shaped funerary monument of the 4th-Dynasty pharaoh Shepseskaf, and the PYRAMIDS OF PEPY II and his queens.

MEMPHIS
TO THE FAIYUM

DAHSHUR, *354*
LISHT, *356*
MEIDUM, *357*
ILLAHUN, *359*
IHNASIYA EL-MEDINA, *360*

1 CAIRO
2 GIZA
3 PYRAMID OF SENWOSRET III
4 RED PYRAMID
5 PYRAMID OF AMENEMHET II
6 BENT PYRAMID
7 PYRAMID OF AMENEMHET III
8 PYRAMIDS OF MAZGHUNA
9 PYRAMID OF SENWOSRET I
10 MEIDUM PYRAMID
11 PYRAMID OF AMENEMHET I
12 PYRAMID OF SEILA
13 ATFIH
14 ILLAHUN PYRAMID
15 SEDMENT EL-JEBEL
16 IHNASIYA EL-MEDINA
17 BENI SUEF
18 DISHASE

One day

◆ **G** C5-C4-D5-D6

DAHSHUR

"As the Nile widens out once again and flows between the slopes of Jebel Moqattam and a curtain of date palms, all the pyramids are visible. The Pyramid of Giza is almost out of sight, the old Pyramid of Saqqara is level with the boat and the Pyramids of Dahshur are drawing closer. Cairo has completely disappeared."
Eugène Fromentin

The site of Dahshur stands on the left bank of the Nile, about 16 miles south of Giza, in a restricted military zone. It is hoped, however, that the recent re-allocation of land will enable the site to be opened to the public in the not-too-distant future. The site includes two 4th-Dynasty stone pyramids and three 12th-Dynasty mudbrick pyramids, both groups lying parallel to the Nile, as well as the remains of necropolises and an Old-Kingdom town.

PYRAMID OF SENWOSRET III. The original 12th-Dynasty monument, now a 98-foot-high mudbrick hillock with a central (excavated) crater, had a limestone revetment and stood 328 feet square and 256 feet high. An outer access shaft, opening to the west, led to the granite-lined funeral apartments (robbed during Antiquity and today inaccessible) whose burial vault contains a red granite sarcophagus. An underground corridor to the northeast linked the four tombs dug to the north of the pyramid where Jacques de Morgan discovered the jewelry of the princesses Sat-Hathor and Mereret, now on display in the Cairo Museum ▲ 276.

Surrounded by a brick enclosure wall, the FUNERARY COMPLEX (annex tombs, north and west chapels) was probably inspired by that of Djoser. Outside the enclosure wall, to the south, was the vaulted chamber which housed the cedar-wood barques and their sled (Cairo Museum). The east temple is in ruins. Scattered across the mountainside to the south are (inaccessible) Old-Kingdom tombs and the remains of the town of the Pyramid of Snefru.

"WHITE" PYRAMID OF AMENEMHET II. The extensively damaged limestone pyramid (12th Dynasty) had eight sand-filled strengthening walls arranged in the shape of a star. The (inaccessible) north entrance opened onto a straight corridor which led down to the split-level funeral chamber, closed by two granite portcullises, which contained a sandstone sarcophagus set in the floor. Inside the rectangular enclosure wall, all that remains of the funerary temple to the east are a few scattered blocks and a paved way leading eastward. The several tombs (including that of Princess Khnumet) to the west contained jewelry and diadems which can now be seen in the Cairo Museum. To the north of the complex is the Old-Kingdom necropolis excavated by Jacques de Morgan, while the limestone blocks and remains of a paved way to the south could belong to a Middle-Kingdom pyramid.

PYRAMID OF AMENEMHET III. The original 12th-Dynasty monument consisted of a pyramid (341 feet square and 266 feet high), surmounted by a black granite pyramidion (Cairo Museum). The underground chambers which open to the east were lined with Tura limestone. They formed a complicated system of three sets of chambers: the royal burial chamber containing a red granite sarcophagus, decorated with projections and redans; the queens' chamber; and a suite of rooms of indeterminate use to the south. Two gates (east and west) were set in the niched, inner enclosure wall. The east funerary temple has virtually disappeared; only its paved way has survived. To the north of the way traces of mudbrick (probably priests') dwellings were discovered. A line of twelve tombs, between the two enclosure walls to the north of the pyramid, have provided some valuable discoveries, including a wooden statue (Cairo Museum) of the *ka* of the 13th-Dynasty king Auybre-Hor. Private tombs dug during the Old Kingdom lie to the southwest. The two tombs of the second, older group of pyramids were constructed during the 4th Dynasty by King Snefru.

RED PYRAMID. The so-called Red Pyramid, to the north, is the earliest example of a "true" pyramid. Built from blocks of the local red stone and originally covered with Tura limestone, it was 722 feet square and stood 325 feet high. The access corridor to the tomb is on the north side and opens onto a suite of three rectangular rooms.

PYRAMID OF AMENEMHET III
The monument looks like a pile of mudbricks emerging from a mound of bricks and sand. The fragility of its construction, indicated by the restoration carried out during the Pharaonic period (supporting beams, limestone blocks) explains why the pyramid was

abandoned in favor of the Pyramid of Hawara ▲ *370* where the pharaoh was buried.

The so-called Red Pyramid is relatively well preserved. Its limestone pyramidion and the remains of the funerary temple were recently discovered to the east.

The northeast corner of the Bent Pyramid at Dahshur.

BENT PYRAMID. At the southern edge of the site this dual-angled pyramid still retains much of its limestone outer casing. Its name is derived from the inexplicable change in its angle of inclination: from 54° 27' to 43° 22' at a height of 160 feet. It has two entrances, each leading to two (inaccessible) series of chambers. The (still visible) brick walls of its upper temple once housed two stelae which stood either side of an offering table set in the floor. The lower temple, surrounded by a brick enclosure wall, consisted of a four-roomed antechamber, a court and, at the far end, a ten-pillared portico leading to six chapels.

MAZGHUNA. About 3 miles south of Dahshur a track leads westward from Mazghuna to a site occupied by two pyramids from the end of the 12th and 13th Dynasties, which are now nothing but heaps of rubble.

The pyramids of Amenemhet I and Senwosret I stand about one mile apart on opposite sides of a *wadi*. They are very badly damaged and look like two mounds of sand on the edge of the plateau. The Pyramid of Senwosret, to the north, looks like a 65-foot-high hill and is a larger version of the Pyramid of Amenemhet.

LISHT

Midway between Dahshur and Meidum the site of Lisht lies on the *jebel* to the northwest of the villages of Lisht and Maharraqa. The remains of Old-Kingdom and 11th-Dynasty tombs are obscured by the ruins of Itytawi, a residential town founded by the two first 12th-Dynasty kings.

PYRAMID OF AMENEMHET I. The pyramid was partially constructed from limestone blocks taken from Old-Kingdom monuments. The (inaccessible) north entrance, which lay behind a false granite door (Cairo Museum) at the back of a chapel, opened onto a corridor leading to an access shaft. The water level in the flooded burial chamber makes it impossible to visit. A few scattered blocks are all that remains of the funerary temple, built on a lower terrace to the east. Inside the double enclosure wall royal tombs lay to the west of the complex and several mastabas, including that of the vizier Antefoker, to the east. Outside the southwest corner of the wall, the (intact) tomb of Senebtisi and a number of papyri were discovered.

PYRAMID OF SENWOSRET I. The pyramid still has part of its limestone outer casing. It is built on a central strengthening framework of stone cross-walls in which the cavities formed by the walls are filled with stone blocks. On the pyramid's north side a chapel concealed the entrance to the (inaccessible) corridor which was lined with limestone and blocked with granite. The flooded burial vault makes excavation impossible. The monument, in the center of the funeral complex, is surrounded by a double limestone (inner) and brick (outer) enclosure wall. Between the two walls are nine pyramids belonging to the royal family. The funerary temple on the east side was based on the design of the Old-Kingdom temples. Part of the paved way of the lower temple has been discovered. The mastabas outside the complex include that of Imhotep, chancellor and high priest of Heliopolis, containing two magnificent statues of Senwosret I.

MEIDUM

The pyramid, reached via the road about 5 miles southwest of the village of Meidum, is known as El-Ahram el-Kaddab ("the false pyramid"). It is thought to have been begun by King Huni (3rd Dynasty) and completed by Snefru (4th Dynasty). It was originally a seven-step pyramid, but another story was probably added prior to the smooth, limestone revetment which made it a "true" pyramid. It was undoubtedly used as a quarry, which accounts for its present appearance: a sort of terraced tower emerging from a huge mound of debris. The limestone funerary temple, located in the center of the east side, consists of two offset rooms leading to an open court where two arched stelae stand on either side of an altar. The outer wall once enclosed two tombs, one to the north and the other to the south, most probably the satellite pyramid. An open way

The entrance of the Meidum Pyramid, on the north side, is about 65 feet above the ground. A descending corridor leads to a rock-cut antechamber once closed by a wooden

door. Beyond the chamber, a square shaft leads to the rectangular tomb (plundered during the New Kingdom) with its vaulted and corbeled roof.

THE GEESE OF MEIDUM
Many tombs dating from the Old Kingdom to the Roman period are scattered north-to-south across the hillside around the pyramid complex. The nearby necropolis is divided into three sectors: the west, northwest and, of particular interest, the north sector with mastabas nos. 1 to 17 from the reign of Snefru. The mastaba of Neferma't and Atet (no. 16) has provided some fine inlaid reliefs and the famous "geese of Meidum" (below).

357

PYRAMID OF SENWOSRET II AT ILLAHUN

The pyramid was built around a 40-foot-high limestone core. Limestone walls in the shape of a star form the framework of the mudbrick structure, which was originally covered with a limestone revetment and surmounted by a black granite pyramidion. It would have been about 157 feet high and 351 feet square with an angle of inclination of

42° 35'. Each side was separated by a sand-filled trench. The monument was surrounded by a niched enclosure wall, partly constructed and partly dug. The (inaccessible) entrance to the southwest opened onto a complex system of four access shafts and two tombs. The deeper, vaulted tomb is lined with granite and contains a sarcophagus.

running east–west for a distance of 230 yards used to lead to the enclosure wall of the pyramid town, Djed-Snefru, to the east. To the south of the way the remains of a construction ramp are still visible.

GERZA AND RIQQA. The site lies on the left bank of the Nile about 3 miles north of Meidum and less than 1½ miles north-west of the village of Riqqa, which has a brick and cement works. Gerza ("Grgt" in Pharaonic Egyptian and "Kerke" in Greek) gave its name to the second half of the pre-Dynastic Nagada (Gerzean) period. The necropolises, spread over a distance of almost 3 miles, were divided into two groups: Gerza and Riqqa. The pre-Dynastic Gerzean tombs were oval pits dug in the sand in which the dead were laid on their side, surrounded by funerary paraphernalia. The nearby cemeteries of Riqqa, to the south, contained the New-Kingdom tombs.

SEILA. Situated about 7 miles to the west of the Meidum Pyramid on the Jebel er-Rus, the three-step Pyramid of Seila is covered with limestone debris. It should have had four steps and probably dates from the 3rd or 4th Dynasty. Its function remains unknown. It is one of a group of seven monuments of this type scattered throughout Egypt. The excavation of Coptic priests' tombs revealed thousands of papyri (some religious) as well as white linen robes.

ABUSIR EL-MELEQ. Turn west off the main Cairo–Beni Suef road at Ishmant and continue for about 6 miles. In addition to pre-Dynastic remains, the site of Abusir el-Meleq had sepulchers from the Hyksos period and, in the secondary necropolis of Ihnasiya el-Medina, priests' tombs from the Saite period. Osiris was worshipped here, and blocks from a temple built by Nectanebo II were used to build the mosque. In 750 the last Ommiad caliph, Marwan II, fled Baghdad but was killed by the Abbasid usurpers. He is buried nearby.

ATFIH. The town of Atfih stands about 2 miles east of the Nile on the ancient site of Aphroditopolis. The Egyptian name "Tp-yhwt", meaning "the first of the cows" (Hathor), became "Petpeh" in Coptic, from which the Arabic "Atfih" was derived. Although infrequent, past excavations have discovered animal necropolises and Ptolemaic family tombs. The recently discovered sepulchers of cows in huge limestone tombs are not open to the public.

ILLAHUN

The Pyramid of Senwosret II stands about 2 miles northwest of the village of Illahun, on the right bank of Joseph's Canal (regulated by two barrage-bridges which have replaced the dam built by the Middle-Kingdom pharaohs). The village lies midway between Beni Suef and Medinet el-Faiyum ▲ *368*. The ancient town of Ro-hent became Lahone ("mouth of the canal") in Coptic. A mudbrick enclosure wall (in addition to that of the pyramid) surrounded the remains of a red granite funerary temple to the east, eight mastabas and the Queen's Pyramid to the north, and four access shafts in the south, three of which led to tombs. The tomb of Princess Sat-Hathor contained a fine collection of gold and silver jewelry, including a beautiful diadem (Cairo Museum). The remains of the lower temple were discovered to the east. The pyramid complex is at the center of a huge complex of buildings.

Necropolises dating from the pre-Dynastic to the Roman period are scattered across the hillsides around Illahun. Beneath a hillock, to the west, the architect of the pyramid, the chancellor Inpy, was laid to rest in a 12th-Dynasty mastaba. The town of Kahun, which was founded by Senwosret II to accommodate the pyramid workers, lay about half a mile to the west, across a *wadi*.

SEDMENT EL-JEBEL. Sedment, which is situated about 8 miles northwest of Ihnasiya, is the seat of a major Coptic pilgrimage. During the 15th century the large Coptic monastery, founded two centuries previously, was abandoned. The present monastery, Deir Mari Girgis ● *107*, was built in 1914.

BENI SUEF

The recently completed museum stands on the edge of the town. The first floor is devoted to Pharaonic (royal statues, Canopic jars, sarcophagi, sphinxes) and Graeco-Roman (funerary stelae, *tanagras*) antiquities which have mostly come from the nearby sites of Abusir and Heracleopolis Magna. However all the second-floor exhibits, comprising Coptic and Muslim antiquities, have come from the Cairo museums.

NECROPOLIS OF
IHNASIYA EL-MEDINA
A necropolis from the
Third Intermediate
period, excavated to
the southeast,
contained limestone
tombs. Numerous
fragments from the

Roman period
provide evidence of
buildings arranged
round a forum which
was later bordered by
churches. The four
granite columns at
Kenissa are thought
to belong to a temple
later converted into a
church.

IHNASIYA EL-MEDINA

Outside Beni Suef a secondary road leaves the main road and heads west (10 miles) to Ihnasiya el-Medina, also known as Ihnasiya Umm el-Kimam ("mother of the shards"). Nen-nesu or Hwt-nen-nesu ("house of the royal child"), capital of the Twentieth Nome of Upper Egypt, became the Greek town of Heracleopolis Magna and then Hennes in Coptic and Ahnas in Arabic. The site increased in importance during the 9th and 10th Dynasties when its princes controlled a large part and then the whole of Lower Egypt before being ousted by the Theban princes. During the Graeco-Roman period the capital of the nome of Heracleopolis worshipped a local ram-headed god, Herishef, who became Arsaphes, or Heracles in Greek. The ancient site covers an area of 165 acres, but there are no buildings between the town in the northeast and the villages to the west and south. The TEMPLE OF HERISHEF, built by Ramesses II, stood in a depression to the southwest. Its scattered blocks were hewn out of fine quartzite, but the present state of the site makes it difficult to see the original layout: a columned court, a columned portico with palm capitals and decorated with two seated colossi of Ramesses II, a hypostyle hall with twenty-four columns, which opened onto a pronaos and the sanctuary. Recent excavations to the south, near the Roman ramparts, have revealed an Archaic period cemetery, bricked-up officers' tombs from the First Intermediate period and a necropolis from the Third Intermediate period.

DISHASHA. The necropolis is situated on the west bank of Joseph's Canal, about 6 miles south of Ihnasiya el-Medina. Turn west off the Beni Suef–El-Minya road at Biba (Coptic church). Dishasha village lies about 14 miles northwest. A vast necropolis dating from the end of the Old Kingdom contains rock tombs and mastabas. Two are of particular interest: the rock tomb of Inty, whose chapel, cut out of three niches, is decorated with Old-Kingdom scenes and texts, and the tomb of Iteti, with its pillared canopy, rock-cut chapel and vaulted ceiling, and vertical access shaft.

THE FAIYUM

KOM USHIM, *366*
SHAKSHUK, *366*
DIMAI, *366*
DIONYSIAS, *366*
MEDINET MADI, *368*
MEDINET EL-FAIYUM, *368*
UMM EL-BRIGAT, *369*
DEIR EL-MALAK GHOBRIAL, *369*
PYRAMID OF HAWARA, *370*

At less than an hour's drive from Cairo, the
Faiyum offers an extremely rapid and restful
change of scenery. Since 1993 it has been
linked to the capital by a four-lane toll
expressway and can easily be visited in a day,
although a longer stay is certainly justified.
The Faiyum is in fact a microcosm of Egypt,
bringing together the most beautiful aspects
of the country's landscapes: fields and palm
trees, water and desert, mountains and
ruins. Its several outstanding natural
features include the vast salt lake BIRKET
QARUN. The many, mainly Ptolemaic and
Roman, archeological sites may not have
the imposing splendor of the sites of
Upper Egypt, but they do have the
charm of isolated and almost
forgotten ruins. The Faiyum, in spite
of appearances, is not in fact an
oasis. Although it is surrounded by
desert, the vast depression (692
square miles) in which it
lies is linked to
the Nile by one

1 KARANIS
2 SHAKSHUK
3 DIMAI
4 QASR EL-SAGHA
5 QASR QARUN
6 MEDINET MADI
7 MEDINET EL-FAIYUM
8 UMM EL-BRIGAT
9 DEIR EL-MALAK GHOBRIAL
10 PYRAMID OF HAWARA
11 PYRAMID OF ILLAHUN

One/two days
◆ H B5-B6-C5-C6

of its tributaries, JOSEPH'S CANAL or Bahr Yussuf, which runs
parallel to the Nile for a distance of 275 miles. The Faiyum
was originally a lake, the ancestor of Lake Qarun, which is
barely one tenth (just under 83 square miles) of the area
covered several million years ago. During the Middle
Kingdom the lake's water supply was cut off when the Nile
was canalized and diverted for irrigation. As evidenced by its
fauna this was originally a freshwater lake but, exposed to
constant evaporation and used extravagantly for irrigation,
the water has reached a level of above 3 percent salinity.
Although few fish can tolerate such high salt levels, it is
traditionally maintained that specimens up to 6 feet long
inhabit the depths of the lake (55 feet). Fishing (closed season
between March and June) is a vital supplementary activity for
the local inhabitants. The Greeks called the lake Moeris,
while the Egyptians called it Pa Yom ("the sea") from which
the modern name of the province was derived.
HISTORY. The Faiyum is
renowned for its

THE GOD SOBEK
All the towns of the
Faiyum had a temple
dedicated to the
crocodile god Sobek,
protector of the
nome. A crocodile
mummy (below).

363

prehistoric
remains, with
Neolithic man in
particular leaving traces of early populations of hunters and
fishers. During the Old Kingdom the marshlands and reed
beds of To-She ("land of the lake") were rich with fauna and
were a favorite hunting-ground for the pharaohs and nobility.
Crocodiles abounded, the embodiment of the god Sobek who,
until the end of the Roman occupation, remained the
protector of the nome. Each town dedicated a temple to
him and he was worshipped as Suchos, Soknopaiou,
Petesuchos and Pnepheros. But this fertile region could
not remain purely a place of leisure and enjoyment and,
on the initiative of Senwosret II, the powerful rulers of the
Middle Kingdom began a systematic development of the
land with irrigation systems, canals and a dam on the
Joseph's Canal. The Faiyum became the most fertile region
in Egypt and received particular attention from its
principal benefactor, Amenemhet III, who was so
enchanted by its beauty that he abandoned his pyramid at
Dahshur ▲ *354* in favor of one he had built at Hawara. The
inhabitants of the Faiyum deified the pharaoh who was
worshipped for the next two thousand years.
GRAECO-ROMAN PERIOD. Many centuries later the Faiyum
had a second protector, Ptolemy II Philadelphus (3rd century
BC), the first of the Lagides to adopt the Egyptian tradition
(convenient from the dynastic point of view) of marrying his
own sister. He named the most beautiful province of Egypt
after this beloved sister, Arsinoe, a name which it kept until
the end of the Roman Empire. Ptolemy II transformed the
Faiyum by settling the Greek veterans of his army there. This
new population brought prosperity to the province by
developing and perfecting its irrigation system. At the time
the surface area under cultivation (almost 618 square miles)
represented 10 percent of fertile Egypt. Although the present
level of the lake is 33 feet lower, which has released half its
surface area, the area of cultivated land in the modern Faiyum
is less than it was in the nome of Arsinoe. The province,
which was closely associated with the city of Alexandria, was
always regarded by the Ptolemies as a sort of experimental
region, under Greek control, for the development of crops
and the introduction of new species such as the apricot tree.

The Roman occupation gradually reduced Arsinoe's golden age to nothing. Subjected to a colonial-type economy and overwhelmed by a system of absurd and ruinous taxation, the *fellaheen* were forced to leave their villages. The province, which began to decline in the middle of the 3rd century, was finally and completely ruined by the 4th and only recovered some of its former glory during the reign of Mohammed Ali (1805–49).

PAPYRUS. According to a custom particularly associated with the nome of Arsinoe, human and crocodile mummies were covered with a thick binding of used or new papyrus. This layer, made up of all kinds of texts (including everyday writings, letters, accounts and exercises) was complemented by the discovery of piles of old archives. Together they provide a detailed description of every aspect of the daily life of the nome.

▲ THE FAIYUM

TEMPLES OF KARANIS
The TEMPLE OF THE SOUTH (below) is the older of the two temples of Karanis. Built of stone, it is dated by a still-legible, Greek inscription on the lintel of the main doorway in which the name of the original dedicatee, Nero, has been altered to that of his uncle, Claudius. The temple includes

three rooms linked by a wide vestibule. The TEMPLE OF THE NORTH is almost a total ruin, but pools and steam rooms of the Roman baths can still be seen.

DIMAI
The ruins of Dimai are both striking and mysterious. They are buried beneath great tumuli, red with shards of glass and pottery and strewn with all kinds of fragments.

KOM USHIM: RUINS OF KARANIS. After the Avenue of the Pyramids follow the signs for Alexandria and then turn off left onto the road to the Faiyum. The NEW MUSEUM OF ANTIQUITIES is due to be built at this intersection to replace the museum in the Midan at-Tahrir ▲ *280*. After crossing an expanse of desert, as the road begins to be bordered by trees, the ruins of Karanis lie over to the left. A small museum houses relics from excavations in the region. Of all the towns in the nome of Arsinoe, Karanis is undoubtedly the one for which there is the most information, because of the well-preserved state of the everyday objects and papyrus. The town was founded during the reign of Ptolemy II around a temple dedicated to Petesuchos, a crocodile god. As it spread northward a second temple was built. After a period of decline the town prospered until the 3rd century BC before finally disappearing in the early 5th century.

SHAKSHUK. About 2 miles after Karanis turn right and follow the signs for the inn known as the *Auberge du Lac*, once a favorite winter resort and hunting lodge with King Farouk, along a road which follows the shores of Lake Qarun. The village of Shakshuk stands at the far end of a small bay and its main street forms a corniche below which brightly colored fishing boats, decorated with images and prayers, bob at their moorings.

DIMAI. Although it is possible to travel overland by four-wheel drive to Dimai (there is a track opposite Karanis), the best way to approach the arid shores and mudbrick walls of SOKNOPAIOU NESOS ("the island of the crocodile god") is across the lake from Shakshuk. This former fishing village and caravanserai, on the northern boundary of the nome, was the first to be deserted by its inhabitants. A processional way whose remains can still be seen to the south of the site led from the gates of the TEMPLE OF SOBEK to the god's primordial habitat. About one hundred yards outside the walls, the cellars used for storing oil and wine still have their vaulted ceilings. The remains of two temples, one built of stone and one of brick, can still be seen inside the precinct. A few miles east is the limestone TEMPLE OF QASR EL-SAGHA which, although never completed, has retained its seven chapels. It is one of the few examples of Middle Kingdom religious building, but there is no indication as to its function.

DIONYSIAS. After Shakshuk take the road which runs parallel to and sometimes along the shores of the lake. Follow it for a few miles and then take the direction of QASR QARUN, leaving the point of the lake on your right. Turn left after crossing a canal and follow a road bordered by large dovecotes until, about 8 miles after the village of El-Shawasna, the roof of the Temple of Dionysias comes into view. This was the most westerly town in the nome and may have been a staging post on caravan routes from the Libyan Desert. It was founded in c. 3rd century BC and, because of its strategic position and incursions by the Bedouin tribesmen known as the Blemmyes, was fortified by the emperor Diocletian. A Roman fort similar to those in the Kharga Oasis ▲ *260* housed a large garrison.

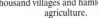

ORCHARD OF EGYPT

The Faiyum is famed for the abundance and quality of its fruits and vegetables, but also, and more poetically, for its roses, jasmine and orange blossom. Its one million inhabitants, scattered across the province in more than two thousand villages and hamlets, live by agriculture.

The Faiyum is also a protected site and harbors a rich and varied population of waterfowl.

367

▲ THE FAIYUM

To the south, the avenue leading to the Temple of Narmuthis is guarded by sphinxes and lions.

When Leo Africanus visited Medinet el-Faiyum in the early 16th century he described it as "civilized and well populated; it has many craftsmen, especially weavers".

The first excavations (1948) uncovered thermal baths, houses decorated with frescos and glassworks which are today once more engulfed by sand. Unusually for the Faiyum the so-called "TEMPLE OF STONES" dedicated to Sobek still has its roof, while in the shadowy interior fourteen rooms are arranged either side of a central corridor leading to three chapels.

MEDINET MADI: NARMUTHIS. Continue southward from Qasr Qarun. Archeologically speaking Medinet Madi (ancient Narmuthis) is considered to be the most interesting site of the Faiyum, although it is so vast that it has not yet been completely excavated. Narmuthis stood next to a Middle Kingdom city and its Ptolemaic extension. The Middle Kingdom temple, dedicated to Sobek, Ernutet (the serpent goddess associated with Isis) and Horus, was built by Amenemhet III and extended by the Ptolemies. Like the rest of the site it is under threat from the sand. Its interior walls are covered with hieroglyphics and bas-reliefs depicting Amenemhet III and his son, Amenemhet IV, presenting offerings to the gods. The far end of the temple is extended by a small Ptolemaic temple which would have been linked to the city's north gate by a processional way and porticos.

MEDINET EL-FAIYUM

Medinet el-Faiyum, known first as Crocodilopolis and then Arsinoe, is the modern capital of the province. It stands at the center of the Faiyum basin and is the point of convergence for road, canal and rail networks.

Medinet el-Faiyum is crossed by Joseph's Canal and eight tributary canals and has been described, by its more enthusiastic reviewers, as the Venice of Egypt. The city where the writer and traveler Maxime Du Camp marveled at "bazaars [which were] of a cleanliness unusual for the East" has all the charm of a rural Egyptian town. Bridges and footbridges link quays which are bustling with trade. Among the main attractions are the huge wooden waterwheels (built by the Greek settlers) which creak and groan as they raise water from one level

to another. The great stone obelisk (more like a stele) which stands at the city's north entrance was erected in honor of Senwosret I (12th Dynasty). Not much remains of the ancient capital of the nome at Kiman Fares, a few miles outside Medinet el-Faiyum, as the site has been extensively developed. This was the home and principal place of worship of the crocodile god, Sobek, and a sacred lake harbored enormous crocodiles which, according to Strabo, were fed on meat and honey cakes and adorned with gold by the priests. The city has a substantial Coptic community, but during the 1980's became a stronghold of Muslim fundamentalism.

UMM EL-BRIGAT: TEBTUNIS. Head south out of Medinet el-Faiyum and turn left, after the bus station, toward Itsa. The brick remains of a ROMAN AQUEDUCT lie scattered in the fields. At Tutun a sign on the right indicates the direction of Umm el-Brigat. The road follows the edge of a broad canal and after about 4 miles comes to the site and modern village of Umm el-Brigat. Although partially covered by sand, the extensive remains of ancient TEBTUNIS are extremely impressive, and enhanced by this beautiful setting.

DEIR EL-MALAK GHOBRIAL. Several ancient monasteries,

TEBTUNIS
The ruins lie on the edge of the desert. Tebtunis, founded during the 22nd Dynasty, was developed by Greek and Roman settlers. It was here, in the late 19th century, that a *fellaheen* discovered the first papyri scrolls in Greek, Latin and demotic script. A broad and still partially paved way crosses the ruins under the watchful gaze of two huge limestone lions. All that remains of the vast temple complex are some of the lateral rooms in beautiful, honey-colored stone.

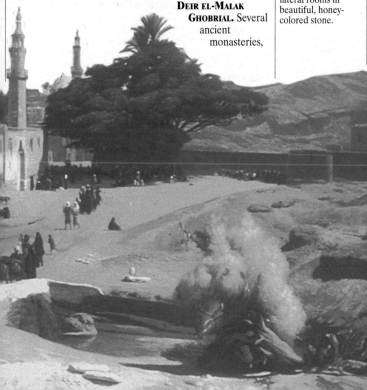

Detail of a fresco depicting Adam and Eve, from one of the many Coptic monasteries of the Faiyum.

A MAGNIFICENT FIND
An exceptional discovery gave an added dimension and restored some of the former glory to the Faiyum which suffered so much over the ages. In 1888 a total of 146 magnificent portraits painted on wood were discovered during excavations carried out in the Roman cemetery to the north of the pyramid by the archeologist Sir Flinders Petrie.

situated at the southern edge of the Faiyum, are evidence of a Christian presence which dates back to the 3rd century. These monasteries (there were still thirty-six in the Middle Ages) are today being given a new lease on life by a revival of Coptic monasticism. The oldest and most interesting to visit is the DEIR EL-MALAK GHOBRIAL, or the Monastery of the Archangel Gabriel, built on the high slopes of the Jebel Naqlun. The mystical associations of this austere, arid landscape, so close to the cool freshness of trees and plots of green vegetables, go back a very long way. According to the Christian historian Abu Salih, Jacob, the grandson of Abraham, settled here. The original monastery was probably built in the 4th century AD by the Bishop Aur, acting upon the instructions of the Archangel Gabriel, who had commanded him to build a sanctuary in these mountains where people "would gather in crowds more numerous than doves in a dovecote". In fact between the 4th and 6th centuries the monastery was the center of the religious life of the Faiyum, with Saint Samuel numbering among its many illustrious visitors. Before it was rebuilt in 1968, all that remained was a church with six Corinthian columns supporting a beautiful wood ceiling decorated with geometric designs. Just below the ridge of the mountain, southeast of the monastery, cells hewn out of the rock (the work of Bishop Aur) enabled monks to retreat in accordance with the eremitic tradition of the Egyptian desert. **PYRAMID OF HAWARA.** (The route is signposted from the obelisk of Medinet el-Faiyum.) Today it is hard to imagine that the Pyramid of Hawara and its funeral complex were among the most renowned and most visited sites of the Ancient World. The brick infrastructure is all that remains of the pyramid, once covered in bonded stone, while the labyrinth where Herodotus claimed to have counted three thousand rooms (the site, he said, defied description) has been reduced to a confused expanse of shards. The legend associated with the complex was linked with that of its founder, Amenemhet III, who was also said to have created Lake Moeris.

EL-MINYA TO THEBES

EL-MINYA, *372*
BENI HASSAN, *374*
HERMOPOLIS, *376*
TUNA EL-JEBEL, *377*
TELL EL-AMARNA, *378*
ASSIUT, *380*
ABYDOS, *386*
DENDERA, *388*

1 EL-MINYA
2 BENI HASSAN
3 ANTINOE
4 HERMOPOLIS
5 TUNA EL-JEBEL

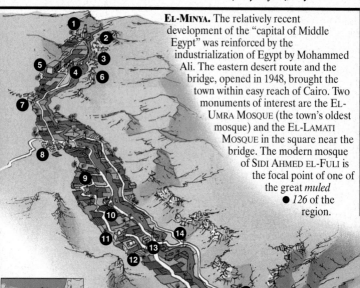

EL-MINYA. The relatively recent development of the "capital of Middle Egypt" was reinforced by the industrialization of Egypt by Mohammed Ali. The eastern desert route and the bridge, opened in 1948, brought the town within easy reach of Cairo. Two monuments of interest are the EL-UMRA MOSQUE (the town's oldest mosque) and the EL-LAMATI MOSQUE in the square near the bridge. The modern mosque of SIDI AHMED EL-FULI is the focal point of one of the great *muled* ● *126* of the region.

▣ Two–four days
◆ D F

The minaret of the el-Lamati mosque and the Muslim cemetery of el-Minya at the foot of the Libyan mountain range.

The municipal museum, currently being refurbished, houses a collection of Egyptian antiquities.

TIHNA EL-JEBEL. Acoris was the Greek name for the Pharaonic town of Dehenet ("the forehead") whose name was undoubtedly inspired by the promontory around which the town has developed. Tihna el-Jebel is one of the sites where, under the Lagides and then the Romans, the Pharaonic and Greek cultures co-existed: the ancient gods were honored with Greek names, the dead were buried according to Egyptian tradition and their epitaphs were written in Greek or Latin. The temple is reached via the steeply sloping sacred way, once lined by altars, statues and columns. Amun and Suchos (the Greek name of the crocodile god Sobek ● *61* ▲ *362*) were the two main divinities of the temple. The hieroglyphic inscriptions are in the name of Nero. On the columns several calligraphic Greek texts, written in ink, give thanks for the Nile floods: "(Year) two and (year) one of our Lords Diocletian and Marcus Aurelius, the welcome waters, regenerating and life-giving with their fertile mud, rose to the sanctuary of Suchos, Amun, Hermes and

Hera and the gods who share their temple, amidst general happiness and rejoicing" (based on a translation by Bernand). To the right a chapel, perched on the cliff, combines the Egyptian (images of the gods) and Greek (dedication) styles. The cross in the niche at the back of the chapel is an indication that the building was used for Christian worship. About 100 yards southwest of the temple, amidst the rubble of collapsed houses, are the remains of a GREEK-STYLE TEMPLE dedicated to Zeus-Helios-Serapis, a part-Greek, part-Egyptian god of the Ptolemies. A relief representing the Dioscuri standing either side of Helena, high up behind the promontory, was meant to protect boatmen passing along the Nile below. The necropolis stretches along a valley to the east.

DEIR EL-ADRA. The "Monastery of the Virgin" stands on the cliff opposite the town of SAMALUT on the so-called JEBEL EL-TEIR (Bird Mountain) where the Holy Family is said to have stayed. The church, which according to tradition was founded by the Empress (Saint) Helena, mother of Constantine, stands above a tomb from the Archaic period. During pilgrimages (January 29 and August 22) the

One of the ancient mosques of El-Minya.

monastery, no longer inhabited by monks, becomes an encampment for the Faithful. To the north are the ancient quarries, which spared the speos of Merneptah and a low relief of Ramesses III.

ZAWIYET EL-MAYTIN. The remains of a 3rd-Dynasty pyramid, a mound of red shards and the façade of the tomb of Nefersekheru (18th–19th Dynasty) are more or less all there is to see at Zawiyet el-Maytin or Kom el-Ahmar (Red Hill), the modern name of Hebenu, the capital of the Sixteenth Nome of Upper Egypt. The walk along the Arabian mountains (currently being quarried by dynamite) is extremely beautiful and runs along the edge of one of the largest Muslim cemeteries in Egypt.

"The steep banks of the river often consist of broad, straight lines one above the other. The white mountain (*sharab*) is covered with rounded hillocks striped with gray, striped like the back of a hyena; at other points it is a smooth, white cliff."
Gustave Flaubert

BENI HASSAN

Beni Hassan could be described as a typical Middle-Kingdom
necropolis. The time had passed when high-ranking
government officials were buried near their king (Saqqara
▲ *344*, Giza ▲ *334*): the upheavals of the First Intermediate
period (2140–2022 BC) gave a certain independence to local
governors (nomarchs) and it was from then on that they
tended to be buried in their own nome. Twelve of the thirty-
nine great rock-cut tombs are decorated and five of these are
truly remarkable, not only for their architectural beauty, but
also for their vast, vaulted chambers and their choice of
columns. Champollion ▲ *216* classified the columns with cut-
off corners as "proto-Doric" and believed he had discovered
the ancestor of the Greek Doric order. The name of Baqet,
one of the architects, was found. These tombs are also
remarkable for the richness and originality of their décor. The
tombs of Amenemhet (no. 2), "prince of the Oryx Nome",
Khnumhotep III (no. 3), "the hereditary lord", Khnumhotep I
(no. 14), Baqit III (no. 15) and Khety (no. 17) feature
traditional scenes of agricultural life, hunting in papyrus
thickets, pilgrimages by boat to Abydos ▲ *386* and Busiris,
and the presentation of offerings to the deceased who is
represented in "heroic" proportions, seated on a chair. The
desert hunting scenes on the north wall of tomb no. 2 depart
from the classical repertoire and, on the north wall of tomb
no. 15, include the hunting of four fantastical creatures: a
"Sethian" animal, a griffin, a serpent-headed quadruped and
a unicorn. These creatures are clearly a representation of the
belief that the desert was the home of the evil forces of chaos
and that hunting in the desert helped to preserve cosmic
order. The training of men in violent sports and military
exercises was a constant preoccupation of the suzerains of the
Oryx Nome, who had to maintain their power by force (the
east walls of tombs nos. 2, 15 and 17 depict scenes of the
fortress under siege). In tomb no. 2 (on the north wall)
Asiatic tribesmen, led by their chief Abisha, have come, with
their donkeys, to sell kohl (of which the Egyptians used a
great deal). This is the most famous representation of these
nomadic Bedouins, who lived and traveled along the eastern
borders of Egypt. There are two biographical inscriptions in
the necropolis that are essential to an understanding of the
political and economic situation of Egypt at that time, when
the country was emerging from over a century of serious
upheavals. One of these is a thirty-two-line inscription on the
interior uprights of the door of tomb no. 2; the other is an
inscription of 222 columns of text which can be found
within tomb no. 3.

"SPEOS ARTEMIDOS". The Cave of Artemis, situated in a *wadi* (Batn el-Baqara) about 2 miles to the southwest of Beni Hassan, was hewn out of the rock for the lion-goddess Pakhet ("she who scratches"), alias Artemis, by Hatshepsut. These *wadi* mouths were the preserve of wild beasts who sometimes left the desert and made incursions into the valley.

ANTINOE. Antinoe was founded by the emperor Hadrian in AD 130 . Little is known of the town's Pharaonic past, of which the temple dedicated by Ramesses II to the god Shepsy, the avatar of Thoth of Hermopolis, is the only visible legacy. All that remains of Hadrian's town is a pile of shards interspersed with architectural fragments. It was used as an ancient quarry and capitals from Antinoe have been found in a 15th-century mosque in Cairo. Legend has it that Salah ad-Din ▲ *271* had the enclosure wall dismantled and used it to build the wall of the capital. The mosque in the village of Sheikh Abada is said to have been built on the site of the house of Mary the Copt, who was the Prophet's concubine. The early Christians established orthodox monasteries in the mountain quarries.

One of the views of Antinoe that appeared in *La Description de l'Egypte* ● *140* ▲ *315*. The triumphal arch which stood on the site at the time of the French expedition has since disappeared (used in the construction of a sugar refinery).

THE FOUNDATION OF ANTINOE
Founded by Hadrian on October 30, AD 130, Antinoe is said to have been built in memory of his favorite, Antinus, who threw himself in the Nile to save the emperor from a deadly omen.

"Phlegon gathered the architects and engineers of my entourage together on the shores of the river; sustained by a sort of lucid intoxication, I led them along the rocky hillsides; I explained my plan, the construction of the forty-five sections of an enclosure wall; I marked the position of the triumphal arch and the tomb in the sand. Antinoe was about to be created."
Marguerite Yourcenar, *Memoirs of Hadrian*

Gayet's excavations at Antinoe (left).

375

BIRTH OF HERMOPOLIS
The word for "eight" in Ancient Egyptian is *shmun*. It was one of the town's two ancient names and has survived in the modern name of Ashmunein. It refers to the eight "ancestors of very early times" who formed four couples of frog-males and serpent-females, the incarnations of the primordial waters, spatial infinity, shadows and the invisible. A muddy hillock emerged from the primordial waters. On it grew a lotus

with golden stamens and petals in lapis-lazuli. In the form of four bulls, the males fertilized the flower which opened and revealed a child, a finger held to its mouth: the sun was born which, in its turn, would create the world.

DEIR ABU HENNES. Deir Abu Hennes (St John's Monastery), to the south of Antinoe, is famous as the orthodox monastery founded in the quarries exploited during the reign of Amenhotep III. Crosses, Greek and Coptic graffiti and prayer niches attest to the presence of this eremitic community centered around the tiny church which is traditionally thought to date from the time of Empress Helena.

MELLAWI. Before El-Minya became the regional capital at the beginning of the 19th century, Mellawi was an important town whose revenues were dedicated to Mecca. The streets of the old town have retained their original layout with two fine ancient mosques standing next to each other at the center: the EL-YUSUFI MOSQUE (1623), whose columns and capitals came from ancient sites in the region (including Antinoe), and the EL-ASQALANI MOSQUE, which dates from 1779. The Mellawi Museum houses an admirable collection of antiquities which have come mainly from the necropolis of Tuna el-Jebel. They include bronzes, ibis mummies and sarcophagi, plaster coffin masques (which are in fact portraits), and huge sarcophagi from the necropolises of Meir and Assiut and a fine head from a New-Kingdom royal statue.

HERMOPOLIS

With the other Ancient Egyptian cities of Heliopolis ▲ *285*, Memphis ▲ *332* and Thebes ▲ *394*, Hermopolis shares the rare privilege of being one of the "birthplaces of the world". As well as being a "cosmogenetic" capital it was also the capital of the Fifteenth (Hare) Nome of Upper Egypt. Its patron was the god Thoth, incarnated in the form of the ibis and baboon, the scribe who presided over all forms of knowledge: language and sacred writings, laws, the measurement of time and the calendar. He became Hermes in the Greek pantheon, the Trismegistus of the hermetic texts.
REMAINS. The ruins of the city lie in the center of the plain at the point where it widens out. Huge columns surmounted by Corinthian capitals lend a particular charm to the site. They are the remains of a basilica (built on the site of a 3rd-century Ptolemaic temple), the town's monumental covered market during Ptolemaic and Roman times. Earlier remains are rare and we can only guess at the layout of the great temple of Thoth. The two colossal quartzite baboons at the entrance to the site, bearing the name of Amenhotep III, would certainly have stood before a gateway. The great column bases, sculpted with the cartouches of Philip III Arrhidaeus, belong to a portico that was still standing at the time of the Egypt

The so-called "Ptolemaios" funeral temple at Tuna el-Jebel.

Expedition. Among clumps of tamarisk to the west, a small pylon marks the entrance to a temple dedicated to Amun-Re, built by Ramesses II, using limestone *talattat* ▲ *402* taken from Tell el-Amarna, and decorated during the reigns of Merneptah and Sety II. The two scenes in the gateway show Sety II being welcomed by Amun-Re and Thoth (with the head of an ibis). To the south of the site the large peasant houses of the village, built on the rest of the *tell*, have great charm and character. The mosque, built from the debris of the ancient town, replaced a church.

TOMB OF PETOSIRIS Inside the tomb (whose entrance is seen below) the religious and funerary scenes are executed in accordance with Egyptian principles, while scenes of everyday life interpret the traditional repertoire in Greek style (vestibule). In the chapel the plinth decorated with bearers of offerings is a true masterpiece.

TUNA EL-JEBEL

On the surface Tuna el-Jebel consists of the chapels of the Ptolemaic and Roman tombs belonging to the notables of Hermopolis. Below ground is the necropolis of the sacred baboons and mummified ibis offered to Thoth. Well before the cemetery the northwest boundary stele of the town of Akhenaten stands alone on the face of a low cliff. The king and Nefertiti, along with three of their daughters, are shown worshipping the solar disk.

TOMB OF PETOSIRIS. The originality of the family tomb of Petosiris, the high priest of Thoth and contemporary of Alexander the Great, lies in the combined Egyptian and Greek styles of its décor. The tombs found beyond the Tomb of Petosiris are characterized by the same blend of styles, with the Greek ornamental front sometimes replacing the (Egyptian) grooved cornice and the capitals varying from Pharaonic composite to Corinthian.

TOMB OF ISADORA. Isadora drowned during the reign of Hadrian. The sculpted shell decorating her tomb is echoed in the lines of Greek verse painted on the wall: "In fact, it was the nymphs, oh, Isadora, the nymphs, daughters of the river, who built this chamber for you. Nilo, the eldest daughter of the Nile, began the work, fashioning a shell like those he [the Nile] harbors in his watery depths" (based on a translation by Perdrizet). The Roman access shaft to the west of the tomb is 112 feet deep.

NECROPOLIS OF SACRED ANIMALS. The galleries of the *ibiotaphon* extend for several hundred yards. Here, as elsewhere, the cult of the animal incarnation of a particular divinity became widespread during the last centuries of pagan worship.

EL-BERSHA. During the 11th and 12th Dynasties the nomarchs of the Fifteenth Nome of Upper Egypt were buried at El-Bersha. The tombs have fallen prey to quarriers and are in an advanced state of disrepair. Of the ten tombs on the site only one is open to the public: the Tomb of Thuthotep, famed for its scene depicting the transporting of a colossal statue.

SHEIKH SAÏD. During the 5th and 6th Dynasties the governors of Hermopolis were buried at Sheikh Saïd. The names of the princes can still be seen in the ruined necropolis.

The sacred animal necropolis contains chapels (the best preserved is in the name of Ptolemy I), stone baboon sarcophagi and corridors filled with jars where there are two mummified ibis (above, left and right).

BOUNDARY STELAE
To mark the boundaries of his new city Akhenaten had fourteen monumental stelae carved in the cliffs, three on the west bank and eleven on the east bank. The scenes show the royal family worshipping the solar disk, while the texts praise the divine star, outline the construction program and undertake not to exceed the boundaries defined by the stelae.

TELL EL-AMARNA

Virtually everything there is to say has been said about what has become known as the "Amarnian experience". Hypotheses and fantasies aside, it basically concerned a king and queen involved in a political experience which was, to a certain extent, at variance with tradition. Their decision to identify a single, sufficient god, concentrated within the solar disk, their creation of a new city on land which, according to the texts, did not belong to any divinity, their adoption of the esthetic principles which characterized all their works and, finally, the brutal return to orthodoxy by their successors, with a *damnatio memoriae* which left no stone standing, are the main features of what was an exceptional period in Egyptian history.

AKHETATEN. In his fifth regnal year Amenhotep IV changed his name to Akhenaten, meaning "favorable to the Aten" (the solar disk) and founded his capital, Akhetaten ("Horizon of the

"The beauty of the land and the legacy of its history seem insignificant when compared with the magnificence of the evening sky which I awaited as if it were the sole event of the day."

Edouard Schuré

Aten"), in the vast cirque of Tell el-Amarna, which covers an area of 6 miles (north–south) by 2 miles (east–west). The king built temples for his new cult, palaces for himself and the royal princesses, administrative buildings, houses for his subjects and a village for the necropolis workers, marking the perimeters with fourteen BOUNDARY STELAE. The necropolis is divided into two sections which lie to the north and south of the cirque. Of particular interest in the north are the tombs of HUYA (no. 1), MERYRE (no. 2), AHMOSE (no. 3), another MERYRE (no. 4) and PANEHSY (no. 6) and, in the south, of PARENNEFER (no. 7), TUTU (no. 8), MAHU (no. 9) and AY (no. 25) who became pharaoh and succeeded Akhenaten. To the attentive visitor scenes from the everyday life of the ancient city are revealed in the reliefs of the tombs. The royal couple form the leitmotif and are shown "in their public appearances and in the privacy of the palace, accompanied by their daughters, breathing, eating, walking, at leisure, making offerings and worshipping, beneath a huge sun whose rays are vibrant with life. These epiphanies of the Trinity are the central theme of huge compositions showing the foundation festivals, offerings placed in open sanctuaries, visits to sanctuaries, the receiving of tributes, the rewarding of ministers, the dedication of the worshippers and the activities of their subjects, living images with a wealth of picturesque detail" (P. Vernus and J. Yoyotte, *Les Pharaons*).

MEIR AND EL-QUSIYA. During the Old and Middle Kingdoms, the notables of Cusae (modern El-Qusiya) were buried in the necropolis of Meir. Cusae was the capital of the Fourteenth Nome of Upper Egypt and the town of the goddess Hathor ● *62* who became the Greek goddess Aphrodite Urania. Recent renovation work in the tombs has restored the texture and color of their images. The hallmark of this necropolis, especially in the CHAPELS OF SENBI AND UKHHOTEP, is the extremely realistic style in which traditional scenes are represented. Here, more than anywhere else, one is aware of the artists' sense of the present, of details that surprise and amuse. The hirsute herdsman (below), bent like his staff, verges on caricature.

KOM DARA. Kom Dara is the name of a huge brick construction (over 393 feet square) covered with sand and bordered by the houses on the outskirts of the village. Whether mastaba or pyramid ● *82*, this Old-Kingdom tomb is the largest in its necropolis.

Tell el-Amarna as it is today.

"Each of these streets ...was conceived, traced by Akhenaten. We watched, together, as each of the buildings was constructed. Now, all I have to do is close my eyes and I see its towering temples and houses, its living gardens and its network of streets."
Andrée Chedid
Nefertiti et le Rêve d'Akhenaten

379

ON THE CARAVAN ROUTE

"From the time of the Arab conquest to the reign of Mohammed Ali, Assiut prospered owing to its position at the end of the caravan

route from Nubia, Sannar, Dongola and Darfur. Its markets sold 'gold dust, elephants' tusks, ebony, musk, civet, ambergris, ostrich feathers, various types of gum and a host of other expensive merchandise. But its most valuable commodity was the two or three thousand black slaves that the caravans brought back to sell in Egypt'."

Benoît de Maillet
La Description de l'Egypte

ASSIUT

Assiut, Syut to the Ancient Egyptians, was the fief of the jackal gods Wepwawet ("Opener of Ways") and Anubis, after whom the Greeks renamed it Lycopolis ("city of the wolf"). Although the geographical position of the capital of the Thirteenth Nome of Upper Egypt meant that it was of strategic interest in the recurrent struggles between Upper and Lower Egypt, it never played a role of any national importance. The modern city center stands squarely on the *kom* of the ancient city and nothing is directly known about the monuments buried beneath several feet of accumulated ruins.

FAMOUS NAMES. Plotinus, the neo-Platonist philosopher, was born in Lycopolis in 205. He left the provincial capital for Alexandria and became a disciple of Ammonius, founder of the famous neo-Platonist school. From there he went on to Rome where he taught a doctrine based on the "union of the soul with God through ecstasy and contemplation". Some two hundred years later the town became the birthplace of one of the greatest saints of Christian Egypt: John of Lycopolis, a carpenter who withdrew to the desert of the nearby mountains. Among those drawn by his gift of prophesy was the Roman emperor Theodosius who learned of his forthcoming victories over the tyrants (Magnus Clemens) Maximus and Eugenius, his death and the succession of his sons to the Empire. John died in 394.

MODERN ASSIUT. Today Assiut is a large town, the seat of a governorate and capital of the province of Saïd (Upper Egypt), with the third largest university in Egypt (whose students occasionally give the government cause for concern). The covered market, on top of the *kom*, has a certain charm. The museum of the former Assiut College houses a modest collection of antiquities from all periods, which come from the region's various sites.

NECROPOLIS OF ASSIUT. The TOMB OF HAPIDJEFA, Prince of Assiut during the reign of Senwosret I, was dug on the first terrace of the cliff, but he died and was buried in Nubia, and his tomb in Assiut remained empty. A long inscription lists the ten clauses of the contract concluded with the priests to ensure that his funeral cult was properly performed. The southernmost of the three tombs situated on a second terrace is that of ITYBI. The tomb of his son KHETY, in the center, is decorated with scenes of the battles fought by the

"Two o'clock. The sun, already high in the sky, takes [Assiut] from behind. The entire town is steeped in grayish purple and stands in a vast stretch of pale lilac water. Behind the town the lofty, unyielding silhouette of a mountain is bathed in the same light, completely immersed and indistinct in the softest and most even tones of purplish-gray imaginable. One senses, in the distance that separates the town and the mountain and in the sudden change of tone, the vast expanse that lies between them. In fact you can see water flowing around the town. To the right, to the left, a vast, double lake. A bridge links the two branches . . . A huge town, a city of mud walls and monumental constructions; pyloned houses, clean, regular and new-looking; the streets are dusty but free of rubbish."
Eugène Fromentin, 1835

kings of Heracleopolis against the Theban princes, while the TOMB OF (another) KHETY, to the north, has images of the hydrological work carried out by the owner to use the Nile floods to best advantage. The view from the terrace takes in modern Assiut (whose suburbs are encroaching onto agricultural land) and, to the north, one of the largest Muslim necropolises in Egypt.

DEIR DURUNKA. About 6 miles south of Assiut, on the road which runs parallel to the Libyan mountains, a town suddenly appears on the cliff face. Its buildings, constructed in recent years by the Coptic orthodox see of Assiut, are evidence of the importance of the pilgrimage of the Virgin of Deir Durunka (August 22). The Holy Family is believed to have stayed in the site's oldest CHURCH, which stands in an ancient quarry in the middle of the cliff. Its monastery is the most famous in a region where Christianity is particularly deeply rooted.
The churches of several nearby

The great temple that once stood at Qaou el-Kebir is lavishly illustrated in *La Description de l'Egypte* (above). In 1821 it was washed away when the Nile altered its course. Its blocks were reused for a palace in Assiut.

The entrance and interior of the church of the Red Monastery.

The god Min at the Temple of Athribis.

monasteries were dedicated to Saint Athanasius, Saint John the Baptist, Claudius, Philotas and Moncurius. About 300 yards to the north a rectangular opening, clearly visible against the white rock face, is traditionally believed to be the hermitage of Saint John of Lycopolis.

ABU TIG. Abu Tig is derived from the Greek *apotheke* (shop, warehouse). The town stands at the center of a region whose agricultural landscape has a very particular charm. Land re-allocation has had a different effect on the plain of Abu Tig where the boundaries between the (often terraced) fields appear as irregular curves rather than as the straight lines seen on the plains in the rest of the valley. The region gives some idea of the cultivated face of Egypt from Antiquity to the construction of the Aswan High Dam.

EL-BADARI. The term "Badarian" was derived from the village of El-Badari. The nearby cemetery in fact revealed a considerable amount of material (dating from between 5500 and 3800 BC), which made the Badarian stage (during which the inhabitants of the Nile Valley perfected their stock-breeding and agricultural skills) the earliest stage of the pre-Dynastic period.

QAOU EL-KEBIR. The two names of the Pharaonic town known as Antaeopolis (town of Antaeus) in Graeco-Roman times are translated as "The Two Sandals" and "High Mountain". The (now non-existent) great temple that once stood at Qaou el-Kebir is mentioned in *La Description de l'Egypte*: "Travelers will be amazed, as we ourselves were, at the sight of these beautiful columns and palm capitals (visible from the river through groups of palm trees of the same height), standing, as it were, amongst the trees whose image they faithfully reproduce." THE NECROPOLIS can still be seen, perched high on the mountain. Three 12th-Dynasty tombs (two Wakhas and an Ibu) are the most interesting monuments on the site. The rock-cut CHAPEL consists of several porticoed terraces opening onto a series of underground rooms. The long access ramps from the valley add to the monumental aspect of the complex. Most of its tombs are later (30th Dynasty), from the Roman period.

TAHTA. Commemorative scarabs are evidence of the gift made by Amenhotep III to his queen Tiyi of a 150-acre domain at Djarukha, in the region of Tahta, her family home. It was inundated during the Nile floods and the royal sovereigns used to sail aboard the royal barque (the *Shining Sun*). Blocks found in the fields by local *fellaheen* are all that remain of the temple, dedicated to Horus, that once stood at Tahta.

WHITE MONASTERY. According to the life of Shenute as told by his disciple, Besa, the Coptic abbot was born in 348, took monastic orders at the age of seven and soon withdrew into the desert where he lived as a hermit. He took part in the Council of Ephesus in 431 and died in 466. He built the Deir el-Abyad or White Monastery, of which only the church has survived. The building materials for the monastery were provided by local temples as Shenute vented his fury against the pagan gods. The age, size and state of preservation of the church make it an important landmark in the history of ancient Christian art: a nave with a basilican layout, reused columns and, to the east, a "tri-conical" sanctuary. Several fires have detracted from its original splendor. The festival of "Amba Shenuda" is held on July 14.

RED MONASTERY. The 6th-century Deir Amba Bishoi is also known as the Red Monastery because of the burnt brick from which it was built. It lies about 2 miles north of the White Monastery and, like the latter, only the church remains.

AKHMIM. On his pilgrimage to Mecca in the 12th century Ibn Jobeir passed through Akhmim and was greatly impressed by one of its temples: "Apart from its walls, this huge temple is supported by forty columns . . . The ceiling of the entire temple is made of stone paving admirably arranged to form a

"And the angel said to Apa Bgoul: 'When you rise in the morning, put the robe that you find before you on the little boy Shenute, . . . the Lord Jesus has sent it to you so that you may dress him in it; for verily I say unto you, he will be a just and chosen man . . . he will build a monastery, he will be

an inspiration and a protector for anyone who comes to him in his dwelling-place and his church will last for generations'."
Vie de Schnoudi
(based on the translation by Amélineau)
The White and Red monasteries (above).

383

NECROPOLIS OF EL-HAWAWISH
The Old-Kingdom tombs of this necropolis are decorated with figures and scenes from everyday life. A butchery scene (right).

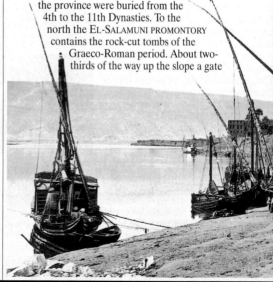

single unit ... Inside and outside ... the figures are all different in shape and appearance; there are figures horrible to behold, of inhuman aspect, which make those who look upon them tremble with fear, filling them with apprehension and wonder" (based on a translation by Gaudefroy-Demombynes). In the 14th century El-Khatib destroyed the temple and built a college, the remains of which are found inside the houses: its granite columns have been transformed into millstones and the limestone is used in the lime kilns. Akhmim is the town of the ithyphallic god Min who, as well as being the god of fertility, was also master of the deserts between the Nile and the Red Sea. The Greeks recognized him as Pan and duly called the town Panopolis: "The Pans and Satyrs who live near Chemmis [Akhmim] were the first to learn of the death of Osiris and spread the news. This was how the sudden fear that grips a multitude became known as panic" (Plutarch). The ancient history of the town which, during the Pharaonic period, was called Ipu or Khent-Menu, is told by its necropolises. The Arabian mountains open up into a cirque, delimited to the south by the NECROPOLIS OF EL-HAWAWISH where the governors of the province were buried from the 4th to the 11th Dynasties. To the north the EL-SALAMUNI PROMONTORY contains the rock-cut tombs of the Graeco-Roman period. About two-thirds of the way up the slope a gate

GIRGA
"It is an unremarkable, modern town; as big as El-Minya and Mellawi, smaller than Assiut and less pretty than all of them. The name Girga or Dgridga comes from the great monastery, built before the town existed and dedicated to Saint George, pronounced "Gerge" in the local dialect ... The Nile washes against the buildings of Girga and each day demolishes them a little more ... The town's only interest is its position, equidistant from Cairo and Syene, and the richness of the surrounding region."
Dominique Vivant Denon

stands out clearly against the hillside, conspicuous because of its regular shape and imposing size. This is the GROTTO OF PAN, a rock-cut temple dedicated to Min and Amun-Re during the reign of Ay, the successor of Tutankhamun. It is one of the few monuments attributed to him. The architect of the speos was a certain Nakhtmin, whose name means "Powerful-is-Min".

EL-BIRBA AND GIRGA. It is not known for certain which of these two towns is the site of ancient This (or Thinis), capital of unified Egypt during the 1st and 2nd Dynasties and capital of the Eighth Nome of Upper Egypt throughout Egyptian history. When visitors used to travel by *dahabiya* ● *122*, the approaches to Girga were famed for the beauty of the landscape. The town is named after Saint George (Girgis) to whom the monastery was dedicated. An extremely picturesque, paved *suq* and the so-called Porcelain Mosque (El-Sini), which was almost washed away by the Nile, have all the characteristics of the "Orientalist" tradition. At BEIT QALLAF, the site of one of the This-Thinis necropolises, five (3rd Dynasty) mudbrick tombs have been excavated.

NAGA EL-DEIR. The necropolis known as Naga el-Deir stretches for several miles along the cliff of the Arabian mountains. The dead were buried there from the pre-Dynastic period to the Middle Kingdom. The Reisner papyri (named after the man who discovered them) were found on a sarcophagus in one of the 12th-Dynasty tombs. For such an early period, they provide remarkably detailed information on the organization of a building site and give the names and relationships of at least seven hundred workers and overseers.

COLOSSUS OF MERIT-AMUN
In 1981 a magnificent 21-foot colossus of Merit-Amun, daughter of Ramesses II (whose lips were still painted red), was discovered during excavations at Akhmim: "she of the beautiful brow, crowned with a rearing cobra, the beloved of her Lord . . ., she of the perfect countenance, the beauty of the palace, the beloved of the Master of the Two Lands, she who stands beside her Lord, as Sirius is beside Orion, she whose words are a delight [to hear] when she opens her mouth to soothe the Master of the Two Lands" (text, back pillar).

Colossus of Ramesses II (top).

385

ABYDOS

TEMPLE OF SETY I. The site of Abydos is vast. Virtually nothing remains of the ancient town which lies beneath the village of Beni Mansur, of the metropolitan temple which stood at the place known as Kom el-Sultan, or of the desert necropolises.

The fame of Abydos is based on one monument: the cenotaph-temple of Sety I, the only royal structure built on the god's territory which is still well preserved. The bases of the walls are all that remains of the two courts built by Ramesses II. Today visitors enter the temple via the portico which precedes the first hypostyle hall. Among the temple's special features are the SEVEN AXIAL CHAPELS dedicated, from left to right, to Sety I deified, Ptah, Harmachis (Horus on the Horizon), Amun-Re (central chapel), Osiris, Isis and Horus. These rooms and the suite of rooms leading off the chapel of Osiris are decorated with reliefs which number among the most beautiful in Egyptian art. Following the hiatus of the Amarnian experience ● 42, ▲ 378, the reign of Sety I (and at Abydos in particular) marks the birth of what was to become the Ramesside style. Along the right-hand wall of the corridor opening off the left wall of the second hypostyle hall a sculpted tableau gives a selective list of seventy-six pharaohs to which Sety I pays homage: one of the few "royal lists" compiled by the Egyptians. This so-called "Gallery of Lists" is of greater value as a self-view of Egyptian history than as a means of reconstructing the royal line of succession.

OSIREION. The strange structure of huge blocks that Sety I had built behind his temple was supposedly the fictitious tomb of Osiris. According to Strabo: "At the far end [of the temple] is a well into which you descend via spiral galleries formed by monoliths of extraordinary size and structure. A canal diverted from the great river flows to this place where it is surrounded by a sacred wood of acanthus, dedicated to Apollo." This artificial underground island may have contained the sarcophagus and Canopic jars of the god. The complex was covered by a mound planted with trees, a distinctive feature of Osirian sanctuaries. The smaller and less well-preserved cenotaph-temple of Ramesses II lies about 200 yards to the north of that of his father.

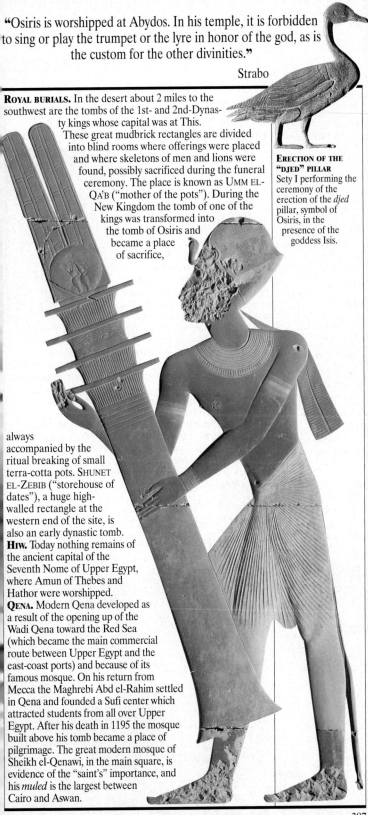

> "Osiris is worshipped at Abydos. In his temple, it is forbidden to sing or play the trumpet or the lyre in honor of the god, as is the custom for the other divinities."
>
> Strabo

ERECTION OF THE "DJED" PILLAR
Sety I performing the ceremony of the erection of the *djed* pillar, symbol of Osiris, in the presence of the goddess Isis.

ROYAL BURIALS. In the desert about 2 miles to the southwest are the tombs of the 1st- and 2nd-Dynasty kings whose capital was at This. These great mudbrick rectangles are divided into blind rooms where offerings were placed and where skeletons of men and lions were found, possibly sacrificed during the funeral ceremony. The place is known as UMM EL-QA'B ("mother of the pots"). During the New Kingdom the tomb of one of the kings was transformed into the tomb of Osiris and became a place of sacrifice, always accompanied by the ritual breaking of small terra-cotta pots. SHUNET EL-ZEBIB ("storehouse of dates"), a huge high-walled rectangle at the western end of the site, is also an early dynastic tomb.

HIW. Today nothing remains of the ancient capital of the Seventh Nome of Upper Egypt, where Amun of Thebes and Hathor were worshipped.

QENA. Modern Qena developed as a result of the opening up of the Wadi Qena toward the Red Sea (which became the main commercial route between Upper Egypt and the east-coast ports) and because of its famous mosque. On his return from Mecca the Maghrebi Abd el-Rahim settled in Qena and founded a Sufi center which attracted students from all over Upper Egypt. After his death in 1195 the mosque built above his tomb became a place of pilgrimage. The great modern mosque of Sheikh el-Qenawi, in the main square, is evidence of the "saint's" importance, and his *muled* is the largest between Cairo and Aswan.

387

Detail of the capitals
of the Temple of
Hathor

The ceiling of the
Court of the New
Year (above right).

DENDERA

"Re opened his eyes inside the lotus as it emerged from
primordial chaos and his eyes began to weep and droplets fell
to the ground: they were
transformed into a beautiful woman
who was named Gold of the Gods,
Hathor the Great, Mistress of
Dendera" (based on a translation
by Sylvie Cauville). And so Hathor
was born. She presided over
amorous pursuits; music, dance and
enjoyment were her preserve and it
was through them that she was
honored. This pan-Egyptian
divinity also took the form of a
fierce lioness who killed humans, a
celestial cow and life-giving flood
waters. Dendera was only one of

her many temples, but it is today among the best preserved
and the best known in Egypt. Virtually everything inside the
mudbrick enclosure wall is designed to evoke divine
influence. The entrance is through a huge gateway preceded
by public fountains. The monuments are all relatively recent
since, as in many sanctuaries throughout Egypt, the ancient
temples of Dendera were entirely rebuilt during the
Ptolemaic and Roman periods.

TEMPLE OF HATHOR. The main temple, which was begun
during the reign of Ptolemy XII Auletes (80–51 BC) and
continued until the reign of Nero (AD 54–68) remained
unfinished. Today visitors enter directly via the pronaos with
eighteen columns arranged in the form of a sistrum, the

instrument associated with the goddess, whose head, with its cow's ears, is reproduced on the capitals. The astronomical ceiling is decorated with the daily course of the sun, the lunar cycle, the decans, the Twelve Hours of the day and night and the signs of the zodiac. Along the walls is the sinuous body of the sky-goddess Nut who swallows the solar disk in the

evening and gives birth to it in the morning. After this comes the HYPOSTYLE HALL flanked by six rooms which were the service chambers where offerings were received. The priests arranged these offerings on huge tables in the offering hall. This led into the vestibule with the "robing room" and finally the central SHRINE of the "Great Seat". The huge granite naos with bronze doors inlaid with gold, which housed the goddess' statue, is no longer there. The sanctuary also contained the sacred barques of Hathor, Horus, Isis and Harsomtus who are represented on the walls (the goddesses with women's heads and the gods with falcons' heads). The sanctuary is separated from the rest of the temple and protected from the outside world by a corridor and the ELEVEN DIVINE CHAPELS that it services. The chapels are dedicated (from the left as you face the sanctuary) to Hathor, Isis, Sokar (the falcon-headed funeral god of Memphis associated with Osiris), Harsomtus (son of Hathor and Horus), the next four chapels to Hathor, the ninth to Horus of Edfu and the last two to Hathor. Crypts are built into the walls of the temple on three sides and at three levels. Some are richly decorated and one, entered through chapel no. 8, is mainly devoted to the representation and the description of the divine statues and the sacred objects of the temple.

CLEOPATRA AND CAESARION
The exterior back wall of the temple has become famous for its representation (in a style which, it is true, does not distinguish them from other kings and queens) of the legendary Cleopatra and the son she bore Caesar, Ptolemy XV Caesar, known as Caesarion.

"This monument seems to me to have something primitive about it, the character of a temple *par excellence*. . . . Nothing simpler and more precisely calculated than the few lines which compose its architecture. Since the Egyptians borrowed nothing from other cultures, they did not add 'foreign' ornaments or superfluous elements to what was dictated by necessity. Their principles were order and simplicity, and they elevated these principles to the very highest level."
Dominique Vivant Denon

COPTIC BASILICA
Inside the temple, to the left of the entrance, are two *mamissi*. Between them is the Coptic basilica which was added in the 5th century.

FESTIVAL OF THE NEW YEAR. The tower of the central shrine ends in the Court of the New Year and the Pure Place, which lies beyond through the right-hand door of the vestibule. Every temple had these two rooms, used for the New Year ceremonies, which involved the presentation of offerings in the court and the exposure of the divine statues in the Pure Place. On the ceiling, as in the pronaos, are images of Nut swallowing and giving birth to the sun, whose rays light up the temple, symbolized by the face of Hathor. The procession ascended the stairs to the roof: the king was followed by the priests bearing symbols and portable chapels, who were in turn followed by the divinities bearing offerings. Once on the roof they made their way to the chapel whose twelve columns represented the face of the goddess turned toward the four points of the compass. The divine statues were exposed to the sun's rays and were recharged with its divine energy for another year (the hippopotamus-goddesses on the columns personified the twelve months of the year).

RESURRECTION OF OSIRIS. On the roof the six chapels, in two groups of three, are dedicated to the basic myth of the resurrection of Osiris, who was murdered and cut into pieces by his brother Seth. Isis searched Egypt for the pieces and put them together to recreate the body of her husband. She then bore him a son: Horus, the supreme royal heir. These chapels guaranteed the annual resurrection of the god during a festival held as the waters of the Nile subsided. This ancient ritual, described in every detail on the walls, was a commemorative ceremony which involved the creation, by re-enacting the gestures, of a replica of Osiris's body from a paste in which barley was the main ingredient. The image, sprinkled with pure water, germinated and was later buried in one of the chapels. All the provinces, which each possessed a reliquary containing a piece of the god's body, were invited to attend. The process was so delicate and so decisive that, in order to ensure its success, the powers of the protecting spirits were invoked, whose assembled hosts can be seen in the chapels. One of the chapels contained the molding of the famous zodiac, bought by France in 1823 (Louvre Museum ▲ *476*). A staircase (a metal one has replaced the original) leads to the roof of the pronaos, which offers a view of the various monuments on the site, the desert (where the necropolis was located) and countryside beyond.

"MAMISSI". On the way back to the entrance of the temple, two *mamissi* stand on the left. The first, dating from the reign of Nectanebo I (380–63 BC) is the oldest building on the site. The second is unfinished and bears the cartouches of Trajan and Antoninus Pius (138–61). Both of these *mamissi* are dedicated to the birth of the divine heir Harsomtus, son of Hathor and Horus. The scenes decorating the exterior south wall, against which a Coptic basilica (far left) was built in the 5th century, are true masterpieces of bas-relief carving from the later period. They are skillfully executed, and their attention to detail is quite meticulous.

The sacred lake is the most beautiful of Egypt's surviving temple lakes. During the festival of the resurrection of Osiris 34 barques and 365 tiny "boats", each containing a candle, were set afloat on its waters.

The town of El-Ballas still produces the large earthenware jars (used for carrying water) for which it is famed (above). However, plastic (Egypt is one of the world's largest per capita consumers) will soon replace this age-old craft industry.

QIFT. The ruins of ancient Koptos, in the center of Qift, give little idea of the importance of the town during antiquity. It rebelled during the reign of Diocletian and was razed to the ground. The geographical position of Koptos guaranteed its economic prosperity before it was superseded, during the Mameluke period, by Qus and, in modern times, by Qena. The town stands at the mouth of a *wadi* which opened it up to the desert. Koptos and its god Min ● 63 both date from the beginning of Egyptian history. In Koptos Min was the protector of the gold mines, quarries and caravan routes. All that remains of his temple are a few foundations and fragments of the enclosure wall. The best preserved

One of the gates (right) of the Temple of Harwer in Qus.

Pilgrims from the Maghreb, Cairo and Alexandria passed through Qus on their way to Mecca. The age and beauty of its mosque are an indication of its prosperity. Detail of the decoration of the mosque and a ruined palace (below).

monuments are concentrated in the southern part of the town: a solitary gateway dating from the reign of Claudius, the uprights of a door set in a farmyard (Ptolemy XII and Caligula) and the chapel of the legendary Cleopatra with an image of three concentric naos containing the sacred barque. North of the suburbs of the modern town is the small TEMPLE OF EL-QAL'A, which dates from Roman times, dedicated to Isis and Harpocrates.

NAGADA. Nagada made a valuable contribution to Egyptian prehistory. Excavations revealed a vast cemetery of small, rectangular tombs just below the surface of the sand. The deceased lay curled up on their side, surrounded by pots, schist offering basins and terracotta figurines. Since this discovery the last stages of prehistory in Upper Egypt (3800–3100) have been known as I, II and III.

QUS. The two ruined gates of the TEMPLE OF HARWER (Horus the Elder) are all that remains of the ancient town of Apollinopolis Parva, the rival of Koptos in the Fifth Nome. The opening of an alternative route to the Red Sea during the 13th century meant that Qus replaced Qift as Upper Egypt's main commercial center trading with Africa, India, Arabia and the Yemen.

THEBES

TEMPLE OF LUXOR, 397
TEMPLE OF KARNAK, 404
VALLEY OF THE KINGS, 417
TOMB OF TUTANKHAMUN, 418
TEMPLE OF SETY I, 424
DEIR EL-BAHRI, 426
NECROPOLIS OF SHEIKH
ABD EL-QURNA, 430
RAMESSEUM, 432
MEDINET HABU, 434
DEIR EL-MEDINA, 438
VALLEY OF THE QUEENS, 440
QURNA, 442

1 TEMPLE OF AMUN-RE
2 KARNAK: TEMPLE OF MONTU
3 TEMPLE OF MUT
4 TEMPLE OF LUXOR
5 BIRKET HABU
6 MALKATTA
7 MEDINET HABU
8 TEMPLE OF AMENHOTEP III
9 TEMPLE OF HOREMHEB
10 DEIR EL-MEDINA

Restitution of the Theban region to the Middle Kingdom.

The celebrated Egyptian city of Thebes was described by Homer as "the city of a hundred gates" because so many of its temples had the monumental entrances favored by contemporary Greek architecture. Known to the Ancient Egyptians as Waset, Thebes was twice the Egyptian capital. It was from Thebes that Ahmose restored the unity of Egypt and inaugurated the New Kingdom, one of the most glorious periods in the history of the Two Lands. Even when it was not the capital, Thebes nonetheless played a key role in the history of Egypt. From the Middle Kingdom to the end of antiquity it was the sacred city of Amun-Re, the supreme god and source of Pharaonic legitimacy, and one of the main spiritual, intellectual and economic centers in Ancient Egypt.

11 Temple of Merneptah
12 Ramesseum
13 Temple of Thutmose
14 Deir el-Bahri
15 Temple of Sety I

🔼 **Six days**
◆ **K L**

EGYPTOMANIA ✪
There is an unusual atmosphere at Luxor, no doubt due to the swarm of tourists. Enter into the spirit: take a ride in a horse-drawn carriage, admire the sunset on board a felucca, browse through the bazaars and sample the local cuisine... Allow two hours for a visit to the temple and museum in Luxor. It will take much longer for a visit to the temple at Karnak (1½ miles away) which was built over a period of more than 1,300 years.

CITY OF THEBES. The ancient city of Thebes stood at the center of a vast cultivated region, bordered to the east and west by the arid peaks of the Arabian and Libyan mountains. It was divided by the Nile into two very distinct parts. The city proper lay on the east bank now occupied by the town of Luxor (from the Arabic El-Uqsur, meaning "the palaces"). It was built entirely of mudbrick and consisted of a series of districts, suburbs and villages organized around the temples of Karnak and Luxor and linked by a *dromos*, a straight, paved way bordered by sphinxes. On the west bank the necropolis, funerary temples and embalming rooms, which were known during the Roman occupation as *memnonia*, were built into the cliff.

Foundations of houses, some of the few remains of the city of Thebes.

THE CORNICHE
The Temple of Luxor is situated on the Corniche, whose promenade has just been entirely rebuilt by a Chinese company. It owes its somewhat irregular layout to the fact that it was built on the site of a quay which followed the line of the river. To the east of the Corniche a garden has recently been restored after years of neglect. It is surrounded by bazaars which were relocated here as part of a campaign to smarten up the town.

The first pylon: the temple entrance is flanked by two colossi of Ramesses II and one of the two original obelisks.

THEBES: EAST BANK

By the mid-19th century Thebes was a shadow of its former self. It was nothing but a small town ranged against the Temple of Amenhotep III, a pile of ruins amidst a pile of more ancient ruins, which was under threat from the Nile floods and the lime kilns. Luxor, a town of 11,000 inhabitants in 1900, now has a population of 150,000 and is governed by a special statute which grants it an administrative autonomy unique throughout Egypt. The center of the town revolves around the Temple of Luxor. About 2 miles to the north lies the ruined Temple of Karnak. Some sections of the ancient paved way bordered by sphinxes, which used to link the temple to Luxor, have been excavated.

"EGYPTOMANIA". Following the successive waves of "Egyptomania" that swept Paris and London, and even reached the United States, there was an understandable attempt in this Ancient Egyptian capital to bring official buildings into line with a traditionally "Egyptian" form of architecture, especially after the discovery of the Tomb of Tutankhamun. The National Bank of Egypt near the Winter Palace, the spa south of the *Novotel*, the police station and the 1960's railway station are just a few examples. During the period when Upper Egypt was visited by train, the neo-Pharaonic stations of Edfu ▲ *448* and Kom Ombo ▲ *452* were obligatory stops on the itinerary.

COLONIAL ARCHITECTURE. At the northern end of the temple site are two ocher-colored houses belonging to the descendants of one of Luxor's old Coptic families. These houses have probably survived because they were sequestered after the 1952 revolution. The center of Thebes still has a few Art Deco and Italianate apartment blocks near the station and, in the Shari' el-Markaz, neo-Arabic-style wooden balconies. At the airport road intersection are three tropical-style, "Nubian" sandstone buildings with huge wooden verandahs: the villa of the head of Luxor Town Council, the "rest-house" of the Egyptian Ministry of Irrigation and the Anglican Coptic School.

TEMPLE OF LUXOR

This monumental complex was linked to Karnak by the long, straight *dromos* completed during the reign of Nectanebo I. The paved way, which is extremely well preserved in front of the temple, crossed the city and ended before a huge sandstone gate, of which only the eroded remains can be seen today. The gate opened onto a forecourt in the corner of which stands a small Roman chapel of burnt brick, dedicated to the god Serapis during the reign of Hadrian. The Temple of Luxor used to be called Ipet Resyt, which has often been translated as "Harem of the South". More broadly speaking it was a southern palace where the god resided like a king, attended by his servants, the priests. The temple was first excavated in 1881 by Gaston Maspero and the work was continued by his successors. Over a century later, during the excavation of the court of Amenhotep III (whose columns were in danger of collapsing), workmen found five carefully preserved royal statues from the New Kingdom buried in the sand about 3 feet below the level of the courtyard. Another twenty or so statues of pharaohs and divinities from different historical periods were discovered buried haphazardly beneath them. They are on display in the Luxor Museum, in a room shaped like a tomb.

Although the site was cleared by Gaston Maspero ● 96 in 1881 and studied by his successors, the Temple of Luxor has not yet been completely excavated because the Abu el-

Hagag Mosque stands on a solid mass of earth in the corner of the first court.

ABU EL-HAGAG MOSQUE. The mosque, dedicated to Sheikh Yussef Abu el-Hagag, is one of the oldest in Luxor. The sheikh, who came from Baghdad in the 12th century, was descended from the Prophet via Hassan, son of the Prophet's daughter Fatima. The Fatimid-style mosque has survived several attempts to demolish it and release the site. It has a beautiful mudbrick minaret to which a second was added in the early 20th century by the khedive Abbas Helmi.

"MULED" OF ABU EL-HAGAG. The *muled* ● 126 of Abu el-Hagag is the most important annual feast in Luxor and one of the best known in Upper Egypt. It is held on the fourteenth of the month of Sha'ban, the presumed date of the sheikh's arrival in the town. The *muled* is characterized by a procession of *feluccas* ● 122 carried by the Faithful, which is thought to be a ritual dating back to the ancient procession of the sacred barque of Amun from the Temple of Luxor to Karnak. For the Faithful the boats represent the one used by Abu el-Hagag on his journeys. Another special feature of the *muled* is a dish of minced meat, onions and crushed corn.

THEBAN TRIAD: AMUN, MUT AND KHONSU

The development of the domain of Amun-Re is linked to that of Thebes, the capital of Egypt from the 18th Dynasty. Each pharaoh recorded his devotion in stone. Karnak was first discovered in the 16th and studied from the 18th century, with the Donati excavations (1759) and Napoleon Bonaparte's Egypt Expedition (1798). The first Egyptologists appeared with Champollion (1828) while the excavation of the Temple of Amun, directed by Mariette (1858), marked the beginning of systematic research.

SACRED BARQUE OF AMUN
During the Beautiful Feast of the Valley and the Festival of Opet, Amun journeyed in his sacred barque carried by thirty priests. The vessel, in gilt and inlaid wood and decorated at the prow and stern with divine symbols, supported an openwork naos surmounted by a dais.

Temple of Montu

Eastern temple

Temple

Sacred lake

Seventh pylon

Eighth pylon

TEMPLE OF LUXOR
The Temple of Luxor, linked to Karnak by a *dromos* (1½ miles) built by Nectanebo, was where the Feast of Opet was celebrated. During the reign of Amenhotep III, the edifice consisted of a south sanctuary preceded by a peristyle court and a colonnade. The entrance pylon and first court were added by Ramesses II.

Ninth pylon

Tenth pylon

Temple of Khonsu

Temple of Opet

PLAN OF KARNAK
The largest enclosure in the center, with its nine gateways, was dedicated to Amun. The enclosure to the north contains the Temple of Montu, whose original layout is reminiscent of the Temple of Luxor. To the south, and linked to the Temple of Amun by a *dromos*, lies the temple of his wife Mut.

The chapel which served as a shrine for the sacred barques dates from the reign of Hatshepsut and was reused on this site by Ramesses II.

COURT OF RAMESSES II
On the south side of

PYLON AND COURT OF RAMESSES II. The great pylon forming the façade of the temple was preceded by colossi and two obelisks, of which only one remains. The other was transported to Paris in the 19th century and now stands in the Place de la Concorde. On the walls are scenes of the Battle of Kadesh, fought by Ramesses II against the Hittites in Syria. A chapel whose façade has four fasciculate granite columns stands in the corner of the first court behind the pylon. It was a triple shrine for the sacred barques of Amun, Mut and Khonsu, which were brought in through a western side door in direct line with the way leading from the quay. In the northeastern corner of the court the massive structure of a Coptic church (whose walls are still standing) provides the foundations of the ABU EL-HAGAG MOSQUE: three very different places of worship whose proximity makes a striking historical summary. Although the south side of the court, where "closed" papyrus columns alternate with pink granite colossi, was open to the public, this was as far as they could go. From here they watched the arrival of processions which then moved on into the part of the temple built during the reign of Amenhotep III.

THE COLONNADE. Two huge, black granite colossi representing Ramesses II seated on his throne and wearing the double crown of Upper and Lower Egypt mark the entrance to the

the court, alternate "closed" papyrus columns and pink granite colossi create a powerful effect. The statues on the left show Ramesses II walking majestically. At his side his queen, Nefertari, scarcely reaches to his knee.

great colonnade whose interior decoration dates from the short reign of Tutankhamun ▲ *418*. The young king's face appears in the sculpted groups (usurped by Ramesses II) at the entrance to the hall. Although the side walls have been reduced to less than one third of their original height, their decoration is extremely interesting because it depicts the first of Thebes' two most important religious festivals, the OPET FEAST (the name of the month in which it was held, the second month of the season of the Nile floods). The king had to take part in the feast at least in the first year of his reign since it confirmed that he was indeed the son of Amun-Re. Originally, during the reign of Hatshepsut, six chapel-shrines served as a "way station" for the sacred barques during their overland journey from Karnak to Luxor.

Only the return journey was made along the Nile. But from the reign of Amenhotep III, the festival was continually extended in size and duration (from eleven days to over three weeks) and both journeys were made by river. On the west wall of the columned court are scenes depicting the progress of the outward journey and, on the east wall, the return journey to Karnak. After it had passed through the colonnade, the procession of sacred barques entered the Court of Amenhotep III.

COURT OF AMENHOTEP III. The Court of Amenhotep III, with its fasciculate porticos, is virtually complete. The south side of the court opens onto a long hall, the pronaos of the temple. Two of the side chapels set in the back wall housed the barques of Mut and Khonsu, which ended their journey here. A central door led into an outer hall where there are signs of a large axial niche, remains of frescos and traces of the chapel (which venerated the insignia of the Roman legion that pitched camp around the temple in AD 301). The frescos represented a speech made by the emperor Diocletian at the time of his reorganization of the defense of Upper Egypt. In front of the niche, a canopy supported by four columns (of which only two remain) surmounted the altar. A door appears to have been recently pierced at the back of the niche to allow access into the temple. The door led into the offering hall whose decorations have retained some of their original colors. In the center of the next hall is a chapel built by Alexander the Great who is represented on its walls as a pharaoh, a status conferred on him after his victory by the priests of Amun of Siwa Oasis ▲ 256. The sacred barque of Amun ended its journey here and was placed on a pedestal, while Amun of Karnak entered all the side chambers of the eastern part of the temple. Today visitors enter beneath the Roman arch added to the entrance by Amenhotep III.

"MAMISSI". The ceremonies culminated in the next room, the so-called *mamissi* or "birth room", with the symbolic annual union of the queen mother and Amun-Re. Ancient texts explain how the god charmed the queen with his scent. The aim of this union was to engender the newborn child and consequently the king himself and his *ka*, which was the expression of his specific function: his royalty. This ceremony symbolized the

The great colonnade, seen from the Court of Amenhotep III.

THE PROCESSION OF SACRIFICIAL BULLOCKS
In the southwest corner of the Court of Ramesses II are reliefs showing the procession of sacrificial bullocks brought to the temple by shaven-headed priests dressed in pleated linen robes (above). At the head of the procession the pharaoh's many sons are recognizable by their long sidelocks. The scene depicts their entry into the temple. The pylon is shown from the front while all its original statues are seen in profile.

Detail from a papyrus scroll representing one of the sacred gods of Karnak.

"TALATTAT"
Talattat are the blocks of stone of equal size used for building during the reign of Akhenaten ● 42 and reused in

the construction of more recent edifices. The Luxor Museum has a wall (59 feet by 10 feet) of *talattat* blocks originally used in one of Akhenaten's temples at Thebes. The blocks were taken from the ninth pylon of the Temple of Karnak. The wall (detail right) was painstakingly reconstructed and shows Akhenaten and Nefertiti paying homage to Aten.

rebirth of the king's royal person and the confirmation of his power, since he was simultaneously re-engendered and recognized by Amun-Re. So when the pharaoh emerged from his temple, he appeared rejuvenated and invested with new strength and wisdom. Although the annual cycle would be repeated, he would remain the guarantor of order. The world would continue to function and Egypt would prosper.

APARTMENTS OF AMUN OF LUXOR. The rooms at the far end of the temple constituted the apartments of Amun of Luxor. They were arranged around the great transverse colonnaded hall. In the axial sanctuary chamber traces of the platform which supported the divine naos can still be seen. It may seem strange to the modern mind that Amun could reside simultaneously at Karnak, Luxor and in other temples. Amun was in fact omnipresent throughout the world and was represented in these sanctuaries in a special "concentrated" form. He could only be apprehended in his multiple aspects, each one of which was not only a reflection but also a part of the Great Whole. The Great Whole could not be expressed directly: his inconceivable magnitude, his power and his nature could only be glimpsed through symbols.

TOWARD KARNAK. The ancient route to the Temple of Karnak follows the SHARI' EL-MARKAZ, the main street, which runs parallel to the Corniche. This busy street is bordered by bazaars, restaurants and cafés with brightly colored signs. Near the Pharaonic-style police station is the oldest mosque in Luxor, the EL-MEKASHKESH MOSQUE, which contains the 10th-century remains of a saint who had come to Upper

Egypt to spread the teaching of Islam. The mosque has been restored many times and is often visited by pilgrims because of the miraculous powers attributed to the saint who, according to tradition, was a monk before converting to Islam. Opposite the mosque is the Franciscan Church and its adjacent schools (girls on the right and boys on the left), founded in 1889 and run by Franciscan nuns. Beyond the courthouse and the Coptic church stands the great Coptic basilica.

LUXOR MUSEUM

The Luxor Museum, which is situated midway between Karnak and Luxor on the Nile Corniche, is a useful complement to a visit to the two temple sites. In the great basement rooms, to the right of the entrance, are the remarkable discoveries made in 1989 in the great Court of Amenhotep III. These include an amazing quartzite reproduction of a life-size royal statue of Amenhotep III, which stands on the sled on which it was moved. Other fine statues include the goddesses Iwnit and Hathor

and, on a single pedestal, a group depicting Horemheb kneeling before Amun. On the first floor is an extremely fine basalt statue of Thutmose III, found in the "Hiding Courtyard" at Karnak, followed by an alabaster group representing the god Sobek and Amenhotep III. Against the wall the great stele of King Kamose depicts the decisive Theban victory over the Hyksos, which heralded the birth of the New Kingdom. On the second floor are scenes reconstructed from the *talattat* blocks taken from the ninth pylon, and a fine head of Amenhotep IV (Akhenaten) also taken from the edifices built by this king to the east of the great Temple of Amun-Re. Near the ramp is a colossus of Senwosret I in the guise of Osiris, which is thought to have come from the façade of the Middle Kingdom temple at Karnak. At the intersection, the Shari' el-Markaz becomes the SHARI' EL-KARNAK and, after crossing a small bridge, the remains of the recently excavated *dromos* that once linked the Temple of Luxor to the Temple of Karnak gradually come into view, lower down, in the middle of a village. From the ruined Temple of Mut, on the left-hand side, a second *dromos* leads to the gateway of the tenth pylon. It passes the great *pisé* enclosure wall, the gateway of Ptolemy III Euergetes and several houses which can be seen on the left before it finally arrives at the domed tomb of two saints (Sidi Ahmed and Sidi Ali). A road running past the Department of Antiquities leads to the main entrance of the temple.

"Anyone who has drunk of the waters of the Nile, seeks to return to the Nile, for no other water can slake their thirst. Anyone born in Thebes seeks to return to Thebes for no other city in the world can compare with Thebes. Anyone born in a street in Thebes seeks to return to that street; in cedarwood palaces, they long for a hut built of clay; amidst the scent of myrrh and perfumed unguents, they long for the smell of dried cow-dung burning on the fire and the aroma of fried fish ... Would that I were a swallow or crane with powerful wings to fly in the face of my guards toward the land of Kemi. I would build my nest on the marbled columns of the Temple of Amun, amidst the dazzling, golden brilliance of the obelisks, the scent of incense and the aroma of fatted sacrificial victims."
Mika Waltari
The Egyptian

403

Only priests and
those who served the
god were allowed into
the inner sanctum of
the temple, which was
a veritable "holy city"
enclosed by a high
mudbrick wall. The
temple was not so
much a place of
worship for the
ordinary rank and file
as one where
mysterious
ceremonies involving
precise and complex
rituals were held, with
a view to maintaining
cosmic harmony. All
that ordinary
Thebans saw of the
temple were its gates,
its enclosure wall and
the paved access
ways. What could be
more impressive than
the permanent
presence of this
awesome, hidden
power?

TEMPLE OF KARNAK

GREAT TEMPLE OF AMUN-RE. The ancient name of Karnak,
Ipet Sut ("the most hallowed of places"), designates the
"center of the world" where Amun, the creator of the
universe, first created himself and then all things and living
beings. He combined the power of the Theban demiurge
(Amun) with that of the supreme sun-god of Heliopolis (Re).
He was the guarantor of the continued survival of the
universe that he had created and therefore of the kingdom
ruled by his "beloved son" pharaoh, the only official priest.
Mankind, by worshipping in the temple, could help preserve
the cosmic harmony so essential to life, and encompassed by
the Egyptian concept of *ma'at* ● *63* which signified truth,
order and justice. All this was part of the pharaohs' duty.
Their watchword was "Life, Stability and Strength".
ORGANIZATION OF THE TEMPLE. Amun resided in his temple
and was served by a hierarchy of priests who not only
performed the sacred rites but also carried out the intellectual
and material tasks associated with the running of the most
important sanctuary in Egypt. Among other things, this
involved managing a
vast agricultural
domain. A total of
eighty thousand

people served the temple during the reign of Ramesses III and the High Priest of Amun was a prominent figure who attended all the important events in the life of the kingdom. For more than two thousand years, from the end of the second millennium BC, the pharaohs erected monuments at Karnak as an offering to their divine father Amun-Re to ensure his good offices. Each one modified, embellished and extended Karnak, often demolishing the edifices of his predecessors to dedicate a new building, while Amun-Re, present in the small gold statue which stood in a monolithic kiosk (naos) in the depths of the temple, shone in the darkness.

ARRIVING AT THE TEMPLE: THE QUAY. Karnak is reached along an access road built on the site of the canal that once linked the Temple of Amun to the Nile. All that remains of the dock (now filled in) is the quay and the central raised dais. In ancient times the quay and its approaches were planted with trees and groves. Below the quay to the right (south of the dais) and beyond a Roman dock in red brick are two parallel paved ramps bordered by stone parapets, built during the reign of Taharqa ● 44, which once led down to the river bank. Beyond the ramps lies the CHAPEL OF ACHORIS, a columned structure with screenlike walls received the sacred barque of Amun on the occasion of its ceremonial voyages. The western *dromos* leading to the temple entrance is bordered by crio-SPHINXES, creatures with the body of a lion (the epitome of vigilance and guardianship and the symbol of royalty) and the head of a ram (the symbolic animal of Amun and the embodiment of physical strength and procreant energy). Nestling between the feet of the god is a statue of his son Ramesses II. To the right, just before the entrance, are the remains of a Roman chapel dedicated to imperial worship.

"I know that Karnak is the horizon above the earth, the glorious first ascension, the sacred eye of the Master of the Universe": an inscription by Hatshepsut ● 426 on one of the obelisks.

Details of the great enclosure wall.

THE "DROMOS"
The sphinxes lining the processional way were thought to protect the journey of the sacred barques leaving the temple.

405

HYPOSTYLE HALL
One can only imagine the splendor of the axial aisle when twelve papyrus columns supported the 82-foot-high ceiling. Light flooded in through the high traceried windows, which opened onto the central nave, while the side aisles remained in the shadows. Here and there a fine pencil of light penetrated the few square openings pierced in the stone ceiling. This "thicket" of giant papyri symbolized the force of life which abounds near its creator. Their "roots" plunged into the water of the *nun* (underground water table), while their stems thrust upward and their corollas opened toward the sky of the blue-painted ceiling.

The steps of the chapel, front colonnade and walls are red brick. Inside are pedestals (once surmounted by statues) inscribed with the names of Roman emperors. The emperors, often represented in the guise of pharaohs on the bas-reliefs of later temples, were honored during the first three centuries AD. The great temple entrance has lost its granite lintel (weighing about 440 tons), whose fragments lie strewn on the ground. It is flanked by two sandstone piers attributed to Nectanebo I. The building was never completed, and the walls have a rough appearance. The pylon, the largest in Egypt, is thought to have once stood about 105 feet high. The piers of a pylon represented the mountain chains which bordered the fertile valley (the only inhabitable part of the region), the two horizons between which the sun (often carved on the cornice in the center of the entrance) ran its course. The pylon protected the temple entrance and gave access to the sacred area. Near the top of the gateway, to the right, an inscription commemorates the visit of the members of the Egypt Expedition ● *140* in 1799.

COLUMN OF TAHARQA
The giant papyrus column is all that remains of the kiosk of Taharqa, which stood in the center of the temple's first court.

FIRST COURT. The KIOSK OF TAHARQA, in the middle of the first court, has one remaining column. At its center is the alabaster pedestal on which the sacred barque of Amun-Re rested. The sides of the court are bounded by colonnades from the Bubastite period. At the foot of these columns are traces of a row of rams, the remains of the eastern section of the *dromos* which was removed when the court and kiosk were built. Behind the pylon, to the right, a pile of mudbrick is all that remains of the ramp used to build the edifice. Above the ramp, in the stone façade, a Coptic niche and rows of horizontal holes into which floors were fitted are the legacy of one of the monasteries built inside the temple from the 7th century onward. On the left of the court is the edifice built by Sety II whose three chapels served as a way station for the sacred barques of Amun, Mut and Khonsu. The CENTRAL CHAPEL, preceded by two royal statues (only the pedestals have survived), accommodated the barque of Amun, which was decorated on the prow and stern with rams' heads. At the far end of the building are three niches which held royal devotional statues. On the right is the CHAPEL OF KHONSU, whose sacred barque was decorated at both ends with a falcon's head surmounted by a crescent moon and disk. On the left is the CHAPEL OF MUT, whose barque was decorated with the statue of a woman wearing the crowns of Upper and Lower Egypt. To the south of the court, a temple built by Ramesses III includes a pylon preceded by colossi, a court and covered halls. It has no shrine, but three rooms which accommodated the barques. At the far end of the great court are the damaged piers of the second pylon, built by Horemheb. The shattered statue of Pinedjem I has been reinstated in front of the entrance. The pylon's gateway,

An impression of strange strength and beauty is created by the superhuman proportions of the hypostyle hall which formed the antechamber (pronaos) of the temple. It was here that the sacred barques gathered before leaving the temple and where part of the coronation ceremonies were held, strikingly depicted in the bas-reliefs decorating the walls. The far wall of the right side aisle includes a scene showing Ramesses II receiving his "jubilees" (promising many years on the throne) from the hands of Amun-Re.

Detail of a fresco representing the procession of the sacred barque.

THUTMOSE III
A row of royal colossi representing Thutmose III stands along the west wall of the "Wadjyt Hall". The king is standing with his arms crossed and is wearing the tight-fitting costume of the *sed,* or jubilee, celebrations. This is a reminder of the original function of the hall, which was used for one of the stages of the coronation ceremony: the apposition of the crowns of Upper and Lower Egypt.

rebuilt during the Ptolemaic period and flanked by two colossi of Ramesses II, leads into the great colonnaded hall begun by Sety I and completed by Ramesses II.

COURT OF THE OBELISKS: THE TEMPLE GATE. As you leave the great hypostyle hall through the gateway of the badly damaged third pylon, you come into a narrow court where several symmetrical obelisks once stood. This was the main point of intersection of the two main axes of the temple, just in front of the entrance to the covered halls. Only one of the obelisks erected by Thutmose I remains, alongside the granite plinths of two of its neighbors, erected by Thutmose III. The eastern gate of the temple, built by the architect Ineni, was preceded by a lightweight canopy supported by two gold-plated columns. As you pass through the gateway of the pylon, you are left to imagine the dark, covered halls. The first, "Wadjyt ('verdant' or 'flourishing') Hall", was refurbished several times. The colossi of Thutmose I are a reminder of its original function: the apposition of the crowns of Upper and Lower Egypt. It was then converted for a short time into a narrow court where Queen Hatshepsut erected two magnificent obelisks. Thutmose III, who wanted to overshadow his co-regent, restored the columned hall.

BARQUE SHRINE AND PALACE OF MA'AT. The next pylon leads into the inner part of the temple and the central chapel-shrine built of huge granite blocks whose final stage (which can still be seen today) dates from the time of Philip III Arrhidaeus, half-brother and successor of Alexander the Great. It is preceded by a vestibule comprising two pillars carved with the symbolic plants of the Two Lands: the papyrus (north) of Lower Egypt and the lotus (south) of Upper Egypt. The chapel has two sections: a vestibule to the west and then the shrine proper, whose central pedestal is extremely well preserved. It was here that the sacred barque of Amun-Re rested when the god was not traveling. The walls are decorated, on four registers, with scenes showing the king making offerings to Amun-Re represented in his two most common guises (as a king walking and as an ithyphallic, mummiform being). The reliefs on the south wall of the chapel have retained some of their colors. The sacred barque is represented as it appeared during the ceremonies of the "Beautiful Feast of the Valley", which took the divine procession to the west bank of the Nile. The chapel stands in the center of a monumental complex known as the "Palace of Ma'at", which included a suite of offering halls. In front of a stele (in the form of a false door) inlaid with lapis lazuli and

Colossal statue of
Ramesses II.

a huge offering table (neither of which have survived), the
god received his "meal" in the form of an offering of food
which was recovered and redistributed by the priests once he
had "eaten his fill". As you make your way round the outside
of the chapel, from south to north, you come across a door
with black granite uprights which opens onto a series of small
rooms. The first shows the ritual purification of Hatshepsut by
Horus and Thoth. The water they pour over her is
represented by a double line of "crosses of life". In the upper
register is the "royal ascent" of the queen accompanied by the
gods. The queen's effigy and name have been hacked out,
another example of Thutmose III's campaign against the
memory of the queen who, for more than twenty years, had
overshadowed him by retaining the regency entrusted to her
on the death of her husband, Thutmose II.

"MIDDLE KINGDOM COURT": THE LOST SANCTUARY. Below the
chapel, to the east, is an area which today resembles a sort of
court. It is in fact the site of a former sanctuary and its
annexes, built at the time of the foundation of the temple
during the Middle Kingdom. The monumental complex,
constructed in fine limestone by Senwosret I, constituted the
heart of the temple and was hallowed for as long as the latter
was in use. It disappeared into the limestone kilns of the
inhabitants who occupied the site when the temple was
abandoned. A court must have preceded the series of gates
(the "Gates of the Hereafter", of which only the granite
thresholds have survived) while a huge alabaster
platform is probably all that remains of the naos,
the kiosk which contained the god's statue. The
daily rites of worship were performed here. Every
morning the duty priest broke the seal affixed the
previous night and opened the wooden shutters of
the naos. The officiating priest dressed and
prepared the god, reciting the appropriate prayers
and making offerings while he ministered to his
"needs". He then withdrew, discreetly removing
every trace of his footsteps on the thin layer of
sand on the floor. Everything in this dark, silent
place was steeped in an air of mystery and respect.

THE "AKHMENU" AND ITS ANNEXES. Since the walls have been destroyed it is possible to pass directly into the annexes built by Thutmose III against the east wall of the temple. The most prominent feature of this monumental complex is the great columned hall, known during antiquity as the "Akhmenu" ("jewel of monuments"). It is better to approach it through the entrance to the complex, which lies to the south between two polygonal columns. One of the Osiride colossi that flanked the entrance is still standing. In the southern part of the complex a long corridor leads to a series of small side rooms. The first seven were used to preserve the ritual offerings of food and the last two were split-level magazines. A square hall decorated with images of the sacred barques of Amun, Mut and Khonsu leads back to the great hall. The great hall of the Akhmenu has retained its stone revetment

and most of its original wall-paintings, particularly its azure ceiling scattered with gold stars. On the right of the entrance is the "Chamber of the Ancestors", a tiny chapel dedicated to the royal ancestors of Thutmose III, whose walls have been restored using casts made from the original blocks in the Louvre Museum in Paris. The room is basilican in design and comprises a raised, central "nave" illuminated by high windows and two side aisles whose roof is supported by columns in the form of ancient jubilee tent-pegs, a reference to the function of the monumental complex. The mysterious ceremonies associated with the jubilee celebrations were in fact performed here, beginning in the southern suite of rooms, which could be reached through the side door opening onto a well-preserved, eight-columned hall. This was the chthonian part of the complex associated with the journey through the Underworld in which the god Sokar, the main participant in the nocturnal regeneration of the sun, interceded. The ceremonies took place inside the great hall of the Akhmenu where the sacred barques were placed. The fifteen bays of the great hall are noticeably unequal. The central bay is much wider than the others and the texts are arranged symmetrically on the architraves along its axis, which is aligned with the great solar axis of the temple. An axial door to the east opens onto a series of three rooms ending in a narrow door whose raised threshold once stood above an alabaster pedestal. This discrete side entrance is like the doorway to a hidden crypt and leads into a vestibule with four well-preserved, fasciculate columns whose walls are decorated with flora and fauna: the "botanical garden" of Karnak. It is situated opposite the secret sanctuary which consisted of a long hall with niched side walls (most of the niches have since been destroyed). By contrast, the immense red quartzite pedestal which supported the naos at the far end of the hall is well preserved. In front of it stands a huge, granite offering table. To the north of the Akhmenu are three parallel chapels. A staircase on the right leads to the "upper room", which is open to the sky and where a central altar is aligned with the four points of the compass. The room symbolized the victory of the sun, which, having journeyed through the Underworld, rose in the east in the form of the scarab beetle Khepri, pushing the shining disk between its front feet. The union with the solar disk, one of the closing ceremonies of the jubilee, was performed here and was repeated on the occasion of each new annual cycle. During this ceremony the divine and royal statues were exposed to the rays of the rising sun so that they assimilated its vital energy.

EASTERN BUILDINGS. A wooden gallery runs across the rear of the temple toward the east. Along the axis the nearby ruins of the small TEMPLE OF THE HEARING EAR can be found, so called in ancient times because it was here that the Thebans were able to present their prayers to Amun. The single, axial obelisk which used to stand on the site of the sanctuary is now in Rome. It is one of the largest of its kind.

SACRED LAKE. A tour of the temple takes you, a little further south, to the vast stretch of water known as the sacred lake. To the east, below the stands used for the Sound and Light Show, is the area where the temple priests lived. By following the edge of the lake you come to the remains of a temple built by Taharqa. At one corner of this crumbling edifice with its misshapen walls is the huge granite scarab beetle representing the god Khepri, whose pedestal is engraved with the name of Amenhotep III.

SACRED LAKE
Water from the sacred lake, thought to be a resurgence of the *nun* (primordial water), was used for ablution, purification and the preparation of offerings in the rooms on the far side of the lake. The lake was also the scene of the "sacred voyages" made by statues of the gods in small boats.

AKHMENU
The ceiling of the Festival Court of Thutmose III is supported by two rows of ten columns and a row of thirty-two pillars. It has retained much of its polychrome decoration.

411

Gateway of the seventh pylon, flanked by statues of Thutmose III.

Statue of the god Amun in the four-columned hall in the Temple of Khonsu.

PROCESSIONAL WAY. The north–south axis of Karnak consists mainly of a series of pylons and courts. The entrance is through the side gate of the first court, the so-called "Hiding Courtyard", which was the scene of an amazing discovery in the early 20th century of thousands of statues and bronzes. These had been removed from the inner rooms of the temple during the Ptolemaic period to release space and facilitate the restoration of the walls, and hidden beneath the pavement of the court where they remained for thousands of years. The finest of the statues can be seen in the Luxor ▲ *403* and Cairo ▲ *276* museums. To the south lies the seventh pylon, built by Thutmose III. Two obelisks used to stand in front of the south façade until the western obelisk was removed in AD 330 on the orders of Constantine. Today it stands in Istanbul, not far from the Church of St Sophia, on the site of the Constantinople Hippodrome where it was relocated. A little further on stand the eighth and ninth pylons, built by Hatshepsut and Horemheb respectively. Inside the ninth pylon tens of thousands of *talattat* were discovered, which had come from edifices built to the east of the temple by Amenhotep IV (Akhenaten) at the beginning of his reign. About one hundred of these blocks have been reassembled and are on display on the second floor of the Luxor Museum. On the east side of the next court is a jubilee structure, built by Amenhotep II, comprising a porticoed façade and an axial ramp. Finally the tenth pylon, begun by Amenhotep III and completed by Horemheb, marks the southern boundary of the site. Huge statues of Amenhotep III once stood in front of it.

TEMPLE OF KHONSU. The Temple of Khonsu, built by Ramesses III, is certainly the most complete and the most revealing of Karnak's architectural structures. Its main entrance was through the great gateway built by Ptolemy III, set in the southern section of the enclosure wall. The edifice is virtually intact. Engraved on the cornice is a solar disk flanked by two protective cobras facing each of the two horizons. It is framed by two great, extended wings which symbolize its heavenly flight. The entrance to the court of the temple is through the gateway of the pylon, which is on the whole well preserved. Beyond the covered hypostyle hall are the remains of a central pedestal for the barque of Khonsu and, beyond that, a four-columned hall with a central altar. The shrine is situated right at the back of the temple. The Temple of Khonsu offers visitors the opportunity to see the most secret part of the temple, no longer possible in the Temple of Amun. It is also a very good example of the general layout of an Egyptian temple, in which the rooms become progressively smaller from the entrance to the inner sanctum: the shrine containing the god's statue.

TEMPLE OF OPET. The remains of the Temple of Opet lie to the west and at right angles to the Temple of Khonsu. The later section, built during the Ptolemaic period, is the best preserved. Its external decoration was never completed. In the temple forecourt is a statue of the lioness Sekhmet and nearby an altar and a pool. This layout was linked to the healing powers of the goddess whose help was solicited by those who were sick and infirm through their prayers and magic.

OPEN-AIR MUSEUM. A visit to Karnak should be complemented by a walk to the Open-Air Museum, which can be reached before leaving the site through the north gate of the first court of the Temple of Amun. It has a collection of monuments mainly discovered during excavations carried out inside the third pylon. First of all, blocks from the "RED CHAPEL" of Hatshepsut, a beautiful building which served as a shrine for the barque of Amun and whose site is today occupied by the chapel of Philip Arrhidaeus, are presented course by course on ledges. Further on, in the shade of some trees, the magnificent "WHITE CHAPEL" of Senwosret I, the most elegant and ancient structure in Karnak, has been reconstructed from the blocks of stone recovered. Built in the style of a jubilee kiosk, it has a roof, openwork sides and two entrances, and stands on a raised platform. Its delicately carved scenes show the king making offerings to Amun-Re and Amun in his ithyphallic form. The different nomes (the administrative areas of Egypt) are listed in the form of columns on the parapet. Thus the entire region is represented on the chapel of the king who took possession of it, the pharaoh and guarantor of the order established by Amun. A little further north the "ALABASTER CHAPEL" of AMENHOTEP I, the oldest known barque shrine, has been rebuilt. Inside the shrine, the king is shown presenting offerings to the sacred barque. Finally, beyond the reconstruction of the summit of a small limestone pylon constructed by Thutmose II is that of the "Festival Court" built by Thutmose IV, which used to be situated in front of the fourth pylon on the site of the eastern side of the hypostyle hall.

Detail of a fresco in the Temple of Khonsu.

THE "RED CHAPEL"
The shrine of the sacred barque was built by Hatshepsut entirely in red quartzite, apart from its black granite foundations and doors. The queen is depicted throughout as a pharaoh (below) and is either alone or precedes Thutmose III, intentionally stressing her ascendancy over her co-regent.

413

TEMPLE OF MUT

In the courts of the Temple of Mut rows of strange statues of Sekhmet stand among clumps of alfa-grass. There must have been at least one for each day of the year.

"Walking into Karnak was like walking into one of Piranesi's Prisons, solidified suddenly into stone, and grown to natural, nay to heroic size . . . . Beyond the aisle, a vast space littered with fallen masonry lay open to the sky. Cavernous openings, porticos, colonnades, blocks of masonry; obelisks, statues of Pharaohs, some upright, some prone; and beyond them, beyond this magnificent desolation, shrilled the thin piping of the frogs . . . It crushed the mind, since it was not the human mind that had conceived it as it now appeared, but such inhuman factors as time upon earth."

Vita Sackville-West

TEMPLE OF PTAH. The sunken path opposite the north entrance of the great hypostyle hall runs past two chapels dedicated to the "Divine Votaresses of Amun" and leads to the Temple of Ptah, the great god of Memphis who also had a shrine in Thebes. The statue of Sekhmet (his wife), found on the site, has been reinstated in one of the rooms at the back of the temple. The light filters down onto the statue of the powerful woman who was once no stranger to the innermost chambers of the great Temple of Amun-Re.

TEMPLE OF MONTU. The Temple of Montu, the warrior god of Thebes, lies beyond the gate of the great precinct situated opposite the entrance to the Temple of Ptah. The edifice, built by Amenhotep III, is fairly extensively ruined and is not open to the public. It is possible, however, to admire the huge Ptolemaic gateway of the precinct, opposite which there was once a *dromos* and a quay.

TEMPLE OF MUT. South of the tenth pylon and less than 450 yards from the Precinct of Amun is the Temple of Mut, the wife of the great god of Thebes. The now-ruined temple, built by Amenhotep III, has a special romantic charm. On the sides of a ruined colonnade are reliefs representing the god Bes, a bearded and beneficent dwarf and, in the court, rows of strange statues of Sekhmet. The temple is surrounded on three sides by the waters of the crescent-shaped sacred lake (Asheru), which shine and sparkle through clumps of reeds. Beyond the lake is the TEMPLE OF RAMESSES III, preceded by "walking" royal colossi. To the left of the great entrance, in the northeast corner of the precinct, another badly ruined temple, dating from the reign of Amenhotep III and dedicated to Amun-Re, still has some of its painted scenes. Outside the Precinct of Mut is the recently excavated *dromos* which once linked the temple entrance to the great paved way (1½ miles long) which led to Luxor.

MODERN BUILDINGS. On the left as you leave the temple is the Franco-Egyptian Center which, since 1967, has been responsible for the conservation, study and restoration of the temples. The traditional, Nubian-style residence of the permanent CNRS (Centre National de la Recherche Scientifique) mission which constitutes the French team stands lower down on the shores of the Nile. The Epigraphic Survey of the Oriental Institute of the University of Chicago, generally known as Chicago House, has a research library renowned for its photographic collection, which includes an important 19th-century section. Chicago House, founded in 1924 by James Breasted and based in Luxor, gathers information on the sites of Upper Egypt using photogrammetric techniques.

CROSSING THE RIVER

All the other important remains in Thebes are found on the opposite bank, which is reached, as in ancient times, by boat. The crossing, which is today one of the main attractions of a visit to Luxor, once had symbolic significance. For the Ancient Egyptians, the westward crossing was not so much a journey to the shores of the Dead (an unthinking, modern interpretation) but more the voyage to the land of Life.

THE GODDESS SEKHMET
Inside the right-hand (south) chapel of the Temple of Ptah stands a black granite statue of Sekhmet, the wife of Ptah. The lion goddess (whose name means "powerful") sometimes unleashed her anger against mortals, especially on the last five days of the year, and was only appeased by long prayers recited by priests. She also possessed healing powers.

THE SACRED VALLEY ✪
You would need more than one visit to fully cover the biggest funeral complex in Egypt. It extends over 18 miles and you should alternate walking with taxis. Start with the Valley of the Kings (the tombs are opened in turn from year to year) then rejoin the temples of Deir el-Bahri by the path and finish with the tomb of Ramesses II. Keep the Valley of the Queens for a second visit (of the twenty-four tombs of queens and their children, five are visible), together with the complex of Medinet Habu and Deir el-Medina, the village and necropolis of those whose lives were dedicated to the building of these monuments.

THEBES: WEST BANK

For the Ancient Egyptians the west was not the direction of finality and death but rather the way to the "kingdom of the West" where the deceased could be admitted by Osiris to the Day of Judgment. It was also the direction taken by the setting sun before it journeyed through the Underworld. When it disappeared into the shadows the heavenly body was gradually regenerated and reappeared each morning as a new being. These two aspects of rebirth (Osirian and solar) are represented in all the funerary monuments, tombs and temples on the west bank of Thebes. The Egyptians who cultivated this fertile valley believed that the kingdom of Osiris resembled this earthly kingdom of fields, canals and agriculture. It was a sort of familiar, earthly paradise where the deceased could enjoy a happy life for eternity. They could only recover their completeness, temporarily lost at the moment of death, by gathering together all the various elements which made up their identity during their earthly life: their body, their *ka* (vital energy which was both preserving and creative), their *ba* (spiritual element), their *ankh* (immortality), their shadow and their name.

FUNERARY RITES. The body, in particular, was essential to the life that mummification aimed to preserve. The mortal remains, brought by boat from the east bank, were prepared more or less carefully, depending on the family's financial resources. Specialist priests, imitating the rites originally performed by Anubis on the body of Osiris, removed the entrails which were preserved in four Canopic jars (whose stoppers represented each of the four sons of Horus) and placed in the tomb near

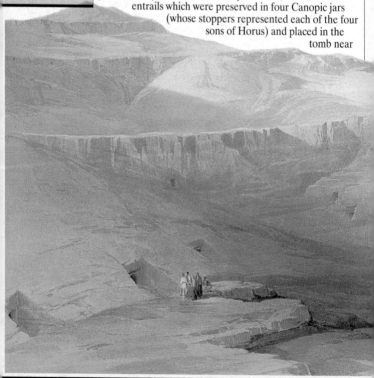

the sarcophagus. Once the body was cleaned, dried out with natron and coated with ointments, it was tightly bound in strips of cloth. There were many embalming rooms between the Nile and the Theban necropolis.

VALLEY OF THE KINGS

The royal necropolis, known in ancient times as "the Place of Truth", is a logical place to start a visit to the west bank. None of the tombs in the western valley is open to the public and only the present Valley of the Kings enables visitors to discover the very singular world of the 18th- and 19th-Dynasty pharaohs. The mountain of Thebes at the far end of the valley in fact forms a

natural pyramid both in terms of its shape and its function since it contains sixty or so royal tombs.

THE GREAT ROYAL HYPOGEA. Today it is only possible to visit about a dozen of the great royal tombs. They are opened in turn from year to year to limit the amount of damage caused by the vast numbers of visitors and enable restoration work to be carried out. The tomb of Ramesses II (a large part of which has collapsed) and that of his father, Sety I, are not open to the public. The latter tomb is famed not only for the quality but also for the extent of its decoration (details above and right), which must be protected and preserved. The royal tombs were entirely hewn out of the living rock, sometimes penetrating deep through alternating layers of limestone and flint.

"THE BOOK OF THE DEAD"
Sacred texts containing the formulae to be pronounced in the presence of the guardians of the gates of the Twelve Hours of the night were placed in the tombs. These formulae were found in the chapters of what is known today as *The Book of the Dead* but which the Egyptians called *The Book of the Coming Forth by Day*.

Although one of the smallest in the necropolis, the Tomb of Tutankhamun is undoubtedly the most famous of the Egyptian tombs as a result of the extraordinary discoveries made there in the early 20th century. It had been protected by a particular set of circumstances. An attempt to plunder it during antiquity had proved unsuccessful; the thieves must have been surprised and the tomb closed up again. The debris from the later excavation of the nearby hypogeum of Ramesses VI covered and disguised the entrance to such an extent that the tomb remained exceptionally well concealed from would-be plunderers for centuries. In 1922 Howard Carter directed excavations on the site under the sponsorship of Lord Carnarvon. He was about to abandon his search when a small flight of steps suddenly appeared . . .

THE SITE
Having explored the Valley of the Kings fairly unsuccessfully for several years, Howard Carter decided, and with good reason, to concentrate on the ancient workers' huts located at the foot of the Tomb of Ramesses IV.

LORD CARNARVON
For several years Lord Carnarvon (1866–1923) financed excavations in the Valley of the Kings which ended with the discovery, by Howard Carter, of the Tomb of Tutankhamun. He died before the tomb had been completely excavated, a task which took almost ten years.

Howard Carter (1873–1939) began his career in Egypt as a draftsman. In 1899 he was appointed inspector general of monuments in Upper Egypt.

DISCOVERY OF THE TOMB

When the door of the tomb was cleared on November 4, 1922 the fact that it had been re-sealed gave rise to fears that the tomb had been plundered. One can imagine Carter's amazement when, on November 25, he got his first glimpse of the priceless contents of the sepulcher: "At first, I could see nothing. The flame of the candle flickered as hot air was released from the chamber. Then, as my eyes grew accustomed to the darkness, shapes gradually began to emerge: strange creatures, statues, and, everywhere, shining gold. For a few seconds – which must have seemed like an eternity to my companions – I was speechless." Carter had just discovered the greatest treasure ever bequeathed by Pharaonic Egypt.

INSIDE THE TOMB

Everything a king could possibly need in the Hereafter was arranged in these small rooms: dismantled chariots, furniture, chests, vases, statues and various kinds of food. The initial impression created by so many objects piled up in this cramped space was that of a strange collection of bric-a-brac rather than a logical arrangement.

THE FUNERAL MASK

On the forehead were carved Nekhbet (the vulture) and Bruto (the serpent), the symbols of the Two Lands governed by the king. On the chin was the beard symbolizing Osiris and, around the neck, a three-tiered necklace of gold and blue faience.

THE MUMMY

Inside the third sarcophagus was a mummy whose hands – covered in gold, crossed on its chest and sewn to the linen shroud – held a flail and crook, the emblems of Osiris. On the outer linen shroud was a representation, decorated with gold elements, of the flight of the Ba (the spiritual element).

The items were obviously of more value for their physical, effective presence than for the way in which they were arranged. In the tomb they were fulfilling their role mystically, just as ordinary objects fulfilled their role in the world of the living. Today the treasure of Tutankhamun can be seen in the Cairo Museum ▲ 276.

THE SARCOPHAGUS

The wooden chests which slotted inside one another, and the successive sarcophagi, or coffins, formed protective layers around the royal mummy. The first coffin was in gilt wood and measured just over 7 feet. The second coffin (6½ feet), covered in gold and inlaid with glass to imitate precious stones, symbolized Osiris. The third and final coffin (6 feet) was wrapped in a reddish linen shroud. It was in solid gold and represented the pharaoh as a boy. The neck and chest were encircled by a neckpiece of seeds and flowers sewn on papyrus. Inside the coffin was a mummy whose head was covered with a gold mask representing Tutankhamun with the attributes of Osiris.

421

ROYAL TOMBS

In this dark, enclosed world the themes represented on the walls were usually allusions to different chapters of the sacred books: the *Book of the Opening of the Mouth*, the *Book of What is in the Underworld*, the *Book of Gates*, the *Book of Caverns*, the *Litany of Re*... Their purpose was to help the deceased to overcome the obstacles encountered during the journey through the Underworld. There are many images of the difficult route through the darkness, which is depicted as a combat fought by the dead, with the help of the appropriate ritual formulae and guided by the gods, before being finally reborn in the manner of Osiris and Re.

Plaster revetments evened out the irregularities of the walls. The occasionally carved but mainly drawn decorations were painted and it was not uncommon for this type of tomb ornamentation to be completed at the time of the king's death. A large royal tomb had a main staircase (carefully sealed after the burial) and then a descending corridor. During the 18th Dynasty this led onto an interior gallery which was sometimes interrupted by a huge well and might also make several sharp turns before reaching the burial chamber. During the 19th Dynasty the route was generally more rectilinear in design. The burial chamber, situated at the furthest point on this route, housed the sarcophagus containing the royal mummy. Furniture was arranged around it and in small adjoining rooms. The most logical visitor's route from the entrance to the end of the Valley of the Kings cannot take into account the chronological order of the tombs.

TOMB OF RAMESSES IX. This is the first tomb (no. 6) on the route. Its corridor is flanked by four rooms decorated with scenes from the sacred books, while beautiful astronomical images are painted on the blue background of the ceiling. Priests dressed in panther skins are depicted in the furthest room. A four-pillared room precedes the burial chamber where only the mark of the sarcophagus remains on the floor.

TOMB OF MERNEPTAH. The tomb (no. 8) of the son and successor of Ramesses II has a steeply sloping corridor which crosses the first room. In a pillared side room opening off the first, the king is depicted in the presence of various gods. The corridor crosses another room before finally reaching the

422

vaulted burial chamber, which contains a pink granite sarcophagus.

TOMB OF RAMESSES VI. This is one of most complete and best preserved tombs (no. 9) in the necropolis. The first section of the corridor is decorated with images from the *Book of Gates*. The sky goddess Nut (who swallows the solar disk in the evening and gives birth to it each morning) is depicted among the various constellations on the great vault of the sarcophagus chamber.

TOMB OF RAMESSES III. On either side of the entrance to the tomb (no. 11) are two sculpted heads of Hathor, goddess of the Theban necropolis. The decoration of the small side rooms is remarkable for the sheer variety of scenes represented: the preparation of offerings, sailing boats, Nile gods, divinities of the various nomes and two blind harpists singing the king's praises. The next rooms have scenes from the *Book of What is in the Underworld* and the pillared room from the *Book of Gates*. The sarcophagus has been removed from the eight-pillared burial chamber and is today housed in the Louvre Museum ▲ *476* in Paris.

TOMB OF RAMESSES I. The short reign of the founder of the 19th Dynasty explains the small size of his tomb (no. 16). The funeral chamber is decorated entirely with scenes depicting the king in the presence of various divinities and extracts from the *Book of Gates*.

TOMB OF HOREMHEB. In the lower part of the tomb (no. 57), where the scenes are depicted against a blue-gray background, it is possible to see the various stages of the wall paintings. Once the general outline had been established, the drawing was painted in red and then corrected in black by a more expert hand before the different colors were added.

TOMB OF AMENHOTEP II. The scenes in the first rooms of the tomb

TOMB OF RAMESSES III
The variety of scenes depicted in the side rooms is remarkable. The next rooms have scenes from the *Book of What is in the Underworld*, the pillared room from the *Book of Gates* and the corridor from the *Litany of Re*. The goddess Hathor, the Nile god, and Ramesses III (opposite, below).

423

TOMB OF THUTMOSE III
A very steep wooden staircase (below) leads to the concealed entrance of the Tomb of Thutmose III (no. 34) high on the hillside. The very stylized decoration (right) is like that of Amenhotep II's tomb. The rounded corners of the funeral chamber and the tomb's overall design evokes that of a royal cartouche.

(no. 35) show the king in the presence of Osiris, Anubis and Hathor. The extremely stylized decoration of the funeral chamber (painted in black against an ocher background) is reminiscent of the writing on a huge papyrus and evokes the *Book of What is in the Underworld*. The mummy was still in its sarcophagus when the tomb was discovered. In ancient times the small side room to the right was used to conceal nine royal mummies from further plunder following the desecration of their respective tombs.

TOMB OF SETHNAKHT. The Tomb of Sethnakht (no.14) was originally the Tomb of Queen Tawsert (wife of Merneptah-Siptah and then of Sety II). Sethnakht extended it and covered the parts decorated by the queen with plaster, but these are now showing through in places, especially in the corridor. In the funeral chamber decorated with scenes from the *Book of Gates* are a few remaining fragments of the sarcophagus. The nearby TOMB (no. 15) OF SETY II has a particularly fine carved decoration at the entrance to the corridor evoking the *Litany of Re* and the *Book of What is in the Underworld*.

TEMPLE OF SETY I

The portico of the fasciculate, colonnaded façade of the extremely well-preserved Temple of Sety I occupies the entire western side of the second court.

Stretching to the north and east at the end of the road to the Valley of the Kings is Thebes' oldest necropolis, the necropolis of Tarif, or Antef (after the 11th-Dynasty princes who founded it). Some of the tombs, most of which have been destroyed, can still be seen along the side of the road leading to the Temple of Sety I. Once through the present gate of the precinct, the ruined gate of the axial pylon which opened onto the

> "These hieroglyphs, these figures, undoubtedly represent the history of human knowledge: the priests of Egypt only consigned them to the sepulchral depths to protect them from the catastrophes of the world."
>
> Comte de Forbin

first court can be seen on the left. On the south side of the court are the remains of a palace. To the north of the temple the mudbrick walls of a complex of vaulted magazines have been rebuilt to a height of about 3 feet. The walls of the annexes have virtually been leveled. Inside the mortuary temple the ceremonies designed to guarantee the survival of the king in the Hereafter were performed. The road continues south along the side of the necropolis of Dra-Abu el-Naga, which lies on the slopes of the Western Desert. None of the sometimes well-preserved tombs belonging to 18th-Dynasty priests and scribes is open to the public.

ASASIF NECROPOLIS

After skirting round the necropolis Dra-Abu el-Naga the road continues westward into the Valley of Asasif where only two of the 25th- and 26th-Dynasty tombs can be visited.

TOMB OF PASABA. The tomb of Pasaba, the steward of Nitocris, the Divine Votaress of Amun, has a long flight of steps leading to a pillared court where there is a bee-keeping scene on one of the pillars. The first court leads into a second, which in turn leads to the underground rooms and the gallery opening onto the tomb. To the west of the tomb is the pylon of the TOMB OF MONTUEMHET, one of the largest tombs in Thebes, which is currently being restored.

TOMB OF KHERUEF. The Tomb of Kheruef (no. 192), steward of Queen Tiyi during the reign of Amenhotep III, stands about 100 yards southeast of the tombs mentioned above. Although it is very badly damaged it has a series of raised reliefs which are truly remarkable not only for their expressive quality but also for their portrayal of movement in the figures participating in the festival of the erection of the *djed* pillar.

TEMPLE OF SETY I
The central entrance opens onto a six-columned, hypostyle hall (above) whose walls are decorated with scenes in which Sety I and Ramesses II make offerings to Amun-Re. The shrine lies on the axis of the temple. The north entrance opens onto a court with a solar altar, while the south leads to a suite of rooms dedicated by Sety I to his father, Ramesses I, and completed by Ramesses II.

Senenmut, chief steward and architect to Queen Hatshepsut, had his own figure included in the statue niches of the central corridor of the temple. His tomb (no. 353) lies to the north of the road as you leave the temple.

MURALS
Beneath the double portico situated between the complex of Anubis and the ramp is a series of scenes depicting the birth and education of the queen, her accession and divine ancestry. Beneath the opposite portico, south of the ramp, are the celebrated scenes of the maritime expedition sent by the queen to the land of Punt

(modern Somalia). Scenes on the low wall forming the southern boundary of the portico show the houses on stilts (above) and flora of these distant lands, as well as the amply proportioned Queen of Punt. (The present relief is a cast of the originals which can be seen in the Cairo Museum ▲ 276.)

DEIR EL-BAHRI

Deir is the Arabic word for "monastery". It is often used in Thebes to designate the site of an ancient Coptic monastery built on the ruins of a Pharaonic structure. The far end of the Valley of Asasif is blocked by the cliff of Deir el-Bahri at the foot of which a series of three temples was built.

TEMPLE OF MENTUHOTEP I. The Temple of Mentuhotep, built during the Middle Kingdom, is the oldest temple in the group and stands on the left. It is characterized by its outer porticos and its ramp leading to a terrace whose center was once occupied by a massive pyramidal, or more probably mastaba-type, structure ● *82*. Behind the temple lay a court open to the sky and a hypostyle hall built against the cliff. A long underground corridor led deep into the mountainside to the tomb. In the rocky spur which closes the mountainous cirque to the left of the temple is the (inaccessible) entrance shaft which led to the cache of royal mummies (including the mummy of Ramesses II) discovered by Gaston Maspero ● *96* in 1881.

TEMPLE OF HATSHEPSUT. The temple stands on the axis of the present access road, formerly the site of the ancient *dromos* which once crossed the entire Asasif depression to the Nile Valley. Several of the limestone sphinxes which stood along its edge are now in New York's Metropolitan Museum. The first part of the uprights is all that remains of the entrance to the first court. To the left of the ramp, beneath one of the square-pillared porticos that border the terrace to the west, is a carved scene depicting the transportation of two great obelisks that the queen had brought by river from the Aswan quarries to Karnak ▲ *404*.

Detail (far left) of the great corbeled vault, painted with a starry blue sky, of the shrine in the Temple of Hatshepsut, and detail (left) of a wall painting.

Detail of a scene depicting the queen's birth.

The ramp leads to a second court also bordered by a double porticoed façade of square pillars. The precinct situated in the northwest corner is dedicated to Anubis, the jackal-headed god who presided at the embalming ceremony and who is represented on the walls of the twelve-columned vestibule. In the center of the far wall is the narrow, vaulted corridor which led to the shrines. The north side of the court is occupied by a polygonal-columned portico, while to the south is a monumental annex, with its own access ramp, dedicated to Hathor. THE THIRD TERRACE (not open to the public) consists of a central court bordered by a colonnade on three sides and, to the north, a smaller court with a square solar altar in the center. On the other (south) side of the central court is a suite of vaulted rooms dedicated to the royal funeral cult. THE SHRINE OF THE TEMPLE was built into the side of the cliff. Its last room and vestibule were additions dating from the Ptolemaic period.

TEMPLE OF THUTMOSE III. Scarcely anything remains of the temple built by Thutmose III between those of Mentuhotep I and Hatshepsut. Only the first section of the ramp, the remains of the terrace and fragments of the walls and columns are still visible. It was designed to dominate the Temple of Hatshepsut and must have been a fine edifice, judging by the decorated blocks; two are in the Luxor Museum ▲ 403.

The extremely powerful architectural composition of the temple, designed as a series of terraces and horizontal porticos which stand out against the vertical rock face, was probably inspired by the nearby Temple of Mentuhotep.

▲ DEIR EL-BAHRI

The funeral temple of Queen Hatshepsut (1490–68), on the west bank of the Nile, was built by the architect Senenmut. This hemi-speos, which lies along a southeast/northwest axis, was inspired by the nearby Temple of Mentuhotep whose terraces and porticos it has reproduced. Its originality lies in the way in which the edifice blends with the natural surroundings. Discovered in 1743, it was the subject of several research programmes. The first excavations, carried out by the Egypt Exploration Fund in 1893, were followed by excavations, consolidations and restorations by the American (1911) and Polish (1961) missions.

"PROTO-DORIC" COLONNADE
The sixteen-sided columns of the north portico of the second terrace evoke the Greek architectural tradition, causing them to be wrongly described as "proto-Doric". However the abacus (with no capital), molding and groove are typically Egyptian.

HATSHEPSUT
This painted limestone head of Queen Hatshepsut, now in the Cairo Museum ▲ 276, came from an Osiride statue of the upper terrace portico.

EXPEDITION TO THE LAND OF PUNT
The painted bas-reliefs of the south portico of the first terrace tell the story of the trading expedition to the land of Punt (Somalia) during the ninth regnal year. The King of Punt and his wife are accompanied by bearers of offerings.

The figures are realistically portrayed, with the Queen of Punt easily recognizable by her obesity.

HATHOR CAPITALS
The columns of the chapel of Hathor are decorated with capitals representing the goddess of the Theban necropolis. The cow's ears, the sistrum and the house of Horus are the attributes of the goddess.

From left to right: an agricultural scene (Tomb of Menna), the presentation of offerings by envoys from the land of Punt (Tomb of Rekhmire), four agricultural scenes (Tomb of Menna) and a barber's scene (Tomb of Userhet).

NECROPOLIS OF SHEIKH ABD EL-QURNA

After leaving the Asasif, the road runs past the hill of Khokha and turns south to necropolis of Sheikh Abd el-Qurna, which lies beyond the ruined temples of Ramesses IV and Thutmose III. The necropolis has dozens of tombs belonging to 18th-Dynasty dignitaries and stretches across the surrounding hills. The entire area is dotted with hundreds of holes, interspersed with the houses of the village.

TOMB ARCHITECTURE. Although they vary in terms of detail and size, the tombs of these dignitaries are built according to a general principle that differs from that of royal tombs. Their doors, which originally had a movable leaf, opened toward the east where the light of the rising sun symbolized rebirth. The upper section was surmounted by a small mudbrick pyramid (the remains of some of these can still be seen). The façade sometimes opened through a series of closely placed doors, which meant that the first vestibule remained accessible. In the court in front of the façade stood the biographical stelae of the deceased. Inside the tomb a vestibule wider than its depth opened onto a long, narrow room, at the end of which a niche contained statues of the deceased and his relatives. The rest of the tomb was inaccessible and consisted of a rock-cut corridor leading to an underground tomb which housed the sarcophagus and the funeral paraphernalia. It is impossible to predict the number of tombs open to the public. The six tombs that are generally open give a complete and varied idea of the beauty of this necropolis.

TOMB OF RAMOSE. The Tomb of Ramose (no. 55), vizier and governor of Thebes during the reign of Amenhotep IV, is preceded by a court and is famed for the quality of the bas-reliefs in the vestibule. On the east wall the beauty of the outlines and the fine texture of the braided hair illustrate the degree of refinement of the art of the period. The south wall is painted with scenes depicting the funerary procession. The construction of the tomb was interrupted when Ramose had to follow the king to Tell el-

Amarna. The various stages of the drawing, carving and painting of the scenes are can be seen on the walls.

TOMB OF USERHET. The Tomb of Userhet (no. 56), a royal scribe during the reign of Amenhotep II, lies to the south of the Tomb of Ramose. The most remarkable scene shows Userhet in a chariot, hunting desert animals with a bow.

TOMB OF NAKHT. About 100 yards to the north a path climbs steeply to the tomb (no. 52) of the scribe and astronomer of Amun during the reign of Thutmose IV. On the west wall, to the right of the door, are scenes depicting fishing, hunting and the harvest in the Nile Delta where Nakht probably had an estate. To the left of the door is one of the most beautifully painted scenes (the funerary banquet) in Thebes, but there are no illustrations of the astronomical activities of Nakht.

TOMB OF MENNA. About 50 yards further up the path, the Tomb of Menna (no. 69), an inspector of estates during the reign of Thutmose IV, contains some extremely realistic agricultural scenes and very detailed funeral scenes.

TOMB OF REKHMIRE. About 100 yards to the south a path climbs to the tomb (no. 100) of the governor of the town and vizier during the reign of Thutmose III. On the west wall, to the left of the door, are scenes of foreign tribute from Punt (Somalia), Khefti (Crete), Kush (Sudan) and Retenu (Syria), while those in the chapel illustrate Rekhmire's economic and administrative activities. Beyond these, scenes showing the polishing of statues, the making of bricks and goldsmiths and carpenters at work provide a great deal of information on the various attitudes, tools and accessories which characterized these trades.

TOMB OF SENNEFER. Near the Tomb of Rekhmire is the Tomb of Sennefer (no. 96), whose title was "Mayor of the Southern City" (Thebes) during the reign of

TOMB DECORATIONS
On the walls of the vestibule, painted scenes illustrate the private life and professional activities as well as the funeral procession and banquet of the tomb owner. These images are a remarkable source of information on the civilization of Ancient Egypt both in terms of the wealth of details provided and the meaning and degree of sophistication of representation. At the far end of a narrow room opening off the center of the vestibule was a niche containing statues of the deceased and his relatives.

BATTLE OF KADESH

Beneath the east portico of the second court of the Ramesseum is one of the finest-known representations of the Battle of Kadesh (Syria) where Ramesses II fought the Hittites in 1299 BC. The scene depicts Ramesses II's heroic counterattack. Standing in his chariot the young king fires arrows with deadly precision at the fleeing Hittites, many of whom are drowning in the Orontes. On the left the river reaches Kadesh, which is surrounded by ramparts and water. The intact banner means that the city was not captured. There were other encounters during the Hittite war until the first great peace treaty was concluded in the twentieth year of Ramesses' reign. To the east of the portico other episodes of the Battle of Kadesh are illustrated on the first pylon.

Amenhotep II. Its upper section is inaccessible. A long, underground corridor leads to the tomb, whose ceiling is painted with luxuriant vines and grape clusters, while the walls are decorated with scenes of offerings made to Sennefer by his daughter, the singer of Amun Muttawi.

RAMESSEUM

Below the necropolis the monumental complex of the Ramesseum, built by Ramesses II, stretches along the edge of the fertile valley. It was started at the beginning of his reign and took twenty years to complete. It has been used as a quarry since antiquity. As the walls of the façade have been pulled down the entrance leads straight into the inner area of the second court.

SECOND COURT. The court is flanked to the east and west by pillared porticos with engaged Osiride statues of Ramesses. The king is shown with his arms crossed, holding his scepters and tightly wrapped in a shroud (in imitation of Osiris), being summoned to rebirth in a new life. Beneath the eastern portico is an illustration the Battle of Kadesh. In the last register, at the top of the wall, is the grand procession of the annual festival of Min. The entrance to the second court of the Ramesseum was blocked by the fall of a huge granite colossus on whose shoulder an inscription

> "It is melancholy to sit on the piled stones amidst the wreck of this wonderful edifice, where violence inconceivable to us has been used to destroy what art inconceivable to us had erected."
>
> Harriet Martineau

describes Ramesses as the "sun of princes". The statue must have stood originally about 69 feet high. On the south side of the court was a royal palace whose lower wall sections and column bases can still be seen. The interior of the temple is reached via the east side of the court, beyond the very badly damaged first pylon.

HYPOSTYLE HALL. The central part of the hall (whose ceiling is well preserved) was lit by traceried windows. Behind the façade, on the interior (south) wall of the hall is a scene showing the capture of the Syrian fortress of Dapur. Across the hall, at the far end of the west wall, Ramesses II receives his scepters from Amun-Re. Below this scene is a procession of Ramesses' many sons. On the walls of the next room are the sacred barques of the Theban Triad and the royal barque which came here in procession from Karnak during the "Beautiful Feast of the Valley". In the mysterious shadows of the shrine (which now no longer exists) the king's statue was placed in the presence of a statue of Amun, the source of all life. This annual union invested the dead king with new energy. On the ceiling of the hall are images of the months and seasons of the year. In the center Thoth, master of both writing and time, is represented as a baboon on top of a *djed* pillar, the symbol of renewal.

SMALL TEMPLE. On the north wall of the Ramesseum is a small temple dedicated to Ramesses' mother, Tuya, and wife, Nefertari. Its foundations date from the reign of Sety I and it has retained some of its original paving and column bases.

ANNEXES. The mudbrick annexes of the Ramesseum, which extend for a distance of 20 yards or so around the shrine, are better preserved than in other Egyptian temples. They give a clear idea of the magazines, workshops and service chambers built inside the sacred precinct.

ANNEXES
The wealth of the temple, such as cereals, cloth, earthenware jars and precious metals, was stored in the magazines (some still have their original vaults) in the northwest section of the Ramesseum. A sacerdotal necropolis was founded here in the 10th century BC and the chapel walls and entrances to the many tombs scattered across the site make it difficult to distinguish the original layout of the annexes.

OSIRIAN ROOMS

The south door of the second hypostyle hall leads into a first chamber, which in turn leads into a small, two-columned room decorated with scenes of the king's coronation renewed in the Hereafter. The next room is a sort of vestibule which has a long bench (where offerings were probably placed) and opens onto two connecting rooms. A second door in the vestibule led into the Osirian chapel proper, which was linked to the other world by the false door carved on the far wall.

MEDINET HABU

The road runs alongside the ruined temples of Thutmose IV, Merneptah, Ay and Horemheb before reaching the monumental complex of Medinet Habu. The entrance, with its square towers, glacis and rounded merlons, imitates the gateways of oriental fortresses: a reminder of battles fought by Ramesses III during a troubled period in Egyptian history. This fortified entrance was part of a square, mudbrick building which no longer exists.

CHAPELS OF THE "DIVINE VOTARESSES OF AMUN". Inside the complex, on the left, are the adjoining funerary chapels of the "Divine Votaresses of Amun" who were 25th- and 26th-Dynasty queens and princesses. Each chapel has a court leading to a shrine covered, unusually in Egypt, by a vault of bonded stone.

SMALL TEMPLE. Opposite the chapels, to the north, is the Small Temple (18th Dynasty). The main part of the temple (built on a substructure) dates from the reign of Thutmose III and can still be seen today. At the far end, the shrine is preceded by a central barque shrine and surrounded by a gallery with a series of windows set in the outer wall. The temple originally possessed its own mudbrick enclosure whose

stone gates, built by Taharqa, have survived.
Over the centuries a series of additions were
made to the east side of the temple. A kiosk
dating from the reign of Nectanebo I was added
to the court and small pylon built by Taharqa. This
was followed by the construction of a Ptolemaic pylon on
which the outer lintel of the gateway has retained part of its
painted decoration. Finally a pronaos preceded by a court
was begun during the reign of Antoninus Pius. The walls of
this unfinished complex were built from reused blocks, as
demonstrated by the fragments of bas-reliefs which can be
seen on the inner walls. The temple stands on the sacred
hill of Djeme, the site of the sepulchers of the eight
primordial divinities of Hermopolis and joint creators
of the world. Subtle and complex connections, based
on the myths of the origins and renewal of creation,
linked Amun-Re to this site where important
ceremonies were held every year.

GREAT TEMPLE. The virtually intact pylon of the Temple of
Ramesses III stands at the center of the site. It is
decorated with scenes depicting the king adopting
the traditional stance of the "massacre of the
enemy". The north façade of
the temple evokes the war
fought by Ramesses III against
the "Sea Peoples" in the Nile
Delta. In the FIRST COURT, in
front of each pillar of the
north portico, is a colossus of
the standing king. Across the
court is the outer colonnade of
the palace with the king's
"Window of Appearances".
A ramp leads to the SECOND
COURT, whose southwest
corner is also decorated with
battle scenes. However, the
quality and state of
preservation of the images of
the sacred barques of the
Theban Triad, in the western
section of the north wall, are
far superior. Although most of

the inner rooms have lost their ceiling, the lower section is
intact. A series of hypostyle halls led, along the central axis of
the temple, to the sanctuary. In the north section, near the
second hypostyle hall and the staircase leading to the terrace,
is the entrance to the complex dedicated to Re-Harakhti.
It is arranged around an open courtyard which
used to have a central solar altar. On the
lintel of the west portico, the king is
shown in front of a group of chattering
baboons (animals devoted to the rising
sun), worshipping the solar barque. On
the south side of the central axis is the
suite of Osirian rooms.

ROYAL PALACE. The overall layout of the
royal palace built against the temple is
clearly visible. The central hypostyle hall

One of Ramesses I's
sons (west wall of
the main court of the
Great Temple),
the sacred barque
of the Theban Triad
(west wall of the
hypostyle hall) and
the pharaoh on the
River Nile (right-
hand side chapel).

435

▲ MEDINET HABU

Ramesses III chose the sacred site of Medinet Habu to build his jubilee and funeral temple. Although inspired by the Ramesseum it is unlike other religious edifices in that it is surrounded by a fortified enclosure wall. Following the death of Ramesses III it became the administrative center of the priests of Amun. After the excavations of Mariette and Morgan in 1859, it was not until the work carried out by the Oriental Institute of Chicago (1927–60) that the site became the subject of extensive research which involved a systematic study of the temple.

"MIGDOL" FORTIFIED ENTRANCE

Of the two gateways in the enclosure wall, only the east gate has survived. The first floor consists of solid masonry, pierced by a central gateway. The upper floors house apartments reached via a ramp situated beyond the gateway.

18TH-DYNASTY BARQUE SHRINE
The oldest building on the site is a square-pillared, peripteral temple. It was built by Queen Hatshepsut and completed by Thutmose III as a shrine for the sacred barque of Amun during the Beautiful Feast of the Valley.

MAIN PART OF THE TEMPLE

ANNEXES

NAVAL BATTLE
The bas-reliefs on the north outer wall depict the first great naval battle in history. It shows Ramesses III defeating the Sea Peoples who swept along the eastern Mediterranean coast in c. 1200 BC, destroying the Hittite empire and the coastal towns and cities. The Philistines were driven back by Ramesses III and settled on the Palestinian coast to which they gave their name.

SHOPS
Shops were vaulted and built in brick.

ENCLOSURE WALL

PRISONERS
These faience panels from the Palace of Ramesses III show Egypt's traditional enemies taken prisoner by the pharaoh. They can be recognized by their dress and headgear: a Libyan, a Nubian, a Syrian prince, a Bedouin and a Hittite.

The Temple of Medinet Habu covers an area of 20 acres. A text written during the reign of Ramesses III states that 62,626 prisoners of war worked in the temple.

TOMB OF SENNEDJEM
On the east wall of the tomb was a beautifully painted image of the "fields of Ialu", a sort of map of the kingdom of the Hereafter (detail above). On the west wall the deceased and his wife adore twelve gods, including Osiris (right), in a naos.

On the south wall Nephthys and Isis, in the form of birds, watch over the mummy. All the scenes have the characteristic yellow background of most of the many tombs of Deir el-Medina.

(the bases of the columns can still be seen) opens to the north toward the first court of the temple, while a door to the south leads to the throne room. The throne dais, behind which the "false door" stele once stood, is still in place. Beyond this are three apartments consisting of a vestibule, chamber and washroom. This was above all a symbolic residence where the dead king would continue to be present and be served within his mortuary temple.

ENCLOSURE WALLS AND ANNEXES.
The second enclosure wall of Medinet Habu is the wall of the Temple of Ramesses III, which surrounds a complex of annex buildings. The remains of the houses of the Coptic town of DJEME, which occupied the entire site, gives the outer enclosure wall an irregular outline.

DEIR EL-MEDINA

The workmen's village of the royal necropolis, situated in the little valley behind the hill of Qurnet Murai, has been completely excavated. The master quarriers, masons, painters and sculptors who worked on the royal tombs lived within the enclosure wall with their families. They could reach the Valley of the Kings via the mountain path which passed above the cliff of Deir el-Bahri. Their houses, clustered together on either side of the village street, consisted of a main room in which there was a sort of bench with steps and a second, smaller room. Beyond this was an open kitchen with a stove and often a cellar hewn out of the rock. A small flight of steps led to the terrace.

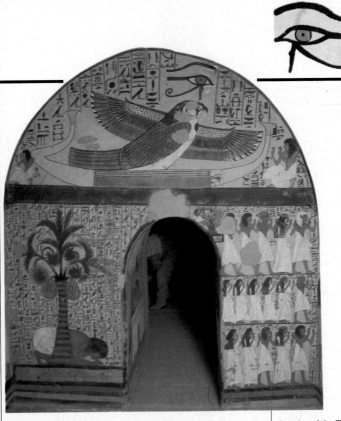

TEMPLE. The temple dedicated to Hathor and Ma'at that stands to the north of the village was completely rebuilt during the Ptolemaic period. It consists of a small court and pronaos (whose columns have composite capitals), a central sanctuary and two side chapels. The south wall in the left of the two chapels is engraved with a beautiful scene depicting the weighing of the heart in the presence of Osiris. The heart of the deceased (the seat of thought), placed on one pan of the scales, should be balanced by the light feather of Ma'at (goddess of Truth). The result was recorded by Thoth. A monstrous creature, Ammit "the Devourer", waited by the scales for those who were rejected, while the successful candidates could attain the Kingdom of the Blest. To the north of the temple lies the Great Pit, an excavated site over 130 feet deep which yielded almost five thousand *ostraca* ● *59*. These have provided very useful information on life in Deir el-Medina during the Ramesside period. Only two of the tombs in the hillside necropolis to the west of the ancient village can be visited.

TOMB OF SENNEDJEM. The Tomb of Sennedjem (no. 1), a servant in the royal necropolis during the 19th Dynasty, was discovered intact in 1866. The tomb has a beautiful vaulted ceiling decorated with vignettes from the *Book of the Dead*.

TOMB OF INHERKAU. The tomb (no. 359) of the "foreman of the mayor of the Two Lands" consists of two vaulted rooms. The second is decorated with vignettes from the *Book of the Dead* superposed on three registers. Inherkau is shown adoring the Phoenix and the cat of Heliopolis slaying the serpent Apophis.

Interior of the Tomb of Pashed (left), from the Ramesside period.

LAYOUT OF A TOMB
The tombs of Deir el-Medina tended to follow the same basic layout. An entrance in the form of a small pylon opened onto a court at the far end of which was the funerary chapel in the form of a small, steep-sided pyramid (one has recently been restored near the two tombs open to the public). In front of the chapel stelae and statues of the deceased were protected by a canopy. The access shaft to the tomb was dug either in the floor of the court or the chapel.

439

COLOSSI OF MEMNON

After several hundred yards the road leading back to the Nile passes the famous Colossi of Memnon (the Greek form of the name of Amenhotep III). These two huge, pink quartzite statues representing the king seated on his throne (which bears the symbol of the union of Upper and Lower Egypt) have not always stood alone on the plain as they do today. They once stood before the façade of the mudbrick pylon of a huge mortuary temple. Few of its remains can still be seen but its layout has been established by taking soundings. The temple was demolished during antiquity and a number of its blocks reused in Karnak and in some of the temples of the west bank.

A number of Greek inscriptions (which can be seen on the lower part of the colossus) were carved by the illustrious visitors who came to hear the famous "singing" statue of the Roman period. Some are dated and the oldest originates from the reign of Nero. While most visitors were content to write simple prose, some have composed elaborate poems.

VALLEY OF THE QUEENS

Only a few of the eighty tombs on this site at the southern edge of the Theban necropolis are open to the public. During the 18th Dynasty it received the remains of princes and princesses, while in the 19th Dynasty certain queens were also buried here. Unfortunately the famous TOMB OF NEFERTARI (no. 66), decorated with scenes of exceptional high quality, is not accessible. The TOMB OF AMENHIKHOPESHEF (no. 42), a son of Ramesses III, shows the young prince accompanied by his father in the presence of Thoth, Ptah and other divinities. At the far end of the tomb is the sarcophagus and the remains of a still-born baby. The TOMB OF QUEEN TITI (no. 52), probably one of the wives of a 20th-Dynasty king, consists of an entrance corridor where the queen is depicted with sidelocks, the sign of extreme youth. Several divinities are represented, including Ptah in his naos, Thoth, Atum,

QURNA
Most of the population of the west bank is concentrated in a series of hillside villages near the tombs. The largest of these villages is Qurna, which continues to flourish in spite of damage to the tombs, the ban on further building and a number of rehousing projects.

Isis and Nephthys. In the second chamber the queen presents an offering to the Hathor cow as it emerges from the sacred mountain. In the furthest chamber offerings were placed before the gods. On the far wall Osiris is depicted between Neith and Selqit, Nephthys and Thoth. The TOMB OF KHAEMWESE (no. 44) shows the young prince dressed in a linen robe and wearing a necklace, with the characteristic sidelock of princes. He first makes a lone offering to the gods and is then presented with his father to the guardians of the gates of the Hereafter.

MALKATTA. A track leads south and skirts round the western edge of Medinet Habu. After about half a mile the sparse remains of the mudbrick walls of the various monumental complexes of the Palace of Malkatta, Amenhotep III's royal residence, can be seen on the right and then the left of the track. It is the only known Theban palace and certainly the only one to have been built on the west bank. The construction of the vast lake (Birket Habu) to the east of the palace created the regularly spaced mounds that extend for about 1¼ miles. Near the far end of the ancient lake is the small Roman temple of Deir Shelwit, built at the end of the 1st century AD.

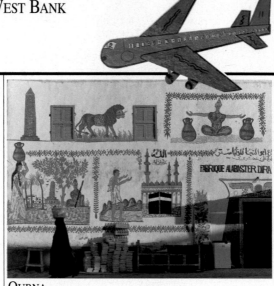

When villagers from Qurna make the journey to Mecca, their houses are decorated with images of pilgrimage. The lion is often featured, symbolizing the difficulties of the journey and the courage of the pilgrim. Appropriate Koranic verses, prayers and the pilgrim's name complete the decorations. The interior of the house is also decorated with paintings and *surah*. Garish banners, which combine Pharaonic and Islamic images, are hung on the walls of the town.

HASSAN FATHI
The Egyptian architect Hassan Fathi (1900–89), winner of the 1980 Aga Khan Award for Architecture, researched and completed several projects in the region.

QURNA

Qurna is a fine example of traditional Egyptian rural architecture. The houses, built of mudbrick mixed with straw and cemented together with mortar made from mud, seem to blend with their surroundings. The mud revetment is earthcolored in the plains and ocher in the mountains. Facades are decorated with brick crenelations and raised and rounded corners. The flat roofs are made of planks supported by palm beams or trunks and covered with an insulating layer of earth. The façades are roughcast in bright colors, made from iron oxide-based paints (yellow, ocher, red and blue).

QURNA EL-GEDIDA (NEW QURNA). One reason given for the relocation of the inhabitants of Qurna (still very much on the agenda) was the deterioration of the tombs. The best known of the many projects generated by the proposal was Hassan Fathi's pilot scheme, completed in 1948. It was not, however, appreciated by the mountain-dwellers, who made their living from tourism and the sale of (genuine or fake) antiques favored by the location of their villages, and they refused to leave. The project was inspired by traditional Nubian housing and makes generous use of vaults and *pisé* domes, architectural features that are used in the rest of Egypt only for tombs. Some buildings were eventually inhabited, but only after some major alterations. Finally the project overlooked the fact that rural dwellings must be flexible and able to be constantly altered, which is virtually impossible in New Qurna where now only the mosque remains intact.

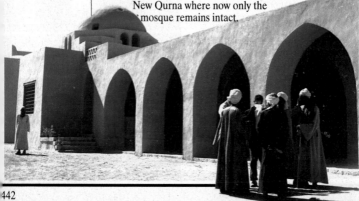

THEBES
TO ASWAN

ESNA, *446*
EL-KAB, *447*
EDFU, *448*
KOM OMBO, *452*

THEBES TO ASWAN

ARMANT. The village of Armant (the ancient Greek settlement of Hermonthis), which stands near the Nile about 12½ miles south of Thebes, is steeped in history. The flourishing Middle Kingdom town, with its large necropolis, was extended during the 18th Dynasty by the construction of huge temples (now destroyed). Much later Cleopatra VII made it the capital of the nome. It was still flourishing at the beginning of the Christian era but was subsequently neglected. Although nothing much remains of the Temple of Cleopatra (its blocks were used in the 19th century to build the Armant sugar refinery), the temple dedicated to the local god Montu, represented here in the form of a Buchis bull, has survived. Buchis bulls, the earthly representation of the god, were buried in the sacred vaults of the Bucheum near the Temple of Montu. Among the scattered blocks and foundations which still exist (pylon of Thutmose III) is the image of a

Detail of hieroglyphs and general view of the ruined Temple of Tod.

rhinoceros. The four sanctuary towns of Hermonthis, north Karnak ▲ 404, Medamud and Tod, situated in the vicinity of Thebes and dedicated to Montu, enclosed an area known as the "Palladium of Thebes", the ancestral land placed under the god's protection.

TOD. Across the Nile from Armant, on the edge of the Arabian Desert, the village of Tod stands on an ancient site which is still mostly buried beneath its houses. Although the first religious settlement dates back to the Old Kingdom, the temple (as it stands today) and sacred lake date from the Ptolemaic period. At the back of the temple, in the area of the pronaos, are scenes commemorating its foundation.

Today little remains of the Temple of Cleopatra at Armant, since most of the blocks were reused to build the local sugar refinery.

On the right the chapel-shrine of Thutmose III, designed to receive the sacred barque of Montu, houses a statue of the falcon-headed god surmounted by a solar disk, two *uraei* and two tall feathers. A vast hoard of treasure consisting of gold and silver ingots, silver chalices and lapis lazuli was found in four chests buried beneath the

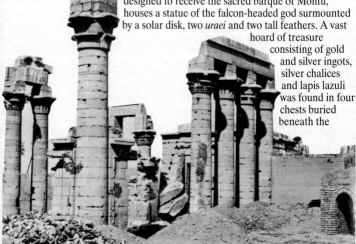

🚗 🚶 **Three days**
◆ F B2-C3-C4

original Middle Kingdom sanctuary. The pieces are now on display in the Cairo Museum ▲ *276* and the Louvre ▲ *476* in Paris.

JEBELEIN. To reach Jebelein (whose name, derived directly from Ancient Egyptian, means "the two mountains"), cross the Nile from the east to the west bank at El Shagab, about 17½ miles south of Luxor. The (higher) east mountain is dominated by the Tomb of Sheikh Mussa and has a Ptolemaic temple dedicated to the goddess Hathor. The remains of a mudbrick structure (a 20th-Dynasty fort) can be seen on the summit of the mountain, but the main reward for the effort spent climbing up this limestone mass is the magnificent view from the top. The ancient town of CROCODILOPOLIS used to lie on the small plain at the foot of the mountain, but now only the necropolis remains, on the west mountain opposite. The tombs, which were built between the Middle Kingdom and the Ptolemaic period, have been repeatedly plundered and the site is strewn with debris. Across the Nile from Jebelein, at MOALLA, there are openings on the hillside which mark the entrances to tombs dating from the First Intermediate period and belonging to dignitaries who achieved a degree of independence from a centralized power weakened at the end of the Old Kingdom. A text from the tomb of the nomarch Ankhtifi explains the administration of the region during the famine that had occurred during this time.

"The alien and mysterious Nile, that gigantic serpent that winds so fabulously, so ungraspably, back through history."
Rose Macauley,
Pleasures of Ruins

445

ESNA

A barrage lies just outside the town of Esna, which stands on the west bank of the Nile. The town's Greek name was Latopolis because the fish (*lates*), the embodiment of the goddess Neith, was its sacred animal. Esna became increasingly important during the 18th Dynasty when Egypt developed its commercial relations with the Sudan, and an Esna–Derr route was established. The original temple of Esna was built during the reign of Thutmose III. There was a renewal of interest in the town during the 26th Dynasty. Under the Ptolemies and the Romans it became the capital of the Third Nome of Upper Egypt and a second temple was built. Most of the edifice has remained unexplored since the modern town has developed on the site of the ancient city, and its roof, surrounded by modern urban development, is on a level with the floors of the houses. The temple was dedicated to the ram-god Khnum who, at the dawn of time, fashioned mankind from the mud of the Nile on his potter's wheel. His divine companions included the lioness Menhyt (his consort), Nebtu (the goddess of the countryside), and the god Heka (the manifestation of vital energy). A special place was reserved for the androgynous divinity Neith (represented armed with a bow and arrows) who, according to local mythology, was the primordial creator of the world.

TEMPLE OF ESNA The hypostyle hall, the only part of the temple that has survived, dates from the reign of the Roman emperor Claudius. An image of the god Bes at Esna (below).

HYPOSTYLE HALL. The scenes and texts in the hypostyle hall, executed between the Graeco-Roman period and the reign of Decius in AD 250, were never completed. The style of the period is reflected in the bas-reliefs, whose figures have a more rounded appearance. The rectangular hall (the roof is still intact) opens to the west through an entrance flanked by columns. Inside, a wide variety of scenes illustrating the surrounding countryside is depicted on the capitals of twenty-four columns, while the shafts are reserved for images of the town's three main festivals: the creation of the universe by Neith, the raising of the sky by Khnum, and his victory over the human rebels. The columns support a ceiling, on which all these events are circumscribed by the course of the sun and the constellations. Outside the hall, on the frame of one of the lateral doors of the façade, two cryptographic texts dedicated to Khnum and Neith use only two (ram and crocodile) hieroglyphs.

The necropolis of El-Kab. The entrances to the excavated tombs can be seen on the mountainside.

Coptic statues found among the ruins of the Temple of Esna, which was converted into a church.

Fresco from the tomb of Paheri, grandson of Ahmose and nomarch of Nekheb, representing scenes from everyday life.

EL-KAB

From the pre-Dynastic period two religious centers developed in the region of El-Kab, one on either side of the River Nile. On the east bank, near the shores of the river, stood the ancient Egyptian city of Nekheb (the Greek city of Eileithyiapolis) and, on the west bank, ancient Nekhen (the Greek city of Hieraconpolis) also known as Kom el-Ahmar ("the red hill") where vast pre-Dynastic cemeteries stretch across the desert. Nekheb el-Kab, one of the oldest towns in Upper Egypt, was placed under the protection of the vulture-goddess Nekhbet. She was also known as "the white goddess" because she offers the White Crown of the south to the pharaoh and presides over royal and divine births. When the capital was moved to Memphis, El-Kab lost its importance even though it was the birthplace of the noble Middle Empire families who reconquered the country after the Hyksos invasion ● 40. Two sectors of El-Kab lie on a vast plain situated at the mouth of a *wadi*. The first, the town proper, includes temples, a *mamissi* (birth house) and a sacred lake (now a large depression to the east of the town) protected by a thick brick enclosure wall (1,740 feet square) with lateral gates. Today visitors use the west entrance, which provides the opportunity to see various architectural elements. In a smaller enclosure is the main temple dedicated to Nekhbet, a religious establishment dating from the Old Kingdom which was maintained and then converted at the beginning of the New Kingdom until the 30th Dynasty. In front of this crumbling temple the remains of the *mamissi* dedicated to Nekhbet (the embodiment of Hathor) can still be seen. The second sector is centered around the necropolis, on a rocky outcrop. The most important tombs (those of Ahmose, Renni, Paheri and Se date from the 18th Dynasty and the Ramesside period.

THE GOD HORUS
The Temple of Edfu is inhabited by the falcon-headed god Horus, also depicted crowned with a solar disk whose two spread wings represent the falcon soaring in the skies. As the protector and divine symbol of royalty, the falcon is associated with Re, the solar star, and becomes the guarantor of universal cosmic harmony. The

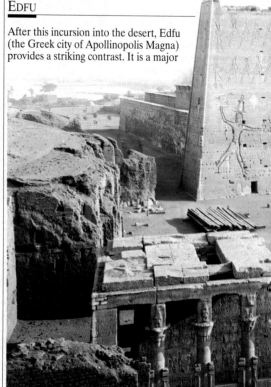

Temple of Horus at Edfu is a fine example of a typical temple layout which is best understood by working inward from the entrance to the sanctuary (or naos) situated in the darkest and most secret recesses of the temple. As well as being a place for the daily worship of the god, the temple was also the focal point of the great annual festivals which constituted the official ceremonies of Horus, as evidenced by the Egyptian calendar. The festival of the coronation guaranteed the annual renewal of Horus' royal status and reaffirmed the power of his earthly representative, the pharaoh, and was held on the esplanade in front of the first pylon. Every year a falcon was chosen for the occasion from a sacred aviary in the Temple of the Falcon (now destroyed).

TEMPLE OF THOTH. Leave the tombs on the left and follow the *wadi* (about 1½ miles) to the Temple of Thoth. The chapel was built by Setau, viceroy of Nubia, during the reign of Ramesses II at the place known locally as El-Hammam ("the bath"). A nearby cave-temple in the mountainside is dedicated to Nekhbet, who was transformed into the lioness Hathor-Tefnut. According to an ancient myth, the disappearance of the moon is linked to the lioness' flight into the desert, from where she was brought back into Egypt after being pacified by the god Thoth. A flight of steps carved out of the rock leads to the Ptolemaic speos. Two vestibules lead into a small, rock-cut chamber with a vaulted ceiling. The temple was converted into a Coptic monastery during the Christian era. Further along the *wadi* is the crag known as "Vulture Rock", which is covered with drawings and inscriptions, some dating from prehistoric times. Beyond the rock is the TEMPLE OF AMENHOTEP III, dedicated to Nekhbet-Hathor. The portico of the façade has disappeared, and one enters the temple directly. The reliefs were mutilated by Amenhotep IV and then restored by Sety I.

EDFU

After this incursion into the desert, Edfu (the Greek city of Apollinopolis Magna) provides a striking contrast. It is a major religious and commercial center which stands at the nucleus of the road network and the end of the desert and gold-mine routes. The pile of rubble to the west of the Temple of Horus is probably the original site of the village of DJEBA. Although French and Polish teams were keen to excavate the site and have uncovered Old Kingdom mastabas and Byzantine houses, the nerve center of the town is undisputedly the temple of the falcon-god Horus.

TEMPLE OF HORUS. Access to the site is from the back of the temple. There has been a succession of structures built on this sacred site from prehistoric times (when the falcon-god was housed in a wicker hut) to the New Kingdom. The temple owes its imposing appearance to Ptolemy III Euergetes who began to rebuild the original temple completely in 237 BC. The work was not completed until 57 BC. Today visitors pass beneath the pylon and cross the court bordered on three sides by a colonnaded portico. Beyond the court is the FIRST HYPOSTYLE HALL (or pronaos) whose façade honors Horus and Hathor and whose gates were opened only for festivals. The high priest used to enter the temple through this gate and purify himself in the "ROBING ROOM" (on the left of the entrance to the pronaos) before taking the papyrus bearing the day's order of worship from the library (on the right of the entrance). The SECOND HYPOSTYLE HALL, darker than the first, opens, on the west side, onto the "CHAMBER OF THE NILE" (which contained the pure water from the well used for the priests' ablutions) and

THE ARCHETYPAL PHARAONIC TEMPLE ✪
The temple of Edfu, one of the best preserved in Egypt, stands in the center of the village of the same name. Although comparatively recent, it gives a fairly accurate idea of what temples were like in the Pharaonic period. Ideally make a half-day trip, leaving from Luxor or Aswan.

The court of the temple is bordered to the south, east and west by identical colonnaded galleries with "open" capitals. The columns in the same gallery are all different.

HYPOSTYLE HALL
On the columns were images of the various divinities of the nome to whom offerings were made and who represented all the sanctuaries of Egypt. The south and west walls illustrate the ritual of the founding of the temple. The king is seen choosing the site with the goddess Seshat (crowned with a star), marking out the boundary with a cord and stakes, digging the foundations and filling them with sand before dedicating the divine residence to its master, Horus.

the "laboratory" (where the ointments and perfumes were prepared for the daily anointment of the statue). On the opposite (east) side it opens onto the treasure-house where valuable and religious items were kept. Then comes the OFFERING HALL where food offered to the god was placed on dressers and altars and from where staircases led up to the temple terrace. On certain occasions (transitional periods such as the Festival of the New Year) the god had to be united with the solar disk in the "Court of the New Year", which opened off the so-called "Pure Place" (whose ceiling traced the voyage of the solar barque through the Twelve Hours of the day). The statue, the god's earthly medium, had to be recharged with divine energy by being carried up the side staircase to the temple terrace; here it was exposed to the sun's rays before being taken down again by the opposite staircase. The bas-reliefs on the walls of these staircases show the procession of priests and standard-bearers carrying the cases containing the god's statues up to the court of the New Year on one side and down again on the other. The vestibule opens onto the SANCTUARY and its stone naos, which also contained the sacred barque of Horus. The god (his statue) residing in the temple enjoyed the services of the priests who woke him each morning, dressed him, offered him meals and sang hymns in his honor. They returned in the evening to prepare the god for the night's repose. A corridor ran round the outside of the naos to various CHAPELS reserved for special rites, for storing the cloth used to clothe the god's statues and to welcome divinities, including Hathor, who usually resided in Dendera ▲ 388. Her visit to her husband, the Horus falcon, for a fortnight every year was an occasion for great public celebration, and the two gods emerged regenerated from this encounter (the "Feast of the Beautiful Meeting").

Leave the darkness of the sanctuary and make your way to the inner, eastern section of the enclosure wall on which the sun-god is depicted destroying his enemies. These events were performed as part of an annual ritual known as the "Triumph of Horus", which ended with Horus seizing power and taking possession of his earthly heritage. The ritual of the "ten harpoons" (which ended with the slaying of the hippopotamus, the symbol of Seth, enemy of the sun and Horus) and Horus sailing victoriously on the sacred lake of Edfu (now buried beneath the village to the east of the temple) were the two main elements of the festival. Another annual ritual performed in the MAMISSI situated in the forecourt of the great temple was the birth scene of the divine child Harsomtus, the son of Horus and Hathor, in the form of the god "Horus who unites the Two Lands", embodied on earth by the pharaoh Horus.

JEBEL SILSILA. About 90 miles south of Edfu, the Nile flows between the rocky shores of Jebel Silsila ("the mountain of the chain"). According to legend, the river was once barred at this point by a chain stretching between two rocks on either side of the river. Jebel Silsila marks the boundary of the Egyptian region of Nubia where the Nile was believed to rise and where the Nile god was worshipped. The site was quarried early on in history because of the excellent quality of the sandstone and the proximity of the Nile. The vast sandstone quarries on the eastern shore provided the stone for the monuments of Dendera ▲ *388*, Thebes ▲ *394*, Esna ▲ *446*, Edfu and Kom Ombo. Three thousand workers toiled to provide stone for the Ramesseum ▲ *432*. Quarrymen's marks and inscriptions provide evidence of the gargantuan tasks carried out by the Pharaonic workforce: the great STELE OF AKHENATEN, for example, hewn out of the rock north of the shore. Amenhotep IV (Akhenaten) ▲ *378* worshipped Amun here (at the beginning of his reign) and the inscription below the stele indicates that a large workforce brought back stone for the sanctuary of Karnak ▲ *404*. Closer to the shore are the remains of a great (unfinished) sandstone sphinx and a chapel of Amenhotep III.

JEBEL SILSILA QUARRIES
Many of the (mostly open) quarry faces are as much as 65 feet high. The stone was quarried from a straight or echeloned face (above). The quarry on the eastern shore was worked from the 18th Dynasty to the Graeco-Roman period. The quarry was abandoned in AD 200 and was only reopened in 1906 when the Esna barrage was built.

View of the rock-cut grottos at the entrance to the ancient quarries.

WEST BANK

The west bank can now be reached along the road which runs from Edfu, along the canalized section of the Nile, to the old Aswan ▲ *456* dam. Although it, too, has quarries, it is first and foremost the site of a speos and the Nile shrines. The largest SHRINES were built by Sety I, Ramesses II and Merneptah and there is also a stele of Ramesses III with its hymn to the Nile. The kings made offerings during the festivals held in honor of the Nile floods.

SPEOS OF HOREMHEB. The façade of the speos (with its five openings formed by four pillars) is visible from a distance. At one time a flight of steps climbed from the river to a forecourt. The speos itself consists of a vaulted, transverse hall whose far wall opens onto the sanctuary containing seven statues, including Amun (in the center) and Horemheb. The decoration was completed during the reign of Ramesses II. On the southwest wall Horemheb is shown being suckled by the goddess Taweret (represented by a hippopotamus, the embodiment of the Nile and its life-giving floods) who imparts her divine strength and power in her milk, thus enabling him to vanquish the Nubian enemy. As you leave the speos of Horemheb, follow the river south to the great stelae which consecrate offerings from Ramesses III, Ramesses V and Shoshenq I to the gods of Thebes, Heliopolis and Memphis. Beyond the stelae some of the small chapels which line the route (the chapel of Sennefer, for example) are in fact tombs, although most are commemorative monuments erected in honor of the Nile.

KOM OMBO

The road continues southward along the east bank to Kom Ombo, passing through the villages of New Nubia, where some of the Nubian refugees were relocated when their homes and villages were drowned following the construction of the Aswan High Dam ▲ *460*. The region is typically Nubian, with its brightly colored houses, its fields of sugar cane and, as you approach Kom Ombo, orange groves.

TEMPLE OF KOM OMBO. The Temple of Kom Ombo can be seen from a distance. It is situated on top of a hillock, on the ancient site of Ombos, which was occupied from prehistoric times. The elevated position of the temple offers a splendid view (from the terrace, facing away from the sanctuary) of the modern village of Kom Ombo, which lies to the east, opposite the island of Mansuria on a bend in the Nile. The great temple has some impressive ruins. When it was abandoned by the priests, it was engulfed by sand (the color of the stone is an indication of the level of sand on the inside). The Copts who inhabited it destroyed some of the reliefs, before the edifice was used as a quarry. Finally the Nile completed its destruction by eroding part of the temple's ancient terrace. In spite of the ravages of time and mankind, it is difficult to remain indifferent to the beauty of the site. One very singular feature of the temple's layout and elevation is the double row of doors leading to a DOUBLE SANCTUARY, which is emphasized by a wall-cum-screen separating the two sections. The northern section is dedicated to the falcon-god Harwer, or "Horus the Elder", and the southern section to the crocodile-god Sobek. The two gods are accompanied by their "families": Harwer's wife Tesentnefert ("the Good Sister") and son Panebtawy ("Lord of the Two Lands") and Sobek's consort Hathor and son Khonsu, although the two triads often tend to merge and combine in an extremely complex theology. The overall layout is that of a divine temple during the Ptolemaic period. A few foundations are all that remain of the PYLON whose southern section develops the theme of the king entering the temple, followed by spirits bearing the products of the land of Egypt and the Sobek triad. Beyond the pylon and inside the court the king is shown leaving his palace escorted by standards. In the southwest corner of the court a staircase once led to the roof terrace.

The paved COURT has a columned portico and central altar. As you approach the sanctuary there is a scene showing the purification of the king in one of the intercolumniations of the façade of the pronaos. Three

A crocodile relief on one of the temple walls.

CITY OF GOLD
The name Kom Ombo (the ancient Greek settlement of Ombos) is derived from the Ancient Egyptian word *nubt*, which means "city of gold". In fact the town occupied a strategic position at the mouth of the *wadis,* which led to the regions in which gold was mined.

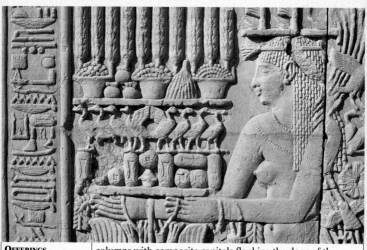

OFFERINGS
It was the pharaoh's duty to uphold the worship of the gods and present them with offerings in return for their protection. These offerings are usually depicted in the lower register of temple decorations.

SURGICAL INSTRUMENTS
On the inner face of the second enclosure wall is a unique illustration of several surgical instruments. These Roman instruments should be related to the healing powers usually associated with Harwer.

columns with composite capitals flanking the door of the PRONAOS are inscribed with the motifs of the lotus (south) and the papyrus (north), the symbols of the Two Lands. Inside the pronaos the arrangement of the capitals echoes this duality with the exception of one (southwest) column, while the intercolumniations illustrate the king's coronation. The ceiling is decorated with astronomical images, and the scenes on the walls of the hall show the king's purification and his consecration of the temple. On the west wall of the papyrus-columned HYPOSTYLE HALL, between the two doors of the central axis, is an inventory of the sacred places of Egypt, the gods of the main towns and the local and national festivals. In the next room the construction and foundation of the temple are prefaced by a scene showing the goddess Seshat "stretching the cord". This is followed by the purification of the newly erected temple where the king is shown throwing grains of natron. Traces of circles on the paving in front of the entrance to the hall indicate the original position of the offering table. In the OFFERING HALL, a lion goddess, appointed to oversee the offerings made on each day of the year, was accompanied by bull- or ram-headed spirits. Only the south staircase leading to the roof terrace (where the temple statues were exposed to the sun) remains. In the last room before the sanctuary were the statues of the gods and the temple-builder kings who were worshipped there. Although the "Court of the New Year" (to the north of the last room) no longer exists, part of the ceiling of the "Pure Place" (where the statue was dressed for the Festival of the New Year) still remains, decorated with two images of the sky-goddess Nut. On the body of the first are winged solar disks and, on the second, the different phases of the moon, while a barque of the night sails between the two. The pedestals that once supported the sacred barques and some of the chapels of the sanctuary can still be seen. To the south of the temple the CHAPEL dedicated to HATHOR by Domitian houses the crocodile mummies from the nearby crocodile necropolis (about half a mile to the southeast) and some recently discovered sarcophagi. The *mamissi* near the pylon of the temple has been largely destroyed.

Aswan and Abu Simbel

Aswan, *456*
Aswan High Dam, *460*
Philae, *462*
Abu Simbel, *464*

1 ASWAN ✪ 2 KITCHENER'S ISLAND 3 ELEPHANTINE ISLAND 4 TOMB OF THE AGA KHAN 5 MONASTERY OF ST SIMEON 6 SEHEL ISLAND 7 FIRST DAM 8 PHILAE 9 HIGH DAM

A TASTE OF AFRICA ✪
At Aswan the desert closes in again on the Nile, changing the ambience and scenery – now you are truly in Africa! A stay of two to three days is ideal to look around the town on foot, explore the spice market, supplied by caravans for millennia, go on an excursion to the island of Aqilqilla to see the temple of Philae, saved from the water, and examine at close quarters the famous Aswan dam, constructed by the builders of the pyramids.

ASWAN

Aswan is situated about 130 miles south of Luxor on what was once the southern border of Ancient Egypt. It lies on the east bank of the Nile at a point where the river cuts its way through the granite rock of the first of the cataracts

surrounding the ISLAND OF SEHEL, where Anukis (daughter of Khnum) was worshipped. About 250 inscriptions (dating from the 4th Dynasty to the Ptolemaic period), engraved on the rocks of the island, commemorate particular expeditions and events: for example, the famine which raged for seven years during the reign of Djoser was ended only by the intervention of the god Khnum. At Aswan the green, fertile belt of the Nile Valley is interrupted and replaced in mid-desert, behind the great dam, by the vast LAKE NASSER. Sandstone is replaced by granite in the form of two rocky barriers which hold back the Nile and also harbor the quarries

10 KERTASSI
11 KALABSHA
12 MAHARRAKA
13 DAKKA
14 WADI ES-SEBUA
15 AMADA
16 ABU SIMBEL ✪

⚐ **Four days**
◆ **F** C4-B5-B6-A6

exploited early on in history by the great builder-pharaohs. Khnum is the lord of the cataract and master of a gulf which was believed to be the source of the Nile floods. From ancient times Aswan was a huge market situated at the crossroads of the routes from Africa, the western deserts of Egypt and India. This frontier trading-post, visited by people from a number of different countries, was also an important strategic point. It has served as a base for Roman garrisons, for the Turkish troops of the Ottoman sultan Selim in 1517, for the army of General Kitchener during the conquest of the Sudan (1896–8) and is now a major garrison for the modern Egyptian army.

ELEPHANTINE ISLAND. Syene, the Ancient Egyptian name of Aswan, was derived from "syenite" (the name was wrongly applied to granite and today reserved for another type of rock). It is the modern counterpart of the first market town situated on the island of Elephantine (from the Egyptian word *abu* meaning "elephant") so called because of the extensive trade in ivory during antiquity. The island, with its Nubian villages, is reached by *felucca*. The ancient quays and landing-stage on the eastern side of the island once gave access to the temples of Thutmose III and Amenhotep III, destroyed in 1822 by the Turkish government. Only the Roman NILOMETER remains. Near the Nilometer the ELEPHANTINE MUSEUM houses objects discovered on the island and in the surrounding area, including prehistoric schist basins and the mummies of the sacred rams of Khnum, with their richly decorated and gilt casings. The ruins of the ancient city were discovered beyond the museum, in the south part of the island. They include the temples dedicated to Khnum and Satis by Queen Hatshepsut and the temple in honor of Hekayib (governor of Elephantine Island during the 6th Dynasty and deified posthumously) by his successor Sarenput I (whose tomb is at Gharbi Aswan). Several chapels containing statues represent the largest complex devoted to private worship.

NILOMETER
The Nilometer on Elephantine Island was described by Strabo in the 1st century AD as "a steeply graded staircase that plunges down into the river". The graduated scale on the walls was used to measure the flood levels which were certified by inscriptions in demotic script, Greek, Arabic and French.

KITCHENER'S ISLAND
The British general Horatio Kitchener (1850–1916) was sent to Egypt in 1883 to reorganize the Egyptian army, which he then led against the Sudanese Mahdi. After his victory in 1898 he discovered an island off the shore of Aswan where he planted a wide variety of exotic plants, which are still flourishing today.

Detail (right) of frescos in the Tomb of Sarenput I (12th Dynasty).

On the side of the hill known as Qubbet el-Hawwa (named after the *marabut* buried there) are two rows of rock-cut tombs belonging to the princes and dignitaries of Elephantine.

Mummies from the ram necropolis found nearby can be seen in the Elephantine Museum.

KITCHENER'S ISLAND. Geziret el-Nabatat or Plantation (formerly Kitchener's) Island is also reached by *felucca*. It is famed for its botanical gardens, which include many African and Asiatic species.

GHARBI ASWAN

Opposite the town of Aswan, on the west bank, the steep cliff of Gharbi Aswan (west Aswan) is surmounted by the tomb of a *marabut*, QUBBET EL-HAWWA, erected in honor of a local saint.

HYPOGEA OF THE PRINCES OF ELEPHANTINE. The tombs of dignitaries who held office between the end of the Old and the Middle Kingdoms can be seen halfway up the cliff. They are reached by flights of steps equipped with a form of chute for hoisting sarcophagi from the Nile to the tomb entrance. When the tombs, discovered between 1889 and 1969, were excavated they revealed texts describing expeditions into the Sudan and Central Africa. They are also of interest from the architectural point of view, with the huge speos highlighting the veining and colors of the rock. They include the TOMBS OF SABNI AND HIS FATHER, MEKHU, who died during the reign of Pepy II on a voyage to Lower Nubia (probably assassinated by local tribesmen). His son organized an expedition to bring back the prince's body and punish the inhabitants. On the left section of the door Mekhu and his wife receive offerings. The TOMB OF SARENPUT II is remarkable for its six-pillared chamber and the niches containing a statue of Sarenput in the guise of Osiris. THE TOMB OF HARKHUF, the great 6th-Dynasty explorer who traveled to Central Africa and brought back a "dwarf" (who was probably a Pygmy) for the king, contains a text giving details of the letter from the king thanking Harkhuf for his present. The TOMB OF HEKAYIB AND HIS SON has a double-columned façade as well as reliefs which depict hunting and fishing scenes and a bullfight.

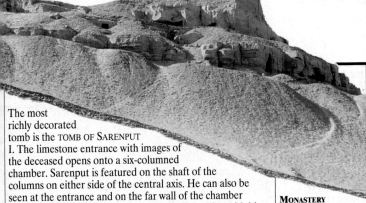

The most richly decorated tomb is the TOMB OF SARENPUT I. The limestone entrance with images of the deceased opens onto a six-columned chamber. Sarenput is featured on the shaft of the columns on either side of the central axis. He can also be seen at the entrance and on the far wall of the chamber followed by his sandal-bearer and his dogs, hunting with his family and being entertained by singers. On the same bank the TOMB OF THE AGA KHAN is a reminder of the latter's presence in Aswan. The forty-eighth imam, Mohammed Shah Aga Khan (who died in 1957) is buried here.

MONASTERY OF ST SIMEON. The Monastery of St Simeon lies about twenty minutes' climb from the Mausoleum of the Aga Khan. However, a better line of approach is to follow the path which runs along the ridge (about fifty minutes' walk), for it offers a magnificent view of Aswan. The monastery was built in the 6th century in honor of a local saint, Amba Hadra (or Amba Samaan), but the problems of keeping it supplied with water, along with repeated Bedouin attacks, led to its being abandoned at the end of the 12th century. It has all the features of a Coptic monastery ● *106*: the church built according to the classic layout of a nave flanked by side aisles and dissected by a transept leading to the choir (whose vaulted ceiling had a fresco showing Christ seated on a throne, surrounded by angels) and the sacristies, monks' cells, attics and tombstones. It was one of the largest Coptic monasteries in Egypt.

EAST BANK. On the east bank the town of Aswan and its bazaar stretch along the Corniche, which is the departure point for the road to the granite quarries. En route it passes

the FATIMID CEMETERY whose high-domed mausoleums commemorate the saints of Islam and, in particular, Sayyida Zeinab ▲ *314*. In the northern sector of the quarries, exploited from the 6th Dynasty to the Graeco-Roman period, is the so-called UNFINISHED OBELISK, which, had it been completed, would have weighed over 1,320 tons and stood some 118 feet high. To extract the blocks (often carved on three faces) the Egyptians chipped out holes along the line of the stone to be removed into which they inserted wooden wedges. These wedges were kept well soaked and, as they swelled, they shattered the block of stone. To the south two lidless Graeco-Roman sarcophagi and an unfinished royal colossus lie in the sand.

MONASTERY OF ST SIMEON
Once one of the great Coptic monasteries in Egypt, the Monastery of St Simeon was surrounded by a high enclosure wall made of brick with stone foundations.

The veritable forest of cupolas surmounting the tombs of venerated and important people in Aswan's vast Fatimid cemetery is an impressive sight.

MUSEUM OF NUBIA
Built in 1998, the museum is noted for its modern approach. The exterior is sober gray, in the tradition of the region. It gives a complete overview of the Nubian civilization since the time of the pharaohs, with a mass of archaeological material, including a reconstruction of a Nubian house.

HIGH DAM
A barrage of gravel, earth and rocks almost a mile deep at its base, 2½ miles long and 375 feet above the level of the water retains the vast artificial lake (which stretches for about 312 miles beyond the Egyptian border) formed by its construction. A huge hydroelectric power station has been built on the right bank.

Construction work in progress (above).

TEMPLE OF WADI ES-SEBUA
The eight pairs of sphinxes lining the *dromos* of the Temple of Ramesses II (below) evoked the

name of the site: the Valley of the Lions. They led to a pylon flanked by two colossi of Ramesses II. An Osiride court precedes the excavated part of the temple.

FIRST DAM. The first dam, built in Aswan granite and inaugurated by the British in 1902, soon proved unequal to the task of controlling irrigation downstream. It was widened and heightened several times but was finally replaced by the High Dam.
HIGH DAM. The construction of the Aswan High Dam (Sadd el-Aali) was overshadowed by political difficulties. The initial financing was to have come from the United States but in the end it was built and brought into use by Russian capital and engineers.
SAVING THE TEMPLES. The shores of the Nile between Aswan and Abu Simbel were lined with temples. An international rescue operation organized by UNESCO saved these divine residences from the flood waters. Some were transferred to museums in Berlin, Leiden, Madrid, New York and Turin, while others remain in situ, on the west bank (now LAKE NASSER), as proof of the value of these Nubian edifices.
KALABSHA. The Temple of Kalabsha, originally situated over 30 miles from Aswan, now stands about 6 miles from the first dam. Most of the temple was built during the reign of Augustus, although the remains of a chapel at the northwest corner date from Ptolemy IX. The temple is dedicated to the god Merwel (the Greek god Mandulis), the Nubian version of Horus associated with Isis, goddess of Philae. Its layout is the same as that of the Temple of Edfu ▲ *448*. Starting from the pylon, a double enclosure wall in brick and stone delimits the divine complex. The pylon, reached via a ramp, opens onto a courtyard with colonnades on three sides. On the façade of the pronaos intercolumniations alternate with columns whose capitals take the form of the lotus, papyrus and vines. The naos (later converted into a church) consists of three adjoining rooms. The roof beyond the first room of the sanctuary offers a good view of the site and the nearby TEMPLES OF KERTASSI and BEIT EL-WALI (governor's house), a speos preceded by a court whose walls celebrate the military victories of Ramesses II.

WADI ES-SEBUA. Wadi es-Sebua ("valley of the lions") is the site of the ancient temple of Wadi es-Sebua and the temples of DAKKA and MAHARRAQA. The Graeco-Roman temple of Dakka, dedicated to the god Thoth of Pnubs, was begun in the 3rd century BC by the Ethiopian king Arkamani. Several Ptolemies and Roman emperors worked on the temple, which was finally completed by Augustus. The axis of the temple, runs parallel with the river. A great pylon leads into the complex where the sanctuary lies beyond the pronaos and two rooms. The TEMPLE OF WADI ES-SEBUA was completely dismantled and rebuilt 2½ miles to the west. The small Temple of Horus which originally stood there is now destroyed and only the Temple of Ramesses II remains.

AMADA. The southern section, comprising the Temple of Derr and the Tomb of Penne (a governor), has developed around the TEMPLE OF AMADA, a hemi-speos dedicated to Amun-Re and Re-Harakhti by Thutmose III and Amenhotep II. The speos part of the temple was detached from the ground and lifted in one 990-ton block which was then moved 2 miles across the desert on rails to its new site about 330 feet above the first. In 1966 the constructed part of the pronaos was dismantled, course by course, and then reassembled and rebuilt near the speos. The TEMPLE OF DERR, which had originally stood on the east bank, was dedicated to Re-Harakhti by Ramesses II. THE TOMB OF PENNE (Penne was the governor of the region which lay between the first cataract and the second) was located in a necropolis containing Middle Kingdom and New Kingdom tombs at Aniba.

"But I am left with the impression that the Nile itself, with its great flow of water and its ever green banks and eternal youth is the really interesting thing, far finer than its monuments. These are interesting as part of the river's history, not the Nile because of them."
Wilfred Scawen Blunt

TEMPLE OF MAHARRAKA
The temple, which dates from Roman times and was dedicated to Isis and Serapis, was never completed. The most important remains are those of the hypostyle hall.

RESCUE OPERATION
With the advent of the 20th century the island of Philae was submerged for part of the year by the waters of the artificial lake created by the first dam. The building of the High Dam would have completely submerged it. So a rescue operation was mounted, financed by the Egyptian government and UNESCO. The temples were dismantled and moved to the island of Agilkia, which was leveled and extended to receive them.

PHILAE

According to tradition it is from Philae ("Pilak" in Egyptian), the smallest of the islands, that the goddess Isis watches over the tomb of Osiris on the neighboring island of BIGA, declared sacrosanct because its earth was considered part of the god's mummified body. Only priests and temple servants were permitted to live on the island to perform the sacred rites of Isis and Osiris.

TEMPLE OF ISIS. The Temple of Isis and Horus the Child (Harpocrates) dominates the group of monuments erected on the island between the 26th Dynasty and the Roman period. Beyond the *dromos* scenes on the great pylon show the sovereign addressing the divinities Isis, Horus and Hathor. Two granite lions, once joined to two obelisks, stand guard. Inside the gate of the first pylon an inscription attests to a visit by members of the Egypt Expedition in 1799. The central court opens, to the east, onto a series of rooms and, to the west, onto a *mamissi* comprising a pronaos and three rooms

where Isis the Elder is worshipped as the mother of Hathor. The second pylon, slightly offset to the east, opens onto a pronaos (later converted into a Coptic church) with a decorated ceiling on which the vulture of Upper and Lower Egypt circles in the central bay while the barques of night and day sail down the lateral bays. The sanctuary is composed of several rooms and forms an independent suite. The granite naos still exists. A staircase in the first room leads to the roof and the Chapel of Osiris, where the sacred rites of the god were performed and whose walls are covered in devotional scenes based on the myth of his death and resurrection. As you leave the naos continue westward to the 2nd-century GATEWAY OF THE EMPEROR HADRIAN and the source of the Nile. A vulture and a falcon are perched above a grotto where the Nile god is depicted entwined by a serpent, pouring water from two vases. To the north is a temple dedicated to Harendotes and, to the south, a Nilometer.

TEMPLE OF HATHOR. The columns of the temple dedicated to Hathor by Ptolemies VI (Philometor) and VIII (Euergetes II) have scenes of harpists, flutists, monkeys playing the lyre and the god Bes playing a small drum, distractions designed to placate the goddess. The nearby KIOSK OF TRAJAN received the sacred barque of Isis when the goddess returned to the island. Although unfinished, it is remarkable for its capitals.

Philae seen by a traveler: (from top to bottom) a reconstruction of the island and its monuments during the Graeco-Roman period; the flooded Temple of Isis; rescuing the temples; the island of Agilkia today (right).

The pronaos of the great temple of Abu Simbel with its pillars and engaged statue of Ramesses II, invaded by the sand.

Scenes of the famous Battle of Kadesh, engraved on the walls of the pronaos.

ABU SIMBEL

The delightful islands of Aswan and Philae are the prelude to the grand finale of a voyage up the Nile: the great rock temples of Abu Simbel. While air links offer a quick and easy way to reach the site (built 175 miles from Aswan), with the added bonus of an aerial view of the vast Lake Nasser, the road crosses a relatively flat and dazzlingly colored stretch of desert. In 1968 the Egyptian government, in association with UNESCO, undertook a truly "Pharaonic" task. The two speos of Ramesses II and Nefertari were cut into sections, strengthened, dismantled and reconstructed on the summit of a rocky outcrop of the Libyan mountains which overlooks the Nile at this point. The original site, at the foot of the cliff, was completely submerged following the construction of the Aswan High Dam.

TEMPLE OF RAMESSES II. The more southerly speos sets the tone with its façade (108 feet high x 125 feet wide) of four colossal statues of Ramesses II facing the east. The smiling king sits enthroned, wearing the double crown of Upper and Lower Egypt. His subjects, including princesses, princes, the queen mother and his first queen Nefertari, are depicted on a much smaller scale, standing at his feet. The power of Ramesses II extending over the enemies of Egypt is represented on the sides of the thrones where the conquered nations are placed to the north or south according to their geographical position. As if to greet the rising sun, twenty-two baboon statues stand

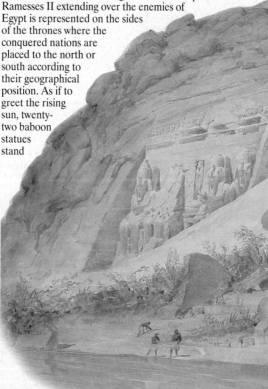

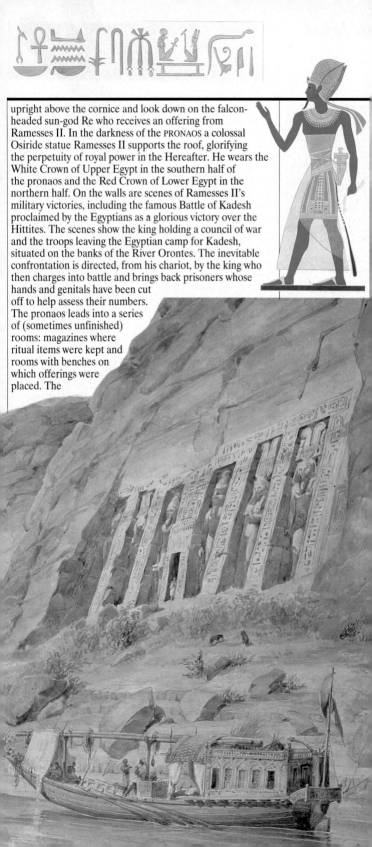

upright above the cornice and look down on the falcon-headed sun-god Re who receives an offering from Ramesses II. In the darkness of the PRONAOS a colossal Osiride statue Ramesses II supports the roof, glorifying the perpetuity of royal power in the Hereafter. He wears the White Crown of Upper Egypt in the southern half of the pronaos and the Red Crown of Lower Egypt in the northern half. On the walls are scenes of Ramesses II's military victories, including the famous Battle of Kadesh proclaimed by the Egyptians as a glorious victory over the Hittites. The scenes show the king holding a council of war and the troops leaving the Egyptian camp for Kadesh, situated on the banks of the River Orontes. The inevitable confrontation is directed, from his chariot, by the king who then charges into battle and brings back prisoners whose hands and genitals have been cut off to help assess their numbers. The pronaos leads into a series of (sometimes unfinished) rooms: magazines where ritual items were kept and rooms with benches on which offerings were placed. The

RELOCATING THE TEMPLES
The delicate rescue operation of Abu Simbel lasted for three years (1963–6). The two temples were disengaged from the cliffs in which they were carved, dismantled into 1,036 numbered blocks, transported and reassembled in an artificial cliff according to the original layout, in a new setting which recreated their original environment.

vestibule, covered with offering scenes, opens onto another room with a central door leading into the sanctuary and two others opening onto side chapels. In the sanctuary are four seated statues carved out of the rock: Re-Harakhti (red), Ramesses II deified (red), Amun-Re (blue) and Ptah (white). The divine patrons of Egypt's three great cities (Heliopolis, Thebes and Memphis) surround the deified king. Twice a year (on October 20 and February 20) at daybreak, the sun's rays fell on and "revitalized" the statues in the sanctuary. Only Ptah, the source of chthonian life, remained in the shadows. At the center of the sun's regenerating light the king was reinvigorated with divine energy. On either side of the façade two chapels (one of which contains a solar altar) are dedicated to the worship of the sun, while three stelae stand at the southeast corner of the façade. One of these, the so-called "Marriage Stele", illustrates the marriage of Ramesses II with the daughter of the king of the Hittites.

TEMPLE OF NEFERTARI. The façade of the Temple of Nefertari echoes the theme of the royal colossus of Ramesses II, which

alternates with statues of his first queen Nefertari, in the guise of Hathor-Satis, and their children. The pronaos, whose six Hathor pillars replace the Osiride pillars of the speos of Ramesses II, is decorated with scenes which show the king massacring the various enemies of Egypt in the presence of Nefertari while the queen herself makes offerings to the goddesses Mut and Hathor (far wall). Three doors in the pronaos open onto the vestibule preceding the sanctuary set deep in the hillside. Inside this rocky "womb" the goddess Hathor appears as the Hathor cow, protecting the breastplate of Ramesses II, while on the south wall the king glorifies his own image and that of his deified queen. On the north wall Nefertari performs the rites of divine worship under the watchful eye of Mut and Hathor.

EGYPT IN THE MUSEUMS
OF THE WORLD

ITALY, *468*
GERMANY, *470*
UNITED STATES, *472*
UNITED KINGDOM, *474*
FRANCE, *476*
EUROPE, *478*
OBELISKS, *480*

In 1824 the French refused the collection put together by the Piedmontese French consul in Egypt, Bernadino Drovetti (1776–1852). It was subsequently acquired by Charles Felix of Savoy, King of Piedmont and Sardinia, who decided to found the first great Egyptian museum. Since then the 5,300 pieces (which came from surface excavations and date mainly from the New Kingdom) have been exhibited at the Accademia delle Scienze in Turin. It was not until the Italians Schiaparelli and Farina, who were following in the footsteps of Mariette, Maspero and Petrie, undertook systematic archeological excavations and scientific studies that the different stages of Egyptian history, from prehistory to the Coptic period, were explored.

Treasure from the tomb of Kha.

EGYPTIAN MUSEUM, TURIN

After Cairo, the city of Turin has the largest collection of Egyptian antiquities in the world. Its rooms are organized according to themes or by provenance. A magnificent collection of colossal statues representing gods, kings and nobles, acquired by Drovetti in 1815, came from the Temple of Amun at Karnak. Ernesto Schiaparelli's early 20th-century excavations at Deir el-Medina ▲ 438 discovered the (intact) 18th-Dynasty tomb of the architect Kha and his wife, complete with all the funeral paraphernalia, furniture and statues which were intended to accompany the deceased on their voyage into the Hereafter. There is another intact (although anonymous) tomb from the 5th Dynasty, as well as the richly painted 11th-Dynasty tomb of Ity from Gebelein.

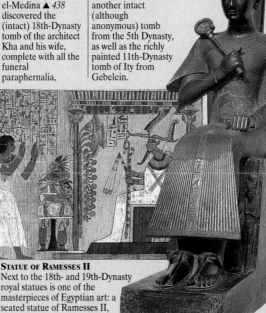

The Turin museum houses a fine collection of ceramics, amulets, papyri and cloth as well as a number of figurines made of wood.

STATUE OF RAMESSES II

Next to the 18th- and 19th-Dynasty royal statues is one of the masterpieces of Egyptian art: a seated statue of Ramesses II, wearing a pleated tunic with, on his left, the sculpted image of his wife.

One of the rooms in the Turin museum,
painted by Delleani (1881).

ARCHEOLOGICAL MUSEUM, FLORENCE AND THE VATICAN MUSEUM

The National Archeological Museum in Florence possesses a comprehensive collection of Egyptian antiquities. Its exhibits consist mainly of pieces which were brought back from Ippolito Rossellini's expedition to Egypt with Champollion ▲ 216 in 1828, and the later discoveries of Ernesto Schiaparelli.

The Vatican Museum in Rome founded in 1839 by Pope Gregory XVI houses, amongst other treasures, a head of the pharaoh Mentuhotep IV (11th Dynasty) and a colossal granite statue of Queen Tuy, mother of Ramesses II. Much of the Vatican's Egyptian collection (like that of the Capitol museums) has come from excavations carried out within the city of Rome, which highlights the importance of the cult of Isis, introduced from Egypt at the time of the Roman conquest.

HEAD OF MENTUHOTEP
This sandstone head of the pharaoh Mentuhotep is one of the key exhibits in the Vatican's Egyptian collection.

CHAPEL OF ELLEJISSA
Following the Nubian rescue operation which was mounted by UNESCO during the 1960's, the museum at Turin acquired Nubia's most ancient rock chapel. It was built at Ellejissa by Thutmose III in 1450 BC, restored two centuries later by Ramesses II and converted into a church with the advent of Christianity.

EGYPT IN THE MUSEUMS OF ITALY
Italy has collections of Egyptian antiquities in Bologna, Naples, Palermo and Trieste, as well as in Turin, Florence and the Vatican.

USEFUL INFORMATION
MUSEO ARCHEOLOGICO NAZIONALE DI FIRENZE
Via della Colonna, 38
Florence
Hours: 9am–2pm

MUSEO GREGORIANO EGIZIO
Cortile del Belvedere
Citta del Vaticano
Vatican, Rome
Hours: 9am–2pm

MUSEO EGIZIO DI TORINO
Via Accademia delle Scienze, 6
Turin
Hours: 9am–2pm

465

In 1846 Frederick William IV, King of Prussia, chose a small island in the River Spree, in the center of Berlin, as the site for the city's Egyptian Museum, which would house, in particular, the 1,500 pieces brought back from an expedition led by the Egyptologist Karl Richard Lepsius (1810–84). The pieces were added to Berlin's existing collection of Egyptian antiquities, formed thirty years earlier by Frederick William III. Its director was Giuseppe Passalacqua, an adventurer from Trieste who had brought back a surprising number of antiquities from the Nile Valley.

HISTORY OF THE EGYPTIAN MUSEUM, BERLIN

The Egyptian Museum of Berlin was opened in 1850 and run under the joint directorship of Karl Richard Lepsius ● 94 and Giuseppe Passalacqua until the death of the latter in 1865. From the end of the 19th century two Egyptologists, Johann Peter Adolf Erman and Ludwig Borchardt, promoted the study of Egyptology and enriched the museum's collection. Erman began to write a dictionary of the Egyptian language in Berlin while Borchardt carried out excavations in Egypt where he discovered the famous limestone bust of Queen Nefertiti at Tell el-Amarna ▲ 378. The museum also received donations of pieces discovered during the excavations financed by two patrons of the arts from Berlin: Baron von Bissing and the wealthy merchant James Simon.

During World War Two the museum collections, stored in the city and the neighboring provinces, sustained considerable losses. All the sarcophagi and mummies were destroyed, as were one hundred crates of exhibits and over five hundred stone items. Five warehouses remained undamaged. The contents of three of these, recovered by the Russians, were returned to the Bodenmuseum in East Berlin in 1958. The contents of the other two warehouses, which were returned to West Germany by the Allied troops, formed the nucleus of the Egyptian Museum of West Berlin, opened in 1967.

USEFUL INFORMATION

ÄGYPTISCHES
MUSEUM
Schlossstr. 70
14059 Berlin
Hours: 9am–5pm
Closed: Friday

ÄGYPTISCHES
MUSEUM UND
PAPYRUSSAMMLUNG
BODENMUSEUM-
MUSEUMSINSEE
10178 Berlin
Hours: 9am–5pm
Closed: Monday

There are also important collections at Leipzig, Munich (efficient acquisitions policy), Hamburg, Hanover, Heidelberg and Hildesheim.

SARCOPHAGUS OF KEN-HOR
Painted wood sarcophagus from the Third Intermediate period, surrounded by its funeral paraphernalia.

COLLECTIONS OF THE EGYPTIAN MUSEUM

A number of pieces from Borchardt's excavations at Tell el-Amarna can be seen at the palace of Charlottenburg in former West Berlin. They include the bust of Nefertiti and the plaster head of Akhenaten ● 42. A bronze statue, thought to be that of the priest Khonsu-Met, and the statue of Meres, "singer in the Temple of Amun", date from the Third Intermediate period. The sacred cat, also in bronze, of the lion-goddess Bastet, and the family group, in wood (which had originally been painted red), of Psamtick, are both fine examples of works from the Archaic period. Another particularly rare piece is the so-called "green head", which was sculpted in green *pierre dure*, and dates from the early Ptolemaic period.

HEAD OF QUEEN TIYI
This head of Queen Tiyi (mother of Akhenaten), delicately carved in yew, is an 18th-Dynasty masterpiece.

HEAD OF AKHENATEN
Among the twenty or so plaster heads exhibited in the museum is a head of Akhenaten, probably used as a model for other portraits of the pharaoh.

REORGANIZATION
After World War Two Germany's Egyptian collections were located on both sides of the Iron Curtain. This was particularly apparent in Berlin where they were divided between the monumental Pergamon in East Berlin and the palace of Charlottenburg in West Berlin. Since reunification the collections are being completely reorganized.

BUST OF NEFERTITI
This painted limestone bust of Queen Nefertiti, wife of Akhenaten, was discovered by Borchardt in 1912 in the workshop of the sculptor Thutmose at Tell el-Amarna.

471

The decision made in 1906 to create an Egyptian Department of Antiquities at the Metropolitan Museum in New York, coincided with the first American expeditions to Egypt, and to Thebes and Lisht in particular. As well as being mainly supplied by the discoveries made during these excavations, the museum's collections were also enriched by the reproductions of more than four hundred copies of wall-paintings made by the team of epigraphists accompanying the expeditions. Lord Carnarvon, Theodore M. Davis and Albert Gallatin are three of the prominent names associated with the sales, donations and bequests made by private collectors to the Metropolitan Museum.

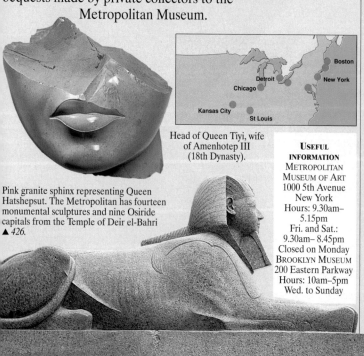

Head of Queen Tiyi, wife of Amenhotep III (18th Dynasty).

Pink granite sphinx representing Queen Hatshepsut. The Metropolitan has fourteen monumental sculptures and nine Osiride capitals from the Temple of Deir el-Bahri ▲ 426.

USEFUL INFORMATION
METROPOLITAN MUSEUM OF ART
1000 5th Avenue
New York
Hours: 9.30am–5.15pm
Fri. and Sat.: 9.30am– 8.45pm
Closed on Monday
BROOKLYN MUSEUM
200 Eastern Parkway
Hours: 10am–5pm
Wed. to Sunday

Fragment of a wall painting, showing fishing with a net, from a Theban tomb.

The museum has a fine collection of Old- and Middle-Kingdom sarcophagi, including this 21st-Dynasty, painted wood sarcophagus.

Limestone funeral stele of Senu (18th Dynasty).

Reconstruction of the temple at Dendera (1st century BC), a gift from Egypt in recognition of the American contribution to the Nubian rescue operation ● 98.

OTHER UNITED STATES MUSEUMS

The Brooklyn Museum in New York also possesses a significant collection of Egyptian antiquities, as well as a major center of Egyptology: the Wilbur Library. Also worth a visit are the Museum of Fine Arts in Boston (one of the largest museums in the United States), the Philadelphia University Museum, the Walters Art Gallery in Baltimore, the Oriental Institute Museum and Field Museum of Natural History in Chicago, the Cleveland Museum of Art and the museums of Detroit, Kansas City, New Haven and St Louis.

The magnificent neoclassical building of the British Museum, which superseded Montagu House, stands in Bloomsbury, in the heart of London. Among its many other treasures it houses one of the four or five leading collections of Egyptian antiquities in the world. Like the other major European collections, it was initially based on an older, existing collection, and formed from the shrewd acquisitions of those veritable "forwarding agents" of antiquities who enjoyed more or less unrestricted access to Egypt and its treasures during the first half of the 19th century: in particular the British consul in Cairo Henry Salt (1780–1827) and the adventurer Giovanni Battista Belzoni (1778–1823).

HISTORY OF THE BRITISH MUSEUM COLLECTION

Systematically organized and scientifically conducted excavations, particularly under the aegis of the Egypt Exploration Fund (later the Egypt Exploration Society), made it possible to build up varied and comprehensive collections. The reliefs and statues of Deir el-Bahri ▲ 426 are one such example. The British archeological missions were extremely active on a number of sites and kept the museum supplied with coherent archeological material, not just "beautiful objects". In this respect, the material from the site of Qasr Ibrim (in Nubia), is particularly interesting.

ORGANIZATION OF THE COLLECTION

Exhibits are organized on the basis of an outstanding, revised presentation. Generally speaking, statues, reliefs, sarcophagi and heavy pieces, with some extremely dark and evocative side galleries, are on the first floor, while smaller items and thematic classifications are on the second.

BUST OF RAMESSES II

Most of the major exhibits were either purchased by or donated to the museum during the 19th century: for example the granite bust of Ramesses II (right), taken from the Ramesseum ▲ 432 by Belzoni and the "royal list" of Abydos, as well as paintings and small, luxury, funerary items.

Mock Canopic jars in painted wood, made in the 21st Dynasty. By this time the internal organs were being embalmed and then replaced in the mummified body.

THE PAPYRUS COLLECTION

The museum has an entire series of important papyri, including an account of the enquiry into the plundering of the royal tombs during the reign of Ramesses IX (Abbott Papyrus), the mathematical Rhind Papyrus and the great Harris Papyrus.

"BOOK OF ANI"

The museum also has some splendid examples of *Books of the Dead*: for example the 19th-Dynasty, painted papyrus book of the scribe Ani (left), and the books of Hunefer and Nakht.

ROSETTA STONE

This huge, black basalt stele is one of the "jewels" of the museum's collection. It is inscribed with the bilingual text, in Greek and Egyptian (hieroglyphs and demotic script), which provided the key for the deciphering of Egyptian writing.

Edinburgh
Glasgow
Manchester
Liverpool
Cambridge
Oxford
London

USEFUL INFORMATION

BRITISH MUSEUM
Great Russell Street
London WC1

Opening hours:
10am–5pm
Sunday: 2.30–6pm

Closed on public holidays.

475

New-Kingdom "horse" ring in
gold, cornelian and *cloisonné*.

Jean-François Champollion,
sometimes described as founding
father of Egyptology, became the first
curator of the Egyptian Department of
Antiquities of the Louvre Museum,
founded by Charles X in 1826. On the
second floor of the south wing of the Cour
Carrée, the architect Fontaine designed the rooms destined to
house one of the most prestigious collections of Egyptian art in
the world. The pieces which comprised the first acquisition,
approved by the king in 1824, were presented against a décor
which reproduced Egypt's legendary magnificence and
grandeur. Champollion gave precedence to the historical and
scientific view, imposing a new concept of museology which
broke with the traditional esthetic demands of the period.

HISTORY OF THE LOUVRE COLLECTION

When Champollion
▲ 216 died in 1832,
the department
already had a
considerable number
of exhibits which had
come mainly from
the purchase of the
collection of the
British consul in
Alexandria, Henry
Salt, in 1826, and of
the second
collection of
Drovetti, the
French consul in
Egypt, in 1827.
Drovetti's first
collection, refused by

France in 1824, is now
in the Egyptian
Museum in Turin.
The antiquities that
Champollion brought
back from Egypt in
1828, although few in
number, were of
extraordinarily high
quality. The second
half of the 19th
century heralded a
new type of
acquisition from the
French excavations in
Egypt carried out by
Auguste Mariette
● 96. The foundation
of the Cairo branch

of the French
Institute in 1880
strengthened the links
between
archeological
missions and national
institutions. The more
recent additions
mainly resulted from
the transfer of reserve
collections from the
Bibliothèque
Nationale in 1922 and
the Musée Guimet in
1946, as well as from
donations from
private collectors.

MADJIA SARCOPHAGUS
The painted wood
sarcophagus found at
Deir el-Medina
▲ 438 is an example
of the new type of
sarcophagus used at
the time. Various
objects, pieces of
furniture and items of
jewelry were found
during the same
excavations.

**USEFUL
INFORMATION**

MUSÉE DU LOUVRE
34, quai du Louvre
Opening hours:
9am–6pm
Monday and
Wednesday:
9am–10pm
Closed on Tuesday.

Paris

Quartzite
statue of Nefertiti: a
fine example of the
humanization of
figures during the
Amarnian period.

In recognition of the collaboration of the French teams during the Nubian temple rescue operation, Egypt donated the colossal statue of Amenhotep IV (Akhenaten) to the Louvre Museum. Today, the Louvre's Egyptian collection contains some 5,000 pieces covering 4,000 years in the history of the Nile Valley.

PECTORAL OF RAMESSES II

The brilliance and prosperity of the New Kingdom is reflected in the sumptuousness of the exhibits, as illustrated by the gold cup of the Egyptian general Djehouty and the pectoral of Ramesses II.

TREASURES OF THE LOUVRE

Remains from the royal tombs of the Nile Valley exhibited in the Louvre include the pink granite sarcophagus of Ramesses III and a fragment of a wall-painting representing Sety I and the divinity Athor. The Archaic period is represented by a number of illustrated papyri and bronze statues. The Faiyum museum also has some fine pieces from the Saite period: the Posno Horus, the life-sized limestone statue of the Apis Bull from Mariette's excavations at Memphis in 1852, and some fine examples of the Faiyum portraits. With the remains of Christian churches and the famous linen and wool weaving, the Louvre's Coptic rooms cover the eight most productive centuries of Christian art in Egypt.

SEATED SCRIBE

The museum has a collection of Old-Kingdom statues of which the oldest are in limestone and archaic in their rigidity. The "seated scribe" (in limestone, alabaster and rock crystal), found at Saqqara, is a fine example of their stylistic development.

CHANCELLOR NAKHTI

Outstanding among the Middle-Kingdom pieces are the remains of funerary items and the magnificent acacia statue of the chancellor Nakhti, found in the provincial necropolis of Assiut.

477

As well as the leading national museums, which have entire wings and series of rooms devoted to Egyptian antiquities, there is an impressive number of smaller museums and foundations throughout the world which have their own Egyptian collection, put together from purchases and donations. As it would be impossible to provide an exhaustive list, here are some of the best known.

FRANCE

In Paris, apart from the Louvre, the small collections of the Musée Rodin, the Petit Palais and the Bibliothèque Nationale are well worth a visit. The Clot-Bey (doctor to the *pasha* of Egypt in the 19th century) collection in Marseilles has been transferred from the Château Borély to the magnificent building of La Vieille Charité in Le Panier district. The collection of Egyptian antiquities in the new art museum in Grenoble, where Champollion grew up and began his research, includes the stele of the Princess of Bakhtan. The Musée des Beaux-Arts in Lyons also has a fine collection of objects which have come mainly from the excavations of Coptos but also from the collections of such national institutions as the Musée Guimet and the Louvre. In Strasbourg the collection of the Palais Universitaire (the University Institute of Egyptology) is, unusually for France, an extremely valuable university collection built up primarily during the German Imperial period (1870–1914) but also during the period when the university sponsored the French excavations at Tanis (limited access).

Statue of a bearded man (Nagada period), Musée des Beaux-Arts, Lyons.

COLLECTIONS IN THE FRENCH MUSEUMS

Nantes: Musée d'Archéologie

Avignon: Musée Calvet (currently being refurbished)

Cannes: Le Suquet

Orleans: Musée Historique et d'Archéologie de l'Orléanais

Toulouse: Musée Georges-Labit

Bas-relief from the Temple of Kalabsha ▲ 460 in Nubia, showing Augustus in Egyptian dress (Musée Champollion, Figeac).

A small exhibition of objects on loan from the Louvre Museum can be seen in the recently converted Musée Champollion in Figeac, originally the house where the Egyptologist was born.

Wooden model of a boat (12th Dynasty) and heads of Semite prisoners (20th Dynasty) in the Kunsthistorisches Museum, Vienna.

Faiyum portrait (2nd century). Pushkin Museum, Moscow.

OTHER LEADING EUROPEAN MUSEUMS

BELGIUM
In Brussels the collections of the Musées Royaux d'Art et d'Histoire were put together from major Belgian excavations and purchases. The Queen Elisabeth Foundation has made Brussels one of the international centers of Egyptology.

AUSTRIA
The Kunsthistorisches Museum in Vienna has a very large and long-standing collection of stelae, reliefs and statues, including a remarkable

13th-Dynasty statue of the Sobekemsaef and Theban sarcophagi. There are also some fine reliefs from the tomb of Meryre (presented in major exhibitions devoted to Amenhotep III in the United States and Paris), recently discovered at Saqqara ▲ 344 by the French Bubasteion mission.

THE NETHERLANDS
The large collection in Leiden was put together by the Swedish consul Giovanni Anatasi at the beginning of the 19th century. It

consists mainly of pieces from Thebes ▲ 394 and Memphis ▲ 332 and includes, in particular, the magnificent reliefs from the Tomb of Horemheb and the statues of Maya.

Funerary statuette in polychrome wood. Gulbenkian Museum, Portugal.

Make-up dish in the shape of a fish. Barbier-Mueller Museum, Geneva.

EGYPTIAN COLLECTIONS THROUGHOUT THE WORLD
CZECH REPUBLIC
Náprstkovo Muzeum
DENMARK
National Museet
Ny Carlsberg

Glypotek
THE NETHERLANDS
Pierson Museum
Rijksmuseum
SWEDEN
Mediterranean Museum
SWITZERLAND
Museums in Geneva, Neuchâtel, Basel
PORTUGAL
Calouste-Gulbenkian Foundation
RUSSIA
Pushkin Museum
Hermitage Museum
JAPAN
University Museum of Archeology, Kyoto

Obelisks appeared on the European scene in 1585 when the Vatican obelisk was erected opposite St Peter's in Rome. However, they tended to lose their specifically Egyptian characteristics. On October 22, 1836 the Luxor obelisk, a gift from the Egyptian government to France, was erected in the Place de la Concorde during a ceremony attended by the people of Paris.

THE OBELISKS OF ROME
The city of Rome has five obelisks (right and left). The obelisk of Ramesses II from Heliopolis ▲ 270, which used to stand in the center of the Circus Maximus (above), today stands in the Piazza del Popolo.

THE OBELISK OF CONSTANTINOPLE
The 197-foot obelisk of Thutmose III (far right) broke as it was being unloaded in Constantinople. Only the upper section (85 feet) was erected by Theodosius the Great on the site of the Roman hippodrome, today the At Meydani.

"CLEOPATRA'S NEEDLES"
In 1877 John Dixon built a cylindrical metal container surmounted by a deck and fitted with masts and sails, to transport one of "Cleopatra's Needles" from Alexandria to London. The second of the two obelisks, a gift from the Egyptian government to the United States in 1879, today stands in New York's Central Park.

Practical information

482 Getting there
484 Getting around
486 Daily life
493 Useful words and phrases
494 List of addresses
507 Places to visit
516 Bibliography
517 List of illustrations
528 Index
539 Map section

KEY

■ Credit cards
🏠 Quiet
🅿 Parking
≋ Swimming pool
⬆ Terrace
⬆ Garden
🌿 View
🇨 Town center
✪ Editor's choice

Prices

Hotels		Restaurants	
▪	< $25	▪	$5 to $25
▪▪	$25 to $80	▪▪	$15 to $30
▪▪▪	$80 to $150	▪▪▪	$25 to $40
▪▪▪▪	> $150	▪▪▪▪	> $40

◆ GETTING THERE

USEFUL ADDRESSES
The official website for tourist information for Egypt is: www.touregypt.net

→ UNITED KINGDOM
■ **Egyptian Embassy**
26 South Street
London
W1Y 6DD
Tel. 020 7499 2401
■ **Egyptian Consulate**
2 Loundes Street
London
SW1X 9ET
Tel. 020 7235 9777
■ **Egyptian Tourist Authority**
168 Piccadilly
London W1
Tel. 020 7493 5282

→ UNITED STATES
■ **Egyptian Embassy**
2300 Decatur Plaza
NW
Washington DC
20008
Tel. 202 232 5400
■ **Egyptian Consulate**
1110 Second Ave.
New York
NY 10022
Tel. 212 759 7120
3001 Pacific Ave.
San Francisco
CA 94115
Tel. 415 346 9700/2
■ **Egyptian Tourist Authority**
630 Fifth Ave.
Suite 1706
New York
NY 10111
Tel. 212 332 2570
San Vincente Plaza
Suite 215
83 Wilshire Bld
Beverley Hills
CA 90211
Tel. 213 653 8815

TRAVEL AGENTS
Some travel agents offer package or personalized tours to Egypt.
■ **US**
MISR Travel
630 Fifth Ave.
NY 10011
Tel. 800 22-EGYPT (34978)
■ **UK**
Trailfinders
194 Kensington
High Street
London W8 7RG
Tel. 020 7938 3939

MONEY
→ CHANGE
E£1 = GP£0.2 = US$0.3 = 0.3 Euros
It is illegal to take £E out of the country. You are therefore advised to hold on to all the receipts for your exchange transactions in order to change Egyptian money back into your own currency upon departure.

→ CREDIT CARDS
Are accepted by major hotels and many stores.

→ TRAVELER'S CHECKS
Can be exchanged at most banks, and are accepted by all stores for tourists.

→ FOREIGN CURRENCIES
European currencies and US dollars are accepted almost everywhere.

TRAVELING BY AIR
→ REGULAR FLIGHTS
■ **British Airways**
Direct flights from London to Cairo.
UK
Tel. 0345 222 111
■ **TWA**
Operates direct flights to Cairo.
US
Tel. 800 892 4141
■ **Egypt Air**
Operates direct flights from London and the US to Cairo.
UK
Tel. 020 7734 9490
USA
Tel. 800 334 6787
ALEXANDRIA
19 Midan Saad Zaghlul
El Raml Station
Tel. (03) 483 33 57
CAIRO
9 Shari' Tal'at Harb
Tel. (02) 393 28 36
LUXOR
Shari' el-Nil
Tel. 380 580/1/2/3/4

■ **London–Cairo**
Prices from around £300
Duration: 5 hours
New York–Cairo
Prices from around $1,400
Duration: 10½ hours

→ CHARTER FLIGHTS
Direct charter flights from London/New York to Cairo and Luxor, Sharm el-Sheikh or Hourghada. Flights are often included as part of a package deal.

TRAVELING BY SEA
From Jordan (Aqaba to Noueiba)

→ STANDARD FERRY
Daily sailings at 10am and 6pm
Duration: 3 hours
Prices vary according to the type of car.

→ FAST FERRY
Daily sailing
Duration: 1 hour
Cost: $42
Information
Canal Tours
Abd-el-Khaled Sarwat (Cairo)
Tel. (02) 574 57 55

TRAVELING BY CAR
→ BY ROAD FROM ISRAEL
There are two border posts (North and South) between Israel and Egypt. A visa for Egypt must be obtained in your own country. As there are no direct bus services between points in the two countries at the moment, it is necessary to change buses or travel by car. Check all the necessary formalities before setting off.

INSURANCE
It is recommended that you take out travel insurance with your travel agents, insurance brokers, credit card company, etc. Avoid doubling up on insurance.

→ CREDIT CARDS
Gold, Premier and Mastercard offer insurance schemes that cover repatriation under certain conditions.

→ TRAVEL AGENTS
Can usually arrange additional insurance to cover loss or theft of luggage, repatriation and third-party liability.

FORMALITIES
→ VISAS
■ **United Kingdom and United States**
Issued by the Egyptian Consulate.
■ **Egypt**
Visas can be obtained by EC members at the airport on arrival in Egypt ($20).
■ **Other documents required:**
Passport with a minimum validity of 6 months, photographs, proof of travel (return flight ticket or other).
■ **Validity and extension of visas**
Visas are issued for 3 months, but are only valid for 1 month if obtained in Egypt. Extensions can be obtained for a fee at the Mogammaa (Central Government Building) ▲ 280 in Cairo within 14 days after your visa has expired.

→ SPECIAL VISA FOR SINAI
A 14-day visa can be obtained for Sinai if traveling to the country overland.

VACCINATIONS
No vaccinations are required.

However, it is recommended that you bring an adequate supply of any prescription medication that are needed. Vaccinations against hepatitis A and B are advisable. For further information on vaccinations, cost and the countries for which they are required, ask your general practitioner.

HEALTH

■ **Medicine**
Before leaving home ask your doctor to prescribe drugs for sunstroke, fever and an upset stomach.
There is some risk of malaria between May and October, so make sure you take some sort of preventative treatment with you (Delta region and Upper Egypt).

■ **Hygiene and treatment**
High-protection suncream and aftersun lotion, insect repellent, antiseptic cream and water purifying tablets are also indispensable.

WHEN TO GO

■ **Alexandria and Cairo**
Avoid in summer, at Easter and during the New Year festivals which are the busiest periods.

■ **Nile Delta, Mediterranean and Red Seas**
Ideal temperatures in spring and in the fall.
WARNING:
Many hotels close in Mediterranean areas during the low season.

■ **Oases and deserts, Nile Valley**
Best conditions are between November and March.

■ **Sinai**
Avoid in winter as nights in the mountains are bitterly cold.

CLIMATE

Desert climate in most of the country.

■ **December–March**
Northern Egypt can be really cold and wet; afternoons in the south are hot, but nights can be cold.

■ **April–November**
Temperatures begin to rise in April and remain high until October. They do vary according to latitude and reach a maximum of 120°F/ 50°C in the south.
WARNING:
Sandstorms (Khamsin) in March and April.

→ TEMPERATURES IN F°

	Cairo min/max	Aswan
Jan.	46/65	46/76
Feb.	48/68	48/80
Mar.	52/76	56/88
Apr.	58/82	64/96
May	63/90	70/105
June	64/96	78/108
July	70/96	80/110
Aug.	72/96	77/110
Sep.	68/92	76/108
Oct.	64/86	70/99
Nov.	58/78	60/88
Dec.	50/70	50/80

WHAT TO TAKE

■ Torches and spare batteries are indispensable items for visiting temples and tombs.

■ Take spare films with you for cameras and movie cameras. High-sensitivity films are recommended for taking photographs or for filming inside museums and tombs (the use of flashes is not allowed).

■ Clothing that covers the body well and that can be put on and taken off easily (long-sleeve shirts, pareos), comfortable walking shoes and sandals. Dress to suit the climate and customs. Some form of sun hat and sunglasses (to protect your eyes from both light and dust) are essential.

COST OF LIVING

→ AVERAGE BUDGET
■ **Cheap**
Hotel: £E30–50
Restaurant: £E20
■ **Average**
Hotel: £E250
Restaurant: £E30
■ **Luxury**
Hotel: £E700
Restaurant: £E50

→ COST
■ **Admission to a site or a museum**
£E8–30
■ **Coffee or tea**
£E1–5
■ **Gasoline (Super)**
£E1 (1 liter)
■ **Foreign-language newspaper**
£E0.50
■ **Large bottle of mineral water**
£E2–5
■ **Postcard**
£E1
■ **Pack of Egyptian cigarettes**
£E0.50–4
■ **Airfare**
Cairo–Aswan or Luxor–Cairo
£E1,100

TIME DIFFERENCE

Egypt is two hours ahead of Greenwich Mean Time.
When it is noon in Cairo, it is 10am in London and 5am in New York.

ELECTRICITY

Alternating current 220 volts.

STUDENTS

→ INTERNATIONAL STUDENT CARD
Entitles the holder to 50% reduction when visiting museums and archeological sites, as well as on certain train journeys. Non-international student cards are not accepted.

TELEPHONE

■ **To call Egypt from the UK**
00 20 + city code + number
■ **To call Egypt from the US**
01 20 + city code + number
■ **Egyptian city codes**

Cairo	2
Alexandria	3
Luxor	95
Aswan	97
Sharm el-Sheikh	62
el-Faiyum	84
Ismailiya	64
el-Minya	86
Port-Said	66
Suez	62

MOBILE PHONES

→ "ROAMING" OPTION
Depending on the type of service you subscribe to in the UK or US, you may be able to apply for an international option, which will enable your mobile to be connected to a local mobile telephone line as soon as you arrive in Egypt.
WARNING:
*The cost of communications is very high.
Not available in Nubia.*

→ CARD OPTIONS
Rental-free formula: GSM cards (Alo or Click cards) can be purchased.
Cost: £E1,090 with £E50 worth of calls to be used within 20 days. Can be recharged with £E50, 100, 200 and 300 cards.

◆ GETTING AROUND

AIRPORTS
→ ADDRESSES
■ Alexandria
International
airport
3 miles south of
Alexandria
Tel. (03) 420 20 21
or (03) 420 10 36
■ Cairo
International
airport
Heliopolis
Tel. (02) 291 42 55,
(02) 291 42 66
or (02) 291 42 77
Lost luggage:
(02) 291 42 89
WARNING:
*There are two
airports in Cairo:
the old one and
the new one.*
■ Luxor
International
airport
12½ miles from the
city center
Tel. (095) 37 46 55
■ Sharm el-Sheikh
airport
Tel. (062) 60 11 40/
41/42/43
■ Hurghada airport
Naama Bay
Tel. (065) 44 26 31
■ Kharga airport
New Valley
Tel. (088) 90 04 57
■ Aswan airport
14 miles south of
the center
Tel. (097) 48 03 07
■ Other airports
There are smaller
airports in
Abu Simbel,
El-Arish, Taba
and St Catherine's.

→ TRANSFER
■ Cairo airport
Free shuttle bus
service between the
old and new
airports.
– BUS
Bus no. 400 goes
to Midan at-Tahrir

(center of Cairo)
– AIRPORT
SHUTTLE BUS
Takes travelers to
whatever
destination they
may require. Before
setting off,
the driver draws
up an itinerary
according to the
various destinations
requested by the
passengers.
– TAXI
Without any doubt
the fastest and most
practical means of
transport for the
city center or any
other destination.
Check the official
tariffs at the
tourist office,
and agree on the
price before getting
into the car.
■ Alexandria
airport
Buses 203 and 310,
minibuses 703 and
710 go from the
airport to Midan
Orabi.
■ Other airports
Taxis are generally
the best form of
transport between
the airports and
the city centers.

BY AIR
→ DOMESTIC AIRLINES
■ Egyptair
6 Shari' Adli
Cairo
Tel. (02) 392 7649
Connections
between Cairo,
Alexandria, Luxor,
Aswan, Abu Simbel,
Hurghada and
Kharga.
■ Air Sinai
(Egypt)
Tel. (02) 578 03 22
or 578 03 23
Connections
between Cairo,

Hurghada, El-Arish,
Taba, Sharm
el-Sheikh and
St Catherine's.

BUSES
→ CITY BUSES
Bus terminals are
usually situated
outside railway
stations or in main
squares.
■ Cost
10–25 piastres.
■ In Cairo
Abd el-Monem Riad
terminal, behind the
Egyptian Museum.
WARNING:
*There are no maps
of bus routes, stops
are badly indicated
and buses are
usually crowded.
It is essential to
obtain first-hand
information.*

→ MINIBUSES
They leave from
the same terminals
and follow the same
itineraries as
ordinary buses, but
are not as popular
because of their
higher fares. You
cannot stand during
the journey.
■ Ticket
25–50 piastres.

→ COACHES
■ Companies
– EAST DELTA
Midan Ard el-
Torgoman
Cairo
Tel. (02) 574 28 14
or 576 22 93
Services between
Cairo and Sharm
el-Sheikh, Dahab,
Nuweiba, Port-Said,
Ismailiya, Rafah,
St Catherine
– SUPER JET
Midan Ard
el-Torgoman

Cairo
Tel. (02) 579 81 81
Services between
Cairo and
Alexandria,
Hurghada, Mersa
Matruh (in summer),
Port Said
– UPPER EGYPT
Midan Ard el-
Torgoman
Cairo
Tel. (02) 556 15 43
or 576 02 61
Services between
Cairo, Luxor, Aswan,
Hurghada.
– WEST DELTA BUS
COMPANY
Behind Midan Giza
Giza
Tel. (02) 290 48 51
Services between
Cairo and
Alexandria
and the Delta
region.
Make reservations
in advance and
confirm times.

CARRIAGES
In Luxor and
Aswan carriages are
the best form of
transport. You
should agree on the
price before getting
into one.

ROADS
Drive slowly and
always be on the
look-out as red
lights, pedestrian
crossings, traffic
priority, etc., are not
always respected in
Egypt. When
driving outside
the main cities
or town, do not
stray from the
main roads or
tracks. Avoid
driving at night.
Do not drive alone
into the Nile Valley
(prohibited).

STATIONS AND TERMINALS

→ RAILWAY STATIONS

■ **Alexandria**
Midan el-Gumhuriya, at the southern end of Shari' Nabi Daniel
■ **Aswan**
At the end of the street where all the souks are.
■ **Cairo**
Midan Ramses
■ **Luxor**
Midan Station

→ BUS TERMINALS

■ **Alexandria**
– BUS AND COMMUNAL TAXIS:
Midan el-Gumhuriya, next to the railway station.
■ **Cairo**
– TERMINAL FOR MAIN COACH COMPANIES:
Midan Ard el-Torgoman, behind Midan Ramses
– TERMINAL FOR BUSES AND COMMUNAL TAXIS (northern destinations):
Midan Ahmed-Helmi, behind Midan Ramses
■ **Luxor**
– BUS TERMINAL
Shari' el-Karnak north exit toward Horus Hotel.
– COMMUNAL TAXIS TERMINAL
Shari' Television, north exit out of town.
■ **Aswan**
– BUS TERMINAL
Shari' at-Tahrir, near the railway station and the government buildings.
– COMMUNAL TAXIS TERMINAL
Midan Station

CAIRO SUBWAY

For the time being, there is only one

subway line (north–south), which is useful for getting to the Coptic district (Mari Girgis).
A second line is due to be opened in the near future.
■ **Cost**
From 50 piastres to £E10, according to the length of the journey.
Subway stations are indicated by a large, red-colored letter M. A map is available at the main stations.

DIRECTION OF TRAFFIC

→ ON THE ROAD

Only the direction is indicated, except on freeways ("autostrades") between Cairo and Alexandria or the Suez Canal.

→ IN TOWN

Street names appear in Arabic and English on a blue plaque.
Use your own maps as local town plans are not available.

ON THE NILE

→ CRUISES

Travel agents in the UK and the US, as well as in Egypt, offer various cruises down the Nile. The departure point is usually Luxor with stops at Esna, Edfu, Kom Ombo, Aswan, and even Dendera, further up. Long cruises (Cairo–Aswan–Cairo) are available only in summer under strict police escort as they have to go though

Middle Egypt, a military zone forbidden to tourists.

→ FELUCCAS

It is possible to hire feluccas for a few hours or for the day at Luxor and Aswan, and visit the sites around the region.

TAXIS

→ INDIVIDUAL TAXIS

Numerous and cheap (more expensive outside hotels). For an extra charge you can hire a taxi for the whole day. Agree on the price before setting off on any journey.

→ COMMUNAL TAXIS

Outside railway stations and in main public squares.
WARNING:
In some regions, such as Middle Egypt (el-Minia to Thebes ▲ 371 ◆ 508), cars carrying foreign passengers must travel in convoy. The tourist police must be notified the day before the journey is to take place.

TRAIN

→ NATIONAL SERVICES

■ **Cairo–Alexandria**
– FAST TRAINS
11 trains daily from 6am until 8pm. Duration: 2 (direct trains) to 3 hours.
– SLEEPER-CARS
Twice a day.
■ **Cairo–Southern Egypt**
– SLEEPER-CARS
Dinner/breakfast and two-bed sleeper.

Daily at 7.40pm
To Luxor: 8 hours
To Aswan: 13 hours
– "EXPRESS" TRAINS
Are half the price but take from 4 to 10 hours longer!

→ RESERVATIONS

Tel. (02) 348 46 33 or (02) 348 73 54

STREETCARS

Streetcars are an excellent way of exploring Alexandria and its surroundings ▲ 196. The blue line follows the coast eastward, while the yellow and white line goes in a westward direction. Times: 5.30am until midnight (1am in summer)
Cost: 10 piastres

BICYCLE

A particularly popular means of transportation in Luxor, but also in Aswan, Hurghada and Siwa. Hotels can make the necessary rental arrangements. *Beware of the heat!*

CARS

All international car rental companies can be found at Cairo airport. Average cost per day: US$45
You must have a valid driving license and be over 25.
You can also hire chauffeur-driven cars or limousines at most of the major hotels or through representatives.

USEFUL ADDRESSES

→ ALEXANDRIA
■ **British Consulate General**
3 Shari' Minas
Kafr Abdon
Roushdi
Ramley
Tel. (03) 546 7001/2
■ **US Consulate General**
3 Shari' al Faraana
Tel. (03) 472 1009

→ CAIRO
■ **British Embassy**
Shari' Ahmed Ragheb
Garden City
Cairo
Tel. (02) 354 0850
■ **US Embassy**
5 Shari' Latin America
Garden City
Cairo
Tel. (02) 355 7371

ACCOMMODATION

→ HOTELS
■ **Categories**
Only 4- or 5-star hotels are on a par with their European equivalents for levels of comfort. Facilities can vary a lot from one hotel to another in lesser categories. These criteria also apply to cruise-boats.
Large chains such as the Hilton, Sheraton, Marriott, Sofitel, Novotel, P.L.M. or Mövenpick can be found in Cairo, Alexandria, in the Nile Valley and near the Red Sea.
■ **Cost**
More attractive than in Europe and the US: $300–550 for full-board in a luxury hotel on a weekly basis. Prices are slightly cheaper in the summer, except in Cairo and Alexandria.
■ **Reservations**
Reservations and confirmation are highly advisable.
WARNING:
The Abu Simbel site (2 hotels) and Middle Egypt

(currently not recommended because of the political situation) sometimes experience difficulty in coping with the high demand during the popular seasons.

→ HOLIDAY VILLAGES
Water sports facilities.
■ **Mediterranean**
Sidi Abd el-Rahman, Mersa Matruh
■ **Red sea**
Hurghada, Port Safaga, Sharm el-Sheikh, Dahab, Nuweiba

→ YOUTH HOSTELS
Can be found in all the main towns, but they tend to be quite far from the center.
■ **Opening times**
Closed noon–2pm (or 10am–noon) and 11pm at the latest.
■ **Cost**
Around £E10 per person (breakfast included) in a double room and £E5 for a meal.

AIR CONDITIONING AND HEATING
Most restaurants for tourists have air conditioning. Hotels with 3 stars or more are usually air-conditioned. Lesser categories do not offer this facility. Only 4- or 5-star hotels have heating, which is essential for the cold winter nights.

BEHAVIOR

→ CLOTHING
Both in town and outside, avoid clothes that are too tight, short or figure-hugging (women especially).
■ **When visiting mosques**
Always wear suitable clothing (no shorts, and your arms should be covered), and take

off your shoes on the way in (have a tip ready for the shoe keeper). Women should wear a scarf to cover their hair.
■ **When visiting churches**
Same attire as for mosques.
You can leave a small contribution upon leaving.

→ **PHOTOGRAPHY**
As a general rule, always ask for permission before taking a picture of a person or a place. Never take pictures of "street life" without permission from the people involved.

→ **THINGS NOT TO DO**
■ Refuse to buy an object after having agreed to a price
■ Get annoyed with a slow official
■ Criticize the country (religions, organization, cleanliness, bakshish, etc.)

→ **THINGS TO DO**
■ Give small presents (photographs, perfume, etc.), which are much appreciated.
■ In queues, let women go first as they always have priority.

CRAFTS AND SOUVENIRS
→ **ANTIQUES**
Bona fide antiques are extremely rare, while there is no shortage of copies.
WARNING:
Antique dealing is prohibited and it is illegal to take valuable objects out of Egypt.

→ **CRAFTS**
■ **Alabaster**
There are several types of alabaster, ranging from milky white to dark

brown. Handcrafted items have a rough appearance, while those made by machine are much smoother. You can find them in front of Luxor, and in Cairo.
■ **Blown glass**
This is Cairo's specialty. You will find beautiful vases, glasses, ewers, etc., in shades of blue, green or brown behind the Khan el-Khalili souk, near Bab el-Futuh.
■ **Carpets**
There are weaving schools near Saqqara where you can see the famous naive carpets inspired by rural life ▲ 345. Traditional silk or woolen carpets are also on sale there.
■ **Copper**
The greatest choice of copper trays, plates, boxes and other items can be found in the souks of Cairo.
■ **Cotton**
Many boutiques sell both Middle-Eastern and Western clothing (T-shirts, shirts, etc.) made of good-quality cotton, as well as printed or damask tablecloths.
■ **Gold**
18-carat gold items can be bought at reputable jewelers. Copies of Pharaonic jewelry abound, the most famous being the cartouche (a pendant with the person's name in hieroglyphs) as well as Western jewelry.
■ **Silver jewelry**
Jewelry and other silver objects (such as boxes, mirrors, keyholders, etc.) are relatively inexpensive.
■ **Turquoise and lapis-lazuli**
Genuinely beautiful.

→ **PAPYRUS**
The most beautiful papyrus can be found in the "Papyrus Institutes", with decorations from ancient tombs or papyrus (Ave. of the Pyramids at Giza: *Ani, New Pharao, Sobek*...).
Street vendors offer mediocre (and even fake) papyrus, at very low prices.

→ **PERFUME**
■ Most essential oils (jasmine, musk, amber, etc.) can be found in Nazlet el-Semman, a village near the pyramids at Giza. You can choose and mix your favorite scents. Wide choice of perfume bottles.
■ There are many boutiques in Luxor, Aswan and Sharm el-Sheikh.

DRINKS
→ **WINES**
Wines are often disappointing, except for the following:
■ Obélisque (red, white and rosé)
■ Omar Khayyam (red)
→ **BEERS**
■ Stella (light)
■ Export (light)
■ Löwenbrau (light)
■ Saqqara (light)
■ Premium (ginger)

→ **COFFEE**
Coffee is usually boiled, Turkish style, and served *sada* (without any sugar), *mazbout* (with some sugar), or *ziada* (with a lot of sugar).

→ **FRUIT JUICES**
■ Guava, mango, orange, lemon, strawberry, according to the fruit in season. Try cane juice (*assab*) as well.

→ **"KARKADE"**
Infusion of hibiscus leaves. Excellent for high blood pressure. It is sometimes mixed with tamarind juice.

→ **TEA**
Tea is served black, rarely with mint, and can sometimes be extremely sweet.

→ **WATER**
■ **Tap water**
Tap water is usually drinkable in large cities but tends to be heavily chlorinated.
It is best to avoid drinking it; you should buy water in sealed bottles instead.
Outside major cities or in the desert, it is highly advisable to filter and boil the water, and use purifying tablets.
■ **Mineral water**
The main brands are Baraka, Aqua, Siwa and Minéral. Quite inexpensive.

FESTIVALS
→ **RELIGIOUS FESTIVALS**
Are basically family affairs, even if there's much animation in the streets ● 74.
■ **Coptic festivals**
– COPTIC CHRISTMAS January 7
– COPTIC NEW YEAR September 11
– COPTIC EASTER Date varies
■ **Islamic festivals**
Dates vary from one year to the next as most festivals are determined by the lunar calendar.
– MULED EL-NABI Anniversary of the Prophet's birthday (month of Rabia)
– AID EL-SAGHIR (Small festival), also known as Aid el-Fitr, marks the end of Ramadan and goes on for three days. People usually exchange presents

◆ DAILY LIFE

and families get together.
– AID EL-KEBIR (Big festival), also known as Aid el-Adha (festival of the sacrifice). During the festival, a sheep is slaughtered in remembrance of Abraham's sacrifice.

→ **GENERAL FESTIVALS**
■ **Cham el-Nessim** (Spring festival) Takes place the day after Coptic Easter.
■ **Muled d'Abu el-Haggag** (In Luxor) Traveling festival dating back from the Pharaohs' time. The saint is carried in a small boat during a procession through the city, from the mosque built inside the temple of Luxor ▲ 397.
■ **Abu Simbel** celebrations February 20 and October 20 are the times of the year when the sun rays penetrate the temple ▲ 464.

FOOD
→ **MEZES**
Traditionally, these are a multitude of small dishes into which everyone dips with pieces of Arab bread. The most common are:
■ *Tahina*, sesame paste, sometimes mixed with aubergine (*baba ghanug*) or chick peas (*hummus*)
■ Stuffed vine leaves

→ **DISHES**
■ *Mulukhiya,* soup with coriander and garlic, and served with rice
■ *Taamiya* or *falafel*, balls of fried broad beans with herbs
■ *Kuchari*, rice with lentils

and macaronis, served with tomato sauce and onions
■ *Fuul*, dish based on broad beans ● *134*
→ **MEAT**
■ *Kebabs*, grilled meat
■ *Koftas*, grilled minced meat
■ *Shawarma*, slivers of marinated and grilled meat
■ *Hamaam*, roasted pigeon

→ **PATISSERIES**
■ *Basbussa*, pastry with a semolina base
■ *Baklava*, almond pastry
■ *Konafa*, vermicelli and cheese pastry
■ *Um-ali*, pastry cooked in almond milk and raisins with cinnamon

GOING OUT
There are many clubs, cabarets, casinos and movie theaters in Cairo and Alexandria

→ **CAFÉS**
Cafés have a friendly atmosphere and are very lively in the evening. Tea, Turkish coffee and anis are popular drinks. One can watch television, play dominos or *taula* (a national game), smoke *chicha* (hookah) while taking part in a conversation. In general, these places and activities are reserved for men, with the exception of the Khan el-Khalili café in Cairo ▲ 286.

→ **MOVIE THEATERS**
■ **Movie theaters in Cairo**
The larger theaters are worth going into for their traditional style of décor and their

large screens. The most famous movie theaters are located in the city center ▲ 272. Check the *Métro*, the *Radio* and the *Miami*, Shari' Qasr an-Nil ▲ 275 and Shari' Tal'at-Harb; the *Rivoli*, Shari' 26th July; the *Lido* and the *Pigalle*, Shari' Imad ad-Din ▲ 273; the *Tahrir*, Shari' at-Tahrir.

→ **BELLY-DANCING AND CABARETS**
■ **Places**
Many dancers have left the cabarets of the pyramids in order to perform in Cairo's larger hotels. There are still a few cabarets that offer excellent shows, although apart from in Cairo and some hotels in Alexandria, most places are not worth the bother.
■ **Times**
Shows never start before midnight or even 1am. In general, one can dine there as well.

→ **DANCING DERVISHES**
Not to be missed. Free shows at 9.30pm on Wednesdays and Saturdays at the El-Ghuri medersa ▲ 296.

GUIDES
Should be registered with the Ministry of Tourism. In general, they know their subject very well.
■ **Organized tours**
A guide is usually

assigned to a group of visitors by a local agency representing a foreign one and obtains all necessary authorizations for admission to sites in Upper and Lower Egypt. This guide alone is allowed to give explanations on the sites. Unless special permission is granted, a stranger is not allowed to take a group around; it is considered a serious offense for which he can be fined or expelled from the country.
■ **On the sites**
No local guide is ever attached to a site or a museum. Individual visitors have no other option but to apply to a local agency if they require a guide.
■ **Cairo's Museum of Egyptian Antiquities** ▲ 276
The only museum with its own resident guides (next to the ticket office).

HAGGLING
→ **FIXED PRICES**
Certain areas of trading or sectors are more controlled.
■ Stores in the large cities (other than the souks)
■ Hotel boutiques
■ Jewelers
■ Papyrus Institutes
■ Restaurants

→ **VARIABLE PRICES**
Apart from the above-mentioned places, you are expected to haggle. Depending on the vendor, prices can sometimes be three times higher than they should be. Never get irritated or angry as haggling is supposed to be part of the pleasure of buying. There's a great number of peddlers who follow

tourists around and keep lowering the prices of the items they are selling in the hope of tempting the visitor into buying them.

HEALTH
→ DRUGSTORES
Are found all over the country and drugs are very cheap. You will find basic products, such as sun protection cream and insect repellents.
In Cairo, there is 24-hr drugstore in every district.

→ HOSPITALS
In case of emergency it is best to go to one of the private hospitals in the large cities.
■ **Alexandria**
– COPTIC HOSPITAL
Shari' Muharram Bay
Tel. (03) 49 35 706
Near Midan Gumhuriya
– MEDICAL CITY HOSPITAL
S. Mustafa Kamel
Tel. (03) 85 21 50
■ **Cairo**
– ANGLO-AMERICAN HOSPITAL
Cairo-Gezira Tower
Tel. (02) 340 61 62
Kubri at-Tahrir
– HELIOPOLIS HOSPITAL
Shari' Hegaz
Tel. (02) 243 31 85
Between the airport and Swisshotel Cairo el-Salam Hotel
– MISR INTERNATIONAL HOSPITAL
Midan Fini, Doqqi
Tel. (02) 349 40 05 or (02) 371 65 55
At the end of Shari' Fini, on the right, past Midan el-Gala'
– QASR EL-AINI HOSPITAL
Roda Island
Tel. 02 362 93 90
Northern end of the island, on the coastal road toward the south, near Manial Bridge.
■ **Luxor**
– AN-NIL COASTAL ROAD HOSPITAL

Tel. (097) 37 20 25
Past the museum, in the direction of Karnak

HOLIDAYS
■ Jan. 1
New Year's Day
■ Jan. 7
Coptic Christmas
■ May 1
Labor Day
■ June 18
Liberation Day
■ Jul. 26
Commemoration of the 1952 revolution
■ Oct. 6

Commemoration of the 1973 War
■ Cham el-Nessim
In spring, the day following Coptic Easter

HORSES AND CAMELS
→ HORSES
Arab thoroughbreds
● *136.*
■ **Rental**
Apply to the Saqqarah Country Club, Saqqarah Road
Tel. (02) 381 12 82 or (02) 381 14 15
Fax (02) 381 05 71
■ **Rental of horses at the foot of the pyramids**
Opposite the Mena House Hotel, at Giza, to visit the site or to travel as far as Saqqara

through the desert. Negotiate a price on the basis of E£20–25 per hour (and don't forget to add a tip of E£10).
WARNING:
*For safety reasons, this activity is not recommended to young women on their own.
Also, the 7-hour-long ride may be too arduous for amateur horseriders.*

→ CAMELS
Many excursions on camel-back are also available at Giza, Saqqara, and along the coasts of Sinai and Aswan.
Always negotiate a price on the basis of E£20–25 an hour.

HYGIENE
■ **Food**
Large restaurants are under proper control. Other places may not be as strict. Avoid salads and fried foods. Cooked meat is generally safe to eat.
■ **Dehydration**
The problem is only likely to occur in the desert. You should try to drink at least four pints of water a day in the summer.

■ **Swimming**
Avoid contact with Nile water, as you could contract bilharzia, a serious disease that affects the liver. Springs in oases do not, in general, present any danger.

INTERNET
Most large hotels offer computer facilities and access to Internet facilities. The number of cyber cafés is growing in larger cities.

MARKETS AND SOUKS
→ MARKETS
Markets are mostly fruit and vegetable as well as cattle markets. They are worth a visit for the special atmosphere they exude.
WARNING:
Tourists are easily spotted and those who don't buy anything will tend to feel a bit conspicuous. Avoid taking pictures of people and places without permission from the persons involved.
■ **Alexandria**
– FRUIT, VEGETABLE AND POULTRY MARKET
Sunday morning in the streets close to Pompey ▲ *194.*
– FISH MARKET
Near the harbor, toward the end of the morning when the fishing boats return with their catch ▲ *174*
■ **Cairo**
– VEGETABLE AND POULTRY MARKET
Permanent. Behind the El-Azhar mosque ▲ *294.*
– SPICES SOUK
Permanent, near Shari' El-Muizz ▲ *288.*
Its narrow little streets hold an incredible number of herbalists. It is one of the most picturesque places in medieval Cairo.

– MEAT MARKET
Every morning,
Midan el-Ataba
el-Khadra ▲ 275
– CAMEL MARKET
On Friday and
Monday morning
at the souk of El-
Gamal, beyond
Charia el-Soudan
near Imbaba airport
(left bank).
Tourists are charged
admission.
The animals come
from western Sudan
along the Forty-
Eight-Day route
which leads to
Aswan through the
Nubian desert.
From there, trucks
carry them to Cairo.
A camel is worth
between $1,200
and $3,000.
WARNING:
*The district is
currently sealed off
by the police until
further notice as it is
a fundamentalist
stronghold.*
■ **Luxor**
–CATTLE MARKET
Takes place every
Tuesday morning
outside town on the
way to the airport.
It is very popular
and extremely lively.
■ **Other markets**
Other markets are
held occasionally in
other cities (Edfu,
Kom Ombo).

→ **KHAN EL-KHALILI**
Khan el-Khalili
▲ 286, Cairo's main
souk and one of the
largest in the
Middle East. Since
1382, when a
caravanserai was
established there,
all sorts of crafts
and goods can be
found there. It is as
much a place for
visiting and
discovering, as it is
for buying.
■ **How to find it**
Between S. el-Azhar
el-Khadra, S. el-
Muizz and Midan el-
Hussein. It is divided
into several, not
clearly defined,
areas of activities.

■ **Opening times**
The stores in Khan
el-Khalili stay open
until very late.
Cafés, amongst
which is the famous
el-Fishawi ▲ 287,
remain packed until

the early hours of
the morning. During
the month of
Ramadan, stores
remain open until
11pm, and cafés
until midnight.
ADVICE:
*Haggling is
expected. Never
agree to a price
until you know the
true value of the
object you wish to
purchase.
Never give a price
unless you are
ready to pay it.
There are many
tourists traps, so it is
up to the visitor to
judge a situation
and to distinguish
real craftsmen from
fake ones. It's
all a matter of
tact and
diplomacy.*

MEDIA
→ **FOREIGN PRESS**
European
newspapers are
on sale just about
everywhere. Expect
a two-day delay for
a daily newspaper.

→ **LOCAL NEWSPAPERS**
English-language
Egyptian Gazette,
daily
Egypt Today,
monthly

→ **RADIO**
RFI and BBC

→ **TELEVISION**
Available in large
hotels
**English-language
channels**
*CNN, Super Channel
Euro News,
Eurosport, Movie
Channel*
Channel 2
Broadcasts a daily
news bulletin in
English at 8pm.

MONEY
There are 100
piastres (pt) in
each Egyptian
pound (£E). There
are 100, 50, 20, 10, 5
and 1 pound notes;
50, 25, 20, 10 and
5 piastre coins.
Egyptian bills are
printed in roman
letters on one side
and Arabic
characters on the
other.

→ **EXCHANGE**
Cash and traveler's
checks can be
changed at banks
and major hotels.

→ **CREDIT CARDS**
Becoming
increasingly
more useful when
visiting Egypt. If
your credit card is
lost or stolen when
in Egypt, call the
following numbers:
American Express
Tel. 570 3411
Visa and MasterCard
Tel. 357 1148/9

→ **TRAVELER'S CHECKS**
A very secure
means of payment,
accepted by many
stores.

→ **FOREIGN
CURRENCIES**
Most European
currencies and US
dollars are accepted
in most places.

OPENING TIMES
■ **Office and
government offices**
Closed on Friday, the
day for communal
prayer.
■ **Stores**
Usually open
9am–2pm, and
5–8pm
Tend to stay
open at lunchtime
in tourist areas and
in large cities. Many
are closed on
Sundays in cities.
■ **Monuments and
archeological sites**
Opening times can
vary. They are
usually open daily
7am–5pm, except
Fri. (11.30am–
1.30pm).
■ **Museums,**
Usually open daily
9am–4pm, except
Fri. (11.30am–
1.30pm).
■ **Mosques**
The largest
mosques are
regarded as
monuments and
are open to
visitors 8am–5pm.
Out of respect,
avoid the times
for prayer
(dawn, noon,
around 4pm, sunset
and evening), and
above all Friday at
noon ● 74.
■ **Churches
and monasteries**
Open daily, except
during services,
Lent, and the
most important
Christian festivals.
**Churches in
Cairo**
Open daily 9am–
4pm, but often
closed on Sun.
during prayer
▲ 318.

PHOTOGRAPHY
100- and 200-ASA films are available. Processing is cheaper in Egypt, but the quality is not as high as in Europe. You have to declare video equipment upon entering and leaving the country.
REMEMBER:
Protect equipment from the dust!

POST OFFICE
Post offices are open daily 8am–2.30pm, except on Friday.

→ COST
There is only one rate (1.25 piastres for a letter or a postcard).

→ MAILING TIME
Mail takes from 4 to 10 days to be sent from the Post Office, and from 3 days to 3 weeks to arrive!

→ STAMPS
You can also buy stamps at hotels and from postcard vendors at a slightly higher price.
■ **Cairo's central post office**
Midan Ataba, behind Midan Opera

SPORTS
→ SCUBA-DIVING
The Red Sea and its two lighthouses, Hurghada ▲ *267* and Sharm el-Sheikh ▲ *248*, are especially popular with divers.
■ **DIVING SPOTS**
Most of them are situated halfway between Hurghada, on the West Coast and Sharm el-Sheikh, at the opening of the Gulf of Aqaba.
– RAS MOHAMMED
Located at the southern tip of the Sinai, and classified as a nature reserve. Wonderful 2,000-foot-deep marine garden of coral and

colorful fish. Access to the site is restricted. Check with diving clubs.
– TOWER OR TEMPLE
Respectively 200-feet and 66-feet deep.

These sites got their names because of their exceptional underwater architecture.
– CHEDUAN ISLAND AROUND DAHAB BLUE HOLE SITE
Steep, 263-feet deep. For experienced divers only.
– CANYON
Dark and narrow. Relatively easy access.
■ **Level**
Diving spots are accessible to divers of all levels of ability. Underwater visibility of 100 feet. Beginners must content themselves with a simple diving mask and a snorkel. For more experienced divers, the falls offer a

magnificent spectacle.
■ **Diving license**
Diving classes are available. An international diving license can be obtained at the

end of your stay.
■ **Accommodation**
The region offers suitable hotel facilities, from simple pensions to luxury hotels.
■ **Equipment**
The various establishments provide their clients with all the basic equipment.
WARNING:
Diving suit and shoes are essential as the corals are sharp and some quite toxic. Beware of the stonefish's sting, as it is deadly.
■ **Underwater photography**
Underwater photography classes and rental of equipment are also available at the various sites.

→ FUNBOARD
Following in the wake of the popular diving centers, funboard centers have also sprung up along the Red Sea.

→ WALKING
Egyptian deserts and oases, as well as the Sinai, offer a multitude of walks. Bear in mind that the desert is a dangerous place, so you should never leave the main roads and venture out on your own. Apply to agencies that offer specialized walks, camel rides, four-wheel drives or mountain bike rides in your own country or once you are in Egypt (arrangements can sometimes be made to suit your personal requirements).
WARNING:
A special permit is required for an individual journey through the desert.
■ **Lybian Desert Tours** ▲ *254*
6-, 7- and 12-day tours; 900- and 1,250-mile tracks
Arabian Desert ▲ *264*.
2-day tour
Sinai ▲ *238*
A walker's paradise. Pharaonic remains, biblical and natural sites, climbing of Mount Serabit (2,625 feet), etc. Approximately $700 per person for a 6-day tour and $1,150 for the 12-day tour.
ADVICE:
Take light, comfortable clothing (cotton) for the day and warmer garments (wool) for the night, high-top shoes or boots to protect yourself from vipers and scorpions, a proper hat and sunglasses.

TEMPERATURES IN HURGHADA, RED SEA		
IN FARENHEIT		
	Air	Sea
	min/max	max
Jan./Feb.	50/70	68
Mar.	54/74	70
Apr.	62/80	74
May	70/86	78
June/Jul.	76/97	80
Aug.	78/97	82
Sep./Oct.	68/92	82
Nov.	62/80	70
Dec.	54/74	68

TELEPHONE
Communications are good except in Western oases.
■ **Telephone centers**
Can be found in all the major towns. Just give the number you wish to call to the operator.
■ **Telephones with cards**
You can purchase £E5, 10, 15, 20 and 30 cards.
■ **Rates**
You pay for the first 3 minutes, then for each additional minute.
Night rates apply from 8pm to 8am (–25%).
There will a 40 to 50% increase for calls made from your hotel.

→ CODES	
UK	**00 44**
US	**00 1**
Egyptian towns	
Cairo	02
Alexandria	03
Luxor	095
Aswan	097
Sharm el-Sheikh	062
Faiyum	084
Ismailiya	064
Minia	086
Port-Said	066
Suez	062
Police	**122**
Information	
Cairo	140
Others	10

TIPPING
■ **Bakshish**
Expected whenever something is done for you (parking lot attendants, or shoe keepers at mosques.)
■ Taxi drivers always expect a tip on top of the established fare. The service is included in hotels and restaurants, but it is customary to round up the bill.
■ Children usually beg for objects or change.
ADVICE:
Avoid giving money to children. Do not give

anything to a child who does not ask for anything. Do not give anything to children in groups, to avoid fights.

TOURIST OFFICE
There is one in every major tourist town, but the literature on offer tends to be rather poor. The town maps and leaflets for tourists are quite basic.

TOURIST POLICE
The purpose of the tourist police is to inform and protect touristst. They can be found at or near the main tourist sites. The officers are easily recognizable thanks to their green armband bearing the words "Tourist police", and most of them speak English. The Tourist Police are there to help you should you encounter any problem, including theft.
■ **Alexandria**
– MONTAZA
Tel. (03) 547 33 95
– CITY CENTER
Tel. 03 86 38 04
■ **Abu Simbel**
At the end of the coastal road, before the post-office.
Tel. (097) 32 31 63
There is a Tourist Police station at Abu Simbel airport.
■ **EL-Minia**
El-Nil Corniche
Tel. (086) 32 45 27
■ **Cairo**
5 Shari' Adli
Next to the Tourist Office
Tel. 126
– EGYPTIAN MUSEUM
Midan at-Tahrir
Tel. (02) 574 43 19
– RAMSES STATION
Midan Ramses
Tel. (02) 575 35 55
■ **Luxor**
Luxor International airport
Tel. (097) 38 21 20

USEFUL WORDS AND PHRASES ◆

COMMON EXPRESSIONS

Yes: naam, aywa
No: la
Perhaps: yemken
Necessary: daruri
Please: men fadlak (m.) men fadlik (f.)
Thank you: shukran
Sorry/excuse me: afuan
Good morning: sabah el-kheir; marhaba
Good evening: masa el-kheir
Goodbye: saïda
My name is: esmi
What is your name?: shu esmak?
How are you?: ez zayyak? (masc) ez zayyek? (fem)
Today: en-nahar da
Tomorrow: bukra
Yesterday: imbarih
I speak English: ana batkallam englizi
I don't speak Arabic: ma-batkallamsh 'arabi
I don't understand: ana mish fahem
Do you speak English?: batkallam englizi?
Can you help me?: mumken tsaadni?
Information: istiilamat
What time is it?: el-saa kam?

DAYS

Monday: el-etnein
Tuesday: el-talata
Wednesday: el-arbaa
Thursday: el-khamis
Friday: el-gumaa
Saturday: el-sabt
Sunday: el-had

MONTHS

January: yanayer
February: febrayer
March: mars
April: abril
May: mayu
June: yunyu
July: yulyu
August: aghustus
September: september
October: oktober
November: nofanber
December: dissanber

SEASONS

Winter: sheta
Fall: kharif
Spring: rabia
Summer: seif

NUMBERS

One: wahad
Two: tnein
Three: talata

Four: arbaa
Five: khamsa
Six: sitta
Seven: sabaa
Eight: tamania
Nine: tesaa
Ten: ashara
Fifty: khamsin
One hundred: mia
Five hundred: khams mia
One thousand: alf

TRAVEL

Airplane: tayara
Airport: matar
Ticket: tazkara
Change: sarf
Customs: gumruk
Station: mahatta
Porter: hammal
Train: trein
Suitcase: shanta
Departure: dahab
Arrival: wussul
Delay: taakhkhor
Travel agent: wikalat safar
Bus station: mahattet el-otobus
When does the ... arrive?: emta wussul?
When does the ... leave?: emta qiyam ...?
I want to go to ...: ayez aruh a ....
Stop here, please: waeff hena men fadlak
Wait: intazir

FINDING YOUR WAY AROUND

Where is ....?: fein ....?
Is it near?: qarib?
Is it far?: baïd?
(On the) left: shmal
(On the) right: yamin
Above: fuq
Below: taht
In front of/outside: uddam
Behind: uara
Here: hena
Over there: henak
Before: abl
After: baad
South: janub
North: shamal
East: sharq
West: gharb
Street: shari'/sharia
Village: qaria
Town: medina
Sea: bahr

GETTING AROUND

Car: sayara
Driver: sawaa
Petrol/Gas station: mahattet benzine
Petrol/Gas: benzine

Pump up: nafkh
Oil: zeit
Hire: ajar
Bridge: kubri
Gate: bab
Wheel: dulab
Road: tariq
Taxi: taxi

AT THE HOTEL

Hotel: fundoq
Room: ghorfa
Key: meftah
Bathroom: hammam
Towel: futa, manchafa
Sheet: sharshaf
Blanket: hiram
I would like a room: mumken oda
I have reserved a room: hagazt oda
How much does a room cost?: bi kam el-oda?

AT THE RESTAURANT

Restaurant: mataam
Breakfast: ftur
Lunch: ghada
Dinner: asha
Water: mayya
Mineral water: mayya maadania
Wine: nebid
Juice: assir
Glass: kas
Plate: sahn
Bread: aïsh
Butter: zebda
Olives: zeitun
Cheese: jibna
Salad: salata
Vegetables: khodra
Meat: lahma
Chicken: dajaj
Fish: samak
Dessert: helu
Fruit: fakiha
Ice-cream: buza
Coffee: ahua
Coffee without sugar: ahua sada
Tea: shay
Sugar: sokkar
Milk: halib
Hot: sokhn
Cold: bared
May I have the tab, please?: mumken lehsab men fadlak?

VISITS

Visit: ziara
Open: maftuh
Closed: msakkar
Ticket office: shubbak
Ticket: tazkara
Town: medina
Quarter: hay
House: beit
Garden: hadiqa
Theater: masrah

Cinema: cinama
Museum: mathaf
Mosque: gamea

THE POST OFFICE

Where can I telephone?: fein mumken atalfein?
Post office: el-barid
Postage stamp: tabea baridi
Telephone: talifon
Telegram: barqiya

EMERGENCIES

Police: shurta
Fire brigade: atfaïya
Infirmary: mashfa
Hospital: mustashfa
Pharmacy: saydaliya
Doctor: tabib; hakim
Please call the doctor: tlob el-tabib men fadlak

SHOPPING

Bureau de change: maktab es-sarf
Money: fuluss
I would like to change some money: ayez asarref fuluss
Change (coins): fakka
Have you any change?: andokom fakka?
Price: el-taman
Where can I buy...?: fein mumken ashtari ...?
How much?: kam?
How much is this?: bi kam da?
It's too expensive: ghali awi
A little: shuaya
A lot: ktir
That's fine/perfect: tamam
Baker: khabbaz
Grocer: baqqal
Butcher's: majzara
Shop: mahal
Photographer's: mahal suar
Bookshop: maktaba
Newspaper: jarida
Book: kitab
Antique dealer: tajir athariyat
Jeweler: sayegh

MATERIALS

Gold: dahab
Silver: fodda
Copper: nhas
Terracotta: fokhar
Silk: harir
Cotton: qotn
Synthetic: tarkibi
Wool: suf
Glass: ezaz
Imitation: taqlid
Original: assli

◆ LIST OF ADDRESSES
ALEXANDRIA

Towns are listed in alphabetical order
▲ refers to the "Itineraries", while ◆ refers to the map section of this guide.
For a full list of symbols, see page 481.

ALEXANDRIA
▲ 174 ◆ A, B
→ FOR THE GOURMET
✪ Pastroudis
◆ **B** C2
39 Shari' Gamal
Abd el-Nasser
Tel. (03) 492 96 09
*In the street running
past the Graeco-
Roman Museum
Worth a visit for its
excellent Oriental
and Western
patisseries and its
unique atmosphere.*
🅐🅒

✪ Pâtisserie Délices
◆ **B** B2
Midan Saad Zaghlul
Tel. (03) 486 14 32
*One of Egypt's most
famous patisseries
and tearooms. Pre-
1940s atmosphere.
Very good Western
and Oriental
patisseries.*
🅐🅒

→ RESTAURANTS
✪ Adhura
◆ **A** B2
*In a narrow street
between the
Western Harbor
and the Abu el-
Abbas mosque
Open
noon–midnight
The tables are set
out at the end of a
narrow street that is
scattered with
sawdust. This fish
store-cum-
restaurant, where
customers choose
their own fish and
seafood, is an
example of the basic
"eating house" in its
simplest form. The
food is delicious,
helpings are
generous and the
prices reasonable.
One of the best
restaurants in
Alexandria.
No alcohol.*
🅒⬆🅓

L'Entrecôte
◆ **G** A1
Muntazah Sheraton
Hotel
Corniche, el-Muntaza
Tel. (03) 548 05 50
Open 7–11pm

*Sophisticated French
restaurant,
renowned for its
excellent meats.*
🅐🖃🅿🅓

Le Plat d'Or
◆ **B** B2
Sofitel Cecil Hotel
16 Midan Saad
Zaghlul
Ramleh Station
Tel. (03) 483 71 73
*On the Corniche.
International and
Egyptian cuisine in
the fine setting of
the Cecil Hotel.*
🅒🖃🅓

China House
◆ **B** B2
Sofitel Cecil Hotel
16 M. Saad Zaghlul
Ramleh Station
Tel. (03) 483 71 73
*Traditional Chinese
cuisine.*
🅒🖃🅓

✪ San Giovanni
◆ **G** A1
San Giovanni Hotel
205 Shari' el-Gaisha
Stanley
Tel. (03) 546 77 74
or (03) 546 77 75
Open noon–4pm and
8.30pm–midnight
*On the Corniche,
past Stanley beach
Good hotel-
restaurant, offering
a wide variety of
Middle-Eastern and
European fish and
seafood dishes.
Pleasant.*
🅐🅒🍴🖃🅿🅓

✪ Tikka Grill
◆ **A** B2
26 Shari' el-Gaisha
Tel. (03) 480 51 19
or (03) 480 51 14
Open noon–4pm
and 8–11pm
*At the end of the
Corniche, before
Qaitbay Fort
An elegant
restaurant in a
wonderful position
(huge bay windows
overlooking the
harbor and Qaitbay
Fort). Fish and
seafood specialties.
Other dishes on
request. Good value.*
🅐🍴🖃🅿🅓

**✪ Zéférion
Restaurant**
◆ **G** A1
Abukir
(East of Alexandria)
Tel. (03) 562 13 19
*Excellent fish and
seafood restaurant.
Quiet, with a good
location by the sea
and reasonably
priced, this
restaurant is
becoming one of
Alexandria's most
popular restaurants.*
🅓

→ ACCOMMODATION
El-Haram Hotel ★★★
◆ **G** A1
162 Shari' el-Gaisha
Tel. (03) 546 40 59
or (03) 546 39 84
Fax (03) 546 45 78
Corniche
*Very well-kept hotel
near the public
beaches. Facilities
are rather limited.*
🅒🅿🅓

**✪ El Salamlek
San Giovanni Hotel**
◆ **G** A1
Muntaza Palace
Tel. (03) 547 79 99
Fax (03) 547 35 85
*Former palace of the
royal harem, very
near the Muntaza
Palace. Ideally
located and
very luxurious (all
the suites are
magnificent), this
hotel is undisputably
Alexandria's most
beautiful hotel.*
🍴🖃🅿🅓

**✪ Helnan Palestine
Hotel ★★★★★**
◆ **G** A1
Muntaza Palace
Muntaza
Tel. (03) 547 40 33
Tel. and fax
(03) 547 35 00
*At the end of the
Corniche
Near the beach and
surrounded by the
el-Muntaza Park.
Spacious rooms with
balcony and sea view.*
🅐🍴🖃🅿🅓

Landmark Hotel ★★★★
◆ **G** A1
163 Shari' Abdel

Salam Aref
San Stefano
Tel. (03) 588 05 00
or (03) 586 18 50
Fax (03) 588 05 15
*Small street to the
right of the
Corniche, before
San Stefano Beach
Near the city center
and the sea. No
private beach.
Very good service.
Busy in summer.*
🅒🖃🍴🅿🅓

**Mercure
Romance ★★★★**
◆ **G** A1
303 Shari' el-Gaisha
Saba Pasha
Tel. (03) 588 09 12
or (03) 588 09 11
Fax (03) 587 05 26
*Good, centrally
located hotel with
nearby sports club.
All rooms are suites.*
🅒🖃🍴🅿🅓

**Montazah Sheraton
Hotel ★★★★★**
◆ **G** A1
Corniche
Montaza
Tel. (03) 548 05 50
or (03) 548 12 20
Fax (03) 540 13 31
*12½ miles from
the center, at
the end of the
Corniche, just before
el-Montaza Park
Friendly atmosphere
and efficient service,
but the rooms are
small and the hotel
is noisy in summer
(outside nightclub).
The beach is across
the road.*
🍴🖃🍴🅿🅓

**Ramada
Renaissance ★★★★★**
◆ **G** A1
544 Shari' el-Gaisha
Sidi Bishr
Tel. (03) 548 39 77
or (03) 549 03 35
Fax (03) 549 76 90
*On the Corniche,
in the direction of
el-Muntaza
Large, centrally
located hotel (rather
noisy). Good service,
but the rooms are
rather small. Near
the beaches.*
🅒🖃🍴🅿🏠

Regency Hotel ★★★
◆ G A1
696 Corniche Miami
Tel. (03) 557 15 47 or (03) 548 69 73
Fax (03) 559 71 08
Small, very reasonably priced hotel close to the public beaches. Good value for money.
🄲🄴🄿🄿·

Semiramis Hotel ★★★
◆ G A1
80 Shari' el-Gaisha
Tel. (03) 483 08 24 or (03) 482 78 37
Fax (03) 484 68 37
Corniche
Reasonable, near the public beaches and Alexandria's main places of interest.
🄲·

✪ Sofitel Cecil Hotel ★★★★
◆ B B2
16 Midan Saad Zaghlul
Tel. (03) 483 71 73 or (03) 483 14 67
Fax (03) 483 64 01
Alexandria's most famous early-20th-century hotel has retained all its original charm. The rooms have been renovated and the central location is ideal.
🄲·

Windsor Hotel ★★★★
◆ B B2
17 Shari' el-Shohada
Tel. (03) 480 87 00 or (03) 480 81 23
Fax (03) 480 90 90
Street overlooking the sea, behind the Pullman Cecil Hotel and Midan Saad Zaghlul
All the comfort and charm of a traditional hotel, vast rooms and a friendly atmosphere.
🄲·

Youth Hostel
◆ G A1
32 Shari' Port Said Chatby
Tel. (03) 597 54 59
In the street running parallel to Shari' el-Gaisha, in the direction of Montaza

---

ABU SIMBEL
▲ 464 ◆ F A6
→ACCOMMODATION
Nefertari Abu Simbel★★★★
Tel. (097) 40 05 08

ASWAN STREET MARKET

or (097) 40 05 09
Fax (097) 40 05 10
Five minutes from the airport in the direction of the temples.
The hotel is divided into a main wing and a series of chalets. Magnificently situated on Lake Nasser. It is the only hotel near the temples, but unfortunately it is not very well run (not very clean, the service is slow and the reservations are often not kept).
·

ASWAN
▲ 456 ◆ M
→ RESTAURANTS
✪ Club 1902
◆ M A3
Sofitel Cataract Hotel
Near Ferial Gardens
Tel. (097) 31 60 00
This British colonial-style restaurant – the best in Aswan – provided the setting for a scene from the film Death on the Nile (1978).

Very luxurious, excellent service, orchestra, good dance cabaret. European cuisine.
·

✪ El-Masry
◆ M B2
Shari' Abdel Magid Abu Zid
Open noon–midnight
Street leading into the souk, in the direction of the station
A well-known, well-kept and extremely popular restaurant. Good Egyptian

cuisine (generous helpings and inexpensive). The El-Masry "Whisky" – a cold spiced vegetable soup – is highly recommended.
·

Orangerie
◆ M B2
Aswan Oberoi Hotel
P.O. Box 62
Tel. (097) 31 46 67 or (097) 31 46 66
Open noon–3pm and 7–9.30pm
Elephantine Island
Luxury restaurant, offering European, Egyptian and Indian cuisine. Not particularly original, but in a beautiful setting.
·

Panorama
◆ M B2
El-Nil Corniche
Open 10am–midnight
South end of the Corniche, just before the Eastmar jetty
Small, unpretentious restaurant, well situated on the Nile. Friendly welcome. Rather ordinary Egyptian cuisine.
·

→ ACCOMMODATION
✪ Amun Hotel ★★★
◆ M A3
Amun Island
Tel. (097) 31 38 50 or (097) 31 38 00
Fax (097) 31 71 90
Boat-cum-ferry from the end of the Corniche (near Ferial Gardens)
Remarkable location on an island beyond Elephantine. Very comfortable hotel with a magnificent garden that really warrants an additional star. Run by the Club Méditerranée.
·

◆ LIST OF ADDRESSES
CAIRO

Towns are listed in alphabetical order
▲ refers to the "Itineraries", while ◆ refers to the map section of this guide.
For a full list of symbols, see page 481.

✪ Aswan Oberoi Hotel ***
◆ M B2
Elephantine Island
P.O. Box 62
Tel. (097) 31 46 67
Fax (097) 31 35 38
Free ferry service
every 10 mins from
the Corniche
Hotel with
huge, comfortable
rooms and a
swimming
pool. Situated in a
magnificent garden
on Elephantine
Island.
🏠🍴🖃🏊♿

**Basma Hotel
Aswan *****
◆ M A3
Shari' el-Fanadek
Tel. (097) 31 09 01
or (097) 31 09 02
Fax (097) 31 09 07
Hotel situated at
some distance
from the center.
Reductions if you
stay more than
three days.
🏠🖃🏊♿

Horus Hotel **
◆ M B2
El-Nil Corniche
Tel. (097) 31 33 13
Small, lacking in
comfort but
inexpensive and
well situated.
🄲🍴⦁

**Isis Hotel
Aswan *****
◆ M B2
El-Nil Corniche
Tel. (097) 31 51 00
or (097) 31 52 00
Fax (097) 31 55 00
Comfortable
chalets on the
shores of the Nile.
Near the souk.
🄲🍴🖃🏊♿

**Sofitel
New Cataract *****
◆ M A3
Near Ferial
Gardens
Tel. (097) 31 60 00
Fax (097) 31 60 11
Heavy 1960's
architecture but
the rooms are
comfortable.
Good buffets.
🏠🍴🖃🏊♿

✪ Sofitel Old Cataract Hotel ***
◆ M A3
Near Ferial Gardens
Tel. (097) 31 60 00
Fax (097) 31 60 02
Former colonial
hotel. Absolutely
charming with a
magnificent view
of the Nile and
Elephantine Island.*

OLD CATARACT HOTEL, ASWAN

*Truly wonderful.
It is a pleasure to
stay there.*
🏠🍴🖃🏊♿

Youth Hostel
◆ M C1
96 Shari' Abtal at-
Tahrir
Tel. (097) 32 23 13
Near the station in
the direction of the
Corniche

CAIRO

▲ 270 ◆ H, I, J
→ FOR THE GOURMET
Groppi
◆ I B3
Midan Tal'at-Harb
Open 9am–10pm
Before the
Revolution, Groppi's
was a famous
meeting place
for Cairene
intellectuals. Today
it is rather old-
fashioned, but has
retained its original
charm. A haven of
peace in the city
center. Specialty:
dates stuffed with
chocolate. Excellent
croissants.
🏠🄲

Koueder
◆ I B3
42 Shari' Tal'at-Harb
Open 10am–9pm
Famous city-center
patisserie offering a
wide selection of

*Western and
Oriental
confectionary
(konafa, basbussa,
etc.). Customers
eat standing.*

⦿ Patisserie El-Abd
◆ H C2
Shari' Tal'at-Harb
Excellent Egyptian
specialties at

*reasonable prices.
Take out or eat at
the counter.*

→ RESTAURANTS
Aladin
◆ H B3
Cairo Sheraton Hotel
Midan el-Gala'
Doqqi – Giza
Tel. (02) 336 98 00
or (02) 336 97 00
Open 12.30–4pm
and 8pm–1am
Good-quality
Lebanese and
Middle-Eastern
cuisine. Evening
entertainment
(music, dancing).
🄲🖃🔲

Andrea
◆ G C4
Canal road
The Pyramids
Tel. (02) 383 11 33
Open 11am–11pm
Opposite the road
to Saqqara, at the
end of the Avenue
of the Pyramids
Egyptian food
(excellent chicken
grilled with herbs).
Simple and
inexpensive.
🏠🖃🖃🔲🔲⦁

✪ Arabesque
◆ I B4
6 Shari' Qasr el-Nil
Tel. (02) 578 88 96
or (02) 575 98 96
Open noon–3pm

*and 7–11pm
Before you get to
Midan at-Tahrir
One of Cairo's
best Egyptian
restaurants. Set up
in an art gallery.
Delightful Oriental
décor (mashrabiya
works, copper and
brass).*
🏠🄲🖃⦁

✪ Asia House
◆ I A5
Helnan Shepheard
Hotel
El-Nil Corniche
Garden City
Tel. (02) 355 38 00
or (02) 355 39 00
Open noon–3.30pm
and 7–11pm
*Excellent Indian and
Chinese cuisine in a
superb setting
(interior fountain,
Mogul-style décor).*
🏠🄲🖃🔲

The Bird Cage
◆ I A5
Hotel Semiramis
Intercontinental
Tel. (02) 355 71 71
*Small and very
pleasant Asian
restaurant with a
view of the Nile.
Good cuisine.*
🖃🍴🔲

Chandani
◆ G C4
(Omam Restaurants)
5 Shari' Wissa-
Wassef
Omam Tower
Giza
Tel. (02) 570 12 26
*One of the two
restaurants of the
Omam Tower.
Luxurious Indian
décor. Good-
quality cuisine
but expensive.
No alcohol.*
🏠🄲🅿🔲

Christo
◆ H A6
Ave. of the Pyramids
Tel. (02) 387 35 82
Open noon–
midnight
At the end of the
Avenue of the
Pyramids, on
the corner of the
desert route to

Alexandria
*Very simple setting
with a terrace
overlooking the
Pyramid of Khufu.
Grilled fish and
seafood restaurant.
Excellent value for
money.*
⊞⊟▣◼

Ciao Italia
◆ **H** B3
El-Gezirah
Sheraton Hotel
Gezira Island
P.O. Box 264
Orman-Giza
Tel. (02) 341 13 33
or (02) 341 15 55
Open 7pm–midnight
*Southern tip of
Gezira Island
Tiny, traditional
Italian restaurant
(reservations
essential)
overlooking the
Nile. Extremely
good, but the
service tends to be
slow.*
▣⊞⊟▨▣◼

Citadel Grill
◆ **I** C2
Cairo Ramses
Hilton Hotel
1115 El-Nil Corniche
Maspero
Tel. (02) 575 49 99
Open 7–11.30pm
*Meat is a specialty in
this establishment.
Serves enormous
(imported) steaks,
but also some
seafood dishes.*
▣▣⊟▨◼

Da Mario
Nile Hilton
◆ **I** A4
El-Nil Corniche
Midan at-Tahrir
Tel. (02) 578 04 44
or (02) 578 06 66
Open noon–2am
*Small Italian
restaurant.
Good, traditional
cuisine. Quick
service. Evening
entertainment
after 8pm.*
▣⊟▨◼

✪ **Don Quichotte**
◆ **H** B1
9 Shari' Ahmad
Heshmet

Zamalek
Tel. (02) 340 64 15
or (02) 341 54 96
Open 7–11pm
Behind the Algerian
Embassy
*Small, friendly
restaurant.
Very good
international
cuisine. Particularly
delicious fish dishes*

KUBRI AT-TAHRIR, CAIRO

*(reservations
essential).*
▣⊟◼

El-Ezba
◆ **G** C4
Road to Saqqara
Tel. (02) 384 03 08
Open noon–3.30pm
and 7.30–11pm
*Generous helpings
of inexpensive
Egyptian food in a
delightful setting
(typical interior of
an Upper-Egyptian
house). Large
garden with
animals. This
country restaurant is
a popular lunchtime
place for groups.
Reservations are
recommended.*
▣⊞▣⊟▣◼◼

El-Fanus
(Omam Restaurants)
◆ **G** C4
5 Wissa Wassef
Omam Tower
Giza
Tel. (02) 570 12 26
Open 7pm–
midnight
*For those who like
couscous. Cairo's
best Moroccan
restaurant. The
setting is
magnificent.
No alcohol.
Reservations
essential.*
▣▣⊟▣◼

El-Yotti
◆ **H** B1
44 Mohy el-Din
Abu el-Ezz
Mohandissine
Tel. (02) 349 49 44
Open 12.30–3pm
and 7–11.30pm
At the end of Shari'
at-Tahrir on the
right, before Shari'
Sudan

*Renowned
restaurant in a
pleasant setting.
Good Egyptian and
international cuisine.*
▣⊟◼

✪ **Falafel**
◆ **I** A3
Cairo Ramses
Hilton Hotel
1115 El-Nil Corniche
Maspero
Tel. (02) 575 49 99
Open 8pm–midnight
*An excellent setting
in which to enjoy
Egyptian food.
Cabarets every
evening (Egyptian
dancing, belly
dancing) at 8pm and
midnight. Very
pleasant atmosphere.*
▣⊟▣◼

✪ **Felfela**
◆ **I** B4
15 S. Huda Shaarawi
Tel. (02) 392 27 51
Open 11am–1am
Near Midan Tal'at
Harb
*One of the most
famous restaurants
in Cairo. Amazing
décor resembling an
Aladdin's cave of
wood paneling
and paintings.
Inexpensive
Egyptian cuisine
(good meze and
pigeons). Very busy.*
▣◼

La Gondola
◆ **G** D4
Sonesta Hotel
4 Shari' el-Tayaran
Nasr City
Tel. (02) 262 81 11
Open 7pm–
midnight
*Excellent fish
restaurant.*
⊟◼

Grill Gezira
◆ **H** B1
Cairo Marriott Hotel
Shari' Saraya el-
Gezira
Zamalek
Tel. (02) 340 88 88
Open 7–11pm
*Luxury restaurant
serving excellent
meat dishes.*
▣▣◼

✪ **Justine's**
(Four Corners
Restaurants)
◆ **H** B2
4 Shari' Hassan Sabri
Zamalek
Tel. (02) 341 29 61
or (02) 340 75 10
Open 7pm–midnight
On the right, after
the 6-October
Bridge
*Luxurious French
restaurant – one
of the best in
Cairo. The setting
is on a par with the
cuisine.*
▣⊞⊟▣◼

✪ **Kebabgy**
◆ **H** B3
El-Gezira
Sheraton Hotel
P.O. Box 264
Gezira Island
Orman-Giza
Tel. (02) 341 13 33
or (02) 341 15 55
Open noon–3.30pm
and 7pm–midnight
*Ideally located on
the Nile, with a
delightful Egyptian
décor. One of the
best restaurants in
Cairo for Egyptian
cuisine.*
▣⊞⊟▨▣◼◼

✪ **Khan**
el-Khalili
◆ **I** F4
5 Shari' El-Badistan
Khan el-Khalili
Open noon–3pm

Towns are listed in alphabetical order
▲ *refers to the "Itineraries", while* ◆ *refers to the map section of this guide.*
For a full list of symbols, see page 481.

and 7–11pm
*This magnificent,
almost palatial
restaurant comes as
quite a surprise in
the souk of Khan el-
Khalili. Delicious
Egyptian cuisine. No
alcohol. Rather
expensive.*
🄲 ⬛ ▣ ⊡

La Mamma
◆ H A3
Cairo Sheraton
Hotel
Midan el-Gala'
Doqqi – Giza
Tel. (02) 336 98 00
or (02) 336 97 00
Open 12.30–3.30pm
and 8pm–1am
*Very good Italian
restaurant
with evening
entertainment.
Rather expensive.*
🄰 🖾 ▣ P ⊡

**La Piazza
(Four Corners
Restaurants)**
◆ H B1
4 Shari' Hassan-Sabri
Zamalek
Gezira Island
Tel. (02) 341 29 61
or (02) 340 75 10
Open noon–4pm
and 7–11.30pm
*Popular Italian
restaurant.
Extremely good
menu and pleasant
surroundings.
Regular evening
entertainment.*
⬛ P ⊡

La Terrasse
◆ H B1
President Hotel
22 Shari' Dr. Taha-
Hussein
Zamalek
Tel. (02) 340 07 18
or (02) 340 06 52
Open 1–4pm
and 7pm–1am
*Fairly ordinary lunch
(cold buffet), but à
la carte menu with
very good meat
dishes and theme
buffets (Chinese,
grills, fondue
bourguignonne)
in the evening.
Very reasonably
priced.*
⬛ ▣ P ⊡

**Le Chalet (Swissair
Restaurants)**
◆ H A6
El-Nasr Building
Shari' El-Nil
Giza
Tel. (02) 361 01 65
or (02) 337 10 05
*Rural Swiss cuisine
in luxurious
authentic setting
(you could easily be
in Switzerland).
Disorientation
guaranteed.*
🖾 ⬛ P ⊡

Le Champollion
◆ J A1
Le Méridien Cairo
Hotel
Roda Island
Tel. (02) 362 17 17
Open 12.30–3.30pm
and 7–11.30pm
*One of the best-
known French
restaurants in Cairo.
Excellent cuisine and
muted atmosphere.
View of the Nile.
Special business
lunches.*
🄰 🄲 🖾 ⬛ P ⊡

**Le Château (Swissair
Restaurants)**
◆ H A6
El-Nasr, Shari' El-Nil
Giza
Tel. (02) 361 01 65
or (02) 337 10 05
*Above Le Chalet
restaurant. Excellent
French restaurant.
Beautiful décor and
delightful setting.
Very expensive
French wines.*
🄰 🖾 ⬛ P ⊡

Le Marco Polo
◆ H F1
Le Méridien
Heliopolis Hotel
51 Shari' Oruba
Heliopolis
Tel. (02) 290 50 55
or (02) 290 18 19
Open 1pm–1am
*Luxury international
restaurant.
Impeccable gourmet
cuisine. Popular.
Dinner reservations
advisable.*
🄰 ⬛ P ⊡

✪ Moghul Room
◆ G C4
Mena House

Oberoi Hotel
Route of the
Pyramids
El-Ahram
Tel. (02) 383 32 22
or 383 34 44
Open noon–3pm
and 7–11pm
Open Fri. noon–3pm
At the foot of the
Pyramids
*A wonderful little
restaurant – Indian
statues to greet
you at the entrance,
warm and friendly
atmosphere, Indian
music in the evening
and excellent cuisine
(quite spicy and
truly delicious).
Reservations
essential.*
⬛ ⊠ P ⊡

✪ Nile's Maxim's
◆ H B1
Marriott Hotel
Tel. (02) 340 88 88
Boats: two cruises
every evening at
7pm and 9pm
(duration: 2 hours)
*Superb floating
restaurant. Good
cuisine and
high-quality
entertainment
(Oriental dancing).*
🖾 ⬛ ⊡

Nubian Village
◆ J A1
Le Méridien Cairo
Hotel
Roda Island
Tel. (02) 362 17 17
Open 8pm–midnight
Closed Dec.–Feb.
*Terrace restaurant
overlooking the
Nile. Egyptian
and Middle-
Eastern cuisine.
Entertainment
and Eastern music
every evening.*
🖾 ⬛ ⊡

✪ Paprika
◆ I A3
El-Nil Corniche
Tel. (02) 578 78 87
or (02) 578 94 47
*Small Egyptian
restaurant.
Simple and
inexpensive.
Some international
dishes.*
🄲 ⬛ P ⊡

Rubayyat
◆ G C4
Mena House
Oberoi Hotel
Road to the
Pyramids
El-Ahram
Tel. (02) 383 32 22
or (02) 383 34 44
Open noon–3pm
and 8pm–midnight
At the foot of the
Pyramids
*A vast, magnificent
dining room. Lunch
buffets are not
exceptional, but
a good evening
menu with
traditional Egyptian
entertainment at
9.30pm.*
⬛ ⊠ P ⊡

Rumours
◆ H B3
Sheraton Hotel
Gezira
Tel. (02) 341 13 33
or (02) 341 15 55
Open 9pm–2am
*Superb setting with
one of the best
views of Cairo by
night. Piano bar.
Sophisticated
international cuisine.*
🄲 P ⬛ 🖾 ⊡

**Sakkura
(Omam Restaurants)**
◆ G C4
Omam Tower
5 Wissa Wassef
Giza
Tel. (02) 570 12 26
*Friendly
atmosphere.
Reproduction of a
Japanese interior
where the cooking is
done in front of the
customers. Excellent
cuisine. No alcohol.*
🄰 🄲 ⬛ P ⊡

✪ Silver Fish
◆ H A3
39 Shari' Mohy el-
Din
Abu el-Ezz, Doqqi
Tel. (02) 349 22 72
Open noon–3pm
and 7.30–11pm
*The best fish
restaurant in the
city center. An
extremely varied
menu and pleasant
surroundings.*
🄰 🄲 ⬛ ⊡

Sushiyama
◆ I A2
World Trade Center
El-Nil Corniche
Maspero
Tel. (02) 578 51 61
*Currently the most
sophisticated
Japanese restaurant
in Cairo.*
⬛⬛⬛

Les Trèfles
◆ I A2
El-Nil Corniche
Opposite the World
Trade Center
Tel. (02) 579 65 11
*New French
restaurant with a
superb view of the
Nile. Excellent
cuisine. Rather
expensive.*
⬛⬛

Tandoori
◆ H A3
11 Shari' Shehab
Mohandissine
Tel. (02) 348 63 01
Open 7–11.30pm
*Very good Indian
restaurant which
competes with the
nearby Taj Mahal.
Good menu and
pleasant setting.*
⬛⬛⬛⬛

✪ **The Terrace**
◆ H B1
Cairo Marriott Hotel
Shari' El-Saraya el-
Gezira
Zamalek
Tel. (02) 340 88 88
Open 7pm–midnight
Closed Dec.–Apr.
On Gezira Island
*In the magnificent
gardens of the
Marriott Hotel
(former palace of
the Khedive Ismail).
Excellent Egyptian
food (grills).
Entertainment.*
⬛⬛🅿️⬛⬛⬛

→ **ACCOMMODATION**
**Cairo Heliopolis
Mövenpick *****
◆ H F1
On the road to Cairo
International Airport
Heliopolis
Tel. (02) 291 94 00
or (02) 247 00 77
Fax (02) 418 07 61
Luxury hotel with

*good restaurants
and a pleasant
garden. Ideal for
short stays (or
between airport
connections).*
⬛⬛🅿️⬛⬛

**Cairo Jolie-Ville
Mövenpick *****
◆ G C4
On the desert road
to Alexandria
P.O. Box 1, Giza
Tel. (02) 385 26 66
*Beautiful hotel.
Comfortable and
quiet. Ideal for a
longer visit to the
Pyramids of Giza
and Saqqara.*
⬛⬛⬛🅿️⬛⬛

✪ **Cairo Marriott
Hotel *****
◆ H B1
Shari' Saraya el-
Gezira
Zamalek
Tel. (02) 340 88 88
Fax (02) 340 66 67
On Gezira Island via
Kubri at-Tahrir
*Former palace of the
Khedive Ismail with
a beautiful garden,
bars and magnificent
restaurants (huge
19th-century
paintings). The very
spacious rooms are
located in two huge
modern towers at
either end of the
palace. Excellent
service and the
height of luxury.
Avoid the wing at
the far end of the
garden as it
overlooks the street.*
⬛⬛⬛⬛🅿️⬛⬛

**Cairo Ramses Hilton
Hotel *****
◆ I A3
1115 El-Nil Corniche
Maspero
Tel. (02) 575 49 99
Fax (02) 575 71 52
*A top-category
hotel overlooking
the Nile, with a full
range of facilities.
Next to the hotel is
a famous shopping
mall. Several
restaurants and a
bar with a
magnificent view.*
⬛⬛⬛⬛🅿️⬛

**Cairo Sheraton
Hotel *****
◆ H A3
Midan el-Gala'
Doqqi – Giza
Tel. (02) 336 98 00
or (02) 336 97 00
Fax (02) 336 46 01
At the far end of
Kubri el-Gala', at the
intersection leading
to the Avenue of the
Pyramids
*Large, luxury hotel
with a modern wing
added to the "old"
wing. Spacious rooms
with all mod cons.
Bars, restaurants.*
⬛⬛⬛⬛🅿️⬛

Carlton Hotel *
◆ I B2
21 Shari' 26-July
Ezbekiya
Tel. (02) 575 51 81
or (02) 575 50 22
*Comfortable hotel
but situated in a
rather noisy district.
The rooms and the
hotel are well-kept.*
⬛⬛⬛⬛🅿️⬛

✪ **Cosmopolitan
Hotel ***
◆ I B4
1 Shari' Ibn-Tahlab
Tel. (02) 392 38 45
Midan Tal'at-Harb,
then Shari' Qasr el-
Nil, second on the
right
*Well-situated in
the city center.
Comfortable hotel
with a great deal of
early 20th-century
charm. Very good
value for money.*
⬛⬛⬛🅿️⬛

**El-Gezirah Sheraton
Hotel Cairo *****
◆ H B3
Gezira Island
P.O. Box 264
Orman Giza
Tel. (02) 341 13 33
or (02) 341 15 55
Fax (02) 340 50 56
Southern tip of
Gezira Island, near
Kubri at-Tahrir
*A fine piece of
architecture in a
splendid position.
All the rooms
overlook the Nile.
Several restaurants.*
⬛⬛⬛⬛⬛⬛

Grand Hotel *
◆ I C2
17 Shari' 26-July
Ezbekiya
Tel. (02) 575 77 00
or (02) 575 75 09
Fax (02) 575 75 93
*Large, centrally
located hotel, but
rather noisy. Large
rooms and very
friendly welcome.
Competitively priced.*
⬛⬛🅿️⬛

✪ **Helnan Shepheard
Hotel ****
◆ I A5
El-Nil Corniche
Garden City
Tel. (02) 355 39 00
or (02) 355 38 00
Fax (02) 355 72 84
On the Nile, behind
the Mogammaa and
near Kubri at-Tahrir
*Probably doesn't
warrant four stars,
but has a great
deal of charm with
its traditional
architecture and its
huge, Moorish-style
rooms. Top-quality
restaurants.
Tends to be rather
noisy so ask for a
room overlooking
the Nile.*
⬛⬛⬛⬛⬛🅿️⬛⬛

**Le Méridien
Cairo Hotel *****
◆ J A1
Roda Island
Tel. (02) 362 17 17
Fax (02) 362 19 27
Beyond Midan at-
Tahrir, toward Maadi
*Luxury hotel with
several restaurants,
indoor and outdoor
bars, and huge,
comfortable rooms.
Excellent position on
the northern tip of
Roda Island. Ask for
a room overlooking
the Nile.*
⬛⬛⬛⬛⬛🅿️⬛⬛

**Le Méridien
Heliopolis Hotel
*****
◆ H F1
51 Shari' Oruba
Heliopolis
Tel. (02) 290 18 19
Fax (02) 291 85 91
Main road to the
airport, opposite

Towns are listed in alphabetical order
▲ *refers to the "Itineraries", while* ◆ *refers to the map section of this guide.*
For a full list of symbols, see page 481.

"old" Heliopolis
Very luxurious,
French-style hotel,
conveniently
situated for visiting
Heliopolis and the
City of the Dead
(20 mins' drive from
the city center).
▨✷P♠▦

○ **Le Méridien**
Pyramids Hotel *****
◆ **G** C4
P.O. Box 25
The Pyramids
Tel. (02) 383 03 83
Fax (02) 383 17 30
Desert road to
Alexandria
Excellent hotel.
Remarkable service.
Several restaurants
(including a
renowned Lebanese
restaurant).
Spacious, well-
decorated rooms.
▨◻✷P♠▦

Lotus Hotel **
◆ **I** B3
12 Shari' Tal'at Harb
Tel. (02) 575 09 66
or (02) 575 06 27
Fax (02) 575 47 20
Conveniently
situated but devoid
of all luxury.
Inexpensive and
clean.
C◻

○ **Mena House**
Oberoi Hotel *****
◆ **G** C4
On the road to the
Pyramids
El-Ahram
Tel. (02) 383 32 22
or (02) 383 34 44
Fax (02) 383 77 77
At the intersection
of the desert road
to Alexandria
Former palace of
the Khedive Ismail.
All the crowned
heads of Europe
have stayed here
(including French
Empress Eugénie for
the opening of the
Suez Canal). Charlie
Chaplin and
T.E. Lawrence were
amongst its many
regular guests. One
of the finest hotels
in the world.
▧▨◻✷P▦

Nile Hilton
Hotel *****
◆ **I** A4
El-Nil Corniche
Midan at-Tahrir
Tel. (02) 578 04 44
or (02) 578 06 66
Fax (02) 578 04 75
The most famous of
Cairo's city-center
hotels, next to the
Antiquities Museum.
Beautiful rooms,
excellent restaurants
and bars, but
unfortunately
very noisy. Large
Egyptair office.
The rooms
overlooking the
garden are quieter.
C▧◻✷P♠▦

Nitocrisse Hotel *
◆ **I** C3
171 Shari'
Mohammed Farid
Tel. (02) 391 51 66
or (02) 391 57 38
Near Shari' Adli, one
of the main streets
in the city center
Ideal for lower-
budget vacation.
Basic comfort but
clean. One of the
more reasonable
one-star hotels.
C◻

Novotel Cairo Airport
Hotel ****
◆ **H** F1
Cairo Airport
P.O. Box 8
Heliopolis
Tel. (02) 291 85 77
or (02) 291 85 20
Fax (02) 291 47 94
Rather charmless,
but ideal for a stop-
over between
flights.
◻✷P♠▣

Oasis Hotel ****
◆ **G** C4
P.O. Box 44
The Pyramids
Tel. (02) 383 17 77
or (02) 383 27 77
Fax (02) 383 09 16
On the outskirts of
Giza, on the desert
road to Alexandria
Some distance from
the center but quiet,
comfortable and
close to the
Pyramids of Giza.
▧◻✷P♠▣

○ **Pension**
Roma Cairo
◆ **I** C3
169 Shari'
Mohammed Farid
Tel. (02) 391 10 88
or (02) 579 62 43
City center
Not luxurious but
a very well-kept
boarding house.
Extremely friendly
welcome. In an
ideal location for
visiting the city
center and very
reasonably priced.
C◻

President Hotel***
◆ **H** B1
22 Shari' Dr. Taha-
Hussein
Zamalek
Tel. (02) 341 67 51
or (02) 341 31 95
Fax (02) 341 17 52
Via the Kubri
26 July
Very reasonable,
good value for
money and relatively
quiet for a hotel in
the city center. Has a
good French
restaurant and a
popular nightclub.
▧C◻P▣

Pyramids Park ****
◆ **G** D4
Tel. (02) 383 86 66
Fax (02) 383 90 00
On the outskirts
of Cairo, on the
desert road to
Alexandria
Pleasant place for
a vacation. The
extensive park
has a number of
chalets in a large
garden and the
finest swimming
pool in the Middle
East. The rooms
are spacious,
but the small and
badly positioned
"cabanas" should
be avoided.
▧◻✷P♠▣

Safir Cairo
Hotel ****
◆ **H** A3
Midan el-Missaha
P.O. Box 138
Doqqi
Tel. (02) 348 24 24
or (02) 348 28 28

Fax (02) 360 84 53
Near Gezira
Island, via the
Kubri el-Gala'
More like a good
three-star hotel.
Located near
the center but in a
district devoid of
interest.
C◻✷P▣

Semiramis Inter
Continental *****
◆ **I** A4
El-Nil Corniche
Garden City
Tel. (02) 355 71 71
Fax (02) 356 30 20
At the end of Kubri
at-Tahrir, behind the
Mogammaa
Extremely
comfortable, but
a very unfriendly
atmosphere.
The building is
of station-like
proportions.
Ideal for business
conferences.
Ask for an upper-
floor room
overlooking
the Nile.
C◻✷P▦

Siag Pyramids
Hotel Cairo ****
◆ **G** C4
Road to Saqqara
P.O. Box 107
Ahram
Tel. (02) 385 60 22
or (02) 38 50 05
Fax (02) 385 74 13
At the Cairo end of
the road to Saqqara,
as you leave
the Avenue of
the Pyramids
Became famous as
the starting point
for the Pharaoh's
Rally. Ideally located
for visiting Saqqara
and Giza. Very
comfortable but
doesn't really
warrant four stars.
▧▨◻✷P▣

Sofitel Maadi
Towers Hotel*****
◆ **G** D4
29 El-Nil Corniche
Maadi
Tel. (02) 526 06 01
or (02) 526 06 02
Fax (02) 526 11 33
Very comfortable

hotel, some distance from the center near the residential district of Maadi. Swimming pool on the terrace. Very pleasant in summer. The hotel has an excellent French restaurant.
Ask for a room overlooking the Nile.
🏊 ▣ ⛤ P ▦

Sonesta Hotel ***
◆ H F1
4 Shari' El-Tayaran-Medinet Nasr
Tel. (02) 262 81 11
or (02) 261 71 00
Fax (02) 263 57 31
Road from the airport to the city center. Turn left after the Air Force barracks
Situated in Heliopolis. Very comfortable. Luxury boutiques.
▣ ⛤ P ▦

✪ **Swisshotel Cairo El-Salam Hotel *****
◆ H F1
Shari' Abdel-Hamid Badawi
Heliopolis
Tel. (02) 297 40 00
or (02) 297 60 37
Fax (02) 245 57 55
Road from the airport to the city center, then turn to the right toward Ismailiya
Extremely well-kept with an early-20th-century charm (featured in Jacobs' movie Mystery of the Great Pyramid). Beautiful rooms and excellent restaurants.
Quite possibly the finest airport hotel in Egypt.
🏠 ▣ ⛤ P ♁ ▦

Youth Hostel
◆ J A5
135 Shari' Abdel-Aziz
el-Seoud-el Manial
Roda Island
Tel. (02) 364 07 29
Near Gamaa Bridge

→ **NIGHTCLUBS**
After 8
◆ I B3
Shari' Qasr el-Nil near the Qasr el-Nil movie theater
Tel. (02) 574 08 55

Piano Piano
◆ I A2
World Trade Center
Boulak
Tel. (02) 76 28 10

Regina
◆ H B3
El-Gezirah Sheraton Hotel
Tel. (02) 341 13 33

Sultana
◆ I A4
Semiramis Inter Continental
Tel. (02) 355 71 71

The Cellars
◆ H B1
President Hotel Zamalek
Tel. (02) 341 67 51

The Harris Pub
◆ H B1
Cairo Marriott Hotel Zamalek
Tel. (02) 340 88 88

The Zinc
◆ H B1
Zamalek
Tel. (02) 340 96 40

→ **CABARETS (BELLY DANCING)**
Casino El-Lel
◆ G C4
Avenue of the Pyramids
Tel. (02) 585 42 52

Salt and Pepper
◆ H B1
Shari' Abul-Fedda Zamalek
Tel. (02) 342 05 29

The Parisiana
◆ G C4
Avenue of the Pyramids
Tel. (02) 383 39 11

The Tivoli
◆ H F4
Midan Almaza Heliopolis
Tel. (02) 290 64 96

→ **CAFÉS AND BARS**
Fichawi Café
◆ I F4
Shari' Gohar el-Qaid Khan el-Khalili
Oriental café inside the souk.

Club 36
◆ I A3
Cairo Ramses Hilton Hotel
Tel. (02) 575 49 99
Trendy piano bar, with a superb panoramic view over the city.

→ **SHOPPING**
Akhenaton Carpets & Tapestry
◆ G C4
Tel. (02) 20 14 88
or (02) 20 15 02
Road to Saqqara, just before the actual site
Carpets, tapestries. Good quality. Haggling.

Ani Papyrus
◆ G C4
Avenue of the Pyramids
Giza
Open 9am–9pm
Before you get to the Pyramids, on the left-hand side of the street
Good-quality papyri. Beautiful designs. Set prices.

Dr Ragab Papyrus
◆ H B3
3 Shari' El-Nil
Giza
Open 9am–9pm
Set prices.

Galal
◆ I F4
Shari' el-Muski
Tel. (02) 588 26 66
or (02) 588 27 77
Khan el-Khalili
Main street of the souk district
Luxury jewelry.

Karanak Bazaar
◆ G C4
Pyramids
16 Avenue of the Pyramids
Tel. (02) 383 00 47
or (02) 383 43 45
An Aladdin's cave. All types of Egyptian souvenirs of variable quality. Haggling.

L'Orientaliste
◆ I B4
15 Shari' Qasr el-Nil
Tel. (02) 575 34 18
Near Midan Tal'at-Harb
Reputable bookstore (old editions in English and French, prints, old postcards of Egypt).

Maat Papyrus
◆ G C4
Avenue of the Pyramids
Giza
Open 9am–9pm
On the left, before the Pyramids
Set prices.

Mobaco
◆ I B3
18 Shari' Tal'at-Harb
Tel. (02) 347 37 91
Branches:
– CAIRO RAMSES HILTON HOTEL
1115 El-Nil Corniche
Maspero
Tel. (02) 575 49 99
– NILE HILTON HOTEL
El-Nil Corniche
Midan at-Tahrir
Tel. (02) 578 04 44
– SEMIRAMIS INTER CONTINENTAL
El-Nil Corniche
Garden City
Tel. (02) 355 71 71
Very good quality, Western-style, cotton clothing at competitive (set) prices which do, however,

◆ LIST OF ADDRESSES
DAMIETTA

Towns are listed in alphabetical order
▲ *refers to the "Itineraries", while* ◆ *refers to the map section of this guide.*
For a full list of symbols, see page 481.

---

increase from one
month to the next.

**New Pharaoh
Papyrus**
◆ G C4
Avenue of the
Pyramids
Giza
Open 9am–9pm
On the left, before
the Pyramids
*Good papyrus store.
Set prices.*

Octopus
◆ H F1
15 Shari' Baghdad
Heliopolis
Tel. (02) 664 33 78
*Western-style cotton
clothing. Set prices.*

Safari
◆ H B1
10 Shari' Lutfallah
Zamalek
Tel. (02) 340 19 09
*Western-style cotton
clothing. Excellent
quality. Set prices.*

Sobek Papyrus
◆ G C4
Avenue of the
Pyramids
Giza
Open 9am–9pm
On the right, before
the pyramids
*Good-quality
papyrus. Set prices.*

The Old Shop
◆ I F4
Shari' Sikkit el-
Badestan
Main street in the
Khan el-Khalili
*Well-known antique
dealer. Mostly bric-
a-brac rather than
genuine antiques.
Haggling.
Warning:
It is illegal to export
pre-Revolution
items.*

DAMIETTA
▲ 222 ◆ G E1
→ACCOMMODATION
El-Manshy hotel *
5 Shari' el-Nokrashy
Tel. (057) 32 33 08
City center
*Basic comfort. This
is the only hotel in
a town of little
touristic interest.*
◘ P ▢

EL-ALAMEIN
▲ 204 ◆ C E1
→ACCOMMODATION
Alda Beach *****
13½ miles west of
Alexandria
Tel. (03) 410 28 02
*Extremely
comfortable
luxury hotel.
Half-board only.*
◘ ▨ ▢ ✿ P ▣

**Atik Hotel
el-Alamein**
65½ miles from
Alexandria
Tel. (03) 410 61 83,
(03) 410 61 84
or (03) 410 61 85
Fax (03) 410 61 82
*Comfortable
seaside hotel.
Ideal for a relaxing
vacation. Several
restaurants (closed
in winter). Prices
are considerably
lower out of
season.*
▨ ▢ ✿ P ▣

EL-ARISH
▲ 252 ◆ D E1
→ACCOMMODATION
**El-Arish Oberoi
Egoth Hotel** ****
Shari' el-Fateh
Tel. (068) 35 13 21
or (068) 35 13 22
Fax (068) 35 23 52
*The best hotel
in El-Arish.
Sports facilities.
Reservations
essential in
summer.*
◘ ▨ ▢ ✿ P ▣

THE FAIYUM
▲ 362 ◆ G C6
→ACCOMMODATION
**Auberge of Lake
Faiyum** ****
Tel. (084) 70 00 02
or (084) 70 07 30
On Lake Qarum,
via the road to
Medinet el-Faiyum
*Luxury hotel with
splendid English
lounges. Ideal for a
relaxing vacation.*
◘ ▨ ▢ ✿ P ▣

**New Panorama
Shakshuk village
Lake Karoon** ***
Shakshuk
Tel. (084) 70 17 46
or (084) 70 13 14

Fax (084) 70 17 57
Road to Shakshuk,
via Medinet el-
Faiyum
*Very pleasant hotel
with spacious,
comfortable rooms.
Friendly welcome.*
◘ ▨ ▢ ✿ P ▣

Youth Hostel
Building no. 7
El-Hadeka
Tel. (084) 32 36 82
or (084) 35 00 05
Near the main
square

HURGHADA
▲ 264 ◆ D E6
→ACCOMMODATION
**Coral Beach
Village** ****
13½ miles along the
road to Safaga
Tel. (065) 44 71 60
or (065) 44 71 66
Fax (065) 44 71 70
*Ideal for a vacation
by the Red Sea.
Full range of sports
facilities.*
◘ ▨ ▢ ✿ P ▣

**Hurghada
Hilton Plazza** *****
Main Street
Gabal El-Harem
Tel. (065) 44 21 16,
(065) 44 21 18
or (065) 44 21 19
Fax (065) 44 21 13
*Luxurious hotel
near the city center,
with all the comfort
and water sports
facilities one could
wish for.*
▨ ▢ ✿ P ▣

**Hurghada
Marriott Beach
Resort** *****
On the Corniche
Tel. (065) 44 69 55
or (065) 44 69 60
Fax (065) 44 69 70
*Luxurious hotel,
recently built in
a seaside town
that resembles
a perpetual
construction site.
All comforts and
water sports
facilities.*
▨ ▢ ✿ P ▣ ▣

**Hurghada Sheraton
Hotel** ****
Tel. (065) 44 20 00

or (065) 44 20 01
Fax (065) 44 33 33
On the Corniche
*Excellent hotel,
although
architecturally
disapppointing
(looks rather like
a blockhouse).*
◘ ▨ ▢ ✿ P ▣

ISMAILIYA
▲ 236 ◆ G F3
→ACCOMMODATION
**Mercure Hotel
Etap Forsan
Island** ****
P.O. Box 77
Tel. (064) 33 80 40
or (064) 33 80 41
Fax (064) 33 80 43
On the Corniche, in
the direction of the
Suez Canal
*The only good hotel
in Ismailiya. View of
the canal and very
good restaurants,
especially the
Eugénie. Small
rooms.*
◘ ▨ ▢ ✿ P ▣ ▣

LUXOR
▲ 397 ◆ L
→RESTAURANTS
Bella Donna
◆ L A3
Shari' Khaled Ibn
el-Walid
Tel. (095) 38 08 50
Open 12.30–2pm
and 8–9.30pm
*Situated in an
inner courtyard
of the Club
Méditerranée.
Excellent
international
buffets. À la carte
dinner menu.*
◘ ▢ ✿ ▣ ▣

Class
◆ L A3
Shari' Khaled Ibn
el-Walid
Open noon–3pm
and 7–11pm
At the end of
the Corniche,
just below the Isis
Hotel Luxor
*New restaurant on
the second floor of
a bazaar. A selection
of European and
Egyptian dishes.
Good value for
money.*
◘ ▢ P ▢

☉ **Dakka**
◆ **L** A3
Mercure Hotel
El-Nil Corniche
Tel. (095) 37 49 44
Open 9am–11pm
*Small restaurant
on the edge of a
swimming pool.
An ideal place to
relax after visiting
the sites. Small
international menu.*
⬜🅰◻⬚❋⬆◻

☉ **El-Madiriya**
◆ **L** A3
Shari' Khaled Ibn
el-Walid
Open 7pm–midnight
*Narrow street at
right angles with
Shari' Khaled,
before the Isis Hotel
Luxor
Excellent Egyptian
restaurant with a
varied menu and
friendly service.
Simple setting
and modestly
comfortable.
Inexpensive.*
⬜◻⬆❖◻

Fellah's Tent
◆ **F** B2
Mövenpick
Jolie-Ville Luxor
Crocodile Island
Tel. (095) 37 48 55
Open Thur. and Fri.
5–9pm
*As you leave Luxor,
in the direction of
Esna
The tent offers an
Egyptian buffet and
a dance cabaret. The
island – near the
hotel – is reached by
"felucca" upon
request.*
⬜🅰◻⬚❋⬆❖◻

☉ **Felucca**
◆ **L** A3
Luxor Hilton
Hotel
Tel. (095) 37 49 33
or 37 49 46
Open 1–3pm
and 7–9pm
*On the Corniche,
past the Karnak
temples
Lunch- or dinner-
trips on a "felucca".
Order before you
leave.*
⬜🅰◻❖◻

Haty
◆ **L** B3
Station Road
Open noon–11pm
*Small, unpretentious
and inexpensive
restaurant serving
a wide variety of
Egyptian dishes.*
🅲◻

TEMPLE OF LUXOR

TEMPLE OF EDFU

☉ **La Mamma**
◆ **L** A3
Luxor Sheraton
Hotel and Resort
Road to El-Awamiya
Open noon–11.30pm
*The most delightful
Italian restaurant in
Egypt. Situated in a
small park where
peacocks, geese
and pelicans preen
themselves near a
pond. Excellent
seafood risotto.*
⬜◻⬚❋⬆❖◻

The Marhaba
◆ **L** A3
Corniche
Open 11am–11pm
*Between the
Temple of Luxor
and the New Winter
Palace Hotel
Its main attraction is
its central location.
Unimaginative
European cuisine
and basic Egyptian
dishes (broadbeans).
View of the Nile.*
⬜🅲❋⬆◻

☉ **Sheherazade
Terrace**
◆ **F** B2
Mövenpick
Jolie-Ville
Luxor
Crocodile Island
Tel. (095) 37 48 55
Open 7.30–11pm
*As you leave
Luxor, in the
direction of Esna
Grills and theme
buffets (Italian,
Egyptian, Indian,
Swiss) in the
splendid gardens of
"Jolie-Ville".
Magnificent setting
with a view
of the Nile.*
⬜🅰◻❖◻

→ACCOMMODATION
**Akhetaton Village
Belladonna ★★★★**
◆ **L** A3
Shari' Khaled Ibn
el-Walid
Tel. (095) 38 08 50
Fax (095) 38 08 79
*In the direction
of Esna
Club Méditerranée
village in a beautiful
lush setting.
Swimming pool,
lovely rooms
and a popular
discotheque.
View of the
Nile.*
⬜🅰❋⬆❖◻

Horus Hotel ★★
◆ **L** B1
Shari' el-Karnak
Tel. (095) 37 21 65
*Small, well-kept
and inexpensive
hotel.*
◻◻◻

☉ **Isis Hotel
Luxor ★★★★★**
◆ **L** A3
Shari' Khaled Ibn
el-Walid
Tel. (095) 37 33 66
or (095) 37 01 00
Fax (095) 37 29 23
*On the Corniche,
in the direction of
Esna
Well-situated
on the Nile with
spacious rooms
and various
restaurants and
bars. Splendid
swimming pool
and basement
nightclub.
Ask for a room
overlooking
the Nile.*
⬜🅰◻⬚❋◻⬆◻

**Luxor
Hilton ★★★★★**
◆ **L** A3
El-Nil Corniche
New-Karnak
Tel. (095) 37 49 33
Fax (095) 38 65 71
*Beautiful rooms
and excellent
atmosphere.
Delightful setting
with a magnificent
view of the Nile.*
⬜🅰◻⬚❋◻⬆◻

☉ **Luxor
Sheraton Hotel &
Resort ★★★★★**
◆ **L** A3
Road to
el-Awamiya
Tel. (095) 37 45 44
or (095) 37 40 13
Fax (095) 37 49 41
*At the end of the
Corniche
Stands in an
attractive lawned
park on the banks
of the Nile.
The rooms are
large and pleasant.
Restaurants
and outdoor
bar, theme buffets
and nightclub.*
⬜🅰◻⬚❋◻⬆◻

Towns are listed in alphabetical order
▲ refers to the "Itineraries", while ◆ refers to the map section of this guide.
For a full list of symbols, see page 481.

✪ Mercure
Hotel ★★★★
◆ L A3
El-Nil Corniche
Tel. (095) 38 09 44
or (095) 37 49 44
Fax (095) 37 49 12
*Haven of peace in
an attractive setting.
Several restaurants
and bars. Small,
comfortable rooms
and a fine
swimming pool.*
🏠🅲⬜🏊❄🅿🔼🎦

✪ Mövenpick Jolie-
Ville Luxor ★★★★★
◆ F B2
Crocodile Island
Tel. (095) 37 48 55
Fax (095) 37 43 96
Corniche, then the
main road to Esna
*Large, comfortable
chalets surrounded
by trees and flowers.
Splendid swimming
pool and children's
play area with
animals (monkeys,
camels, etc.).*
🏠🏊⬜❄🅿⊞

Novotel Evasion
Luxor Hotel ★★★★
◆ L A3
Shari' Khaled ibn
el-Walid
Tel. (095) 38 09 25
Fax (095) 38 09 72
*Original architecture
with a central light
well. Pleasant rooms.*
🏠🏊⬜❄🅿🔼🎦

Philippe Hotel
Luxor ★★★
◆ L B1
Shari' Dr. Labib-
Habachy
Tel. (095) 37 22 84
or (095) 37 36 04
Just before the
Luxor Mercure Hotel
*Small, clean hotel.
Not luxurious but
conveniently
situated between
the Nile and the
souks. Famed for its
jewelers.*
🅲⬜🎦

Sofitel
Winter Palace ★★★★
◆ L A3
El-Nil Corniche
Tel. (095) 38 04 22,
(095) 37 11 94
or (095) 38 24 25

Fax (095) 37 40 87
*Two hotels run by
Pullman: the Old
Winter Palace has a
traditional "English"
charm with exposed
beams in the bars
and huge rooms.*

APHRODITE BEACH, MERSA MATRUH

SUEZ CANAL

*The New Winter
Palace is more
recent; it has less
charm but is more
comfortable.
Both currently
share the same
reception.*
🏊⬜❄🅿🔼⊞

Sonesta
St-Georges Hotel
◆ L A3
Sonesta St-Georges
El Nil Corniche
Tel. (095) 38 25 75
Fax (095) 38 25 71
*Comfortable hotel
close to the city
center. Ask for a
room with a view
of the Nile, as the
others tend to be
rather noisy.*
🏊⬜❄🅿⊞

Youth Hostel
◆ L B1
16 Shari' el-Karnak
Tel. (095) 37 21 39
Between the
Corniche and the
road to the airport.

→SHOPPING
Philippe Jewels
◆ L B1
Philippe Hotel
Luxor

Tel. (095) 37 22 84
*This is a very
good jeweler's
with a wide choice
of gold, silver,
turquoise and lapis
lazuli. Bank inside
the store.*

Radwan
◆ L A3
Shari' Khaled Ibn
el-Walid
Tel. (095) 38 16 55
or (095) 37 46 43
Opposite the Isis
Hotel Luxor
*The second best
jeweler's in Luxor.
Excellent quality and
a wide selection.
Below the boutique,
cotton clothing (very
nice T-shirts). Bank
inside the store.*

MERSA MATRUH

▲ 204 ◆ C C1
→ACCOMMODATION
Beach House Hotel
★★★
Shari' el-Shatee
Tel. (03) 393 51 69
Corniche,
Mersa Matruh
*Good hotel by the
sea. Suites only.
Full-board.*
🏠🏊⬜❄🅿⊞

Miami Hotel ★★★
Corniche
Tel. (03) 93 58 91
*Good hotel
overlooking the
beaches. No
private beach.*
🏠🏊🅿🎦

Negresco Hotel ★★★
Corniche
Tel. (03) 493 44 92
or (03) 493 44 91
*Hotel overlooking
the sea. Ideal for a
short stay. No
restaurant.
Breakfast only.*
🏊⬜🅿🎦

Radi Hotel ★★★
Corniche
Tel. (03) 493 48 28
or (03) 493 31 93
*Full-board only.
Good value for
money.*
🏊⬜❄🅿🎦

Rommel House
Hotel ★★★
Corniche
Tel. (03) 93 54 66
*Comfortable hotel
with competitive
prices.*
🏠🏊🅿🎦

Youth Hostel
4 Shari' el-Gala'
P.O. Box 51512
Tel. (03) 49 32 33

EL-MINIA

▲ 372 ◆ D B5
→ACCOMMODATION
Mercure
Nefertiti ★★★★
El-Nil Corniche
Tel. (086) 34 15 15
Fax (086) 36 64 67
*The best hotel in
Middle Egypt.
Opposite the main
building, chalets
overlooking the Nile.
Good restaurants
and pleasant bar.
Departure point for
visits to Beni Hassan.*
🏠🏊⬜❄🅿🔼🎦

NUWEIBA

▲ 249 ◆ D F4
→ACCOMMODATION
Bawaki Beach
Hotel ★★★
11¼ miles from
Nuweiba
Tel. (062) 50 04 70
Fax (062) 50 04 71
*As you leave
the town, in the
direction of Taba
Excellent hotel. Well-
equipped for water
sports and good
value for money.
Half-board only.*
🏠🏊⬜❄🅿🎦

El-Salam Village **
Hotel district
Tel. (062) 50 04 41
Fax (062) 50 04 40
Pleasant vacation village. Well-equipped and reasonably priced.
🏠 ♨ ⛱ 🅿 📶

✪ El-Sayadeen Touristic Village ***
Hotel district
Tel. (062) 52 03 40
or (062) 52 03 41
Lovely vacation village. Recently built, comfortable, and with a full range of sports activities.
🏠 ♨ ⛱ 🅿 📶

El-Waha Touristic Village **
Hotel district
Tel. (062) 50 04 20
Fax (062) 52 04 20
Well-equipped vacation village. Excellent value for money.
🏠 ♨ 🅿 📶

Hilton Coral Hotel ***
Tel. (062) 52 03 20
or (062) 52 03 21
Fax (062) 52 03 27
Hotel district
The best hotel in Nuweiba (and the most expensive). Recently built, extremely comfortable and offering a full range of watersports.
🏠 ♨ ⛱ 🅿 🔔 📶

PORT SAFAGA
▲ 265 ◆ D E6
→ ACCOMMODATION
Holiday Inn Resort****
Holiday Inn Safaga
Tel. (065) 45 28 21,
(065) 45 28 22
or (065) 45 28 23
Fax (065) 578 35 85
With the resort of Hurghada having reached saturation point, the Safaga hotel district is now undergoing rapid development. New luxury hotel with all mod cons. Very comfortable.
♨ ⛱ 🅿 📶

Menaville Village ***
Tel. (065) 45 17 61
Fax (065) 45 17 64
Hotel district
Luxury vacation village in a relatively undeveloped tourist region. A full range

of watersports facilities and marina. Half-board.
🏠 ♨ 🅿 ⛱ 🅿 📶

Safaga Paradise Village ****
Tel. (065) 45 16 33
or (065) 45 16 34
Fax (065) 45 16 30
Hotel district
Very comfortable hotel, ideal for a vacation in this region. Half-board compulsory.
🏠 ♨ 🅿 ⛱ 🅿 📶

Shams Safaga Village ***
Tel. (065) 45 17 81,
(065) 45 17 82
or (065) 45 17 83
Fax (065) 45 17 80
Hotel district
Ideal for a family vacation. General comfort and standard Red Sea activities.
🏠 ♨ 🅿 ⛱ 🅿 📶

PORT SAID
▲ 236 ◆ G F1
→ ACCOMMODATION
Helnan Port Said Hotel *****
Corniche
P.O. Box 1110
Tel. (066) 32 08 90
or (066) 39 08 98
Fax (066) 32 37 62
Ⓒ ♨ 🅿 ⛱

New Regent Hotel ***
Shari' Gumhuriya
Tel. (066) 22 48 91
Very comfortable hotel near the harbor. One of the few hotels in Port Said with a swimming pool.
Ⓒ ♨ 🅿 🛗

Sonesta Port Said Hotel
Shari' Sultan Hussein
Port Said
Tel. (066) 32 55 11
or (066) 32 64 10
Fax (066) 32 48 25
New, very pleasant hotel standing directly opposite the Suez Canal. Splendid view. Excellent general comfort.
♨ 🅿 ⛱ 🅿 🛗

Youth Hostel
Shari' El-Amin
Corniche
Tel. (066) 22 87 02
Fax (066) 22 64 33

ST CATHERINE'S
▲ 244 ◆ D E4
→ ACCOMMODATION
Daniela Village ***
Tel. (062) 47 03 79
Tel. in Cairo (res.):
(02) 348 26 71
The second of St Catherine's hotels. Lacks comfort, but clean and reasonably priced. Half-board only.
🏠 🅿 📶

St Catherine Tourist Village ****
Wadi el-Raha
Tel. (062) 47 03 31
or (062) 47 03 24
Fax (062) 47 03 23
Pleasant, comfortable chalets scattered over a wide area. Dominated by the hillside restaurant. No alcohol.
🏠 🅿 🅿 📶

Sin Plaza
Tel. (062) 47 02 93,
(062) 47 02 94
or (062) 47 02 95
Fax (062) 47 02 95
Hotel with comfortable chalets.
🏠 🅿 📶

SHARM EL-SHEIKH
▲ 248 ◆ D E5
→ ACCOMMODATION
Coral Bay Hotel *****
Tel. (062) 60 16 10,
(062) 60 16 40
or (062) 60 16 90
Fax (062) 60 08 43
New luxury hotel, comfortable. Ideal for a vacation near the Red Sea.
♨ 🅿 ⛱ 🅿 📶

Gafi Land Tourist Village ***
Na'ama Bay
Tel. (062) 60 02 11
or (062) 60 02 12
Fax (062) 60 02 10
Hotel district
15 mins from the airport
Delightful hotel with beautiful rooms. Very competitive prices.
🏠 ♨ 🅿 🅿 📶

Ghazala Hotel
Na'ama Bay ****
Tel. (062) 60 01 50
or (062) 60 01 56
Fax (062) 60 01 55
Hotel district
All mod cons and sporting facilities on the Red Sea.
🏠 ♨ 🅿 🅿 📶

Towns are listed in alphabetical order
▲ *refers to the "Itineraries", while* ◆ *refers to the map section of this guide.*
For a full list of symbols, see page 481.

Hilton
Al Fairuz *****
Tel. (062) 60 01 40
or (062) 60 01 37
Fax (062) 60 10 43
Hotel district
*Luxury hotel
offering all types
of watersports
facilities.*
⬜🏄🟰🎿🅿️📶

⭕ **L.T.I. Seti
Sharm Hotel**
Sharm El-Mayah Bay
Sharm El-Sheikh
Tel. (062) 66 18 30,
66 18 31, 66 18 32
or 66 18 39
Fax (062) 66 08 77
*Delightful hotel
with chalets by the
sea. Pleasant 1940s-
style reception
area. This hotel is
excellent value for
money. A wide
range of watersports
facilities.*
🏄🟰🎿🅿️📶

⭕ **Marriott** *****
Tel. (062) 60 01 90
Fax (062) 60 01 88
*Originally called the
Mövenpick, this
hotel was reopened
in 1996. Magnificent
hotel offering first-
class comfort and
services, as well as all
types of watersports
facilities. Beautiful
rooms and reception
area. Exquisite
location.*
⬜🏄🟰🎿🅿️📶

**Mövenpick
Sharm el-Sheikh**
*****
Naama Bay
Tel. (062) 60 01 00
or (062) 60 01 01
Fax (062) 60 01 11
Hotel district
*One of the two
most beautiful
hotels in Sharm
el-Cheikh and near
the Red Sea.
Luxurious rooms,
entertainment and a
full range of
sporting activities.*
⬜🏄🟰🎿🅿️📶

⭕ **Novotel
Aquamarine
Hotel** ****
Tel. (062) 60 01 72

or (062) 60 01 73
Fax (062) 60 01 93
Hotel district
*Series of one-
storied chalets.
Well-situated,
several outdoor
restaurants, evening
entertainment,
and a full range
of watersports
facilities.*
⬜🏄🟰🎿🅿️📶📶

Youth Hostel
B.P. 46619
Tel. (062) 60 03 17
and (062) 66 03 17

SIDI ABD EL-RAHMAN
▲ *202* ◆ C E1
→ACCOMMODATION
⭕ **El-Alamein
Hotel** ****
Tel. (03) 492 12 31
or (03) 492 12 30
On the outskirts
of Sidi Abd el-
Rahman in the
direction of El-
Alamein

*Beautiful location
with chalets
overlooking the
beach. Sports
facilities still rather
limited. Usually fully
booked throughout
the summer.*
⬜🏄🅿️📶

SUEZ
▲ *236* ◆ G F4
→ACCOMMODATION
**Green House
Hotel** ***
Shari' Port Said
Tel. (062) 33 15 53
or (062) 33 15 54
Near the Suez
Canal
*New, comfortable
hotel with
swimming pool and
a good restaurant.
Way station on the
Sinai route.*
🖥️🟰🎿🅿️📶

Red Sea Hotel ***
13 Shari' Riad
Port Tawfiq

Tel. (062) 33 43 02
or (062) 33 43 03
Fax (062) 33 43 01
*Luxury hotel on the
port of Toufik. All
rooms overlook
the canal.*
⬜🖥️🅿️📶

**Summer Palace
Hotel** ***
Port Tawfiq
Tel. (062) 22 44 75
Fax (062) 32 19 44
*Good hotel, well-
positioned on the
port.*
⬜🅿️📶

Youth Hostel
Shari' el-Hurriya
P.O. Box 171
Tel. (062) 33 90 69
Opposite the
stadium

TABA
▲ *249* ◆ D F3
→ACCOMMODATION
**Hotel Hilton
Taba** *****
Taba Beach
Tel. (062) 53 01 40
or (062) 53 03 00
Fax (062) 57 87 044
*Extremely
comfortable,
luxury hotel
offering watersports
facilities. Close
to the Israeli
border.*
⬜🏄🖥️🎿🅿️📶

TANTA
▲ *210* ◆ G C2
→ACCOMMODATION
Arafa Hotel ***
Midan Station
First Tanta
Tel. (040) 33 69 52
Fax (040) 33 18 00
*Very reasonable
hotel.*
🖥️🖥️🅿️📶

**Green House
Hotel** ***
Shari' el-Borsa
Gumhuriya
Tel. (040) 33 07 61
or (040) 33 07 62
Fax (040) 33 03 20
*Very reasonable
hotel.*
🖥️🖥️🅿️📶

Youth Hostel
2 Shari' Ahmed-
Aly
Tel. (040) 33 79 78

Please note that the times indicated below are not always strictly applied

NECROPOLISES, PHARAONIC TOMBS AND TEMPLES

BEWARE
Necropolises (such as Ramesseum and Valley of the King) are ticket operated. You will need to decide in advance which tombs you wish to visit. Plan your journey.

Necropolises and tombs are generally open daily 7am–5pm.
Temples are open daily 8am–5pm and sometimes earlier in summer when it is advisable to go early in the morning in order to avoid the heat.

CHURCHES, MONASTERIES AND CHRISTIAN CONVENTS

Churches are usually open daily 9am–4pm. Monasteries and Christian convents have no fixed opening times and no set admission fees. They are not regarded as places of touristic interest and do not fall under the management of the Ministry of Antiquities.

MOSQUES AND ISLAMIC MONUMENTS

The same goes for mosques, except for those listed as places of interest, such as the largest mosques in Cairo. They are usually open daily 8am–5pm; ticket offices close at 4pm.

MIDDLE EGYPT

Assiut, Minia, Beni Hassan, Sohag, Mallawi, Beni Sueif

Some regions are not readily accessible to tourists, such as Middle Egypt, which is placed under military control. An official escort is necessary in order to visit this region. Visiting times are approximate and listed here for information only.

ISOLATED REGIONS

Western oasis, Delta region, Northern Sinai and desert regions east of the Nile

Although they may be accessible, some regions still remain outside the usual tourist routes. Opening times are approximate and can change according to unexpected visitors.

ABU RUDEIS

MAGHARA TURQUOISE MINES
Snefru hieroglyphs, Khufu; Hathoric statues

Open daily 7am–4pm.
Zone under military control.
The Tourist Police must be informed of your itinerary the day before.

▲ 242
◆ D D4

ABU SIMBEL

TEMPLE OF RAMESSES II AND NEFERTARI

Access through the airport or by cruise-boat.
Open daily 7am until the arrival of the last flight (sometimes 8pm).

▲ 464
◆ F A6

ABU ZENIMA

TEMPLE OF SARABIT EL-KHADIM
Sinai

Temple of Hathor.
Normally open daily 7am–4pm; not often visited.

▲ 242
◆ D D4

ABYDOS

TEMPLES OF SETY I AND RAMESSES II

Open daily 7am–4pm. Access under military escort only. The Tourist Police must be informed of the visit the day before.

▲ 386
◆ F B1

ALEXANDRIA

ANTONIADIS GARDENS
Next to Nuzha Gardens

Open daily 8am–4pm.
Old Greek house and Roman ruins.

▲ 190
◆ C F1

FINE ARTS MUSEUM
1 Shari' Menasce
Muharram Bay

Open daily except Fri. 9am–1pm, 5–6pm.
Art collection and concert/exhibition hall.

▲ 189
◆ A C2

◆ PLACES TO VISIT

CAVAFY MUSEUM 4 Shari' Sharm-el-Sheikh	*Open daily except Mon. 9am–2pm.* *Tue. and Thur. 6–8pm.* *Museum housed in the apartment where the poet* *Constantin Cavafy resided and wrote during most* *of his life.*	▲ 185 ◆ B B2
GRAECO-ROMAN MUSEUM 5 Shari' el-Mathaf-el-Romani (Shari' Museum)	*Open daily except Fri. 9am–5pm.* *A collection of over 40,000 Pharaonic, Greek and* *Roman antiquities.*	▲ 186 ◆ A C2
KARM ABU MENAS 25 miles west of Alexandria	*Open daily. No specific times.* *Ruins of Saint Menas Monastery (3rd century).*	▲ 202 ◆ C F1
KOM EL-DIKKA AMPHITHEATER	*Open daily 9am–4pm.*	▲ 183 ◆ B C3
KOM ES-SHOGAFA CATACOMBS	*Open daily 9am–4pm.; summer 9am–5pm.*	▲ 192 ◆ A B3
ANFUSHI NECROPOLIS	*Open daily 9am–4pm; summer 9am–5pm.* *Ptolemaic catacombs dating back to the* *2nd century BC.*	▲ 177 ◆ A A2
NUZHA GARDENS Antoniadis	*Open daily 8am–4pm. Small zoo.* *Green area suitable for family outings.*	▲ 190 ◆ C F1
POMPEY PILLAR	*Open daily 9am–5pm.*	▲ 194 ◆ A B3
QASR EL SAFA **ROYAL JEWELS MUSEUM** 21 Shari' Ahmed-yehia-Glim	*Open daily 9am–4pm. Fri. 9–11.30am, 1.30–4pm.* *Superb collection of jewels belonging to the* *Egyptian royal family.* *Beautiful presentation.*	◆ C F1
QAITBAY FORT Alexandria harbor	*Open daily 9am–5pm.* *Mameluke fort located in the site of Alexandria's* *former lighthouse. Small maritime museum.*	▲ 177 ◆ A B1
TOURIST OFFICE MAIN OFFICE Midan Saad Zaghlul ANNEX Main station Midan Gumhuriya	*Open 9am–6pm.* *Although incomplete, maps of the city do list the* *main places of interests.*	

ASSIUT

ASSIUT MUSEUM Shari' el-Ghumhuriya	*Closed.*	▲ 380 ◆ D B6
ASSIUT NECROPOLIS	*Closed.*	▲ 380 ◆ D B6

AKHMIM

EL-HAWAWISH NECROPOLIS	*No specific visiting times. Visits are only possible* *under military escort. The Tourist Police must be* *notified the day before.*	▲ 384 ◆ D B6

ASWAN

ELEPHANTINE ISLAND	*Open daily except Mon. 9am–4pm.* *Fine vestiges of the Temple of Khnum, nilometer,* *museum.*	▲ 457 ◆ F C4
HIGH DAM	*Open daily 7am–5pm; summer 7am–6pm.*	▲ 460 ◆ M C3
KITCHENER'S ISLAND	*Open daily 8am–5pm.* *Magnificent botanical gardens on the Nile.*	▲ 458 ◆ M A2
HYPOGEA OF THE **ELEPHANTINE PRINCES** West bank Aswan	*Open daily 7am–4pm; summer 7am–5pm.* *Tombs of the Governors of Aswan* *(Old and Middle Kingdoms).*	▲ 458 ◆ M A1

MUSEUM OF NUBIA	Open 9am–1pm, 5–9pm; summer 5–10pm. A complete overview of Nubian civilization, from prehistory until the present time.	▲ 459 ◆ M A3
PHILAE TEMPLE Aguilika Island	Open daily 7am–4pm. Famous temple dedicated to the goddess Isis.	▲ 462 ◆ M C2
MONASTERY OF ST SIMEON	Open daily 8am–4pm. 4th-century monastery.	▲ 459 ◆ M A2
UNFINISHED OBELISK	Open daily 6am–5pm. Pink-sandstone obelisk dating back from the Hatshepsut period.	▲ 459 ◆ M B3

BEHBEIT EL-HAGAR

RUINS OF ISEUM	No details of opening times.	▲ 220 ◆ G D2

BENI SUEF

IHNASIYA EL-MEDINA Temple and necropolis 10 miles from Beni Suef	Usually open daily 7am–4pm. Visiting permit required from the military authorities as this temple is in a military zone. Old Heracleopolis.	▲ 360 ◆ D B3
BENI SUEF MUSEUM	Open 9am–4pm. Unpretentious museum that does not receive many visitors.	▲ 359 ◆ D B3
DISHASHA Necropolis on the road from Beni Suef to el-Minia	Open daily 7am–4pm. Visiting permit required from the military authorities. Necropolis dating back to the Old Kingdom.	▲ 360 ◆ D B4

CAIRO

ABDIN PALACE Midan Qasr Abdin	Open daily 9am–3pm. Former royal palace. Access to parts of the palace only.	▲ 281 ◆ I D4
BEIT AS-SINNARI Harret Monge	Open daily except Fri. 9am–2pm. Exhibition of applied arts, from Pharaonic times up to the present day.	▲ 315 ◆ J D1
BEIT AS-SUHAYMI 19 Shari' Darb-el-Asfar	Open daily except Fri. 9am–3pm.	▲ 291 ◆ I F3
BEIT EL-HIRAWI	Open daily 9am–4pm. 16th- and 17th-century merchant house.	▲ 295 ◆ D B3
BEIT GAMAL AD-DIN EL-DAHABI 6 Shari' Hara Hoch Qadam	Open daily 9am–4pm. 17th-century Ottoman house.	▲ 297 ◆ I F4
BEIT ZEINAB KHATUN	Closed.	▲ 295 ◆ D B3
CHURCHES IN THE COPTIC DISTRICT Old Cairo near the Coptic Museum	Open daily 9am–4pm, except Fri. and Sun. 11am–1pm (services). Church of St Sergius, St Barbara's church and synagogue.	▲ 319 ◆ J A6 J B6
CITADEL	Open daily 8am–5pm. Museums: 9am–3pm. The visit includes Mohammed Ali Mosque, the Police and Military museums and the Qasr el-Gawhara (palace).	▲ 304 ◆ J F1 J F2
COPTIC MUSEUM Coptic quarter	Open daily. 9am–4pm. Closed Fri. 11am–1pm Beautiful presentation of Egyptian Christian art.	▲ 321 ◆ J A6
EGYPTIAN MUSEUM, CAIRO Midan at-Tahrir	Open daily 9am–4pm. Museum of Pharaonic civilization.	▲ 276 ◆ I A3
EL-GHURI **MAUSOLEUM AND WAKALA**	Open daily 8am–4pm. 16th-century Mameluke palace. Dancing dervishes shows some evenings. Exhibitions of crafts in the Wakala el-Ghuri opposite.	▲ 296 ◆ I F4

◆ PLACES TO VISIT

GAYER-ANDERSON MUSEUM Near Ibn Tulun Mosque	*Open daily except Fri. 8am–4pm.* *Closed Fri. 11.30am–1pm.* *The combination of two houses dating back* *respectively to the 16th and 18th centuries, where* *Mayor Gayer-Anderson lived and which he* *restored. Themed décor in every room: Persian,* *Turkish, Chinese, etc.*	▲ 313 ◆ J E2
GEZIRA MUSEUM 1 Shari' el-Marsafist	*Open daily except Fri. 9am–4pm.* *Egyptian crafts.*	▲ 282 ◆ H B2
MAHMUD-KHALIL MUSEUM 1 Sheikh-Marsafy St.	*Open daily except Mon. 10am–5.30pm.* *Vast collection of Impressionist paintings.*	
MUKHTAR MUSEUM Gezira Center for Modern Arts, Gezira, near Kubri el-Gala'	*Open Tue.–Sun. 10am–1pm and 5–9pm.* *Closed Fri. 9am–noon.*	▲ 282 ◆ H B2
MANIAL PALACE Shari' Ali-Ibrahim Roda Island	*Open daily except Fri. 9am–4pm.* *19th- and 20th-century furniture in a former royal* *palace. Small Museum of Hunting.*	▲ 283 ◆ J A2
MUSEUM OF MODERN ART Cairo Opera Complex	*Open daily except Mon. 9am–4pm; closed Fri.* *11.30am–1pm.* *20th-century Egyptian paintings and sculptures.*	▲ 282 ◆ H B2
MUSEUM OF AGRICULTURE **AND COTTON** Dokki	*Open daily except Mon. 9am–4pm.* *Closed Fri. 11.30am–1pm.* *The history of agriculture from its origins until* *today.*	◆ H A4
MUSEUM OF CARRIAGES Bulaq	*Open daily 9am–4pm.* *Annex of the Museum of the Citadel's Carriages.*	◆ H C1
MUSEUM OF ETHNOLOGY 109 Qasr-el-Aïni	*Open daily except Fri. 9am–4pm.* *Closed public hols.* *Collection of 19th-century Nubian and African* *objects.*	
MUSEUM OF HYGIENE As-Sakakini	*Closed.*	
ISLAMIC MUSEUM Port Said	*Open daily 9am–4pm.* *Closed Fri. 11am–2pm.*	▲ 316 ◆ I D4
POSTAL MUSEUM Midan el-Ataba el-Khadra 2nd floor of the main post office	*Open daily except Fri. 9am–1pm. History of the* *postal system in Egypt and impressive collection* *of stamps.*	▲ 275 ◆ I D3
RAILWAY MUSEUM Ramses Station	*Open daily except Mon. 8.30am–1pm,* *Fri. 8.30am–noon.* *Fine collection of train engines and carriages,* *including that of the Khedive Ismail.*	▲ 273 ◆ I C1
1973 WAR PANORAMIC SHOW Heliopolis Road to the airport	*Closed Tue. Exhibition of tanks and aircraft from* *the Kippur War. Panoramic shows at 9.30am,* *11am, 12.30pm, 6pm, 7.30pm.* *Open daily 9am–3pm.*	
TOURIST OFFICE Misr Travel Tower Midan Abbassiya Tel. (02) 282 84 56 Fax (02) 285 43 23		
CITY OF THE DEAD		
BARQUQ MAUSOLEUM Shari' El-Sultan-Ahmed	*Open daily 9am–4pm.*	▲ 329 ◆ J F3
IMAM AS-SHAFI'I MAUSOLEUM Shari' Imam as-Shafi'i	*Open daily 9–4pm. Place of pilgrimage.*	▲ 330 ◆ J F5

QAITBAY MAUSOLEUM Shari' el-Sultan-Ahmed	Open daily 9am–4pm.	▲ 328 ◆ J F4

DASHUR

PYRAMIDS OF DAHSHUR	Open daily 7am–4pm. Pyramids of the Ancient and Middle Empires, including the Bent Pyramid, those of Senwosret III, Amenemhet II and Amenemhet III.	▲ 354 ◆ D B3

DAKHLA OASIS

BALAT	Open daily 7am–4pm. Neolithic and mastaba site of the Old Kingdom.	▲ 259 ◆ E D2
DEIR EL HAGAR	Open daily 7am–4pm. Ancient Roman temple converted into a monastery.	▲ 259 ◆ E D2
EL-MUZAWAKA TOMBS	Open daily 7am–4pm. Roman necropolis.	▲ 259 ◆ E D2

DAMIETTA

COPTIC MONASTERY OF ST DAMIENNE	Open daily except during Christian holidays.	▲ 223 ◆ G E1

DENDERA

TEMPLE OF DENDERA	Open daily 7am–5pm. Magnificent Hathoric, Ptolemaic and Roman temple.	◆ F C2

DISUQ

TELL EL-FARAÏN Nile Delta	Opening times may vary.	▲ 212 ◆ G C1

EDFU

TEMPLE OF HORUS	Open 7am–5pm. Ptolemaic and Roman temple.	▲ 449 ◆ F C3

EL-ARISH

MUSEUM OF BEDOUIN TRADITION On the coastal road leading to Rafah	Open daily 10am–6pm in winter and 8am–8pm in summer. Museum of Bedouin life in the Sinai Desert.	▲ 252 ◆ D E1

EL-KAB

NECROPOLIS OF EL-KAB	Open daily 7am–5pm. Police escort. The Tourist Police must be notified the day before.	▲ 446 ◆ F C3

ESNA

TEMPLE OF KHNUM	Open daily 7am–5pm.	▲ 447 ◆ F B2

THE FAIYUM

DEIR EL-MALAK GHOBRIAL	No specific opening times. Not frequently visited.	▲ 370 ◆ G C6
KARANIS	No specific opening times. Not frequently visited.	▲ 366 ◆ G C6
MEDINET MADI	No specific opening times. Not frequently visited.	▲ 368 ◆ G B6

GIZA

PYRAMIDS	Open daily 6am–5pm. Warning: Only 150 visitors are admitted to the Pyramid of Khufu every day.	▲ 334 ◆ G D5

| SPHINX | Open daily 9am–4pm. | ▲ 342 ◆ G D5 |
| **SOLAR BARQUE** At the foot of the Pyramids | Open daily except Tue. 9am–4pm (last admissions 3.30pm). Magnificent cedar-wood boat that belonged to Pharaoh Khufu. | ▲ 337 ◆ G D5 |

HURGHADA

| **MONS CLAUDIANUS** | Archeological site. No specific opening times. Quarries dating back to Roman times. | ▲ 267 ◆ D D6 |
| **MONS PORPHYRITES** | Archeological site. No specific opening times. Quarries dating back to Roman times. | ▲ 267 ◆ D D6 |

ISMAÏLIYA

| **MUSEUM OF ANTIQUITIES** Mohammed Ali Quay | Open daily 9am–4pm. Small museum of objects from Pharaonic times up to the present day. | ▲ 236 ◆ G F3 |

KHARGA OASIS

DUSH 50 miles south of Kharga	No specific opening times. Ruins of a Roman temple dedicated to Isis and Serapis.	▲ 263 ◆ E E2
EL-DEIR 18 miles north of Kharga	No specific opening times. 3rd- to 4th-century Roman fort.	▲ 262 ◆ E E2
MUSEUM OF THE NEW VALLEY	Open daily 9am–4pm. Very small museum.	▲ 260 ◆ E E2
EL-BAGAWAT NECROPOLIS	Open daily 8am–5pm. Christian necropolis. Tombs with cuppula.	▲ 261 ◆ E E2
QASR EL-GHUEIDA 15½ miles south of Kharga	No specific opening times. Remains of a Ptolemaic temple.	▲ 262 ◆ E E2
QASR EL-ZAIYAN	Usually open daily 8am–5pm. Remains of a temple to Amenetis.	▲ 263 ◆ E E2
TEMPLE OF HIBIS	Open daily 8am–5pm. Temple to Amun, Persian era.	▲ 260 ◆ E E2

KOM OMBO

| **TEMPLE OF KOM OMBO** | Usually open daily 6am–5pm. Double temple from Ptolemaic times. | ▲ 452 ◆ F C3 |

LAKE NASSER

	Visit of Nubian temples (rebuilt into three groups). A visit to the last two groups is part of a cruise on Lake Nasser.	
AMADA GROUP	Open daily 6am–5pm; summer 6am–6pm. Temples of Amada, Derr and tomb of Penne.	◆ 461 ◆ F B6
KALABSHA GROUP Behind the Aswan high dam	Open daily 6am–5pm. Accessible by motor boat. Temple of Kalabsha, Temple of Beit el-Wali and Temple of Kertassi.	▲ 460 ◆ F C4
WADI ES-SEBUA GROUP	Open daily 6am–5pm; summer 6am–6pm. Temples of Wadi es-Sebua, Maharraqa and Dakka.	▲ 461 ◆ F B5

LISHT

PYRAMID	Open daily 7am–5pm.	▲ 356 ◆ G D5

LUXOR/THEBES

DEIR EL-BAHRI	Open daily 6am–5pm. Temple of Hatshepsut.	▲ 426 ◆ K A2
DEIR EL-MEDINA	Open daily 6am–5pm. Valley and city of craftsmen, Ptolemaic temple and magnificent tomb of Sennedjem.	▲ 438 ◆ K A3
LUXOR MUSEUM	Open daily 9am–1pm and 4–9pm in winter, 4–10pm in summer. Modern design, exceptional pieces.	▲ 403 ◆ L B1
MEDINET HABU	Open daily 6am–5pm. Funerary temple of Ramesses III.	▲ 434 ◆ K A4
ASASIF NECROPOLIS	Open daily 6am–5pm. Tombs from the New Kingdom.	▲ 425 ◆ K B2
NECROPOLIS OF SHEIKH ABD EL-QURNA	Open daily 6am–5pm. Valley of the Nobles.	◆ 430 ◆ K A2
RAMESSEUM	Open daily 6am–5pm. Funerary temple of Ramesses II.	▲ 432 ◆ K B3
TEMPLE OF KARNAK	Open daily 6am–6pm in summer; 7am–5pm in winter. Great temple to Amun and "open-air museum".	▲ 404 ◆ K F
TEMPLE OF LUXOR	Open daily 6am–9pm. Illuminated at night.	▲ 397 ◆ L A3
TEMPLE OF SETY I	Open daily 6am–5pm. Funerary temple of Ramesses II's father.	▲ 424 ◆ K C2
TOURIST OFFICE Nile Corniche Between the temple and the New Winter Palace Hotel Tel. (095) 37 32 94	Open daily 9am–3pm and 6–9pm. Warning: out of season, the ferry linking the east bank and west bank does not necessarily operate. Take a taxi rather than an unofficial` small boat, which can be more expensive.	
VALLEY OF THE KINGS	Open daily 6am–5pm. New Kingdom pharaohs' tombs, including the tomb of Tutenkhamun.	▲ 417 ◆ K A1
VALLEY OF THE QUEENS	Open daily 6am–5pm. Tombs of the queens and princes of the New Kingdom. Tomb of Nefertari: daily 8am–noon. Number of visitors limited to 150 per day.	◆ 440 ◆ K A3

MANSURA

RUINS OF MENDES	No specific opening times. Remains of 21st-Dynasty temple.	▲ 221 ◆ G D2

MEIDUM

PYRAMID OF MEIDUM	Usually open daily 6am–5pm. Not frequently visited.	▲ 357 ◆ G C6

MEMPHIS

MIT RAHINA 19 miles south of Cairo Left bank of the Nile	Open daily 7am–4pm. Remains of Memphis, capital of the North. Sphinx of Hatshepsut, Granite colossus of Ramesses II.	▲ 332 ◆ G D5

◆ PLACES TO VISIT

EL-MINIA AND SURROUNDINGS

	Warning: region under military control. No specific visiting times. Visits limited.	
BENI HASSAN Abu Qurqas	Usually open daily 6am–5pm. Military escort obligatory.	▲ 374 ◆ D B5
DEIR EL-ADRA Opposie the city of Samalut known as Jebel el-Teir	Usually open daily 6am–5pm. 4th-century monastery.	▲ 373 ◆ D B5
MINIA MUSEUM	Closed.	▲ 372 ◆ D B5
SPEOS ARTEMIDOS Near Beni Hassan	Cave of Artemis. No specific opening times.	▲ 375 ◆ D B5
TIHNA EL-JEBEL	Closed.	▲ 372 ◆ D B5
ZAWIYET-EL-MAYTIN Kom el-Ahmar	No specific opening times. Necropolis from the 18th and 19th Dynasties.	▲ 373 ◆ D B5

MELLAWI

ASHMUNEIN AND TUNA EL-JEBEL	No specific opening times. Ancient Hermopolis.	▲ 377 ◆ D B5
ANTINOE Village of Sheikh Abada	No set opening times. Considerably damaged.	▲ 375 ◆ D B5
DEIR ABU HENNES South of Sheikh Abada	No specific opening times. Just go to the church door.	▲ 376 ◆ D B5
MELLAWI MUSEUM	Usually open daily 9am–4pm. Not frequently visited.	▲ 376 ◆ D B5
TELL EL-AMARNA	Usually open daily 8am–4pm. Badly damaged tombs. Amazing site.	▲ 378 ◆ D B5

PORT SAID

HISTORY MUSEUM	Open daily 9am–4pm. Collection of objets from pre-Dynastic times.	▲ 236 ◆ GF1
MILITARY MUSEUM	Open daily 9am–4pm. Presentation of Arab-Israeli wars.	▲ 236 ◆ G F1

QUSEIR

WADI HAMMAMAT	No specific opening times. Rupestrian inscriptions dating back from the Old and Middle Kingdoms.	▲ 268 ◆ F C2

RAS MOHAMMED

RAS MOHAMMED NATIONAL PARK Sinai	Open daily 7am–4pm. Beautiful diving site.	▲ 248 ◆ D F3

RAS ZA'FARANA

MONASTERY OF ST ANTHONY Track 20½ miles west of Ras Za'farana on the desert road.	Open daily except on religious festivals and Lent 9am–5pm. Food and overnight accommodation available.	▲ 265 ◆ D C3
MONASTERY OF ST PAUL Track 15½ miles south of Ras Za'farana on the Suez-Hurghada route	Open daily except on religious festivals and Lent 9am–5pm. Food and overnight accommodation available.	◆ 265 ◆ D C3

ROSETTA

QAITBAY CITADEL	Open 7am–4.30pm. 15th-century Mameluke citadel.	▲ 215 ◆ G B1

ST CATHERINE'S

| ST CATHERINE'S MONASTERY | Open daily 9.30am–12 noon. Closed Sun. and on Christian and Muslim holidays. | ▲ 244 ◆ D E4 |

SAQQARA

| PYRAMIDS AND NECROPOLIS OF SAQQARA | Open daily 6am–5pm. Great Memphis necropolis. The stepped pyramid of Djoser, Serapeum. | ▲ 344 ◆ G D5 |

SIWA

| JEBEL EL-MAWTA | No specific opening times. | ◆ 257 ◆ C A3 |
| TEMPLE OF AGHURMI | Open daily 7am–4pm. Remains of the temple of Jupiter-Amun. | ▲ 256 ◆ C A3 |

SOHAG

| RED MONASTERY: DEIR AMBA BISHOI | Just go to the convent door. Closed on religious festival days. | ▲ 383 ◆ F A1 |
| WHITE MONASTERY: DEIR EL-ABYAD | Just go to the convent door. Closed on religious festival days. | ▲ 383 ◆ F A1 |

TABA

| SALAH AD-DIN FORT | Open daily 8am–5pm. On Pharaoh's Island, restored medieval fort with breathtaking view of the four neighboring countries. | ▲ 249 ◆ D F3 |

TANIS

| RUINS AND NECROPOLIS OF TANIS | Open daily 7am–5pm. Opening times vary because of current excavation works. | ▲ 224 ◆ G E2 |

WADI NATRUN

| MONASTERIES OF WADI NATRUN | No specific opening times. Just go to the doors of the monasteries. | ▲ 208 ◆ C F2 |

◆ BIBLIOGRAPHY

ESSENTIAL READING

◆ ALDRED (C.): *Egyptian Art in the Days of the Pharaohs*, London and New York, 1980
◆ IDRIS (B.H.): *Egypt from Alexander the Great to the Arab Conquest*, Oxford, 1948
◆ MURNANE (W.J.): *Penguin Guide to Ancient Egypt*, London and New York, 1983

ANCIENT EGYPT

◆ ALDRED (C.): *The Egyptians*, London, 1984
◆ ALDRED (C.): *Akhenaten and Nefertiti*, London, 1973
◆ BAIKIE (J.): *Egyptian Antiquities in the Nile Valley*, Methuen, 1932
◆ BAINES (J.) and MALEK (J.): *Atlas of Ancient Egypt*, Oxford, 1980
◆ BEVAN (E.): *A History of Egypt under the Ptolemaic Dynasty*, London, 1927
◆ BREASTED (J.H.): *History of Egypt*, London and New York, 1905
◆ BUNSON (M.): *The Encyclopaedia of Ancient Egypt*, New York and Oxford, 1991
◆ DAVIES (W.V.): *Egyptian Hieroglyphics*, London, 1987
◆ DESROCHES-NOBLECOURT (C.): *Tutankhamen*, English trans., 1963
◆ EDWARDS (I.E.S.): *Tutankhamen, his Tomb and its Treasures*, New York, 1977
◆ ERMAN (A.): *The Ancient Egyptians, A Sourcebook of their Writings*, English trans., New York, 1966
◆ GARDINER (A.H.): *Egypt of the Pharaohs*, Oxford, 1961
◆ GRIMAL (N.): *A History of Ancient Egypt*, Oxford, 1992
◆ HARRIS (J.R.): *The Legacy of Egypt*, Oxford, 1971
◆ HOBSON (C.): *The World of the Pharaohs: A Complete Guide to Ancient Egypt*, New York and London, 1987
◆ JAMES (T.G.H.): *An Introduction to Ancient Egypt*, London, 1964
◆ MONTET (P.): *Lives of the Pharaohs*, English trans., London, 1968
◆ SIMPSON (W.K.): *The Literature of Ancient Egypt*, New Haven, 1972

HISTORY OF THE DISCOVERIES

◆ BELZONI (G.): *Narrative of the Operations and Recent Discoveries*, London, 1820
◆ CARTER (H.): *The Tomb of Tutankhamun*, London, 1923–33
◆ CLAYTON (P.): *The Rediscovery of Ancient Egypt*, London, 1982
◆ FAGAN (B.M.): *The Rape of the Nile*, London, 1977
◆ GREENER (L.): *The Discovery of Egypt*, London, 1966
◆ JAMES (T.G.H.): *Excavating in Egypt, the Egypt Exploration Society 1882–1982*, London, 1982
◆ JAMES (T.G.H.): *Howard Carter, the Path to Tutankhamun*, London and New York, 1992
◆ LEPSIUS (R.): *Discoveries in Egypt, Ethiopia and the Peninsula of Sinai*, London, 1853
◆ MAYES (S.): *The Great Belzoni*, London, 1959

ART AND ARCHITECTURE

◆ EDWARDS (I.E.S.): *The Pyramids of Egypt*, 3rd ed., London, 1972
◆ KISCHKEWITZ (H.): *Egyptian Drawings*, London, 1972
◆ OTTO (E.): *Egyptian Art and the Cult of Osiris and Amon*, London, 1968
◆ SCHÄFER (H.): *Principles of Egyptian Art*, English trans. Oxford, 1974
◆ SMITH (W.S.): *The Art and Architecture of Ancient Egypt*, Harmondsworth, 2nd ed. 1981
◆ TERRACE (F.L.B.) and FISCHER (H.G.): *Treasures of the Cairo Museum*, London, 1970
◆ Wilkinson (R.H.): *Reading Egyptian Art*, London, 1992

EGYPTIAN RELIGION

◆ CERNY (J.): *Ancient Egyptian Religion*, London, 1952
◆ MORENZ (S.): *Egyptian Religion*, English trans. London, 1973

◆ RUNDLE-CLARK (R.T.): *Myth and Symbol in Ancient Egypt*, London, 1978
◆ SAUNERON (S.): *The Priests of Ancient Egypt*, London, 1960
◆ SHORTER (A.W.): *The Egyptian Gods*, London, 1937
◆ WAINWRIGHT (G.A.): *The Sky Religion in Egypt*, Cambridge, 1938

LATER HISTORY

◆ BAKER (R.W.): *Egypt's Uncertain Revolution under Nasser and Sadat*, Harvard, 1978
◆ BLUNT (W.S.): *The Secret History of the English Occupation of Egypt*, London, 1923
◆ BUTLER (A.J.): *The Arab Conquest of Egypt*, Oxford, 1902
◆ CAMERON (D.A.): *Egypt in the 19th Century*, London, 1898
◆ COOPER (A.): *Cairo in the War 1939–1945*, Hamish Hamilton, 1989
◆ DODWELL (H.H.): *The Founder of Modern Egypt, Mohammed Ali*, Cambridge, 1931
◆ ELGOOD (P.G.): *The Transit of Egypt*, London, 1928
◆ HEROLD (J.C.): *Bonaparte in Egypt*, London, 1963
◆ HOLT (P.M.): *Egypt and the Fertile Crescent, 1516–1922*, London, 1966
◆ ISSAWI (C.): *Egypt in Revolution*, Oxford, 1963
◆ KYLE (K.): *Suez*, London, 1992
◆ LACOUTURE (J.): *Nasser, A Biography*, London, 1973
◆ LANE (E.W.): *Manners and Customs of the Modern Egyptians*, London, 1836
◆ LANE-POOLE (S.): *History of Egypt in the Middle Ages*, London, 1925
◆ LLOYD (C.): *The Nile Campaign: Nelson and Napoleon in Egypt*, Newton Abbot, 1973
◆ RUSSELL (D.): *Medieval Cairo*, London, 1962
◆ SANDERSON (G.N.): *England, Europe and the Upper Nile, 1822–1899*, Edinburgh, 1965

◆ VATIKIOTIS (P.J.): *The History of Egypt from Mohammed Ali to Sadat*, London, 1980
◆ WATERFIELD (G.): *Egypt (New Nations and Peoples)*, London, 1967
◆ WOODWARD (P.): *Nasser*, London, 1992

TRAVEL WRITING AND FICTION

◆ BURKHARDT (J.L.): *Travels in Nubia*, London, 1819
◆ CHRISTIE (A.): *Death on the Nile*, London, 1937
◆ DURRELL (L.): *The Alexandria Quartet*, London, 1985
◆ EDWARDS (A.): *A Thousand Miles up the Nile*, London, 1877
◆ FLAUBERT (G.): *Flaubert in Egypt*, English trans. by Francis Steegmuller, London, 1972
◆ FORSTER (E.M.): *Alexandria, a History and a Guide*, Alexandria, 1922 (many later editions)
◆ GAUTIER (T.): *L'Orient*, Paris, 1877
◆ GORDON (Lady D.): *Letters from Egypt, 1862–1869*, London, 1969
◆ KINGLAKE (A.W.): *Eothen*, London, 1844 (and later editions)
◆ MAILER (N.): *Ancient Evenings*, London and New York, 1983
◆ NIGHTINGALE (F.): *Letters from Egypt*, London, 1987
◆ PRESCOTT (H.F.M.): *Once to Sinai: the Further Pilgrimage of Friar Fabri*, London, 1957
◆ WALTARI (M.): *Sinuhe the Egyptian*, English trans., London, 1949

GUIDES

◆ HART (G.): *Pharaohs and Pyramids, a Guide through Old Kingdom Egypt*, London and New York, 1991
◆ MARTINENGO (L.): *Egypt (Odyssey Guides)*, Hong Kong, 1994
◆ ROCHESTER (D.) and O'BRIEN (K.): *Egypt (Rough Guides)*, London, 1993
◆ SETON-WILLIAMS (V.) and STOCKS (P.): *Egypt (Blue Guides)*, London and New York, 1990

LIST OF ILLUSTRATIONS

Front cover (US & UK):
Pyramids of Giza, F. Frith, photo, 1858–9. © The Royal Photographic Society, Bath. Temple of Luxor, © P. Chapuis/ Railway Museum, Cairo. *Tourists on the Pyramid of Khufu*, photo, c. 1900. Coll. Van Léo, Cairo. *The Sphinx*, E. Prisse d'Avennes, watercolor. Bibl. nat. © Édimédia. Church of Abu Seifen, icons, details. © J. L. Aunos.
Spine: *Goddess Hathor receiving Sety I*, painted bas-relief (US), Sarcophagus of Imenenimet, outer casing and interior. Louvre. © RMN, Paris.
Back cover: Reconstructed Island of Philae © W. Louvet (US). Temple of Khonsu, detail © J. Livet (UK). Sabil Kuttab, illus. Claude Quiec (UK). Lamp. Coll. Islamic Museum, Cairo. © S. Sharouni. *Zikr dancing*, engraving, in Gaston Maspero's *l'Égypte*, 1881. *Portrait of a man*, painting/wood, 2nd century. Egyptian Museum, Cairo. *Ibsamboul*, detail, Champollion, litho, in *Monuments de l'Égypte et de la Nubie*, 19th century. © Bibl. nat., Paris.
1 *Ibsamboul, great temple of the South*, Béato, photo, 19th century. Gallimard archive.
1–11 *Boats on the Nile*, Boyer, photo. © Roger-Viollet.
11 *Tourists returning from Karnak*, detail, photo, early 20th century. *Idem.*
12–13 *Tourists picnicking in a temple*, photo, c. 1900. *Idem.*
7 *Colossal sculptures, Philae. Idem.*
16 Nile Valley. © Y. Travert
18 Sakia. © Denis Roche.
24 White Desert. © N. Levallois.
Tulul el-Beled © J.-L. Bovot.
25 Arabian Desert, Kharga. © N. Levallois. Mount Sinai in winter. © P. Giambone/Bonechi
26 Lake Nasser. Ph. F. Bony/Gallimard
28–29 Red Sea © B.C.

Rives/Ardoukoba/ C.E.D.R.I. Red Sea © K. Amsler/C.E.D.R.I. Red Sea © A. Folley/ C.E.D.R.I.
30 Ras Muhammed. Ph. F. Bony/Gallimard
33 Mount Sinai. © C. Rausch/Rapho
37 *Sety I and Horus*, Belzoni, litho, copy of a fresco from the tomb of Sety I. Collège de France, Paris. Ph. Delebecque/ Gallimard.
38 Knife, Nagada period. Louvre. © RMN, Paris. Terracotta vase, Nagada period. *Idem.* Figurine of a woman, crocodile bone, Nagada I. *Idem.*
39 King Djoser, painted limestone, Old Kingdom. Egyptian Museum, Cairo. Stela of the Serpent-King, bas-relief/limestone, c. 3000 BC Louvre. © RMN, Paris. *Saqqara*, P. Coste, watercolor, 1819. Bibl. Saint-Charles, Marseilles.
40 Casket and cylindrical seals of King Mentuhotep, alabaster and schist, bronze and silver, Middle Kingdom. Louvre. © RMN, Paris. Amenemhet III at prayer, black granite, Middle Kingdom. Louvre. *Idem.* Statue of Senwosret III, diorite, Middle Kingdom. Louvre. © RMN, Paris.
41 Scarabs, glazed schist, New Kingdom. Louvre .© RMN, Paris. Statue of Hatshepsut and of Sennefer, painted sandstone, New Kingdom. Louvre. © RMN, Paris. Tomb of Inherkau, fresco. © J. Livet.
42 *Akhenaten and his family worshipping*, painted limestone slab, New Kingdom. Egyptian Museum, Cairo. Coffin of Ramesses II, painted wood, New Kingdom. *Idem. Ramesses fighting the Hittites*, Prisse d'Avennes, litho, 19th century. © Bibl. nat., Paris.
43 Fallen colossus, Tanis. © J.-L. Bovot. Statuette of King Taharqa worshipping the falcon-god Horus, gold, silver and bronze, 25th Dyn. Louvre. © RMN, Paris. Stela of'Apis, painted limestone, "Late" Period. *Idem.* Cat wearing the cartouche of Psamtik I, bronze and gold, Saite period. *Idem.*
44–45 *Nile scenes*,

mosaic, 1st century BC Palestine Archeological Museum. © Édimédia.
44 Profile of Cleopatra, bas-relief, Temple of Kom Ombo. © Stilin/Artephot. *Alexander the Great*, G. Zumpe, engraving. © Bibl. nat., Paris. Roman emperor represented as a pharaoh, marble 1st century AD Louvre. © RMN, Paris. The god Osiris, detail, gold, 9th century BC Louvre. © RMN, Paris.
45 *Title page of a Bohairic gospel-book*, Coptic period. © Bibl. nat., Paris. *The Roman emperor Justinien*, mosaic, Ravenna. © Roger-Viollet.
54 Model of fellah ploughing. Coll. British Museum, London. *Working in the fields*, fresco, Valley of the Kings. © Dagli-Orti. *Harvesting grain and ploughing*, paint/mud, c. 1450 BC Louvre. © RMN, Paris. *Harvesting figs*, facsimile of a painting from the tomb of Knumhotep at Beni Hassan. © British Museum, London. Inspecting cattle. *Idem.*
55 *Hunting scene*, fresco, Thebes. British Museum, London. *Preparing to tread wheat*, fresco, tomb of Menna. Ph. Gallimard. *Transporting grain*, fresco. Egyptian Museum, Turin. © SCALA. *Inspecting work in the fields, detail of the harvest*, fresco, tomb of Khaemwese. © British Museum, London.
56 *Mesyankh and his two daughters*, painted limestone , Old Kingdom. Egyptian Museum, Cairo. *The lady Madja and her husband*, painted wood. Louvre. © RMN, Paris. Model of a house, limestone, New Kingdom. *Idem.*
56–57 Banquet scene, fresco. © British Museum, London.
56 *Garden with an ornamental pool*, fresco. *Idem.* Ancient Egyptian furniture, wood and ivory. *Idem.*
57 El-Kab, tomb of Paheri, seated couple, detail of a bas-relief. © J. Livet. *Inkherkhau seated with his wife and children*, fresco, Deir el-Medina. © E. Lessing/Magnum.

Ancient Egyptian furniture. © British Museum, London. Make up applicator, painted wood, 18th dynasty. Louvre. © RMN, Paris.
58 Writing materials, Louvre. © RMN, Paris. *Story of the Battle of Kadesh*, papyrus, New Empire. *Idem.* Papyrus. © British Museum, London. *Seated scribe*, painted limestone, Old Kingdom. Egyptian Museum, Cairo.
59 Scribe's casket, painted wood, New Kingdom, Louvre. © RMN, Paris. *Monkey playing a flute and scribe praying*, ostraca, limestone. *Idem. Goldsmith's workshop*, tomb of Rekhmirr, fresco, 18th dynasty. © Gallimard. *Carpenters and sculptors at work*, details of a fresco, tomb of Rekhmire, 18th dynasty. © E. Lessing/ Magnum. Painter's materials. Egyptian Museum, Cairo.
60 *Sun god Harakhti*, detail of the stela of Taperet, painted wood, c. 900–800 BC Louvre. © RMN, Paris. The god Bes, temple of Dendera. © J. Livet. *The goddess Meretseger followed by the goddess Taweret*, limestone stela. Egyptian Museum, Turin. *The goddess of fertility suckling a child*, bas-relief, tomb of Khaemhet, Valley of the Nobles. © Dagli-Orti. *Khepri*, tomb of Nefertari. © J. Livet.
61 *The god Anubis*, detail of a fresco. Ph. Gallimard. *The god Sobek*, bas-relief, temple of Kom Ombo. J. Livet. *Ramesses III addressing the gods of Karnak, the consort of Amun*, facsimile of the Harris papyrus. British Museum, London.
62 *Nekhbet*, detail, J.-Champollion, litho in the *Monuments de l'Égypte and de la Nubie*. © Bibl. nat., Paris. *Book of the Dead of Khonsumes*, papyrus, c. 1000 BC Louvre. © RMN, Paris. Statuette of Bastet. © British Museum, London. *Nile God*, tomb of Ramesses II. © J. Livet. *Horus*, detail, J.-Champollion, litho in the *Monuments de l'Égypte et de la Nubie*. © Bibl. nat., Paris. *Thot and Ptah*, tomb of Nefertari

◆ LIST OF ILLUSTRATIONS

J. Livet. *Goddess Hathor receiving Sety I*, painted bas-relief. Louvre. © RMN, Paris.
63 *Allegory of the World*, funeral papyrus of Nespakashuti. Louvre. © RMN, Paris. *Khnum*, tomb of Nefertari. © J. Livet. *Ma'at.* © J. Gallimard. *Sekhmet.*© J. Livet. *The God Min*, bas-relief.
© P. Chapuis/Rapho. *Amun*, detail of the facsimile of the Harris papyrus. British Museum, London. Ph. Gallimard.
64 Mummification, sarcophagus, © Hildesheim, Pelizaeus Museum. Book of the Dead of Ani. © British Museum, London.
64–65 *Weighing of the heart*, papyrus of Junefer. *Idem.*
65 Sarcophagus of Menenimet, outer casing and interior. Louvre. © RMN, Paris. *"Opening of the mouth" of mummies*, tomb of Pairy. © J. Livet. canopic jars of Anpuhotep of Anpuhotep, limestone and painted wood. Egyptian Museum, Cairo. *The soul of the deceased descending into the tomb*, papyrus of Nebqed. Louvre. © RMN, Paris.
66 Abbassid coins. © Bibl. nat., Paris. *Saladin's calvacade*, ilumination, 14th century. © *Idem.* *Saladin*, Egyptian postage stamp, 1957. Gallimard archive.
67 *Egypt and the Nile*, Arabic manuscript of Al-Idrissi, 1182. Nat. Library, Cairo. © Dagli-Orti. *Mamelukes*, Wilkinson, watercolor, 19th century. © Bibl. nat., Paris.
68 *Alexandria captured by Napoleon Bonaparte*, engraving, 19th century. Musée Carnavalet. © J.-L. Charmet. *Muhammed Ali*, litho from a drawing by M. de Forbin, 1818. Bibl. des Arts déco, Paris. © H. J. Park/Tapabor.
69 *Arrival of the imperial yacht "l'Aigle" at Ismaïliya for the opening of the Suez Canal*, engraving from a sketch by A. Marc, in *l'Illustration*, 19th century. Gallimard archive. *Turkish invasion of Egypt*, J.A. Beaucé, watercolor engraving, 1847.

© Édimédia. *The British presence in Egypt*, cartoon, in *Puck*, 1896. Library of Congress, Washington. © Édimédia.
70 *Egyptian women demonstrating at the opening of the first Parliament*, photo, in *Le Monde illustré*, 1924. Bibl. des Arts déco, Paris.
© J.-L. Charmet. *New Egyptian ministers*, *idem.*
© L. of Selva/Tapabor. Saad *Zaghlul Pasha*, photo, early 20th century. © Roger-Violet. *Train riddled with bullets during the Six-Day War at El-Qantara*, 1973. © Gerster/ Rapho. *"We are ready" cover of a French newspaper, Images*, May 20, 1967. © Roger-Violet.
71 *Nasser at the Bandung conference*, photo, April 1955. © Roger-Violet. *Signing of peace agreement between Israel and Egypt in Washington* , photo, 1978. © Keystone. *Hosni Mubarak*, 1980's poster 1980. © H. Labib, Cairo.
72 Coptic manuscript. Coptic Museum, Cairo. © S. Sharouni. Covers of Egyptian novels. Gallimard archive.
73 Coptic manuscript. © Bibl. nat., Paris. *Decoration on a Koran*, P. d'Avennes, litho, in *l'Art arabe*, 19th century. *Idem.*
74 Coptic manuscript, detail. Coptic Museum, Cairo. © S. Sharouni. *Saint Mark preaching in Alexandria*, Bellini, oil/canvas. Brera, Milan. © Giraudon. *Pope Shenute.* © Abbas/ Magnum.
75 *At prayer in the mosque*, detail, Mahmud Saïd, oil/canvas, 1934. Museum of Modern Art, Cairo. *Egyptian prayer mat embroidered with the one hundred names of Allah.* Private coll. © J.-L. Charmet. *At prayer in the mosque.*© S. Grandadam. *The Sufadegs*, Mahmud Saïd, oil/canvas, 1960. Museum of Modern Art, Cairo.
76 *Muslim Brotherhood*, poster, 20th century. © J.-L. Charmet. *Al Azhar*, Lehnart & Landrok, early 20th century. Gallimard archive. *Friday prayer in the El-Hussein mosque.*

© Abbas/ Magnum. *Sign outside Allah's bakery.* © J.-L. Godeau.
77 *Sphinx*, litho in *Description de l'Égypte.* Gallimard archive.
84 *Naos at Edfu*, litho, in *Description de l'Égypte.* Gallimard archive.
85 *Capitals at Kom Ombo, Ramesseum, Sphinx*, lithos, in *Description de l'Égypte.* Gallimard archive.
86 *Tomb of Queen Mer-Neith, J. P. Lauer.* © IFAO. *Cenotaph of Queen Mer-Neith, J. P. Lauer.* © IFAO. *Pyramid of Djoser, J. P. Lauer.* © J. P. Lauer.
89 *Tomb of the vizier Bocchoris and Tomb at Tuna al-Jebel*, lithos, in *Description de l'Égypte.* Gallimard archive.
92 *Gate of Medinet Habu*, litho, in *Description de l'Égypte.* Gallimard archive.
94 *Belzoni drawing the pyramids* and *They set to work to clear away the sand*, drawing, 1823. © Bibl. nat., Paris. *H. Salt*, J. J. Halls, litho. Gallimard archive. *Champollion le Younger*, drawing, 1829. All rights reserved.
95 *Scholars of the Egypt Expedition*, watercolor, in *Commission d'Égypte*, 1899. © Bibl. nat., Paris. *Sarcophagus discovered at Thebes*, J.-J. Rifaud, litho. Centre Golénischeff. Ph.Delebecque/Gallimard d.
One of the Arabs cried out and *Arabs with torches*, engravings, in *L'Égypte et la Nubie*, 1823. © Bibl. nat., Paris.
96 *Bulaq Museum*, photo, early 20th century. Archives dept. of Alpes-de-Haute-Provence. *Auguste Mariette*, photo, 19th century. © Roger-Violet.
97 *Excavating the tomb of Amenhotep II* and *Excavations at Dahshur*, engravings, 1898. 1894. © Keystone. *Petrie*, photo, 1822. Gallimard archive
98 *Christiane Desroches Noblecourt.* © Stock. *Dismantling the temple of Abu Simbel.* © Nenadovic/ Unesco. *Work at Philae.* © A. N. Vorontzoff/Unesco. *Abu Simbel, dismantling a fresco*, drawing. © D. Roger/Unesco.

99 *Abu Simbel, reconstructing the great temple.* © Nenadovic/ Unesco.
100 *Abu Simbel, photogrammetric survey.* © Unesco.
101 *Abu Simbel*, © Hervé Champollion/Top.
103 *Restoring the Sphinx, Restoring a statue*, © P. Chapuis/MAFB. *Restoring the Pyramid of Djoser.* © P. Chapuis/ Rapho.
104 *Chapel of Amenhemet I* © J. Livet *Restoring the tomb of Montuemhet and Detail.*© P. Chapuis/ Rapho.
105 *Restoring the sarcophagus of Aper-El. Sorting "pâte de verre" fragments. Cleaning a mummified cat.* © P. Chapuis/MAFB. *Restoring the tomb of Montuemhet, detail.*© P. Chapuis/Rapho. *Sorting pottery shards* © A. Zivie/MAFB.
114 *Tombs and cupulas*, lithos, in *Description de l'Égypte.* Gallimard archive.
119 *Schooling with the aid of a stick*, Ahmed Ibn Al Hasan Ibn Ahnaf, manuscript, in *The Book of Horses*, 1227. Nat. Library, Cairo.
120 *Filling the Cairo canal*, litho, in *Description de l'Égypte.* Gallimard archive.
121 *Feluccas on the Nile.* © R. Burri/Magnum.
122 *Boat on the Nile at Ibrim, Nubia*, L. de Bellefonds, watercolor, 1827. V. & A. Museum, London. © Édimédia. *Bateau*, photo. © N. Henein and C. Gaubert. *My boat on the Nile*, P. d'Avennes, watercolor, 1859. V. & A. Museum, London. © Édimédia.
123 *Boat on Lake Manzala.* © J. L. Bovot.
124 *Barber's sign advertising circumcision*, photo, 1st half 20th century. *Publicity hoarding for bridal wear, wall painting*, 20th century. © J. G. Ross/Rapho. *Muslim wedding ceremony in Egypt*, engraving, 19th century. L. of Selva/ Tapabor. © Roger-Violet.
124–125 *Bridal caravan.* © Roger-Violet.
125 *Coptic baptism* © Barbey/Magnum. *Funeral procession*, L.

LIST OF ILLUSTRATIONS

A. Crapelet, watercolor drawing, 19th century. Bibl. des Arts graphiques, Louvre. Ph. P. Léger.

126 *Idem*, detail. *Idem. Festival of Cham el-Nessim*, engraving from a drawing by Darjou, 1873. © Roger-Violet. Luxor, Festival of Spring. © R. Burri/Magnum.

126–127 Qurna, painted house. © J. Livet.

127 *Muled*, Al Gazzar, oil/canvas, 20th century. © C. Roussillon. Cairo, waiting for sunset and festival to celebrate the end of ramadan. © H. Gruyaert/ Magnum. *The Holy Carpet*, R. Dalton, engraving, in *Antiquities & Views in Greece and Egypt*,1741. © Bibl. nat., Paris.

128 *The Musician*, L. Deutch, oil/wood, late 19th century. © ACR Éditions, Courbevoie. *Traveling musicians in an Arab café in Cairo*. © Roger-Violet. Umm Kalsum. © B. Barbey/ Magnum.

129 *Belly dancing*, Cairo, postcard, early 20th century. Gallimard archive. *Samia Gamal at 16*, photo, 1940's. © Mary Mollo. *Lute, "qanun" and flute*, lithos, in *Description de l'Égypte*. Gallimard archive. Musical group in Siwa Oasis. © G. Sioen/Rapho.

130 *The Basket Maker*, litho, in *Description de l'Égypte*. Gallimard archive. Making donuts. © G. Degeorge. "Fuul" seller. © S. Grandadam. Knifegrinder in Cairo. © Revault/IREMAM, Aix-en-Provence. *Licorice-syrup seller*, M. Naghi. oil/canvas, c. 1950. *Public scribe*, postcard, early 20th century. © L. of Selva/Tababor.

131 *Mat makers*, litho, in *Description de l'Égypte*. Gallimard archive. © C. Roussillon. *Lime juice seller*, postcard, c. 1900. Gallimard archive. Shoe shiners in Cairo, Naya, 19th century. © Société française de photographie, Paris. Potter at Balas. © J. Livet. Street barber. © E. Lessing/Magnum. *The furniture maker*, L. Deutch, oil/wood, 1900. Private coll. © ACR Éditions, Courbevoie. Ironer in Cairo. © G.

Degeorge.

132 Long-handled *kanaka*, used for making coffee. Islamic Museum, Cairo. *Coffee seller*, detail, postcard, early 20th century. *Arab café* E. Girardet, oil/canvas, 2nd half 19th century. Musée D'Orsay. © RMN, Paris.

133 *Interior of Arab café*, T. Frère, oil/canvas, late 19th century. Coll. MAAO. © RMN, Paris. *Café scene*. Cairo. © G. Degeorge. Interior of a café in Cairo. © Wessam Mehanna. *Arab making coffee*, engraving, 19th century. Bibl. des Arts déco, Paris. © L. of Selva/ Tababor. *Arab café*, postcard, early 20th century. Coll. L. Claude. *Arab café*, detail, Naya, 19th century. © Société française de géographie, Paris.

136–137 *Horsemen*, lithos, in *Description de l'Égypte*. Gallimard archive.

136 *Horsemen accompanying a procession in Cairo*, Richard Dalton, litho, in *Antiquities & Views of Greece & Egypt*, 1791. © Bibl. nat., Paris. *Schooling with the aid of a stick*, Ahmed Ibn Al Hasan Ibn Ahnaf, manuscript, in *The Book of Horses*, 1227. Nat. Library, Cairo. © Dagli-Orti.

137 *Grooming a horse. Idem. Pilgrim to Mecca and Muhasseb, responsible for the security of markets*, engraving. Bibl. des Arts déco, Paris. © L. of Selva/ Tababor. *Arab horsemen practising equestrian skills*, Richard Dalton, litho, in *Antiquities & Views of Greece and Egypt*, 1791. © Bibl. nat., Paris.

138 *Horus*, litho, in *Description de l'Égypte*. Gallimard archive. *Young falconer and his falcon*, Arab miniature, 17th century. © Bibl. nat., Paris. Sparrowhawk and goshawk. © Jacana. *Arabs hunting with hawks*, Eugène Fromentin, oil/canvas, 1865. Musée Condé, Chantilly.

139 *Interior of Deir el-Medina*, David Roberts, litho, 19th century. Gallimard archive.

140–141 *View of the ruins of Elephantine*

Island, watercolor in *Commission d'Égypte*, 1799. © Bibl. nat., Paris.

140 *Pompey's Pillar*, Vivant Denon, watercolor, 1799. V. & A. Museum, London. © Édimédia.

141 *The Faiyum, detail, jewelry, ancient remains, tunic found in a tomb at Saqqara, ancient remains*, tinted drawings and watercolors, in *Commission d'Égypte*, 1799. © Bibl. nat., Paris.

142–143 *Cairo seen from one of its gates*, David Roberts, watercolor, 19th century. © V. & A. Museum, London.

142 *Sultan Hassan Mosque*, Cairo, idem.

143 *St Catherine's Monastery*, Adrien Dauzats, oil/canvas, 1845. Louvre. © RMN, Paris.

144 *The Carpet Suq*, C. Robertson, watercolor, 1887. Private coll.© Édimédia. *Carpet Seller in Cairo*, J.-L. Gérôme, oil/canvas, 1886. © ACR Éditions. *Bazaar in Khan el-Khalili, detail*, C. Robertson, watercolor, c.1880. *Idem*.

145 *Residence of the Mufti Sheikh al Mahdi*, Frank Dillon, watercolor, 1873. V. & A. Museum, London. © Édimédia. *The Midday Meal in Cairo*, Lewis, oil/canvas, 1875. © ACR Éditions, Courbevoie.

146 *Cairo*, Kees Van Dongen, oil/canvas, 20th century. Coll. par. © Édimédia. *P. Klee*, photo, early 20th century. All rights reserved.

147 *Ad Parnassum*, Paul Klee, oil/canvas, 1932. © P. Lauer/Musée Des Beaux-Arts of Berne. *Pyramid*, Paul Klee, watercolor, 1934. *Idem. The Legend of the Nile* , Paul Klee, pastel/cotton and jute, 1937. *Idem*.

148 *Funeral procession*, Saïd Al-Adawi, ink/paper, 1970. © I.M.A., Paris. *Mersa Matruh*, Mahmud Saïd, oil/canvas, 20th century. © Museum of Modern Art, Cairo. *View of the Nile and Roda Island*, Mohamed Naghi, oil/canvas. *Idem*.

149 *Zouheir Kamel*, oil/canvas, illustration from a novel by Naguib Mahfouz.

150–151 *Alexandria*

and its Lighthouse, engraving, 16th–17th century. Bibl. nat., Paris © J. L. Charmet.

150 C. Cavafy, drawing. Coll. restaurant l'Élite, Alexandria. © R. Zéboulon. Lawrence Durrell. © Éditions Buchet Chastel.

151 Stratis Tsirkas. Coll Éditions du Seuil.

152 Édouard Al-Kharrat. All rights reserved. *Alexandria*, tram station, detail. © Roger-Violet.

153 Tewfik el-Hakim, photo, 1985. © F. El-Khoury/ Rapho. *Threshing machine*, litho, in *Description de l'Égypte*. Gallimard archive. *A. Dumas*, photo, 19th century. © Bibl. nat., Paris.

154 *Mont Jebel, from Wadi Feiran*, V. Guérin, litho, in *La Terre sainte* (The Holy Land), 1884. © Édimédia.

155 *View of Lower Egypt*, D. Vivant Denon, engraving. Gallimard archive. *Pierre Loti*, photo, 19th century. Coll Archives Dépt. of La Rochelle. *Camel driver*, litho, in *Description de l'Égypte*. Gallimard archive.

156–157 *Manuscript on papyrus*, litho, in *Description de l'Égypte* Gallimard archive.

157 *Water carrier*. *Idem*

158–159 *View of western end of the Midan Ezbekiya. Idem.*

158 *View of the main square in Cairo*, L. Mayer, litho, in *Vues d'Égypte* (View of Egypt), 1802. © Bibl. nat., Paris.

159 *Taha Husein*, Egyptian postage stamp, 1973. Gallimard archive. *Islamic Cairo*, litho, 19th century. © Bibl. nat., Paris.

160 Naguib Mahfouz, photo, 1985. © F. El-Khoury/ Rapho. *Dancer musicians*, lithos, in *Description de l'Égypte* Gallimard archive.

161 A. Cossery, photo, 1986. © F. El-Khoury/ Rapho. *At the barbers, detail*, Naya, photo, 19th century. © Société française de photographie, Paris. Gamal Githani. Coll. Éditions du Seuil. All rights reserved. *Dancer* litho, in *Description de l'Égypte*. Gallimard archive.

162–163 El-Minya, E.

iceri, litho, 19th century. © Bibl. nat., Paris.

62 Logo of the newspaper *Al-Ahram*. Michel Butor, photo, c. 1950. Coll. Grasset. All rights reserved.

63 G. Flaubert, engraving/wood, 19th century. © Bibl. nat., Paris. *Dancer*, engraving, in *Description de l'Égypte*. Gallimard archive.

64 Ruins on *Elephantine Island*, D. Vivant Denon, litho, in *Voyage Dans la Basse and Haute-Égypte*, 1802. Gallimard archive.

65 *The Pyramids of Giza*, David Roberts, litho, 19th century. Gallimard archive.

66 Pyramids of Giza, *Temple of Wadi es-Sebua*, Necropolis of Thebes. © Y. Arthus-Bertrand/ Altitudes.

67 Philae, *Deir el-Bahari, the Temple of Hatfu.* © *Idem.*

68 *Mineral formations* near a lake near Siwa, *Cemetery in the Nile Delta*, *Sand dunes.* © *idem.*

69 Shores of *Lake Nasser*, *Harvesting and bailing wheat, Valley of the Kings.* © *idem.*

70 *The citadel*, *Market in the Faiyum*, *Cemetery in Aswan.* © *idem.*

71 *Alexandria lighthouse*, A. Manesson Mallet, engraving, in *Description de l'Unic.*, 1683. © J.-L. Charmet.

72–173 Frontispiece *Valley of the Nile from Alexandria to the Second Cataract*, H. Moreau, litho, in *Panorama d'Égypte and Nubie*, 1841. © Bibl. nat., Paris.

74 Alexandria, *the harbor.* © G. Degeorge.

75 *The Foundation of Alexandria*, Spinello Aretino, fresco, 16th century. Sienna, Pallazzo Pubblico. © Giraudon.

76 *The Capture of Alexandria*, image d'Épinal, 19th century. Coll. musée Carnavalet, Paris. © J.-L. Charmet. *Façade of a house in the Turkish quarter.* © G. Degeorge.

77 *Fort Qaitbay*, photo, early 20th century. © Roger-Viollet. *Fort Qaitbay*. © G. Degeorge.

78 *Abu el-Abbas el-Mursi Mosque.* © R.

Zéboulon. *Idem, entrance.* © Explorer. *Abu el-Abbas Mosque*, photo, early 19th century. © Roger-Viollet.

179 *Menasce Temple , Jacob Sasson Temple, Elianou Hazan Temple*, postcards, early 20th century. © R. Zéboulon. *Street in the Turkish quarter*, photo, early 20th century. © Roger-Viollet.

180 *British bombardment of Alexandria* , image D'Épinal, 19th century. © J.-L. Charmet.

181 *Royal Stock Exchange*, photo, early 20th century. © Roger-Viollet. *House of Azir Osman Aga*, P. Coste, watercolor, 1820. Bibl. Saint-Charles, Marseilles. Ph. J. Bernard/ Gallimard. *Midan at-Tahrir (Liberation Square)*, photo. © Roger-Viollet.

182 *Map of Alexandria*, 17th century. Private coll. © Édimédia. *Attarine Mosque*, photo, early 20th century. © Roger-Viollet.

183 Roman theater. © P. Chapuis/Rapho. Roman excavations. © G. Degeorge. *Cleopatra's obelisk*, D. Vivant Denon, watercolor, late 18th century. A. & V. Museum. © Édimédia.

184–185 *View of Alexandria from the fort of Kom el-Dikka with the Nabi Daniel mosque*, photo. © Roger-Viollet. **184** Midan Saad Zaghlul. © G. Degeorge. Synagogue, interior © R. Zéboulon. Alexandria, synagogue. © F. El-Khoury/ Rapho.

185 *Portrait of Constantine Cavafy*, drawing, 20th century. Coll. restaurant l'Élite. © R. Zéboulon. Graeco-Roman Museum, façade. *Idem.*

186–187 Hadrien, Harpocrates, Alexandria glass, funeral mask, tanagra, mosaic, goblet, grotesque figurines, tanagra. © Éditions Sérapis, Alexandria.

188 *Bab Rosetta*, L. Mayer, litho, in *Vues d'Égypte*, 1802. © Bibl. nat., Paris.

189 Museum of Modern Art, Alexandria. © P. Chapuis/Rapho. *Mosque, ancient*

Alexandria, L. Mayer, litho, in *Vues d'Égypte*, 1802. © Bibl. nat., Paris.

190–191 *Mahmudiya Canal*, photo, early 20th century. © Roger-Viollet. **191** *Tent of Ibrahim Pasha, camp for directing work on the great canal*, P. Coste, watercolor, 1820. Bibl. Saint-Charles, Marseilles. Ph. J. Bernard/ Gallimard. Faculty of Engineering, façade and details. © P. Chapuis/Rapho.

192 *Exterior of the catacombs*, L. Mayer, litho, in *Vues d'Égypte*, 1802. © Bibl. nat., Paris. Catacombs of Kom el-Shogafa, doorway and entrance hall. © Dagli-Orti.

193 *Idem*, details. © G. Degeorge.

194–195 *Pompey's Pillar*, L. Mayer, litho, in *Vues d'Égypte*, 1802. Coll. Bibl. Arts déco, Paris. © J.-L. Charmet.

195 Alexandria beach, beach huts, cabins and façade of an apartment building on the Corniche. © Explorer.

196 Mosaic. © Éditions Sérapis, Alexandria.

196–197 *Ruins of the Ptolemaic (Great) Library*, L. Mayer, litho, in *Vues d'Égypte*, 1802. © Bibl. nat., Paris.

197 Alexandria. © Aunos/Gamma. Entrance to Ramleh Station. © R. Zéboulon.

198–199 *Fort and harbor at Abukir*, L. Mayer, litho, in *Vues d'Égypte*, 1802. © Bibl. nat, Paris.

198 Hypogeum at Mustafa Pasha. © Dagli-Orti. Shatby cemetery. © R. Zéboulon.

199 *Murat defeating the Turks at Abukir*, oil/canvas, 19th century. © Édimédia. Abukir, carrioles. © R. Zéboulon.

200 Hypogeum of El-Ouardian. © Dagli-Orti. Palace of El-Mex, Bonfils, photo, 1870. © Bibl. nat., Paris.

201 Villa Lachin. © M. Volait. Agami beach. © J. Marthelot/Scope.

202 Karm Abu Mina, interior of basilica, general view, wine press. © Éditions Sérapis, Alexandria.

203 Icon of Saint Menas. Coptic Museum, Cairo. Lake Mariut.

© J. Marthelot/Scope. **204** El-Alamein, after Rommel's retreat, photo, 1942. © Tallandi, Paris. German cannon recovered on the El-Alamein. Vanino archive, idem. Villa. © M. Volait. German troops at El-Alamein, photo, in *L'Illustration*, 1942. © L. of Selva/Tapabor.

205 Suez Canal, Henri de Montant, litho, in *Le Petit Parisien*, 1870. © L. of Selva/Tapabor.

208 *Deir Amba-Bischoi*, interior, watercolor, in *Commission d'Égypte*, 1799. © Bibl. nat., Paris, crown used for mass © W. Louvet. Kellia. © MSAC.

209 *Views of Deir es-Suriani*, Deir Amba Bishoi and Deir Abu Makaryus, *communion bread*, watercolors, in *Commission d'Égypte*, 1799. © Bibl. nat., Paris. Church of Deir Amba Baramus. © W. Louvet.

210 *Dancing at Ned Sile* and *Nile ferry near Ned Sile*, L. Mayer,lithos, in *Vues d'Égypte*, 1802. © Bibl. nat., Paris.

210–211 *Egyptian summer residence on the Menuf Canal*, idem.

211 Tanta, mosque Sidi Ahmad el-Badawi, postcard, early 20th century. Gallimard archive.

212 *The Market at Dessouk*, G. Ebers, litho, in *l'Égypte*, 1880. © Édimédia. Fuwa, P. Coste, watercolor, 1820. Bibl. Saint-Charles, Marseilles. Ph. J. Bernard/ Gallimard.

213 Buto, Sekhmet. © Burgunder. Bouto, Ramesses II, Sekhmet and stela of Thutmose III. © Burgunder. Bouto. © J. L. Bovot.

214 Rosetta, café and minaret. © G. Degeorge.

214–215 *Rosetta*, L. Mayer, litho, in *Vues d'Égypte*, 1802. © Bibl. nat., Paris.

215 Houses in Rosetta, litho, in *Description de l'Égypte*. Gallimard archive.

216 *Fish, serpent and figure*, J.-F. Champollion, hieroglyphs, in *Principes généraux de l'écriture sacrée egyptianne*, facsimile of the 1841 edition, Institut d'Orient. *Portrait of Champollion the Younger*, L. Cogniet, 19th century. Louvre. © Giraudon. Title page of *Monuments de l'Égypte et de la Nubie*, Champollion the Younger, 1845. Ph. Delebecque/ Gallimard. Table of phonetic symbols of hieroglyphics and demotic script, J.-F. Champollion. © Bibl. nat., Paris.

217 The Rosetta Stone, 196 BC British Museum, London. © Dagli-Orti. Figure, J.-F. Champollion, hieroglyphs, in *Principes généraux*. Paris. Manuscript of the *"Grammaire égyptienne"*, idem. © Bibl. nat., Paris.

218–219 Amenhotep III, Nekhbet and Horus, J.-F. Champollion, litho, in *Monuments de l'Égypte et de la Nubie*. © Bibl. nat., Paris.

218 Manuscript of the *"Grammaire égyptienne"*. © idem.

219 Sallier papyrus, detail. © British Museum, London. Example of demotic script, J.-F. Champollion. © Bibl. nat., Paris.

220 Behbeit el-Hagar, stela and ruins. © J.-L. Bovot. *Mansura, the port of Talkha*, photo, early 20th century. © Roger-Violet.

221 Mansura, general view and Salih Ayyub Mosque, idem.

222–223 View of Damietta, J.-J. Rifaud, litho, 1830. Coll. centre Golénischeff.

222 Battle between Saracens and Christians, manuscript. © Bodleian Library. *Early morning in Damietta*, R. Talbot-Kelly, watercolor, in *Égypte*, 1912. © Édimédia.

223 The tomb of the Sheikhs at Damietta, idem.

224–225 View of Belbeis, litho, in *Description de l'Égypte*. Gallimard archive.

224 Zagazig, general view, postcard, early 20th century. © P. Geday. Bubastis. © E. Lessing/ Magnum.

225 Zagazig region, saqia and pigeon loft. © J. Marthelot/Scope. Tanis, entrance of the Temple of Amon and statue of Ramesses II. © E. Lessing/Magnum.

226 Tanis: tomb of Psusennes, bas-relief, sarcophagus, tomb of Osorkon-Takelot,

painted bas-relief, colossus from the Great Temple. © J.-L. Bovot.

227 Tanis: granite block, Ramessid colossus, tomb of Psusennes, bas-relief. © J.-L. Bovot.

228 Portrait of Saïd Pasha, photo, 19th century. © Bibl. nat., Paris. *The Suez Canal*, map, in *Qui est l'ennemi de la France à trac. l'Histoire*, anti-British review published during World War Two. © Édimédia. *Canal of Suez*, G. Nicole, map in *Voyage pittoresque à trac. The Suez Canal*, 1869. © L. de Selva/Tapabor.

229 Panoramic view of the Isthmus of Suez showing the route of the Canal, engraving based on plan by Linant and Mougel, 1856. © Bibl. nat., Paris. *Pavilion of the Isthmus of Suez, a lecture by M. of Lesseps*, engraving, 1867 (World Fair). © L. of Selva/Tapabor.

230 Office of the Suez Canal, postcard, late 19th century. Coll. S. Noweir. *Ferdinand de Lesseps*, engraving, in *L'Illustration*, 1864. © Keystone.

231 Mobile machine used during the excavation of the Suez Canal, *Transporting a dredger on the Isthmus of Suez, Cutting through the Isthmus of Suez*, engravings, in *L'Illustration*, 1864–61–59. © Keystone. *A trench on the Suez Canal*, engraving, in *Les Grands travaux du siècle*, J. B. Dumont, 1891. *Ship canal at Kantara*, engraving, in *L'Illustration*, 1869. Gallimard archive.

232–233 Official convoy for the inauguration of the Suez Canal at El-Guisr, J. Didi after Riou, litho, c. 1870. Bibl. des Arts déco, Paris. © J. L. Charmet.

232 Inauguration of the canal of Isthmus of Suez, litho, 19th century. Bibl. des Arts déco, Paris. © J.-L. Charmet. *The Final Blow delivered by Ali Pasha to unite the two seas*, engraving after Riou, in *L'Illustration*. © Keystone.

233 The fleet at anchor

in the Bitter Lakes, litho after Riou, 1869. © L. of Selva/Tapabor. *The Suez Canal*, H. of Montant, litho, in *Le Petit Parisien*, 1870. © L. of Selva/Tapabor.

234–235 Port Said, the port and Terrace of the Casino Palace Hotel, photos, early 20th century. © Roger-Violet.

234 Port Said, houses. © Éditions Sérapis, Alexandria.

235 Suez, postcard © L. of Selva/Tapabor.

236 Ismaïliya, villa of Ferdinand Lesseps. © J.-L. Bovot. *The Bazaar of Suez*, J. Didi after Riou, litho, c. 1870. Bibl. des Arts déco, Paris. © J. L. Charmet. *Suez, Colmar Street, Ismaïliya, The Canal*, postcards © L. de Selva/Tapabor.

237 St Catherine's Monastery © G. Degeorge.

238 Bedouin women from the Aleiqa tribe. © N. Levallois. Bedouin family in their tent. © G. Sioen/ Rapho.

240 Desert landscape, Léon Bonnat, oil/canvas, 19th century.© House of Pierre Loti, Rochefort. *The Ten Commandments* psalter of Ingborg of Denmark. Musée Condé, Chantilly. © Giraudon. *General view of the oasis of the Springs of Moses*, photo, early 20th century. © J. Boyer/Roger-Violet.

241 The Flight of the Israelites, G. Mastaert, oil/canvas. © Édimédia.

242 Qal'at el-Gindi. © Levallois. Stela from the Temple of Hathor at Sarabit el-Khadim. © J. P. Garcin/ Diaf. Qal'at el-Jundi. © Éditions Sérapis, Alexandria. Oasis of Feiran.© Sioen/Rapho.

243 Oasis of Wadi Feiran.© Gerster/Rapho. View of Sinai. © R. Zébouloum. Monastery of Mount Sinai photo, early 20th century. © Roger-Violet.

244 St Catherine's Monastery, details. © G. Degeorge. St Catherine's Library, detail. © N. Levallois. *Monks from St Catherine's Monastery*, photo, early 20th century. © Harlingue-Violet.

244–245 St Catherine's Monastery, David Roberts, litho, 19th

century. Gallimard archive.

245 St Catherine's Monastery. © G. Degeorge. *Ancient means of entering St Catherine's*, photo, early 20th century. © Harlingue-Violet.

246 Moses receiving the Ten Commandments, Brother Jacques Le Grant, miniature, in *De bonnes Mœures*, 15th century. © Bibl. nat., Paris.

246–247 View of Mour Sinai, E. Lear, oil/canvas, 19th century. © ACR Éditions.

247 Garden of Elijah, Mount Sinai.© C. Sénéchal/Diaf. Chapel on Mount Sinai. © W. Louvet. *Crossing the Red Sea*, illuminated French Bible. Assise, Bibl. communale. © Roger-Violet. From the path on Mount Sinai. © C. Sénéchal/Diaf. Steps to the summit of Mount Sinai. © idem. Summit o Mount Sinai. © Garcin/Diaf. *Father Elijah at the top of the steps t the summit of Mount Sinai*. © Roger-Violet.

248 Nuweiba region, Colored Canyon © Sénéchal/Diaf. Nuweiba region. idem. Bedouin fishermen. © Gerster/ Rapho.

249 Aqaba, Léon Bonnat, oil/canvas, 19th century. © Musée Francisque-Mandet, Riom.Geziret Pharaon. © Gerster/ Rapho. Coral Island. © B. Degroise/Diaf. Geziret Fara'un.© N. Levallois.

250 El-Qantara, postcards, early 20th century. © L. of Selva/ Tapabor

250–251 Bedouins from El-Qantara, postcard Coll. L. Claude, Paris.

251 Coronation of Baldwin I, William of Ty illumination in *Histoire Du Passage Outremer*. © Bibl. nat., Paris, western manuscripts. Bedouin from El-Qantara, postcard Coll L. Claude, Paris.

252 Sinai, detail. © B. Régent/Diaf. El-Arich, Date harvest. © M. Bar Am/Magnum. *View of North Sinai*, Wilkinson, watercolor, 19th century. © Bibl. nat., Paris.

253 The Oasis, Léon Belly, oil/canvas, 1863. Coll. Alain Lesieutre,

LIST OF ILLUSTRATIONS

aris. © ACR Éditions, Courbevoie.
54 Date Palm. © N. Levallois. Oasis of Siwa, rying dates. © C. énéchal/Diaf.
55 Palm, papyrus. © N. Levallois.
56 Siwa Oasis, bridal own and jewelry. © N. evallois. Siwa Oasis, eneral view. © C. énéchal/Diaf.
57 Temple of Umm l-Ubeydah. © C. énéchal/Diaf. Minaret nd temple of Aghurmi. © N. Levallois. 'leopatra's ool. © C. Sénéchal/ iaf.
58 Hot springs of arafra.© C. Munoz. arafra Oasis. © M.-C. ordaz. White Desert. © C. Munoz.
59 El-Qasr, nausoleums. © C. Aunoz. Balat. © evault/IREMAM, Aix-n-Provence. Dakhla, ninaret. © C. Munoz.
60 Desert, "melons". © G. Gerster/Rapho. I-Bagawat, Nestorian hapels. © N. Levallois.
60–261 Kharga Oasis, Frédéric Cailliaud, engraving, in Voyages à l'Oasis de hebes et dans les éserts, 1818. © Bibl. nat., Paris.
61 Umm el-Dabadib, ortress and village. © N. Levallois.
262 Umm Labakha, oman fortress. © N. Levallois. Kargha, uq. © W. Louvet.
63 Qasr el-Ghueida, tolemaic temple. © N. Levallois. Dush, emple. © W. Louvet. ush, treasure. © J.-F. Gout/IFAO.
64 Monastery of t Antony, interior. © Revault/ IREMAM, ix-en-Provence.
64–265 Deserts of ower Thebaid, Daniel icard, watercolor map, 717. © Bibl. nat., Paris.
66 View from the rabian mountains, atercolor, in ʻommission d'Égypte, 799. © Bibl. nat., Paris. emple of Sérapis. © N. evallois.
67 Shores of the Red ea, nets. © N. evallois. Hurghada. © of Selva/ Tapabor.
lons Claudianus. © N. Levallois.
68 Emerald mines of ʻebel Zabarah, detail, rédéric Cailliaud, litho, ↑ Voyages à l'Oasis de ʻhebes et dans les

déserts, 1818. © Bibl. nat., Paris. Wadi Hammamat.
© N. Levallois. Quseir, hotel and port. © P. Chapuis/Rapho. Quseir, William Princep, watercolor, 1842. Private coll. © ACR Éditions, Courbevoie.
269 The Pyramids of Giza. © Y. Travert.
270–271 Three Arabs from Cairo, watercolor, in Description de l'Empire turc, c. 1600. © J.-L. Charmet. Map of Cairo, engraving, late 16th century. © Bibl. nat., Paris.
270 Initial "O" with Saladin brandishing his sword, in Tauner Manuscript © Bodleian Library. Horsemen practising with lances, illumination, in Manuscrit mamelouk sur la Chevalerie, 15th century. Islamic Museum, Cairo. Ph. Gallimard.
271 View of the aqueduct, Cairo, P. Coste, engraving in Architecture arabe, © Bibl. nat., Paris. Obelisk at Heliopolis, anonymous, watercolor,18th century. © Cabinet des Arts graph., Louvre. Ph. P. Léger. Battle of the Pyramids, Château de Cailles (dup. Gallimard).
272 Qasr el-Nil barracks, Zangaki, photo, 19th century. Coll. D. Roche.
273 Hind Rostom in "Cairo Station" directed by Yussef Shahin, 1957. © Yves Thoraval. Hind Rostom and the "Diana" cinema, idem, photo by Studios Dorès, Alexandria, 1933. Coll. Mercèdes Volait.
274 The Old Opera House, Van-Léo, photo, 1946. Midan Ezbekiya, © P. Chapuis/Rapho, 1992. Clot Bey and Shari' Mohammed-Ali. idem.
274–275 Midan Ezbekiya, engraving, in Description de l'Égypte. Gallimard archive.
275 Shepheard's Hotel, photo, in Burton Holmes Travelogues, 1910. Gallimard archive. Smoking room in Shepheard's Hotel, detail, engraving, in The Graphic, 1880. © Roger-Viollet.
276 Egyptian Museum, main gallery. © P. Chapuis/Rapho. tomb of Tutankhamun, fresco, detail. © A. Held/Ziolo.

Chair of Sitamun, wood inlaid with gold and bronze. © E. Lessing/ Magnum.
276–277 Monumental statue. © P. Chapuis/ Rapho.
277 Chest of Tutankhamun, detail. © A. Held. Funerary mask of Tutankhamun. © S. Grandadam. Chest of Tutankhamun, fishing with bow and arrow. © M. Babey/Artephot. Canopic jar, cover repr. Tutankhamun. © E. Lessing/Magnum.
278 Head of Nefertiti. © E. Lessing/Magnum. Statue of Prince Rahotep and his wife Nofret, autochrome, 1914. © Musée Albert-Kahn. Akhenaten, illustration in The Mystery of the Great Pyramid, E. P. Jacobs. © Éditions Blake & Mortimer.
278–279 Model from the tomb of Meketre, inspection of cattle, painted wood . © Babsy/ Artephot.
279 Sarcophagus, autochrome, 1914. © Musée Albert-Kahn, Dept. of Hauts-de-Seine. Nefertiti, unfinished head. © Ph. Roland/Artephot.
280 Midan at-Tahrir and the Egyptian Museum, postcard, c. 1960. © J.-L. Arnaud. Cairo, Société of Géographie, detail of the façade and conference.hall © P. Chapuis/Rapho. Abdin Palace, Zangaki, photo, 19th century. © Bibl. nat., Paris. Abdin Palace. © L. of Selva/Tapabor.
281 Boats on the Nile, engraving, 19th century. Coll. Société de Géographie. © P. Chapuis/Rapho. Saad Zaghlul, Egyptian postage stamp, 1977. Certificate of subscription to Saad Zaghlul Mausoleum El Mosawar no. 171. Coll. C. Roussillon.
282 Modern Cairo © P. Chapuis/Rapho. Fêtes de Ghezireh, A. Birck, poster, 1886. © L. of Selva/Tapabor. Gezira Palace Hotel, postcard, early 20th century. Coll. CEDEJ, Cairo.
283 Plan of Roda Island, F.-L. Norden, engraving, in Voyage D'Égypte et de Nubie, 1755. © Bibl. nat., Paris. Manyal Palace, ext. and int. © P. Chapuis/

Rapho. The Nilometer engraving, early 19th century. Coll. Bibl. Arts déco. © J.-L. Charmet.
284 Mohammed Hassanein Haykal in 1940. Coll. of the Newspaper Al-Ahram, Cairo. Journal Al-Ahram, title. Offices of Al-Ahram. Ph. P. Godeau/Gallimard. Shubra Palace, detail of fountain. © P. Chapuis/ Rapho.
285 Heliopolis, basilica, villa and palace, postcards, early. 20th century. Coll. CEDEJ, Cairo. Villa of Baron Empain (detail of décor and elevation), G.-L. Claude, watercolor model, 1910. Coll Louise Claude. Ph. D. Doyle/ Gallimard.
286 Cover of El-Suqariya, a novel by Naguib Mahfouz, Egyptian edition. Friday prayer in the El-Hussein Mosque. © Abbas/Magnum, 1989. El-Hussein Mosque. © Y. Arthus-Bertrand/ Altitude.
287 Naguib Mahfouz, caricature by Salah Enani. © P. Godeau. El-Fishawi. © B. Barbey/Magnum.
288 An-Nasir Muhammed Medersa, detail. © G. Degeorge. Qala'un Medersa, W. Bartlett, watercolor, 1848. © V. & A. Museum, London.
289 Qala'un Medersa: detail of the mihrab, and funeral chamber of Qala'un. Barquq Medersa: prayer hall and fountain. © G. Degeorge. Le Kaaba and surrounding area, decoration in the Katkhuda Sabil-kuttab, Prisse D'Avennes, litho, in L'Art arabe, © Bibl. nat., Paris.
290 Bab el-Futuh, courtyard of Beit as-Suhaymi. © G. Degeorge. Beit el-Suhaymi, detail, 1978. © Revault/IREMAM. Beit el-Suhaymi (qaa). © G. Degeorge.
290–291 Ruins of the Caliph Hakim Mosque, Cairo, P. Marilhat, oil/canvas, Louvre. © Lauros-Giraudon.
291 Bab el-Futuh. © G. Degeorge. El-Aqmar Mosque . © Revault/ IREMAM. El-Hakim Mosque . © L. of Selva/ Tapabor.

LIST OF ILLUSTRATIONS ◆

292 Baibars Khanqa . © B. of Saint-Martin. *Lamp from the tomb of the Sultan Baibars II*, Prisse D'Avennes, litho, in *L'Art arabe.* © Bibl. nat., Paris. Qaitbay Wakala, façade and gateway, Emir Qara Sunqur Medersa. © G. Degeorge.

293 *Bab an-Nasr*, David Roberts, watercolor, 1839. © Christie's Colour Library, London. Musafirkhane Palace.© G. Degeorge.

294 Cairo, El-Azhar suq. © C. Roussillon.

295 El-Azhar Mosque, minaret 1 & 3. © G. Degeorge. *idem*, 2 & 4 © S. Grandadam. *Minarets of the El-Azhar Mosque*, Zangaki, photo, c. 1870. Coll. Denis Roche.

296 El-Ghuri Medersa. © G. Degeorge. *El-Ghuri Mosque and Medersa*, watercolor photo, in *Mosques of Egypt*, 1949. Coll. S. Noweir.

297 *Cairo, int. courtyard of Gamal el-Din*, G.-L. Claude, watercolor, 1910. Coll. L. Claude. Ph. D. Doyle/ Gallimard. Gamal el-Din, gateway and courtyard. © Revault/ IREMAM.

298 *El-Mu'ayyad Mosque*, photo. © Roger-Viollet. El-Mu'ayyad Mosque. © G. Degeorge.

298–299 *El-Mu'ayyad Mosque, external view , sanctuary and prayer hall with mihrab and minbar.* P. Coste, litho, in *Architecture arabe.* © Bibl. nat., Paris.

299 *Palace of Radwn Bey*, Frank Dillon, watercolor, c. 1860.© V. & A. Museum. *As-Salih Talai Mosque*, photo, in *Mosques of Egypt*, 1949. Coll. S. Noweir. Mosque Salih Talaï, capital. © G. Degeorge.

300 El-Mihmandar Mosque, Umm el-Sultan Sha'ban Medersa. Ph. P. Godeau/Gallimard. *Qijmas el-Ishaqi Mosque* , photo, in *Mosques of Egypt*, 1949. Coll. S. Noweir.

301 El-Maridani Mosque, entrance. © S. Grandadam. El-Maridani Mosque. Ph. P. Godeau/ Gallimard. Kiriani mosque. © J. G. Ross/ Rapho. er-Razzaz Palace, 1978. © Revault/IREMAM, Aix-en-Provence.

302 *At prayer in the Blue Mosque, detail*, W. C. Horsley, oil/canvas, 1878. Private coll. © ACR Éditions, Courbevoie. Aqsunqur Mosque, minbar and mihrab. © G. Degeorge. View of Cairo from the Blue Mosque. © S. Noweir.

303 Mosquéth D'Aqsunqur, detail of ceramics. © G. Degeorge. El-Mu'ayyad mauristan. © Revault/IREMAM, Aix-en-Provence.

304 Citadel, tower on the enclosure wall. © Travert/ Gallimard. Lions' Tower, detail. Ph. P. Godeau/ Gallimard.

304–305 *View of the Midan el Rumeyleh and the Citadel*, engraving, in *Description de l'Égypte.* Gallimard archive.

305 Mohammed Ali Mosque. Ph. Y. Travert/ Gallimard.

306 *An-Nasir Mohammed Mosque*, postcard, early 20th century. Coll. S. Noweir. An-Nasir Mohammed Mosque. © G. Degeorge. *Gate of the Citadel*, L. A. Crapelet, watercolor, c. 1870. Dépt. Arts graph., Louvre. Ph. P. Léger.

307 Suleyman Pasha Mosque, cupola. Ph. P. Godeau/Gallimard. *Suleyman Pasha*, Lassalles, litho, 19th century. Bibl. Arts déco, Paris. © J.-L. Charmet. Suleyman Pasha Mosque, int. and entrance to the mausoleum. Ph. P. Godeau/Gallimard.

308 Amir Akhur Mosque, minbar and detail. © G. Degeorge. Cairo. © Silvester/Rapho.

309 In the Sultan Hassan medersa. © S. Grandadam. *View of Grand Cairo*, Henry Salt, litho, 1809. © Bibl. nat., Paris.

310 Yashbak Min Mahdi Palace, photo, 1976. © Revault/IREMAM, Aix-en-Provence. Yachbak Min Mahdi Palace. Ph. P. Godeau/ Gallimard. Amir Taz Palace. © Revault/ IREMAM, Aix-en-Provence. Hassan Bodega Mosque . © G. Degeorge.

311 *Zikr dancing*, engraving, in *L'Égypte* de Gaston Maspero, 1881. *Dervish Monastery*, P. Coste, watercolor, 1822. Bibl.

Saint-Charles, Marseilles. Ph. J. Bernard/Gallimard. Sheikhu Medersa, ceiling. Ph. P. Godeau/Gallimard. Sheikhu Khanqa © G. Degeorge.

312 Ibn Tulun Mosque, details of the mihrab. © G. Degeorge. Ibn Tulun Mosque. © Burri/Magnum.

312–313 *General view of the ruins of Ibn Tulun Mosque*, F. Mason-Good, photo, 1868. Coll. D. Roche.

313 Ibn Tulun Mosque, detail of the mihrab, Sangar el-Gaouli Mausoleum. © G.Degeorge.

314 *French Institute in Cairo*, detail, watercolor, in *Commission d'Égypte*, 1799. Bibl. nat., Paris. Midan as-Sayyida Zeinab. © S. Noweir. As-Sayyida Zeinab. CL. Gallimard. *As-Sayyida Zeinab Mosque*, photo, in *Mosques of Egypt*, 1948. Coll. S. Noweir

315 *French Institute*, Balland, engraving, 19th century. © Roger-Viollet. *View of casinos on the El-Khalig Canal*, Pascal Coste, litho, in *Architecture arabe.* © Bibl. nat., Paris. *Tram in the Midan as-Sayyida Zeinab*, photo, c. 1930. © Roger-Viollet.

316 *Façade of the Islamic Museum*, autochrome, 1914. © Musée Albert-Kahn, Boulogne. Terracotta dish. Coll. Islamic Museum, Cairo. © S. Sharouni, Cairo. Sculpture of a donkey, Astrolabe. © *Idem.*

317 Ceramic tiles decorating a Persian mihrab, 14th century. © G. Degeorge. Lamp. © S. Sharouni. Mameluke gateway, detail of decoration, 14th century. © G. Degeorge. Glass lamp from mosque. *Medicinal plants*, miniature, Coll. Islamic Museum, Cairo. © S. Sharouni.

318 *View of Old Cairo*, Norden, engraving, in *Voyage de Norden*, 1755. © Bibl. nat., Paris. Ruins of the fortifications of Babylon. © O. Brésard. Ruins of Babylon below the El-Muallaka church. © W. Louvet.

319 El-Muallaka church, ext. view © O. Brésard. El-Muallaka church, interior. Ph. P. Godeau/Gallimard. Icons of El-Muallaka church. © Roussillon.

320 Convent of St George, detail of door, Church of the Virgin, façade and detail. Ph. P. Godeau/Gallimard.

321 St Barbara's Church, detail. Ph. Gallimard. St Barbara's Church. Ph. P. Godeau/Gallimard. Synagogue, Tora © O. Brésard. Synagogue, detail. Ph. P. Godeau/Gallimard.

322 Coptic cloth, detail, icon showing two saints Abrakaad and Ogbani wearing animal masks. © S. Sharouni. Wall fresco. © W. Louvet. Icon representing St Mercurius. © S. Sharouni. Parchment of magical texts, detail. © G. Degeorge.

323 Bronze oil lamp. © S. Sharouni. Coptic cloth.© *idem.* Coptic cloth, detail. © G. Degeorge.

324 *General view of Cairo*, autochrome, 1914. © Musée Albert-Kahn, Dépt of Hauts-de-Seine.

324–325 Church of Abu Seifen, icons, details, marquetry, details. © J.-L. Aunos.

326 *The Tombs of the Caliphs*, D. Vivant Denon, engraving, in *Voyage Dans la basse et la Haute-Égypte*, 1802. © Bibl. nat., Paris. Khound Toughay Mausoleum. © Wessam Mehanna/Gallimard.

327 *Qaitbay Mosque*, postcard., early 20th century. Coll. S. Noweir. *Interior view of Qaitbay Mosque*, Pascal Coste, litho, in *Architecture arabe.* © Bibl. nat., Paris. *Minaret of the Qaitbay Mosque*, L. A. Crapelet, watercolor drawing, c.1870. Louvre, Dépt. Arts graph. Ph. P. Léger.

328–329 *Tombs of the Sultans Barsbey, Inal and Ounas*, minaret of the Sultan Inal, G.-L. Claude, watercolors and oil/canvas (3 and 5), 1910. Coll. L. Claude, Paris. Ph. D. Doyle/Gallimard.

328 Mausoleum of Qaitbay, prayer hall and detail of mirhab.

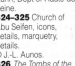

◆ LIST OF ILLUSTRATIONS

© G. Degeorges. **329** *Arab wedding at the Tombs of the Caliphs*, photo, early 20th century. © Roger-Viollet.
330 El-Bacha Hoch. © W. Mahanna/Gallimard. Sultaniya. © Revault/ IREMAM. Khalwati. © Hicham Labib, Cairo.
331 *Jebel Mokkatam*, Lehnart & Landrock, photo, c. 1930. Gallimard archive. Mameluke Tombs, general view and details. © P. Chapuis/Rapho.
332–333 Reconstruction of the site of Memphis, J.-Ph. Golvin, watercolor drawing.
333 Memphis, ruins of the temple of Ptah. © P. Chapuis/Rapho. *Ramesses II*. © S. Grandadam.
334 Reconstruction of the site of the Pyramids of Giza, J.-C. Golvin, watercolor drawing.
334–335 *Tourists at the Pyramids*, label, c. 1914. Private coll. © J. L. Charmet.
335 *Road to the Pyramids*, autochrome, 1914. © Musée Albert-Kahn, Dépt. of Hauts-de-Seine. Site of the pyramids. © Y. Arthus-Bertrand/Altitude.
336 *Plan of the interior of the Great Pyramid*, B. de Maillet, engraving, in *Description de l'Égypte*, 1735. © Bibl. nat., Paris. *Pyramids of Memphis*, litho, in *Description de l'Égypte*. Gallimard archive.
336–337 *The Pyramids of Giza*, F. Frith, photo, 1858–1859. © Royal Photographic Soc., Bath.
337 *Tourists climbing the Pyramid of Khufu*, photo, c. 1900. Coll. Van Léo, Cairo.
338 *View from the top of the Great Pyramid of Giza, Underground chamber near the Pyramids, chamber and sarcophagus in the Great Pyramid, first and second pyramids of Giza*, L. Mayer, lithos, in *Vues d'Égypte*, 1802. Coll. Collège de France, Paris.
339 *Interior of the Great Pyramid*, idem. © Bibl. nat., Paris.
340 *Pyramids of Giza*. © Yvan Travert. *Great chamber and entrance of the second pyramid of Giza*, Belzoni,

engraving, 1810. Coll. Collège de France, Paris.
341 *The Sphinx*, J.-P. Sebah, photo, c. 1880. Coll. L. Claude.
342–343 *Head of the Great Sphinx*, L. Mayer, litho, in *Vues d'Égypte*, 1802. Coll. Collège de France, bibl. Champollion. *Oedipus*, Jean-Léon Gérôme, oil/canvas, 19th century. Club des Diplomates, Cairo. © P. Chapuis/Rapho. *The Sphinx*, Emile Prisse D'Avenue, watercolor. Bibl. nat. © Édimédia. *Head of the Great Sphinx and the Pyramids of Giza*, David Roberts, litho, 19th century. © S. Grandadam. *Profile of the Head of the Great Sphinx*, Frederick Ludvig Norden, engraving, mid 18th century. The Schuster Gallery, London. © Édimédia. *View of the Head of the Great Sphinx and the Second Pyramid* , L.-F. Cassas, c. 1801. © Musée Des Beaux-Arts, Tours. *The Sphinx and the Pyramid of Giza*, Louis-Amable-Crapelet, drawing, 1853. Cabinet des Arts graphiques, Louvre. Ph. P. Léger. *"Simoon" in the Desert*, David Roberts, print, 19th century. © S. Grandadam.
344 Reconstruction of the site of Saqqara, J.-C. Golvin, watercolor drawing. Wissa Wassef workshops. © L. de Selva/Tapabor. Carpets from the Wissa Wassef workshops. © J.-C. Aunos.
344–345 *Nile landscape*, litho, in *Description de l'Égypte*. Gallimard arch.
345 Pyramid. © Dagli-Orti.
346 Saqqara: monastery of St Jeremiah and Pyramid of Djoser. © Y. Arthus-Bertrand/Altitude. Columns of the chapels. © P. Chapuis/Rapho.
346–347 J.-P. Lauer behind the "cobra" wall. © P. Chapuis/Rapho.
347 Temple and pyramid, excavators on the site of Saqqara, reopening of the Step Pyramid, idem.
348 King Djoser, painted limestone, Old Kingdom. Egyptian Museum, Cairo. **349** Plan of Saqqara,

entrance wing and façade of the House of the South J.-P. Lauer. Egyptian Department of Antiquities, Cairo. The "cobra" wall. © P. Chapuis/ Rapho.
350 *Entrance of the Serapeum*, engraving, in *Album of Mariette*, 19th century. Private coll. Serapeum, int. © P. Chapuis/Rapho.
351 Tomb of Nefer and Ka-Hay, bas-relief, the making and baking of bread. © Giraudon. *Interior of the Serapeum*, engraving, in *Album of Mariette*, 19th century. Private coll.
352 Pyramid of Mernere, detail of ceiling. © P. Chapuis/Rapho. Tomb of Aper-El. © P. Chapuis/ MAFB. Pyramid of Mernere. © P. Chapuis/ Rapho. Sarcophagus, Tomb of Aper-El. © A. Zivie/MAFB.
353 Pyramid of Meidum. © J. Marthelot/Scope.
355 *Pyramids of Dahshur*, P. Coste, watercolor, 1819. Bibl. Saint-Charles, Marseilles. Ph. J. Bernard/Gallimard. Dahshur, Pyramid of Amenemhet III, detail and general view from the east, Valley Temple and the Red Pyramid. © J.-L. Bovot.
356 *Dahshur, the Bent Pyramid*, watercolor, in *Commission d'Égypte*, 1799. © Bibl. nat., Paris. the Bent Pyramid, detail. Lisht, Pyramid of Senwosret I (from the south), Pyramid of Amenemhet I (north side), Pyramid of Amenemhet (from the northeast), Pyramid of Senwosret I (from the southwest). © J.-L. Bovot.
356–357 *The Geese of Meidum*, fresco, Pyramid of Meidum. Egyptian Museum, Cairo. © Held/Artephot.
357 Pyramid of Meidum. © Y. Arthus-Bertrand/ Altitude. Meidum, Pyramid of Snefru, access corridor. © J.-L. Bovot.
358–359 Pyramid of Illahun. © J.-L. Bovot.
358 Pyramid of Illahun. © Burgunder. Pyramid and mastabas. © J.-L. Bovot.
359 *Beni Suef on the*

Nile, Prosper Marilhat, oil/canvas, 1st half 19th century. Wallace collection, London. © Édimédia. *Beni Suef, the post office*, postcard, early 20th century. Coll. S. Noweir.
360 Necropolis of Ihnasiya el-Medina, general view, tomb, necropolis, columns. © J.-L. Bovot.
361 *Portrait of a young man*, painting/wood. Musée Du Louvre. © Held/ Artephot.
362 The god Sobek. © J. Livet.
363 The Faiyum. © P. Beuzen/Scope. Crocodile mummy, engraving, in *Description de l'Égype*. Gallimard archive.
364 *Portrait of two brothers*, painting on wood. Egyptian Museum, Cairo. © Faillet/Artephot. Artémidore, idem. Coll. British Museum,London.
365 *Portrait of a man and portrait of a woman*, painting on wood, 2nd century. Egyptian Museum, Cairo. *The Athlete*, idem. British Museum, London. Crocodilopolis, J. J. Rifaud, litho, in *Tableau de l'Égypte*, 1830. Gallimard archive.
366 Karanis, temple of the South and crocodile pool. © Burgunder.
367 Fishermen on the lake. © A. Gérard/Hoa-qui. The Faiyum, landscape. © Beuzen/Scope. The lake. © A. Gérard/Hoa-qui. The Faiyum. © Kumasegawa/Artephot. The Faiyum, village. © Beuzen/Scope. Lake Qarun. © Godeau-Aunos/Hoa-Qui. The Faiyum. © Kugasegawa/ Artephot.
368 Temple of Narmuthis, avenue of lion and sphinxes . © E. Charri.
368–369 *View of Medinet el-Faiyum*, J.-L. Gérôme, oil/wood, c. 1870. Private coll. © ACR Éditions, Courbevoie.
369 *View of an Egyptian temple near Birket el-Qarun*, Jomard, watercolor, in *Commission d'Égypte*, 1799. © Bibl. nat., Paris. Tebtunis. © E. Charri.
370 *Adam and Eve*, detail, fresco from the Faiyum, 10th century. Coptic Museum, Cairo. © Dagli-Orti. Pyramid of

Hawara. © Dagli-Orti.

371 *Dendera*, detail, David Roberts, litho, 19th century. Gallimard archive.

372 *El-Minya*, ancient mosque, autochrome, c. 1914. © Musée Albert-Kahn, Dépt. of Hauts-de-Seine. Arab cemebery near El-Minya. © Sioen/ Rapho.

373 *El-Minya, minaret of the Oudha Mosque*, autochrome, c. 1914. © Musée Albert-Kahn.

374 Beni Hassan, interior of the tombs, fresco. © J. Livet. Beni Hassan. © Marthelot/ Scope. *Rock-cut tombs at Beni Hassan*, Charles Vacher, watercolor, 1863. V. & A. Museum. © Édimédia.

375 *Antinoe*, litho, in *Description de l'Égypte*. Gallimard archive. *Gayet's excavations at Antinoe*, engraving, in *Supplément du "Petit Journal illustré"* © L. of Selva/Tapabor.

376 *Ruins of the Temple of Hermopolis*, anonymous, 19th century. V. & A. Mus., London. © Édimédia.

377 Tomb of Isadora. © Magnum. Tuna el-Jebel, painting. © J. Livet. tomb of Petosiris, interior. © Kumasegawa/Artephot. tomb of Pétosiris, exterior. © Burgunder.

378 Tell el-Amarna. © *idem*. Tell el-Amarna, stela and bust of Akhenaten. Egyptian Museum, Cairo. © E. Lessing/Magnum.

379 Site of Tell el-Amarna. © Sioen/Rapho Meir, the herdsman. © J. Livet.

380–381 *Saout*, photo, early 20th century. © Roger-Viollet.

380 Assiut region. © Marthelot/Scope. *Assiut*, the main mosque, David Roberts, litho, 19th century. © S Grandadam.

381 *Saout, plan and decorative details of the hypogea*, watercolor, in *Commission d'Égypte*, 1799. © Bibl. nat., Paris.

382–383 *Qaou el-Kebir, view of the temple*, litho, in *Description de l'Égypte*. Gallimard archive.

382 Monastery, entrance, interior and Temple of Atrhibis, the god Min. © P. Chapuis/Rapho.

383 Coptic monk and monastery. © P. Chapuis/ Rapho. Deri Amba Bishoi. © Sioen/Rapho.

384 El-Hawawish, tombs, frescos. © P. Chapuis/ Rapho.

384–385 *Girga*, Béchard, collotype, in *L'Égypte et la Nubie*, 1887. © Bibl. nat., Paris.

385 Akhmin, colossus of Ramesses II, colossus of Merit-Amon. © P. Chapuis/ Rapho.

386–387 Temple of Abydos, bas-reliefs, Isis, bee, Osiris, duck. © J. Livet.

388 Dendera, ceiling of the hypostyle hall. © Burgunder.

388–389 Dendera, Temple of Hathor. © Babey/Artephot.

389 Dendera, Cleopatra and Caesarion. © Dercheron/Artephot.

390 *Dendera*, David Roberts, litho, 1838. V. & A. Museum, London. © Édimédia. Dendera, Coptic Museum inside the Temple of Hathor. © Kumagesawa/Artephot. Dendera, court of the New Year. © J. P. Garcin/Diaf. Dendera, sacred lake. © J. Livet.

391 *Under the portico of the Temple of Dendera*, David Roberts, litho, 1838. V. & A. Museum. © Édimédia.

392 El-Ballas, earthenware jars. Qus, remains of the temple. © J. Livet. *Cathedral mosque of Qus, tympanum*, Prisse D'Avenue, litho, in *L'Art arabe*, 19th century. © Bibl. nat., Paris. Qus, ruins of a palace. © J. Livet.

393 *Avenue of Sphinxes* photo, early 20th century. © Roger-Viollet.

394–395 Reconstruction of Karnak and Luxor, J.-C. Golvin, watercolor drawing.

394 Countryside near Luxor. © J.-P. Garcin/ Diaf. Valley of Thebes. © P. Chapuis/Rapho.

395 Old Karnak. © J. Livet.

396–397 *The Ruins of Luxor on the Nile*, David Roberts, litho, 19th century. Gallimard archive. Luxor, entrance to the temple. © J. Livet.

397 Annual *muled* of Abu l-Hagag. © F. Gilson/ Gamma. *Mosque of Abu' el-Hagag*, photo, early 20th century. © Roger-Viollet.

398–399 *Theban Triad, Amun, Mut and Khonsu, Procession of the Sacred Barque*, lithos, in *Description de l'Égypte*. Gallimard archive. *The Temples of Luxor and Karnak looking toward the north, Temple of Karnak*, watercolor drawings. © J.-C. Golvin.

400 *Barque shrine* G.-L. Claude, watercolor, 1910. Coll. L. Claude, Paris. Ph. D. Doyle/ Gallimard. Court of Ramesses II. © I. Morath/ Magnum.

401 Luxor, photo, late 19th century. Coll. L. Claude, Paris. Procession of sacrificial bullocks, bas-relief. © J. Livet. *Obelisk of Luxor*, David Roberts, 19th century. © Édimédia.

402–403 *Temple of Karnak*, David Roberts, litho, 19th century. Gallimard archive.

402 The god Amun, detail from the Harris papyrus. Coll. British Museum, London. Talattat. © S. Grandadam. Talattat, Nefertiti. © J. Livet.

403 Bazaar in Luxor. © B. Barbey/Magnum. Café. © P. Chapuis/Rapho.

404 Reconstruction of Karnak, J.-C. Golvin, watercolor drawing.

404–405 *The Avenue of the Sphinxes*, Hector Horeau, watercolor, 19th century. Griffith Institute. © Édimédia.

405 Gate in the north enclosure wall and detail of the great enclosure wall. © J.-C. Golvin.

406–407 *Thebes, the great hypostyle hall*, David Roberts, litho, 19th century. V. & A. Museum, Paris. © Édimédia.

406 *Taharqa's column*, G.-L. Claude, watercolor, 1910. Coll. L. Claude. Ph. D. Doyle/Gallimard.

407 *General view of the Temple of Karnak*, Belzoni, litho, 19th century. Collège de France.

408 *Wall of Philippe Arridhaeus*, fresco. © J.-C. Golvin. Court of the Obelisks. © J. Livet.

409 The fallen obelisk of Hatshepsut and Court of the Obelisks, pillars.© J. Livet.

410–411 Karnak, general view. © J. Livet.

410 *Botanical garden*, the "Akhmenu", bas-reliefs and view of the chamber. © J. Livet.

411 The "Akhmenu" fresco. © J. Livet. The "Akhmenu" column. © J.-Cl. Golvin.

412 *Memorial of Thutmose III*, photo, 20th century. © Roger-Viollet. Temple of Khonsu, four-columned hall. © J. Livet.

413 Temple of Khonsu, detail. *Idem*. Open-air Museum, block from the chapel of Hatshepsut. *idem*.

414 Temple of Mut. © J. Livet.

414–415 *The quay at Luxor*, F. Frith, photo, 1858–59. © Royal Photographic Society, Bath.

415 Temple of Ptah, statue of Sekhmet. © J. Livet.

416–417 *Entrance to the Tombs*, David Roberts, litho, 19th century. V. & A. Museum. © Édimédia.

417 Hunefer papyrus. Coll. British Museum, London. Papyrus. © Bibl. nat., Paris.

418 Lord Carnarvon, photo. All rights reserved. *View of the royal necropolis, entrance to the Tomb of Tutankhamun, Carter and a workman bringing the bed of Taweret out of the tomb*, photos, 1923. Collège de France, Paris.

419 *Burial chamber*, photo, 1923. Collège de France, Paris. *Howard Carter, idem.* © Bibl. nat., Paris. *Carter and an assistant wrapping one of the statues*, photos, 1923. Coll. of France, Paris. *Carter opening the door of the last chapel, idem.*

420– 421 Axonometric perspective of the Tomb of Tutankhamun, J.-C. Golvin, ink drawing.

420 *Carter unwrapping the shroud covering the second sarcophagus, mummy of Tutankhamun*, photos, 1923. Coll. of France, bibl. Champollion.

422 Tomb of Sety I, and Tomb of Ramesses III, details. © J. Livet.

423 *Idem.*

424 Tomb of Thutmose III, fresco and entrance. © J. Livet.

424–425 *Valley of the Nile with the ruins of the temple of Sety I*, P. Marilhat, oil/canvas,

19th century. Musée Du Louvre. © RMN, Paris.
425 Memonium, litho, 19th century. © L. of Selva/Tapabor.
426 Deir el-Bahari, Temple of Queen Hatshepsut, frescos, details. © J. Marthelot/Scope. Deir el-Bahri, portrait of Senenmut and houses on stilts, bas-reliefs, details. © J. Livet.
426–427 Deir el-Bahari, Temple of Hatshepsut, photo, 1944. © Mary Mollo.
427 Deir el-Bahari, Birth of Hatshepsut, bas-relief. © J. Livet. Hathor pillar. © S. Grandadam.
428 Head of Hatshepsut, Egyptian Museum, Cairo.
429 Hathor capital. Gallimard archive. Queen of Punt, porters from the Land of Punt, bas-reliefs. © J. Livet.
430 Tomb of Menna, frescos. © J. Livet. Idem. © IBM.
431 Tomb of Rekhmire, of Menna, Rekhmire, of Userhet, frescos. © IBM. Cross-section of hypogeum at Qurba. Gallimard archive Ph. Delebecque/Gallimard.
432 Ramesseum, G. Belzoni, litho, 19th century. Collège de France, Paris. Ph. Delebecque/Gallimard.
432–433 How Memnon was transported, G. Belzoni, watercolor, 19th century. Ph. P. Clayton.
433 Ramesseum. © Burgunder.
434 Reconstruction of the Temple of Medinet Habu, J.-C. Golvin, watercolor drawing. Medinet Habu, David Roberts, litho, 19th century. V. & A. Museum, London. © Édimédia.
435 Son of the king, detail. Gallimard archive. Medinet Habu, side chapel and hypostyle hall, bas-reliefs, details. © J. Livet.
436–437 Naval Battle of Medinet Habu, in Description de l'Égypte, Gallimard archive. Temple of Medinet Habu, J.-C. Golvin, watercolor drawing. Prisoners, bas-reliefs, Egyptian Museum, Cairo.
438 Tomb of Sennedjem, frescos. © J. Livet.
439 Tomb of Pashed, fresco. © J. Livet.

Temple, David Roberts, litho, 19th century. Gallimard archive.
440–441 The Colossi of Memnon, D. Roberts, litho, 19th century. Gallimard archive.
440 Colossus of Memnon, photo, 1944. © Mary Mollo.
441 Qurna, inhabited tomb and general view. © P. Chapuis/Rapho.
442 Qurna, frescos painted on houses. © J. Livet. Hassan Fathi, photo. © Fondation Agha-Khan, Geneva. Qurna, photo.© Roger-Viollet.
443 Interior of the temple of Esneh, K. R. Lepsius, litho, 19th century. Gallimard archive.
444 Tod, remains of the temple. © J. Livet. Tod, general view of the temple.
© J. Marthelot/Scope. Cleopatra's Temple at Arment, F. Frith, photo, 1857. © Bibl. nat., Paris.
446 Esna, Temple of Hathor and the god Bes. © J.-D. Sudres/ Scope. El-Kab, necropolis. © Burgonder. Esna, coptic funeral stelae . © J. Livet.
447 El-Kab, tomb of Paheri. © J. Livet.
448 Temple of Edfu, the god Horus. © J. Livet.
448–449 Edfu, photo, 20th century. © Roger-Viollet.
449 Edfu, village. © G. Degeorge. Edfu, mosque, autochrome, 1914. © Musée Albert-Kahn, Dépt. of Hauts-de-Seine.
450 Outer courtyard of the Temple of Edfu, David Roberts, oil/canvas, 1840. Coll. part. © ACR Éditions, Courbevoie. Temple of Edfu, hypostyle hall. © J. Livet.
451 Temple of Edfu, corridor, detail of east wall. Jebel Silsile quarries, quay, t. © J. Livet. Silsila, in Commission d'Égypte, 1799. © Bibl. nat, Paris.
452 Temple of Kom-Ombo, detail. © G. Degeorge.
452–453 Kom Ombo, David Roberts, litho, 1838. Coll. V. & A. Museum, London. © Édimédia.
453 Temple of Kom Ombo, Sobek. © G. Degeorge. Village near Kom Ombo.
© Beuzen/Scope. Kom-Ombo. © Pratt-

Pries/Diaf. Kom-Ombo. © S. Grandadam.
454 Kom Ombo, detail. © G. Degeorge. Kom-Ombo, surgical instruments. © J. Livet. Kom Ombo, column. © G. Degeorge.
455 Excavation of the Temple of Abu Simbel, David Roberts, litho, 19th century. Gallimard archive.
456 Aswan, village on Elephantine Island. © G. Degeorge. Aswan, the nilometer, photo, 19th century. Coll. D. Roche, Paris.
458 Aswan, botanical garden. © P. Beuzen/ Scope. tomb of Sarenput I, details. © J. Marthelot/ Scope.
459 Tombs of the princes of Elephantine, © Pratt-Pries/ DIAF. West bank of the Nile. © J. Livet. Muslim cemetery.© G. Degeorge. Unfinished lake. © Y. Arthus-Bertrand/Altitude.
460–461 Construction of the Aswan High Dam, photo. © L. of Selva/ Tapabor. Construction of the Aswan High Dam. © R. Burri/Magnum. Temple of Wadi es-Sebua. © Y. Arthus Bertrand/ Altitude.
461 Temple of Maharraka, Hector Horeau, watercolor, 19th century. Coll. Griffith Institute, Oxford. © Édimédia.
462–463 Philae, the flooded Temple of Isis and Kiosk of Trajan. © Babey/ Artephot.
462 Philae, blocks of stone before reconstruction. © E. Lessing/Magnum.
463 The Island of Philae, W. H. Bartlett, watercolor, 19th century. Coll. V & A. London. © Édimédia. Reconstruction of the Island of Philae, J.-C. Golvin, watercolor drawing. Reconstruction of the ruins of Philae. © E. Lessing/ Magnum. The reconstructed Island of Philae. © W. Louvet.
464 View of the Great Temple of Abu Simbel, Richard Lepsius, litho, 19th century, Gallimard archive. Grand temple, The Battle of Kadesh, bas-relief. © G. Degeorge.
464–465 Temples of Abu Simbel, Hector Horeau, watercolor, 19th century. Coll. Griffith

Institute, Oxford. © Édimédia.
465 Ibsamboul, great chamber, east wall, detail, Champollion, litho, in Monuments de l'Égypte and de la Nubie, 1835.
© Bibl. nat., Paris.
466 Reconstruction of the Temples of Abu Simbel.
© Gerster/Rapho. The Temples of Abu Simbel. © M. Gotin/ Scope. Ibsamboul, great chamber, east wall detail, Champollion, litho, in Monuments de l'Égypte and de la Nubie, 19th century. © Bibl. nat., Paris.
468 Toilet chest in painted wood, tomb of Kha at Deir el-Medina. Egyptian Museum, Turin. © Dagli-Orti. The dead arriving before Osiris, Book of the Dead and statue of Ramesses II. idem.
© SCALA.
469 Egyptian Museum, Turin, Delleani, oil/canvas, 1881. © Dagli-Orti. Head of the pharaoh Mentuhotep. Egyptian Museum, Turin. © SCALA.
470 Sarcophagus of the priest Ken-Hor, painted wood. Staatliche Museum, Berlin.
471 Head of Queen Tiyi, head of Queen Nefertiti, head of Akhenaten. © AKG, Berlin.
472–473 Fresco from a tomb tebaine. Metropolitan Museum, New York © Édimédia.
472 Fragment of the head of Queen Tiyi, Hatshepsut represented as a sphinx. Idem.
473 Sarcophagus, funeral stela of Senu. Idem. Temple of Dendur. © R. Burri/ Magnum.
474 Portrait of Belzoni, litho, 19th century. © P. Clayton.Amulets, fresco from the tomb of bust of Ramesses II. © British Museum, London.
475 Canopic jars, Harris papyrus, papyrus of Ani. Rosetta stone. © Dagli-Orti.
476 "Horse" ring, gold and cornelian. Louvre. © RMN, Paris. Fragment of a statue of Queen Nefertiti, sandstone. Idem. Sarcophagus of Madja, painted wood. idem.
477 Make-up applicator, wood, ebony and ivory. idem. Pectoral

LIST OF ILLUSTRATIONS ◆

of Ramesses. Louvre. © Scala. Statue of a dignitary, bronze. Louvre. © RMN, Paris. *Seated scribe*, painted limestone . *idem.*
478 Statue of a bearded man, Nagada period. Musée de Lyon. © Bulloz. Augustus in Egyptian dress, bas-relief. Musée Champollion, Figeac. © Dagli-Orti.
479 Boat with figures, wooden model from a tomb. Kunsthistorisches Museum, Vienna. © E. Lessing/Magnum. Heads of Semite prisoners, glazed clay. *idem. Dark-skinned woman*, Faiyum portrait, painting on wood. Pushkin Museum, Moscow. © Cercle D'art/Édimédia. Make-up dish. Barbier-Mueller Museum, Geneva. Ph. Guillemot/CdA. © Édimédia. Egyptian funerary statuette, wood polychrome. Gulbenkian Museum, Lisbon. Ph. Hinous/CdA. © Édimédia.

Illustrators:
Nature:
16–23: François Desbordes
20–23: Gilbert Houbre
26–27: Gilbert Houbre François Desbordes, Claire Felloni, Jean Chevali
28–29: François Desbordes
30–31 Bruce Pearson François Desbordes, Claire Felloni, Jean Chevali
32–33: François Desbordes, Claire Felloni
34–35: Anne Bodin
36: François Desbordes, Jean Chevalli
Architecture:
82–83: Jean-Claude Sené
84–85: Jean-Claude Sené

86–87: Jean-Claude Sené, François Brosse
88–89: Jean-Claude Sené, François Brosse
90–91: François Brosse
92–93: Jean-Claude Sené
102: Jean-Pirre Lange
104: Jean-Pire Lange
106–107: François Brosse
108–109: Philippe Biard, 110–111: Philippe Candé
112–113: Claude Quiec
114–115: Jean-Claude Sené
116–117: Jean-Claude Sené
118: Jean-Claude Sené
Art and Tradition:
60–61: Nathalie Fonteneau
120–121: Philippe Biard
122–123: Maurice Pommier
Itineraries:
218: Jean-Pire Lange
348: Philippe Biard
418: Gilbert Houbre.
418: Jean-Claude Sené

Acknowledgments:
We would like to thank the following for permission to use the literary excerpts from pages 150 to 164:

◆ CURTIS BROWN: Excerpt from *Passenger to Teheran*, by Vita Sackville-West, copyright © 1926 by Vita Sackville-West (The Hogarth Press, London, 1926). Reprinted by permission of Curtis Brown London, on behalf of the author's estate.
◆ JONATHAN CAPE LTD and TWEEDIE & PRIDEAUX: Excerpt from letter of January 23, 1912 from T.E. Lawrence to Mrs Rieder from *The Letters of T. E. Lawrence*, edited by David Garnett (Jonathan Cape Ltd, 1938). Reprinted by permission of Jonathan Cape Ltd, and Tweedie

& Prideaux for the Trustees of the Seven Pilgrims of Wisdom Trust.
◆ DOUBLEDAY: Excerpt from *Palace Walk*, by Naguib Mahfouz, translated by William Maynard Hutchins and Olive E. Kerry (1991). Reprinted by permission of Doubleday, a division of Bantam Doubleday Dell Publishing Group, Inc.
◆ DUTTON SIGNET and FABER AND FABER LIMITED: Excerpt from *Clea*, by Lawrence Durrell, copyright © 1960 (renewed 1988) by Lawrence George Durrell. Rights in Canada administered by Faber and Faber Limited, London. Reprinted by permission of Dutton Signet, a division of Penguin Books U.S.A. Inc., and Faber and Faber Ltd.
◆ FABER AND FABER INC. and FABER AND FABER LTD: Excerpt from *An Egyptian Journal*, by William Golding, copyright © 1985 by William Golding. Rights outside the United States administered by Faber and Faber Ltd, London. Reprinted by permission.
◆ HARPERCOLLINS PUBLISHERS LTD: Excerpt from *On the Shores of the Mediterranean* by Eric Newby (Harvill, 1984). Reprinted by permission of Harvill, an imprint of HarperCollins Publishers Ltd.
◆ HARVARD UNIVERSITY PRESS: Excerpt from *The Letters of Gustave Flaubert*, edited by Francis Steegmuller, Cambridge, Mass.: The Belknap Press of Harvard University Press, copyright © 1979, 1980 by Francis Steegmuller. Reprinted by permission.

◆ JOHN MURRAY (PUBLISHERS) LTD: Excerpt from *East Is West* by Freya Stark (1946). Reprinted by permission.
◆ PENGUIN BOOKS LTD: Excerpt from *The Histories* by Herodotus, translated by Aubrey de Sélincourt, copyright © 1954 the Estate of Aubrey de Sélincourt. Reprinted by permission.
◆ PETERS FRASER & DUNLOP GROUP LTD: Excerpt from *Labels - A Mediterranean Journey*, by Evelyn Waugh (Duckworth 1930). Reprinted by permission.
◆ PRINCETON UNIVERSITY PRESS: Excerpt from two journal entries of Dec., 1856, and Jan., 1857, from *Journal of a Visit to Egypt and the Levant*, by Herman Melville, edited by Howard C. Horsford (1955). Reprinted by permission.
◆ RANDOM HOUSE, INC.: Excerpt from "Nasser's Egypt" from *United States: The Complete Essays* by Gore Vidal, copyright © 1993 by Gore Vidal. Reprinted by permission.
◆ WATSON LITTLE LTD: Excerpt from letter from Edward Lear to his wife on "The Knack of Riding Camels" from *Edward Lear Selected Letters*, edited by Vivien Noakes (The Clarendon Press, 1988). Reprinted by permission.
◆ WEIDENFELD AND NICOLSON: Excerpt from Rudyard Kipling letter of Feb. 1913, to his children from *O Beloved Kids – Rudyard Kipling's Letters to His Children*, edited by Elliot L. Gilbert (1983). Reprinted by permission.

◆ INDEX

A

Abar (el-), zawia (Cairo) 310
Abbas II, khedive 185
Abbas, khedive Abu el- 182, 211, 229
Abbas, khedivial tomb of 331
Abd el-Qurna, necropolis of sheikh (Thebes) 430
Abdin, palace (Cairo) 274, 281, 307
Abu el-Abbas el-Mursi, mosque (Alexandria) 178
Abu el-Dahab, mosque (Cairo) 295
Abu el-Dahab, mosque 111, 295
Abu el-Fatah, mosque (Alexandria) 178
Abu el-Hagag, mosque (Thebes) 397, 400
Abu el-Maati, mosque (Damietta) 223
Abu el-Naga, mosque (Fuwa) 213
Abu Ghurob 39
Abu Ghurob, temple of 82
Abu Menas, monastery 202
Abu Rudeis 242
Abu Sarga, church (Old Cairo) 320
Abu Simbel 26, 35, 95, 217, 464
Abu Simbel, temple of 98, 99
Abu Sir Bana, town 220
Abu Tig 382
Abukir 198, 199
Abukir, battle of 199
Abukir, gardens 199
Abusir 39, 201, 344
Abusir el-Meleq, site 358
Abydos 374–86
Abydos, town 386
Achoris, chapel of (Karnak) 405
Adda complex (Alexandria) 188
Adra (el-), church (Old Cairo) 320
Aga Khan Award 201, 290, 442
Aga Khan, tomb of (Gharbi Aswan) 459
Agami, town 200
Aghion, villa (Alexandria) 190
Aghurmi, temple of 256
Agilkia, island 99, 462
Aguiba, beach 204
Ahmed Pasha, sabil-kuttab (Cairo) 286
Ahmediya brotherhood 211
Ahmose, Theban ruler 41
Ahmosids, the 41
Ahram (al-), newspaper 284
Aïn Musa (Sinai) 240
Aïn Umm el-Dabadib, village 261, 262
Aïn Umm Labakha, fortress of 262
Akhenaten 278, see

Amenhotep IV
Akhenaten, great stele of 451
Akhmenu, columned hall (Karnak) 410
Akhmim, town 72, 383, 384
Alabaster Chapel (Karnak) 413
Alamein (el-), battle of 204
Alamein (el-), town 204
Alexander the Great 44, 57, 174, 408
Alexandria 44, 68, 174–204
– amphitheater 183
– tram 197
– canal 213
– cisterns 188
– city center 182
– corniche 195
– Greek quarter 188
– harbors 174
– Stock Exchange 180
– suq district 179
– Turkish quarter 176
Ali, Mohammed 67, 68, 69, 174, 176, 184, 190, 206, 212, 229, 261, 271, 305, 365, 372
Alin Aq, palace (Cairo) 303
Almaza (singer-dancer) 128
Amada, temple of (Aswan) 461
Amarnian period 42, 104
Amba Shenuda, church (Old Cairo) 325
Amba Shenuda, festival 383
Amenemhet I, pyramid of (Lisht) 356
Amenemhet II, "white" pyramid of (Dahshur) 355
Amenemhet III 40, 364, 370
Amenemhet III, pyramid of (Dahshur) 355
Amenhikhopeshef, tomb of (Thebes) 440
Amenhotep I, tomb of 88
Amenhotep II, tomb of (Thebes) 423
Amenhotep III 383, 399, 400, 412, 425, 440, 441
– court of (Luxor) 400, 403
– palace of 91
– temple of (El-Kab) 396, 448
– tomb of 96
Amenhotep IV (Akhenaten) 42, 350, 352, 378, 403, 412, 430
Ammit the Devourer 65, 439
Amr Ibn el-As, mosque (Old Cairo) 223, 324
Amun
– apartments of of Luxor 402
– god of Thebes 41, 63, 84, 263, 372, 398, 399, 404, 412, 413, 425, 452
– great temple of 225, 227

– sacred barque 74, 397, 398, 400, 401, 407, 410, 436
– second temple of 257
– temple of (Karnak) 468
Amun-Re
– chapel (Abydos) 386
– god 377, 385, 398, 394, 402, 405, 407, 413, 425, 433, 435, 466
– great temple of (Karnak) 83, 404
– sacred barque of 406, 408
Andalusian Gardens (Cairo) 282
Anfushi, bay (Alexandria) 176
Anfushi, district (Alexandria) 176
Anfushi, necropolis (Alexandria) 177, 291
Ankishariya (el-), or Northern Enclosure (Cairo) 305
Antinoe, town 375
Antiquities, Egyptian department of 96, 214, 276, 348, 350
Antiquities, new museum of (Faiyum) 366
Antoniadis Gardens (Alexandria) 190
Antoniadis, palace (Alexandria) 191
Antoniadis, Sir John A. 191
Antoninus Pius, emperor 263, 391
Anubis, jackal-headed god 35, 61, 193, 424, 427
Aper-el, tomb (Saqqara) 352
Apis Bulls 333, 351
Apis, god 43, 193
Aqaba, gulf (Sinai) 238, 248
Aqbughawiya, medersa (Cairo) 294
Aqmar (el-), or Gray Mosque (Cairo) 108, 290, 291
Aqsunqur, or Blue Mosque (Cairo) 302
Arab World, university of the (Cairo) 294
Arabian Desert 264
Arcadius, basilica of 202
Architecture 77–119
Areg (el-), track 258
Arish (el-), town (Sinai) 249, 250, 252
Armant, village 444
Arsinoe, town see
Medinet el-Faiyum 364
Arsinoe-Crocodilopolis, town 365
Artemis, cave of 375
Artisans, Egyptian 58
Arts and traditions 119–38
Asasif, necropolis (Thebes) 425, 430
Ashmunein 72
Ashraf Barsbey (el-), sultan 287
Ashrafiya, medersa (Cairo) 287

Askar (el-), district (Cairo) 270, 324
Assiut
– necropolis 380, 381
– town 260, 380
Aswan
– first dam 69, 452, 460, 461
– High Dam 26, 71, 98, 234, 452, 460, 462
– quarries 426
– town 170, 456
Ataba el-Khadra (el-), midan (Cairo) 275
Atfih, town 358
Atrach, Farid el- (singer) 128
Attarine
– district (Alexandria) 182
– mosque (Alexandria) 182
– suq 183
Aytmishi, mosque (Cairo) 303
Azab (el-), or Lower Enclosure (Cairo) 304
Azhar (el-), district (Cairo) 210, 294
Azhar (el-), mosque 74, 325
Aziz (el-), caliph 291
Azzuz, baths (Rosetta) 215

B

Bab an-Nasr, or Victory Gate (Cairo) 289, 292
Bab el-Azab (Cairo) 306
Bab el-Futuh, or Gate of Conquest (Cairo) 289
Bab el-Hadid (Cairo) 273
Bab el-Muzayini (Cairo) 294
Bab el-Nabi, or Gate of the Prophet 211
Bab Rosetta, district (Alexandria) 188
Bab Rosetta, mosque of the (Alexandria) 189
Bab Zuwaila (Cairo) 110, 291, 298
Babylon 318
Babylon, fort 270, 319
Badawi, Sidi Ahmed el- 126, 210
Bagawat (el-), oasis 260, 261
Baghdad 66, 270, 358
Bagur (el-), village 210
Baguri, sheikh Ibrahim el- 210
Bahariya, oasis 254, 258
Bahrein, oasis 258
Balat, village 260
Barai (el-), village 382
Bardawil, lake (Sinai) 251
Barquq, complex of Sultan (Cairo) 289
Barquq, khanqa of Sultan Farag Ibn 110, 111, 329
Barquq, sultan 220
Barrage, Delta (or El-Qanatir el-Qahiriya) 206
Barsbey, complex of Sultan 328

Barsbey, sultan 224, 328
Bastet, god 35, 62
Bawiti (el-), town 258
Baybars el-Jashankir, khanqa 113, 292
Bazaara wakala (Cairo) 293
Beaches of Alexandria 195
Bedouins 238
Beit as-Sinnari (Cairo) 315
Beit as-Suhaymi (Cairo) 116, 290, 291
Beit el-Qadi 117
Beit el-Qadi, midan (Cairo) 288
Beit el-Qadi, shari' (Cairo) 288
Beit el-Umma, residence (Cairo) 281
Beit er-Razzaz (Cairo) 301
Beit Gamal ad-Din (Cairo) 297
Beit Shabshiri (Cairo) 297
Bellefonds, Linant de 206, 229
Belzoni, Giovanni Battista 95, 340, 464
Ben-Ezra, synagogue (Old Cairo) 321
Beni Hassan, necropolis 87, 374
Beni Mansur, village 386
Beni Suef, village 359
Bent pyramid (Dahshur) 356
Berlin, Egyptian museum in 95, 470
Bersha (el-) 377
Bes, god 60, 446, 462
Beshtak, palace (Cairo) 290
Bey, Ali 68
Bey, Murad 325
Bilbeis, ancient city 224
Birba (el-) town, 385
Birket Habu, lake 441
Birket Qarun, lake (Faiyum) 362
Bitter, lakes 228, 229, 250
Blemmyes, Barbarian tribe 255
Boats 120
Book of the Dead, the 65, 417, 439
Botanical garden (Karnak) 410
British Museum (London) 474
Brotherhoods, Muslim 70, 76
Bulaq, suburb (Cairo) 276, 284
Burg el-Arab, village 201, 256
Burg el-Turfa, tower (Cairo) 307
Buseiri (el-), mosque (Alexandria) 178

C

Caesarion, son of Cleopatra 389
Cafés 132–3

Cairo 269–325
– Bulaq Museum 96
– Carriage Museum 307
– cemeteries 326
– Citadel 67, 170, 304
– city center 272
– Coptic Museum 322
– Egyptian Museum 276–9, 322, 354, 412, 421, 428, 445, 426
– Mukhtar Museum 282
– Opera House 274
– Postal Museum 275
– Railway Museum 273
Camp David Agreements 71, 240
Carriage Museum (Cairo) 307
Carter, Howard 418
Catacombs (Alexandria) 192
Cavafy, Constantine (poet) 185
Cavafy, museum (Alexandria) 185
Cecil Hotel (Alexandria) 184
Cemeteries (Old Cairo) 326
Cerisy, Lefèbure de (engineer) 177
Champollion, Jean-François 38, 94, 216, 217, 374, 398
Chevrier, Henri (architect) 104
Church of the Virgin, *see* el-Adra
Citadel (Cairo) 67, 170, 271, 304
Claudianus, Mons 267
Cleopatra 44, 204, 392, 398
Cleopatra's needles (Alexandria) 183, 197
Cleopatra's Pool, spring 257
Cleopatra, temple (Armant) 444
Colored Canyon (Sinai) 248, 249
Constantine, emperor 45
Constantius II 197
Coptic church 45, 74, 322
Coptic Museum (Old Cairo) 321, 322
Coptic quarter (Old Cairo) 320
Coptic script 219
Coptic, basilica (Dendera) 390
Coste, Pascal 110
Craft trades 130–1
Crocodilopolis, town *see* Medinet el-Faiyum

D

Dahab, village (Sinai) 248
Dahshur, pyramids of 39, 345, 354
Dahshur, site 97, 354, 364
Dakhla, oasis 254, 259
Dakka, temple of (Aswan) 461
Damietta, town 222

Daqahliya, province 221
Darb el-Ahmar, district (Cairo) 300
Darb el-Hajj (Sinai) 249
Darb el-Qirmiz, shari' (Cairo) 290
Darb el-Sindadiya, village 261
Darfur, town 254
Darius I 228, 260
Dauzats, Adrien (painter) 143
Deir (el-), Roman fortress 262
Deir or monastery:
Deir Abu Hennes 376
Deir Abu Makaryus 208, 209
Deir Amba Baramus 208, 318
Deir Amba Bishoi 208
Deir Amba Bishoi, or "red" monastery 383
Deir Durunka, town 381
Deir el-Abyad or "white" monastery 383
Deir el-Adra 373
Deir el-Bahri (Thebes) 83, 121, 167, 279, 426, 428–9, 438
Deir el-Hagar (Dakhla) 259
Deir el-Malak Ghobrial (Faiyum) 369
Deir el-Medina (Thebes) 88, 90, 438, 468
Deir es-Suriani 106, 208, 209
Deir Mari Girgis *see* St George's Monastery
Deir Shelwit 441
Delta, barrage 229
Delta, the 206–36
Dendera
– town 388, 450
Derr, temple of (Aswan) 461
Dervish theater (Cairo) 311
Deserts, 253–68
Desroches-Noblecourt, Christiane 98
Dikheila (el-), military camp 200
Dillon, Frank (painter) 145
Dimaï, ruins (Faiyum) 366
Din, Salah ad- 67, 249, 270, 271, 304, 330, 375
Dinocrates, architect 174
Dionysias, temple (Faiyum) 366
Dishasha, necropolis 360
Disuq, town 211, 212
Djeba, village 449
Djed pillar (Abydos) 387
Djedededfre, pyramid of 344
Djoser
39, 348, 456
– funeral complex of (Saqqara) 78, 346, 347
– pyramid of (Saqqara) 86
Dongen, Kees van (painter) 146, 147
Dra-Abu el-Naga, necropolis (Thebes) 425

Dumaqsis, mosque (Rosetta) 215
Durrell, Lawrence 162
Dush treasure, the 263
Dush, site of 263

E

Eastern Cemetery, (Cairo) 289
Edfu
– temple of 449, 460
– town 84, 396, 448
Egyptian Civilization, museum (Cairo) 282
Egyptian Museum (Cairo) 276–9
El-Fishawi Café (Cairo) 287
Elephantine Museum (Aswan) 457
Elephantine, hypogea of the princes of 458
Elephantine, island 457
Eliahu Hanabi, synagogue (Alexandria) 184
Elite, restaurant (Alexandria) 185
Enaton, monastery 200
Esna, barrage 451
Esna, temple of 446
Esna, town 446
Europe, Egyptian antiquities in 478
Expedition, Egypt 94, 140, 228, 241, 315, 377, 406, 464
Ezbekiya (el-), district (Cairo) 274

F

Fahmi, Mustafa 281, 308
Faiyum, the 40, 185, 362–70
Fakahani (el-), mosque (Cairo) 297
Fakhri, Ahmed (archeologist) 258
Falconry 138
Family, Egyptian 56–7
Farafra, oasis 254, 258, 259
Farouk, khedivial tomb 331
Farouk, king 199, 281
Fathi, Hassan 109, 201, 260, 263, 442
Fatimid cemetery 459
Fatimids, dynasty 66
Feiran, oasis (Sinai) 242, 243
Feluccas 122
Festival Court (Karnak) 411, 413
Festivals 126–7
Fine Arts, museum of (Alexandria) 189
Flaubert, Gustave 161
Florence, archeological museum of 469
Forster, E.M. 163
French Cultural Center (Alexandria) 184
Fuad, king 70, 199, 240
Funerary rites 64–5
Fustat 66, 270, 324
Fuwa, town 213

◆ INDEX

G

Gabari, palace 200
Gamia el-Fath, mosque (Damietta) 223
Gamia el-Nasser, or Victory mosque 220
Gastronomy 134–5
Gawhara el-Lala (el-), mosque (Cairo) 308
Gayer-Anderson Museum (Cairo) 313
Geographical Society (Cairo) 280
Gérôme, Jean-Léon (painter) 144, 342
Gerza, site 358
Gezira
– island (Cairo) 282
– Museum (Cairo) 282
Geziret Fara'un, or Pharaoh's island (Sinai) 249
Gharbi Aswan 458
Ghuri (el-)' mausoleum 296
Ghuri (el-)' mosque 111, 296
Ghuri (el-') wakala 296
Ghuri (el-), gate (Cairo) 286
Ghuri, Sultan Qansu el- 67
Girga, town 384, 385
Giza
276, 334, 374
– pyramids of 39, 146, 166, 334
Gods, Egyptian 60–3
Gold mines 268
Golding, William 162
Graeco-Roman Museum (Alexandria) 185, 186–7
Greek hospital (Alexandria) 190
Greek quarter (Alexandria) 188
Groppi café (Cairo) 275
Gumrok, district (Alexandria) 176

H

Hadrian 375
Hafez, Abd el-Halim (singer) 128
Hakim (el-), mosque (Cairo) 291, 329
Hakim (el-), sultan 67
Hammamat, wadi 268
Hamuli, Abdul el- (singer) 128
Hapidjefa, tomb of (Assiut) 380
Hara el-Rum, or Christian quarter (Cairo) 297
Haramlik, palace 199
Harem, palace (Cairo) 307
Harrania, village 345
Harsomtus 389
Harwer, temple of (Qus)
Hassan Sadaqa, mausoleum (Cairo) 310
Hassan
– medersa of Sultan (Cairo) 110, 289, 309
– sultan 143, 298

Hathor
– chapel (Deir el-Bahri) 429
– goddess 35, 62, 379, 424, 445, 453, 462, 466
– temple of (Dendera) 388
– temple of (Thebes) 438, 462
Hatshepsut, obelisks of (Karnak) 409
Hatshepsut
– queen 41, 121, 400, 426, 428, 457
– tomb of (Thebes) 426
Hawara, pyramid of (Dahshur) 355
Hawara, pyramid of (Faiyum) 370
Hawawish (el-), necropolis 384
Hearing Ear, temple of the (Karnak) 411
Heliopolis (Cairo) 224, 270, 285, 288, 357, 376, 452
Helwan, suburb (Cairo) 284
Heracleopolis 40, 360
Herishef, temple of 360
Hermonthis, village 444
Hermopolis 376
Herodotus 158
Hibis, temple of 260
Hiding Courtyard (Karnak) 412
History 37–77
Hittites 42
Hiw, town 387
Horemheb 42
Horemheb, speos of 452
Horemheb, temple of 434
Horemheb, tomb of (Thebes) 423
Horses 136–7
Horus
– chapel (Abydos) 386
– falcon god 34, 43, 62, 84, 138, 193, 383, 448, 451, 462
– temple of (Edfu) 167, 449
Hotel Continental (Cairo) 274
Hotel Métropole (Alexandria) 197
Hurghada 31, 267
Hurriya (el-), shari' (Alexandria) 188
Hussein (el-), district (Cairo) 286
Hussein (el-), mosque (Cairo) 76, 286
Hyksos 41, 358, 447
Hypogea, great royal (Thebes) 417

I

Ibn el-As, Amr 45, 66, 173, 191, 196, 228, 270, 324
Ibn el-Nabi, cistern (Alexandria) 188
Ibn Tulun, mosque (Cairo) 66, 110, 121, 312
Ibrahim 272
Ibrahim el-Qaïd, mosque (Alexandria) 178, 198
Ibrahim, khedivial tomb 331
Ihnasiya el-Medina, necropolis 358, 360
Ihnasiya el-Medina, town 360
Ikshidid, dynasty 66
Illahun, village 359
Imam as-Shafi'i, cemetery 330
Imam as-Shafi'i, mausoleum 330
Imam as-Shafi'i, mosque 110
Imhotep (architect) 86, 348
Inal el-Yusufi Atabaki, mosque (Cairo) 299
Inal, complex of Sultan 114, 115, 329
Inherkau, tomb of (Thebes) 439
Irrigation, museum of 207
Isadora, tomb of 377
Ishaqi (el-), mosque (Cairo) 109, 300
Isis 62
Isis, chapel (Abydos) 386
Isis, temple of 462
Ismaïl, khedive 128, 181, 232, 280, 307
Ismaïliya 68, 250
Ismaïliya
– canal 224, 236

J

Jebel Abu Dukham 267
Jebel Dakrur 257
Jebel el-Mawta 257
Jebel el-Raha (Sinai) 241
Jebel el-Sheikh 262
Jebel el-Tarif 262
Jebel el-Teir 373
Jebel el-Zeit 266
Jebel Fatira 267
Jebel Hammam Fara'un (Sinai) 242
Jebel Katherina 32
Jebel Moqattam (Cairo) 270, 305, 331
Jebel Musa 32
Jebel Musa, or Mount Sinai 247
Jebel Serbal (Sinai) 243
Jebel Silsila, quarries 451
Jebel Umm el-Ghanayin 262
Jebel Yashkur (Cairo) 312
Jebelein, village 445
Joseph's Canal, or Bahr Yussuf (Faiyum) 359, 363, 368
Joseph's Well (Cairo) 306
Jubilee chapels (Saqqara) 347
Jupiter Amun, oasis 204
Jupiter Amun, temple of 257

K

Kab (el-) 447
Kadesh, battle of 432, 464
Kahun, town 90

Kalabsha, temple of (Aswan) 99, 460
Kalsumm, Umm (singer) 128
Kamil, (el-), sultan 289
Kamiliya, medersa (Cairo) 289
Karanis, temples of (Faiyum) 366
Karnm Abu Menas 202
Karnak
– temples of (Thebes) 84, 102, 104, 404, 412
Katkhuda, Abd el-Rahman 314
Katkhuda, *sabil-kuttab* of Abd el-Rahman (Cairo) 289
Kellia, site 107, 209
Keniset Mari Girgis *see* St George's Church
Khafre, pyramid of 38, 95, 334, 340–1
Khalig (el-), canal (Cairo) 122, 315
Khan el-Khalili, district (Cairo) 144, 286
Khanqa (el-), mosque 224
Kharga, oasis 25, 254, 260
Kharga, town 262
Khayrbay, mosque (Cairo) 302
Khedivial buildings (Cairo) 273
Kheruef, tomb of (Thebes) 425
Khnum, ram-god 63, 446, 456
Khodari (el-), mausoleum (Cairo) 313
Khodari (el-), mosque (Cairo) 313
Khonsu, chapel of (Karnak) 407
Khonsu, god 263, 398, 453
Khonsu, sacred barque 400, 401, 407, 410
Khonsu, temple of (Karnak) 84, 412
Khufu 38
Khufu, funeral barque 120
Khufu, pyramid of 335–40
Khund Tughay, mausoleum 326
Kings, Valley of the 88, 90, 169, 350, 417, 418
Kipling, Rudyard 153
Kitchener's Island 458
Klee, Paul (painter) 146
Kom Dara, tomb 379
Kom el-Ahmarsee Zawiyet el-Maytin
Kom el-Dikka, amphitheater (Alexandria) 183, 185
Kom es-Shofaga (Alexandria) 192
Kom es-Shogafa, necropolis 89
Kom Ombo
– temple of 452
– village 85, 396, 451, 452
Koptos *see* Qift
Kumma, fort 92, 93

L

Lamati (el-), mosque 372
Language 72
Lashin, villa (Agami) 201
Lawrence, T.E. 152
Laymun (el-), okelle (Alexandria) 179
Lear, Edward 157
Lesseps, Ferdinand de 229, 230, 236
Lewis, John Frederick (painter) 145
Liberation Square, see Tahrir (Midan at-)
Library, Great Alexandria 194
Libyan Desert 254
Lisht, site 356
Lisht, town 334
Louvre Museum (Paris) 140, 390, 476

Luxor
– (el-Uqsur) 395
– Museum 402, 403, 412, 427
– temple 396, 397, 399, 403

M

Ma'at, goddess of Truth 63, 439
Ma'at, palace of (Karnak) 408
Ma'at, temple of (Thebes) 438
Madbuliya, mosque (Damietta) 223
Maghara, turquoise mines (Sinai) 242
Mahalla el-Kubra (el-), town 220
Maharraka, temple of (Aswan) 461
Mahdi, sheikh el- 145
Mahfouz, Naguib (writer) 72, 160, 286
Mahmud el-Kurdi, mosque (Cairo) 299
Mahmud Muharram, mosque (Cairo) 293
Mahmudiya Canal 175, 190, 213
Mahmudiya, medersa (Cairo) 308
Malik el-Kamil (el-), sultan 221
Malkatta, palace 441
Mameluke cemetery 331
Mameluke, sultans 67
Mamura (el-), gardens 199
Manshiya, district (Alexandria) 180
Manshiya, midan (Alexandria) 177, 180, 181, 182
Mansur (el-), Abbasid caliph 228
Mansura, town 221
Manyal, palace (Cairo) 283
Manzala, lake 35, 123
Mareotis, lake (now Mariut) 174, 203
Maridani (el-), mosque (Cairo) 301

Mariette, Auguste 96, 226, 276, 342, 350, 396, 436
Mark Anthony 204
Markaz (el-), shari' (Thebes) 402
Marzuq el-Ahmedi, mosque (Cairo) 293
Maspero Gardens (Cairo) 282
Maspero, Gaston 96, 322, 397, 426
Mazghuna 356
Medamud, village 444
Medinet el-Faiyum 170, 359, 368

Medinet Habu
– (Thebes) 91, 92, 277, 434, 436
– Great Temple 435
– Royal Palace 435
– Small Temple 434
Medinet Madi (Faiyum) 368
Medinet Madi, temple of 83
Meidum 35, 278, 357
Meidum, pyramid (or El-Ahram el-Kaddab) 39, 357
Meir, necropolis 379
Mekashkesh (el-), mosque (Luxor)
Mekhu, tomb of (Gharbi Aswan) 458
Mellawi, town 376
Melville, Herman 152
Memnon, colossi of (Thebes) 440
Memphis 39, 270, 332, 376, 447
Memphis, necropolis 345
Mendes, town 221
Menkaure, pyramid of 38, 334, 341
Menna, tomb of (Thebes) 431
Mentuhotep I, tomb of (Thebes) 426
Mentuhotep, king 40
Mentuhotep, temple of 83, 428
Mer-Neith, tomb of Queen 87
Merneptah 42, 226, 452
Merneptah, temple of 434
Merneptah, tomb of (Thebes) 418
Mersa Matruh 148, 200, 204, 256
Metropolitan Museum in New York 472
Mex (el-), village 200
Mihmandar (el-), mosque (Cairo) 300
Military Museum (el-Alamein) 204
Military prison (Cairo) 306
Min 63, 382, 385, 392
Minet el-Bassal, district (Alexandria) 175
Minya (el-), town 372
Misr el-Gadida (or New Cairo), see Heliopolis
Mithqal medersa, see Sabiqiya
Mitwali (el-), mosque 220

Modern Art, museum of (Alexandria) 189
Modern Art, museum of (Cairo) 282
Moeris, lake 365, 370
Mohammed Ali, barrage 207, 213
Mohammed Ali, midan (Alexandria) 180
Mohammed Ali, or Alabaster Mosque (Cairo) 305
Mohammed, prohet 75
Mohammed, Saïd 182
Montu, god 34, 444
Montu, temple of (Karnak) 414
Montuemhet, tomb of (Thebes) 103, 104, 425
Moses 200, 241
Mu'ayyad (el-), mauristan 303
Mu'ayyad (el-), mosque 110, 298
Mu'ayyad (el-), or Red Mosque (Cairo) 298
Muafi (el-), mosque (Mansura) 220
Muallaqa (el-), or St Mary's Church (Old Cairo) 319
Mubarak, Hosni 71
Muizz (el-), shari' (Cairo) 288
Mukhtar Museum (Cairo) 282
Mukhtar, Mahmud (sculptor) 184, 273
muled 126–7
muled el-Nabi, or muled of the Prophet 127, 211
muled of Abu el-Hagag 126, 397
muled of Sayyida Zeinab 314
muled of sheikh el-Qenawi 387
muled of Sidi Ahmed el-Bagawi 211
Mummification 64
Muntaza (el-), gardens 199
Muntaza (el-), village 195
Murabak, Ali (historian) 189
Musafirkhana, palace (Cairo) 293
Museum Gayer-Anderson (Cairo) 313
Museum of Egyptian Civilization (Cairo) 282
Museum of Fine Arts (Alexandria) 189
Museum of Irrigation (the Delta) 207
Museum of Luxor 402, 403, 412, 427
Museum of Modern Art (Alexandria) 189
Museum of Modern Art (Cairo) 282
Museum of Natural History (Alexandria) 191
Museum of Port Said 236
Museum of Tanis 226
Museum of Tanta 211
Museum, Berlin Egyptian 470
Museum, British (London) 474

Museum, Bulaq (Cairo) 96
Museum, Coptic (Cairo) 322
Museum, Egyptian (Cairo) 276–9, 322, 354, 412, 421, 426, 428, 445
Museum, Elephantine (Aswan) 457
Museum, Florence archeological 469
Museum, Gezira (Cairo) 282
Museum, Louvre (Paris) 140, 390, 476
Museum, Mellawi 376
Museum, Metropolitan (New York) 472
Museum, Open-Air (Karnak) 413
Museum, Open-Air (Memphis) 333
Museum, Vatican 469
Museums of the world, Egypt in the 468–80
Museum of Nubia 459
Music 128–9
Mussa, tomb of sheikh 445
Mustafa, sabil-kuttab of Sultan (Cairo) 314
Mut, chapel of (Karnak) 407
Mut, goddess 61, 227, 263, 398, 466
Mut, sacred barque 400, 401, 407, 410
Mut, temple of (Karnak) 414
Mutubis, bridge 213
Muzawaka (el-), tombs of 259

N

Nabi Daniel, mosque (Alexandria) 184
Nabi Daniel, shari' (Alexandria) 184
Nadura, temple of 261
Nafisa el-Beida, wakala (Cairo) 298
Naga el-Deir, necropolis 385
Nagada, town 392
Naghi, Mohammed (painter) 148
Naguila (el-), Roman town 204
Nakhl, town (Sinai) 249
Nakht, tomb of (Thebes) 431
Napoleon Bonaparte 68, 94, 271, 324, 398
Nasir, Mohammed (an-) 292
Nasir Mohammed (an-), complex of Sultan (Cairo) 289
Nasir Mohammed (an-), medersa 288
Nasir Mohammed (an-), mosque (Cairo) 306
Nasr ad-Din, mosque (Alexandria) 178
Nasr ad-Din, mosque (Fuwa) 213
Nasser, Gamal abd el- 70, 98, 180, 234
Nasser, lake 26, 169, 456, 460, 464

INDEX

Natural History, museum of (Alexandria) 191
Nature 15–36
Necropolises 86–7
Nectanebo 44
Nectanebo II 358
Neferefre, pharaoh 344
Neferirkare, pharaoh 344
Nefersekheru, tomb of 373
Nefertari 433, 464
Nefertari, speos of (Abu Simbel) 464
Nefertari, temple of (Abu Simbel) 466
Nefertari, tomb of (Thebes) 440
Nefertiti 278
Nekhbet, "white" goddess 34, 62, 447
Nekheb el-Kab, town 447
Nephthys 62
New Kingdom, cemetery of the (Saqqara) 350
New Valley 260
New Year, festival of the (Dendera) 390
Newby, Eric 150
Nile
– delta 185, 206
– floods 54
– shrines 452
Nilometer (Aswan) 457
Nilometer (Cairo) 283
Niuserre, pharaoh 82, 344
Niuserre, temple of 345
Nua Missa, oasis 258
Nur ad-Din, mosque 331
Nut, sky-goddess 61, 389, 454
Nuweiba, port (Sinai) 249
Nuzha Gardens (Alexandria) 190

O

Obelisks 480
Obelisks, court of the (Karnak) 408
Okelles 181
Old Cairo 319
Omar, caliph 66
Open-Air Museum (Karnak) 413
Open-Air Museum (Memphis) 333
Opet, religious festival 400
Opet, temple of (Karnak)
Opra complex (Cairo) 282
Orabi, midan (Alexandria) 181
Osireion (Abydos) 386
Osirian rooms (Thebes) 434
Osiris 40, 44, 62, 358, 386, 416, 421, 424, 432, 439
Osiris, chapel (Abydos) 386
Osiris, resurrection of 390
Osiris, tomb of 462

Osorkon, tomb of 226, 227
Ostraca 59

P

Papyrus 58, **511**
Pasaba, tomb of (Thebes) 425
Pasha, Ali 232
Pasha, governor Mahmud 308
Pasha, Mohammed 213
Pasha, Saïd 184, 207, 276
Pasha, Sinan 68
Pelusium, ancient site (Sinai) 250
Pepy I 39
Pepy I, pyramid of 332
Pepy II, funeral complex of 87
Petosiris, tomb 377
Petrie, Flinders 97
Pharos, lighthouse (Alexandria) 110, 176, 177, 201
Philae, island 462
Philae, temple of 45, 98, 99, 167, 462
Police Museum (Cairo Citadel) 306
Pompey's Pillar (Alexandria) 194
Porphyrites, Mons 266, 267
Port Said, shari' (Cairo) 315
Port Said, town 232, 234, 236
Port Tawfiq, town 235
Postal Museum (Cairo) 275
Press district (Cairo) 284
Psusennes I 226
Psusennes I, tomb of (Tanis) 89, 227
Ptah, chapel (Abydos) 386
Ptah, god 62, 193, 440, 466
Ptah, sanctuary of (Memphis) 333
Ptah, temple of (Karnak) 414
Ptolemy I Soter 196
Ptolemy II Philadelphus 201, 220, 228, 364
Ptolemy III 220, 262, 413, 449
Ptolemy XII Auletes 388
Pyramids, avenue of (Memphis) 335

Q

Qaa Muhid ad-Din, *see* Uthman Katkhuda palace
Qahira (el-), the Triumphant One 66
Qaitbay cemetery (Old Cairo) 328
Qaitbay mausoleum 328, **509**, **529**
Qaitbay, complex of Sultan 326
Qaitbay, fort (Alexandria) 176, 177, 178, 195, 215

Qaitbay, medersa (Cairo) 314
Qaitbay, palace 301
Qaitbay, *sabil-kuttab* (Cairo) 311
Qaitbay, *wakala* (Cairo) 292, 295
Qal'a (el-) or Citadel (Cairo) 305
Qal'a (el-), temple (Qift) 392
Qal'a el-Saidiya, barrage 207
Qala't el-Jundi, town (Sinai) 241, 242
Qala'un, complex of Sultan (Cairo) 289
Qala'un, mausoleum (Cairo) 289
Qala'un, sultan 67, 303
Qanibey Emir Akhur, medersa (Cairo) 308
Qantara (el-), town (Sinai) 250
Qaou el-Kebir, village 382
Qara Sunqur, mausoleum (Cairo) 292
Qasr (el-), village 259
Qasr an-Nil, bridge (Cairo) 282
Qasr an-Nil, palace (Cairo) 272
Qasr an-Nil, shari' (Cairo) 275
Qasr el-Ablaq, palace 304, 305
Qasr el-Gawhara, or Jewel palace (Cairo) 305
Qasr el-Ghueida, temple 262
Qasr el-Zaiyan, temple 263
Qasr es-Sagha, temple of 83
Qatai' (el-) 324
Qatai' (el-), mosque (Cairo) 312
Qena, town 387
Qenawi, sheikh el- 387
Qift, town 392
Qijmas el-Ishaqi, mosque (Cairo) 109, 300
Qizlar, sabil-kuttab (Cairo) 310
Quarries, imperial 266, 267
Queens, Valley of the 440
Qurna el-Gedida (new Qurna) 442
Qurna el-Gedida, mosque 109
Qurna, village 441, 442
Qurqumas, complex of Sultan 114, 115
Qus, town 392
Qusun, palace of Emir (Cairo) 310

R

Radwan Bey, kasbah (Cairo) 299
Rafah, town (Sinai) 252
Rahim, Abd el- 387
Railway Museum (Cairo) 273
Ramadan 126, 127

Ramesses I, tomb of (Thebes) 423
Ramesses II 42, 194, 213, 225, 273, 377, 407, 432, 448, 452, 466
– colossi of 333, 360, 385, 396, 460
– court of (Luxor) 400
– palace of 90
– speos of (Abu Simbel) 464
– statue 468
– temple of (Abu Simbel) 101, 464
– tomb of (Thebes) 417
Ramesses III 43, 431, 436
– funerary temple *see* Medinet Habu 434
– palace of 91
– temple of (Karnak) 415
– tomb of (Thebes) 423
Ramesses IV, tomb of (Thebes) 423
Ramesses V 452
Ramesses IX, tomb of (Thebes) 418
Ramesseum
– (Thebes) 85, 432, 451
Ramesses Square 333
Ramesses Station (Alexandria) 192
Ramesses Station (Cairo) 273
Ramesside, dynasty 42
Ramose, tomb of (Thebes) 430
Ras el-Sudr, town (Sinai) 241
Ras el-Tin, necropolis (Alexandria) 177
Ras el-Tin, palace (Alexandria) 176, 177
Ras el-Tin, shari' (Alexandria) 176, 177
Ras Mohammed (Sinai) 30, 248
Ras Nusrani (Sinai) 248
Re, solar god 34, 60, 344, 417, 448
Re-Harakhti, falcon-headed sun god 340
Red Chapel (Karnak) 413
Red pyramid (Dahshur) 355
Rekhmire, tomb of (Thebes) 431
Religion 74–6
Renenutet, serpent-goddess 60
Rifa'i (ar-), mosque (Cairo) 308
Riqqa, site 358
Roberts, David (painter) 143, 342, 343
Robertson, Charles (painter) 144
Roda, island (Cairo) 283, 315
Rosetta, houses of 215
Rosetta, mosques of 215
Rosetta, palm grove 213
Rosetta, town 214, 217
Rossi, Mario (architect) 178, 198
Royal necropolis (Tanis) 227

S

Saad Zaghlul, mausoleum (Cairo) 281
Saad Zaghlul, midan (Alexandria) 184, 197
Sabiqiya, medersa (Cairo) 290
Sabni, tomb of (Gharbi Aswan) 458
Sackville-West, Vita 151
Sacred lake (Karnak) 411
Sadat, Anwar el- 71, 210
Safiyya, mosque 108
Sahure, pharaoh 344
Saïd, citadel (the Delta) 207
Saïd, Mahmud (painter) 148
Saint Menas 202, 203
Sais, or Zaou, town 212
Sais, town 43
Sakakini (as-), suburb (Cairo) 284
Salah ad-Din, citadel (Sinai) 241
Salah ad-Din, midan (Cairo) 308
Salam (el-), canal 238
Saliba, shari' (Cairo) 311
Salih Talai (as-), mosque (Cairo) 109, 299
Sallum, port 204
Samalut, town 373
Sangar el-Gawli, mausoleum 111
Sangar Salar, mosque (Cairo) 313
Saqqara 86, 332, 344, 374
Sarabit el-Khadim, temple (Sinai) 242
Sarenput I, tomb of 458
Sarenput II, tomb of (Gharbi Aswan) 458
Sarghatmish, medersa (Cairo) 313
Sayyida Zeinab (as-), midan (Cairo) 314
Sayyida Zeinab (as-), mosque (Cairo) 314
Sayyida Zeinab, district 270
Scott-Moncrieff, Sir Colin 206
Sedment el-Jebel 359
Sehel, island of 456
Seila, "three-step" pyramid 358
Sekhmet, goddess 35, 63, 415
Semenud, town 221
Semna, fort 92, 93
Senenmut 426, 428
Sennedjem, tomb of (Thebes) 438, 439
Sennefer, tomb of 431
Senwosret I 268, 369
Senwosret I, kiosk of (Karnak) 83
Senwosret I, obelisk of 271
Senwosret I, pyramid of (Lisht) 356, 357
Senwosret I, "white" chapel (Karnak) 104, 413
Senwosret II 364

Senwosret II, pyramid (Illahun) 358, 359
Senwosret III 40
Senwosret III, pyramid of (Dahshur) 90, 354
Serapeum (Saqqara) 96, 350
Serapeum, temple (Alexandria) 194
Serapis, temple of 266, 267
Seth, god 451
Sethnakht, tomb of (Thebes) 424
Sety I 42, 386, 433, 448, 452
Sety I, chapel (Abydos) 386
Sety I, temple of (Thebes) 424, 425
Sety I, tomb of (Thebes) 95, 417
Sety II 377, 407
Sety II, tomb of (Thebes) 424
Shaba, village 212
Shakshuk, village (Faiyum) 366
Shali, town 256
Shallalat, gardens (Alexandria) 188, 190
Sham el-Nessim, festival 126
Sharm el-Sheikh, town (Sinai) 248
Sharqiya, province 225
Shatanuf, village 210
Shatby, cemetery (Alexandria) 198
Sheikh Mutahar, mosque (Cairo) 287
Sheikh Sinan, mausoleum (Cairo) 290
Sheikhu, mosque (Cairo) 311
Shepheard's, hotel (Cairo) 275
Shorbagi, mosque (Alexandria) 179
Shoshenq I 452
Shoshenq III, gate (Tanis) 226
Shoshenq V 213
Shubra, suburb (Cairo) 284
Sicard, Father Claude 226, 264
Sidi Ahmed el-Badawi, mausoleum (Tanta) 210
Sidi Ahmed el-Fuli, mosque 372
Silahdar (el-), wakala (Cairo) 287
Silahdar, mosque of Suleyman Aga el- (Cairo) 291
Silsila, cape 195, 196
Sinai 32, 237–52
Sinai, mountains 238, 243
Sinan Pasha, mosque (Cairo) 284
Sitra, oasis 258
Siwa, oasis 44, 129, 254, 256, 401
Sobek, crocodile-god 61, 83, 363, 372, 453
Sobek, statue of 403
Sobek, temple of (Faiyum) 366
Sokar, falcon-headed god 34, 389, 410

Sphinx of Giza 340, 342
St Anthony, monastery 106, 264, 265
St Barbara, church (Old Cairo) 321
St Catherine's
– monastery (Sinai) 32, 33, 143, 242, 244–5
St Damienne, monastery (Damietta) 223
St David's building (Cairo) 275
St George's
– church of (Old Cairo) 320
– convent of (Old Cairo) 320
– Greek church of (Old Cairo) 320
St George, monastery of 107, 359
St Mercurius, church and convent (Old Cairo) 325
St Paul, monastery 265
St Saba, church of (Alexandria) 188
St Sergius, church of see Abu Sarga
St Simeon
– monastery (Gharbi Aswan) 459
– monastery 107, 459
Stark, Freya 159
Step pyramid 39, 346, 348
Suez
– canal 68, 69, 180, 228, 229, 230–3, 236, 238
– crisis 70, 198, 234
Suleyman Pasha, mosque (Cairo) 307
Suleyman, mausoleum of sheikh 242
Sultaniya (el-), mausoleum 330

T

Taba, town (Sinai) 249
Taghri Bardi, medersa (Cairo) 311
Taharqa 43
Taharqa, column of (Karnak) 406
Taharqa, kiosk of (Karnak) 406
Tahrir (at-), midan (Alexandria) 180, 181
Tahrir (at-), midan (Cairo) 276, 280
Tahta, village 383
Tanis 43, 226
Tanis, temple of 89
Tanta, museum 211
Tanta, town 126, 210
Tarabay as-Sharifi, mausoleum (Cairo) 303
Tarif or Antef, necropolis (Thebes) 424
Tatar el-Higaziya, medersa (Cairo) 293
Taweret, goddess 34, 60, 452
Tawfiqiya, fort 199
Taybarsiya, medersa (Cairo) 294
Taz, palace of Emir (Cairo) 310

Tebtunis, ancient town 369
Tell Basta, or Bubastis, site 224
Tell el-Amarna 91, 279, 378
Tell el-Faraïn, or Pharaoh's Hill 212, 213
Tell el-Kebir, battle of 69
Terbana, mosque (Alexandria) 178
Thackeray, William M. 150
Thebes 40, 376, 393–444, 451
Thebes, corniche 396
Thebes, necropolis 166
Thermal basilica 202
Thmuis, town 221
Thoth, god 34, 35, 193, 377, 433, 440
Thoth, temple of (El-Kab) 448
Thutmose I 41, 408
Thutmose II 41
Thutmose III 403, 410, 436, 444, 446
Thutmose III, temple of (Thebes) 427, 430
Thutmose III, tomb of (Thebes) 424
Thutmose IV 341
Thutmose IV, temple of (Thebes) 434
Ti, mastaba of 351
Tih (el-), desert 238, 249
Tih (el-), plateau 241
Tihna el-Jebel, town 373
Titi, tomb of Queen (Thebes) 440
Tod, village 444
Tomb, architecture 430
Tomb, decorations 431
Tombs, royal (Thebes) 418
Tor (el-), town (Sinai) 240, 241
Trajan 194, 228, 270, 391
Trajan, kiosk of 462
Tulun, Ahmed Ibn 66, 214, 270, 312
Tulunids, the 66
Tuna el-Jebel, temple 377
Tuna el-Jebel, town 377
Turin, Egyptian museum of 468
Tussun Pasha, sabil (Cairo) 298
Tussun, khedivial tomb 331
Tutankhamun 43, 400
Tutankhamun, tomb of 276, 418–21

U

Umm el-Brigat (Faiyum) 369
Umm el-Qa'b (Abydos) 387
Umra (el-), mosque 372
Unis, pyramid of (Saqqara) 347
University, American (Cairo) 280
Userhet, tomb of (Thebes) 431
Ustadar, medersa of

Gamal ad-Din el-
(Cairo) 293
Uthman Katkhuda,
palace (Cairo) 288

V

Vatican Museum 469
Vidal, Gore 164
Vivant Denon,
Dominique 94, 140,
384, 390
Votaresses of Amun,
chapels of the Divine
Thebes) 434

W

Wadi es-Sebua, temple
of 166, 460, 461
Wadi Moqatteb (Sinai)
242
Wadi Natrun,
monasteries of 208
Wadi Sidri 266
Wadi Watir, delta 249
Wafd 70, 281
Wahab, Mohammed
Abd el- (singer) 128
Waqf 178, 302
Wardian (el-),
necropolis 200
Waugh, Evelyn 154
White Chapel of
Senwosret I (Karnak)
404, 413
Wilkinson, John G., 95
Wissa Wassef, Ramses
282, 321, 344

Z

Zagazig, town 225
Zaghlul, mosque
Rosetta) 215
Zaghlul, Saad 69, 70,
184, 213, 281
Zahiriya, medersa
Cairo) 288
Zanqat el-Sittat, or
Ladies' Alley
Alexandria) 179
Zawiyet el-Maytin 373
Zeinab, Sayyida 459
Zifta, town 220
Zoological Gardens
Alexandria) 191
Zulfiqar, wakala (Cairo)
293

HOTELS

Alda Beach
El-Alamein) 502
Akhetaton Village
Belladonna
Luxor) 503
Amun Hotel
Aswan) 495
Arafa Hotel
Tanta) 506
Aswan Oberoi Hotel
Aswan) 496
Atik Hotel
El-Alamein) 502
Auberge of Lake
Faiyum (The Faiyum)
02
Basma Hotel Aswan
Aswan) 496
Bawaki Beach Hotel
Noueiba) 504

Beach House Hotel
(Mersa Matruh) 504
Cairo Heliopolis
Mövenpick
(Cairo) 499
Cairo Jolie-Ville
Mövenpick
(Cairo) 499
Cairo Marriott Hotel
(Cairo) 499
Cairo Ramses Hilton
Hotel (Cairo) 499
Cairo Sheraton Hotel
(Cairo) 499
Carlton Hotel
(Cairo) 499
Coral Bay Hotel
(Sharm el-Sheikh) 505
Coral Beach Village
(Hurghada) 502
Cosmopolitan
Hotel (Cairo) 499
Daniela Village
(St Catherine) 505
El-Arish Oberoi Egoth
Hotel (El-Arish) 502
El-Gezirah Sheraton
Hotel Cairo
(Cairo) 499
El-Haram Hotel
(Alexandria) 494
el-Manshy
(Damiette) 502
El Salamlek San
Giovanni Hotel
(Alexandria) 494
El-Salam Village
(Noueiba) 505
El-Sayadeen Touristic
Village (Noueiba) 505
El-Waha Touristic Village
(Noueiba) 505
Gafi Land Tourist Village
(Sharm el-Sheikh) 505
Ghazala Hotel
Na'ama Bay
(Sharm el-Sheikh) 505
Grand Hotel
(Cairo) 499
Green House Hotel
(Suez) 506
Green House Hotel
(Tanta) 506
Helnan Palestine Hotel
(Alexandria) 494
Helnan Port Saïd Hotel
(Port Saïd) 505
Helnan Shepheard
Hotel (Cairo) 499
Hilton Al Fairuz (Sharm
el-Sheikh) 506
Hilton Coral Hotel
(Noueiba) 505
Holiday Inn Resort (Port
Safaga) 505
Horus Hotel
(Aswan) 496
Horus Hotel
(Luxor) 503
Hotel el-Alamein (Sidi
Abd el-Rahman) 506
Hotel Hilton Taba
(Taba) 506
Hotel Méridien
Pyramides (Cairo) 499
Hurghada Hilton Plazza
(Hurghada) 502
Hurghada Marriott
Beach Resort
(Hurghada) 502
Hurghada Sheraton
Hotel (Hurghada) 502

Isis Hotel Aswan
(Aswan) 496
Isis Hotel Luxor (Luxor)
503
Landmark Hotel
(Alexandria) 494
Le Méridien Heliopolis
Hotel (Cairo) 499
Le Meridien Cairo Hotel
(Cairo) 499
Lotus Hotel 500
L. T. I. Seti Sharm Hotel
(Sharm el-Sheikh) 506
Luxor Hilton
(Luxor) 503
Luxor Sheraton Hotel &
Resort (Luxor) 503
Marriott (Sharm el-
Sheikh) 506
Mena House Oberoi
Hotel (Cairo) 500
Menaville Village
(Port Safaga) 505
Mercure Hotel
(Luxor) 504
Mercure Hotel Etap
Forsan Island
(Ismaïliya) 502
Mercure Nefertiti
(Minia) 504
Mercure Romance
(Alexandria) 494
Miami Hotel (Mersa
Matruh) 504
Montazah Sheraton
Hotel (Alexandria) 494
Mövenpick Jolie-Ville
Luxor (Luxor) 504
Mövenpick Sharm
el-Cheikh (Sharm
el-Sheikh) 506
Nefertari Abu Simbel
(Abu Simbel) 495
Negresco Hotel (Mersa
Matruh) 504
New Panorama
Shakshouk Village Lake
Karoon (The Faiyum)
502
New Regent Hotel
(Port Saïd) 504
Nile Hilton Hotel
(Cairo) 500
Nitocrisse Hotel
(Cairo) 500
Novotel Cairo Airport
Hotel (Cairo) 500
Novotel Aquamarine
Hotel
(Sharm el-Sheikh)
506
Novotel Evasion Luxor
Hotel (Luxor) 504
Oasis Hotel 500
Pension Roma Cairo
(Cairo) 500
Philippe Hotel Luxor
(Luxor) 504
President Hotel
(Cairo) 500
Pyramids Park
(Cairo) 500
Radi Hotel
(Mersa Matruh) 504
Ramada Renaissance
(Alexandria) 494
Red Sea Hotel
(Suez) 506
Regency Hotel
(Alexandria) 495
Rommel House Hotel
(Mersa Matruh) 504

Safaga Paradise Village
(Port Safaga) 505
Safir Cairo Hotel
(Cairo) 500
St Catherine
Tourist Village (St
Catherine) 505
Semiramis Hotel
(Alexandria) 495
Semiramis Inter
Continental 500
Shams Safaga Village
(Port Safaga) 505
Siag Pyramids Hotel
Cairo (Cairo) 500
Sin Plaza
(St Catherine) 505
Sofitel Cecil Hotel
(Alexandria) 495
Sofitel Maadi Towers
Hotel (Cairo) 500
Sofitel New Cataract
(Aswan) 496
Sofitel Old Cataract
Hotel (Aswan) 496
Sofitel Winter Palace
(Luxor) 504
Sonesta Hotel 501
Sonesta Port Saïd Hotel
(Port Saïd) 505
Sonesta Saint-Georges
Hotel (Luxor) 504
Summer Palace Hotel
(Suez) 506
Swisshotel Cairo
El-Salam Hotel 501
Windsor Hotel
(Alexandria) 495

MUSEUMS

Alexandria, Fine Arts
Museum 189
Alexandria, Graeco-
Roman Museum 186,
188, 199
Beit el-Umma, Museum
of (Cairo) 281
Beni Suef, Museum of
359
Berlin, Egyptian
Museum in 95, 470
British Museum, London
474
Cavafy Museum
(Alexandria) 185
Elephantine, museum
457
Florence, archeological
museum 469
Cairo
- Coptic Museum 321-
323
- Egyptian Museum,
Cairo 276, 340, 346,
352, 354-356, 412, 421,
426, 428, 445
- Gayer-Anderson
Museum 313
- Islamic Museum 316,
317
- Mukhtar Museum 282
- Museum of Modern Art
282
- Postal Museum 275
Ismaïliya, Museum of
Antiquities 326
Luxor, Museum of 403
Kharga, Museum of the
New Valley, 260
Louvre, musée du 390,
423, 445, 468, 476, 477

Metropolitan Museum, New York 426, 472
Port Saïd, Historic Museum 236
Port Saïd, Miltary Museum 236
Turin, Egyptian Museum of 468
Vatican Museum 469

RESTAURANTS

Adhura (Alexandria) 494
Aladin (Cairo) 496
Andrea (Cairo) 496
Arabesque (Cairo) 496
Asia House (Cairo) 496
Bella Donna (Luxor) 502
Bird Cage (Cairo) 496
Chandani (Cairo) 496
China house (Alexandria) 494
Christo (Cairo) 496
Ciao Italia (Cairo) 497

Citadel Grill (Cairo) 497
Class (Luxor) 502
Club 1902 (Aswan) 495
Da Mario Nile Hilton (Cairo) 497
Dakka (Luxor) 503
Don Quichotte (Cairo) 497
El-Ezba (Cairo) 497
El-Fanus (Cairo) 497
El-Madiriya (Luxor) 503
El-Masry (Aswan) 495
El-Yotti (Cairo) 497
Falafel (Cairo) 497
Felfela (Cairo) 497
Fellah's Tent (Luxor) 503
Felucca (Luxor) 503
Gondola (La) (Cairo) 497
Grill Gezira (Cairo) 497
Groppi (Cairo) 496
Haty (Luxor) 503
Justine's (Cairo) 497
Kebabgy (Cairo) 497
Khan el-Khalili (Cairo) 497

Koueder (Cairo) 496
L'Entrecôte (Alexandria) 494
La Mamma (Cairo) 498
La Mamma (Luxor) 503
La Piazza (Cairo) 498
La Terrasse (Cairo) 498
Le Chalet (Cairo) 498
Le Champollion (Cairo) 498
Le Château (Cairo) 498
Le Marco Polo (Cairo) 498
Le Plat d'Or (Alexandria) 494
Les Trèfles (Cairo) 499
The Marhaba (Luxor) 503
Moghul Room (Cairo) 498
Nile's Maxim's (Cairo) 498
Nubian Village (Cairo) 498

Orangerie (Aswan) 495
Panorama (Aswan) 495
Paprika (Cairo) 498
Pastroudis (Alexandria) 494
Pâtisserie Délices (Alexandria) 494
Patisserie El Abd (Cairo) 496
Piazza (La) (Cairo) 498
Rubayyat (Cairo) 498
Rumours (Cairo) 498
Sakkura (Cairo) 498
San Giovanni (Alexandria) 494
Sheherazade Terrace (Luxor) 503
Silver Fish (Cairo) 498
Sushiyama (Cairo) 499
Tandoori (Cairo) 499
The Terrace (Cairo) 499
Tikka Grill (Alexandria) 494
Zéférion Restaurant (Alexandria) 494

Map section

540 Cairo street index

541 Alexandra

542 Northeast Egypt

544 Northwest Egypt

546 Libyan desert

548 Southeast Egypt

550 Nile Delta

552 Cairo

554 North Cairo

556 South Cairo

558 Thebes

560 Luxor, Aswan

Key

Freeway	Christian cemetery
Main road	Muslim cemetery
Secondary road	Tourist attraction
Trail	Airport
Railroad	Subway station
International boundary	Hospital
Urban area	
Main town	
Secondary town	

◆ CAIRO STREET INDEX

Abd el-Aziz (Shari')
D3-D4
Abd el-Aziz Es Su'ud
(Shari') **H** B4-B6
Abd el-Aziz Radwan
(Shari') **H** A2-A3
Abd el-Khaliq Sarwat
(Shari') I B3-I C3
Abdel Rahim Sabri
(Shari') **H** A2-A3
Abd el-Mun'im Riyad
(Shari') **H** A1
Abou el-Maati (Shari')
H A1
Abu el-Mahasin
el-Shazli (Shari') **H** A1
Abu Sayafin (Shari') **J** B4
Adli (Shari') I C3
Ahmed Mahir (Midan)
D4
Ahmed Mahir (Shari') I
E4
Ain el-Sira (Shari') **J** D6-
E6
A-K Hamza (Shari') I A4
Ali-Ibrahim (Shari') **J** B2
Amin Bey ar-Rafi'i
(Shari') **H** A3
as-Saad al-Ali (Shari')
H A3
as-Sheikh Ali Yousef
(Shari') **J** B1
at-Tahrir (Midan) I B4
at-Tahrir (Shari')
H A3-I B4
Bab-el-Bahr (Shari')
I D1-D2
Baghala (Shari') I F2
Beiram el-Tunsi (Shari')
H C2-C3
Beit el-Qadi (Midan) I F3
Birket el-Rati (Shari')
I E1
Champollion (Shari') I B3
Clot-Bey (Shari') I D2
Doctor M. Shaheen
(Shari') **H** A2
Duqqi (Shari') **H** A3-A4
el-Ahram (Shari') **H** A6-A5
el-Ashraf (Shari') **J** E3

el-Ataba el-Khadra
(Midan) I D3
el-Auribiya (Shari') **J** E2
el-Azhar (Shari') I D3-E4
el-Bahr el-Azam (Shari')
H A6
el-Bustan (Shari') I B4-C4
el-Corniche (Shari')
J A4-**H** B1
el-Darb el-Ahmar
(Shari') I F5
el-Falaki (Midan) I B4
el-Falaki (Shari') I B5-B6
el-Falonga (Shari') **H** A1
el-Fardus (Shari') **H** A2
el-Gabalaya (Shari') **H** A1
el-Gala' (Kubri) **H** B3
el-Gala' (Shari') I B2
el-Gamia (Kubri) **H** B4
el-Gamia (Shari') **H** A4
el-Geish (Shari') I D3-F1
el-Gezira (Shari') **H** B2
el-Giza (Kubri) **H** B5
el-Giza (Shari') **H** A3-A5
el-Gumhuriya (Midan)
I C4
el-Gumhuriya (Shari')
I C1-C3
el-Hadaiq (Shari') **H** A2
el-Hilmiyan (Shari')
I E6-**J** E1
el-Khalig el-Masri
(Shari') **J** C1
el-Mahatta (Shari') **H** A6
el-Malik (Kubri) **J** A4
el-Malik el-Salih (Shari')
J A4-A5
el-Mansuri (Shari') I B1
el-Manyal (Shari')
J A2-A5
el-Manyal (Kubri)
H B4-C4
el-Misaha (Shari') **H** A3-
A4
el-Misaha (Midan) **H** A3
el-Muizz (Shari') I F3-E5
el-Nasiriya (Shari') I C6
el-Nil (Shari') **H** A2-A5
el-Qa'la (Shari') I D4-E6
el-Qolali (Shari') I B1-C1

el-Roda (Shari') **J** A4
el-Sabtiya (Shari') I C1
el-Sadd el-Barrani
(Shari') **J** B2-C2
el-Sammakin (Shari')
I F1-F2
el-Sahafa (Shari') I B2
el-Sheikh el-Arusi
(Shari') I E2
el-Zahir (Shari') I E1-F1
el-Zahirar (Shari') I B1
el-Zamalek (Kubri) **H** A1
Gamiat el-Qahira
(Shari') **H** A5
Ghait (Shari') **H** A1
Gohar el-Qaid (Shari')
I E3
Hasan el-Anwar (Shari')
H B4-B5
Hasan Sabri (Shari')
I B1-B3
Ibn Yazid (Shari') **J** C3
Imad ad-Din (Shari') I C2
Imam as-Shafi'i (Shari')
J F2-F4
Irabi (Shari') I C2
Isa Hamdi (Shari') **H** A2
Ismail Abaza (Shari') I B6
Kamil Sidqi (Shari')
I D1
Kassab (Shari') **H** A3
Khairat (Shari') I B6
Kubri el-Gala' (Midan)
H B3
Latin America (Shari')
I A4
M. Kamel (Midan) I C3
M. Sabri Abu el-Alam
(Shari') I B4-C4
Maglis el Sha'ab (Shari')
I B5-C5
Magra el-Uyun (Shari')
J B3-D4
Matbaa el-Ahliya (Shari')
I A1-A2
Mathaf el-Zira (Shari')
H A2
Mogammaa (Shari') I A4
Mohammed Faird
(Shari') I C5

Mohammed Izz el-Arab
(Shari') I B6
Murad (Shari') **H** A5
N. Rihani (Shari') I D2
Nadi as-Said (Shari')
H A3
Nawal (Shari') **H** A2
Nubar (Shari') I B6-C4
Port Said (Shari')
J D1-I F1
Qarafet (Shari') I F6
Qasr an-Nil (Shari')
I B3-B4
Qasr el-Aini (Shari')
I A6-**J** B2
Rafaa (Shari') **H** A4
Ramses (Shari') I B2-B3
Ramses (Midan) I C1
Rushdi (Shari') I C4
Sa'ad Zaghul (Shari')
H A6
Salah ad-Din (Midan)
J F1
Salah Salim (Shari')
J B4-**H** F2
Sami el-Barudi (Shari')
I D4
Saray (Kubri) **J** A2
Sarwat (Shari') **H** A4
Shanan (Shari') I B1
Sheikh Rihan (Shari')
I B5-D5
Sherif (Shari') I C3
Sidi Oqba (Shari')
J F5-F6
6 October (Kubri)
I A3-**H** B2
6 October (Shari') I B2-
C2
Sulaimane Gohar
(Shari') **H** A3
Tal'at Harb (Midan) I B4
Tal'at Harb (Shari') I B3
Tawfiq (Midan) I C2
26 July (Kubri) **H** C1
26 July (Shari')
H A1-I C3
Usef Suliman (Shari')
I E1

A

MEDITERRANEAN SEA

FORT QAITBAY

EL-ATTA FORT

FORT SILSILA

CASIN

CHATE NECROPOL

NEW LIBRARY

ANFUSHI

EASTERN HARBOR

See below

ANFUSHI BAY

ABU EL-ABBAS MOSQUE

S. RAS EL-TIN

S. BANDROSHA

TERBANA MOSQUE

26 JULY

S. CHAMPOLLION

(CORNICHE)

SAAD ZAGHLUL

S. I. EL-RAHMAN RUSH

GRAECO-ROMAN MUSEUM

SULT. HUSSEIN

ANFUSHI NECROPOLIS

RAS EL-TIN

EL-SHORBAGI MOSQUE

Midan at-Tahrir

SHARI'

SHARI' EL-HURRIYA

SHARI' LUMOMBA

FINE ARTS MUSEUM

RAS EL-TIN PALACE

MARITIME STATION

MANTHIYA

SHARI' EL-MITWALI

S. NABI DANIEL

STATION

WESTERN HARBOR

SHARI' EL-AKHDAR

SHARI' BAB

SHARI' EL-JUWAL

SHARI' EL-MUHAFAZA

SHARI' EL-AUWA

SHARI' MUHARRAM BAY

UNIVERSITY

GUROK

ATTARINE

SHARI' IBRAHIM

SHARI' EL-KHEDIWI EL-AUWAL

SHARI' IRFAN PASH

VARMUZ

POMPEY PILLAR

SHARI' EL-RAHMA

AS-SAWARI

RAGHIB PASHA

0   500   1000 m
0   1650   3300 feet

GABARI

SHARI' EL-MEX

KOM ES-SHOGAFA CATACOMBS

MAHMUDIYA CANAL

LAKE MARIUT

AIRPORT - EL-ALAMEIN

B

EASTERN HARBOR

(CORNICHE)

26 JULY

S. ES-SAYID MUHAMMAD ABD EL-KARIM

ZAGHLUL

EL-QAÏD MOSQUE

CHAMPOLLION

EL-SHORBAGI MOSQUE

SOUK

Midan Orabi

(CORNICHE)

Midan Saad Zaghlul

RAMLEH STATION

Midan Ramleh

SAAD

SHARI'

ST MARK'S

SHARI'

Midan at-Tahrir

SHARI'

SALAH

AHMED

SALEM

TOURIST OFFICE

SHARI' NABI

ZAGHLUL

SHARI' SAFIYA

AMIN

SULTAN

FIKRY

HUSSEIN

GRAECO-ROMAN MUSEUM

EL-GAZAIR

EL-AUWAL

MANSHIYA

CAVAFY MUSEUM

SHARI' TALAAT HARB

SHARI' EL-HURRIYA

LUMOMBA

SHARI' IBRAHIM

SHARI' EL-QAÏD

GOHAR

ORABI

TAWFIQ

ST CATHERINE'S

ED-ERDA

NABI DANIEL MOSQUE

ROMAN THEATER

SHARI'

ATTARINE

EL-MITWALLI

KOM EL-DIKKA AMPHITHEATER

STATION

SHARI' ABI

SHARI' M. BAY SALAM

AIRPORT - EL-ALAMEIN

EL-MUHAFAZA

ATTARINE

Midan Gumhuriya

0   150   300 m
0   500   1000 feet

SHARI'

C

A B C

Sallum

Sidi
Barani

M E D

Mersa
Matruh

LIBYA

*LIBYAN
DESERT*

1

2

QATTARA DEPRE

*SIWA
OASIS*

Siwa

3

LIBYA

4

5

0	25	50 km
0	15	30 miles

6   A B   C

D

Rosetta
Abukir Idku
BAHA EL-BURULLUS
Damietta
Faraskur
Damietta
LAKE MANZALA
Port Said
Alexandria
Fuwa Sidi Salim
El Hamul
Shirbin
el-Matariya
SUEZ CANAL
TELL EL FARA
(Pelusium)
Kaff el-Dauwar
Disuq
Kafr el-Sheikh
Dikirnis
el-Manzala
el-Ameriya
Damanhur
el-Mahalla el-Kubra
Mansura
TANIS
DAPHNAE
Hosh'lsa
Mah Marham
Sebennytos
el-Simbillawein
Ismailia
Kafr el-Zaiyat
Tanta
Zifta
Abu Kebir
BAHRA EL-TIMSAH
EIR AMBA BARAMUS
DEIR ES-SURIANI DEIR AMBA BISHOI
Tala
Shibin El Kom
Mit Ghamr
Faqus
Zagazig
TELL EL-MASUHUTA (Pithom)
BITTER LAKES
Minya el-Qamh
Benha
Bilbeis
Medinet Ashara Ramadan
DEIR ABU MAKARYUS
Minuf
Shibin el Qanatir
AHMED HAMDI TUNNEL
El-Khanka
Shubra El-Kheima
Cairo
Giza
El-Sh...
Suez
Ain Musa
SPRING OF MOSES
PYRAMIDS OF GIZA
El-Hawamdiya
El Badrshein
SAQQARA
el-Minia
QASR EL-SAGHA
KOM USHIM
PYRAMIDS OF LISHT
(Socnopalos) DIMAI
BIRKET QARUN
Sinnuris
FAIYUM OASIS
el-Faiyum
MEIDUM PYRAMID
PYRAMID OF HAWARA
PYRAMID OF ILLAHUN
el-Gharaq el-Sultani
Ihnasiya el-Medina
Beni Suef
Za'faran
DEIR SAMWEIL
DISHASHA
Sumusta el-Waqf
Sannur
Gabal el-Nour
Biba
el-Fashn
el-Fant
EL HIBA (Ankyronpolis)
WADI SANNUR
Maghagha
(Oxyrhynchos) EL BAHNASA
Sandafa el-Far
Beni Mazar
GEBEL EL-GALALA EL-BAHARÎYA
Matai
WADI EL-TARFA
Samalut
DEIR EL-ADRA
Tihna el-Jebel
ACORIS (Déhenet-Akoris)
ARABIAN DESERT
Idmu
Talla
el-Minia
KOM EL-AHMAR
Abu Qurqas
el-Fikriya
Itlidim
BENI HASSAN
SPEOS ARTEMIDOS
HERMOPOLIS
ANTINOE
TUNA EL-JEBEL
Ashmunein
Mallawi
Dalga
TELL EL-AMARNA
Dairut
Sanabu
Mir
el-Qusiya
Umm el-Qusur
WADI HOUBARA
Manfalut
El-Atamna
Beni Muhammadiyat
Abnub
Manqabad
Assuit
(Lycopolis)
Musha
Abu Tig
El Badari
Tima
QAOU EL-KEBIR (Antaeopolis)
Tahta
El Maragha

60 mls

0   25   50 km
0   15   30 miles

A   B   C

F

E

A B C

Bir Abu Minqar

LIBYAN DESERT

GILF KEBIR

PLATEAU

| 0 | 25 | 50 km |
| 0 | 15 | 30 miles |

A B C

F

A **B** **C**

Tahta

El Maragha

DEIR AMBA BISHOI (RED MONASTERY)
DEIR EL-ABYAD (WHITE MONASTERY) ■
Akhmim

Sohag
El Minsha

(This, Thinis) El Birba   **NAGA EL-DEIR**

Girga

Minshat Bardis El Kushh
El Balyana

ABYDOS

Faw   **Dishna**
Qibli

Nag Hammadi

El Qasr
El Waqf

Hiou (Heou)
(Diospolis Parva)

1

Nagada

DENDERA

Qena

El Ballas

Qift   (Apollinopolis Parva)

Qus

Higaza

WADI
HAMMAMAT

WADI ZAIDUN

VALLEY OF THE KINGS ■   **KARNAK**

El Dabiya   **Luxor**

Armant (Hermonthis)

Jebelein   **TOD**

CROCODILOPOLIS   **MOALLA**

Kiman el Matana

Asfun el Matana

(Latopolis) **Esna**   El Deir

2

el-Sibaiya

WADI EL-MIYAH

el-Mahamid

EL-KULA PYRAMID ■   **EL-KAB** (Nekheb)

(Hierakonpolis) **KOM EL-AHMAR**   el-Kilh

(Apollinopolis Magna)   **Edfu** ● **el-Ridisiya Bahari**

TEMPLE OF HORUS ■

Silwa Bahari

HOREMHEB TEMPLE ■   Kagug   **JEBEL SILSILA**

Faris

OMBOS ■

Bimban   Nasser City

Kom Ombo

3

DUSH ■

El-Aqaba el-Kebira

El Khattara

MONASTERY OF ST SIMEON ■
ELEPHANTINE ISLAND ■
FIRST WATERFALL ■   **Aswan**
FIRST DAM ■

KALABSHA ■   **HIGH DAM**

4

LAKE
NASSER

5

**DAKKA, MAHARRAQA,
WADI ES-SEBUA** ■

AMADA ■

ABU SIMBEL ■

0	25	50 km
0	15	30 miles

A **B** **C**

G

MEDITERRANEAN SEA

El-Borg

Baltim

BAHRA EL-BURULLUS

Borg Migheizil

Rosetta

El-Haddadi

Abukir

Idku

Sidi Salim

Alexandria

Fuwa

El-Maka

Kafr Silim

El-Mahmudiya

TELL EL-FARAIN
(Buto)

Kafr el-Sheikh

**Kafr el-
Dauwar**

Abu Hummus

Disuq

Qallin

El-Amiriya

Damanhur

Shubra Khit

SA EL-HAGAR

**el-Mahalla
El-Kubra**

Zawyet
Sidi Ghazi

Basyun

Hosh'Isa

NAUCRATIS

Mah Marham

Abou en-Matamir

El-Dilingat

Kafr el-Zaiyat

Tanta

El-Santa

Kom Hamada

Tala

Nadir

**Shibin
El-Kom**

Minuf

el-Bagur
Sirs
el-Laiyana

DEIR AMBA BARAMUS

Sadat City

DEIR ES-SURIANI **DEIR AMBA BISHOI**

DEIR ABU MAKARYUS

El-Qanatir
**DELTA
BARRAGE**

**Warraq
el-Arab**

Kirdasa

Giza

PYRAMIDS OF GIZA

PYRAMID OF ABUSIR
PYRAMIDS OF SAQQARA

QASR EL-SAGHA

MEDINET DIMAI

KOM USHIM

Shakshuk

Toamiya

DIONYSIAS

*BIRKET
QARUN*

Sanhur

Sinnuris

El-Roda

**MEIDUM
PYRAMID**

Qasr Qarun

Ibshaway

Eigimin

Seila

Meidum

**MEDINET WATFA
(PHILOTERIS)**

El-Nazla

El-Faiyum

Itsa

**PYRAMID
OF HAWARA**

Qiman
el-Arus

Illahun

Abusir
el-Malau

*FAIYUM
OASIS*

MEDINAT MADI

DEIR EL-MALAK

**PYRAMID
ILLAHUN**

Bush

SEDMENT EL-GEBEL

**AHNAS EL-
MEDINA**

**Beni
Suef**

**UMM
EL-BRIGAT (TEBTUNIS)**

| 0 | 15 | 30 km |
| 0 | 9 | 18 miles |

TANTA - ALEXANDRIA

A B C

ZAMALEK

BULAQ

KUBRI EL-ZAMALEK

SHARI' 26 JULY

SHARI' 26 JULY

KUBRI 26 JULY

SHARI' 26 JULY

EL-AGUZA

GEZIRA ISLAND

NILE

S. MATHAF EL-ZIRA

KUBRI 6 OCTOBER

CAIRO TOWER

EGYPTIAN MUSEUM, CAIRO

Midan At AN-NIL

S. QASR EL-NIL

Midan Tal'at Harb

EL-BUSTAN

BUS STATION

Midan at-Tahrir

Midan el-Falaki

MUSEUM OF EGYPTIAN CIVILISATION

SHARI' AT-TAHRIR

K. QASR EL-NIL

MOGAMMA

BAB EL-LOUK STATION

NADI AS-SAID

SHARI' EL-DUQQI

Midan Kubri el-Gala' EL-GALA'

TAHRIR GARDENS

KUBRI EL-GALA'

PARLIAMENT

EL-DUQQI

AT-TAHRIR

Midan el-Misaha

NILE FOUNTAIN

GARDEN CITY

SHARI' SARWAT

EL-ORMAN GARDENS

KUBRI EL-MANYAL

CAIRO UNIVERSITY

SHARI' EL-GAMIA

KUBRI EL-GAMIA

KUBRI SARAY

ZOO

NILE

MANYAL MUSEUM

RODA ISLAND

SALAD

KUBRI EL-GIZA

S. EL-RODA

KUBRI EL-MALIK

SHARI' SALAH SALIM

GIZA

SHARI' EL-AHRAM

AMR IBN EL-AS MOSQUE

ANCIENT WALLS OF FUSTAT

OLD CAIRO

RUINS OF FUSTAT

NILOMETER

COPTIC MUSEUM

SAQQARA

A B

HELWAN

C

SINAN PASHA
MOSQUE

S. EL-SABTIYA

CENTRAL STATION

MOUBARAK STATION

Midan
Ramses

SHARI' MATBAA EL-AHLIYA

SHARI' EL-MANSURI

SHARI' EL-QOLALI

SHARI' EL-ZAHAR

SHARI'
SHANAN

BULAQ

IRABI STATION

SHARI' EL-GALA'

EL AHRAM

SHARI' EL-SAHAFA

SHARI' RAMSES

SHARI' IRABI

EL-GUMHURIYA

SHARI' 26 JULY

TELEVISION

NASSER STATION

OCTOBER

SHARI' EL-GALA'

EL-EZBEKIYA

SHARI' EL-CORNICHE

Midan
Tawfiq

MAD-AD-DIN

S. EL-GUMHURIYA

KUBRI
6 OCTOBER

SHARI' RAMSES

SHARI' 26 JULY

S. EL-GALA'

6

SHARI' RAMSES

LAW
COURTS

TAL'AT HARB

SHARI' ABD ELKHALIQ SARWAT

TOURIST
OFFICE

SHARI' ADLI

S. GUMHURIYA

NILE

SHARI' CHAMPOLLION

SHARI' SHERIF

Midan
M. Kamel

SHARI' EL-

EGYPTIAN
MUSEUM

Midan
Tal'at
Harb

AN - NIL

SHARI' RUSHDI

SHARI'

BUS
STATION

S. QASR

SHARI'

S. M. SABRI ABU EL-ALAM

SHARI' EL-BUSTAN

KUBRI
QASR EL-NIL

MINISTRY
FOR FOREIGN
AFFAIRS

S.

Midan
at-Tahrir

AT - TAHRIR

Midan
el-Falaki

SHARI' EL - BUSTAN

Midan
el-Gumhuriya

SADATE STATION

MARKET

S. MOGAMMAA

AMERICAN
UNIVERSITY

BAB EL-LOUK
STATION

MOGAMMAA

SHARI'

SHARI' EL-CORNICHE

S. A-K HAMZA

SHEIKH

SHARI' NUBAR

RIHAN

SHARI' MOHAMMED FAIRD

SHARI' SHEIKH

S. LATIN AMERICA

PARLIAMENT

GEOGRAPHICAL
SOCIETY

MINISTRY
OF THE INTERIOR

S. MAGLIS

EL-SHA'AB

S. ISMAIL

SHARI' EL-FALAKI

ABAZA

SHARI' NUBAR

SHARI' KHAIRAT

SHARI' EL-NASIRIYA

GARDEN
CITY

S. QASR EL-AINI

SAAD ZAGHLUL
STATION

S. MOHAMMED

IZZ EL-ARAB

SHARI'

EL-SAIYIDA ZEINAB
STATION

A   B   C

D   E   F

ARMENIAN CHURCH

STATUE OF AMESSES II

JESUIT COLLEGE

SHARI' KAMIL SIDQI

SHARI' BAB-EL-BAHR

SHARI' CLOT-BEY

COPTIC CATHEDRAL

S. N. RIHANI

EL-EZBEKIYA

GARDENS

Midan el-Ataba el-Khadra

POST OFFICE

S. ABD EL-AZIZ

SHARI' EL-QA'LA

S. SAMI EL-BARUDI

ABDIN PALACE

ABDIN

RIHAN

PORT SAID

SHARI' EL-ZAHIR

EL-SAKAKINI

EL-GHAMRA

SULTAN BAIRBAR MOSQUE

ZAHIR

SHARI' EL-

SHARI' USEF SULIMAN

S. BIRKET EL-RATI

SHARI' PORT SAID

SHARI' EL-GEISH

SHARI' EL-SAMMAKIN

SHARI' BAGHALA

BAB EL-SHA'RIYA

SHARI' EL-SHEIKH EL-ARUSI

EL-MUSKI

OLD CITY WALLS

BAB EL-FUTUH

BAB AN-NASR

EL-HAKIM MOSQUE

USUN WAKALA

ABU BAKR IBN MUZHIR MOSQUE

BEIT AS-SUHAYMI

SHARI' EL-GEISH

EL-GAMALIYA

SHARI' PORT SAID

SHARI' EL-MUIZZ

EL-AQMAR MOSQUE

COMPLEX OF SULTAN BARQUQ

BESHTAK PALACE

MUSAFIRKHANA PALACE

COMPLEX OF SULTAN EL-NASSER MOHAMMED

Midan Beit el-Qadi

COMPLEX OF SULTAN QUAL'UN

SABIL-KUTTAB AHMAD PASHA

SHARI' GOHAR EL-QA'ID

SHEIKH MUTAHAR MOSQUE

KHAN EL-KHALILI

EL-HUSSEIN MOSQUE

ASHRAFIYA MEDERSA

EL-SILAHDAR WAKALA

EL-AZHAR UNIVERSITY

SHARI' EL-AZHAR

EL-GHURI MAUSOLEUM

EL-AZHAR MOSQUE

ISLAMIC MUSEUM

Midan Ahmed Mahir

SHARI' A. MAHIR

EL-FAKAHANI MOSQUE

SHARI' EL-MUIZZ

EL-MU'AYYAD MOSQUE

BAB ZUWAILA

BAB EL-KHALQ

SHARI' EL-QA'LA

SALIH TALAÏ MOSQUE

EL-ISHAQI MOSQUE

SHARI' EL-MUIZZ

EL-AHMAR MOSQUE

SHARI' EL-DARB EL-AHMAR

EL-QADI YEHIA MOSQUE

MARIDANI MOSQUE

QUSUN MOSQUE

OLD CITY WALLS

5

SHARI' EL-HILMIYAN

SHARI' EL-QA'LA

DARB EL-AHMAR

BLUE MOSQUE

MOSQUE

TOMBS OF THE CALIPHS

SHARI' QARAFET

S. EL-HILMIYAN

SHARI' EL-QA'LA

AR-RIFA'I MOSQUE

SULTAN HASSAN MOSQUE

0   200   400 m

0   650   1300 feet

D   E   F

6

NILE

A B C

ABDIN

GARDEN
CITY

EL-SAIYIDA ZEINAB
STATION

AS-SAYYIDA
ZEINAB
MOSQUE

SHARI' EL-QASR EL-AINI

S. AS-SHEIKH ALI YOUSEF

SHARI' EL-KHALIG EL-MASRI

SALAH AD-DIN
MOSQUE

KUBRI
SARAY

S. ALI-IBRAHIM

EL-BARRANI

MANYAL
PALACE

SHARI' EL-QASR EL-AINI

SHARI' EL-SADD

SHARI' BEIRAM EL-TUNSI

SHARI' IBN YAZID

SHARI' EL-MANYAL

SHARI' MAGRA EL-UYUN

SALAD AD-DIN

RODA
ISLAND

EL-SALIH

EL-CORNICHE

S. ABU SAYAFYN

EL-ANWAR

EL-MALIK STATION

KUBRI
EL-MALIK

SHARI' SALAH SALIM

EL-RODA

SHARI' EL-MALIK

SHARI'

SHARI' HASAN

CHURCH AND CONVENT
OF ST MERCURIUS

SHARI' EL-MANYAL

SHARI'

AMR IBN EL-AS
MOSQUE

ST
GEORGE'S

OLD CAIRO

ANCIENT WALLS OF FUSTAT

NILOMETER

ST GEORGE'S
CONVENT

ST GEORGE'S
CHURCH

RUINS
OF FUSTAT

MARI GIRGIS STATION

ST BARBARA'S
ST SERGIUS CHURCH
BEN-EZRA SYNAGOGUE

COPTIC MUSEUM

A B C

K

VALLEY OF THE KINGS
18th–20th DYNASTIES

TOMB OF
TUTANKHAMUN

ROYAL TOMBS OF THE
17th DYNASTY

DEIR
EL-BAHRI

TEMPLE OF
HATSHEPSUT

DRA-ABU
EL-NAGA

TEMPLE OF
MENTUHOTEP II

ASASIF

SHEIKH
ABD EL-QURNA

QURNA

TEMPLE OF
THUTMOSE III

TEMPLE OF
RAMESSES IV

TEMPLE OF
SETY I

TEMPLE
OF HATHOR-MA'AT

DEIR
EL-MEDINA

RAMESSEUM
(TEMPLE OF RAMESSES II)

NECROPOLIS
OF THEBES

QURNET
MURAI

TEMPLE OF
THUTMOSE IV

TEMPLE OF
MERNEPTAH

TEMPLE OF
HOREMHEB

TEMPLE
OF AMENHOTEP III

COLOSSI
OF MEMNON

MEDINET
HABU

TEMPLE OF
RAMESSES III

TEMPLE OF
THUTMOSE III

THEBES
WEST BANK

EL-KOM

A   B   C